CHINA TRADE
AND EMPIRE

Jardine, Matheson & Co.
and the Origins of British Rule
in Hong Kong
1827–1843

RECORDS OF SOCIAL AND ECONOMIC HISTORY
NEW SERIES 38

CHINA TRADE AND EMPIRE

Jardine, Matheson & Co. and the Origins of British Rule in Hong Kong 1827–1843

EDITED BY

ALAIN LE PICHON

Published for THE BRITISH ACADEMY
by OXFORD UNIVERSITY PRESS

This book has been printed digitally and produced in a standard specification in order to ensure its continuing availability

OXFORD
UNIVERSITY PRESS

Great Clarendon Street, Oxford OX2 6DP

Oxford University Press is a department of the University of Oxford.
It furthers the University's objective of excellence in research, scholarship,
and education by publishing worldwide in

Oxford New York

Auckland Cape Town Dar es Salaam Hong Kong Karachi
Kuala Lumpur Madrid Melbourne Mexico City Nairobi
New Delhi Shanghai Taipei Toronto

With offices in

Argentina Austria Brazil Chile Czech Republic France Greece
Guatemala Hungary Italy Japan South Korea Poland Portugal
Singapore Switzerland Thailand Turkey Ukraine Vietnam

Oxford is a registered trade mark of Oxford University Press
in the UK and in certain other countries

Published in the United States
by Oxford University Press Inc., New York

Reprinted 2010

ISBN 978-0-19-726337-2

Cover illustration: This is an early nineteenth-century watercolour
depicting a pagoda near Canton (Private collection)

Foreword

The Records of Social and Economic History series contain many volumes relating to the domestic history of Britain, but we welcome also the opportunity to publish materials which throw light on overseas trade and the social and economic dimensions of the British Empire. Previous editions, for example, have included records of commercial links across the Atlantic. Dr Alain Le Pichon is an authority on the China trade in the nineteenth century, and it is fortunate for our better understanding of an important stage in the development of British interests in the Far East that he has edited these letters. Previous historians have made good use of the Jardine, Matheson and Co. archive, but until now a large selection of the correspondence has not been available in edited form. The partnership between Jardine and Matheson was formed in 1827, and this collection takes us through a period of expansion in the volume of trade and a growth in the firm's profits. It ends with the Opium War of 1839–1842.

The letters show Jardine and Matheson dealing with other firms, and with individual traders, in China where the two partners were based, in India where many commodities, including opium, originated, and in London. Letters were also exchanged with ships' captains and officers, who were often trading on their own behalf. Correspondence with London could be concerned with political matters, as legislation, such as the *India Act* of 1833, changed the environment for trade in the Far East. Through the letters the origins and events of the Opium War can be observed, and the foundation of Hong Kong as the main base for British merchants operating in China. There is much of social and human interest in the letters. We appreciate, for example the contrasting, yet complementary characters of William Jardine and James Matheson. The Committee, and the many scholars who will use these sources, owe a considerable debt to Dr Le Pichon for his meticulous editing of this important collection of correspondence.

October 2005

Christopher Dyer
Chairman, Records of Social and Economic History Committee

Contents

List of Illustrations

MAPS

Between pages xix and xxii:

PLATES

Between pages 26 and 27:

Preface

The aim of this volume is to present to the reader a selection of the correspondence from the Jardine Matheson Archive written between the years 1827 and 1843. The selection opens with William Jardine and James Matheson joining forces in Canton in the firm which soon bore their names, and it ends a year after the Treaty of Nanking which marked the end of the Opium War and the start of British rule in Hong Kong. A century later, just after the second World War, Maurice Collis published his *Foreign Mud*, the first book to make extensive use of the Jardine, Matheson Archive. Trade as a subject of historical research had started acquiring a respectability of its own. Since then scholars have published an abundance of historical research on the development of British trade in China, much of which incorporated material from an Archive which has become world-famous. But a gap remained in all this historical production. The primary material was never presented for its own sake. It merely appeared in snippets, serving as the elusive basis for the historian's interpretation. This volume is an attempt at filling the gap.

It is the common fate of projects of this nature to reach the printing stage in a state of relative imperfection. Reasons for delaying putting the final full stop never cease to present themselves. More inspired scrutiny of this or that manuscript might have finally solved the riddle of an illegible group of words. More extensive knowledge of the microcosm of early Victorian traders to the East might have reduced the number of 'unidentified' characters, etc. But, in the end, an imperfect text is better than no text at all, and the editor has to accept the difficulties inherent in the genre as well as his own limitations. It is therefore stating the obvious that what errors and inaccuracies may be found in the following pages are entirely my own.

I have been fortunate in receiving generous assistance and support from a variety of sources, both personal and institutional. The endorsement of the research project in May 2000 by the British Academy was the single most important factor in convincing me that I could bring it to a successful conclusion. My thanks go to Professor Peter Mathias, Professor Michael Thompson, Dr Ken Emond, James Rivington and Janet English. Above all, I am indebted to Professor Peter Dickson for his admirable commitment to the project. I have greatly benefited from his knowledge and historical wisdom and from the invaluable suggestions he kindly made at every stage of the work's progress. *Matheson & Co.* gave me unlimited access to the firm's Archive and supplied the artwork, and it is a pleasure to acknowledge the friendly support I received from its directors, Mr Jeremy Brown, and Mr Martin Barrow, as well as from Mrs Linda Maitland. At the

Cambridge University Library which became my home for several weeks at a time when I pored over the Jardine Matheson manuscripts, my thanks go to Mr D. J. Hall, Deputy Librarian; Dr Patrick Zutshi, Keeper of Manuscripts and University Archives; and in particular to the ever present and helpful Mr John Wells, Under-Librarian, and Mr Godfrey Waller, Superintendent of the Manuscripts Reading Room. Much of my research work was done in the Hong Kong University Library. This was greatly facilitated by my being appointed a Visiting Scholar at the *Centre of Asian Studies* of that university, for which my thanks go to Dr Elizabeth Sinn and Professor Wong Siu-lun. To my own University of Paris-Sorbonne and to my colleagues in the English Department I am greatly indebted for a teaching time-table which has allowed me to complete the project. I am of course most grateful to Professor François Crouzet who, perceiving some historical merit in my initial research on the Jardine Matheson Archive in the late 1990s, was the first to suggest that a case could be made for developing the material and publishing it in the *Records of Social and Economic History* of the British Academy.

Abbreviations

AL — *The Army List*, London, War Office, [1840]. (Published and updated month by month).

BI — *The Bartlett Index*, a manuscript index compiled by Norah Bartlett in the 1950s of in-letters in the Jardine Matheson Archive. (Cambridge University Library Manuscript Reading Room).

BHF — Chris Cook and Brendan Keith, eds., *British Historical Facts, 1830–1900*, London, The Macmillan Press Limited, 1975.

DM — *The Dictionary of Merchandise and Nomenclature, etc. for the use of Counting-Houses*, James Humphreys, Philadelphia, 1805.

DNB — Sir Leslie Stephen and Sidney Lee, eds., *The Dictionary of national Biography* (22 vols. Oxford, reprinted 1959–1960).

DPC — Dodd, Charles D., ed., *The Parliamentary Companion*, London, Whittaker & Co., 1841, 1842, 1843.

EB — Professor Napier Macvey, (ed.), *The Encyclopaedia Britannica*, 7th Edition, Edinburgh, Adam and Charles Black, 1841 1842.

EIRD — *The East India Register and Directory*, London, William H. Allen & Co., 1806 to 1860.

EWH — Stears, Peter N., (ed.), *Encylopaedia of World History*, Cambridge, James Clarke & Co., Cambridge MA, 2001.

GPOAD — Graham, John, (ed.), *The Glasgow Post Office Annual Directory for 1839–1840*, Melville Place, Glasgow.

Hansard — Hansard, Thomas Curson, *Parliamentary Debates*, London, 1839–1843.

JMArch. — The *Jardine, Matheson & Co.* Archive, in the Cambridge University Library.

JRAS	*Journal of the Hong Kong Branch of the Royal Asiatic Society*, Vol.1–40, Hong Kong, 1960–2001
MEB	Boase, Frederic, *Modern English Biography*, Cornwall, privately printed, 1897, London Frank Cass & Co. Ltd., 1965.
NL	*The Navy List*, London, John Murray, (1834–1843).
OED	*Oxford English Dictionary.*
PMSD	Pigot, J., ed., *Manchester and Salford Directory* for 1811, New Cannon Street, Manchester 1811.
PODL	*The Post Office Directory of Lancashire*, London, Kelly & Co., 1858.
PP	*House of Commons Parliamentary Papers*, 1801–1900.
RLD	Robson, William, ed., *London Directory, Street Key and Conveyance List* for 1832, 11, Abchurch Lane, London, 1832.
TLCD	Thompson, R., ed., *London Commercial Directory, Street Guide and Conveyance List* for 1844, 24 College Hill, Cheapside, London, 1844.
Bard, *Traders of Hong Kong*	Bard, Solomon, *Traders of Hong Kong: some Foreign Merchant Houses, 1841–1899*, Hong Kong, Urban Council, 1993.
Bartholomew, *Gazetteer of the British Isles*	Bartholomew, John, (ed.), *Gazetteer of the British Isles*, Edinburgh, (1887), 1962.
Blake, *Jardine Matheson*	Blake, Robert, *Jardine Matheson, Traders of the Far East*, London, Weidenfeld & Nicholson, 1999.
Bulley, *Free Mariner*	Bulley, Anne, *Free Mariner: John Adolphus Pope in the East Indies 1786–1821*, London, Putney, 1992.
Cheong, *Mandarins and Merchants*	Cheong, Weng Eang, *Mandarins and Merchants: Jardine, Matheson & Co, a China Agency of the early nineteenth Century*, London, Curzon Press, 1979.
Choa, *Heal the Sick*	G. H. Choa, *'Heal the Sick' was their Motto, the Protestant Medical Missionaries in China*, Hong Kong, The Chinese University Press, 1990.

Coates, *Macao and the British*	Coates, Austin, *Macao and the British, 1637–1842, Prelude to Hong Kong*, Oxford, Oxford University Press, 1966.
Collis, *Foreign Mud*	Collis, Maurice, *Foreign Mud*, London, Faber and Faber, 1946, reprinted 1965.
Dermigny, *La Chine et l'Occident*	Dermigny, Louis, *La Chine et l'Occident – Le commerce à Canton au XVIIIe siècle*, Volumes I, II, III, IV, Paris, 1964.
Empson, *Mapping Hong Kong*	Empson, Hal, *Mapping Hong Kong, A Historial Atlas*, Hong Kong, Goverment Information Services, 1992.
Endacott, *History of Hong Kong*	Endacott, G. B. *A History of Hong Kong,* Oxford University Press, Hong Kong, (1958), 1993.
Fay, *The Opium War*	Fay, Peter Ward, *The Opium War 1840–1842*, The University of North Carolina Press, Chapel Hill, (1975), 1997.
Fairbank, *Trade and Diplomacy*	John King Fairbank, *Trade and Diplomacy on the China Coast, The opening of the Treaty Ports, 1842–1854*, Stanford, Stanford university Press, 1953, Harvard Reprint, 1969.
Farrington, *Biographical Index*	Farrington, Anthony, (ed.), *A Biographical Index of the East India Company Officers, 1600–1834*, London, The British Museum, 1999.
Farrington, *Catalogue of EIC Ships*	Farrington, Anthony, (ed.), *Catalogue of East India Company Ships, Journals and Logs, 1600–1834*, London, The British Library, 1999.
Garrett, *Heaven is High, etc.*	Garrett, Valery M., *Heaven is High, the Emperor far away, Mandarins in Old Canton*, Hong Kong, Oxford University Press, 2002.
Greenberg, *British Trade*	Greenberg, Michael, *British Trade and the Opening of China, 1800–1842*, Cambridge University Press, 1951.
Hanes & Sonello, *Opium Wars*	Hanes III, W. Travis, and Sanello, Frank, *The Opium Wars*, Naperville, IL., Sourcebooks, Inc., 2002.
Hoe, *The Taking of Hong Kong*	Susanny Hoe, and Derek Roebuck, *The Taking of Hong Kong,* London, Curzon, 1999.
Huang, *China, a Macro History*	Huang, Ray, *China, a Macro History*, Armonk, London, ME., Sharpe, Inc., 1988.

Hucker, *Dictionary of Official Titles*	Hucker, Charles, O., *A Dictionary of Official Titles in Imperial China*, Stanford, Stanford University Press, 1985.
Hunter, *Bits of Old China*	William C. Hunter, *Bits of Old China, 1885*, reprinted Hong Kong, Derwent, 1994, *An American in Canton* (1825–1844).
Hunter, *The Fan Kwae at Canton*	William C. Hunter, *The Fan Kwae at Canton Before Treaty Days* (1825–1844), 1882, reprinted Hong Kong, Derwent, 1994, *An American in Canton* (1825–1844).
Keswick, *The Thistle and the Jade*	Keswick, Maggie, (ed.), *The Thistle and the Jade, A celebration of 150 years of Jardine, Matheson & Co.*, London, Octopus Books Limited, 1982.
Le Pichon, *Origines de Hong Kong*	Le Pichon, Alain, *Aux origines de Hong Kong, Aspects de la civilisation commerciale à Canton, 1827–1839*, Paris, L'Harmattan, 1998.
Low, *Lights and Shadows*	Hodges, Nan P. and Hummel, Arther W., (eds.), *Lights and Shadows of a Macao Life, The Journal of Harriett Low, Travelling Spinster, 1829–1834*, 2 vols., Woodinville, WA, Nan P. Hodges, 2002.
Lust, *Western Books on China*	John Lust, *Western books on China Published up to 1850, in the Library of the School of Oriental and African Studies, University of London, A descriptive Catalogue,* London, Bamboo Publishing, 1987.
McCulloch, *Commercial Dictionary*	McCulloch, J. R. *A Dictionary, Practical, Theoretical, and Historical, of Commerce and Commercial Navigation*, London, Longman, Rees, Orme, Brown, Green & Longman, 1832.
Melson, *Royal Navy in Hong Kong*	Melson, Commodore P. J., ed., *White Ensign, Red Dragon, The History of the Royal Navy in Hong Kong, 1841–1997*, David Tait, Hong Kong, 1997.
Morse, *The Chronicles of the EIC*	Morse, Hosea, Ballou, *The Chronicles of the East India Company trading to China, 1635–1834*, 5 Volumes, Oxford, Clarendon Press, 1926.
Owen, *British Opium Policy*	Owen, David, *British Opium Policy in China and India*, Yale, Yale University Press, 1934, Archon Books, 1968.

Polachek, *The Inner Opium War*	Polachek, James M., *The Inner Opium War*, Cambridge (MA), The Council on East Asian Studies, Harvard University Press, 1992.
Ride, *East India Company Cemetery*	Ride, Lindsay and May, Bernard Mellor (ed.), *An East India Company Cemetery*, Hong Kong, Hong Kong University Press, 1996.
Sutton, *Lords of the East*	Sutton, Jean, *The Lords of the East, The East India Company and its ships, 1600–1874*, London, Cornway Maritime Press, 2000.
Wadia, *Bombay Dockyard*	Wadia, Ruttonjee Ardeshir, *The Bombay Dockyard and the Wadia Master Builders*, Bombay, 1957.

The Jardine Matheson Archive

The Jardine Matheson archive (the 'Archive'), donated to Cambridge University Library by William Keswick in 1934, is of huge extent and is still not completely catalogued. The selection of letters in the present volume (the 'Letters') is only a fraction of the total Out-letters (copies of the firm's letters to correspondents) and In-letters (originals letters from correspondents, including partners when they were absent from Canton). These comprise series C and B respectively of the ten into which the Archive is divided.[1] The principle of selection has been to focus on the main driving forces behind the firm's creation and subsequent business over the period 1827–1843 identified from study of its financial records, contained in series A. These forces include the Calcutta bankruptcies of the late 1820s and early 1830s following widespread speculation in Indian indigo; the ending of the British East India Company's monopoly of the trade in China tea in 1834; the development of a strong banking relationship with the London firm of *Magniac Smith & Co.* from 1836; the acceleration in the 1830s of the trade in Indian opium to China, and the parallel relative failure of exports of English manufactures to China; the Anglo-American banking crisis of 1837; and the collapse of the 'Canton system of trade' between 1836 and 1840, followed by the Opium War of 1840–1842.

[1] See Appendices I and II.

Map of the Far East

Map of China in the early nineteenth century

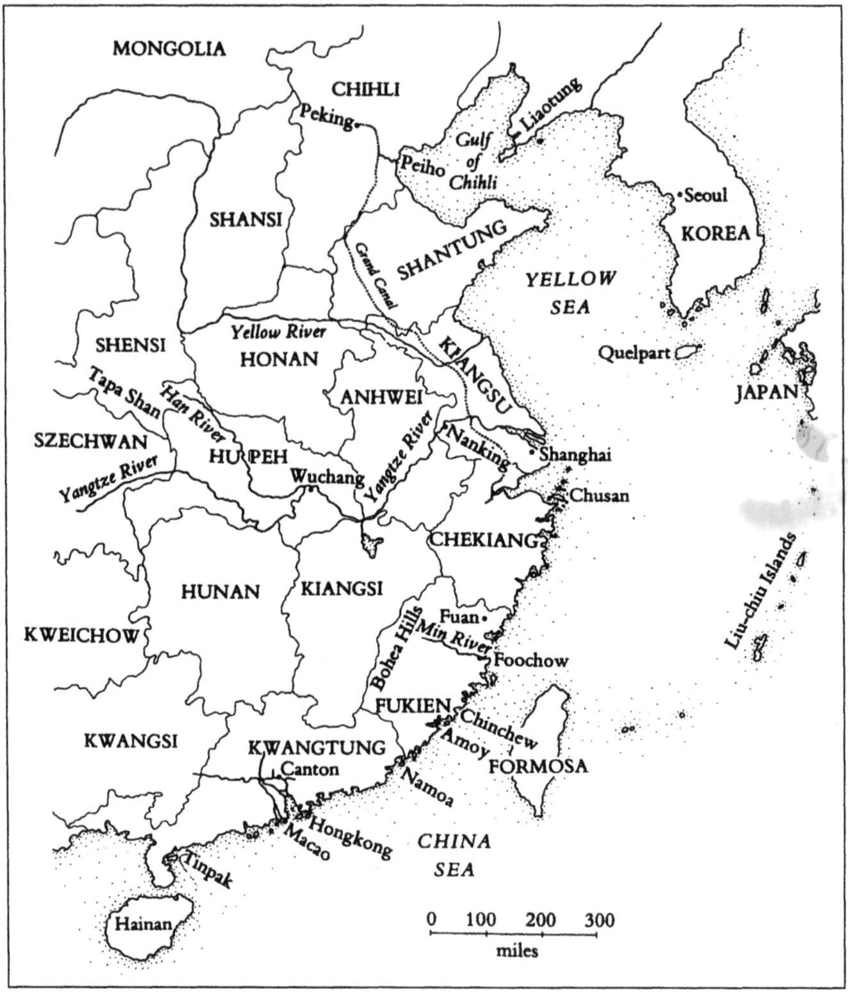

Map of the Pearl River Delta

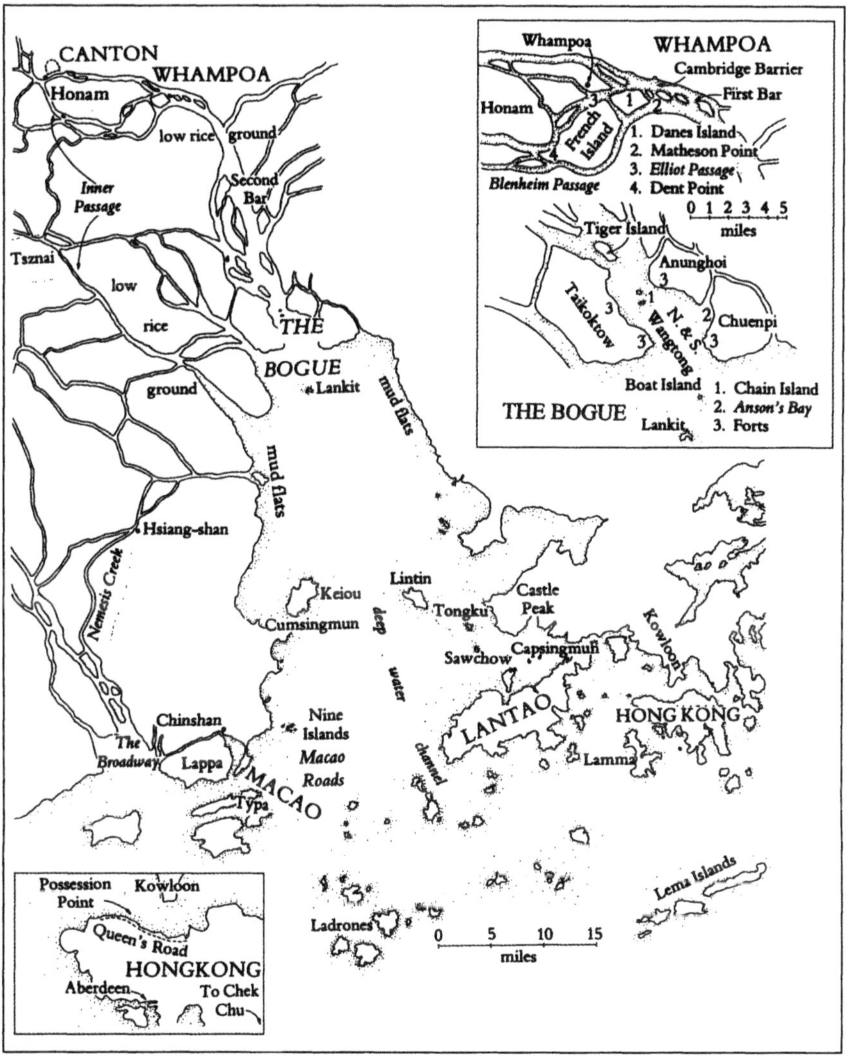

Map of Chusan and the mouth of the Yangtze River

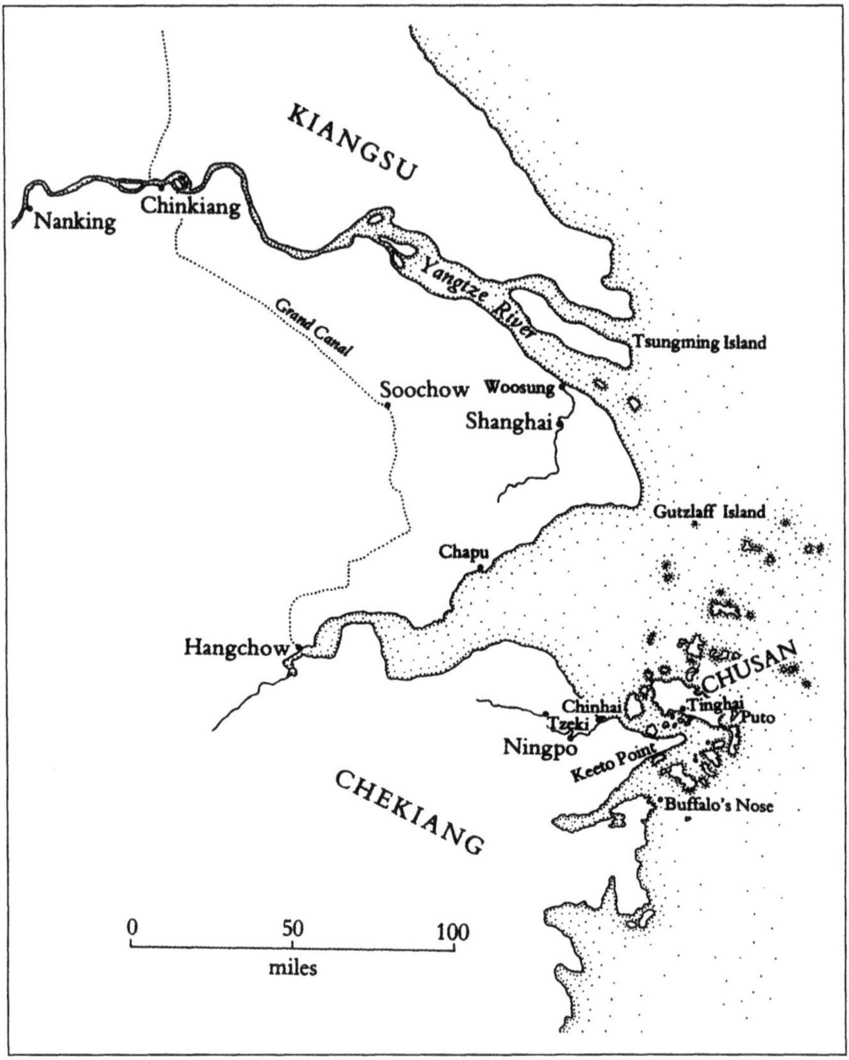

Introduction

1. *Patterns of Eastern Trade, 1784–1834*

The setting for the correspondence in this volume is the Far Eastern trade between Britain, India and China. The English Crown originally granted this trade as a monopoly to the newly-established East India Company in 1600. In the subsequent century and a half, the Company ('John Company') prospered moderately, absorbing the New East India Company of 1698 to become the United East India Company of 1709. It established trading posts ('factories', subsequently Presidencies) at Bombay, Madras and Calcutta, but initially had only limited territorial claims on Indian soil. By the mid-eighteenth century, it was showing a profit of some £600,000 on a turnover around £2 million a year, and paid a dividend of 7–8%.[1] All this changed radically during the Seven Year War of 1756–1763, during which the rival French *Compagnie des Indes*, in alliance with Indian princes, challenged John Company's position. Robert Clive, a writer (clerk) in the Company's service, met the challenge by decisively defeating France's ally, the Nawab of Bengal, at the battle of Plassey on 23 June 1757. In doing so he initiated a complete change in the scale of the Company's trade, and the scope of its territorial power. Cession by the Mogul Emperor of the provinces of Bengal, Bihar and Orissa was followed in August 1765 by his grant to the Company of the *diwani*, or right of revenue collection there. The Company's income soared, enabling Clive and other Company servants to make fortunes. The term 'nabob' for such adventurers is first encountered in 1764. The assumption of the *diwani* also had economic and eventually political consequences far beyond its immediate effect upon the Company's treasury or the winnings of its servants. With the right of collecting land taxes came that of controlling crops to a large extent, and to raise revenue in kind by means of monopolies in articles such as saltpetre and opium.[2] The monopoly over the cultivation of the poppy and the production of opium thus came to the Company with its status as *diwan*. It was subsequently extended to several other parts of India[3] and, by enabling the Company

[1] Marshall, P. J., *Problems of Empire, Britain and India, 1757–1813*, London, George Allen and Unwin Ltd., 1968, p. 82.

[2] Greenberg, *British Trade*, pp. 9–10.

[3] The extension of the monopoly was only partial. Where a full monopoly over the production of opium eluded the Company, it tried—often successfully—to impose a system of transit duties. For a

to control the crop and sell the end-product to merchants for export, it became from the early nineteenth century the principal source of India's ever-increasing opium sales to China, with dramatic consequences, as is explained later.

The promise of immediate prosperity, however, failed to materialize. Against a background of feverish speculation in London in East India stock through the 1760s, the Company's expenses, due to its new territorial power, mounted alarmingly ahead of its revenue. In 1770, they approached £3 million. By 1772, the Company's Indian presidencies had drawn bills which Leadenhall Street[4] lacked the cash resources to meet. Lord North arranged for a state loan of £1.4 million to the Company, saving it from bankruptcy. In return, he asked Parliament to vote the *India Bill* of 1773, or *Regulating Act*. This was 'the first serious attempt to tackle the problem of Indian government by legislation'.[5] Its aim was to restore confidence in the Company by establishing an effective Indian government. It created the post of a Governor-General empowered to rule over the whole of the Company's Indian possessions with the assistance of a council of four men appointed from outside the Company and approved by the directors and the Cabinet. Government was to have access to all correspondence dealing with revenue, political and military subjects. Dividend restrictions were imposed until the state loan was paid back. A Supreme Court was created in Bengal with judges appointed by the Crown.[6] It was unfortunate that the legislation also empowered the Company to demand repayment of English customs duty from American purchasers of re-exported tea. The subsequent Boston Tea Party showed the unwisdom of this. The War of American Independence which followed renewed conflict with the French in India, and drained the Company's resources. By 1780 it was again on the verge of bankruptcy. A new Act, essentially identical to the legislation of 1773, was passed in 1781, but was similarly ineffective. The political will to reform the Company, lacking in 1781, was found by twenty-five year old William Pitt who became Prime Minister in 1783. The *India Act* of 1784 (*Pitt's India Act*) included elements from two rival bills, one of which had been drafted by Fox and Burke, and the other by Dundas. The Company's General Court was finally deprived of its powers to intervene in any question regarding the administration of India. This responsibility was taken over by a Board of Control, made up of six Privy Councillors, including a Secretary of State and the Chancellor of the Exchequer. The Board of Control supervised all matters relating to Indian revenue, administration, war and diplomacy. The Company's Court

discussion of this and related opium monopoly problems, see: Owen, David, *British Opium Policy in India and China*, Yale University Press, (1934), Archon Books, 1968.

[4] The street where India House, the Company's headquarters, was situated.

[5] Marshall, op. cit., p. 33.

[6] John Keay, *The Honourable Company, A History of the English East India Company*, London, Harper Collins, (1991), 1993, pp. 384–386.

continued to oversee trade and patronage. This new legal definition of the relationships between the State and the Company was to remain unaltered until the Company's end in 1858.[7]

From a commercial point of view, however, it was the *Commutation Act* of 1784, a sister piece of legislation to Pitt's *India Act*, which gave the Company a new lease of life. The new Act reduced the duty payable on tea imports from 119% to 12½%. The measure effectively killed tea smuggling, which had become endemic. Annual domestic tea sales which had averaged 6 million pounds soon rose to 19 million pounds as an increasingly urbanized population sustained its demand.[8] The affairs of the Company were now scrutinized in Parliament every year. The increase in consumption and the benefits accruing from the *Commutation Act* enabled it to develop its tea business successfully and to manage this part of its monopoly profitably. In order to pay for ever larger purchases of Chinese tea (China was then the sole producer and exporter of tea in the world), the Company developed its own exports from Europe to Canton and, although it still possessed a theoretical monopoly of all eastern trade, it did not discourage the now growing community of private merchants from shipping their Indian cotton and Bengal opium to China. The proceeds of these private sales in Canton were reinvested in Company bills, and the Company used the cash proceeds of its bill sales to pay for the tea. In 1812, a Select Committee of the House of Commons estimated that between 1793 and 1810 this new triangular China trade had showed a profit of some £17 million pounds.[9] However, the Committee also pointed out that, outside its tea-trading operations, the Company was not prospering. It had accumulated a deficit of £8 million over the years 1792 to 1809, and had borrowed £4 million from the government between 1810 and 1812. Its chronic trade imbalance in favour of India worsened in spite of the large increase in English piece goods shipments from 1786 onwards.[10] Military conflict with France's allies in India between 1793 and 1814 further strained its finances.

[7] Marshall, *Problems of Empire*, op. cit., p. 43.

[8] On the details of the drop in tea duty, see: *PP* 1845 (191) XLVI, pp. 593 and following. On the question of tea smuggling, see: Le Pichon, « L'emploi dans les métiers du thé en Angleterre (1734–1834) », *in* Azuelos, Martine (ed.), 2000, *Travail et Emploi, L'expérience anglo-saxonne, Aspects historiques*, Paris, Presses de la Sorbonne nouvelle, pp. 97–135 ; Mui, Hoh-Cheung, and Mui, Lorna, H., 'Trends in Eighteenth Century Smuggling Reconsidered', *Economic History Review*, Second Series, Vol. 28, 1975, pp. 28–43. More generally on the subject of the Company's handling of its tea monopoly from 1784 to 1834, see: Mui, Hoh-Cheung, and Mui, Lorna, H., *The Management of Monopoly, A Study of the East India Company's Conduct of its Tea Trade, 1784–1833*, Vancouver, University of British Columbia Press, 1984. For the British demand for tea, see also Table 5 below.

[9] Marshall, op. cit., pp. 84–85, quoting *PP* 1812, VI, 11.

[10] Ibid., and p.92, quoting A. Redford, *Manchester Merchants and Foreign Trade, 1784–1858*, Manchester, 1934, p. 112. For a discussion of the trade balance, see the section below, 'The Balance of Trade'.

In this context, the Company applied for parliamentary renewal of its Charter in 1813. Not surprisingly, its overall performance as a trading entity was considered a failure and judged harshly. As a result, the *Charter Act* of 1813 preserved the Company's monopoly only as far as the tea trade was concerned. It allowed British ships to carry other goods freely to and from India. In fact, it legalized what had already happened in practice over a few decades in the eastern sea routes, though not between India and Britain, as is explained below. Now the freedom to trade in products other than tea between London and the Indian ports was obtained by statute, in addition to freedom to trade between India and China and other eastern countries, which had developed outside the law. And it was only a matter of time—twenty years exactly—before the private merchants and the free traders, (William Jardine and James Matheson among them), dislodged the Company from the bastion of its remaining monopoly in the tea trade. In this period, the Company's revenue, though increasing, consistently failed to cover all its expenses. Thus in 1827–1828, its revenue was £23 million, its expenditure £26.1 million, of which nearly £5 million went on debt service. The anomaly of a Company with 'a sword in one had and a ledger in the other', as J. R. McCulloch put it in his *Commercial Dictionary* of 1832, was also unsustainable.[11] With the vote of the 1833 *India Act*, all commerce between Britain and the East as well as within the East itself was finally delivered to British private enterprise as from April 1834. In India, the Company's role had shifted from trader to sovereign. 'Its chief function was now to maintain conditions by which trade could be carried on by others'.[12]

The position of the British in India in the decades before the India Act of 1833 was treated in the older literature as imposition of enlightened Western rule on a backward society; or, in more modern anti-imperial versions, as the insensitive reign of mammon over an ancient culture. Economic development was interpreted as trade with Europe promoted by European East India Companies in general, and John Company in particular. In recent years, these political and economic interpretations have been challenged. Politically, attention has been drawn to the extent of English action within the framework of Mogul rule, often nominally at least as servants of the emperor. As to trade, the fact that Bombay, Madras and Calcutta were all centres of pre-existing local commerce conducted by Indian merchants with links to China and Japan has led historians to the conclusion that increasingly, from 1757 onwards, the threads of indigenous and British capitalism were intertwined, and had started weaving the economic fabric of the 'country trade'.[13] This was essentially the flow of local domestic business

[11] McCulloch, *Commercial Dictionary*, p. 513.

[12] Marshall, op. cit., p. 103.

[13] See the four masterly presidential addresses by P. J. Marshall on 'Britain and the world in the eighteenth century', *Transactions of the Royal Historical Society*, 6th Series, vol. VIII- XI, 1998–2001. See

in which foreigners took an increasing part. The expression later specialized to refer to the flow of imports and exports to and from the Indian ports and the other Asian countries when conducted by Indian and British merchants acting independently from the Company.[14]

The first condition for such ventures was to become rich. The Company's servants had many opportunities of doing so, particularly since Plassey and the assumption of the *diwani* in Bengal. One way was to obtain a sinecure from the Company, such as revenue farming.[15] This was the quickest path to a very large fortune. Another way, often used in conjunction with the first, was to invest jointly with one's banian (a Company servant's or officer's local commercial agent). The Indian banians, as the Muslim mustaddis, and later the Chinese compradors, were all financial and commercial intermediaries whose role was to introduce their foreign masters to lucrative local transactions for their mutual benefit. After Pitt's *India Act* of 1784, Company servants were prohibited from conducting business on their own account alongside their official roles as administrators or agents of the commercial monopoly.[16] It had indeed been a curious paradox of the situation that the first to pursue 'country trade' and to work against the Company's monopolistic interests were in fact its own servants and officers. But once the prohibition of private trading by Company servants became effective, a gentleman could no longer sit on the fence. A choice had to be made—either to remain safely in the Company's service, or to resign and gamble on becoming rich. Many chose to resign and founded Agency Houses.

The first Indian Agency Houses were founded in the 1780s in the three presidencies of India, and the process of their foundation as well as their principal activity is well documented.[17] Typically, a young Company recruit, or the son of a London ship-owning or Company stock-owning family, came to work in India, and after a few years started to buy and sell commodities on his own account.

---

also: Bayly, C. A. *Indian Society and the Making of the British Empire*, Cambridge, C.U.P., 1988; Washbrook, David. A. 'India 1818–1860' in A. Porter (ed.), *The Oxford History of the British Empire III, The Nineteenth Century*, Oxford, O.U.P, 1999.

[14] See C. A. Bayly, *Indian Society and the Making of the British Empire*, p. 46: 'Trade, politics and revenue were so closely intertwined that any successful entrepreneur had to work in all these fields. The British were sucked into the economy by the dynamic of the political economy as much as by their own relentless drive for profit'.

[15] The granting of such farms mirrored the concession of the *diwani* on a smaller scale.

[16] Cornwallis introduced the prohibition in 1786. See: Kumar, Daharma, and Raychaudhuri, Tajan, (ed.), *The Cambridge Economic History of India*, Vol. 2, 1757–1970, p. 816.

[17] See in particular: Sing, S. B., *European Agency Houses in Bengal*, (Calcutta, 1966), p. 240, quoting extracts from the Report to the House of Commons Commission of inquiry of 1832: 'Previously to the present Charter (1813), the houses were chiefly formed of gentlemen who had been in the civil and military services but who perhaps finding their habits better adapted for commercial pursuits, obtained permission to resign their situations and engage in agency and commercial business; they had, of course a great many friends and acquaintances in their respective services who lodged with them their accumulations'.

When he met with success, he registered a new business in partnership with a friend or two. John Palmer, for instance, arrived in Calcutta in the 1780s, and with the fortune he made by speculating in indigo he set himself up as a merchant of independent means. He founded *Palmer & Co.*, one of the oldest Agency Houses in India. When he returned home in 1810 he founded the London firm of *Palmer, Mackillop & Co.*, which started using *Palmer and Co.* as its principal Indian agent, hence the name 'Agency House'. It was indeed a feature of most of the oldest Indian Houses founded by British merchants that they had London parent- or sister-firms which belonged to the same original family and often bore similar names. Conversely, London Houses also sent sons, nephews or younger brothers to India in order to found or assist new Agency operations there. For instance, Palmer's London partner, Mackillop, sent a young relative to Calcutta who, a generation after the founding of *Palmer & Co.*, founded a new Calcutta agency by the name of *Cruttenden Mackillop & Co.*[18]

Much of the business conducted by Agency Houses centred round what would today be called asset- or wealth-management.[19] Company personnel and army officers deposited their savings in the Agency Houses. Rather than acting like modern commercial banks and simply paying depositors a rate of interest, they often 'interested' the depositors in their import and export operations. By pooling resources which belonged to their depositors in order to supplement their own capital, they mounted trading operations, exporting cotton to China, for instance, and reinvesting the Canton proceeds in Indian bills drawn by the Company. Alternatively, if the depositors needed to repatriate their funds to England in view of their approaching retirement, they would reinvest the proceeds of exports to Canton in Company bills drawn in pounds sterling and payable in London. The generic term 'Agency business', implying as it did that the 'agents' were pure intermediaries who were able or willing to shun all ownership risk, and derived their income exclusively from brokerage commissions for their services, was in fact a misnomer. In practice, most agents liked to hasten the process of their own enrichment (or downfall) by mixing speculation in all sorts of commodities with pure or, as the phrase went, 'mere' agency business. (Letter 47).

As Table 1 shows, by the late 1820s, only a few decades after the concept and practice of British 'Agency Houses' had come into existence, there were not less than 10 such firms trading in Madras, 15 in Bombay, and 46 in Calcutta. To this list should be added the 27 principal East India mercantile houses which operated in London. It is of more than anecdotal interest that over half the partners' names

[18] Back in London, the Palmers became ship-owners. In the 1820s, one of the best-known members of the family was Horsley Palmer, the governor of the Bank of England in 1830–1832. (*DNB*). *Cruttenden Mackillop & Co.* was one of *Jardine, Matheson & Co*'s Calcutta correspondents.

[19] On traditional 'agency business', see Greenberg, *British Trade*, pp. 121–124; on the existing variants of what passed as 'agency business', see Le Pichon, *Aux origines de Hong Kong*, pp. 211–277.

Table 1. List of British Agency Houses in India and of London East India Houses in 1830

Madras

Arbuthnot & Co.; Joseph Barrow; *Binny & Co.*; Edward Gordon; *Hall and Bainbridge*; *Parry, Dare & Co.*; William Rutter; *Seth & Gregory*; William Waddell; *Wardrop & Co.*

Bombay

Adam, Skinner & Co.; *Crawford, Thomas & Co.*; *Sir Roger D'Faria & Co.*; *Dirom, Carter & Co.*; *Forbes & Co.*; *Gilder & Co.*; *John Leckie & Co.*; *William Nicol & Co.*; *Saunders & Co.*; *Remington, Crawford & Co.*; *Ritchie, Finlay & Co.*; *Shotton & Co.*; *Stewart, Patrick & Co.*; *Robert Taylor & Co.*; *Owen, Caldecott & Co.*

Calcutta

Alexander & Co.; *Allport & Co.*; *Bagshaw & Co.*; *Barretto & Sons*; Charles Bernard; *Blaney & Co.*; *Bonnaffe & Co.*; *Boyd, Beeby & Co.*; *Breen & Co.*; *Bruce Allen & Co.*; *Buchanan, Munn & Co*; *Carroll & Co.*; George Chisolm; *Colvin & Co.*; *Cruttenden Mackillop & Co.*; *Cumming & Co.*; *Davidson & Co.*; *De Souza & Co.*; Robert Eglinton; *Fergusson & Co*; *Gillander, Ogilvy & Co.*; *Gilmore & Co.*; *Gisborne & Co.*; *Graham & Brewer*; Duncan Ingraham; *Lackersteen & Co.*; *Laprimaunday & Co.*; *J. Mackenzie & Co.*; *Mackintosh & Co.*; *McClintock, Morton & Co.*; *Daniel McDonald & Co.*; *Henry Matthew & Co.*; *Mendieta Uriarte & Co.*; *Ledall & Co.*; *Rennie & Co.*; *Rustomjee Turner & Co.*; *Scott James & Co.*; *Shedden & Co.*; *F. B. Smith & Co.*; *Smithson, Holdsworth & Co.*; *Stewart, Robertson & Co.*; *Sutton & Co.*; *Vrigon & Co.*; *Walker, Rousseau & Co.*; *Wilkinson & Petrie*; *Willis & Earle.*

London

Bazett, Colvin, Crawford & Co.; Henry Blanshard; *William and James Burnie*; *John Campbell; Chalmers & Guthrie*; *J. Cockburn & Co.*; *Cockerell, Trail & Co.*; *Fairlie, Bonham & Co.*; *Fletcher, Alexander & Co.*; *Gregson, Melville, Knight; Hunter & Co.*; *Inglis, Forbes & Co.*; Richard Langslow; *Sir J. W. Lubbock & Co.*; *William Lyall & Co.*; John MacDonald; *Marjoribanks & Ferrers*; *Palmer, Mackillop & Co.*; *William and Thomas Raikes & Co.*; *Rickards, Mackintosh & Co.*; Thomas Saunders Jr.; *Scott, Robert, Fairlie & Co.*; *Small, Colquhoun & Co.*; John Thacker; *Watts & Heath*; Thomas Weeding; *Wigram & Co.*

Source: *EIRD*, 1831.

in these firms were Scottish. William Jardine and James Matheson, whose careers are described later, were therefore often working with fellow-countrymen. Nor does Table 1 include the numerous original Indian, Parsee, and Armenian family firms[20] which were all involved in 'country trade' before country trade even had a name, and with whom the British newcomers had so happily joined forces. As the Company's trading monopoly continued to be eroded, a powerful new group

[20] Members of the Parsee trading community had been established in Bombay for many centuries. They were among traders making their annual visits to Canton in the very first years of the nineteenth century. The 'country trade' was crucially dependent on locally built ships. The Wadias, a Parsee family, had controlled the Bombay ship-building industry since the middle of the 18th century. (See Wadia, *Bombay Dockyard*). Several members of the Armenian community, including the Seths, had settled in Madras. The richest trader in Macao in the late 18th century was an Armenian from Madras, Matheus Joannes. See: Smith, Carl T., 'An Eighteenth-Century Macao Armenian Merchant Prince', *Revista de Cultura*, International Edition, Macao, April 2003, pp. 120–130; Wadia, Rusheed R., 'Colonial Trade and Parsi Entrepreneurs' in Godrej Pheroza J., and Mistree, Firoza Punthakey, (eds.), *A Zoroastrian Tapestry*, Middletown, NJ, Grantha Corporation, 2002, pp. 434–455.

of ambitious independent traders was rising fast in the world of eastern commerce, ready to share the spoils of the tea trade when they became available in 1834.

2. *The Balance of Trade*

To understand the next phase of trade, during which exports of Indian opium to China greatly expanded, creating conditions for the Opium War of 1839–1842, it is necessary to examine India's overall commercial balance. For of all the foreign nations trading in Canton at the time, Britain was alone in being able to exchange not only its own goods for its Canton purchases but also those of its Indian territories. This double-sourcing of 'British' exports to China, of which the lion's share was in fact not Britain's but India's own exports, was paralleled by the dual system of trading just outlined, whereby the Company's official trade was increasingly supplemented by country-traders of all description, including Parsee and Indian merchants, as well as Agency Houses. Both the double-sourcing and the parallel trading helped mask growing trade imbalances with China which eventually led to the Opium War.

The first element in this commercial triangle was the trade between Britain and India. In the decade between 1780 and 1790, India imported British goods worth an annual average of £1.8 million, and exported goods worth £4.2 million to Britain. In spite of its theoretical trade monopoly, the Company carried only 20% of imports and 47% of exports, the rest being shared between the so called 'Clandestine trade' (British traders sailing under foreign flags) and the *bona fide* 'privileged' trading of the Company's supercargoes.[21]

In the first decades of the nineteenth century, India's main imports from Britain were apparel, books and stationery, cotton yarn, cotton piece goods, woollens, manufactured goods, wine and spirits, metals, munitions, dye and paints and maritime stores. The principal exports to Britain were coffee, raw cotton, indigo, silk, and saltpetre. India had long had a lead in cotton goods of all qualities. By 1813, the product of British manufactures started competing successfully with the cheaper ranges of Indian cotton goods. As a result, export of these articles to India grew from 800,000 to 14 million yards between 1814 and 1820.[22] As Table 2 shows, however, this was insufficient to redress the balance of trade to Britain's

[21] Kumar, Dharma, and Raychaudhury, Tajan, (eds.), *The Cambridge Economic History of India*, Vol. 2, 1757–1970, Cambridge, C.U.P., 1983, p. 816. The desire to counter the large share of India's imports carried by the 'clandestine trade' helped gain concessions to the British private traders when the Company's charter was renewed in 1793. Private traders could now claim 3,000 tons of shipping of the Company at reduced freight rates of £5 per ton outward and £15 inward.

[22] Marshall, P. J., *Problems of Empire*, etc., p. 87.

Table 2. India's balance of trade with Britain 1828–29 to 1839–40 (Rupees '000,000)

Year	Merchandise	Bullion	Balance
1828–29	18.9	3.1	22.0
1829–30	30.2	8.1	38.3
1830–31	11.4	5.3	16.7
1831–32	5.6	16.9	22.5
1832–33	14.0	11.6	25.6
1833–34	12.5	4.7	17.2
1834–35	13.9	0.5	14.4
1835–36	21.2	0.1	21.3
1836–37	23.9	0.0	23.9
1837–38	15.1	0.5	15.6
1838–39	15.7	−0.3	15.4
1839–40	25.4	−4.4	21.0

Source: K. N. Chaudhuri, 'India's foreign trade and the cessation of the East India Company's trading activities, 1828–1840, *Economic History Review*, 2nd Series, vol. XIX, 1966, pp. 358–359.[23]

advantage. Trade flows had long shown a balance in India's favour and, over the decade 1828 to 1838, it continued to show a large Indian annual surplus averaging 21.8 million Rupees (over £2 million) in both merchandise and bullion.

India's trade surplus in merchandise with China was even larger than its surplus with Britain. It rose from Rs.21 million in 1828–1829 to Rs.61.9 million in 1836–1837 (or the sterling equivalent of £6 million).[24] As will be shown below, this was largely due to the large increase in opium exports to China over the period. The return to a relatively modest surplus in merchandise of Rs. 10.1 million at the end of the period can be ascribed to the trade disruptions caused by the Opium War.

Where the trading patterns with China proved very different to those with Britain was in the bullion balance. Whereas India was usually a net exporter of bullion to Britain except in the last two years under review, it was a large net importer of gold and silver from China. Bullion imports peaked in the year 1837–1838 at the equivalent of £1.7 million, and still stood at around £400,000 during the first full year of the Opium War. Overall, net imports of bullion from China amounted to the large figure of Rs.139.7 million (or over £13 million) between 1828 and 1840. The Chinese had therefore every reason to feel that silver and gold were being drained out of their country.

[23] A positive figure indicates a balance favourable to India. Conversely, a negative figure indicates a balance favourable to Britain. The figures are expressed in Current Rupees (The Bengal currency). When approximate equivalents are given in £, the rupees (CRs) have been converted at the rate of £1=Sp$4.28=CR10.44. 'Sp$' is the abbreviation for 'Spanish dollars', the currency often used in eastern foreign trade at the time. It is simply referred to below as 'dollars' or '$').

[24] See Table 3.

Table 3. India's balance of trade with China 1828–29 to 1839–40 (Rupees '000,000)

Year	Merchandise	Bullion	Balance
1828–29	21.0	−10.8	10.2
1829–30	22.1	−13.7	8.4
1830–31	21.2	−9.6	11.6
1831–32	33.8	−5.6	28.2
1832–33	29.0	−5.9	23.1
1833–34	42.0	−13.1	28.9
1834–35	31.4	−12.1	19.3
1835–36	50.4	−13.9	36.5
1836–37	61.9	−12.3	49.6
1837–38	40.6	−17.4	23.2
1838–39	40.7	−21.3	19.4
1839–40	10.1	−4.0	6.1

Source: K. N. Chaudhuri, 'India's foreign trade and the cessation of the East India Company's trading activities, 1828–1840, *Economic History Review*, 2nd Series, vol. XIX, 1966, pp. 358–359.

A full appreciation of India's balance of trade can only be reached when individual balances with all the countries with which it traded are taken into account. The general trade figures show that India was a substantial net exporter of merchandise, and a large net importer of bullion. Overall, it recorded a large trade surplus (in round figures) of between Rs. 40 million and Rs.70 million, or *circa* £4 to £6 million (Table 4). Over the period under consideration, however, this trade surplus was counter-balanced by reverse financial flows on the balance of payments. These were made up of India's annual debt service to Britain as its principal creditor, (£3–4 million), loan repayments, and private remittances (£0.5–1.5 million).[25]

The commercial pattern just described was the newest in a much longer history of English trade with China. John Company and other European East India Companies had been trading at Canton since the first half of the 17th century. A few other Chinese ports like Amoy and Ningpo had been open to foreign ships, but over time Canton had become the most active, thanks to the regular system of trading which it developed, known as 'the Canton system'. The system successfully fulfilled two essential requirements: it collected port taxes and other duties which brought a regular flow of funds to the imperial treasury, and it ensured the proper control of foreigners. As a result, the Chinese decided to close down all other ports to foreigners in 1757, and China trade became synonymous with 'Canton trade'.

[25] Chaudhuri, op. cit., p. 359. In both tables 3 and 4 bullion imports by India mostly denote payments by China of an import bill which it could not fully cover by exporting goods. They therefore lessened the amount owed on commodity trade.

Table 4. Overall Indian trade balance 1828–29 to 1839–40 (Rupees '000,000)

	Mechandise			Bullion			
Year	Exports	Imports	Balance	Exports	Imports	Balance	Balance
1828–29	111.3	53.6	57.7	4.6	20.4	−15.8	41.9
1829–30	125.3	50.1	75.2	8.9	21.9	−13.0	62.2
1830–31	105.7	56.5	49.2	5.7	16.7	−11.0	38.2
1831–32	97.8	44.7	53.1	17.9	11.2	6.7	59.8
1832–33	101.3	41.7	59.6	13.1	12.1	1.0	60.6
1833–34	113.7	40.6	73.1	5.5	18.9	−13.4	59.7
1834–35	101.5	42.7	58.8	1.4	20.0	−18.6	40.2
1835–36	138.6	46.0	92.6	0.4	22.4	−22.0	70.6
1836–37	158.7	54.2	104.5	1.1	20.1	−19.0	85.5
1837–38	119.1	48.3	70.8	2.6	26.3	−23.7	47.1
1838–39	126.5	50.7	75.8	1.2	29.9	−28.7	47.1
1839–40	119.5	56.5	63.0	2.8	19.6	−16.8	46.2

Source: K. N. Chaudhuri, 'India's foreign trade and the cessation of the East India Company's trading activities, 1828–1840, *Economic History Review*, 2nd Series, vol. XIX, 1966, pp. 358–359.

The first private traders started arriving in the 1760s. A few came from Britain, (sometimes to collect bad debts as there were as yet no agents on the spot to do this for them),[26] but many more came from India. This was a time when the Company had not yet fully harnessed the exporting potential of Indian commodities, nor adequately responded to the Chinese demand for raw cotton. Indian country traders from the Gujarat and Madras areas were much more nimble. They saw a market opportunity and exploited this cotton export niche successfully. It is also at this time that opium started rising to prominence in Indian exports to China. The Chinese authorities promulgated their first anti-opium edict in 1799, which provides a measure of the Indian country traders' success as opium exporters. The Chinese ban on the exportation of gold and silver, however, came only a decade later, in 1809, reflecting the fact that it took some time for the authorities to establish a causal link between the increasing imports of opium and a parallel increase in bullion exports.[27]

[26] This was the case of John Henry Cox, the son of a famous London clock, automaton, and 'sing-song' maker. The ornate sing-songs adorned with jewels were given as presents to mandarins by those who courted their favours. Cox arrived in Canton in 1787 to collect payments due to his father on earlier shipments. He founded one of the early private British firms in Canton, which was a direct ancestor of *Jardine, Matheson & Co.*

[27] In these developments we follow Cheong, Weng Eang's *Mandarins and Merchants*, pp. 9–16. Cheong's sources include the principal East India Company records of the period, in particular the Canton Consultation papers, the Canton diaries, the Canton Agency Consultations, the Secret Consultations, as well as the Bengal, Bombay, and Madras Consultations, and the Indian Presidencies Reports on private external trade.

At the turn of the nineteenth century, total annual exports from China to India averaged some 1.5 million Taels (or under £500,000).[28] Sugar and sugar products accounted for 25% of the exports; raw silk, silk piece goods, teas and tutenag[29] together made up another 62%. China's imports from India amounted to 4 million Taels (or £1.3 million). Cotton was the first import with 50% of the total, followed by tin and opium. It also imported pepper, camphor, woods and a variety of seafood products. This left China with a negative trade balance of some 2.5 million Taels (£800,000). Over the next three decades China's chronic trade deficit which was mostly caused by the growth in the 'country trade' imports from India, worsened to reach three times this figure.[30]

What accelerated this growing trade gap was the presence in Canton from 1813 of a few permanent Agency Houses modelled on the Indian pattern (see Table 1 above), and active in all sectors of commercial activity, except (until 1834) the tea trade. Before 1813, private traders resident in Canton often lacked a large enough network of constituents and the pooling of financial resources that went with it to be continuously busy throughout the year. By the 1820s, however, five Agency Houses had established positions in Canton and a large flow of recurring business. Three of them were Parsee Houses (M. Framjee, M. Merwanjee, and F. Cursetjee); one was Anglo-Basque (*Yrisarri & Co.*); and two were British (*Magniac & Co., and Dent & Co.*).[31] It was from two of these firms, *Magniac & Co.*, and *Yrisarri & Co.*, that the partnership of William Jardine and James Matheson emerged in 1832, as is shown later.

The trade figures show that China was in credit with John Company before 1833, but in deficit with the private traders. In the seventeen years between 1817 and 1833, China's imports from the Company showed no growth at all and averaged $4.6 million a year (£1.1. million).[32] About half these imports were woollens from Britain. The other half was made up of cotton and cotton goods, some from Britain, and some from India. China's sole export to the Company (apart from bullion) was tea. Exports of various teas rose from 24 to 29 million lbs. between 1825 and 1829 and then levelled off at around 30 million lbs. until 1833.[33] For these teas the Company paid an average of $7.9 million a year (£1.8 million). Seen in the sole light of official Company trade, therefore, Britain was running up a trade deficit with China accumulating at the rate of some £700,000

[28] The exchange rates used are: £1=3.086 Taels; 1Tael = $1.388; £1 = $4.28. (Morse, *Chronicles*, Vol. IV, p. 260).

[29] The term 'tutenag' refers to the zinc imported into Europe from China and the East Indies during the eighteenth century.

[30] See Table 3 above.

[31] These five firms were the principal purchasers of Company bills on India and on England in the 1820s. See: Cheong, op. cit., pp. 97 and 101, compiled from EIC Canton Diaries, vols. 218 to 241.

[32] See Table 5 below.

[33] On tea imports during the period, see *PP* 1845, (191), XLVI, pp. 593 and following.

Table 5. China balance of trade with Britain (Company and private trade) 1817–1833 ($ '000,000)

	Imports			Exports			
Year	EIC	Private	Total	EIC	Private	Total	Balance
1817	5.0	8.7	13.7	6.1	3.6	9.7	−4.0
1818	4.3	8.7	13.0	5.9	4.1	10.0	−3.0
1819	4.2	4.4	8.6	8.0	3.7	11.7	3.1
1820	4.9	10.1	15.0	8.3	5.1	13.4	−1.6
1821	4.9	9.1	14.0	8.0	5.7	13.7	−0.3
1822	3.7	13.3	17.0	8.5	4.2	12.7	−4.3
1823	5.2	10.9	16.1	8.7	4.0	12.7	−3.4
1824	5.2	10.9	16.1	8.0	4.0	12.0	−4.1
1825	5.2	15.7	20.9	8.2	5.3	13.5	−7.4
1826	5.9	15.7	21.6	9.4	4.3	13.7	−7.9
1827	4.5	15.8	20.3	8.5	3.6	12.1	−8.2
1828	4.9	15.4	20.3	7.7	6.3	14.0	−6.3
1829	4.5	18.4	22.9	7.5	6.3	13.8	−9.1
1830	4.2	17.4	21.6	7.8	5.3	13.1	−8.5
1831	3.7	16.8	20.5	7.8	5.2	13.0	−7.5
1832	4.0	18.3	22.3	8.0	4.6	12.6	−9.7
1833	4.4	19.1	23.5	7.7	5.8	13.5	−10.0

Source: Greenberg, British Trade, p. 217. (A compilation and simplification of Morse's balance of trade tables).

a year over a long period of time. In the eighteenth century, the Company had exported silver to China in order to bridge this trade gap, but the practice had been criticised by the British authorities and was discontinued after 1805, save for four subsequent years (1816, 1817, 1821 and 1824).[34]

The figures for the private trade, however, contrast sharply with those of the Company trade. Between 1817 and 1833 Chinese imports from the Indian country trade more than doubled, rising from $8.7 million to $19.1 million (or from £2 million to £4.5 million). Towards the end of the period, some 50% of these were imports of Indian opium and 25% imports of Indian cotton. But whilst China's imports more than doubled, its exports to the private trade remained virtually static, averaging $4.8 million a year (or £1.1 million a year). Raw silk and silk piece-goods were the first items of exports, with over 50% of the total, followed by sugar and other foodstuffs. Overall, therefore, private British trade was accumulating a surplus against China at the average rate of $8.7 million a year (£2.0 million), whilst the Company was running a parallel trade deficit accumulating at the annual average the rate of £0.7 million. It was Britain's good fortune, as sovereign over large parts of India and in sole control of Bengal opium production, to be able to offset the trade deficit resulting from its Chinese tea

[34] See Cheong, op. cit., p. 19.

purchases against the trade surplus resulting from the Indian private trade. In round figures, this set-off exercise resulted in an overall trade deficit against China accumulating at the average rate of £1.3 million a year (£2 million surplus minus £0.7 million deficit), a sum equivalent to China's average annual exports of bullion to India.[35]

The administrative and political complications of trade with China were significant. Examination of the 'Canton system' of trading, as it had developed since 1757, shows that it rested crucially upon the role of the Hoppo, or revenue commissioner. As opposed to his three local peers in rank, the Governor General of the Province (the Viceroy of Canton), the Governor of the City of Canton, and the Tartar General of the Manchu garrison in Canton, the Hoppo was not a professionally trained administrator. He belonged to the 'boyi' class whose members were hereditary servants of the imperial family. He alone was in charge of foreign trade, and his appointment was usually for a period of three years. His principal function was to channel a portion of the earning of the port of Canton to the imperial Treasury. His control of the port activities and revenues was consolidated by the imperial decree of 1760 which accorded legal existence to the hong merchants (trade monopolists, see below) and to the Hoppo's authority over them. When foreign traders were finally prohibited from direct intercourse with the Viceroy and the Governor general in 1782, the Hoppo's control over foreign trade and its growing financial resources was complete.[36] He exercised it through four groups of socio-professional agents who had to be individually licensed—the river pilots, the compradors, the linguists, and the hong merchants.

The Pearl River, with its numerous mud flats and shallows was treacherous to all ships, especially to large Company ships. This provided the Hoppo with the most practical means of subjecting and keeping foreigners under his control. No vessel could sail up from the Macao Roads (the waters near Macao where the River delta meets the open sea) to Whampoa (the port of Canton) without an official pilot being appointed to guide her. Once in Whampoa, (the river was too shallow for ships to sail further up river, though Canton was still 20 miles away), all import goods had to be transhipped to official sampans on their way to Canton, with a parallel process applying to export goods. All transhipping and movement of goods was supervised by the Hoppo's men. The compradors were Chinese caretakers officially licensed to provide food and chandlery services to the thousands of foreigners present in and around Canton during the trading season. The compradors were attached to foreigners' factories and to the captains' ships, and prior to 1842 their role was confined to that of provision suppliers with attendant book-keeping duties. The 'linguists' were Chinese officials appointed by the

[35] The average bullion export from China to India as calculated from table 4 above comes to 11.6 million rupees (£1.1 million).

[36] Cheong, Op. cit., pp. 15–16.

Hoppo to the crucial task of keeping the accounts of export and import duties of all the foreign ships and their cargoes.[37] They were also responsible for handling disputes with foreign traders, organizing meetings with the Chinese authorities, and acting as go-betweens for foreign traders and the Chinese customs service whenever the need arose. The 'hong merchants' were a group of twelve merchants (together the Co-hong) who were exclusively licensed to handle China's foreign trade. As such they were (or were meant to be) the only Chinese merchants dealing with the foreign traders, warehousing and buying their foreign goods and conversely selling them Chinese exports. One of their more important functions was to act as security agents and guarantors for all the amounts due by the foreign merchants. When foreign ships were ready to sail after loading their return cargoes, permission to leave Whampoa had first to be obtained from the Hoppo's office. The Hoppo finally delivered his 'grand chop' once his officers had established that all dues had been paid—port entry tax ('ship measurement'), import and export duties, and all official payments to the pilots, to the compradors, to the linguists, and to the hong merchants.

With the passing of time, a combination of market forces, technical advance, enlarged business flows in illicit trade, and increased financial sophistication undermined the Canton system. By the mid-1830s, flat-bottomed steam boats were leading to the redundancy of the pilots' function. Compradors were becoming closer to the foreigners who paid their salaries and eventually their licence fees than to the Hoppo's men. The linguists' role as financial adjuncts to duty-collection was being undermined by the growth of the hidden opium trade, whilst their translating and communicating function was being overtaken by the prevalence of pidgin-English for the conduct of mercantile transactions. The hong merchants' principal role as guarantors of commercial transactions with foreigners and as upholders of the Hoppo's tax collection system was collapsing under the weight of their own debts and bankruptcies, and the concomitant rise of the 'outside' (unlicensed) Chinese merchants. Thus, in spite of its success and resilience over a long period of years, the Canton system eventually gave way to the forces of modernity imported from the West. Some of its weakest points were its sole reliance on personal virtue in senior personnel and its remarkable lack of checks and balances, both of which were exposed by the quite sudden rise in imports of Indian opium in the 1830s. Not surprisingly, greed and extortion flourished at all levels of the hierarchy as the value of the opium trade accelerated. Imperial edicts against opium imports and consumption were now flouted by the very people who were meant to eradicate the trade. More profoundly, the Canton system was

[37] In this paragraph on the four principal functional aids to the Hoppo's control of foreign trade, we follow the most recent scholarly analysis of the 'Canton system' by Paul Arthur Van Dyke's *Port Canton and the Pearl River Delta*, Ph.D. Dissertation, University of Southern California, Ann Arbor, ProQuest Company, 2003.

essentially the product of a system of political governance which denied the mercantile, money-making class true recognition in society. In a country where mastery of literary, philosophical and artistic skills as sanctioned in the imperial examinations was the only path to social position, administrative monopoly and political power, this system of trading served its purpose for a time. It made a financial contribution to the imperial treasury whilst keeping the mercantile communities, both domestic and foreign, pent up harmlessly in the splendid isolation of their factories. Once those who had become rich from trade and industry (toil) also yearned for power and influence, the Canton system was doomed and China had to start the long process of re-inventing herself.[38]

The growth of the Canton trade which surged at about the time when *Jardine, Matheson & Co.* acquired its name (1832) is inseparable from two financially related world events—England's adoption of tea as one of its national drinks in the late eighteenth century, and China's parallel addiction to opium two decades later.

In 1773, tea imported by the Company and sold to the home consumer amounted to 3.8 million lbs., though the annual average for the ten years to 1773 had been over 6 million lbs. In 1843, with a population which had more than doubled, the total amount sold for domestic consumption had grown to 40.3 million lbs. With the *Commutation Act* of 1784 and the drastic lowering of duties tea consumption soared,—14.8 million lbs. in 1785; 21.3 million lbs. in 1795; 24.3 million lbs. in 1805; 25.9 million lbs. in 1815; 29.2 million lbs. in 1825, etc.—, a trend which was to continue well into the twentieth century.[39] With the English Treasury deriving an annual average of £3.5 million from tea duties in the early decades of the nineteenth century, it was clear that tea had become an addiction not only to the British consumer but also to the government.

A question which arose each year in Canton where the Select Committee of the Company was directing its China trade operations was how to pay for the tea.

[38] In his *Wealth of Nations*, Adam Smith repeatedly alluded to China, to her wealth compared with that of European countries, to the virtual absence of foreign trade, and to its land tax system which he saw as conducive to the development of a good network of roads and canals. He did not criticize the highly monopolistic 'Canton system' of trade as such, his critical analyses of monopolies being aimed at targets much closer to home. See 'China' and 'Monopoly' in the 'Index of subjects' (vol. 2, pp. 439–500) in: Cannan, Edwin, (ed.), *An Inquiry into the Nature and Causes of the Wealth of Nations* by Adam Smith, 2 vols. London, Methuen & Co., 1904.

[39] For the figures of domestic tea consumption, and for the annual amounts of duty paid, see: *PP* 1845 (191) pp. 593 ff. For the effect of the *Commutation Act*, see above, note 14. Production of tea in British India started in the late 1830s and early 1840s and later in Ceylon (Sri Lanka). But Indian tea did not reach the London market in sizeable quantities until the 1870s and 1880s. When large quantities of tea reached the domestic market from the colonies, however, it further fuelled domestic consumption and marked a radical and final decline of Chinese tea exports to Britain. See: Le Pichon, Alain, 'Le premier thé de l'Inde britannique: du rêve à la réalité', *Cahiers victoriens et édouardiens*, No 55, 2002; and : 'Les entrepreneurs et la distribution du thé en Angleterre, 1834–1934', *L'entrepreneur et la dynamique entrepreneuriale, l'expérience anglo-saxone*, Paris, Economica, 2003.

There were four ways in which the Company could and did pay for its tea. It could ship bullion from Britain or from India; it could sell British goods; it could sell Indian goods; and it could borrow. These four methods of payment were usually used concurrently, in varying degrees, although the Company largely stopped shipping bullion as a means of payment after 1805.[40]

The Company also sold British and Indian goods, but this never covered the cost of its tea imports. It left a gap which could be as low as $1.1 million (£260,000) as in 1817, or as high as $4.8 million (£1.1 million) as in 1822.[41] The cumulative shortfall for the period 1817–1833 amounted to no less than $55.4 million (£13 million), giving an annual average shortfall of $3.3 million (approximately £800,000). To cover this shortfall the Company had to borrow. With the growth of the Indian country trade, the development of opium sales, and also the arrival of ever more numerous American traders, there was usually no shortage of liquidity in the Canton market. The exception was during the period 1819–1823, when China's balance of trade showed smaller deficits than usual. This meant that private merchants did not have sufficient liquidity to satisfy both their immediate trade investment needs and the Company's credit requirement. It was this temporary lack of liquidity and resulting difficulty in borrowing which forced the Company to ship bullion to Canton in 1821 and 1824.

Generally, however, the Canton market was highly liquid. Much of this liquidity was immediately re-invested by private traders in Chinese goods like silk and sugar as export 'return' to India. Once these returns had been purchased, the traders and the Agency Houses used up any excess cash either to buy bullion and ship it to India,[42] or to purchase Company bills drawn either on India or on London. They bought Company bills drawn on India when they wanted liquid proceeds of their Canton sales to be available in their respective Indian presidencies; and they bought Company bills drawn on London when they needed sterling in their accounts with their London agents.[43] For a long time the Company was the only entity of sufficient standing and credit-worthiness to borrow in the Canton market. Private bills were occasionally seen in the market, but they were not used as a general means of payment between trading parties. Things started changing in the third decade of the century with the arrival of American bills which fuelled inflation and speculation in the commodities markets. The

[40] See note 34 above.

[41] See Table 5 above.

[42] See Table 4 above, showing the net bullion transfers from China to India.

[43] From an examination of Table 5 can be derived two series of figures which are of special interest here. Subtracting column 4 (Company exports from China) from column 1 (Company imports into China) gives the amount which the Company needed to borrow to cover its tea purchases. Subtracting the figures thus obtained from column 7 (Company plus private balance of trade with China) gives the amount available for the return investment of the private trade. Obviously, such reconstruction has only indicative value.

Americans traders were increasingly present in Canton from 1814, after the end of the 1812 War with Britain. As had happened with the Company, they were unable to cover their tea and other purchases with their exports of goods to China, and they continued shipping bullion to cover their shortfall at the average rate of $3.6 million a year from 1816 to 1833. From 1827, however, they supplemented their declining bullion shipments with bills typically drawn by American cotton exporters on London Houses. When they found that they could easily sell these bills in Canton to private traders and Agency Houses, in order to generate cash used for their Chinese returns, they came back year after year with more bills. With the addition of $4.8 million worth of American bills brought to Canton in 1833 alone, the market became more liquid than it had ever been, and this was a contributory factor to the speculation in opium which then took off.[44]

What funds the Company needed and was able to borrow in Canton largely came from cash sales realized by Indian and British traders speculating in Indian commodities. Over time, the principal source of these cash sales became opium. It is in this sense that Indian opium can be said to have paid for Chinese tea consumed in Britain. Since the acquisition of the *diwani*, the culture, manufacture, and auction sales of opium were a monopoly of the Company in Bengal. Elsewhere in India it had negotiated with the local princes to gain control of the drug's movements and sales. Once sold to private traders, the Company had nothing more to do with opium. Outwardly, it therefore maintained a scrupulous observance of the Chinese imperial edicts which since 1799 had repeatedly banned the import of opium. In reality, it could not have survived financially without the proceeds from opium sales which the private trade invested in its bills. Britain's obligations to China were thus neatly settled through the ability of Indian agriculture to produce a large crop of opium poppy, the eagerness of the Chinese to pay cash for the drug, and the willingness of British and Indian merchants to trust that the paper they took from the Company in exchange for their own cash would eventually be honoured.

As Table 6 shows, it took sixteen years, from 1809 to 1824, for opium shipments to double and reach close to 9,000 chests. From then on, the quantities doubled every seven or eight years to reach over 40,000 chests at the start of the Opium War. In the absence of statistical data about contemporary retail sales and consumption patterns, general factors must be relied upon to account for this huge increase in opium imports by China. These factors include the addictive quality of the drug, the relative decline in its price over the period, the availability of a large and (from the Company's point of view) lucrative supply, the greed of middlemen, and the abundant market liquidity leading to heightened speculation.

[44] For American Imports of Silver and bills, see: Cheong, Op. cit., p.54, quoting figures derived from K. S. Latourette, *Transactions of the Connecticut Academy*, Vol. XXII, 1917.

Table 6. Growth of opium shipments from India to China 1809–1839 (In chests '000 – y/e June)

Year	Bengal	Malwa	Total	Year	Bengal	Malwa	Total
1809	3.2	1.0	4.2	1825	6.0	6.7	12.7
1810	3.1	1.5	4.6	1826	3.8	5.6	9.4
1811	3.6	1.4	5.0	1827	6.6	5.6	12.2
1812	2.8	2.1	4.9	1828	6.7	5.5	12.2
1813	3.3	1.6	4.9	1829	4.9	7.7	12.6
1814	3.2	2.6	5.8	1830	7.4	8.1	15.5
1815	3.0	0.7	3.7	1831	5.7	12.9	18.6
1816	2.7	1.5	4.2	1832	6.8	9.3	16.1
1817	3.4	1.2	4.6	1833	7.6	14.0	21.6
1818	2.9	0.8	3.7	1834	7.8	11.7	19.5
1819	2.6	1.0	3.6	1835	10.2	11.7	21.9
1820	1.7	2.3	4.0	1836	14.9	15.4	30.3
1821	2.6	1.7	4.3	1837	12.6	21.4	34.0
1822	3.3	2.3	5.6	1838	19.6	14.8	34.4
1823	3.2	3.9	7.1	1839	18.2	22.0	40.2
1824	3.4	5.5	8.9				

Source: Cheong, op. cit., p. 21. The compilation is based on series found in the Canton diaries of the East India Company.

It is not possible to assess the precise market value of these opium shipments. Like that of all agricultural commodities, the market price of opium fluctuated wildly from year to year, as indeed within the same trading season. It was dependent on a number of factors, including provenance, quality, packaging, shipping and insurance costs, demurrage, etc. In the year of *Jardine, Matheson & Co.*'s foundation (1832), the overall value of opium exported to China was officially recorded as $11.6 million (£2.7 million),—well in excess of the overall value of tea imported by the Company ($7.7 million, or £1.8 million). During that same year the market price per chest of Bengal opium fluctuated between $940 and $625, and of Malwa opium between $720 and $490.[45] The disappointingly low prices achieved by Malwa led William Jardine to imagine a scheme whereby he would corner the entire market with the help of his Bombay friends (Letter 61). Whilst the scheme was never actually put in practice, the episode says much about the reliance of private traders on opium to make their fortunes quickly.

Although smoking opium was not a native Chinese practice and was probably introduced over time by a combination of Western, Arab, and Javanese sailors and traders, it became established in the late eighteenth and early nineteenth centuries as the standard way of consuming opium in China.[46] Once established, the addiction spread rapidly first along the coast and among the idle rich who alone could

[45] The figures a quoted by Morse in his *Chronicles,* Vol. IV, p. 341.

[46] On the origins of opium smoking in China, see: Booth, Martin, *Opium, A History*, London, Simon & Schuster, 1996, pp. 103–107.

initially afford the expensive luxury, and afterwards, with ever-growing and cheaper supplies from India in the third and fourth decades of the century, to a wider cross-section of China's large population.

A chest contained on average 120 lbs of opium. The 40,000 chests imported or smuggled into China in 1839–1840 contained therefore some 4.8 million pounds of opium. By way of comparison, Britain was at the time importing some 40,000 pounds of the drug annually, mostly from Turkey. Later in the century, during the period 1860–1881, when laudanum was consumed relatively freely, there was not a single year when net imports of opium to Britain exceeded 400,000 pounds.[47] By a most bizarre and irreversible game of international seesaw, tea which had been drunk for two millennia by the Chinese had been adopted—and adapted—by the British for their own use in order to feel better. And opium, which had been known for an equally long time as a pain-killer, and was produced in abundance in Britain's new Indian territories, was conversely adopted by the Chinese as an article that also made them feel better. Both commodities gave rise to an immense flow of clandestine trade. In mid-eighteenth century England, half the tea delivered to the consumer was contraband tea. In the 1830s China, 100% of the banned opium imports represented as much as half of the country's entire imports. Smuggling, an action traditionally conducted under cover of darkness and in great secrecy had developed into an open daytime activity. Pitt's elegant solution had been to kill the smugglers' margin by paring the duty on legal imports to the bone. Having unwisely banned all opium imports without having the means to enforce the ban, the Chinese emperor did not have a similar option open to him and Commissioner Lin's radical cure was eventually to prove more expensive than the disease.[48]

3. *Jardine, Matheson & Co., 1827–1843*

This was the background against which the foundation and rise of *Jardine, Matheson & Co.* must be set. At the time of its official foundation in 1832, the Agency House which became known as *Jardine, Matheson & Co.* had existed, in one form or another, for some forty-five years. The origins of the firm dated back to 1787, with the arrival of John Henry Cox in Canton.[49] In the early nineteenth century, it was run by three partners, Thomas Beale, Alexander Shanks and Charles Magniac. In 1808, the firm made a profit of $96,000 on a turnover of $1.2 million. Over 75% of the profit was derived from the 'Commission account', as was typical of Agency Houses. The firm already had an established business in

[47] McCulloch's *Commercial Dictionary*, article on 'Tariff'. See also *PP*, 1882, (391), lxiv, 571.
[48] See below, in the the section 'The Opium War'.
[49] See above, 'Patterns of Eastern Trade', note 26.

bills, Indian cotton, and Bengal opium. Its flow of business with Bombay was still relatively undeveloped.[50]

Unsuccessful opium speculations bankrupted Thomas Beale personally in 1815, though he continued to live in Macao (Letters 25, 55), and was helped by his former partners and their successors. Alexander Shanks died the following year, leaving an estate of $139,763 dollars.[51] These changes left Charles Magniac, the surviving partner of Huguenot descent, in sole control of a much weakened firm. Its turnover was nearly half what it had been in 1808, and its capital had been amputated by two-thirds following the former partners' withdrawal or demise. The firm was now called *Magniac & Co.*, a name it was to keep from 1817 to 1832.

Charles Magniac started rebuilding his firm's fortunes. In 1819, *Magniac & Co.* started a brisk trade in Bengal opium with a young new merchant who had recently arrived in Calcutta—James Matheson.[52] Charles Magniac's brother, Hollingworth Magniac (Letters 10, 11, 13, 16, etc.), arrived from London to work in the Canton firm and soon became a partner. But another brother, Daniel Magniac, proved unsatisfactory and left under a cloud (Letters 13, 16, 43, 52, 54). When Charles Magniac died, in 1824,[53] the firm was again in disarray, with Hollingworth Magniac as sole partner searching for a capable trader to help him develop the business. He approached the forty-year old William Jardine, whom he knew to be able, steady, and experienced. For the past few years, Jardine had sailed regularly as an independent trader between Bombay and Canton, slowly accumulating capital. When he joined *Magniac & Co.*, in 1825, his entire fortune, including his pro-rata share of the profit for the year, came to $14,225.[54] It was from these relatively modest beginnings that he was to build up a very large fortune over the next fifteen years, showing that special trading circumstances could permit a quite exceptional accumulation of profit.

William Jardine (1784–1843) was one of five children born to a family of small farmholders near Lochmaben in Dumfriesshire.[55] His father died when he was nine. His elder brother, David, supported him through his studies at Edinburgh. There he qualified as a medical surgeon at 18, the normal age at a time when the medical profession was not yet very highly regarded. A year later, in 1803, he obtained an appointment as surgeon's mate in one the Company's ships, the

[50] *JMArch.*, A1–7, Ledger for 1808.

[51] *Ibid.*, Ledgers A4–2 and A4–3.

[52] *Ibid.*, Ledger A4–4.

[53] Charles Magniac left an estate of $274,248. (*JMArch.*, A1–29).

[54] This was the equivalent of £3,324, which would have yielded £133 at 4% p. a., when an annual income of £500 was considered a minimum at the time to lead the life of a country gentleman.

[55] Very little is known with any certainty about William Jardine's family prior to the early nineteenth century. The two principal sources are: Steuart, James, *Jardine, Matheson & Co., An Outline History of a Chinese House*, Hong Kong, privately printed, 1934; and Keswick, *The Thistle and the Jade*.

Brunswick. For the next fourteen years he remained in the Company's employ, rising to the rank of surgeon and serving principally on the *Glatton*, and later on the *Windham*.[56]

Like all Company officers, Jardine was allocated an amount of cargo space appropriate to his rank, and this enabled him to trade in a small way, on his own and on his friends' accounts. The surgeon's mate learned his future business by buying and selling small amounts of cassia, cochineal and musk, bringing back these articles to England from India and China, and developing in the process a keen sense of what sold well, where, and for what profit. Whilst his letters show little evidence that he had a strong sense of the power of market demand, he developed an uncommon familiarity with the market supply mechanisms and an eye for 'quality' in the products and commodities of the trade (Letter 32).

In 1817, after fourteen years as a Company's employee, William Jardine resigned his commission and became an independent country trader, in partnership with two merchants whom he had known over the years. One was Thomas Weeding (Letters 25, 32, 69, 83, etc.), a former surgeon on the *Boddam* and the *Glatton* who now lived in London and had made a great deal of money since becoming a private trader in 1810.[57] The other was a Bombay Parsee, Framjee Cowasjee who was developing Malwa exports from Bombay to Canton. In 1819 the three partners bought the Country ship *Sarah* which regularly plied the Bombay to China route from 1819 to 1825, a period during which annual opium exports from Bombay grew from 1,000 to 6,000 chests.[58] The *Sarah* joint venture continued, and had not been completely unwound by 1841 (Letter 244).

After William Jardine joined *Magniac & Co.* the firm prospered, and an important flow of new business from Bombay was added to that of Calcutta and Madras. Hollingworth Magniac was now thinking of retiring to England. Before he did so, however, he invited James Matheson, now working in Canton, to join his firm. Matheson officially started working at *Magniac & Co.* on 1 January 1828 (Letter 11). With two of the most talented traders in Canton running his family firm, Hollingworth Magniac now returned to England, leaving a substan-

[56] See: Farrington, Anthony, (ed.), *A Biographical Index of the East India Company Maritime Service Officers, 1600–1834*, London, The British Library, 1999, p. 420. A surgeon came fourth in the hierarchy of officers serving in the Company's ships. Below the commander came the chief officer, the second officer, and the surgeon, followed by the third officer and the purser. Below the surgeon's mate were three further ranks: the fifth and sixth officers, the midshipmen, and the boatswains, gunmen and carpenters. A commander was paid £250 a year (excluding privileged shipping); a surgeon's mate £70; and a boatswain £25. See: *JMArch.*, A 7–214, a document on the hierarchy and pay of the officers and men of the Company.

[57] Farrington, *ibid.*, p. 834.

[58] See Table 6 above in 'Patterns of Eastern Trade' The *Sarah* was a 935–ton country ship built by the Bombay Dockyard in 1792. It was recorded as belonging to 'Private Merchants'. A (possibly erroneous) entry suggests, however, that it was 'lost in the French War'. See; Wadia, *Bombay Dockyard*, p. 355.

tial part of his own personal capital ($611,000) to be managed by his new partners. In all but name *Magniac & Co.* had in fact already become *Jardine, Matheson & Co.* The change in name was delayed for technical reasons until July 1, 1832 (Letters 52, 53).[59]

During the following twelve years, William Jardine continued spending most of his time in the firm's Canton factory, in a set of offices and private apartments situated at No 4, the Creek. He got up early, worked all day, making and recording the firm's trades, and usually devoted several hours of the night to his correspondence. He appears to have needed little sleep. His constitution was robust. There was little he hated more in life than idleness. He remained for ever suspicious of rest or recreation. He had all the virtues of application and conscientiousness traditionally nurtured by an austere Calvinist upbringing. In the course of business, he was a man of few words who always maintained a dignified composure. But behind the façade of deliberate indifference (which Matheson thought was particularly useful in his negotiations with the Chinese) his intellect was always alert and his emotions ran very deep. In private, he could flare up with annoyance at hypocritical or unfair behaviour. He detested humbug. He was often generous and had a strong sense of gratitude. Above all, perhaps, he had an uncommon sense of what he owed to himself, and his extreme high-mindedness made it hard to for him to sympathise with men of weaker character or feebler purpose than his own. Hardly anything transpires about his private life. A remark here or there suggests that he might have liked to marry after returning to England. But he remained a bachelor to the end. During his time in Canton he accumulated a fortune which amounted to $1,296,210 in 1837 (over £300,000),[60] and he left for England just before the start of the Opium War, in January 1839.

In London, although nominally retired, William Jardine continued working, trading, and attending to his correspondence. He built himself a large town house in the newly developed Upper Belgrave Street. As is shown later, he became one of the champions of opium merchants whose property had been confiscated at the beginning of the Opium War, and he spared no pains to press their claims against the government, lobbying Parliament for an early payment and the Foreign Secretary, Lord Palmerston, for a military response to China's actions.[61] A great lover of Scotland, he finally fulfilled his dream and bought the Lanrick estate in Perthshire. His hope was to lead the life of the country gentleman he had become. He stood for Parliament in the 1841 elections and was returned a Whig Member

[59] It was decided not to change the firm's name until June 1832 so as not to 'advertise Hollingworth Magniac out'. By this arrangement Hollingworth Magniac continued to draw his share of profits, and this enabled him to build up funds for his brother, Daniel, and for his cousin, Francis Hollingworth, both of whom had disappointed him and failed to become partners in the firm.

[60] *JMArch.*, A1– 36, A1–37. See Table 7.

[61] For these developments and references to Letters, see below the section entitled: 'The Opium War' and in particular the sub-section on William Jardine's role in London.

for Ashburton in Devon. But his health declined rapidly at the end of 1842, and he died on 27 February 1843 (Letters 257, 258). His nephews inherited his estate.

Jardine's business partner, James Matheson (1796–1878), was born in Lairg, Sutherland, the son of Captain Donald Matheson of Shinness and Katherine, daughter of Thomas MacKay, minister of Lairg.[62] He was one of a large family, and had at least two brothers and several sisters (Letters 57, 126, 154, 204, etc.). Several members of the family's collateral branches were involved in international trade in various business centres, including Liverpool, Glasgow, London, and Calcutta.

After attending the Royal High School in Edinburgh, Matheson went on to study at the University of Edinburgh, although it is uncertain what subject he read or even if he graduated.[63] In 1815, aged 19, he obtained the indentures of a 'free merchant' from the Company. This enabled him to start work as an apprentice in an uncle's Agency House in Calcutta, *Mackintosh & Co.*[64] His period of apprenticeship, however, ended abruptly three years later. Whether he was dismissed for being too independent, or whether he forestalled the threat of dismissal by an early resignation is uncertain.[65]

Following his business instinct, he sailed to China in 1818, where the market for Indian exports was growing. As Company rules did not allow him to reside in Canton, he settled in Macao where he formed a partnership with a Robert Taylor, importing Bengal opium from Calcutta. However, the partnership was soon unwound, following the death of Robert Taylor in 1820.[66] Meanwhile, one of Matheson's business friends from Bengal, Xavier Yrisarri—a young country trader of Basque origins who had previously been working in the Calcutta Agency Houses of *Larruleta & Co.* and *Mendieta Uriarte & Co.*,—also set up in business in Macao under the name *Yrisarri & Co.* The two young traders had much in common, and in 1821 James Matheson joined *Yrisarri & Co.* as a partner.

[62] R. J. Grace, art. 'Sir James Matheson' in C.S. Nicholls (ed.), *DNB*, Missing Persons, Oxford, O.U.P., 1993, pp. 452–453. Some commentators have suggested that the land-owning status of the Mathesons in Sutherland made James Matheson the social equal of the Canton Select Committee members; (see: Crisswell, Colin, *The Taipans: Hong Kong Merchant Princes*, Hong Kong, Oxford University Press, 1981, p.21). Collis, (*Foreign Mud*, p. 67), is the only one who refers to James Matheson's father as 'a Scottish baronet'. What land was owned by James Matheson's immediate family, however, did not prove sufficient to provide an income for the young Highlander and his siblings.

[63] In the early 19th century, students enrolled at Edinburgh University from the age of 14.

[64] These dates are given by Alan Reid, in Keswick, pp. 16–18. Steuart, *Jardine, Matheson & Co., etc.*, op. cit.) gives 1813 as the date of James Matheson's arrival in Calcutta, and his age 17.

[65] The apocryphal story, as narrated by Alan Reid (op. cit., p. 18) was that: 'he was sent to the quay with an urgent letter, and missed the ship. Threatened with dismissal, he was easily persuaded to try his luck in China'.

[66] Keswick, *The Thistle and the Jade*, p. 265, ch.1, note 3.

Within a few years, *Yrisarri & Co.* became one the five principal Agency Houses in China. It was not as large or as established as either *Magniac & Co.*, or *Dent & Co.*, but its business in Bengal opium and India bills was sufficiently brisk to create competition for the two older British Houses as well as for the three Parsee Agency Houses.[67] Several practices introduced by *Yrisarri & Co.* point to the fact that its partners were the most inventive foreign traders operating in China at the time. The idea of forming a partnership with a merchant of a different nationality was in itself highly unusual. The development of business relationships with Spanish Manila (Spanish was a language which James Matheson spoke and wrote fluently)[68] and with Singapore, a British settlement which was then in its infancy,[69] were examples of innovations introduced by the young firm. Above all, James Matheson's early substitution (in 1821) of Lintin as the principal opium trading mart for what had traditionally been the role of Macao proved irreversible and invaluable to opium traders. Finally, in 1823, the Yrisarri partnership made the first attempt to sell opium directly to the Chinese in Amoy.[70] This daring act was undertaken by James Matheson in the *San Sebastian*, under Spanish Flag, in blatant defiance of established Chinese rules and precedents, at least since 1757. It was a voyage of seminal influence which *Jardine, Matheson & Co.* was to repeat earlier and more frequently than its competitors (Letters 63, 81, 88, 89, 107).

News that Xavier Yrisarri had died whilst travelling in India reached James Matheson in early 1827 (Letters 1, 2). With the help of Alexander Matheson, a nephew who had recently arrived from Scotland to learn the trade, James Matheson started to unwind the affairs of the partnership and to trade under the name *Matheson & Co.* In the end, no suitable partner could be found to replace Yrisarri. Realizing that it would be impossible to continue operating on his own, he started looking at offers to join other firms. He finally settled on *Magniac & Co.*, judging that William Jardine, who was twelve years his senior, would be an excellent business match. James Matheson worked in *Magniac & Co.* and later *Jardine, Matheson & Co.* without interruption from January 1828 to March 1842.

James Matheson was as hard-working and as single-minded about making a fortune as William Jardine, but his personality was very different and in many ways complementary to that of his partner. He was less austere and had greater indulgence for the weaknesses of fellow human beings. As a young man with an innovative turn of mind, he had been less deferential of authority and tradition.

[67] See above: 'Patterns of Eastern Trade', note 31.

[68] The *JMArch* of that period contains several copies of Spanish out-letters written by James Matheson. It is likely that he had learned Spanish during his stay in Calcutta, and it is certain that he had on-going business connections with the few Calcutta-based Spanish Agency Houses.

[69] Sir Stanford Raffles had claimed Singapore for the British Crown as recently as 1819.

[70] Collis, *Foreign Mud*, p. 67.

His talent found one of its truest expressions in the art of negotiation. There hardly ever seemed to be a difficult business, political, or human situation which could not be solved, or at least disentangled, by the combined power of his keen intellect, his desire to be helpful, and his considerable personal charm. Above all, he was a consummate communicator and, as he was more interested in exercising influence than in being seen to wield power and authority, he was well-liked wherever he went. He was fond of women and enjoyed their company. He married shortly after his return home, and settled down with his wife to enjoy the $1 million dollar fortune he had made in China (£225,000).[71] He arrived in London exhausted from the strain of managing the firm during the Opium War. But one of his first visits was to Scotland where, as his friend Jardine had done before him, he looked for a suitable estate.[72] He soon purchased the isle of Lewis in the Outer Hebrides and other Scottish estates totalling over 200,000 acres.[73] In 1843 he succeeded to Jardine's parliamentary seat at Ashburton until 1847, and was then MP for Ross and Cromarty, 1847–1868. He was made a baronet in 1850 for his generosity to the people of Lewis during the famine of the late 1840s. He enjoyed thirty-six years of retirement, remaining active in politics, business, and philanthropy to the end of his life. He died in Menton, on the French Riviera, in 1878.[74]

The business activities of the partners in the firm must now be analyzed. At the time when they joined forces, their firm[75] had three layers of original constituents—those traditionally associated with the Magniacs; those who did business with the firm because they knew William Jardine; and those who had been clients of *Yrisarri & Co.* and knew James Matheson.

Many traditional constituents did relatively little business with China. They included *Biny & Co.* in Madras, (Letter 35); *Carnegy & Co.* in Penang (Letter 43) and many others. The two principal constituents which had established trading relations with the firm were *Fergusson & Co.* in Calcutta (Letters 30, 80), and its sister company in London, *Fairlie, Bonham & Co.* (Letters 3, 6, 17, 65). Both Agencies had been founded by Henry Bonham, a rich managing owner of several

[71] See Table 7 below.

[72] 'Matheson was well on the 17th Instant (Sept. 1842), and going to look at the island of Lewis but would return to Achany about the 28th Instant'. (*JMArch.*, J.42., Letter of William Jardine in Richmond to John Abel Smith in London, dated 20 September 1842).

[73] Bateman, John, *The Great Landowners of Great Britain and Ireland*, Leicester, Leicester University Press, 1971, (1876, 1878). The acreage owned by Sir James Matheson in Ross alone was 220,433 and had an annual value of £23,223.

[74] Matheson was elected FRS in 1846. He was chairman of the *Peninsular & Oriental Steam and Navigation Company* and Lord Lieutenant and Sheriff principal of the County of Ross. In 1843, he had married Mary Jane, the daughter of Michael Henry Percival, a member of the Quebec Legislative Council. They had no children. (*DNB*).

[75] The firm is now referred to as '*Jardine, Matheson & Co.*', regardless of whether it still was technically *Magniac & Co.*

Portrait of William Jardine (Jardine, Matheson collection)

PLATE II

Portrait of James Matheson (Jardine, Matheson collection)

Portrait of Jamsetjee Jejeebhoy (Jardine, Matheson collection)

PLATE IV

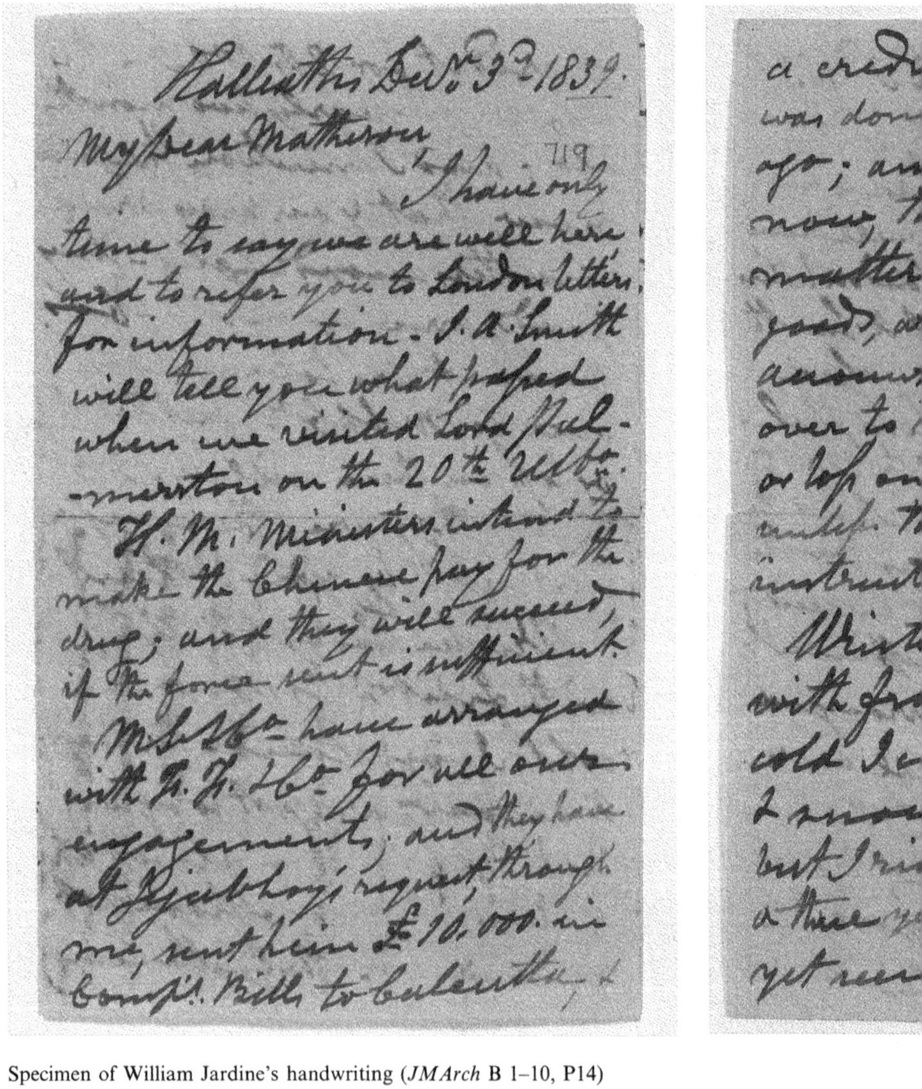
Halleaths Decr. 3d 1839.

My Dear Matheson

119

I have only time to say we are well here and to refer you to London letters for information — J. A. Smith will tell you what passed when we visited Lord Pal-merston on the 20th Ulto.

H. M. Ministers intend to make the Chinese pay for the drug; and they will succeed, if the force sent is sufficient.

M. S. & Co. have arranged with F. F. & Co. for all our engagements, and they have at Jejeebhoy's request, through me, sent him £10,000. in Compy's. Bills to Calcutta, &

a credi
was don
ago; an
now, t
matter
goods, a
account
over to
or loss on
unless. T
instruct
Winte
with fr
cold I c
& snow
but I ri
a three y
yet see

Specimen of William Jardine's handwriting (*JMArch* B 1–10, P14)

0,000 £ – this
ly two months
tion the business
u may arrange
ingly – Any
on S.I. 26 bas.
be handed
; but the profit
will be S.I. 26 ...
otherwise
one & them –
t in here
now – the
nd – the rain
not so agreeable
in about like
– I have not
e Gentlemen

around us – We dine with
General Sharp to day – I've
not yet been to Dumfries
nor seen the Marquis of Queensbury
nor Sir Wm Jardine who
is in Edinburgh –

Tell Andrew his friends
here are all well – excuse
this hurried note & believe
me in haste

Yours very sincerely

W Jardine

J. Matheson Esqr –
Canton or Macao.

PLATE V

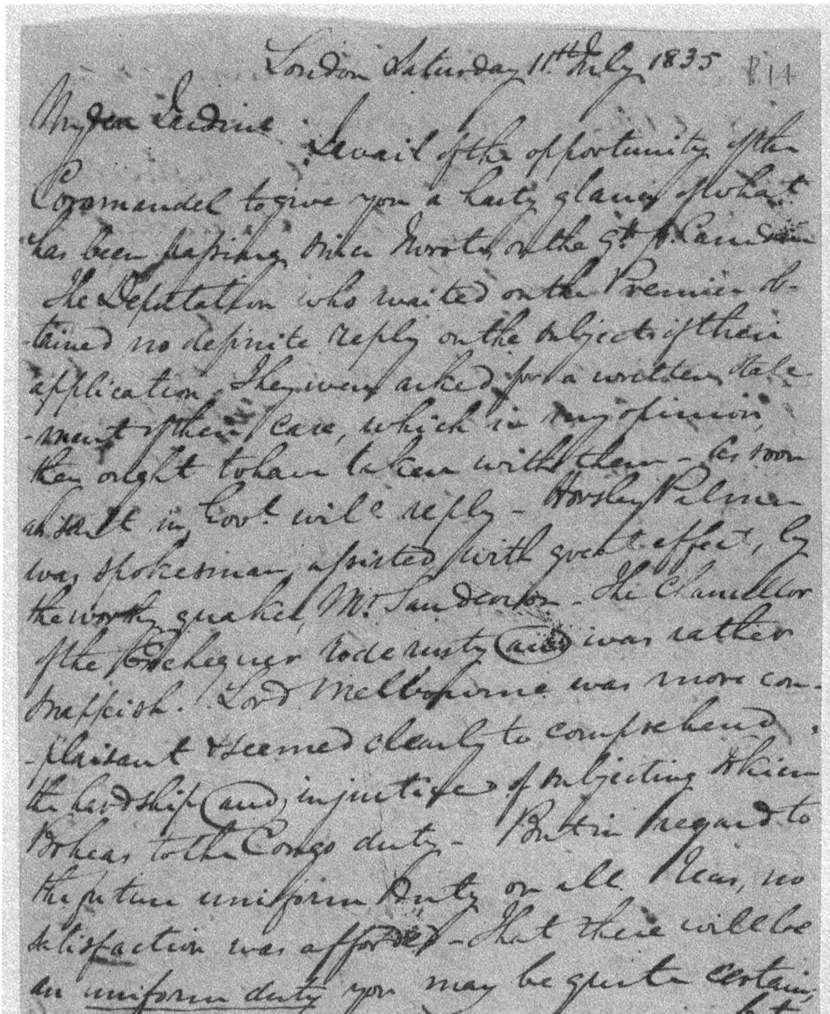
London Saturday 11th July 1835 P.14

My dear Jardine: I avail of the opportunity of the Coromandel to give you a hasty glance of what has been passing since I wrote by the 9th [illegible]. The Deputation who waited on the Premier obtained no definite reply on the subject of their application. They were asked for a written statement of their case, which in my opinion they ought to have taken with them — as soon as it is sent in Govt. will reply — Horsley Palmer was spokesman, assisted with great effect, by the worthy quaker, Mr. Sanderson — The Chancellor of the Exchequer rode rusty (as i) was rather snappish. Lord Melbourne was more complaisant & seemed clearly to comprehend the hardship and injustice of subjecting Boheas to the Congo duty — But in regard to the future uniform duty on all Teas, no satisfaction was afforded — That there will be an uniform duty you may be quite certain but

Specimen of James Matheson's handwriting (*JMArch* B6–8, 719)

I wrote to you ft. Camden, (and) now repeat that Mr
Nicolson is supposed to be a ruined man — You will
of course be cautious in dealing with him. I have
seen Temple who speaks very favorably of our
Tea management — He is looking very ill —
I have also seen Magniac and his Wife looking
remarkable well — He professes himself willing
to abandon all his arrangements, if not agreeable
to us — indeed our good uses his principal motive —
and if we do not like his plans, he is de-
-termined to relinquish them! — This is so
like the little man! — I have a very growling
and disagreeable letter from McLean complaining
of his having no silk — (and) of our not paying more
attention to his business — On the latter point I mean
to try to convince him that we have paid attention
to it (and) having traced our powers to the utmost,
really cannot do more — Should he be incapable
of conviction on this head, I really fear we must be
content to his separating from us — But I shall be
temperate and mean to put myself in the hands of
my (old) friend [illegible] as an adviser & moderator with
McL.

Yours very truly in haste
J Matheson

PLATE VI

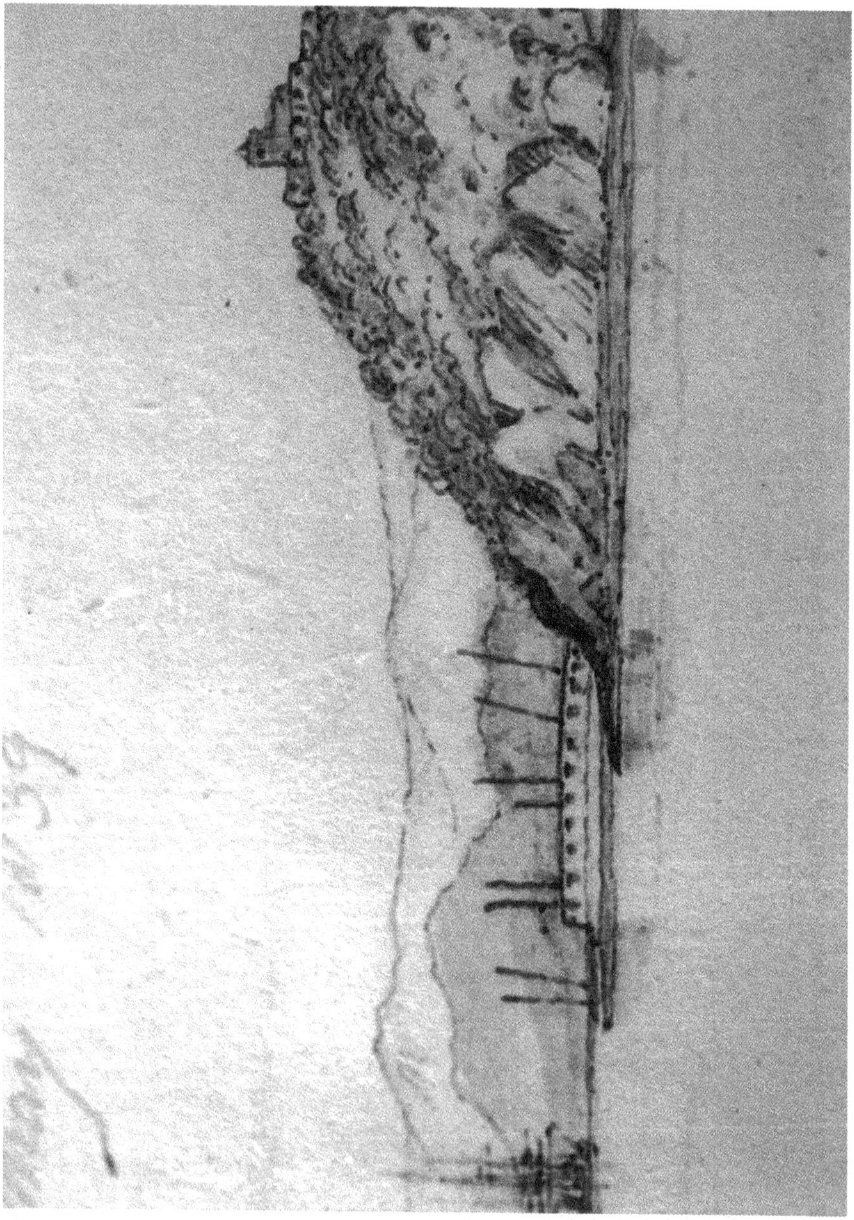

A view of the Chuenpee fort (Private collection)

Company ships from 1800 to 1828.[76] *Jardine, Matheson & Co.* looked after *Fergusson & Co.*'s interests in China, selling its opium and other exports, and buying return cargoes of sugar and silk as well as Company bills. *Fairlie Bonham & Co.* in London was an established East India Agency, and the relationship reflected well on *Jardine, Matheson & Co.*, which was at the time a much smaller and less well-known firm. The firm also traded with the west coast of India, importing cotton and Malwa opium to China. Its principal constituent in Bombay was *Remington & Co.* (previously known as *Remington Crawford & Co.*). Both William Jardine and James Matheson were on friendly terms with its two senior partners, H. P. Haddow (Letters 54, 90, 120) and M. T. D. DeVitre, (Letter 61). The flow of business between the two firms increased substantially in the late 1820s and early 1830s, and the two firms' respective partners exchanged frequent and remarkably candid business letters.

When he joined the firm James Matheson brought his business relationships along with him, many of which continued very active. Among them were the established London East India Agency of *Gregson Melville Knight* (Letter 10); the Macao Agency House of *Calvo & Co.* (Letter 15); John Purvis (Letters 2, 92), and Charles Thomas (Letters 33, 66), both important contacts for the growing flow of transshipping business in Singapore. Because of his oral and written fluency in Spanish, James Matheson also corresponded with the Manila Agencies and with the firm's Spanish and Portuguese clients (Letter 57). More importantly, he was instrumental in helping a nephew, Hugh Matheson (Letters 47, 48), start an Agency House in Calcutta. The new firm, *Lyall Matheson & Co.* (Letters 64, 86), was a partnership with Charles Lyall, with whose cousin James Matheson was on friendly terms (Letter 149). With the failure of *Fergusson & Co.* in 1833 (Letter 80),[77] *Jardine, Matheson & Co.* had lost its principal Calcutta agent. It could have been a serious blow for the Canton firm, save for the recent foundation of *Lyall Matheson & Co.* which became overnight a replacement for the failed agent. Over the years Charles Lyall was entrusted with a great deal of Bengal opium business, even though he was prone to misinterpret James Matheson instructions (Letters 97, 146, 189, 191, 207, 221).

The business relationships which William Jardine had built up over a much longer career as an independent trader were unsurprisingly more numerous than those of James Matheson. They crucially included Thomas Weeding and

[76] Farrington, Anthony, (ed.), *Catalogue of East India Company Ships, Journals and Logs, 1600–1834*, London, The British Library, 1999.

[77] A wave of bankruptcies affected most of the Calcutta Agency Houses between 1830 and 1833. This was due to prolonged speculation in indigo. The first House to fail in December 1830 was also the largest and the most established, *Palmer & Co.* One of the last to fail was *Fergusson & Co.* In the process, its London sister company, *Fairlie, Bonham & Co.*,—later renamed *Fairlie, Clark, Innes & Co.* (Letter **65**)—also failed. For the 1830–1833 Calcutta bankruptcies, see: Le Pichon, *Aux origines de Hong Kong*, 'L'indigo et les faillites de Calcutta', pp. 281–294.

Jamsetjee Jejeebhoy. Thomas Weeding (Letters 25, 32, 69, 83, 103, 148, 167), was William Jardine's earliest business partner.[78] It was with him that the 'triangular business transactions' were so successfully set up and so often repeated. A speculator sent sterling bills from England to Bombay or Calcutta. With the proceeds, his agent bought opium at auction and shipped it to Canton. In China, the cash proceeds of the opium were reinvested in silk and Company bills, and the returns sent to London where, a year after inception, a handsome profit could often be booked. Even when the business relationship deteriorated in 1837, as Thomas Weeding abstained from accepting bills drawn by *Jardine, Matheson & Co.*, William Jardine's bitterness at his old friend's betrayal did not obliterate his long-standing gratitude (Letter 167).

The business relationship with Jamsetjee Jejeebhoy, an independent Parsee merchant from Bombay, dwarfed all the others during the period under review.[79] It started in a small way in the mid-1820s, with the Parsee exporting raw cotton to China. As his business grew, Jamsetjee Jejeebhoy bought more ships with which to export more cotton and more Malwa opium to China. *Jardine, Matheson & Co.* was soon turning over more that $2 million of Jejeebhoy's business annually.[80] The firm was greatly enriched by this large flow of selling and buying commissions and by the proceeds of joint speculative transactions. In turn, Jamsetjee Jejeebhoy made a great deal of money thanks to the regular market reports received from, and the meticulous services rendered by both William Jardine and James Matheson. During the decade 1830 to 1840, this was the constituent relationship which was by far the most lucrative for the firm (Letters 22, 34, 67, 82, 160, 165, 168, 172, 198, 206, 209, 211, 217, 228, 230, 233, 242, 244, 247, 253, 254, 258, 259, 260, 263). The near-partnership with Jejeebhoy illustrates the process of Anglo-Indian symbiosis discussed earlier.

William Jardine's fourteen years in the Company's service also brought to *Jardine, Matheson & Co.* valuable relationships with ships' commanders and officers. Some, like Henry Wright (Letter 106), or Andrew Johnstone, one of Jardine's nephews (Letters 23, 205), joined the firm and became partners. A few had grown into capitalists in their own right, like J. H. Gledstanes (Letters 4, 5, 128) or Henry Templer (Letter 134). Others had turned to commanding (and sometimes owning) country ships, and were both customers of the firm and entrusted with special missions on joint accounts. They include Captains Innes

[78] See above: 'The early firm and its founders'.

[79] According to Alan Reid (Keswick, *The Thistle and the Jade*, p. 14) who follows Midshipman Thomas Eddison's account, *Navy Record Society*, 1902 (Keswick, op. cit., p. 265, note 1), William Jardine and Jamsetjee Jejeebhoy had met and struck a friendship as early as 1804 during an episode of the Napoleonic wars, when the crew of the *Brunswick*, including William Jardine, had been taken prisoner, and exchanged off the Coast of South Africa. From the documents in *JMArch*, however, no business relationship seems to have been struck before 1824–1825.

[80] See Table 7 below.

(Letter 63); Grant (Letters 14, 59, 147, 161); Rees (Letters 104, 142, 157); Jauncey (Letters 116, 155); Ovenstone (Letter 122); Clifton (Letter 124); Larkins (Letter 136), etc.

Finally, both William Jardine and James Matheson retained an extremely close business as well as personal relationship with Hollingworth Magniac after his return home (Letters 11, 13, 16, 31, 37, 40, 44, 45, 68, 102, 113, 123, 143). Not only had they relied on his leaving a large part of his fortune in the firm as working capital, they also depended on his money and influence in London when bankruptcies threatened their principal London correspondents both in 1832 (*Fairlie, Bonham & Co.*) and in 1837 (*Timothy Wiggin & Co.*) (Letters 69, 143, 144). Above all, it was Hollingworth Magniac, through his business partnership with John Abel Smith in *Magniac Smith & Co.*, who delivered to William Jardine and James Matheson the two things they still lacked at the time—access to the financial resources of a distinguished banking family, and social connections at the highest level of British society.

These connections were to be of importance at the time of the Opium War. However, well before this, the partners had recognized that business and politics were connected; that men of business needed to influence political decisions. This was illustrated in the struggle to end the East India Company's monopoly of the tea trade. Adam Smith's views of the Company's monopoly as detrimental to both British foreign trade and the Indian economy took close to sixty years to be shared by a majority of MPs.[81] Eventually, however, the *India Act* of 1833 put an end to the Company's trading activity. This radical deregulation of previous commercial practice had important repercussions on the Canton trade in general and on the business of *Jardine, Matheson & Co.* in particular. It was a change which William Jardine and James Matheson had long hoped and worked for. As early as December 1830, James Matheson had written a strongly worded 'Petition to Parliament'. Forty-seven private merchants trading in Canton had put their signature to the document, (Appendix IV). The petition was a frontal attack on the Canton system of trading and, indirectly, on the Company itself as a trading monopoly. Copies of the petition were sent to various English and Scottish friends in the New Year 1831 (Letter 36).

With 1833 approaching and, with it, the parliamentary vote on the Company Charter, William Jardine arranged for Horatio Hardy, the manager of the *Jerusalem Coffee House* in Cornhill and, from the great number of East India officers and traders who daily patronized his establishment, one of the best informed

[81] In 1776, Adam Smith had written: 'The monopoly of the colony trade, therefore, like all the other means and malignant expedients of the mercantile system, depresses the industry of all other countries, but chiefly that of the colonies, without in the least increasing, but on the contrary diminishing, that of the country in whose favour it is established. (*The Wealth of Nations*, II, 4, Ch. 7; see above, note 38).

men in City, to send the firm regular updates of the vote on the Company Charter (Letters 74, 75, 78, 98). Immediately after the vote in Parliament, Hardy wrote: 'The whole of the [Company's] commercial property is to be immediately given up when the Charter expires in April 1834, viz—warehouses, wharf, Docks, East India House, and the buildings with all commercial property in India' (Letter 75). Jardine and Matheson welcomed this revolutionary news wholeheartedly. They had contributed in words and deed to the birth of the new commercial order. Now they had a vested interest in its success. Suddenly, the firm could buy and sell tea, and ship it to England in its friends' ships. William Jardine and James Matheson took up the challenge and managed to ship the first 'free' tea ahead of their competitors to various newly-opened British ports (Letters 83, 84, 85).

The enacting of the 1833 India Act led to important administrative changes in Canton. The Select Committee of the East India Company was disbanded and replaced by a group of superintendents of British trade appointed by the English Crown. In July 1834, the newly-appointed First Chief Superintendent, Lord Napier, arrived in China. He died three months later, having failed in his mission to open diplomatic relationships with the Canton viceroy (Letters 91, 92). The failure to open official trade between Britain and China was felt as a serious blow by the British traders in Canton. James Matheson took the lead in harnessing their disappointment and with their support he founded the Canton Chamber of Commerce as an official platform to air their views (Letter 93). In December 1834, shortly after its creation, the Chamber promptly dispatched a petition to the King, urging him to send a force to Canton to demand reparation for the insults suffered by Lord Napier (Appendix V). But the cause of British traders in Canton had a better chance of being heard if taken up in England by one of its most ardent advocates, and this was the principal factor in James Matheson's decision to sail to England in March 1835.

He arrived in London in July (Letter 111). During the following thirteen months he made sure that his voice was heard where it mattered throughout England and Scotland. In London, he lobbied MPs on the Canton trade and missed no opportunity to learn more about the baffling new tea trade (Letters 118, 119). He frequently saw Hollingworth Magniac and introduced the China trade to the latter's new partner, John Abel Smith (Letters 113, 140). In the manufacturing districts he visited customers originally introduced to his firm by John Macvicar (Letter 126). He addressed the Chambers of Commerce of Glasgow, Liverpool, and Manchester, and persuaded each of their respective presidents to send petitions to the Prime Minister in support of a muscular trade policy towards China (Appendices VII, VIII, IX). Finally, he found the time to gather his ideas and publish a pamphlet on *The Present Position and Prospects of the British Trade with China, etc.* (Letter 135).

Meanwhile in Canton, William Jardine was managing the firm's growing business single-handedly and coping as best he could in the brave new world of commercial deregulation. Two business areas in particular gave him cause for some concern: the new trade in teas, and the trade in direct British exports of cotton piece goods. The last preserve of the secretive Company, tea was a commodity which no private firm had ever dealt with. Simple questions of quality, price, transport, warehousing, and insurance, which had all long been solved when trading in other commodities, were suddenly problematic with teas. A new tea department had to be created; tea-tasters, who were notoriously difficult to find, had to be appointed; customers' complaints had to be answered, and expert advice sought from more knowledgeable London friends (Letters 101, 111, 114, 125, 150, 156, 159). To make things worse, the rump of the Company in Canton (the 'Finance Committee') set up lending facilities which many thought were illegal (Letter 105). This fuelled severe inflation in tea prices and led to a revolt of the 'tea men', who had traditionally supplied the hong merchants,[82] but who now refused to deliver their goods in the hope of achieving still higher prices (Letters 125, 129, 132). Upon his return from London, James Matheson persuaded a reluctant William Jardine that the way forward was simply to drop the hong merchants and to buy teas directly from the tea-men (Letter 137).

Over the period covered by the Letters, it was a general feature of the Canton trade that virtually no foreign merchant could speak, let alone write, Chinese, and no Chinese hong merchant knew English, except occasionally rudimentary Pidgin English. The handful of scholars who, like Robert Morrison[83] studied Chinese seriously tended to be missionaries. Their aim was essentially to convert the Chinese, not to transact business. All mercantile transactions and business contracts had therefore to be arranged orally, with the help of intermediaries—either an official Chinese 'linguist' or a foreign merchant's comprador. It was a reflection on the fundamental honesty of both the European and Chinese merchant communities that the system of oral contracts in approximate English worked so well for so long. It was also a feature of doing business in this way and of setting up contracts outside the framework of the traditional 'rule of law', that any dispute arising in cases of misunderstanding or occasional dishonesty had to be settled through negotiation rather than through the courts.

The firm's business in direct shipments of cotton-piece goods from British exporters pre-dated by two years the days of 'free' trade. Its instigator had been John Macvicar, 'a plain, intelligent Scotchman' first mentioned in Letter

[82] For the 'hong merchants' see the description of the 'Canton system' above.

[83] Robert Morrison (1782–1834) can be considered as one of the fathers of Chinese scholarship. He was sent to Canton by the London Missionary Society in 1807. He translated the New and the Old Testaments in Chinese. He also compiled a *Chinese Dictionary*. In 1818, he founded the Anglo-Chinese College at Malacca where British and American students were taught Chinese.

29, who quickly built a business out of syndicating exports of British cotton manufactures to China. He formed several joint ventures with *Jardine, Matheson & Co.*, which gave the firm a lead over its competitors in this trade. The first experimental shipment from Macvicar's industrial contacts (Letter 46), was followed by a relentless succession of shipments characterized by their poor profitability and the increasing resistance of the Chinese market, particularly after 1836 (Letters 62, 72, 87, 91, 109, 110, 114, 126, 127, 130, 132, 135, 137). Over time, Macvicar's cantankerous nature soured the relationship almost as much as the lack of profits from this trade, and the former associates parted company (Letters 153, 154). Before this happened, however, the overtrading which had been a hallmark in the market in British piece-goods gave rise to difficulties of a potentially more serious nature. In 1837, Hengtai, the hong merchant who had obligingly 'purchased' the bulk of the piece-goods on credit from *Jardine, Matheson & Co.* went bankrupt, owing the firm over $2 million (Letters 136, 140, 141). One of the strengths of Canton system had been its Consoo insurance fund whereby the foreign creditors of failed hong merchants were made whole over time. But the deterioration of the Canton system which followed the British trade deregulation of 1834 raised some doubt as to the eventual repayment of hong debts.

A few months later, the failure in London of several banks which financed American trade temporarily added to the firm's difficulties. One of the failed banks, *Timothy Wiggin & Co.*, had been *Jardine, Matheson & Co.*'s principal banker since 1833, and it was the drawee of a large amount of the firm's bills outstanding in the market. The firm survived the collapse of its London banker thanks to *Magniac Smith & Co.*, whose partners Hollingworth Magniac and John Abel Smith promptly came to the rescue by accepting all its outstanding bills (Letters 143, 144, 145). In fact, the episode sealed the bond of friendship between the two firms which soon entered into exclusive agency agreements with each other (Letter 150). From then on, John Abel Smith had become the exclusive London banker and correspondent of *Jardine, Matheson & Co.*, a position he was to hold throughout the Opium War years (Letters 150, 153, 156, 163, 166, 175, 178, etc.).

When William Jardine and James Matheson started working together in 1827, their firm was established in the sense that it had local notoriety. It was known for the quality of its services to a number of specialized eastern traders, but its name was unknown in England, except to a small number of East India agents. By 1843, the firm had become truly established as a household name in the City. It was poised for a period of extraordinary growth, following the Opium War and the opening of China to foreign trade. Its two founders had become MPs, and their personal fortunes were on a par with those of the City elite, if not those of the richest landowners. By any standard, these were remarkable achievements over a period of just sixteen years. Their careers, it should be noted, conform to

Cain and Hopkins's model of 'gentlemanly capitalism'.[84] They also exemplify Rubinstein's thesis that nineteenth century large fortunes were more often made in finance and trade than in manufacturing. Finally, they illustrate the investment of business fortunes in land, a practice which was of long standing, though it may have eroded later in the century.[85]

The growth of the firm's business over those sixteen years can be seen from at least three different angles—the volume of transactions with its principal constituents, the volume of transactions in a few selected commodities, and its overall profit record. Table 7, constructed from data in the Archive ledgers, gives less than a full picture of the firm's growth, because of gaps in the material, but enables a general pattern to be identified.

The firm traded on a regular basis with Calcutta, Bombay, and London. The Calcutta business with *Fergusson & Co.* which had averaged $250,000 a year up to 1826, declined with the bankruptcies of the principal Bengal Agency Houses, including the firm's agent, *Fergusson & Co.*, owing to speculation in indigo (1828–1832). When *Lyall Matheson & Co.* took over from *Fergusson & Co.* as principal agent, however, the Calcutta business rapidly grew to average $747,000 in the period 1837–1841. Business from the west coast of India provides an even more remarkable picture of growth. *Remington & Co.*'s transactions which had averaged $250,000 a year to 1829 grew to $622,000 in 1830 and stabilized at around $570,000 after 1837. Nevertheless, it was the other main Bombay constituent, Jamsetjee Jejeebhoy, who provided the bulk of the growth in west coast business. Transactions with the Parsee merchant which amounted to $227,000 in 1827, rose to $526,000 in 1830, to $1.2 million in 1837, and to $2 million from 1838 through to the end of the Opium War years. The picture of turnover growth is broadly similar with the principal London correspondents. The business with *Fairlie, Bonham & Co.* which had been brisk at over $250,000 a year until the firm's failure in 1832, was subsequently taken over by *Magniac Smith & Co.* whose annual transactions rose to $1.0 million in 1837, $1.2 million in 1838, and over $2.0 million in most subsequent years. This more than compensated for the decline in business flow from both Thomas Weeding (down from $380,000 in 1838 to $55,000 in 1841), and John Macvicar (down from $200,000 in 1837 to a trickle in the Opium War years).

Growth in the firm's business can also be assessed from an observation of the volume of transactions in commodities. Some commodities showed a decline in

[84] See: P. J. Cain and A. G. Hopkins, *British Imperialism 1688–2000*, London, Pearson Education Ltd., (1993), 2001.

[85] See: Rubinstein, W. D., *Men of Property, The very wealthy in Britain Since the Industrial Revolution*, London, Croom Helm, 1981. On the subsidiary thesis about the decline in investment in land, see also by the same author: *Elites and the Wealthy in Modern British History, Essays in social and Economic History*, Sussex, The Harvester Press, 1987.

Table 7. The firm's business activity, 1825–1843: Jardine, Matheson & Co. ledger statistics in Sp$ '000, y/e 30 June.

[Ledger Nos.]	1825 [A1–29]	1826* [A1–30]	1827 [A1–31]	1828*	1829 [A1–32]	1830 [A1–34]	1831 to 1836*	1837 [A1–35]	1838 [A1–36] [A1–37]	1839 [A1–38]	1840 [A1–39]	1841 [A1–40]	1842* [A1–41]	1843*
Total profit	152		150			181	†	812	672	419	1,649	1,022		
of which, Commissions	29		70		35	144		305	339	280	395	366		
Reserve fund (y/e)									303	333	410	410		
WJ – starting capital	10					125		992	1296	923	606			
share of profit	4					22		289		101	424			
JM – starting capital						39		738	962	460	435	608		
share of profit						22		229		101	424	367		
Volume of transactions with constituents‡														
Bombay														
Remington & Co.	241		306		253	622		540	544	459	575	715		
Jejeebhoy	54		227		89	526		1,229	2,055	1,344	2,239	2,173		
Calcutta														
Fergusson & Co.	288		67		47	272								
Lyall Matheson & Co.								784	870	762	592	727		
London														
Fairlie Bonham & Co.	265		264		130	1,112								
Weeding						48		724	380			55		
Macvicar (& Burn)								196	288	76	4	68		
Magniac Smith & Co.								1,049	1,182	2,192	2,247	1,490		
Volume of transactions in commodities‡														
Piece goods from England								239	181	84		123		
Raw Silk to England			32			526		2,287	920	798	139	232		
Teas to England						62		256	640	996	1,397	1,567		
Tea account								2,854	1,690		2,413			
Opium account§			1,340		1,406	5,298		5,408	7,298		802	6,807		
Opium to East Coast§								2,210	3,206	1,862		5,023		
Bullion account					138	979		1,098	3,908		6,812	6,046		
Bills on England			3		189	154		487	407	403	1,043	1,054		
Bills on India			17		65	546		913		191	339	378		

* Ledgers missing (when no Ledger number is indicated), or too frail for consultation.

† Cheong gives the following profit figures (in Sp. $ ' 000). 1832: 353; 1833: 439; 1834: 678; 1835: 999; 1836: 1,372. (*Mandarins and Merchants*, p. 264). However, he does not indicate how they were compiled.

‡ The figures given for 'Volume of transactions with constituents' and 'Volume of transactions in commodities' are based on selected headings in the Ledgers. Both constituents and commodities have been selected to be broadly representative of the firm's business.

§ The recorded opium figures for 1839 and 1840 are incomplete, given the disruption of the trade and the fact that the business was conducted out of Manila.

trading, like 'cotton piece goods from England' which were down from an annual $230,000 to $84,000 in 1839. Others showed an erratic performance over the years, like 'raw silk to England' which stood at $526,000 in 1830, rose to $2.3 million in 1837, but declined again to $139 in 1840, in the middle of the Opium War. In all other principal commodities, however,—bullion, bills, tea, and opium,—the growth was sustained and, for selected items, massive. 'Bills to England' (sterling or dollar bills payable in London which had been bought in the Canton market and sent as remittances to London correspondents) rose from an average of $150,000 in the early years to over $1.0 million in 1840 and 1841. The 'bullion account' (the gold and silver proceeds from local and coast sales of mostly opium) which had risen to close to $1.0 million in 1830 averaged $6.0 million in the later years. The 'tea account' which did not exist prior to 1834 rose to close to $3.0 million in 1837 and averaged $2.5 million in the following years. The 'opium account' showed the most relentless growth of all. It stood at an already substantial $1.3 million in 1827; it averaged over $5 million in the following years, to reach over $7.0 million from 1838.

Whilst the transactions in commodities showed a growth which often multiplied turnover by a factor of 5 over a 15-year period, the firm's profit grew at a faster rate still and multiplied by a factor of 10. Profit, which had averaged $150,000 in the early years, reached the extraordinary figure of $1.6 million in 1840. A variety of circumstances accounted for the higher rate of profit growth than of turnover growth. The most important among them was the increasing reliance on proprietary trading, and the *relative* decline of commission earnings. In the early years, the share of commissions in overall profit had rarely been below 50%, and had sometimes reached 80%, as in 1830. From 1837, it averaged only 42% and could be as low as 24%, as in 1840.

By the end of the period, the firm owned a fleet of twelve ships, (Letter 162), where it had owned none outright at the beginning. The fleet was principally devoted to opium sales up the China coast (Letter 155). To keep the fleet active at all times was a business necessity which entailed securing a constant supply of the drug on the firm's own account. By 1843, *Jardine, Matheson & Co.*, which had been a small Agency House sixteen years before, was well on its way to becoming a fully-fledged capitalist enterprise. It had remained wise enough to continue relying on a steady flow of commission income, but it had become strong enough to risk its own capital whenever there seemed a reasonable chance to turn in a good profit.

After the Opium War, *Jardine, Matheson & Co.* continued to prosper as one of the principal 'hongs' (trading houses) in the colony of Hong Kong. Its trading activities spread to many parts of China, Japan and much of the Far East. In time, the firm became one of the largest Western investors in the region with a portfolio of interests in textiles (silk and cotton factories), railways, shipping, and real estate, etc. Until the Second World War it was seen as one of the proud symbols of British capitalism in Hong Kong and in the whole the Far Eastern region. With the rapid growth of local Chinese enterprise since 1945 and the return of Hong Kong to Chinese sovereignty in 1997, the firm has kept a lower profile than it once did, but its business ambitions in the region have remained unaltered.

4. *The Opium War*

From the mid-1830s, the apparently unstoppable growth of opium imports challenged the Chinese government in Peking into serious internal discussions. One faction favoured the legalization of the drug. The other faction, led by Lin Tse-hsu (Commissioner Lin) advocated its eradication and eventually won the emperor's ear.[86] In late 1838 the emperor took his decision and gave Lin full powers to annihilate the trade. Because James Matheson and William Jardine played leading roles within their respective spheres of influence in both Canton and in London, it is necessary to look at the episode in some detail.

The 'Opium War'[87] can be said to have started on 18 March 1839, the day when Commissioner Lin ordered all foreign traders in Canton to deliver their opium and to sign an 'Opium bond', by which they pledged themselves to abstain from dealing in the drug under penalty of death (Letter 170). On the following day all Europeans were forbidden to leave Canton, and this 'durance', as James Matheson describes this forced confinement, was to last for two months. Captain Charles Elliot, the First Superintendent of British Trade,[88] took his momentous decision on 26 March and made it public to the British merchants in Canton on 27 March: he required all British opium to be delivered to the Chinese authorities. By issuing official 'opium receipts' to the traders against delivery of their stocks, Elliot effectively made the British government responsible for ultimate financial compensation for the traders' losses. A month after the event, on 1 May 1839, James Matheson's considered judgment was that Elliot's decision had been a 'statesmanlike measure' (letter 170). When James Matheson wrote this, however, he did not know that he was to stay for another 23 days in this enforced confinement. As one of the leaders of the foreign community, he was also one of the last prisoners to be released, and his release only came after all the foreign opium stocks had been surrendered and destroyed. The total value of the opium surrendered and destroyed was estimated at between two and two and a half million pounds sterling.[89]

[86] On Chinese policy-making in the late 1830s with regard to the opium question, see: Polachek, James M., *The Inner Opium War*, Cambridge, MA, Harvard University Press, 1992.
[87] The name was first given by *The Times*, 15 April 1840. (Fay, *The Opium War*, p. 204).
[88] For the role and function of 'First Superintendent of British Trade' following the 1833 India Act, see the development on the Napier mission above.
[89] Initial estimates ranged from 6 to 10 million dollars. *Ibid.*, p. 163.

The Treaty of Nanking was signed on 29 August 1842. It is traditionally regarded as having put an end to the Opium War. It left many important points unresolved, however, and among them the very question of the opium trade. As a result, a whole year was spent in further negotiations before the so-called 'Supplementary Treaty' could be signed on 8 October 1843 (Letter 262 alludes to the negotiations of the Supplementary Treaty under way in July 1843). The Supplementary Treaty itself failed to address the opium trade question squarely. Opium was neither legalized by the Chinese, nor was its commerce discontinued by the British traders. This legal vacuum on the status of the opium trade continued well beyond the second Opium War of 1858–1860.[90] A further two points of paramount importance for the opium traders which the Nanking Treaty did not solve were the amount of the compensation they would receive for the loss of their property when their opium was surrendered in 1839, and the date when that compensation would be paid. Back in London, William Jardine spared no exertions in this direction. His frustration and that of his fellow traders in the East only increased when the British government refused to pay advances on Elliot's opium receipts (Letters 200, 212, 249). Eventually the British government did pay up,—£1,281,211 in all,—but this was not until August 1843, and at the low rate of compensation of 300 dollars per chest on average—a compensation which Alexander Matheson regarded as 'miserable' (Letters 261, 263).[91]

Between March 1839 and August 1842 the Opium War worked its fitful way between blockades of Canton, stoppages of trade, paroxysms of naval battles on the China coast, periods of calm when trading activity resumed, changes of governments in London, changes of policies in Peking, and eventually the establishment of a colony in Hong Kong which the British government had neither planned nor wanted. The war lasted some forty months which divide roughly equally into two phases, each reflecting the personality of the British plenipotentiary appointed as well as the clarity and forcefulness of the instructions he received from London. For the first twenty months Captain Charles Elliot was in charge of operations. Sir Henry Pottinger succeeded him in August 1841 for the second and final phase of the war (Letter 241).

In directing the British to surrender their opium on 26 March 1839, as already noted, Captain Elliot acted in his capacity as Superintendent of British trade in China. The opium traders felt they had to comply with his orders for fear that, '[they] should otherwise have placed themselves beyond the pale of the

[90] For the Supplementary Treaty, its negotiations, main points and its shortcomings, see Fairbank, *Trade and Diplomacy*, chapter 9, 'The opium Settlement in 1843', pp. 133–154.

[91] For details on the payments made by the British government on the 1839 opium receipts, see Letter **170**, note 42, and Letter **262**, note 36. See also: Fay, *The Opium War*, p. 368; Keswick, *The Thistle and the Jade*, p. 73.

protection of the British government' (Letter 170).[92] James Matheson and others soon came to regard this decision which had initially baffled them as a 'statesmanlike' decision: only such officially sanctioned surrender or property, they reckoned, could eventually force the British government into retaliatory action.

It was not until the end of December 1839 that the Foreign Secretary, Palmerston, decided to demand reparation and to send a naval force to China. In the eleven months between the start of hostilities in March 1839 and February 1840, when he received Palmerston's letter approving his action (Letter 194) and appointing him joint Plenipotentiary with his cousin, Admiral Sir George Elliot.[93], Charles Elliot continued to act as best he could as Superintendent of British Trade. He had only a limited force at his disposal and he often needed to rent vessels from merchant firms. Following an affray in Kowloon in July 1839, Commissioner Lin demanded reparation and 'expulsed [the British] from China' (Letters 174, 175). Elliot retaliated by blockading Canton (Letter 178). The members of the American trading community, having agreed to sign the opium bond, were allowed to return to Canton, while the British had no option but to take up residence on, and trade as best they could from, their own ships in and around Hong Kong. By October 1839, a compromise was found with the Chinese authorities, whereby the British could trade at Chuenpi, a fortified headland outside the Bogue. In November, hostilities started again and trade was interrupted once more. On 2 November, Elliot's two frigates, the *Hyacinth* and the *Volage* opened fire on the fleet of Chinese war junks which was approaching British positions. This was the first real naval battle of the Opium War. It resulted in severe Chinese casualties, including an admiral reported killed but in fact only wounded (Letter 188).

So many disruptions in trade, some of them of a violent nature, started having an impact on the Chinese Treasury. Barely six months after its inception, Commissioner Lin's muscular action against opium backfired: he was recalled to Peking, and was later exiled (Letter 192). A new Commissioner, Kishen, was appointed to succeed him (Letter 191). During the first few months of 1840, the situation was calm again, and trade resumed apace, not only in opium operations up the China coast (Letter 207), but also in teas, which the British government

[92] Elliot's order was specific and clear: 'Constrained by paramount motives affecting the safety of the lives and liberty of all the foreigners here present in Canton, and by other very weighty causes, I, Charles Elliot, Chief Superintendent of the Trade of British Subjects in China. . . do hereby in the name and on behalf of her Britannic Majesty's government enjoin and require all Her Majesty's subjects now present in Canton forthwith to make a surrender to me for the service of Her said Majesty's government, to be delivered over to the government of China, of all opium belonging to them, or British Opium under their respective control; and to hold the British ships and vessels engaged in the trade of opium subject to my immediate direction'. Fay, *the Opium War*, p. 153, quoting *PP, Correspondence relating to China*, 1840, 36, (223), 370.

[93] Fay, *Opium War*, p. 217.

regarded as a 'necessity' (Letter 195), not only for its people, but also for the 'four or five millions sterling [which it yielded] in annual revenue'.[94]

The naval force sent to Elliot reached Macao in late 1840 (Letter 211). It consisted of sixteen war ships, four armed steamers, and twenty-eight transport ships carrying four thousand soldiers.[95] Following the arrival of the British force, Canton was immediately blockaded (Letter 213). Palmerston's instructions were for the fleet to move up north, seize Chusan and threaten Peking into negotiations. Accordingly the two Elliots sailed up north with the force. Chusan surrendered in August 1840. Shortly thereafter Peking appointed Kishen to negotiate with Charles Elliot. Meanwhile, Admiral Sir George Elliot was invalided out, owing to illness. Charles Elliot thus found himself the sole British Plenipotentiary. Kishen invited him to return to Canton to negotiate. Elliot who was keen to see trade restored, failed to push his advantage while he was threateningly close to Peking. He returned to Canton by the end of November, convincing himself that Kishen was in earnest (Letter 219). Meanwhile, Kishen, playing for time, awaited the arrival of the Chinese army.

On 7 January 1841, Charles Elliot finally lost patience at Kishen's procrastination. He attacked the Bogue forts guarding the entrance of the Canton river and destroyed them (Letter 222). Kishen, fearing for the city of Canton, had no alternative but to sit down with Elliot to negotiate a peace treaty, the so-called 'Convention of Chuenpi'. It was signed on 20 January 1841 (Letter 223). China agreed to pay Britain an indemnity of six million dollars, to cede the island of Hong Kong, and to reopen trade at Canton. On the whole, the British community trading at Canton was reasonably satisfied (Letter 224). Six days later, on 26 January, the British flag was raised in Hong Kong. The occasion was witnessed by James Matheson who also toured the island by ship (Letter 226). The mercantile community heaved a sigh of relief: trade could resume at last.

Local traders may have been satisfied, but neither Peking nor London were amused. Both refused to endorse the decisions taken by their respective plenipotentiaries. In February 1841, Peking dismissed Kishen and repudiated the Convention of Chuenpi. 'Hostilities are about to recommence', James Matheson wrote to William Jardine, feeling he had been 'humbugged' (Letter 227). As soon as the details of the Convention reached London, the reaction was similar to what it had been in Peking. On 21 April 1841, Palmerston sat down to write a letter of reprimand to his plenipotentiary and to recall him (Letter 232). Charles Elliot had been instructed 'to obtain freedom for the British to live and trade at the five ports of Canton, Amoy, Foochow, Ningpo and Shanghai ; the cession of an island or islands, of if the Chinese absolutely refused (this was the only area in which Palmerston allowed a little leeway), the establishment of a secure English enclave

[94] See the Liverpool Petition of February 1836, last paragraph but one, in **Appendix VII**.

[95] Blake, *Jardine Matheson*, p. 99.

somewhere on the mainland; above all money—money for the unpaid Hong debts, money for the confiscated opium, money for the expense of the expedition'.[96] Instead of which Elliot had obtained 'a barren island with hardly a house upon it', a totally inadequate amount of money to defray all the costs of war and business losses, and not one additional free port at which to trade up the China coast. Sir Henry Pottinger, an Indian army veteran, recently (1840) created a baronet for his services in the Marratha War, was appointed to succeed him.

Elliot's role did not end at once. Pottinger was appointed British plenipotentiary in May 1841, only a few days before the Whig ministry in London lost the 4 June vote of censure, leading to the dissolution of Parliament (Letter 234), and a victory in the general elections for the Conservative Party. Between the renewal of hostilities following the failure of the convention of Chuenpi and Pottinger's arrival in Macao on 9 August, seven months elapsed. During this time, Charles Elliot continued to direct operations. On 26 February 1841 he again stormed the Bogue forts which had been returned to China a month before (Letter 228). Once more trade had to stop (Letter 230), but Elliot's successful progress up the river encouraged the troops and the senior officers to think they would be allowed to storm the city. On 19 March, British forces seemed in a position to do so. Charles Elliot decided to spare the city in return for the reopening of trade.[97] Trade resumed in April until the end of May, when the Chinese attempted to destroy British ships by fire boats. Once again, hostilities resumed, and Charles Elliot gallantly led the fight, for although he was much criticized for his weakness as a negotiator, his personal courage was never in doubt. Seventy-one junks were sunk, and two thousand four hundred men were landed around Canton. Once more Canton was at the mercy of British guns. And once more Charles Elliot spared the city.[98]

When Sir Henry Pottinger arrived in Macao (Letter 241), he handed Charles Elliot his letter of recall. The new plenipotentiary had a clear mission—to accomplish in as little time as possible the instructions which Palmerston had previously given his predecessor.[99] Pottinger lost no time to get down to his task. On 21 August 1841, the naval force under the command of Rear Admiral Parker sailed

[96] Fay, *Opium War*, p. 270, based on Correspondence Relating to China, PP. 1840, 36, (223).

[97] Blake, *Jardine Matheson*, p. 101.

[98] Ibid. p. 102. Robert Blake holds the view that Charles Elliot was 'naive and gullible' (p. 101). This is a view which was shared by a number of Elliot's contemporaries. However, Robert Blake goes further in his overall character assessment: 'The truth is that Elliot was at heart a 'mandarin'. Just as the real mandarins looked down on the co-hong, so Elliot disliked the Jardines, the Mathesons and the Dents of this world.' (p. 102). There is ample proof in this collection to show that William Jardine came to dislike Elliot intensely (see in particular Letter 229); but there is equally substantial evidence showing that James Matheson and Charles Elliot liked each other (see Letters 219, 231, 242, etc.).

[99] Palmerston was by now out of office until the next Whig government in 1846. During the period from 30 August 1841 to 27 June 1846, the Earl of Aberdeen replaced him at the Foreign Office.

with Pottinger to Amoy. On 26 August, Amoy was occupied. On 6 October, Chusan was recaptured. Chinchai and Ningpo were taken a few days later. In February 1842, after this initial success, Pottinger returned to Macao and started organizing an embryonic government in Hong Kong, where several British traders had moved and were already busy building godowns and reorganizing their businesses. He also assembled reinforcements to accomplish his final push to the north and force Peking to surrender.

On 9 March 1842, five days after James Matheson was 'ordered suddenly off to England by his doctors' (Letter 252), the Chinese, under the command of Iching, launched their counter-offensive to recapture the cities they had lost. In Ningpo, Iching lost five hundred men ; the British, fighting under General Gough, had no casualties. The Chinese assaults on Chinchai were equally unsuccessful. Chusan remained largely quiet. Atrocities were committed on both sides during this episode of the Opium war. They did not come through in the official dispatches, but only surfaced later in soldiers' memoirs and letters. By the end of spring 1842 it was clear that the Chinese counter-offensive had ended in failure.[100]

On 7 May 1842, Pottinger launched his final campaign, the 'Yangtze Campaign'.[101] On 18 May Chapu, the port for Hangchow, was attacked and fell after fierce fighting. On 13 June, the force started moving up the Hwangpu River towards Shanghai. Three days later, Shanghai was taken with hardly any resistance. The way was now clear up the Yangtze towards Chingkiang and Nanjing. Chingkiang fell on 21 July after a major engagement. The fall of Chingkiang and the threat to Nanking, the old capital, alarmed the Chinese authorities. Peking was effectively blockaded. The emperor appointed Kiying (Ch'i-ying) at the end of July, with Ilipu as his assistant, to negotiate a peace. Eventually, on 29 August,

[100] On the Chinese counter-offensive of March-April 1842, see Fay, *Opium War*, p. 319–321.

[101] For contents of this paragraph, ibid., pp. 339–355. In spite of Adam Smith's various remarks on the country (1776), China had hardly been a topical subject among the general British public before 1841. A number of memoirs of the Opium War published after that date contributed to develop public awareness. Among those are the following: Jocelyn, Lord Robert, *Six Months with the Chinese Expedition*, London, 1841 (this book was read by William Jardine and is referred to in Letter 229); K. S. Mackenzie, *Narrative of the Second Campaign in China*, London, 1842; Bingham, Commander J. Elliot, *Narrative of the Expedition to China from the Commencement of the War to the Present Period, etc.*, London, Henry Colburn, 1842; Loch, Granville G., *The Closing Events of the Campaign in China*, London, 1843; Murray, Lt. Alexander, *Doings in China*, London 1843; Belcher, Captain Sir Edward, *Narrative of a Voyage round the World, performed in Her Majesty's Ship Suplhur, During the Years 1836–1842, Including details of the Naval Operations in China, from Dec. 1840 to Nov. 1841*, London 1843, Dawsons of Pall Mall Reprint, 1970; 'A Field officer', *The Last Year in China*, London, 1843; Ouchterlony, Lt. John, *The Chinese War: An Account of All the Operations of the British Forces from the Commencement to the Treaty of Nanking*, London, Saunders and Otley, 1844; Cunynghame, Captain Arthur, *An Aide-de-Camp's Recollections of Service in China*, London, 2 volumes, 1844; and, a few years later, Davis, Sir John Francis, *China, During the War and Since the Peace*, London, Longman, Brown, Green and Longman, 2 volumes, 1852. (*JRAS*, Vol. 39, pp. 231–233).

Sir Henry Pottinger and Kiying signed the Treaty of Nanking in the great cabin of the *Cornwallis*.[102] News of the treaty reached London at the end of November (Letter 254). By then, William Jardine was too ill to write. James Matheson was at his bedside, helping him with his correspondence.

Jardine's activities in London before and during the conflict must now be examined. He was nine months into a leisurely voyage back from Canton to London when he first heard that the Opium War had started in March 1839. He hurried to London from Italy, and by mid-September had contacted many of his friends and acquaintances on the East India and China Association. This had been formed in the aftermath of the 1833 India Act with a view to furthering the interest of the free-traders to the East. It had a membership of over one hundred British firms and individuals and its proceedings were published annually.[103] The twenty-three members of its executive committee were prominent men of business in the City with connections in Parliament and in the government. They included G. de Hochepied Larpent, who was chairman of the Association, Archibald Hasties, MP, John Horsley Palmer, Richard Twining, etc. Among committee members especially well-known to William Jardine were W. T. Copeland, MP, J. H. Gledstanes, William Lyall, Thomas Weeding and several others.[104] On 19 September a General meeting of the China trade was called which was attended by all members of the Association present in London. The General meeting appointed a Committee of nine members, which in turn appointed a Subcommittee of three 'consisting of [G. de H.] Larpent, John Abel Smith, and William Crawford'[105] (Letter 182). The Subcommittee members were to seek an appointment with the Foreign Secretary, Lord Palmerston.

John Abel Smith, who had been William Jardine's close business associate since 1837, had easier access to Palmerston than the other two members of the Subcommittee (Letters 176, 179). It was through him that an initial interview was arranged on 27 September (Letter 180). John Abel Smith introduced William Jardine and Alexander Grant to the Foreign Secretary, who was thus able to obtain independent first-hand knowledge of the general situation in Canton and in

[102] The Treaty of Nanking 'provided that the Chinese pay an indemnity of 21 million dollars, six of these earmarked as compensation for the famous confiscated chests. The five ports of Canton, Amoy, Foochow, Ningpo, and Shanghai were to be open to English residence and trade. Consuls were to be permitted at these five places, the Cohong was to be abolished, and a rational schedule of customs duties arranged. Future relations between England and China were to be on the basis of perfect equality. The island of Hong Kong was to pass to Her Majesty in perpetuity. Chusan and Kulangsu were to remain in English hands until the 21 million had been paid ; indeed, the fleet would not leave Nanking until it had loaded the first six.' (Fay, *Opium War*, p. 362). For the full text of the Treaty of Nanking, see **Appendix X**.

[103] For the 1838 membership list of the East India and China Association, see Letter 151.

[104] *Ibid.*, for the full list of the Association's committee.

[105] William Crawford was the head of the London firm *Crawford, Colvin & Co.*, which had an Agency House in Bombay.

China. Palmerston asked William Jardine many questions about the situation in Canton and in China, but he kept silent about his own intentions (Letter 181). On 10 October Palmerston received the official deputation of the Subcommittee. William Jardine, not being a member of the Subcommittee, was not present at that interview. The contents of the interview were summarized by Larpent in a memorandum appended to Letter 182.[106] Again, Palmerston was extremely guarded in his response: 'Nothing fell from Lord Palmerston to commit him as to the intention of government, nor were the words 'armed Force' used by him' (Letter 182).

In late October, William Jardine took the business-like precaution of instructing W. P. Freshfield to investigate the nature of the opium claims against the government (Letter 185). The big question on all opium traders' minds was: who was to pay for the drug which had been confiscated and destroyed? As the drug had been surrendered at the specific command of Captain Charles Elliot, H. M. Superintendent of British Trade, and as opium receipts had been issued to each respective owner pro-rata to his ownership, it seemed to stand to reason that the British government should pay. But were these receipts enforceable? And if so, how, and when? On 20 November, William Jardine accompanied John Abel Smith on another visit to Palmerston. It transpired during this interview that 'H. M. Ministers intend to make the Chinese pay for the drug'. Commenting on this general declaration of intention, William Jardine added: 'they will succeed if the force sent is sufficient' (Letter 190).

Some time in December 1839, William Jardine sent Palmerston a paper outlining his recommendation for action. The paper argued for the necessity of sending a strong naval force and several thousand men. The force was to proceed north towards Peking and demand reparation from the Emperor. Reparation included payment for the opium confiscated, a real commercial treaty, and the liberty to trade at Amoy, Foochow, Ningpo and Shanghai. This paper must have confirmed Palmerston's opinion that a naval force should be sent to China, although he did not declare his position until two months later, at the end of February 1840.[107]

[106] John Macvicar, leading a deputation from Manchester, was also received by Palmerston a few days before 10 October. He had refused to entrust the concern of the Manchester China traders to the care of the Subcommittee, thus attracting the acid remark from William Crawford: 'On the 27th this Subcommittee saw the deputation which was in Town from Liverpool, they have also entrusted to us, the care of the interests of the People there. It was understood the Manchester people would do the same, but it seems it did not conform with the self-importance of Mr. Macvicar to take that course. He saw Lord Palmerston a few days ago. . .' (Letter 182).

[107] Neither a copy of William Jardine's 'paper to Lord Palmerston of 14 December 1839' nor his 'letter of 19 December 1839 to James Matheson' rehearsing the same arguments were located by this editor in *JMArch*. The two authorities who mention these documents are Collis, *Foreign Mud*, p. 235, and Blake, *Jardine Matheson*, p. 93. Both rely on Gerald J. Yorke's unpublished typescript, *The Princely House*, c. 1937, p. 328. Yorke's full passage, quoting from a letter dated 19 December 1839 by William Jardine to James Matheson, reads as follows: 'My advice is to send a naval force to blockade

Meanwhile, a third interview with the Foreign Secretary had taken place on 4 February (Letter 193). William Jardine took this opportunity to '[bring] to his notice the debts due by the Cohong to the foreign merchants'. This meant that yet more money had to be obtained from the Chinese when they eventually were made to pay up for the confiscated opium.

Parliament had to sanction any expedition to China. By early March 'the China papers were laid before the House of Commons' (Letter 197) leading to the China debate of 7 to 10 April 1840. From then on, William Jardine's role in London was less directly political. Once his advice on how to deal with the China crisis had made its contribution to the formulation of government policy, he returned to lobbying for a full and early payment on the opium receipts. Until his own election

---

the coast of China from the Tartar wall to Tienpack or from 40 to 20 degrees north; the force to consist of two ships of the line, two frigates and two flat-bottomed steamers for river service, with a sufficient number of transports to carry . . . six or seven thousand men. The force to proceed to the vicinity of Pekin, and apply directly to the Emperor for an apology for the insult. . . payment for the opium given up, an equitable commercial treaty, and liberty to trade with northern ports. . . say, Amoy, Foochow, Ningpo, Shanghai and also Kiaochow, if we can get it.

// The two first demands would readily be granted, but the third and fourth may be refused, and then we must proceed to take possession of three or four islands, say Formosa, Quemoy, and Amoy (or at least two. . . and intercept the trade from Formosa). We should also take the great Chusan island, which being near Peking would be a source of great annoyance to the Emperor. Having these islands in our possession, the Chinese would most likely grant all our demands on condition of our giving them up. I observe you are for Formosa, but it is too large, unless the inhabitants are well disposed towards us. *How this advice will be received we know not as we have not yet sent it to Lord Palmerston. . .*' (Our italics).

The last paragraph, with its crucial last sentence, omitted by both Collis and Blake, makes it clear that, if the date of the letter quoted by Yorke was correctly transcribed (i.e., 19 December 1839), no paper of recommendation had been sent by Jardine to Palmerston by that date, neither on 14 December, (Collis's version), nor on 5 December (*DNB*'s version, by Richard J. Grace, referring to Cambridge University Library, *JM correspondence*).

By the end of December 1839, however, Palmerston had completed his consultations and certainly knew about Jardine's recommended course of action. He decided to retain several of Jardine's ideas. It remains that, as Jardine's own letters make clear, Palmerston was careful, throughout this time of consultations as indeed during the whole Opium War period, not to give any hint as to which advisers' arguments he found more convincing than others. Only after the war had been won did he allow himself to write the following to John Abel Smith: 'To the assistance and information which you and Mr. Jardine so handsomely afforded us, it was mainly owing that we were able to give our affairs, Naval, Military and Diplomatic, in China, those detailed instructions which have led to these satisfactory results. It is indeed remarkable that the information which we procured from yourself and various other persons whom we consulted in the Autumn of 1839, which was embodied in instructions which we gave in February 1840, was so accurate and complete that it appears that our successors have not found reason to make any alterations in them, and it has turned out that the decisive operation has been that in the Yang tsi Kiang which we suggested to our Naval Commander as far back as our instructions of February, 1840, and that the conditions of peace imposed upon the Emperor are precisely those which we had instructed our Plenipotentiaries Elliot and Pottinger to obtain'. (Fairbank, *Trade and Diplomacy*, p. 83, quoting a letter of Palmerston to John Abel Smith dated 28 Nov. 1842; and Easton, Harry Tucker, *The History of a Banking House, (Smith, Payne and Smiths)*, London, Blades, East and Blades, 1895, p. 29).

to Parliament in 1841 (Letters 237, 240), he remained passionately though indirectly involved in the works of the China Subcommittee, and the parliamentary China Committee (Letter 200) where he continued to act as John Abel Smith's *eminence grise*. In early March 1840, he joined *Magniac Smith & Co.* as a partner (Letter 196), thus renewing a long-standing business alliance with Hollingworth Magniac and sealing a newer, powerful one with John Abel Smith. Two weeks before the China debate in Parliament, the fact that 'the government [refused] to confirm Captain Elliot's guarantee' confirmed early hints that any payment on the opium would need to come from the Chinese themselves if it was to come at all (Letter 198). Keeping his cards close to his chest, Palmerston had found an elegant solution to the government's China dilemma. There was no likelihood that Parliament would agree to pay opium traders over two million pounds sterling to honour Captain Elliot's guarantee. But Parliament might agree to send an expedition to China to open trade and make the Chinese pay for all the bills.[108] Thus the British government's guarantee on the opium was to be honoured, without any opposition from the Christian anti-opium lobby (the 'High Church party' of Letter 177), or financial strain on the Treasury.

On 2 April 1840, a few days before the China debate in Parliament, John Abel Smith who, as MP, had been appointed a member of the Commons China Committee 'suggested a plan of their arranging the Committee in such a manner as they should advise the House to grant a loan in Exchequer Bills for half the amount of the claim, say, £1,200,000 on the security of Elliot's opium receipts' (Letter 200). The plan raised hope among the opium traders, and it continued being discussed until early June when, to William Jardine's disappointment, the Commons China Committee was too divided to recommend any particular course to Parliament, but instead 'laid the evidence before the House without any observation' (Letter 209). William Jardine was incensed by the petty politics of Parliament and what he regarded as an 'evasion of responsibility' on the part of government (Letters 212, 216). Parliament and Cabinet were much more forceful, however, about military action. In the China debate, which took place over a four day period, from 7 to 10 April 1840, the House agreed to Palmerston's proposed amphibious expedition. This opened the prospect of an eventual compensation paid by China, and an expansion of trading privileges. 'We were relieved by ministers having a majority of nine', William Jardine wrote in his letter describing the debate and its outcome (Letter 204). The vote of censure moved by Sir Robert Peel, attacking the government for 'incompetence rather than

[108] In anticipation to such an agreement, Palmerston sent instructions to Lord Auckland, Governor General of India, on 20 February 1840. Auckland was to assemble a naval force and send it to China. The parliamentary debate occurred only two months later, on 7–10 April. (Fay, *Opium War*, pp. 193–194 ; Blake, *Jardine Matheson*, p. 94).

immorality'[109] was narrowly defeated. Parliament thus finally sanctioned the expedition to China and, with it, the Opium War.

By the time the parliamentary debate on China took place, William Jardine, then aged 56, had less than three years to live. Although officially retired, he remained extremely active. He combined his new life as landowner and MP with his duties as a partner in *Magniac Smith & Co.*, exerting himself on behalf of former constituents, who, like himself and Jamsetjee Jejeebhoy, were impatiently awaiting from government the money due on their opium receipts. Many of his 1841 and 1842 letters contain outbursts of frustration at the fact that the money was still not forthcoming, and of anger at those held responsible, notably Charles Elliot (Letters 229, 232). Many letters are also tinged with anxiety at the thought of the old friends and associates exposed to the perils of war in Canton (Letter 245).

William Jardine and John Abel Smith had at least one further interview with Palmerston. It took place in the first few days of May 1841, at a time when the details of the Convention of Chuenpi had reached London. Unknown to those present at the meeting, Palmerston had decided to recall Charles Elliot for disregarding instructions and for obtaining far too little money from China, not to mention the unwanted island of Hong Kong. During the meeting, William Jardine's own frustration at the inadequacy of the financial compensation negotiated by Elliot led him to attempt a joke. 'When telling [Lord Palmerston] that the compensation was only half the amount due,' he wrote, 'I added unless Captain Elliot has put a high value on the Island of Hong Kong, and if he has, we shall be very happy to consider H.M. Government indebted to us for the other half. His Lordship laughed and said he supposed we would' (Letter 233). Like Palmerston, Jardine was more interested in immediately available cash payments and commercial advantage than in territorial expansion.

Whilst Jardine was manoeuvring in London, Matheson was faced with conducting the firm's business in China. With the many disruptions it entails, a war is not usually a favourable environment for trading firms. Despite the obstacles, however, record profits were booked in 1840 and 1841. Whilst holding the fort as senior partner of the firm from January 1839 to March 1842, James Matheson steered a steady course through difficulties which must occasionally have seemed insurmountable. Many of the letters written in Canton, Macao, Hong Kong, or on board the firm's ships when there was nowhere else to go, bear witness to the habitual conditions of uncertainty, confusion and anxiety under which much business had to be dispatched. The British traders, unlike their American counterparts, refused to sign the 'Opium bond' (Letter 171). They were thus no longer allowed to continue in residence in Canton, where the sales of incoming cargoes and the

[109] Blake, *Jardine Matheson*, p. 95. For Blake's analysis of the China debate itself, op. cit. pp. 94–97.

provision of return supplies for their ships had always been, and continued to be, negotiated. This was the first major handicap to the normal continuation of their business. In order to find a solution *Jardine, Matheson & Co.* employed the services of *James Ryan*, their American Agents in Canton (Letter 201). Never before had the firm had so direct and frequent business dealings with the American firms in Canton (Letter 183, 198, 201).

No sooner was the trade stopped in 1839, than contingency plans had to be put in place (Letter 170, under 'Arrangement for this season's business'). The most important and lucrative part of the business had been the opium trade, and therefore means had to be found at all costs to secure its continuation. To this effect, the opium fleet headquarters were moved from Hong Kong to Manila. As early as November 1839, this strategic relocation had been effected with the help of the local agents, *Otadui & Co.* In the absence of Alexander Matheson who was temporarily back in London helping William Jardine lobby for payment on the opium receipts, the firm's other junior partner, Andrew Jardine, was asked to move to Manila.[110] It was from there that he organized the day-to-day opium operations as well as the sales of the drug up the China coast (Letter 188). The choice of Manila as a hub for the opium fleet in substitution for the Hong Kong waters made economic sense, the voyage from the Indian ports and to the China coast involving few additional miles. The opium ships continued to be commanded by captains who were self-reliant and remunerated on a profit-sharing basis. They could be depended upon to do their best for the firm, even in the occasional absence of instructions. As early as January 1840 good progress had been made in the reorganization of the opium business and James Matheson was able to report to William Jardine that 'affairs under the management of [captains] Reed, Jauncey, etc., continue to go on well' (Letter 194). Nevertheless, 'the *golden* days of the Trade [had] gone by', and competition up the coast had never been so fierce (Letter 202).

Amidst the chaos of makeshift offices, with files missing or inaccessible, suppliers and buyers contactable only through intermediaries, James Matheson remained at the centre of the firm's business web, working incessantly, placing opium orders in India (Letters 207, 221), defending the firm's actions against constituents' complaints (Letter 249), negotiating cotton transactions on a large scale through the American firm *Russell & Co.*, etc. (Letter 198), helping widows in need of financial advice (Letter 187). In fact, it was business in wartime, with a number of additional impediments and contingencies to contend with, including occasional anxiety for personal safety. James Matheson often thought it

[110] Alexander Matheson (later Sir Alexander Matheson) was a nephew of James Matheson. He was made a partner of the firm in 1835. He was managing partner from 1843 to 1852 when the firm's headquarters had moved from Canton to Hong Kong. Andrew Jardine, a nephew of William Jardine, was a partner of the firm from 1839 to 1843. (Keswick, op. cit., p. 264).

prudent to disguise his identity. He would then sign himself off as 'Santiago Thomasen' in order to escape detection in the event his letters were intercepted by the Chinese (Letter 201). Overall, however, as already noted, the difficult trading conditions created opportunities for extremely profitable business.

One of the most difficult aspects was the unpredictability of trade interruption. This was particularly so during the first twenty months of hostilities, when operations were under the direction of Charles Elliot. Interrupting trade had long been a favourite weapon of the Chinese when they wanted to retaliate against foreign merchants for whatever reason. It now became a weapon which was also used by the British plenipotentiaries in the form of port blockades. When the blockades were applied to Canton, repercussions on British trade were immediate and dramatic, though not necessarily long-lasting. The letters James Matheson wrote during the period keep a faithful record of these numerous interruptions. The year 1839 was seriously disrupted, the Chinese having stopped the trade in March to all merchants who would not sign the opium bond. This meant that all British official commerce stopped for eight months until October, when Charles Elliot managed to negotiate with the Chinese authorities the reopening of British trade at Chuenpi (Letter 183). But this resumption was short-lived. In November 1839, Elliot's frigates destroyed war junks, and commercial activity stopped again (Letter 188). Although the official Chinese position did not change with the recall of Commissioner Lin, the mandarins started closing their eyes to the intense smuggling in *bona fide* goods which now occurred and which was to continue throughout the hostilities whenever official trade was interrupted. This long period when the tea trade, could only be conducted through what James Matheson himself describes as 'smuggling', continued throughout the Opium War. For the British traders 'smuggling' in this sense consisted in obtaining cargoes of staple Chinese goods illegally. The 40 million pounds of tea annually shipped from China for Britain's consumption had to come through this channel. American agents would place orders with tea suppliers in Canton on behalf of the British firms, and the tea was eventually transshipped from American to British ships. Alternatively, the Chinese suppliers would take the risk of flouting their own rules and deliver supplies directly to the British ships anchored in the vicinity of Hong Kong. This is what James Matheson described as the British Government 'conniving' in the export of tea (Letter 195).

All in all, the trading difficulties associated with the Opium War had a paradoxical effect. Instead of declining, profits soared. With combined profit for the years 1840 and 1841 exceeding $2.6 million, the firm had never before been so successful.[111] In ten years of trading activity, between 1830 and 1840, profits had been multiplied by a factor of almost 10. Such business achievements against the

[111] See Table 7 above.

backdrop of trade disruptions occasioned by the Opium War are accounted for by two principal factors. First, the firm had a resilient and diversified client base, and it continued to be carefully managed during those difficult years. And secondly, the opium business, because of its early relocation to Manila, was the one that suffered least from the effect of the war. The firm's principal source of profit had been successfully insulated from the disruptions of trade.

The firm's geographical base, owing to the vagaries of war and politics, now changed from Canton and Macao to the newly acquired island on which it was to remain. If by 'British rule in Hong Kong' is meant the officially-sanctioned action of governing a new colony whose ownership had just passed from China to the British Crown, then it cannot be denied that the Treaty of Nanking was that official sanction, and that British rule in Hong Kong started on 29 August 1842, or a few months later, once the Treaty had been ratified, on 31 December 1842 (Letter 255). The beginning of British rule in Hong Kong, however, was the result of a far more complex chain of events, and took place in a much more drawn-out process than has often been realized. Behind the apparently straightforward and univocal birth of a new colony heralded by a new treaty, it is indeed possible to detect three distinct beginnings. Taken individually, none of these beginnings was officially sanctioned by Britain. The first arose independently of British agreement; the second occurred in clear disregard of official instructions; and the third was brought about in open, though understandable, defiance of ministerial orders.

Hong Kong first arose out of the will of free traders like William Jardine and James Matheson. It was first and foremost a conveniently-placed harbour where the opium traders took refuge on their receiving ships as early as 1838 (Letters 162, 164). The year 1838 was pivotal in the opium trade. As the Chinese repression campaign on its own opium networks became increasingly stringent, larger and larger single deliveries were being transacted by the trading firms, and in particular by *Jardine, Matheson & Co.* The safety of the drug in transit could no longer be taken for granted and this became a matter of ever-increasing concern. Hong Kong was an anchorage which afforded much better safety and protection than Lintin[112]. Four years before the Treaty of Nanking, therefore, Hong Kong had been elected by the smartest traders as the *de facto* storing harbour for their far-flung coastal operations. This beginning of Hong Kong as a safe harbour for the traders' opium fleets was entirely independent of any official action by the British government.

The second beginning of Hong Kong was quite another matter. By then Charles Elliot was in charge of negotiations with the Chinese as Britain's plenipotentiary. It was one of his demands that Hong Kong should be ceded to Britain. This was agreed by the Convention of Chuenpi of 20 January 1841. Six days later, without

[112] A small island off Hong Kong in the Pearl River delta, which had been the principal centre of the Opium trade in the 1830s.

waiting for a ratification of the Convention, which in any case never came, the British officially hoisted the Union Flag in Hong Kong (Letter 226). On 29 January 1841, Charles Elliot's proclamation promised 'full security and protection to all British subjects and foreigners residing in and resorting to this island, so long as they shall continue to conform to the authority of Her Majesty's Government'.[113] The island was treated as a possession of the British Crown. An embryonic government was organized, a chief magistrate and a harbour-master were appointed. More importantly still, the first land auctions took place in June 1841. The principal trading houses, including *Jardine, Matheson & Co.* bought land at that auction, and they immediately started building godowns and offices.[114] By 23 August 1841, James Matheson and the other British traders had already invested tens of thousands of dollars in Hong Kong real estate. This gave them a powerful incentive to want to retain Hong Kong despite the official stance of British policy which was leaning towards an opening of trade with China which involved no responsibility for territorial possessions. 'I am not disinterested in advocating [Hong Kong's] retention,' wrote James Matheson, as a result of his real estate investment. 'Many prefer Cowloon[115] Peninsula, but we ought to have both' (Letter 241).

Elliot's recall and the fact that the Convention of Chuenpi was never ratified had immediate repercussions upon Hong Kong. Months after what had first appeared as its official birth, the 'new settlement' of Hong Kong continued unrecognized by both the British and Chinese authorities. It was to remain in this state of legal limbo for over a year, until Sir Henry Pottinger finally secured its official existence as a British Colony in the Treaty of Nanking. Meanwhile, in its second beginning Hong Kong had been born of Charles Elliot's dream—an official dream, no doubt, but one deemed by Westminster to be too closely aligned on the sectoral wishes of the expatriate trading community, and above all lacking in financial realism.

Sir Henry Pottinger was asked to complete the task which Charles Elliot had left unfinished. It is not the least irony of Hong Kong's third and true official beginning that the island which Elliot had obtained in January 1841 at the expense of more pressing British demands, Pottinger was to obtain again in August 1842, but this time in complete disregard of formal instructions. By the spring of 1842, the Foreign Secretary, Lord Aberdeen, had decided against any territorial increase in China. In May, modified instructions were accordlingly dispatched to Sir Henry Pottinger. At the time when he was negotiating the Treaty of

[113] Bard, *Traders of Hong Kong*, pp. 36–37. See also Norton-Kyshe, James William, *The History of the Laws and Courts of Hong Hong from the Earliest Period to 1898*, (1898), Hong Kong, Vetch and Lee Limited, 1971, p 5.
[114] Bard, *Traders of Hong Kong*, p.66.
[115] Original spelling.

Nanking, there was therefore a clear official British position against the retention of Hong Kong, and he was fully aware of that position. Nevertheless, the British plenipotentiary chose to retain Hong Kong against the written instructions of his minister.[116] He was encouraged in that stance by the leading members of the British trading community who, like James and Alexander Matheson, were anxious for the retention of the island. He also realized that, during its year and a half of existence under legal limbo, Hong Kong had started to resemble a real British colony, albeit one like no other. Unlike his predecessor, Sir Henry Pottinger got away with this act of blatant disobedience.[117] When he returned to England in 1843, he was given a hero's welcome.

[116] Subsequently, Sir Henry Pottinger wrote to justify his actions. '. . .The retention of Hong Kong is the only single point in which I intentionally exceeded my modified instructions, but every single hour I have passed in this superb country has convinced me of the necessity and desirability of our possessing such a settlement as an emporium for our trade and a place from which Her Majesty's subjects in China may be alike protected and controlled. ' (Endacott, *History of Hong Kong*, p. 22). In another passage, he adds : 'I had no predilection in raising a colony at Hong Kong, or at any other place in China, [but] this settlement has already advanced too far to admit of its ever being restored to the authority of the Emperor.' (*Ibid*., p. 34).

[117] Sir Henry Pottinger was not the first British plenipotentiary or colonial governor to interpret his instructions freely and get away with it. In February 1819, Sir Thomas Stamford Raffles had also exceeded his brief when, within a week, he had negotiated the purchase of Singapore on behalf of the East India Company from the person whom he decided was the rightful Sultan of Jahore. He had long dreamt of ways to counterbalance the Influence of the Dutch in the Malay peninsula. Suddenly, he saw his chance and took it. Lord Hastings's continued support saved him from potential reprimand or worse. (See: *DNB*; Collis, Maurice, *Raffles*, (1968), Singapore, Graham Brash (Pte), 1982, pp. 133–139). See also George Pottinger's assessment of Sir Henry Pottinger's 'Subversive attitude towards Westminster'. (Pottinger, George, *Sir Henry Pottinger, First Governor of Hong Kong*, Phoenix Mill, Sutton Publishing, 1997, p. 86).

Editorial Method

The transcribed material comes exclusively from the Jardine Matheson Archive in the Cambridge University Library. The text of the out-letters is transcribed from original copies bound in folio letterbooks. The text of in-letters is mostly transcribed from microfilm of the original manuscripts, or from the original manuscripts themselves. The letters retain irregularities in their syntax, spelling, and punctuation, which with the writers of in-letters were undoubtedly their own, but which were perhaps due to copyists' errors in the out-letters. While their sense is usually clear, many of the letters present difficulties for the transcriber. The frequent practice of using both sides of thin rice paper for correspondence can cause its front and back to merge, obliterating the text. Discolouration due to age makes some handwriting faint or illegible. Copyists of the out-letters, besides the errors just referred to, not infrequently omitted words, sentences or even paragraphs. Individual letters may even lack a page or more of their content. In the text, the following editorial conventions are employed to identify these hazards, and lessen unnecessary annotation:

a. [ ] : A word or a few words cannot be transcribed. The omission in the text is left blank.

b. [. . .] : A larger part of the text cannot be transcribed, because it is illegible, damaged, or physically missing. Absence of a page of more, however, will be stated in a footnote.

c. [word(s)] : The editor has supplied one or more words to fill an unintentional omission by the writer or the copyist.

d. {word(s)} : The word or words enclosed are probably, but not certainly, as transcribed.

In the absence of such signs, the following editorial rules apply:

1. *Abbreviations and contractions* of family names, names of firms, and standard abbreviations for titles (e.g. Mr., Messrs., etc.) are retained as written. If necessary, abbreviated names of firms are annotated. Initials for Christian names are retained, except when the person referred to is known for certain, in which case the Christian name is written in full.

2. *Other abbreviations and contractions* are normally expanded. The ampersand is given as 'and', except in the names of firms (*Magniac, Smith & Co.*). The tailed 'p' is given as 'per'. Superscript letters are expanded and lowered to the line, as in 'Captain' for 'Captn.', or 'January' for 'Jany'. Marks indicating repetition are given as 'ditto'. The contractions for currencies, measures, and weight are expanded.

3. *Capitalization* is retained as written. Irregularities due to correspondents changing their practice over time, or even within the same letter, are compounded by copyists introducing their own variants.

4. *Footnotes* clarify passages by identifying people, places or events. Once a person has been identified, the documentation is usually not repeated.

5. *Headings of letters* are transcribed in the following format: first, the number of the selected letter in its chronological sequence, followed by the name of the writer of the letter, the place of writing, the name of the addressee, the addressee's place of residence, and finally the date of writing. (e.g.: **170**. James Matheson in Canton to William Jardine in London, 1 May 1839).

6. *Italics* are used for transcribing words underlined, names of firms, abbreviated names of firms, and names of ships.

7. *Paragraphing* is introduced when clear changes of topic occur. Conversely, paragraphing is not retained if no clear changes of topic occur.

8. *Punctuation* is retained as written, except when dashes are transcribed as full stops or commas. Occasionally, punctuation is supplied when totally absent.

9. *Spelling*, including romanization of Chinese names and words, is retained as written. Similar irregularities in spelling occur as for *Capitalization,* and for similar reasons.

JARDINE MATHESON CORRESPONDENCE 1827–1843

1827

1. James Matheson in Canton to *Magniac & Co.* in Canton,

14 February 1827[1]

Dear Sirs,

As we shall not have occasion for our present Factory N° 7 Imperial Hong[2] after the expiry of the year now in progress, we beg to tender to you on behalf of the Landlords the remaining six years of our Lease, leaving it to the decision of any qualified and indifferent person what compensation if any, should be made to us for the great internal improvements and additional buildings which, as you are aware, have been made at a heavy expense to us, and none to our Landlord.

Should it not suit you to take the lease off our hands, we regret that you will consider this as a notice of our intention to discontinue paying any longer the annual rent of 500 dollars for the ground of Factory N° 6, which we shall place at your disposal as soon as required by you consistent with the terms of the Lease.

Awaiting your determination on the subject, we are, dear Sirs, Your faithful servants.

2. James Matheson in Canton to John Purvis in Singapore, 1 March 1827

Dear Sirs,

We beg to acquaint you that during the absence of our Mr. Matheson, who contemplates making a short trip to Bengal,[3] our business will be conducted by

[1] *JMArch. C2-5*, pp. 171–173. All subsequent Letter references are given in **Appendix III**.

[2] The premises known as 'No 7, Imperial Hong' had been rented by James Matheson (later Sir James Matheson) at the time of his business association with Xavier de Yrisarri. After the latter's untimely death in 1826, they were no longer needed. The 'Imperial Hong', or 'Imperial Factory' was one of the thirteen Canton factories used by foreign merchants both as offices and as private accommodation. They were long buildings whose elegant, narrow fronts faced a square and the Canton river. From west to east, the factories bore the following names: Danish, Spanish, French, Chungqua's, American, Paoushun, Imperial, Swedish, Old English, Miscellaneous, New English, Dutch and Creek. *Jardine, Matheson & Co's* premises were situated in this easternmost factory, at No 4, the Creek. (Hunter, *The Fan Kwae at Canton*, p. 13; and p. 100 for the copy of a survey map of the Canton Factories drawn by Commander W. Thornton Bate, R.N., and published in 1856 in London and Edinburgh by *W. Johnston Limited.*

[3] James Matheson was going to Calcutta, where he had first met Xavier de Yrisarri, and where most of the business of *Yrisarri & Co.* originated from. The purpose of the trip was to sort through his partner's estate so that he could wind up the firm and start a new business. In the event, he subsequently joined *Magniac & Co.*, the firm referred to in this letter as giving 'constant advice and superintendence', whose managing partner was William Jardine. (Le Pichon, *Origines de Hong Kong*, pp. 136–137). On Yrisarri's estate, see the letter written in Spanish by James Matheson to J. A. Fernandez dated 15 January 1827, *C2–5*. The balance on the estate was 27,702.07 Spanish dollars. (*JMArch. Yrisarri Letter Book*, and *A8–34–7–8*).

Mr. Joachim Ybar,[4] who has been several years our assistant, in conjunction with Mr. Alexander Matheson,[5] who has lately joined us, and either of them is authorized to sign for the firm.

As they will have the benefit of the constant advice and superintendence of our good friends *Messrs. Magniac & Co.*, our constitutents may be assured of the most zealous and careful attention to whatever interest may be confided to us. Etc.,

Copy to:

Singapore: Graham McKenzie, *Syme & Co.*, *Morgan Hunter & Co.*, J. A. Maxwell.

Calcutta: *Macintosh & Co., Shedden & Co, Bagshaw Barlow & Co., Mendieta Uriarte & Co., James Scott & Co.*

Bombay: *Ranken & Saunders*, J.A. Pereira.

London: *Gregson Melville Knight.* [6]

3. *Fairlie Bonham & Co.* in London to *Magniac & Co.* in Canton,

14 April 1827

Gentlemen,

We have the pleasure to enclose a Copy of your Account Current[7] balanced to the end of last year and continued in open state to the 10th Instant exhibiting the following totals, viz—

Cash at debit	7,718.1.1.	Pounds sterling	Cash at credit	15,036.15.5	Pounds sterling
Dependencies	2,509.12.2		Dependencies	10.900	
	10,227.13.3.			25.936.15.5	

We hope, on examination, the whole will be found correct.

To the various letters with which you have favored us by the ships lately arrived, we shall have the pleasure of replying in detail, by a separate letter and in the meantime, we remain sincerely, Gentlemen,

Yours Obedient servants.

[4] Not identified, but probably an associate of Yrisarri and, like him, of Spanish or Basque origins.

[5] Alexander Matheson, (later Sir Alexander Matheson) was one of James Matheson's nephews. He was 22 and had come to train for business at his uncle's firm. When James Matheson joined *Magniac & Co.* as a partner in January 1828, Alexander Matheson followed him as book-keeper and writer. When James Matheson returned to London in 1842, Alexander Matheson became the firm's 'taipan' or senior partner.

[6] *Yrisarri & Co.*'s principal bankers in London. (*JMArch. C2–5*).

[7] *Fairlie Bonham & Co.*, acting as one of the firm's main London 'constituents' at the time, would normally send a summary of the year's transactions, or 'Account Current'. 'Dependencies' included unrealized goods in transit, and various contingencies. In the present instance the firm had a positive balance in *Fairlie Bonham & Co.*'s books of 15,709 pounds sterling, two shillings and twopence at year-end 1836. For the 'reply in detail', see Letter **5** written two days later.

4. J. H. Gledstanes in London to William Jardine in Canton, 14 April 1827

My dear Jardine,

This will reach you by the *Kellie* poor Adams's ship—you will have heard that he was dismissed for the foolish obstinacy of not reading prayers and for not objecting to its having been thrice entered in the log Book, it is not possible to excuse Adams's folly in not having apprized his friends of the charge about to be brought against him when all might have been averted, on the other hand we all think the Court[8] have been too severe.

My first endeavors were exerted to dispose of the *Commons* at cost price say 3,800 sterling, but unfortunately all the double voyages being gone, no one would engage. Thus situated I deemed that a sailing Captain would do best and I had several applications from Bristow and others and one Pearson offered through Elliot[9] to sail the ship for nothing, but I deemed it a fair opportunity to serve poor {Shaw}. I gave him the preference, agreeing that instead of going Chief mate of one ship he should go as Captain of another, everything for 500 pounds if direct 1,000 pounds if double voyage, this with his pay and primage making 700 pounds as the voyage now stands. His gratitude was unbounded but alas since the creature has been admired by his low friends his senses have forsaken him, his vanity has turned his brain! He ventured to tell me that I had driven a hard bargain, and this day has written to me one of the most impudent letters you ever saw, I must not answer it at present, but when Adams is out of his power, I shall hand him back his own letter.

I have backed this creature through thick and thin, persuaded Adams to take him after [his employer's] death, after quarrelling with Adams I effected an exchange and got him into the *Bridgewater*, he has long been in my debt, is now 350 pounds, and because I now desire to know how much more he is going to draw before I accept his further draft, he writes me insolently that he is surprised how we venture to expose his credit and his honor—(his honor, he is ever lacking of that)—and he conceived he might draw to the extent of 500 pounds, a new theory this, the servant to be paid before his wages are earned—excuse me, my dear friend, for taking up so much of your time, but it is necessary as a preamble to the requirement I am about to make that you will keep him in order by your advise. I think he will look up to you, so pray keep him in order, I think the creature's intentions are good but his vanity is dreadful, he has nothing whatever to do with the trade and is to sign the Bills of Lading. This I think he will do, but he has traded a little on his own account, [and] should he lose money as a trader it will fall upon poor Adams for the tradespeople will pretend that they did not

[8] The Court of Directors of the East India Company had the power to reprimand or dismiss the ships' captains who misbehaved or who, as was the case with Captain Adams, repeatedly refused to observe the rules.

[9] See *Post-Scriptum* to this letter.

know of the agreement with Adams, so pray talk to him about the necessity of economy. It is strange that so poor a man should require lectures on this head, but what may one not expect from a person in his situation engaging a band of performers. Enough on this subject.

How delighted I am to find our worthy friend Wright[10] brought to safe moorings in your anchorage, you have done a kind act and got an able assistant.

We heard long ago but did not know till we saw your signature that you had joined the first House in China[11] May it long flourish under your auspices.

Our concern[12] has gone on well and is still doing so, but we have had drawbacks too in that Charles {Barker} has eased us of about 18,000 pounds sterling and unless Sam Searle makes 7 or 8,000 pounds this trip he will take away a little more. These two accounts are the only two bad ones we have had and enough too, and what is not to be denied is that we suffer by two fools—one rogue and fool, the other an honest fool. Poor Sam's expenses have been his ruin, his private expenses in two voyages amount to 5,000 pounds.

Now my dear Boy, see if by a little of your authority and advise you can save us a little with Sam. You see how free I make with you. But it is the privilege of friendship!

Adams thanks you for the management of the *Kellie* and wonders he has not heard of the shipment of the raw Silk. This article has risen again from 15 to 18 shillings but is rather heavy at those prices so that it will not do to look for an advance but rather a reduction on those prices. These and teas and perhaps a few good Nankins are all that is saleable from your part of the world.

MacWillie all chin chin yum[13] as does Your affectionate friend.

P.S. Our friend Bob Elliot who is now settled at Rochester has been very ill, but now convalescent.

[10] Henry Wright was, like William Jardine, a former associate of J. H. Gledstanes and a purser on the East India Company ship *Castle Huntly*. William Jardine asked him to come and work in the Canton firm in 1826. He became a partner of *Jardine, Matheson & Co.* in 1835 and retired in 1842. For George Chinnery's portrait of him, see: Keswick, *The Thistle and the Jade*, p. 18.

[11] The reputation of *Magniac & Co.* was very high in London. It was the oldest established 'Agency House' in Canton, dating back to 1787 and its original foundation by John Henry Cox. The other house with an impeccable reputation was *Dent & Co.* (See below, Letter **8**, note 45)

[12] J. H. Gledstanes's concern was *Gledstanes Drysdale & Co.*, a London house which James Matheson describes in letter **58** below as 'as House of property'. The progression shown in Gledstanes career from officer in the employ of the East India Company to shipowner after his retirement, and 'merchant banker' doing business with his circle of friends, was not uncommon at the time. Thomas Weeding, William Jardine's first business partner and one of the firm's main correspondent in London until 1835, had followed a similar path. See letters **25** and **69**.

[13] Pidgin English for 'send their best regards'.

5. *Fairlie Bonham & Co.*[14] in London to *Magniac & Co.* in Canton,
16 April 1827

Gentlemen,

We now beg to address you in reply to the letters we have been favored with from you by the Ships of the Season hitherto arrived, as promised in our respects of the 14th Instant; viz—

4th August 1826:

Informing us that you had directed Mr. William Guthrie to make over to us a bill of 1,912 pounds and 10 shillings, or the proceeds if paid, which you had remitted him on account of Captain Thomas Riddock, contingent upon the payment of your draft upon the latter at Bombay, which had been refused by his agents there after his departure. We immediately wrote to Mr. Guthrie on the subject and he replied to us from Portobello in Scotland,[15] that he had forwarded our communication to Mr. James Allan here, a Co-executor of Captain Riddock, who is dead. Mr. Allan, in consequence of this reference, informs us that he expected Mr. Gray, another Executor, would soon be in London, and would see Mr. Guthrie in the interim; and that should they feel justified in paying over the proceeds of the bill in question, they will do it without delay; but that they first wished to see the letter you were to write to Captain Riddock upon the transaction, which appeared to have been entered into by you without his authority.

This letter, we presume, will have since got to hand by the *H.C.S. Java*,[16] our application having been made before her arrival, upon your duplicate received per the *Thomas Coutts*, so that we trust shortly to learn the result. The bill you had also drawn on Captain Riddock, for balance of account, 331.8.10 pounds sterling, remains in suspense likewise, as Mr. Allan says the Executors have no information relative to the transactions alluded to. They hope, however, soon to hear from Mr. Crawford McLeod[17] of Bombay, who is appointed executor to the property in the East, and should he furnish them with any instructions respecting the draft, they will wait upon us on the subject.[18]

4th August:

An envelope received by the *Java*, with three inclosures For Lisbon we duly forwarded.

[14] *Fairlie Bonham & Co.* was *Magniac & Co's* principal London correspondent until 1832. This letter is typical of the so-called 'House letters' in which a firm's clerk or 'writer' was made to take up each points made in the last batches of letters received from the constituent.
[15] Now a district of Edinburgh.
[16] A ship belonging to the East India Company, 'H.C.S.' standing for 'Honourable Company's Ship'.
[17] Crawford McLeod, also mentioned in Letter **67**, was not identified.
[18] A balance of 1,494.23 Spanish dollars was still due by Captain Riddock's estate at the end of June 1830. (*JMArch. Journals A2/15*).

15th November:

In acknowledgement of our correspondence as far as the 31st May, and we pay due regard to what you say with respect to our observations upon your large drafts against indirect or doubtful remittances. We are happy indeed to infer that they have been taken in the sense by which they were dictated of showing our anxious desire to promote the security and regularity of our operations, and while we make full allowance, as we did at the time, for the unforeseen combination of adverse circumstances, so alarming to the Commercial World, we truly hope that your future precautions will prevent your being exposed to similar disappointments.[19] We observe you were sending Mr. Thomson's Power of Attorney, under which your advances were made upon the Teas, to *Messrs. Perit and Cabot*,[20] and hope the guarantee would bear you harmless for any deficiency, but we have not heard further regarding their proceedings since what we have already advised. We likewise hope Mr. Latimer's failure[21] will not occasion any ultimate loss to yourselves, and since we wrote you on the 8th February, Mr. M. C. Ralston[22] has advised us of some progress being made in the sale of the Silks per *Addison*, on which account he has sent us two farther bills for 217.4/10 pounds and 900 pounds, which will be placed to your credit at maturity. We have given you credit for 4 pounds and 9 shillings, as the cost of the Flower Stands for Mr. Mitford; and on the other hand have debited you 516.2/7 pounds for so much transferred to the credit of Mr. H. Shanks, agreeably to your desire, to close the long-standing affairs of the recovery through Mr. B. C. Willcocks.[23]

We are pleased to notice that you had found your Account Current right, and thank you for the promptness with which you have remitted us the bill on the Court of Directors for 10,000 pounds sterling for your credit at maturity.

Mr. Hearn was unable to pay the small bill of 87 pounds and 10 shillings, and we were in communication with him regarding an arrangement by which he hoped to liquidate it, but as we perceive you have been repaid the money by Captain Fox, we shall not proceed farther with the recovery.

We feel obliged by your attention to our notice of Antonio A. Simones, and have informed Mr. Bramston of the obstacles which prevented his wishes from being immediately accomplished. We have also to thank you for the information

[19] The criticism, whilst carefully worded, suggests that large drafts were drawn by *Magniac & Co.* on *Fairlie Bonham & Co.* against 'doubtful remittances' or perhaps insufficient shipments. The specific transaction referred to was not identified. Unsecured drawings were quite infrequent in Canton private trade before the early 1830s.

[20] Mr Perit is mentioned as a partner of *Goodhue & Co* in Letter **69** (1833) and **145** (1837).

[21] John R. Latimer was an American trader in Canton. He was nicknamed 'the gong' 'from his habit of going to and fro in quest of news and to talk'. (Hunter, *Bits of Old China*, p. 269; *The Fan Kwae at Canton*, pp. 10 and 19) .

[22] A Philadelphia merchant. See Letter **69**.

[23] Benjamin C. Willcocks, another American trading in Canton at the time. He was a friend of Chinnery. His name is spelt 'Willcox' by Hunter, a fellow American. (*Ibid.*, p. 267 and p. 19).

afforded us regarding the introduction of Spelter, and although it is sufficiently discouraging, we are not altogether without hope, from circumstances we have heard, that something may have been done with the article in China, in which case we doubt not you will have enabled our friends at Calcutta and Singapore to avail of the opportunity. The *Price Current*[24] you have sent us is very acceptable, although the state of your markets appears to have been affected by the gloomy advices from hence, and your remarks upon Opium are particularly unfavorable.

16th December:

With an enclosure for Don Manuel Brodetts of Cadiz, which will go to its destination by the first opportunity.

We take this occasion to include a *Price Current* of the last Company's Sale of Raw Silk, held in February. We before mentioned an improvement in this article, but the prices rather drooped as the Sale proceeded, and the Private China Silk[25] therefore went off heavily at an advance compared with the October prices, of 10 per cent in Taysaam and 20 per cent in Tsatlee;[26] the Company having had none to offer. The market has not altered since. You will likewise receive herewith a *Price Current* of the quarterly Piece Goods Sale which took place last month. The quantity of brown and yellow Nankeens having been smaller than usual at this time of the year, and the proprietors having bought in a great proportion, the prices rose 2 pence per piece. The demand for the Blue however is so limited that nearly the whole were refused. The prices of the China Silk Piece Goods are lower still than at the previous Sale, there being no demand for any except the damasks of good heavy quality, crimson, skyblue, yellow and a few white, which are now scarce, as well as fine Crape Shawls, well assorted in colours, 1 and three-quarter to 2 yards squared, weighing from 6 and a half to 7 and a half ounces, but none of a smaller size or light texture will answer.

Cotton Wool continues without improvement, and there is very little doing in the India descriptions. Indeed Trade in general is still alarmingly depressed and almost every article of produce much depreciated, except Bengal Indigo,[27] which maintains a high value in consequence of the ascertained failure in the last Crop.

We remain sincerely, Gentlemen, Your Most Obedient Servants.

[24] On the Jardine, Matheson collection of 'Prices Current' in the Cambridge University Archive, see: Wells, John, 'The Prices Current Series in the Archive of *Jardine Matheson & Co.*', in *Business Archive Sources and History*, Number 78, November 1999, London, Business Archives Council, pp. 51–63.

[25] 'Private China Silk' refers to the silk shipped from China on captains' accounts. Export of silk which had been banned in 1759 by the Qianlong emperor was later authorized but rationed. (Garrett, *Heaven is High*, p. 87). The East India Company allowed its supercargoes a certain volume of hold space for the silk they shipped home. This was known as the 'silk privilege'.

[26] The expressions 'Taysaam' and 'Tsatlee' were common at the time among silk traders. They later fell into disuse. The Chinese words appear to refer to the width of the silk rather than to its quality.

[27] On Bengal indigo, its crops and price fluctuations in the late 1820s, see: Singh, *European Agency Houses in Bengal*, Calcutta, 1966, pp. 231, 240 and 314. Speculation in indigo farms was the principal

6. J. H. Gledstanes in London to Willliam Jardine in Canton,
16 April 1827

My dear Willie,

The bearer of this is Mr. Docker, surgeon of the *Windsor*, a very Gentlemanlike young man. He is the nephew of my old cronie Rob Addison formerly *one* of *you*.[28] I chin chin you to be kind to him.

Thine.

7. Alexander Matheson in Canton to James Matheson in Macao,
28 October 1827

My dear Uncle,

My last was dated the 26th, not having had anything to communicate yesterday. Today Yunhing has paid 1,300 dollars for which I have given him an order for one chest of Malwa marked *M&Co.*[29] Robert Mackenzie[30] has taken in all 53 dollars for which at his own suggestion I made out a set of Bills of which I send you the Original, which you can either use or not as you see proper. I made the Exchange 4 shillings 2 pence.[31] He says that on board they would have charged him 5 shillings. I have procured 4 first chop[32] Rice Paper Picture Books, which are now under his charge. I got him a passage in Captain White's boat this forenoon, but through some awkwardness the boat went off without him. I will however make a point of sending him down tonight, or tomorrow morning.

---

cause of the failure of the Calcutta Agency Houses at the time. The indigo craze gave the world a new invention in 1828, and the dictionary a new word—the 'Indigometer', an instrument devised to ascertain the colouring power of indigo. (*OED*).

[28] This note of introduction, written two days after Letter **4**, is virtually unique in the Jardine Matheson archive for its informality. It suggests that J. H. Gledstanes was closely associated with William Jardine during the latter's early career as surgeon on the East India Company ships, from 1802 to 1817.

[29] The mark *M&Co.* stood for *Magniac & Co.* Yunhing was one several opium brokers operating at the time in Canton. They numbered about 20 in the late 1820s and early 1830s (*JMArch. A7/75*), and double that number in the mid-1830s (*JMArch. A7/76*). Among the opium brokers mentioned in this letter, Awung was one of the four best customers. The practice was that the brokers would first pay for their purchases at the firm's factory against a receipt or delivery order. The delivery order would then be presented to the captain of the *Samarang*, a ship anchored in the vicinity of Lintin. The *Samarang* served as the firm's receiving ship until 1832, when it was replaced by the *Hercules*. (Le Pichon, *Origines de Hong Kong*, pp. 74–79).

[30] A relation of James Matheson's mother. See the penultimate paragraph of this letter.

[31] The exchange rate is expressed here as the sterling value of one Spanish dollar. During the period covered by the present correspondence (1827–1843), the sterling exchange rate against the Spanish dollar fluctuated between 4 and 5 dollars to the pound. The Spanish dollar was the currency prevalent for international trade in Canton, Manila, and Singapore at the time. (Morse, *The Chronicles of the EIC, IV*, p. 260).

[32] On the different meanings of 'chop', see below, Letter **8**, note 40.

Enclosed I send you a letter from Cachator respecting Awung's 20 chests. He begs, if you cannot allow him a month, that you will allow him at least till the 15th to clear it. The opium market is quite at a stand. The prices nominally 1,180 dollars for Patna and 1,380 dollars for Malwa.[33] I have been with all the brokers, but could only get one chest cleared, by Yunhing.

I have just received your letter of 15th by which I am happy to find that you arrived safe, at the same time that I regret exceedingly the Comprador's remissness[34] in providing the Boat. I have spoken to him about it, and he assures me that, besides the cold provisions, he also put on board, 14 catties of raw Beef,[35] 9 ditto of Mutton, and three living fowls, besides an abundance of eggs. The Hallman who is certainly an exceedingly stupid fellow, lays all the blame of wanting claret on your servant, to whom he says he gave all that he asked for. This however is far from ridding him of blame. He is so stupid, that today he swore there was no claret in the House !!![36] Before you return I shall do my best to get another Hallman, but if you do not come up it is hardly worthwhile changing. I shall attend to your orders respecting Beef and the half chest of Beer. Also about Mr. Veiga's Factory.[37]

I have done my best in my bad state of health to amuse Mackenzie, and the best proof of his being well pleased with his entertainment is his being in excellent spirits. I found it impossible to give the party you proposed, as for the last three days I have been almost entirely confined to my room. As a proof that I did not think you over liberal to him, you will perceive that I have exceeded your orders in supplying him with money. Besides its being my duty to pay the utmost attention in my power to anyone about whom you interest yourself, I should deem myself the most ungrateful creature in the world if I did not do so to the Mackenzies, from their near relationship to my aunt Matheson, to whose kindness I feel myself deeply indebted.

[33] Patna and Malwa were the two principal kinds of opium sold to the Chinese. Patna was opium cultivated and processed in Bengal under the official control of the East India Company. It was auctioned off in Calcutta and then shipped privately to Canton. (Owen, *British Opium Policy*, pp. 23, 47). Malwa was cultivated more freely in the north-west of India, and shipped from Bombay. (*Ibid.*, p. 101).

[34] A 'comprador' was a Chinese servant entrusted with the responsibility of keeping the factory's accounts for all domestic and household transactions. The function was essential in an environment when virtually no European trader could speak Chinese. For later developments in the function of the 'comprador', see: Yen-p'ing Hao, 'The Compradors' *in* Keswick, *The Thistle and the Jade*, pp. 86–87, etc.).

[35] A 'catty' was the weight equivalent of 16 'taels', or 1,33 lbs. The 'tael' was the trade name for the Chinese 'liang', or ounce. Hence it became the currency of account, the silver tael coin weighing originally one tael of standard silver. (*OED*).

[36] The firm's cellar was well stocked. It contained several thousand bottles of the finest European wines, including claret, madeira, port, sherry, and champagne. (*JMArch. A7–257*).

[37] Joaquim José Ferreira Veiga was a Macao opium trader (Letters **54, 57, 65, 179, 188**). He was also the father-in-law of Joanna Ullman, one of the four Ullman sisters (Letter **248**).

Linchong has been disappointed of the *good* chop of Hyson he expected, so I fear Mr. Solano's commissions must be put off till the next ship sails for Bengal, as must Mr. Irvington's and [ ] unless they are ready in a day or two. I shall send you a Bill of Lading for Mr. Limond's half chest of Tea tomorrow.[38]

Mackintosh is quite well. He dines at the Company's[39] where I cannot accompany him.

Yours affectionately,

8. Alexander Matheson in Canton to James Matheson in Macao,
9 November 1827

My dear Uncle,

I received yours by Captain [ ] last night, enclosing the Policy of Insurance, which I now return to you, after being registered and copied into the book.

By the bearer of this I send you a round of corned beef supplied by Mr. Willcocks weighing 13 and a half catties. Also 25 catties fresh Beef, and 17 catties Mutton, which I hope will be all found good. I hear of no gentlemen going down in a Chop,[40] I fear. I must have recourse to the money Chop Boat to send you the plated dishes and covers and candlesticks. I shall also send you by the same conveyance 4 pots of jelly, being all that remains, 6 bottles of preserved fruits, 20 bottles Marraschino, 12 ditto Champagne, 12 ditto Burgundy, 3 dozen French Claret, 1 box Tenqua's Tea, I Keg preserve Salmon 5 dollars, 1 ditto Biscuits three quarters of a dollar, the two last articles I found at Pitman's. There are no good anchovies to be had here. Mr. Jardine[41] says that there is an abundance of very fine anchovies in his Cellar, to which you are most welcome, as well as to anything else you can find there. He thinks you will find some good Champagne there. You know the Champagne we have here (Gledstanes') is not to

[38] Although the monopoly of the East India Company over tea lasted until 1834, private traders were allowed to make small purchases for the purpose of making gifts to friends and constituents.

[39] The East India Company had the reputation of entertaining visitors lavishly at its Canton factory, or as here, in its Macao headquarters. 'The 'Factory' entertained with unbounded hospitality and in a princely style' (Hunter, *The Fan Kwae at Canton*, p. 18).

[40] Short for 'chop boat': 'a licensed lighter for transporting goods' (*OED*). Hence, the 'money chop boat': a boat specialized in the transport of treasure, bullion or, as here, silver, between the Canton factories, the ships anchored at Whampoa, the outer anchorages, and Macao. The word 'chop', as used in Canton at the time and in the current set of letters, can have three other meanings, depending on the context. A 'chop' was a seal stamped on an official document. A 'chop house' was a custom house where transit duties or port dues were levied. A 'chop of tea' was a parcel of tea, often amounting to several dozen chests of identical quality and provenance.

[41] Alexander Matheson formally refers to William Jardine as Mr. Jardine, in line with the normal practice of the day. William Jardine rented a house in Macao. In time, James Matheson was to rent one also. They used these houses infrequently, usually for brief holidays, or to convalesce after bouts of illness. From this letter, the reader can infer that William Jardine had temporarily lent his Macao house to James Matheson, pending the latter joining his firm.

be depended on, and I now send you five bottle remaining of a dozen you borrowed of Mr. Jardine at your last party here, and 7 bottles remaining of some you got from Mr. Latimer last year.

I hear of no one going down except Ravenshaw. Mackintosh is undecided. I enclose a letter from Marjoribanks,[42] on whom I called today but missed him.

Our Newspaper[43] is likely to take much better than we expected. We have struck off some more copies today, which are more correct. Mr. Jardine has kindly subscribed for 6 copies, and is to forward 50 to his Bombay friends. He also proposes to curtail the *Price Current*, and to omit *Stores* entirely. Dr. Morrison[44] is quite disappointed that there is little room for original matter but will, I hope, now be satisfied, as we mean, if you approve, to limit the *Price Current* in future to two pages. A smaller type is absolutely necessary. There is no doubt now of the Paper succeeding, if it be conducted with tolerable care. I expect to get several subscriptions in the Fleet. Dent[45] promises every support. None of the Factory has yet subscribed.

Accompanying I send you a copy with the proposed alterations.

Yours affectionately,

[42] Stewart Marjoribanks was one of the three members of the 'Select Committee', or executive committee, of the East India Company in Canton. The chief of the factory was Sir James Urmston. The other two members of the Select Committee were W. H. C. Plowden, and J. F. Davis. (Hunter, *The Fan Kwae at Canton*, p. 18). Marjoribanks subsequently retired to England and with William E. Ferrers he formed the firm of *Marjoribanks & Ferrers*. (See Letter **151**).

[43] *The Canton Register*. James Matheson had temporarily taken up residence in Macao for business reasons, since *Yrisarri & Co.* was being wound up and he had not yet formally joined *Magniac & Co.* It also suited him well to be away from Canton. He could thus avoid being seen as having any responsibility with the foundation and setting up of the *Canton Register*. This newspaper, which he founded with the help of his nephew Alexander and for which he donated a printing press (see Letter **9**) was to become the principal English-language daily in Canton. It contained two pages of *Prices Current*, and was read mostly by the business community. (Greenberg, *British Trade and the Opening of China*, p. 16; *The Canton Register and Prices Current, 1827–1843*, Hong Kong University Library). Until its foundation at the end of 1827, the only English-language newspapers published in China had been *The Chinese Courier and Canton Gazette*, (1813–1833), and *The Chinese Repository*, whose editors were the Protestant missionaries working in Canton. (Collis, *Foreign Mud*, p. 311). In 1831, the *Chinese Courier*, whose views had tended to be more strident that those of the *Canton Register*, adopted a quotation from Marvell as a new exergue: 'Oh! Printing, how hast thou disturbed the peace of Mankind! // That lead, when moulded into bullets, is not so mortal as when founded into letters.' (*The Chinese Courier*, 28 July 1831).

[44] The Rev. Dr Robert Morrison was the first protestant missionary to China and an eminent sinologist (1782–1834). He arrived in China in 1807, and founded the anglo-Chinese College at Malacca in 1818. His death, in August 1834, deprived Lord Napier of invaluable service. (Ride, *East India Cemetery*, p. 232). He was the author of many books on China, including *A Dictionary of the Chinese Language in Three Parts* (1815) and *A Grammar of the Chinese Language* (1815). (Lust, *Western Books on China*, pp. 238, 247).

[45] Probably Thomas Dent, the senior partner of *Dent & Co.* from 1820. The firm had impeccable connections, having been founded around 1809 by George Baring, then as East India supercargo. When the company forbade its supercargoes to trade in opium, Baring took on William Davidson as

9. Alexander Matheson in Canton to James Matheson in Macao,
16 November 1827

My dear Uncle,

I handed your annotations on the *Canton Register* to Mr. Wood,[46] who is highly pleased with the interest you take in the Paper. He writes to you today on the subject. Your suggestion about shipping Lists etc. cannot easily be carried into effect without smaller types. *Smith, Elder & Co.*[47] have sent some small types in their last supply, but by some unfortunate mistake, they are all capital letters, and consequently useless for the present. The field for a newspaper is certainly extensive, and if the *Register* is only properly conducted it may be made the most popular journal in the East. There are already more copies subscribed for than will pay all expenses. An article in N° 2 on the state of the Press in India has occasioned much talk, and some idle people, such as Innes,[48] pretend to say that the Factory have taken offence at it. If such be the case, however, I think they are too wise to express their feelings, as it is impossible they can interfere with Wood.[49] If any of

---

a partner. Davidson was sole partner from 1813 to 1820, the year when Thomas Dent joined the partnership. In 1825 Thomas Dent invited Robert Hugh Inglis to join as a partner. (Robert Hugh Inglis was the son and nephew of Hugh and John Inglis, who were both directors of the East India Company. In 1827, a relation of Thomas Dent, Lancelot Dent, also joined the firm as a partner. (Dermigny, *La Chine et l'Occident*, III, p. 1243). Opinions vary, however, on the identity of the early Dent partners. According to Solomon Bard, three sons of William Dent were active in Canton in the 1820s. They were 'John, Lancelot and Wilkinson'. (Bard, *Traders of Hong Kong*, p. 56). In Canton, *Dent and Co.* became the principal rival of *Jardine, Matheson & Co.* After the Opium War, both firms prospered in Hong Kong, but *Dent & Co.* failed in the commercial depression of 1867. (*Ibid.*, pp. 56–57).

[46] W. W. Wood arrived in Canton in 1825 from Philadelphia. 'He was a person of great versatility, mentally and materially'. After editing the *Canton Register* for a number of years, he worked for the American firm of *Russell & Co.* in Canton. The story of his unhappy romance with Harriett Low is well documented. (See: Low, *Lights & Shadows*). In the mid-1830s he left Canton and settled in Manila where he was 'the first person to introduce the art of photography'. (Hunter, *The Fan Kae at Canton*, pp. 67–69; *Bits of Old China*, pp. 270–272).

[47] The London publishers, *Smith Elder & Co.*, were the regular suppliers of office and printing material to *Magniac & Co.* and later to *Jardine, Matheson & Co.* The Canton firm ordered all its leather bound ledgers from *Smith Elder & Co.*, as well as most of its professional and other books. (See, for instance, Letter **60**).

[48] Hunter describes 'Innes' as 'an 'old school' and eccentric Scotchman' (Hunter, *The Fan Kwae at Canton*, p. 69). Captain James Innes (1787–1841) was the 7th Chieftain of the Innesses of Dunkinty, Scotland. He arrived in Canton in 1825 as a free-trader 'at the unusually advanced age of 38. He soon revealed his contumacious nature in several incidents with the officials of the East India Company and his hatred of privilege. His open dealings in opium contributed to the crisis of 1839'. (Ride, *East India Company Cemetery*, pp. 223–225).

[49] The East India Company and its Select Committee had no jurisdiction over the American residents of Canton. It exercised its authority only on the British traders.

them talk to me about it, I mean to disavow any connection with the paper, further than my having hitherto assisted Wood from motives of friendship. With regard to the Press, it will be proper to state to them, that you made an arrangement with Wood, before the paper was established, that if he chose he might take the Press at prime cost, and that as the paper has been successful beyond our expectation, Wood has availed himself of this arrangement, so that the Press is no longer your property. This will screen you from all responsibility. I should also think it prudent to remove the press to some other place, to make it appear more evident that you are entirely unconnected with the business.[50]

The offensive paragraph will, I have not the smallest doubt, give notoriety to the paper, and gain it many subscribers in India.

I write you separately in reply to your letter of the 12th and remain,

Yours affectionately,

1828

10. James Matheson in Canton to *Gregson, Melville, Knight & Co.* in London, 1 January 1828[1]

Gentlemen,

I beg to refer to the accompanying circular announcing my junction with the House of *Messrs. Magniac & Co.*, in consequence of which the Firm of *Matheson & Co.* is now discontinued and I shall henceforth correspond with you in my individual name regarding the winding up of the concerns of my former partnership.[2] I shall be glad that this takes place with the least practicable delay and trust that final accounts are by this time on their way to me.

It will afford me great satisfaction to establish a relationship in business between my present partnership and your respectable firm, and in this head, I cannot do better than refer you to the head of the House, Mr. Hollingworth Magniac,[3] who is now in London and is well known to our esteemed friend, Mr. {Gregson}.

I hope in a few days to be able to render a final account of the small glassware consignment.

I am, dear Sirs, Your faithful, humble servant.

[50] The scheme seems to have been mostly successful. Recollecting the events in 1882, Hunter wrote in a footnote: 'The late Sir James Matheson was the reputed founder of the foreign press in China (*The Canton Register*); but it was an open question whether it was he or Mr. Wood. I contributed to that paper (translations from Chinese) when started; but in the consequent daily intercourse with Wood, he never hinted that he was not its sole founder. (Hunter, *The Fan Kae at Canton*, footnote p. 67).

[1] James Matheson officially joined *Magniac & Co.* on the first day of the year 1828.

[2] In 1827, whilst *Yrisarri & Co.* was being wound up, James Matheson had traded as *Matheson & Co.*

[3] The head of *Magniac & Co.* who had just retired to London, leaving William Jardine in charge of his family firm in Canton.

11. Jardine in Canton to Hollingworth Magniac in London,
10 January 1828[4]

My Dear Magniac,

Thinking it possible the *Atlas* might reach England before the *Farquharson*, or *Scaleby Castle*, I addressed a few lines to you by that conveyance, three days ago, merely saying we were all well and everything going orright. The *Farquharson* is to be despatched today or tomorrow, and I shall now endeavour to reply to your favor of the 20h June last, the only letter that has reached me, not a line to me or the House having been received by the American ship *Milo*, a circumstance I am at a loss to account for, everyone else having received letters by a regular Company Packet.[5]

It is impossible for me to describe my own feelings or the sensation produced here generally when we first heard of Daniel Magniac's marriage.[6] A vague report reached me from Macao before the letters were delivered, but nothing short of seeing in your own handwriting the details mentioned in your letters could have convinced me that he was capable of acting the way he has done.

It is most fortunate for our interests that I had not announced your recession from the House on the 30th of June last, as the same circular that gives notice of Mr. Daniel Magniac's interest having ceased, announces Mr. Matheson a partner.[7]

He made a proposition to Thomas Dent[8] previous to starting for Calcutta, which was declined at the plea of there being already a sufficient number of Partners in the House. This was exactly what Matheson wanted, as it satisfied his Calcutta friends and left him at liberty to form another connexion. When in Calcutta in June last he wrote to you, informing you that his friends *Messrs. Mackintosh & Co.*[9] were desirous he should join our firm, and promised him

[4] One of several letters dealing with the subject of Hollingworth Magniac's family succession in the Canton firm. See also Letters **13, 16, 40, 43, 52, 54, 240** (penultimate paragraph).

[5] In the absence of a regular postal service, East India Company ships carried general correspondence to India and China and back to London in containers known as 'Company Packets'. The *Scaleby Castle*, a 1,216 ton ship, had been built for the East India Company by the Bombay Dockyard in 1798 (Wadia, *Bombay Dockyard*, p. 355). Note the highly unusual spelling for 'alright' on line 3.

[6] Hollingworth Magniac's elder brother, Charles Magniac, had died in 1824. The third brother mentioned here, Daniel, should have succeeded Hollingworth in Canton. His 'marriage', however, was deemed unsuitable and he resigned from the firm (see paragraph 5 of this Letter).

[7] Hollingworth Magniac's interest in the Canton firm continued until 1832, when he was finally 'advertized out'. The firm then changed its name from *Magniac & Co.* to *Jardine, Matheson & Co.* (Letter **54**).

[8] On *Dent & Co.*, See above, Letter **8**, note 45.

[9] James Matheson was related to the Mackintoshes and he had done his training in their Calcutta Agency, *Mackintosh & Co.* (Keswick, *The Thistle and the Jade*, p. 18).

more cordial support than he had anticipated. This cordiality probably rose from their having been very much dissatisfied with Mr. Dent's management of their affairs in England, as partner of the London House. Enclosed you have a copy of our circular, which has been distributed over India.

Being ignorant of the nature of the notice you had given in England, we thought it advisable to issue a different Circular for Europe, and agreed on announcing Mr. Matheson's admission as the primary object of it, making Daniel Magniac's resignation secondary. Of this document I send you several copies that you may circulate, with any addition you may think advisable. At the present moment when men's minds are turned to the China Trade such notice may prove beneficial.

As regards the division of the advantages that may accrue to the House from July 1st 1827 to the same day in 1828, I am perfectly satisfied with the arrangement you propose. To me it makes no difference whether Daniel or you receive the other share, and the only hesitation I feel is as regards the interest you are to receive on your large capital employed.[10] According to the former arrangement you would have received 8 per cent for part of your funds and twelve for such as were in the hands of the Merchants[11] in your own name, whereas being still a partner you are entitled to 12 per cent per the whole, but even this I prefer leaving you to arrange as you think fit, and to whatever decision you may come to I shall abide by, and be satisfied.

The Books have been up for some time, with the exception of the opium account which Mr. Ullman[12] wishes to examine again before he pronounces it correct; this I have assented to, shall go over it myself with him, and then forward the Balance sheet, by one of the next ships.

I have paid a good deal of attention to the proposal made by James Crawford to you,[13] and see no objection to the arrangement contemplated, provided it brings with it an adequate advantage, in an increase of business, which is likely to be the case, if the contemplated relaxation of the trade between Continental Europe and China take place. Mr. Hadow[14] would be an acquisition to any House, but with Matheson's able assistance and using his indefatigable exertions, we shall not feel at a loss, unless our Business increases very much indeed.

[10] Hollingworth Magniac's capital employed in Canton was over 600,000 Spanish dollars (*JMArch. A2/15*).

[11] The hong merchants, through whom all foreign trade was supposed to be transacted in Canton, paid a higher rate of interest on deposit than any other borrowers (Hunter, *The Fan Kwae at Canton*, p. 24).

[12] J. G. Ullman was *Magniac & Co.*'s book-keeper. He had arrived in Canton in 1776, had worked in the Swedish factory, and was close to 70 years of age at the time of this letter (Hunter, *Bits of Old China*, p. 157; Letter **31**, 4th paragraph).

[13] The proposal was not identified. The Crawford family was prominent in the East India Company and many of its members settled for business in Bombay in partnership with the Colvins. (Letters **182, 234**, etc.)

[14] H. P. Hadow (sometimes spelt with one d, and sometimes with two), was a friend of James Matheson. He was a partner of the *Remington & Co.* in Bombay. (Letters **39, 54**, etc.)

I shall be happy to receive your cousin Mr. Hollingworth[15] on the terms you propose, and to make him as comfortable as circumstances will permit, in a place so different to that he has been accustomed to. You will of course explain to him what the conditions are, that he may not feel disappointed in the event of its proving necessary to keep him in a subordinate situation longer than he may contemplate.

While on the subject of parties coming out to the House I may as well mention to you [what] I intended to have proposed to Daniel Magniac had he come out. My only Brother[16] has a very large family, three or four of them Boys, and as he has not the means of providing for them all, [in] the way I wish to see them provided for, I am desirous of having one of them here, to commence in the office, and work his way, by industry and application to business. He is now at school, and I should wish to put him into some respectable Counting House in London for a year or two, to initiate him into strict business habits, which are not easily acquired here. Many years must elapse before he can in any way interfere with other arrangements, further than occupying a desk in the outer office, and not even that far, for two or three years.

In the absence of letters from you per the *Milo*, I was very much gratified to learn, from Millett,[17] that Mrs. Magniac has got safely over her confinement and you were both in tolerably good health, also that Mrs. Sansom's[18] health was much improved; on all which fortunate occurrence I sincerely congratulate you. Mr. Millett further stated that Daniel Magniac was living at Rouen on an allowance from you of three Hundred pounds per annum, a sum I fear very inadequate to his wants, though much more than he deserves.

I allude to this circumstance with reference to that part of your letter which speaks of his proceeding to China *alone*, where by industry and good conduct to retrieve his character. With regard to his returning here, I am afraid he would have so many mortifications to encounter whether alone or otherwise that I should think it the most revolting to his feelings, of anything you could propose to him, unless he returned as a partner, which I concur with you in thinking a measure by

[15] Francis Hollingworth, referred to below in Letters **13, 16, 20, 24, 40, 44, 51, 53.**

[16] William Jardine's brother, David Jardine, had four sons: Andrew, David, Joseph, and Robert. They eventually all came to Canton or Hong Kong to work for the firm, and all became partners. Andrew Jardine (1812–1889) was a partner of *Jardine, Matheson & Co*. from 1839 to 1843; David Jardine (1818–1856), from 1843 to 1856; Joseph Jardine (1822–1861), from 1845 to 1860; and Robert Jardine (later Sir Robert Jardine), from 1852 to 1882.

[17] Charles Millet was a friend of Hollingworth Magniac (Letters **51, 54**).

[18] Mrs. Sansom's husband was the head of the unidentified 'Sansom banking house' which failed in 1831 (Letter **44**). As the couple's son, Charles, is described as Hollingworth Magniac's 'nephew', it is likely that Mrs. Sansom was Mrs. Hollingworth Magniac's sister (*Ibid.*).

no means admissible, as far as the interests of the House are concerned. Taking all the circumstances into consideration, more particularly his aversion to business and the indifferent health he generally had here, I should think it preferable for him to remain on the Continent on such allowance as you may feel disposed to make him, out of your share of the House, which under different conduct on his part would have been his own.

I feel less hesitation in making this suggestion for professing a knowledge of the liberal provision you had made for him, previous to your leaving China, and the very disinterested manner in which you gave up every prospect of further advantage to your own fortune from the House after the 30th of June last. And even when you wish your name and interest in the Firm to cease, I shall be ready in conjunction with Matheson to appropriate a similar sum for the same object for the advantage we shall derive from our succession to that share. And should you prefer having a certain provision made for him at once we are ready and willing to carry on the business here, setting aside a certain sum annually for the benefit of him and his family. In fact I am ready and so is Matheson to enter into any arrangement for his benefit in Europe in preference to seeing him here wretched and miserable, which he must be if out of the Firm. In any other situation than that of a partner his services would be of little value, and having so abruptly advertised him out of the House, I should think announcing his name again, even years hence, would do harm in place of good to our interests, and even as a partner he would have many drawbacks to his happiness.

You will of course see that these suggestions are founded on the value of his share in the House, which his conduct has forced you to deprive him of, but he is still your Brother, and we are desirous of seeing a provision made for him out of that which ought in process of time to have rendered him independent. After all this, however, should you have sent him out in a manner proposed in your letter, you may rest assured I shall do every thing in my power to comply with your wishes.

Be pleased to present my kind regards to Mrs. Magniac, and believe me, my Dear Magniac,

Yours very sincerely.

12. William Jardine in Canton to Howqua, Senior Hong Merchant, and to the Co-Hong, in Canton,

22 August 1828[19]

Gentlemen,

On the [ ] of the last Moon we presented to His Excellency the Viceroy,[20] through your respectable Body, a Petition, respecting the debts due to us by Manhop,[21] in which we referred to our first petition to his Excellency on the same subject, six months ago, and brought the negotiation down to the date.

From this Excellency's reply, dated the 29th day of the last Moon, we find that some mistake, intentionally or otherwise we know not, has crept in to the Translated Copy of our petitions,[22] and that his Excellency has, for the second time, confounded the Clandestine removal, or theft, of 1820 Bales of Cotton, belonging to *Magniac & Co.*, by Manhop and Elong House[23], with the unfair transfer of 30.549 Bales by Manhop's hidden partners in the City;[24] which we are creditably informed, they appropriated to the payment of their old debts.

[19] The 'co-hong', or 'cohong', was the official body formed by the hong merchants. 'According to the policy of the Chinese government, it is only a limited number of merchants, who are called the hong or security merchants, that are allowed to trade with foreigners. Their number formerly amounted to eight, and sometimes to twelve (. . .) All foreign cargo pass through the hands of these merchants, and by them also the return cargoes are furnished. They become security for the payment of duties, and it is treason for any other merchant to engage in trade with foreigners. This severe law, however, it appears, has from time immemorial been evaded; for other merchants, called 'outside merchants' (. . .) are in the practice of dealing with foreigners'. (*EB, VI, p. 101.*). On the cohong, its formation in 1720 and its evolution, see: Fairbank, *Trade and Diplomacy*, pp. 50–51.

Howqua was the most famous and richest of the hong merchants at the time. Known as Wu Tun-yuan to the Chinese, he was born in 1769 and died on 4 September 1843. He was the senior hong merchant and head of the cohong throughout the period covered by the Letters and, as such, was the normal official intermediary between the Chinese authorities and the foreign merchants. The other principal hong merchants in the late 1820s were Mowqua, Pwankeiqua, Pwansulyan, Chungqua, Kingqua, and Gowqua. (Hunter, *The Fan Kwae at Canton*, pp. 20, 30, 66, 43; *Bits of Old China*, pp. 218, 277).

[20] Hucker's *Dictionary of Official Titles* does not list the term 'viceroy' among English equivalents for Ch'ing official titles. The foreign merchants, however, referred to the senior mandarin, or governor of the Canton province, as the 'Viceroy'. The viceroy (governor general of the Canton province), the governor (of the City of Canton), and the 'hoppo' (the Superintendent of Maritime Customs for the Canton province) were the three most important provincial officials or 'mandarins'.

[21] Manhop was a hong merchant who became bankrupt before Hollingworth Magniac's return to England, owing his firm over 38,000 Spanish dollars (*JMArch.* A2/15). William Jardine objects to the preferential treatment of local creditors, a practice which, in the absence of independent courts could not be challenged legally in Canton.

[22] All official petitions from the foreign merchants had to be presented in Chinese to the authorities. The original texts were translated by official translators or 'linguists' working for the cohong.

[23] The English name of a local business firm.

[24] The city of Canton.

When his Excellency fell in to the same error in his reply of our first Petition, we requested you to explain the difference between Elong's theft of 1,820 Bales, and the unjust appropriation of 30,549 Bales by other parties, and we are not a little surprised and grievously disappointed to find this explanation has not been made. Had you fairly represented the circumstances as requested, His Excellency could not now have affirmed that 'Howqua was ordered to inquire in to the business' and stated that only one shop, Elong, had bought cotton from Manhop.

On application to Howqua he denies having made such statement; and we have to request, therefore, that you explain this inconsistency to His Excellency. We should be sorry indeed wrongfully to accuse any man, or set of men, but we have been so repeatedly assured, by most respectable individuals, of the truth of our original statement, that we should be wanting in justice to ourselves, and in zeal for establishing truth, and correcting false representations, were we to remain silent on the subject. There were no less than 10,000 Bales of said cotton in possession of one of the parties a week ago. You must be very deficient in discernment, if you do not, at one glance, see the injustice of this nefarious transaction; which enables Manhop's Chinese Creditors to pay themselves, immediately, their old debts; while we, foreign Merchants, whose claims by the Laws of the Celestial Empire, come next in order, to those of the Emperor himself, are referred to the Co-Hong to be paid in eight years.[25]

Trusting this application may have the desired effect, of bringing such an act of gross injustice clearly to the notice of His Excellency, and of obtaining us immediate redress for such an unheard of grievance, we remain, Gentlemen, etc.

13. William Jardine in Canton to Hollingworth Magniac in London,

16 November 1828

My Dear Magniac,

[. . .] The most important part of your favor of the 7th April is that which relates to your retiring from the Firm, the admission of your relation Mr. Francis Hollingworth,[26] and the best mode of providing for your Brother Daniel, etc., etc.

When addressing you on the 1st April last I hinted on the probability of your wishing to remain a member of the Firm till you should derive such additional advantages, as you might deem sufficient, to compensate you for the losses sustained by Manhop's disgraceful failure—and I have now, after having seen a good deal of your relation Mr. Hollingworth, not the least hesitation in saying your acting on such hint, could not in the slightest degree, prove prejudicial to his

[25] The practice was that the debts of the failed hong merchants were paid back in instalments to the foreign creditors over an eight-year period.

[26] Francis Hollingworth is also referred to in this letter as 'Mr. Hollingworth' and as 'your cousin'.

interest, provided his qualifying himself to take charge of the affairs of the House, should be deemed essential to his being admitted as a partner in the Firm.

You are aware that there is a something in China and in the mode of conducting business here, unlike anything to be met with, in any other parts of the world and it is with extreme reluctance that I go so far as to say your Cousin does not appear to me to possess that turn of mind and manner, which is necessary to enable a person, at an advanced period of life, to make himself *soon* useful in the situation in which he is placed. He is willing, well disposed, anxious to please, and desirous of making himself useful; but with all these good points, he certainly does not make that progress, that you yourself, were you here, would feel desirous he should do.

It is painful to me, to dwell on this subject, and I should have been more happy could I have passed it over in silence; but had I done so, I should have acted a part unworthy of the confidence you kindly repose in me, and nothing would afford me greater pleasure than to have it in my power conscientiously to declare to you, that the opinion I have now formed, has been formed hastily and erroneously. On making this communication I have no object in view, but that of making you acquainted with such circumstances as I consider intimately connected with the respectability, efficiency, and future prosperity of the House, self interest and personal feelings having nothing to do with the view I take of the business—and but for the uncertainty of Mr. Matheson remaining in China, I should, for the present, have refrained from entering on the subject in hopes that by the end of the season, I might have been able to report more favorably, and to have had my own opinion confirmed or altered by that of Mr. Matheson, after he had seen enough of Mr. Hollingworth, to be able to judge of his habits and knowledge of business.[27]

P.S. Mr. Matheson will write to you about his views, which he feels desirous of making subservient to the interests of the House, and will come to no resolution respecting his Calcutta plans until we hear from you, my advice to him being to give up all thought of them, in which however he himself is not quite prepared to concur, although willing under any circumstances to postpone them.

[27] The copy of this letter ends, not with the usual greetings, but with the simple bracketed mention '(Signed WJ)' followed by the phrase: '*vide* Letter Book page 56 for continuation'. In other words, it was a particularly sensitive section of William Jardine's already 'private' letterbook.

14. Alexander Grant[28] in Lintin to William Jardine in Canton,

6 December 1828

My dear Jardine,

I have the pleasure of receiving yours of yesterday by Wilson's boat [ ]. I think 120 dollars for Baylis's carpenter[29] will be a most handsome remuneration and if you like to give him a piece of silk on account of the ship to make a favor for his old wife he ought to think himself splendidly off. I expected he would have been back by this time as we are now in the thick of the work and have a great many Chinese carpenters employed and only three Europeans to look after them. We shall finish coppering by noon tomorrow and I shall haul out of dock on Monday night—or perhaps earlier if the mud can be sufficiently cleared away. [ ].

It is of no consequence whether the sugar comes alongside on Wednesday or Thursday, but I should like to have only *one chop* on either of these days and then want four or five days for the remainder, as I wish two or more things in the Hold that require room.

I am sorry to hear so poor an account of the Drug Market. It must improve bye and bye. Excuse this scrawl, I am up to my eyes in mud. Templeton is now under the bottom driving nails.

15. James Matheson in Canton to *L. Calvo & Co.*[30] in Canton,

29 December 1828

Dear Sirs,

Will you oblige me with your opinion on the following subject: *Messrs. Mackintosh & Co.* of Calcutta having money to remit to *Messrs. Dent & Co.*[31] of this place on account of *Messrs. Jones & Walker*, advanced the sum of 11,000

[28] Captain Alexander Grant was a close friend and independent business partner of Alexander Matheson and William Jardine. When he wrote this note, he was in the vicinity of Lintin, having the *Samarang* repaired. He was part owner and commander of the *Samarang*, the firm's main opium receiving ship between 1828 and 1832 and, after that date, of the *Hercules* and other opium ships. He remained in China until 1837, when he retired to England (Letter **140**). He died in 1841 (Letter **225**). Lintin, a small island situated in the Pearl River delta some fifty miles from Canton, became an opium anchorage in the early 1820s and was well established as a place for opium deliveries and free-trading business by the time this letter was written (Morse, *The Chronicle of the EIC, IV*, p. 134).

[29] David Wilson and John Templeton (mentioned at the end of the Letter) were both ship captains who had settled in Canton. John Templeton was a shareholder in the *Canton Insurance Company* (Letter **65**). Baylis was an assistant on the opium receiving ship (Letter **162**).

[30] The firm of *L. Calvo & Co.* had been doing business with James Matheson's previous firm, *Yrisarri & Co.* It specialized in *respondentia* loans, which were considered too risky by *Magniac & Co.*

[31] *Mackintosh & Co.* was one of the established Calcutta agency Houses. Its main Canton correspondent was *Dent & Co.* (See above, Letter **8**, note 45).

Rupees to Mr. Jose Joaquim Barros,[32] owner of the ship *Confiancia* on *respondentia*,[33] payable in China taking his bond, of which the accompanying is a copy. Mr. Barros paid the first instalment, but having, as you are aware, made a fraudulent bankruptcy, the second was never recovered, and is still unrealized. *Messrs. Dent and Co.* and *Messrs Jones & Walker* wish to make *Messrs. Mackintosh & Co.* responsible for this amount on the ground of their not having exacted the security of a Bill of Lading for the five chests of Patna opium hypothecated by Mr. Barros. As you have had much experience for several years as well in granting *Respondentia* as in realizing bonds similar to the enclosure, remitted by your agents at Calcutta, will you have the goodness to inform me whether it has been usual in these cases to exact Bills of Lading for the property hypothecated, also whether Mr. Barros was in good credit at the period in question.

Begging your excuse of this trouble, I am, dear Sirs,

Your obedient servant.

1829

16. Jardine in Canton to Hollingworth Magniac in London,

25 February 1829[1]

The Sum of 50,000 dollars placed under a 'separate head' at 6 per cent by you which you left with me, for Daniel Magniac's benefit, proposed to be rendered applicable to Francis Hollingworth when admitted a partner, in your letter of the 7th July 1827 and in your favor of the 25th May 1828 hinted at, as a medium through which Matheson and myself could aid in making a provision for Daniel Magniac, in a manner more agreeable to you than that suggested by us, I have left at 12 per cent per annum for the year 1827–1828 and we propose continuing it at that rate of interest, in conformity with your last proposal. It is necessary to observe here, that in your favor of the 25th May you call this sum 30,000 in place of 50,000 dollars, but this I presume is a mistake. The interest to be carried to you credit is English Interest 5 per cent, leaving 7 per cent accumulate; which with the interest he is likely to derive from his shares in the *Canton office*,[2] will in a

[32] Neither the firm *Jones & Walker* nor the bankrupt individual, Jose Joaquim Barros, have been identified.

[33] The practice of granting *respondentia* loans was highly speculative. Bankers secured their loans on the cargoes shipped, usually opium, and financed 100% of its value. The 'bond' was in fact a secured promissory note. For an example of *respondentia* bond, see *JMArch, A-8-X*.

[1] This extract in William Jardine's hand must have been a draft of a letter of even date.

[2] The *Canton Office*: short for *The Canton Insurance Office*, the principal maritime insurance company in Canton. It was started in 1806 jointly by the members of firms later known as *Jardine, Matheson & Co.* and *Dent & Co.* The arrangement was that each firm managed the underwriting syndicates for successive three-year periods. Thus ten underwriting syndicates operated between 1806

few years amount to a considerable sum without being a burthen on any one, beyond what they are able and willing to bear.

But as this will throw the whole burthen of their immediate support on you, I should strongly recommend your reconsidering the plan suggested in my letter of the 10th January 1828 to which you need feel no objection on the score of delicacy, while we have the benefit of your capital, and your name in the firm, and in the event of this year and the next turning out favorably, you will be able to withdraw in June 1830 with very ample means for yourself and them,[3] while we shall have the gratification of knowing they are comfortably provided for without inconvenience to any one: allow me when on this subject to return you my grateful acknowledgments for your consideration in making your retirement from the firm, subservient to our interests.

Your relation, Mr. Hollingworth,[4] has been here on a salary of 2,500 dollars per annum since his arrival; which with occasional advantages that may occur, should prove a sufficient provision for him for the present.

17. *Fairlie Bonham & Co.*[5] in London to *Magniac & Co.* in Canton,

21 April 1829

Gentlemen,

Having written you fully on 18th instant, we have now merely to transmit you the accompanying copy of Your Account Current for last Year, to which we have as usual added an open continuation of the entries to the latest period we could, viz—18th instant, with lists of the dependencies made up on that day, and presenting the following totals, viz—

Debit	*(in pounds)*	*Credit*	*(in pounds)*
Cash	9,626.6.2	Cash	20,488
Bills accepted	40,595.4.2	Remittances	23,056.12.5
Ditto advised	25,125.18.10	Goods uncertain	[blank]
	75,347.9.2		43,544.12.5

We trust the whole may be found correct and satisfactory on examination, and we remain, sincerely, Gentlemen, Your most obedient Servants.

---

and 1835, when the arrangement between the two firms was discontinued and *Jardine, Matheson & Co* started its own *Canton Insurance Office*. (Le Pichon, *Origines de Hong Kong*, pp. 271–277).

[3] Eventually, the arrangement was continued until the last day of June 1832, when the firm changed its name to *Jardine, Matheson & Co.*, and adequate provisions had been made for both Daniel Magniac and Francis Hollingworth. See Letter **54**, penultimate paragraph.

[4] Francis Hollingworth.

[5] For *Fairlie Bonham & Co.*, see above Letter **5**, note 14. The firm is listed in *Robson's London Directory* under the category of 'East India Agents'. Its partners had offices at 9, New Broad Street, and are sometimes referred to in the Letters as 'our friends of New Broad Street'. (*RLD*).

P.S. The enclosed *Price Current* of China Piece Goods just published by our Brokers, will be of some interest to you, as showing the state of markets for Nankeens[6] at this time.

18. *Finlay Hodgson & Co.*[7] in London to *Magniac & Co.* in Canton, 23 April 1829

Gentlemen,

We had the pleasure of addressing you on the 4th July last, since when we have had no direct opportunity for China, but we have from time to time informed our friends at Bombay of what has occurred since then with regard to the *James Scott* and Captain Richards' protested drafts.

The expectation we entertained that the ship would be brought to this country for sale has not, we regret to say, been realized and our hopes of an early settlement of your claim on Captain Richards have been thus thwarted. You are aware that Mr. Shipton's[8] assignment of the *James Scott* to *Messrs. Ritchie and Steuart*[9] gives us no controal over the ship and that we can only enforce the discharge of the Mortgage Bond out of her proceeds. Captain Richards being, however, personally responsible to us for the amount of his dishonoured drafts, we signified to him our determination to arrest him in case of his leaving the ship and coming to this country, as he has been repeatedly urged to do by Shipton's agents here. Under these circumstances he applied to the Tribunal at Antwerp for authority to sell the ship and thus clear himself of his liability, and we of course expressed our readiness to concur in the Bill of Sale, as holders of the Mortgage Bond, *upon its being discharged.* On the other hand the agents of the *James Scott* have done everything in their power to delay the decision of the court and although the case has twice been brought before the Tribunal, the point remains to this day in suspense.

With regard to your favour of the 18th November in which you express your deep disappointment at our want of promptitude and firmness on this occasion, and your opinion that more determined measures on our part, when the vessel was in the downs, might have placed the parties concerned in a much better situation, we could have wished that you had pointed out at the same time the nature of those measures by which we could, in virtue of the mortgage given by Shipton,

[6] Nankeens were 'a kind of cotton cloth originally made at Nanking from a yellow variety of cotton' (*OED*). They were staple returns to England together with raw silk and silk pieces.
[7] London merchants with offices at 8, St Helens Place, Bishopsgate Street. (*TLCD*).
[8] Not identified.
[9] A Bombay firm listed in the Bartlett Index (*BI-JMArch*). The Bartlett Index also lists two letters from Captain Richards 'of the *James Scott*' in 1827.

assume a control[10] over a ship in the Channel bound for a Foreign Port. Having no instructions from you as to any positive line of conduct we have acted throughout this business under the best legal advice both here and at Antwerp, and with the advantage of Mr. J. R. Steuart's cooperation and have therefore no hesitation in saying that we have hitherto availed ourselves of every power which the law has placed within our reach.

We shall continue to act under the same legal advice and hope that Captain Richards will now shortly obtain the authorization of the court at Antwerp for the sale of the ship and thus be enabled to liquidate his dishonored drafts. At the same time you must be aware that the Law in every country, is but too ready to afford facilities for delay, particularly where either of the parties sees it to his interest to have recourse to such a mode of conduct.

We are, Gentlemen your most obedient Servants.

19. *Spode and Copeland*[11] in London to William Jardine in Canton, 25 May 1829[12]

Dear Sir,

We have much pleasure in renewing a correspondence with you. Having for many years been in the habit of shipping many of the Company's officers with glass tumbler burners and other articles from our manufactures, and those officers having retired from the service we petitioned the Company for freight which they readily granted to the extent of twelve Tons, the same we have shipped on the *Mangles*, Captain Carr, as follows: twelve cases of tumbler burners of three sizes; 6 casks and one cask of close bottom vase lamps; 4 cases of copper mounted ship safety lamps, the whole of which we hope will find ready Sale from native demand, the latter for ships use more particularly. Numbers 24 to 27 contain small Earthenware table sets and Breakfast cups and saucers sent really for an experiment, the latter no doubt will find Sale with the Company's officers for ships stores. The table sets no doubt will sell but we fear not like the Breakfast cups and saucers. Numbers 28 to 32 contain small assortments of glass for table use and 33 various glass for ships use. Numbers 20 to 33 we have sent as a trial and should the result be favorable we shall feel happy to ship you to any extent. We shall feel ourselves obliged by your writing us as soon as you receive this for

[10] After first spelling 'controal' (in the second paragraph), the writer of this letter now opts here for another spelling variant.

[11] London glass and china manufacturers. Twenty letters in all were sent from *Spode and Copeland* to *Jardine, Matheson & Co.* The correspondence between the two firms ended in 1833. (*BI-JMArch*).

[12] William Jardine wrote on the cover of this Letter: 'Received 4th April 1830'. It is at about this date that he started the systematic practice of writing a summary or a commentary on the folded front of each letter received. Before 1829 the practice was infrequent. After 1830 it became virtually standard.

our government in future shipments. Can you recommend our sending two or three pairs of Lustres and if so, to what extent the lights—six, eight, or ten lights?

We wish this shipment disposed of immediately, the returns made in fine silk if obtainable at 400 dollars (say four hundred dollars) per picul[13] of the finest quality shipped from Canton to either your own or our Agents *Messrs. Spottiswoode & Connelly*,[14] Singapore, with orders to forward it to us consigned to order. The sea risk to be insured from Canton to Singapore, having an open policy from India and Indian Archipelago to the United Kingdom. The risk from Singapore to England will be covered here. We should wish that in the event of Silk being above our limits you would ship Nankeens.

We were very sorry to loose[15] you in Bombay for the issue of our goods consigned with Framjee Cowasjee,[16] by his disobeying our orders and sending us pepper so inferior in quality which was truly ruinous. He has behaved very ill to us, we assure you. He has never noticed our letters sending him certificates of the goods deficiency in weight. We merely name this to show you how very ill we are used by him.

Ere we make up our letters finally we shall address a few more lines on the shipment of returns.

We are your very obedient Servants.

20. James Matheson in Canton to William Jardine in Macao,

15 September 1829

My dear Jardine,

I did not write to you yesterday. My transactions were as follows:

sold	Akwan[17]	20 chests Companys's Malwa	900 dollars	} 3 weeks
" "	Lyshing	20 ditto	900 dollars	} 3 weeks
today:	Chungfat	5 ditto	905 dollars	
	Cutcheong	1 Damaun[18] guarantee 102 catties	900 dollars	
		1 Patna	805 dollars	

The time sales of Malwa will perhaps appear to you too low, but with the ideas which we both have that a fall, more probably than a rise in the ensuing two

[13] Picul: 'A measure of weight used in China and in the East generally, equal to 100 catties, i.e. about 133⅓ lbs avoirdupois' (*OED*). For 'Catty' see above: Letter **7**, note 35.

[14] The Archive contains 21 letters from this early Singapore correspondent (*BI-JMArch*).

[15] Original spelling.

[16] A Parsee merchant from Bombay and one of William Jardine's first business partners. For further references to Framjee Cowasjee, see Letters **67**, **206**, and **244**.

[17] Akwan, Lyshing, Chungfat and Cutcheon were Chinese opium brokers (*JMArch*. A7/75; A7/76).

[18] Damaun opium, after the Indian port of Daman or Damao, south of Surat, through which it was shipped to China. For the Malwa and Patna varieties of opium, see above Letter **7**, note 33.

months, owing to the Parsees[19] being obliged to realize, while Russell[20] is selling at 895 dollars, which he has told me he considers a fair price, I had not the courage to refuse the offers made to me, after trying in vain to get a small advance. I must take care however that I am not made to sell too much and I will try to hitch it up as you will see I have done with Chungfat today. With Patna, our stock being small, I will play a little, buying at 860–865 dollars and selling on time at 885 dollars. I cannot get 890 dollars. The difference between 865 and 885 does not pay interest and charges, but it is better to have a little pain in this way than not at all and two months sales will fall due conveniently for remittances to England.

The Cotton market is quiet. Mowqua[21] is waiting for deliveries to sell the *Fort William*'s. Prices without variation. Russell is likely to take 40 or so Peculs[22] of the *Fort William* Silk Privilege.

It is now time to acknowledge you letter of 12th, 13th, by which I was glad to find you got down pleasantly and safe.

I have just been to see Howqua, as you suggest, about Baker's business[23] of which I made as good a story as I could; but as you anticipated, it did not seem to interest his prudential feelings. He abused the Portuguese as a parcel of brutes and began to tell me of their charging Russell 6 per cent duty on the *Washington*'s Quicksilver, which having been merely deposited at Macao while the vessel was aground, he thinks ought to be exempt from the duty, on the same principle on which the Chinese Government had exempted the unfortunate *Navigateur*'s goods. Having said this much I must add *entre nous*, that I know no person (I say it with regret) so ill calculated as myself for conveying such a message to Howqua in a way likely to be successful. I know not what I would not give for as much of the arts of diplomacy as would make me competent to negotiate with a Hong Merchant—some of your command of countenance, and apparent indifference about an object which is very interesting to you. Talking of diplomacy, so you

[19] 'Descendants of those Persians who fled to India in the 7th and 8th centuries to escape Mohammedan persecutions and who still retained their religion (Zoroastrianism)' (*OED*). The Bombay Parsees formed a tightly-knit community, and the merchants from that community had acquired a reputation for business acumen.

[20] Samuel Russell, the American merchant of the Canton firm of *Russell & Co.* The only other partner at the time was Philip Ammidon (Hunter, *The Fan Kwae at Canton*, p. 96).

[21] One of the principal Hong merchants. See above, Letter **12**, note 19. The *Fort William* regularly brought cotton from Bombay. The cargo was owned by Jamsetjee Jejeebhoy and consigned to *Magniac & Co.* In turn, *Magniac & Co.* instructed Mowqua to sell the cotton.

[22] Variant spelling for 'picul'. See above, Letter **19**, note 13.

[23] Baker has not been identified. The obscurity of the paragraph stems both from the difficulty of identifying the protagonists, including 'Mr Gardner', 'Hogg' and 'Loureiro', and from the allusive nature of the writing. 'Baker', 'Mr Gardner' and 'Hogg' may have been country ship captains. Though the general background is tolerably clear—rivalries between the Macao authorities and the East India Company's Select Committee in Canton—the factual details have not been traced.

think it was well judged in the Select[24] to expose themselves to the incivility which they never fail to meet with, whenever they correspond with the Macao Government. I should think a skilful negotiator, such as I take Mr. Gardner to be, would avoid placing himself in a situation to have his authority called in question, where he has no power to make it respected, but rather endeavour to carry his point by personal negotiations in a round about way. Hogg tells me that Baker is detained merely because he will not sign a bond for 5,000 dollars to keep the peace. I asked: 'Why not sign the bond ? he surely does not mean to break the peace again.' Hogg replied: 'I fancy he does. He is not done with Loureiro and thinks 5,000 dollars too much to pay for giving him another thrashing. 500 dollars would be enough. Besides Loureiro anybody meeting him might provoke him with a wink to break the peace for the sake of forfeiting his bond.

I have no hesitation in saying that such a man should not be released, without some security to keep the peace, and moreover he should be expelled for ever from Macao. I do not consider Loureiro's life safe, were so infuriated a man to be at large. But if the business lies in the judge's department old Veiga[25] will settle it for you in five minutes. In the Governor's department some other Channel of mediation must be sought. Barretto[26] is not a bad one. The Governor[27] takes tea with him occasionally. Nothing can be done with the Portuguese, going to work in the dry official way.

I shall long for your promised long letter but almost fear you will be kept in so constant a turmoil, that much of what you have to say will lie over till we meet. I am glad you approved of Alexander having gone down. Hollingworth and Chay[28] are meditating a flight, but when they will move I do not know.

Your landlord Mr. Janerio[29] has just written to Latimer[30] and me to say that that pervese man Dent[31] has paid the demurrage which he claimed, and as we promised to do as others did, he hopes we will pay also. Latimer replies that he

[24] The 'Select Committee', or executive committee of the East India Company at Canton comprised the following at the time: Charles Marjoribanks, first member, (appointed 1812–1813); John Francis Davis, second member, (appointed 1812–1813); James Frederick Nugent Daniell, third member, (appointed 1814–1815); and Thomas Charles Smith, fourth member, (appointed 1815–1816). Fourteen further supercargoes made up the total 'Canton Establishment' of the East India Company in China. (*EIRD, 1831*, p.110).

[25] On J. J. F. Veiga, see Letter **7**, note 37.

[26] Bartolomeu Barretto, the father or uncle of Bartolomeu Antonio Barretto who was at the time one of the firm's two bookkeepers, the other being Alexander Matheson.

[27] Joãn Cabral d'Estefique was governor of Macao from 1829 to 1839. See the 'List of governors of Macao (1557–1999)' in Basto da Silva, Beatriz, *Cronologia da Historia de Macau*, 4 vols., Macau, DSEJ, 1992–1998.

[28] Names for the firm's following assistants: Alexander Matheson, Francis Hollingworth, and Chay Beale.

[29] On William Jardine's house in Macao, see above, Letter **8**, note 41.

[30] On John R. Latimer, see above, Letter **5**, note 21.

[31] An early indication of the tense rivalry between *Dent & Co.* and *Magniac & Co.*

will pay if the majority of consignees do so. I reply by referring him to you. Do as you please, in concurrence with Barretto, who knows all that passes between Sr. Janerio and me. It appeared to me that Barretto was rather disposed to favor Mr. Janerio. If he gets any demurrage, in place of being indiscriminately charged on the whole opium it should be allowed only on what remained on board after a certain date.

I shall let you know tomorrow about the mark on Barretto's copy.

Howqua told me today the Company's answer has been received mentioning that Lord Melville is the man they alluded to as having gone off from Chunqua's Hong.[32] They also advert to the heavy change for measurement duty[33] on small vessels and to the necessity of the Viceroy appointing some clever men as Hong Merchants. At the same time they add they are not unaware of the difficulty of finding any such. Howqua regrets the discussion was not commenced earlier, as it will now be impossible to despatch their ships at the regular time, if kept out longer. The Viceroy is alarmed for the duty on Company's woolens, and has sent down a number of guard boats to Toon Coo,[34] which are a serious obstruction to the Opium boats. Excuse the hurried letter and believe me with kind regards to all.

Yours ever sincerely.

[P.S.] Tell Grant[35] I am sorry to say no word of his boots and shoes nor mine.

21. James Matheson in Canton to William Jardine in Macao,

17 September 1829

My dear Jardine,

Dinner is on the table and a fast boat about to start.

I have only time to tell you that it was in consequence of a trick of friend Aho[36] I was induced to write you yesterday Patna was looking down. He has himself

[32] Obscure reference. See also the following passage in Letter **31** below written by William Jardine to Hollingworth Magniac: '. . . it may be as well to mention how our account stands with your friend Lord Melville who is prevented from returning to his family till some arrangements shall have been made for the settlement of his foreign debt'. The reference to 'his foreign debt' makes it clear that 'Lord Melville' is a nickmame for a bankrupt or dishonest Chinese merchant.

[33] In the old Canton trading system, ships paid Chinese duty according to their size. On arrival at Whampoa, Canton's anchorage outside the Bogue, all foreign ships were 'measured' by officials from the customs house and duties were assessed and charged accordingly. (Fairbank, *Trade and Diplomacy*, p. 48). In the 1820s, East India Company ships paid an average of 4,000 to 4,500 Spanish dollars for their 'measurement'. (Morse, *The Chronicles of the EIC*, Vol. III, p. 389). On ship measurement, see also Van Dyke, Paul, Arthur, op. cit. p. 15, note 37, pp. 72–83.

[34] Toon Coo, or Toong Koo: a small sheltered island situated two miles east of Lintin, west of what is today Hong Kong's Castle Peak district. At the time, Lintin was being developed as a safe opium anchorage.

[35] On Alexander Grant, see above, Letter **14**, note 28.

[36] Aho, Yunhing, Allum, and Afo: Chinese opium brokers.

today bought 14 chests at 870 at a fortnight, but the cunning fellow had the money ready and made it a cash sale. He is a sly, deceiving fellow.

I have been induced to let Yunhing have 20 Company's Malwa at 890 dollars cash, partly payable in Sycee[37] at 6 per cent. Since then Allum has come to negotiate the Damaun at 890 dollars—but he thinks he can squeeze the [buyer] to 895 dollars at which I will close. Here are large transactions and you will perhaps think I ought to raise the price. But the fact is we have a preference of sales. Lots of Parsees would sell at any price, even Latimer, and they will be obliged to sell cheaper or I am very much mistaken. Afo tells me the distant markets are dull. Meanwhile I have plucked up courage to reject Aho's conditional offer price to be fixed bye and bye, having the best reason to think he will make a handle of it to bring down the market.

Yours ever in haste.

[P.S.] The Parsee receipts have come at last! for the opium that you were so bothered about by them.

22. Jamsetjee Jejeebhoy[38] in Bombay to William Jardine in Canton

22 December 1829

My dear Sir,

This few lines I intend to send you by via of Bengal to acquaint you what we are doing here, and beg to express our thanks for the management of our concern under your good care meet our entire satisfaction.[39] Had we perceived a few years before the advantage what are now benefited from your experience we might have been more richer.

Our *Success*[40] arrived here first, from your place September. *Sulimony* and *Cornwallis* after a few days. We sold our Sugar at 5 to 14 Rupees and Sugar Candy for 9 to 10 Rupees per Maund.[41] The other ships not so good prices. We received all your favors per *Castlereagh*, she arrived on the 10th December. *Fort*

[37] Sycee: 'Fine uncoined silver in the form of lumps of various sizes, usually having a banker's or assayer's seal stamped on them, used by the Chinese as a medium of exchange'. (*OED*).

[38] Jamsetjee Jejeebhoy: a Bombay Parsee Merchant and the most important single constituent of *Jardine, Matheson & Co.* throughout the 1830s. He was born in 1783 in Nowsaree, a town in Baroda, and died in 1859. He accumulated a large fortune from trading in cotton and opium, and was later known for his generous philanthropy, endowing hospitals, schools and other charitable institutions. He was knighted in 1842, and in 1857 he became the first Indian baronet. (*MEB, II*, pp. 72–73).

[39] Jamsetjee Jejeebhoy's meaning remains usually clear despite the linguistic idiosyncracies.

[40] The *Good Success* was owned by Jamsetjee Jejeebhoy and shuttled regularly between Bombay and Canton. The other ships mentioned in this paragraph were all country ships, i.e. ships belonging to private merchants trading in the East Indies.

[41] Maund: 'A denomination of weight current in India and Western Asia, varying greatly in local value. The standard maund of the Indian empire is now = 100 lbs. troy, or 82⅐ lbs. avoirdupois'. (*OED*).

William and *Ann* on the 16th Instant. The *Golconda* and *Edmonston* not yet appeared. The Market of Sugar so declining that hardly saleable at 4 and three-quarters Rupees per maund are oblige warehousing. The *Fort William* Cargo stocks will be great and we very glad you not send chow chow[42] goods we commissioned.

On our indent Captain Neish[43] paid in Malacca Treasury the September 2nd You send in our account for bill on Bengal Government, obtained 206 Rupees per cent Dollars which were sold at 109 and three-quarter per cent. We received your Europe bills and also the Bank's bills which we obtained for all at 1 shilling and 9 pence per Rupee. The American Copper we contracted at 60 Rupees per a cent, the Camphor at 24 Rupees per Maund. Cassia is missarable we shipped all to Europe.

I am sorry for Mr. Forbes[44] death who appears to be honest man. In consequence of discouraging state of Cotton market in England the merchants here have nothing to send except bills and Bullion, which will keep up the Exchange. I saw the correspondence you good enough to send me restricting the trade in China,[45] which one hopes will be the good effect at the end and glad to hear the result shortly from you.

I am sorry to hear the discouraging account of the Drug market at your place, peoples who dealing in this articles, always sanguin notwithstanding the prices they pay here and the quantity going annually increasing, still they hope and expect to make profit and consequently they paying high prices at interior which will stand them at Damaun at 1,450 Rupees per Chest including Duty, etc. and we certainly expect more quantity than last year from Damaun. Government agents made some mistake at Malwa, they usually paying some of money to the Natives Princes to prevent the smugglers to pass through their Territory.[46] This year they thinking useless to pay them, as soon as they contracted the quantity for ensuing Season, opened the restriction and let it pass to Foreign places. Consequently the price of Drug Rose up from 30 Rupees to 80 Rupees per a quarter of Maund, and disappointed from their contractors, they unable to fullfill their engagement with

42 The expression 'Chow chow' referred to assorted goods. It is recorded by the *OED* as in use in England by 1845. 'Miscellaneous, mixed, assorted. *Chow chow chop*: the last lighter containing the sundry small packages to fill up a ship'.

43 James Neish was captain of the ship *Fort William* from 1827 on (*BI-JMArch*).

44 A partner of *Forbes & Co*., Bombay merchants. (*EIRD*, 1831 List of Merchants and Agents in Bombay, pp. 64–65).

45 Unidentified reference.

46 In the early part of the nineteenth century The East India Company had great difficulty extending its Bengal monopoly of opium production to the rest of India. When, from 1818 onwards, the competition from Malwa and Damaun opium became a serious and permanent problem, the Company unsuccessfully tried a number of practices, including the payment of money to local princes, as an incentive for them to stop smugglers. This did not work. A solution to the problem was found in 1830, the year after this letter was written, in the form of an opium 'transit tax' which affected all non-Bengal opium. (Le Pichon, *Origines de Hong Kong*, pp. 62–63; Owen, *British Opium Policy*, p. 101).

much difficulty afforded them 50 per cent more upon the first pieces, but even that there is doubt to get the full extent, and now they advertized for sale 2,000 Chests and 2,000 more they contemplate, together 4,000 Chests to be sold in usual Sales, but I am doubt to complete, however you shall hear from us result by the February ships now preparing, the *Sulimony*, *Cornwallis* and *Charlotte* the former to go to Calcutta from China.

This year we all ship owners resolved and agreed to with the concurrence of Government not to allow any screws[47] to any of the ships to sail in Eastern Passage, for three years certain from this year. Now the merchants at your place may safely speculate in the staple. We hope by this arrangement improve your market for Cotton. We will ship some best description to your care by the former ships hope the good result from it. The ensuing crop said to be middling, there was no latterly rain this Season and very little dew in the Night. The price at interior is looking up. We will take care of our puchases this year. Nothing but superior description, we must pay high prices for it. This year one is presented with Conjunction with our European Neighbours to the Authorities here for the Grievance to make a regulation and to be Promulgated at Northward to Punish such person or persons whoever make Fraud or Spoil the Cotton and I am glad to say they granted and now publishing the Same, which you'll receive one from us by the February ships.

Bengal Government declared about 8,700 Chests for Sale commencing from 14th Instant.[48] We with Conjunction with our mutual friends wrote *Messrs. Colvin & Co.*[49] to purchase on our joint account 300 Chests and consign to your goodselves. We also wrote to Nanjir[50] to do the same and requested to give as much as Freight in *Jamesina*[51] as they can procure. Our *Good Success* will require copper sheething which will go to Docks by the next spring and hope to start from this about 1st April to your consignment with New Cotton. I seen your remark of Cotton, but you will find quite different this Season from us, and hoped you will do us justice in obtaining very good prices for it as we oblige to pay very high prices for superior description. Perhaps this will be guidance for you if you can put your hands in the [ ] Goods on our account.

Sugar Candy if can be procured at 6 to 5 buy 4,000 Tubs or if 6 to 7 buy only 2,500 Tubs. Soft Sugar in Bags if can be procured at 4 to 3 buy 4,500 Peculs, if

[47] Cotton screws were commonly used in Bombay to pack cotton bales as tightly as possible before loading. Spontaneous combustion could occur and fires could destroy ships if the cargo was not allowed sufficient time to dry off. (Bulley, *Free Mariner*, pp. 161–162).

[48] The Bengal Government not only had the monopoly of opium cultivation in its territory; it also conducted the periodic Calcutta opium auctions.

[49] A Calcutta House of Agency. (*EIRD*, 1831, p. 152).

[50] Not identified.

[51] The *Jamesina*, a 382 ton opium ship which, with the *Samarang*, served as *Magniac & Co.*'s floating warehouse. (Le Pichon, *Origines de Hong Kong*, p. 100).

4 to 5 only 3,500 Peculs, or if little more buy 2,300 Peculs, but ought to be good grain and whiter than *Fort William* Cargo. Planty leaf for Dammage in the Bag. Camphire if last year price say 25 dollars buy 200 Chests. If little more, only 100 Chests. American Copper if can be procured at 25 dollars buy 1,000 Peculs or if little more, only 700 Peculs. One can get here about 61 Rupees per cent. Jappon Copper 500 Peculs. one can get here about 72 Rupees per cent, therefore you make your calculations. Cochineal[52] is unsaleable here at present. We have large stock but if you can get at 300 dollars per Pecul you may buy 30 to 40 Peculs but no more. Nutmeg and Mace if you can get at moderate, say about 60 dollars buy little. This is the indent for our *Good Success*. You may keep ready if you please.

Importation of Specie this year rather small and consequently the price of dollars now ruling high at 223 Rupees and Sycee at 104½ to 105¼. Exchange on Calcutta will keep up at 109 Rupees.

Mr. J. H Crawford[53] arrived in Civil Service. My thanks and respectful salams to your Mr. Matheson to whom I will write by the ships to sail in february.

I have showed our mutual friends *Messrs. Remington & Co.*[54] your letters for *Canton Insurance Company.*[55] Two shares. The result will acquaint by and bye.

I am afraid to take your valuable time in writing such long letter. Now conclude wishing your long life and Prosperity and remain with much thanks and regard, My Dear Sir,

your most Sincerely,

1830

23. William Jardine in Canton to Andrew Johnstone,[1] *HCS Buckinghamshire*,[2]

21st March 1830

My dear Johnstone,

I addressed a few hurried lines to you from Lintin, per *Atlas*, stating that I had requested Mr. Wright to send you some certificates on my account. According to his account you have received, or will receive,

[52] Cochineal is 'a dye-stuff consisting of the dried bodies of the insect *Coccus Cacti*, found on several species of cactus in Mexico and elsewhere. It is used for making carmine, and as a scarlet dye' (*OED*). See also: *DM*, pp. 86–90.

[53] Probably J. H. Crawford who subsequently became Accountant General, Revenue Service (*EIRD*, 1831, Bombay section, p. 9).

[54] House of Agency and *Magniac & Co.*'s principal Bombay correspondent.

[55] On the *Canton Insurance Company*, see above: Letter **16**, note 2.

[1] Andrew Johnstone, 1798–1857 was William Jardine's eldest sister's son. He was a partner of *Jardine, Matheson & Co.* in Canton from 1835 to 1836. When he retired he bought the Halleaths estate in Scotland. (Keswick, *The Thistle and the Jade*, pp. 262, 264).

[2] A 1,369 ton ship belonging to the East India Company. In 1830 the ship was commanded by Captain R. Glasspoole. (*EIRD*, 1830–1831, pp. viii-ix)

	Mr. Clayton's certificates for	1,148.00 dollars
(sent by Mr. Wright)	Mr. Thomson's ditto for	1,148.00 dollars
(and [also] in this)	Mr. Middlemass' ditto for	862.00 dollars

making together 3,158 dollars, or say 650 pounds sterling at your disposal for the following purposes.

We agreed, I think, that 'Chipnowe'[3] was to have 100 or 200 pounds. Mrs Ratcliff[4] is to have 150 pounds, and the balance, 300 pounds, is for the benefit of the family at Kirkburn—should they require it—if not—you may retain whatever sum they are likely to require, or if you think it right, you may assist the Moorhousehead family;[5] but they are not likely to require it at present.

James Stewart,[6] in one of his letters to me says: 'Chipnowe's son Frank is a fine grown-up lad; and ought to have a farm of his own.' Should you and his father be of this opinion, and assistance is required in the way of money, I am ready and willing to render such assistance, and shall at the shortest notice remit home any moderate sum that may be deemed necessary, say 500 pounds for such purposes. But this assistance must be considered as an advance for the general benefit of the Chipnowe family, not as an advance to him, Frank, individually, which might tend to make him play the fool.

With regard to the Moorhousehead family, I am equally prepared to assist them; and should feel obliged by your getting James Stewart or Charles to interest themselves in judging of the propriety of the youngster [being established] in such farms—always depending on my willingness to assist them, while such assistance may be deemed prudent and beneficial to their interests. You are aware that I can turn money to much better account here than it can possibly be turned to at home; and for that reason I am averse to placing funds in England unnecessarily; but the moment arrangements are made or put in fair training, you may rely on my being prepared, *immediately*, to do the needful, as far as reasonable supplies are required.

You are aware I have a strong objection to extravagance and idleness; and I trust you will impress this on the mind of your young cousins—I never can consent to assist idle and dissipated character, however nearly connected with me, but

[3] James Jardine of Chipnowe had married William Jardine's second sister, Margaret Jardine. (Keswick, *The Thistle and the Jade*, p. 262).

[4] Possibly the mother of Miss Matilda Jane Ratcliff, a London resident. (See the single entry for Matilda Jane Ratcliff in the *Bartlett Index*). When writing to James Matheson in Letter **167**, William Jardine refers to Miss Ratcliff as 'your young friend'.

[5] The 'Moorhousehead' or Muirhousehead family: the family of David Jardine, William Jardine's elder brother, four of whose children—Andrew, David, Joseph and (Sir) Robert—later became partners in *Jardine, Matheson & Co*.

[6] James Stewart and Charles Stewart mentioned in the following paragraph are unidentified relations or acquaintances of William Jardine's.

am prepared to go to any reasonable extent in supporting such of my relatives as conduct themselves prudently and industriously.

Should any of my nephews wish to lead a seafaring life, I think I have the means of ultimately providing for one of them, in our own ship at Lintin and would willingly submit to the expense of one or two preparatory voyages in a smart Company's ship—that is, provided the youngster has a natural turn for a seafaring life.

I am not aware of anything more I can say, on the subject of my readiness to assist my relations, though fully aware of the delicate situation in which I have placed you. Judge and act for the best, consulting your mature friends, already named, and I shall be satisfied.

I shall send you some Teas by the *Windsor*, and *Kellie Castle*, with instructions as to their disposal. In the meanwhile, Believe me, with kind regards to all friends, My dear Johnstone,

Yours very sincerely,

(*Per H.M.S. Windsor* – No duplicate of letter – seconds of certificates *per H.M.S. Waterloo* addressed absent *Messrs. Gledstanes Drysdale & Co.,* who will present them should it be necessary – firsts absent).

24. William Jardine in Canton, to Hollingworth Magniac in Colworth,
14 April 1830

My dear Magniac,

When I addressed you on the 9th instant per *Kellie Castle*, I fully expected to have been able to hand you a balance sheet and copy of your private Account on which you might rely; and such as I felt perfectly satisfied with; but I regret to say this is not the case. The balance sheet, when presented to me by Mr. Ullman,[7] was far from according to the opinion I had formed of the operations of the year; and the opium account, one of about four and a half million dollars was not balanced. Having discovered two or three errors, Mr. Ullman expressed a wish to have time to go over the Accounts again; and has only an hour ago presented me with your private Account; which I have merely cast an eye over, and the packet for the *Larkins* is to be closed in half an hour. Ullman, Chay, and Hollingworth are finishing and copying fair the accounts mentioned; and will, I hope, be in time for the packet. Whether this is or not, I am not satisfied with the result of Mr. Ullman's operations, and from aversion on Chay's part to interfere with closing the Books Mr. Ullman has kept, I find he has not paid that attention to the matter that I could have wished.

[7] For J. G. Ullman: see above, Letter **11**, note 12.

Our opium account is so large, upward of four, nearly 5,000, chests having passed through our books, that it will take me a week to follow Mr. Ullman through his extracts for the opium and cash books, and prove them. The old gentleman's head is so confused with bargain money, forfeitures, advances on opium, etc., that his account cannot be relied on, and he has within the last hour confessed he cannot strike a balance, not can he depend on having extracted correctly from Mr. Wright's opium books, which are fortunately very correct and very regularly kept up. I sincerely pity poor Mr. Ullman who has been deceiving himself and me most completely—never saying one word about his difficulties or giving me to understand that he felt in the smallest degree at a loss; while Chay has been in the same room with him every day assisting him without discovering the confused state in which the old gentleman has been for some time. I do feel dreadfully mortified and annoyed with myself for not having insisted on satisfying myself that the Accounts were up, or as nearly so as Ullman represented them.

The Factory are to dine here at 7 p.m. and embark immediately after dinner for Macao, and Mr. Ullman makes one of the party. I am sadly afraid his utility here is at an end, and we must set about raising a sum to protect him and his family from starvation.

Midnight. My dear Magniac,

I promised you a balance sheet. Mr. Ullman says we had better not send it, as it cannot be depended upon. Your private Account goes by the packet. No balance sheet. This letter in charge of the captain of the *Larkins*. I shall explain as far as I am able.

With a Commission Account[8] of about 122,000 dollars, our profit for the year is about 38,000 dollars, while our Interest Account is about 50,000 or 60,000 dollars against us—and the Charges General Account, which was readily square (a little in our favour) last year, is this year, by Mr. Ullman's showing, very much against us. The Opium Account must be in our favour—to what extent it is impossible to say at present, but that point shall be settled in a few days, I having now little to do till an arrival from India gives us employment.

I must take leave of this, to me very distressing, business, and turn to something more agreeable. We have not remitted any specific sum to England on your account, but have requested *Fairlie Bonham & Co.* to supply you with what funds you may require. We have remitted in raw silk: 22,950 pounds sterling; nankeens: 22,262; tea: 7,300; treasure: 50,132; bills and certificates: 68,488; to be remitted from Hamburg: 2,791—making together at a rough guess about 174,022 pounds.

[8] For a House of Agency like *Magniac & Co.*, the Commission account was the most important single contributor to revenue and ultimately to profit. A standard commission of 3 per cent *ad valorem* was charged on most goods sold or bought on behalf of constituents. A commission of 2½ per cent was charged on returns in goods, and of 1 per cent on returns in bills or in bullion. (Greenberg, *British Trade and the Opening of China*, p. 149).

Bills drawn on them, say at 6 months sterling 133,267—leaving a balance of about 40,755 pounds from which you may draw what you require. The silk is valued at 13 shillings per pound. The nankeens at 2 shillings 6 pence per piece. It is most fortunate that no change in partnership takes place till the 30th June next,[9] before which date all accounts, opium, etc. shall be square.

I expect Matheson from Calcutta early in May, but have no idea when we may have another opportunity of addressing you. I expect G. R.'s brother on with Mr. M. G.[10] And I hope he may prove useful. Excuse this letter, written in a state of mind not the most pleasant. Remember me kindly to Mrs. Magniac, and believe me, My dear Magniac,

Yours,

25. Thomas Weeding[11] in London to *Magniac & Co.* in Canton,

30 April 1830

Dear Sirs,

I wrote to Mr. Jardine on the 2nd of February via Singapore, and gave some intimation in that letter of what I had been able to do with the nankeens received per *Sir Joseph Banks*, which were sent to me by Captain Grant for Account of Thomas Beale[12] of Macao to hold the proceeds to your order and to which you adverted in your letter of the 27th April last year.

I have now the pleasure of handing you two account sales, one of 1,000 pieces of white and the other of 19,800 pieces of the yellow of which the greater part were bought in, as they did not reach the price I expected to get for them. Those sold were such as were more or less damaged partly from sea water, and partly from mildew.

The whole of the Nankeens were put up at the December sale, but 8,894 pieces part of the better sort were taxed at 3 shillings and refused. They were tried again

[9] Eventually the 'change in partnership' was postponed by a further year to June 1832, by which time the accounts were squared, and Hollingworth Magniac's share of profits and overall capital could be set aside for repatriation to England.

[10] G.R. and Mr. M. G. were not identified.

[11] Thomas Weeding, formerly of the East India Company, was William Jardine's first business partner with Framjee Cowasjee of Bombay. He remained one of the firm's principal London constituents until 1835–1837. He was listed in the contemporary London directories as 'Merchant', with offices at 6, Great Winchester Street, Old Broad Street. (*RLD* and *TLCD*).

[12] Thomas Beale had been a partner in the Canton firm of *Shank and Beale*, which later became *Magniac & Co.* In 1815, he lost the fortune he had hoped to retire with in disastrous opium speculations. He was 'the oldest foreign resident in China, having arrived prior to 1785'. At the time of this Letter, he still lived in one of the fine old Portuguese houses and kept a well-stocked garden and an aviary. He eventually probably committed suicide in 1841. (See Hunter's sensitive account of this episode in *Bits of Old China*, pp. 73–78). Thomas Chay Beale, one of the firm's book-keeper who is often referred to in the Letters as 'Chay', was Thomas Beale's nephew.

in March sale and taxed at 2 shillings and 10 pence, and still refused. Of the bought in goods I have sent to Italy altogether 12,100 pieces of which 5,000 pieces have been sold to net about 3 shillings, 4,000 pieces to net about 2 shillings and 10 pence, and the remaining 3,000 pieces, the last shipment, have not arrived, but will I hope realize 3 shillings being part of the better quality. In the whole parcel there were six pieces deficient.

Mr. Beale will no doubt be satisfied that I have done the best for his interest. I could not have got 2 shillings and10 pence per piece for the inferior sort in this market, and when the account sales are made up I trust they will be found to net nearly 3 shillings per piece. The price nominally this day for the better quality does not exceed 2 shillings and 6 pence.

I remain, Dear Sirs, your most obedient Servant.

26. *H. J. & R. Barton*[13] in Manchester to *Magniac & Co.* in Canton,
11 May 1830

Gentlemen,

We last had the pleasure of writing you on the 19th March for duplicate even dated and are since without any of your favors to reply to.

Agreeable with our last we have now the pleasure to hand you enclosed Invoice of MG 36/75 – 40 Cases of Goods amounting to pounds sterling 179.18.8 and YE 81/124 – 44 Bales of Twist amounting to pounds sterling 1,405.9/4 shipped by one of the Company's Vessels sailing from London on joint account of *Messrs. James Finlay & Co.*[14] and ourselves. Expenses of shipment with other particulars will be advised you by *Messrs. Finlay Hodgson & Co.*[15]

The goods consist of 520 pieces of plain Cambrics[16] each piece containing 4 lengths of 12 Yards each, or 59 yards agreeable with your previous suggestions and are invoiced at 21/1 shillings to 32/9 per piece—and 1,000 pieces of 9/8 tape[17] and Long Clothes 41 to 42 yards each at 19/10 to 21/– per piece. The Yarns consist of an assortment of numbers 20s up to 80s all 1+++B quality of very excellent spinning, and we hope you will have no difficulty in realizing early and

[13] *Barton, H. J. & Co*, listed in *PMDS* as 'Merchants' with an address at 'Mulberry Street', Manchester. They were among the very first shippers of English manufactured goods to *Magniac & Co.* in Canton.

[14] *James Finlay & Co.*, listed as 'Merchants' in *GPOAD*, with an address at '63, Queen's street, Glasgow'.

[15] The London office of the Finlays. See above, Letter **18**, note 7.

[16] Cambrics: 'A kind of white linen originally made at Cambray in Flanders. Also an imitation made of hard spun cotton yard'. (*OED*).

[17] Tape: 'A narrow woven strip of stout linen, cotton, silk, etc. used as a string for tying garments, etc.' (*OED*).

profitable sales of the whole. Full particulars of the shipments are enclosed and samples are on board the Vessel.

You will most probably hear from *Messrs. James Finlay & Co.* relative to sales and returns; should their letter however not be in time for this conveyance you will please to follow your previous instructions on this head, by disposing of the goods and Twists at the best market prices and remitting the proceeds to *Messrs. Finlay Hodgson & Co.* in good Bills of Exchange or Specie.

We remain, Gentlemen, your Obedient Servants.

27. William Mathieson in Glasgow to *Messrs. Fairlie Bonham & Co.* in London, 13 July 1830[18]

Gentlemen,

Last night I received a letter from Mr. Hollingworth Magniac Esq., of which the enclosed is a copy. It serves me in the meantime as an introduction to your correspondence.

Having been for some time in communication with Mr. James Matheson of the firm of *Messrs. Magniac & Co.* of Canton, and latterly with the House itself, it occurred to me recently that I might be of use to the Establishment in this City, as I had learned that on American and other account, shipments were making to China by Manufacturers and others here. I accordingly corresponded with Mr. Hollingworth Magniac on the subject, and among other matters noticed the propriety of a reference to a respectable House to satisfy the enquiries of expected shippers. These enquiries when made, I am happy to observe, you are willing to satisfy. But being desirous that you should be saved the trouble of frequent applications, permit me to request your addressing such a letter to me as might be exhibited for the satisfaction of parties here by way of obviating the necessity of individual reference to you.

Allow me to state for your satisfaction that I am connected in partnership here with *James Ewing & Co.*[19] carrying on business as West India merchants, and with the *Muirkirk Iron Co.*[20] in the manufacture of Pig and Bar iron, and that any enquiry respecting me will be satisfactorily answered in the *Glasgow Bank*

[18] *JMArch.*, Reel 249, Letter 57E. This letter is a copy, probably first received, and then on-sent, by Hollingworth Magniac to his friends in Canton. It is interesting to note that enterprising Scots like William Mathieson whose North-Atlantic business involved them habitually in the West Indies and in American trade, still had an eye for business development with the East Indies and China. The same remark applies to the Finlays of Glasgow and the Bartons of Manchester.

[19] William Mathieson, the writer of this letter, was a partner of *James Ewing & Co*, 'Merchants' of Glasgow. (*GPOAD, 183*, p. 166).

[20] The firm was not identified.

Company,[21] the correspondents of whom in London are *Leo Richard Carr Glynn & Co.*[22] and *Messrs. Ransom & Co.*[23]

Accompanying this you will receive mercantile and other statements, and I shall be happy to render you any service in this city.

I have the honour to remain, Gentlemen, your most obedient servants.

Circular: Glasgow July 1830
Sir,

In the prospect of an early extension of the trade between this country and China permit me respectfully to solicit a share of any business you may have to transact at Canton in behalf of *Messrs. Magniac & Co.* of that city,—their long residence there and the ample means they possess recommend them as desirable agents for the sale of goods, or purchase of produce, etc., in attending to which their friends may defend on their most zealous endeavours to promote their interest.

Besides the opportunities at present afforded of limited shipments by the vessels of the Honorable East India Company, consignments may be made via Batavia, Singapore and Manila to Canton. I shall be happy to communicate any information of which I am possessed as to markets, etc., and I am respectfully, etc.

Reference in London : *Messrs. Fairlie Bonham & Co.*

28. William Jardine in Canton to James Matheson in Macao,

8 September 1830

My dear Matheson,

I have just returned from calling on Howqua to inquire after an answer to our petition,[24] and have only five minutes to inform you what passed. Howqua said we must wait a day or two longer; to which I replied my instructions were to wait till tomorrow evening; and then despatch a Boat to say there was no answer—and to carry it down if received. These instructions I must obey, and my relief is one,

[21] Probably the *Glasgow Union Banking Company*, with offices at 15, Virginia Street. The other two Glasgow banks were the *Glasgow & Ship Bank*, of 12 Ingram Street, and the *Glasgow Provident Bank*, of 86 Miller Street. (*GPOAD, 1839*, Appendices, p. 63).

[22] The banking firm was subsequently known as *Sir R. C. Glyn, Mills & Co.*, and operated down to the 1960s. (Hilton Price, F. G., *A Handbook of London Bankers*, London, 1876, enlarged 1891, repr. 1970).

[23] *Ransom & Co.*, London bankers, had offices at 1 Pall Mall East. (*RLD, TLCD*).

[24] The petition was not traced. From the context of this Letter and of Letter **29**, however, the petition to the viceroy is likely to have requested overdue payments from Chungqua, or other Hong merchants in financial difficulty or already bankrupt.

if not two vessels will be immediately despatched for the Yellow Sea.[25] He inquired if we would be satisfied, for the present, by a promise from the Viceroy, that the proceeds of the Hongs etc., should be divided among the Creditors as soon as realized—and the Money from the Uncle[26] also. I told him that would tend to convince the Creditors the Viceroy was inclined to act correctly and not seize every thing for duties, but I could not promise that it would prevent the ship from sailing.

He alleged we were unreasonable as the Viceroy was doing all he could. I urged his having done nothing; but allowed Chunqua to get 50,000 dollars deeper in debt, and now only wanted the proceeds of the Hongs, etc. to make up the duty. That done, we might petition for ever and ever Amen—and get paid by instalments from the Cohong. The Lou Son[27] was passing in full robes, he was called in, received his instructions, and proceeded to the Viceroy. They are evidently sadly afraid of the Yellow Sea. In haste,

Yours sincerely,

29. William Jardine in Canton to James Matheson in Macao,
11 September 1830

My dear Matheson,

I have, this instant, received your favor of the 10th, by Captain White[28] and have five minutes allowed me to reply, by Mr. Brown's fast Boat[29]—and to enclose a chop, received last night late from the Viceroy. I have not seen Howqua since it was issued; but he expresses himself very strongly about the proceeds of the Hongs and Houses being appropriated to the payment of the foreign claims, though the duties must appear first on paper. Could this be relied on, I should prefer not sending a ship to the Yellow Sea; and you must judge for yourselves at Macao, as to the propriety of trusting to Howqua's information on the subject of

[25] The Yellow Sea, a thousand miles north of Canton and facing the province of Shantung, was forbidden to foreign traders and to foreign ships. The remark was meant as a thinly-veiled threat to Howqua, the cohong and even the viceroy that, in retaliation for overdue payments, a complaint was to be lodged directly with the emperor. The '*Eight Regulations*' which were supposed to control the Canton trade practices and the relationships with foreign merchants contained a paragraph stipulating that 'Hong merchants are not to owe debts to foreigners' (Hunter, *The Fan Kwae* at Canton, 'The eight regulations'). By the year 1830, however, this specific regulation was, like most of the others, entirely disregarded.

[26] Probably Chunqua's uncle.

[27] The official serving as intermediary between the hong merchants and the viceroy's office.

[28] The Bartlett Index *(BI)* records the existence of two Captains White,—William and John,—both occasional correspondents from Calcutta.

[29] This Mr Brown was not identified. There was a Samuel Brown who was a resident of Macao at the time. He was a Yale graduate and taught the six Chinese pupils of the Morrison Education Society. (Fay, *The Opium War*, p 136).

the Viceroy's intentions. I am convinced, between ourselves, our cause is much weakened by the coming in of the ships—which information had reached Howqua before the Viceroy's anwer was issued.

Baynes[30] asks *me* to send him a draft of a letter to the Emperor, *he* being very much engaged. I expected the said letter to have been, not only written, but translated by the 10th Instant. The purport of it must be nearly the same as that to the Viceroy—stating the reduced number of the Hongs, our being obliged to deal with them, and them only, and then proceed to our grievances of Manhop,[31] Chunqua, etc. I really have not time to draw up a petition or letter, and you can do it much better, among you at Macao.

I forget if I told you that Cushing[32] is anxious to sell both his schooners—but we could not use the American flag to the Northeast. There is a grand objection to the *Merope*'s taking the drug with her, namely, we want an answer; and how is Parkyns[33] to send it to Canton ? The *Falcon* must be the vessel, I suspect, but I can see plainly we are too late to do the thing properly. I shall see Howqua presently—and write again tonight or tomorrow.

Mr. Milne[34] has delivered his packet safe and in good order. I regret the news you communicate, though we had expected such an event for some time. Mr. Macvicar[35] dined with us yesterday. He is a plain, intelligent Scotchman; and proposes returning home in December or January. I am not certain if I informed you of our having sold the *Fort William*'s remaining cotton to Howqua at 9 Taels, 5 mace[36] and about 1,600 Bales of the *Ann*'s to Linchong[37]—the good at 9 Taels, 5 mace, the old is sad trash, some at 6 Tael, 9 mace or 7 Tales, some at 6 Tales. For some 6 Taels, 3 mace is offered China price. We have had fresh musters taken, etc. . . No news. I shall write again soon.

[30] William Baynes was the second most senior East India Company supercargo in 1830 (*EIRD,* 1831, p. 110), hence William Jardine's surprise at being asked to draft an official letter of complaint to the Emperor.

[31] On Manhop, see above, Letter **12**, note 21.

[32] John Pershing Cushing, an American resident in Canton and Macao between 1803 and 1830. He was a partner of the firm of *Perkins & Co.* (Hunter, *The Fan Kwae at Canton*, p. 10). Ten letters in all from J. P. Cushing are listed in the *BI.*

[33] George Parkyns, captain of the *Merope* in 1830, retired to England in 1831. In 1833 he 'bought the Old Stone Hall, Suffolk'. (*BI*).

[34] William Milne Jr., the eldest son of William Milne who had helped the Rev. Robert Morrison translate the Bible into Chinese at the Malacca College. (Fay, *The Opium War*, p. 210).

[35] This is the first mention of John Macvicar, one of the first syndicators of British exports to China. John Macvicar was to play an important role in developing an awareness among British manufacturers of the potential of the Chinese market. The business relationship with *Jardine, Matheson & Co.* made fast progress in the early 1830s, but did not survive the tensions brought about by difficult trading conditions for British piece goods later in the decade. (See Letters **161, 163, 166, 182,** and **216**).

[36] Mace: 'A weight and money of account equal to one-tenth of a tael.' (*OED*). Contemporaries of William Jardine wrote indifferently 'Taels' or 'Tales'.

[37] Linchong: Chinese private merchant and opium broker.

Do the needful with the enclosures, and oblige,
Yours very sincerely,
P.S. Say to Captain Innes[38] the Mare is at his service—if he feels disposed to ride her with my compliments of course.

30. *Magniac & Co.* in Canton to *Fergusson & Co.*[39] in Calcutta,

16 October 1830

Dear Sirs,

As the *Falcon* will probably arrive at Calcutta about the period of your first opium sales, we avail ourselves of the opportunity to make known to you our views in regard to purchases of the drug on our account during the season.

We propose putting you in funds for this purpose as favourable means of remittance occur, to the extent of four Lacks[40] of Rupees, and assuming the quantity to be brought forward at about 5,000 chests of Patna and 2,200 of Benares,[41]—total 7,200 chests (as stated in a communication from one of our neighbours), while the quantity of Malwa likely to come out under the new system of open trade at Bombay and Damaun is estimated at about 10,000 chests, it appears to us that if your first sales should go at 1,600 Rupees per chest for Patna it will be advisable to purchase freely on our account, say to the extent of about half our proposed investment; on the other hand, should the price approximate 1,700 Rupees less or more, we should think it prudent not to go beyond a quarter of the proposed quantity at your first sales. We hear the quality of the Benares highly spoken of, and if equal in weight to Patna, we should be disposed to give the same price to it to the extent of about a third of our quantity and to a quarter extent if the prices be lower. Should the Patna be decidedly inferior, like that of 1826 (which is possible from the failure of the crop), we should rather not be concerned in it. On this head, we conceive the report of the Company's examiners[42] may be relied on, which will render it unnecessary for you to take into consideration mere

[38] Probably not the notorious James Innes referred to in note 48 of Letter **9** above. The Captain Innes mentioned here is John Innes, captain of the *Abercrombie Robinson*, a 1330 ton East India Company ship belonging to H. Bonham, which was in Canton during the 1830–1831 trading season. (*EIRD*, 1831, pp. viii-ix).

[39] *Fergusson & Co.* was the firm's principal Calcutta correspondent until its failure 1833. See Letter **80**.

[40] Lac or Lakh: '(Anglo-Indian, 1613). One hundred thousand'. (*OED*). One Spanish dollar was worth 2.02–2.04 Bombay (or 'Sicca') rupees. The Calcutta (or 'Current') rupee was worth a little less at 2.44 to one dollar. (Morse, *The Chronicles of the EIC, IV*, p. 260).

[41] Patna and Benares were two variants of Bengal opium.

[42] East India Company officials whose role was to inspect the opium processed under their colleagues' supervision before the Calcutta public auctions. For buyers, the presence of the East India Company seal on opium crates was synonymous with product quality.

conjectural surmises of inferiority, provided the balls[43] are unbroken and have not lost more weight than usual by evaporation up to the date of sale.

You are aware that the quality of the last year's Patna is highly approved of; that repacked in compartments at Calcutta has been found to lose disproportionately in weight upon wanting the usual protection of poppy leaves. The cloth envelopes have not yet been tried, and we should not wish to be concerned in this or any other mode of packing up the drug, unless at a reduced price.

We deem it unnecessary to give minute instructions, as to our idea of safe limits in the event of the supply either on your side or at Bombay being different from what we have supposed, and trust you will do us the favor of exercising your discretion on the occasion, acting for us as you would do for yourselves; about fifteen Rupees difference of price for every hundred chests less or more in the supply of Patna and Benares may be considered a safe basis of calculation. As the *Jamesina* will not go to Calcutta this season we shall be obliged by your sending on such opium as you may purchase from time to time, duly insured by you, according as the state of your account may enable you to clear it from the Company's warehouse, or as you may feel disposed without inconvenience to come under advances for us.

We trust you will excuse our begging the favour of your giving a preference of the Insurance to the *9th Canton office*, being, as you are aware, interested in that association.

The present price of the drug may be quoted as follows—Malwa Company's: 560–565 dollars; Damaun: 540–545 per chest, at which it has remained nearly stationary for some time; Patna and Benares, which remained stationary at 780 to 800 dollars per chest, have advanced within these few days to 830–835 dollars, owing to the stock on hand being comparatively moderate, *viz*—on 1st instant: Patna 2,143, compared with 2,510 chests in stock on 1st October 1829; Benares 463 [compared] with 679.

Sales at three months have been effected at 880 dollars per chest and we think the price is likely to be higher than this on the arrival of the new drug. The Company's treasury for Bills on Bengal has opened at the low rate of 200 Sicca Rupees per 100 dollars. The Company has sold one or two cargoes of their Bengal cotton at 9.5.0. per picul; we have heard of the sale of private Bengal cotton. We are, etc.

[43] Before packing the opium was moulded into balls weighing about three pounds each and protected with poppy leaves to keep them moist. Each crate contained forty opium balls. (For the detail of opium processing, packing and shipping, see : Fay, *The Opium War*, p. 12, etc.; Le Pichon, *Origines de Hong Kong*, pp. 65–77).

31. William Jardine in Canton to Hollingworth Magniac in London,
16 November 1830

My dear Magniac,

I had the pleasure of addressing a few lines to you on the 24th ultimo, per *Royal Charlotte* via Singapore, when we were all a good deal excited by the violent discussion then carrying on between the Select Committee and the Chinese Authorities, which have terminated, as then anticipated, by a few blustering Edicts, and a reference to the Emperor.

Mrs. Baynes[44] and Mrs. Hornhill[45] are quietly in Canton; but Mrs. and Miss Low,[46] two American Ladies, having come up after the implements of war had been removed from the Company's Factory, and peace restored, the Viceroy has taken the business up; as a proceeding in direct defiance of his recently issued orders, and threatens to stop the shipping off of cargo to two American ships at Whampoa, consigned to messrs. *Russell & Co.*,[47] in which Firm Mr. Low, the husband of Mrs. Low, is a partner. The reply has hitherto been: 'send Mrs. Baynes away, and the american ladies will immediately follow'. It is difficult to say what the result may be; much will depend on the firmness of the americans—and the Viceroy will probably proceed cautiously till he receive the Emperor's reply to the reference already made.

By this conveyance you will of course expect a copy of the accounts which should have been sent to you last season, and I feel very much annoyed at being again compelled to disappoint your expectations; but the truth is, we found that Mr. Ullman had so mixed up the sold, but uncleared, drug of the previous season with it, that it became necessary to examine minutely the operations of that also,

[44] Mrs Baynes was the wife of William Baynes, the senior supercargo of the English factory in Canton. A few months earlier, she had been the first foreign woman to visit Canton which was out of bounds to all foreign women. She was determined to see for herself 'the princely grandeur in which her husband lived when in Canton [. . .] and in April 1830 persuaded him to take her to Canton for a visit, with Elizabeth Fearon and the wife of another supercargo, Mrs Robinson. [. . .] Their arrival brought threats from a nonplussed Viceroy that he would stop all trade in the factories and send in soldiers to remove them. Baynes's answer was to position Company cannon at the factory gate and order in a hundred armed men from the Company ships, enough to prevent the Viceroy from matching words with action.' (Ride, *East India Company Cemetery*, p. 47).

[45] Mrs. Thornhill, one of Harriet Low's best friends in Macao, is often mentioned in her diary. (Low, Harriett, *Lights and Shadows*, p. 381, note 111).

[46] Mrs. Low was Abigail Low, the wife of William Low, one of the partners of *Russell and Co.*, the largest American firm trading at Canton. Miss Low was their niece, Harriet Low. The American merchants were threatened with stoppage of their trade, and after eighteen days, the ladies returned to Macao. (Ibid. See also: Coates, *Macao and the British*, pp. 155–157. Prior to the publication of Lows' *Lights and Shadows* in 2002, extracts from her diary could be found only in: Loines, Elma, *The China Post-bag of the Seth Low Family of Salem and New York, 1829–1873*, Falmouth House, Manchester, Me., 1953).

[47] For details on the early partners of *Russell & Co.*, see Hunter, *The Fan Kwae at Canton*, Appendix entitled '*Messrs. Russell & Co.*, Canton, 1823 to 1844', pp. 96–97.

which has not yet been satisfactorily accomplished. Mr. Matheson has however made great progress in this tedious examination: and by one of the later ships of the season, we hope to be able to hand you a statement that may be relied on. In the meanwhile I may safely say Mr. Ullman's balance of about 38,000 dollars will be more than doubled by adding to it the profits arising from the opium account. I have no doubt, when the accounts for the two seasons have been adjusted, the result will turn out to be nearly the same as, from memory, I always supposed it to be.

You may possibly recollect my repeatedly observing to you, that I was satisfied [that] Mr. Ulmann's books were sufficiently correct for practical purposes, but never balanced with nicety; and I am now thoroughly convinced my opinion was correct—but the error appears to have been chiefly in the opium account; and such as concerns ourselves only. The poor old man is at Macao, under the care of Dr. Pearson,[48] and is not likely to be of any further use in the office. We have set a subscription on foot for the benefit of his four daughters,[49] and expect to see them well provided for—say, 800 to 1,000 dollars per annum.

Henry Robinson[50] is also at Macao unwell, having some time ago ruptured a small blood vessel in his lungs; which from his delicate state of health, produced a good deal of alarm.

We have had a very fagging,[51] anxious season; with a very large stock of Opium and Cotton, under our charge, and unusually dull markets for both articles.

The Commission Account will be nearly the same as last Season; and the Opium Account exhibits, so far, rather handsome balance.

We have commenced remitting to *Fairlie, Bonham & Co.* in Bullion by each ship of the first despatch; and if copied in time, you will receive enclosed a copy of our letter to them, on the subject of our London account, which will show you the real state of the case. It appears the Balance of interest is about 900 pounds sterling, in our favor; and the account itself nearly square, after allowing amply for your wants; but this shall not be allowed to interfere with our making further remittances this Season, both on your account and our own; as we are anxious to have your 20,000 pounds set at liberty.

[48] Alexander Pearson (1780–1874) was a ship surgeon of the East India Company. He arrived in Macao in 1805 when he introduced Jennerian vaccination against smallpox (i.e. the vaccination of human beings with pus from cowpox pustules). He first obtained a supply of the vaccine from a Portuguese merchant who had brought it to Macao from Manila, and later obtained supplies directly from Spanish ships. With these supplies he vaccinated the population of Macao. He later published a tract on the subject of smallpox vaccination which was translated into Chinese. He retired from China in 1832, leaving behind a grateful population. (Choa, *Heal the Sick*, pp. 52–53).

[49] The Ullman daughters were: Joanna, Anna-Margarita, Maria-Francesca and Roza-Maria. See below, Letter **248**.

[50] Henry Robinson was a book-writer or clerk employed by *Magniac & Co.*

[51] Fag: 'To do something that wearies one; to toil (1772); to make fatigued, to tire (1826)'. (*OED*).

I shall reply to your letters in detail by the next despatch; and this being in many respects, a duplicate of mine of the 24th. ultimo, it may be as well to mention how our account stands with your friend Lord Melville,[52] who is prevented from returning to his family till some arrangement shall have been made for the settlement of his foreign debt.

We hope for about one half of our claims in the end of the year, and I have agreed to give up the papers of the Dutch Hong, in consequence of Howqua, Mowqua, and {Tenqua} promising to pay us 50,000 dollars with interest.

On the subject of your Factories, I have little to say. They have all been full with the exception of N°3 Creek, and the front of the Imperial—the former being unlet, we have filled it with the commanders of ships, who mess in the house, and shall allow you a moderate rent for the use thereof; the latter is now nearly finished, having been built from the foundations by Howqua. But Mr. Dunn having been obliged to rent the front of the Danish[53] Hong, pending the building of N°1 Imperial, you will lose the rent for the time.

Rents have been so much reduced of late years, say, more than a third, and Mr. Dunn having been desirous of altering the plan, I agreed to pay Howqua 2,000 Taels to induce him to build said factory according to the new plan, on Mr. Dunn[54] agreeing to pay the same rent as before—an arrangement I consider very advantageous to your interests. It is now a good substantially built factory; and should last for many years without repairs of any description. The timber is of the very best description, and the bricks of a larger size than is generally used.

Chay Beale has not yet got his set of books up, and the only chance we have of ever getting over such extreme indifference as pervades part of our establishment is by appointing Mr. Alexander Matheson to commence with, and endeavour to keep up the Books for the current season, though he has the letter book, etc. to attend to—a very annoying state of affairs for a public office; but enough of this.

Be pleased to present my kind regards to Mrs. Magniac, and believe me, my dear Magniac,

Yours very sincerely,

[52] For a previous reference to 'Lord Melville' by James Matheson, see above Letter **20**, note 32. Here, the context makes it clear that 'Lord Melville' is the nickname for a Chinese debtor. Although the language is allusive, Hollingworth Magniac is meant to understand that his debtor is still in prison or under house arrest.

[53] For the names of the factories and their geographical situations, see above: Letter **1,** note 2. Although the factory buildings belonged to the Hong merchants and no foreigner was allowed to own property in Canton, it appears that arrangements had been made for Hollingworth Magniac to collect the rent of certain factory offices, probably as compensation for uncollected funds from failed debtors.

[54] Nathan Dunn, of *N. Dunn & Co.*, Canton, mentioned in Letter **65** as a member of the 10th *Canton Insurance Company*.

32. William Jardine in Canton to Thomas Weeding in London

7 December 1830

Dear Weeding,

In my letter of 16th ultimo I informed you of your report on the quality of the musk[55] under your charge having reached me too late to admit of my buying up a quantity that had been in the market for many months. And I shall now make you acquainted with various particulars connected with its sale and shipment.

While the Company's ships were detained outside, Mr. Turner[56] entered into an agreement with the principal holder to advance a certain sum per pecul and ship the whole to his friends in London. One lot of 25 catties had been shipped off, and a second was partly packed, when he discovered the quality to be very indifferent—the pods much wetted and the flavour more like that which issues from a foul stable than from genuine musk. One of the small caddies, containing about a catty, was sent to me, and I cut open many of the pods which had every appearance of being filled in Canton, and containing a brown coloured clay, mixed up with musk and urine—I believe. As this adulterated article was from the same party from whom I had purchased the two lots sent home, I became apprehensive about the quality of them, and determined to run no further risk till a report should reach me.

Whether Mr. Turner received earlier advices or acted on the principle of saving himself if possible from losing his money previously advanced, I know not, but on receiving your report I found he had some short time before entered into an arrangement for the whole, having found someone to become security for the quality after a very severe examination. There have been two or three small lots in the market since of middling quality, and purchased, I believe, by some of the Company's surgeons.

In consequence to what has occurred to Mr. Turner I determined on gaining whatever information I could on the subject of musk, and commenced by cutting open every pod that was brought to me as a muster; and soon began to have a tolerably good opinion of my powers of discriminating between good and bad pods from their external appearance—a faculty which few of the Chinese dealers are possessed of.

[55] 'Musk is a very strong scented substance, found under the belly of the male, of a species of goat, called *moschus mosciferus*. After killing it the peasants cut off the bag containing the Musk. It is about the size of a hen's egg, and is situated nearer to the organs of generation than the navel. In its original state it is nothing more than putrid blood, which coagulated in this bag. The largest bladder cannot furnish above half an ounce of Musk, generally but little more than a quarter of an ounce. Etc.' (*DM*, p. 231).

[56] Richard Turner (1786–1839), was a China resident from 1826 and a partner in *Turner & Co*. The firm traded in opium and other goods. 'He was one of the group, with William Jardine in the chair, appointed at a public meeting to organize a British floating hospital for seamen at Whampoa'. (Ride, *East India Cemetery*, p. 174).

Mowqua, the Hong merchant, has a share in one of the most extensive drug concerns in Canton; and to which I applied for specimens of genuine musk. At Mowqua's request, his partner supplied me with two pods of what is called by the dealers 'woonam's musk' and several picked pods of what the Chinese term 'Tsune Chay'. Of the latter I pronounced one large pod bad, and on cutting it open, found the contents to be common earth mixed with a very small proportion of musk. One of them, a very small one, I considered good and part of the contents proved so; but two pieces of lead were found in the very center of the pod, each about a quarter of an inch in length; and of the diameter or circumference of an ordinary-sized pencil.

I must describe to you what I consider good musk, unadulterated—an article which I believe you seldom meet with in Europe. The genuine musk is in small, round and oblong particles, from the size of a pea down to that of a pin's head—of a black colour, and very peculiar smell. When chewed, or moistened with water and rubbed on paper they appear smooth, are free from grittiness, and have a dull yellow colour—not bright yellow as often stated. In almost every pod that I have seen, these small particles or globules are surrounded by a smaller or larger proportion (according to the pod being genuine or otherwise, I apprehend) of a soft brownish or yellowish coloured powder, moist and full of shreds of their membranous fibres which must, I think, be an adulteration—as in some these membranous shreds are loosely mixed with the moist powder, when in others they are rolled together in round balls as large as a small bean or large pea. Whether this surrounding powder and membranous fibre are of any real value, I know not, but am anxious to be informed.

To enable you to ascertain the point I have sent in charge of Captain Innes[57] and his purser, Mr. Thomson, a small box with ten pods, and two bottles in it, to be forwarded from the Cape of St Helena by the first ship and to your consignment: in hopes of having a report on the quality of each description by early ships of next Season. Some of the pods are of a description I have never seen before and are said to be genuine. But their being without seam is no proof of the contents being pure musk; as the mouth of the pods may easily be opened. One bottle contains the round and oblong particles, selected from several pods; and the other contains what remained of the pods after these particles had been selected. The first I consider pure musk; and wish to know its value per ounce, and whether it has lost its virtue by being put in a bottle. Part of it remained in my desk in paper for many days previous to its being put into the bottle. I am aware the other bottle contains a good many small particles of pure musk which were too minute to be easily separated.

I should like to know the value of this per ounce as it is; and also the value of the brownish coloured powder by itself, supposing the whole of the little dark

[57] Captain John Innes. See above, Letter **29**, note 38.

particles to be picked out. The shreds of membranes are certainly not musk and must be put in to fill up the pod. If you will furnish me with the particulars requested by the first direct ship, duplicate by the second, I shall feel particularly obliged.

There is no good musk in Canton at present; nor do the dealers know when they are to receive any. There is no want, however, of the common kind, which the Parsees generally purchase for Bombay under the name of 'woonam' or 'Wunnam' musk, with a view of ascertaining the value in your market. Should a lot of good musk arrive I shall endeavour to become the purchaser, though aware that a very considerable supply has been sent home within the last eight months.

Under your good management I am satisfied a handsome profit would be realized on a really genuine article whatever might be the fate of the indifferent parcels in the hands of parties ignorant of the proper mode of bringing them to market.

Etc . . .

33. James Matheson in Canton to Charles Thomas[58] in Singapore,

24 December 1830

My dear Thomas,

Captain Ardlie of the ship *Ganges* being unable to quit this port for want of sufficient funds to pay his port charges, we have been induced as a mere act of charity, to ship in his vessel 492 boxes of cassia[59] for London and to advance the freight here, for the entire voyage to that port, including Singapore transshipping charges. Under these circumstances I trust you will excuse our begging the favour of you to procure his signature to the enclosed fresh set of Bills of Lading to London, forwarding two of them as usual, by different conveyance to Thomas Weeding Esq., and one to us. You will have no further trouble, and no charge to incur in the business. I hope therefore we but anticipate your own view in counting on the transaction being free from commission on your part. I enclose the Bill of Lading for Singapore, blank endorsed by *Messrs. Ilbery Fearon & Co.*[60] who lend their name as shippers for a particular reason, the cassia being ours.

[58] Charles Thomas of *Charles Thomas & Co.*, the Canton firm's principal agent in Singapore in the early 1830s. Charles Thomas's services were used principally for transhipping goods to London or India when freighted on ships plying only local routes.

[59] Cassia or Quassia: 'The root, bark, and wood of this tree, have all places in the material medica. The wood is most generally used, and is said to be a tonic, stomachic, antiseptic and febrifuge'. (*DM*, p. 273).

[60] *Ilbery Fearon & Co.*, a partnership of two country traders resident at Macao and Canton: James William Henry Ilbery—a former business friend of Charles Magniac, (Hollingworth Magniac's brother)—and Christopher Fearon. (Ride, *East India Cemetery*, p. 138).

We have also to enable Captain Ardlie to ballast his ship free of expenses put on board of her 400 bags of sugar, the freight of which depends on it realizing 4 shillings per dollar in London. Under that, it is freight free. The Bills of Lading must be signed freight paid, we having given Captain Ardlie a letter to Mr. Weeding requesting him to pay the freight agreed on, if due. We must beg your attention to this also.

You will receive from us an official letter respecting the *Ganges* with a mortgage bond and copy of our instructions, but the parties in Bombay having defeated their own object by not leaving Captain Ardlie the wherewithal to defray his ship's expenses, you must of course allow him to appropriate a sufficient portion of the freight to clear him of the port. In short, we write to you more as a matter of form than from a wish that you should take any trouble about him, further than forwarding the Bond to the mortgagee in London. You have no doubt heard quite enough in the way of reports to induce the utmost caution for your own interest, in the event of your interfering with his concern.

We declined the consignment of the ship, although we are now induced to step forward to prevent his being indefinitely detained for want of money to pay his port charges. Trusting you will excuse all this trouble, I remain,

Yours sincerely,

34. William Jardine in Canton to Jamsetjee Jejeebhoy in Bombay,

30 December 1830

My dear Sir,

I had the pleasure of addressing you last on the 1st Instant and now avail myself of the departure of the *Jamesina* to add a few words in addition to the correspondence from the House, on the subject of cotton and opium.

Cotton has continued in demand, and prices have advanced a little, but we have not yet closed for your consignments per *Guilford* and *Bannerman*,[61] being desirous of realizing, if possible, nine Taels per picul, while the highest offer we have had is 8.7 Taels at thirty days. The cotton is of good quality and we shall persist in our demand for a few days longer, though we may ultimately be contented with 8.8 Taels per picul, by way of closing the account of your cotton consignment.

The stock on hand is large, and we feel averse to running the risk of an Eastern passage ship from Calcutta dropping in before we have disposed of the whole of our cotton now on hand. A friend of Howqua's has been the principal purchaser lately and is now so deeply interested in maintaining present prices, that we have little apprehension of a decline in price for some time to come; but should the

[61] Ship named after the Bannermans, a family connected with the East India Company. The supercargo James Bannerman was residing in Canton at the time.

demand in February and March fall short of expectation, an anxiety to realize may have the effect again of reducing the present still very moderate prices. We should therefore recommend you to do everything in your power to reduce the Bombay rates previous to making your purchases for next season.

On the subject of opium I have little to add to what has been already stated. Patna is in some demand at 910 dollars per chest, at a fortnight or three weeks, and at these prices we should ere now have disposed of your remaining 25 chests, but for a prejudice that exists against the mode of packing in canvas;[62] convinced that they must ultimately come into use, we have refused making the sacrifice demanded of 40 or 50 dollars per chest, and preferred waiting the result of time and a diminished stock. We shall not, however, allow this delay to interfere with the closing of your account as we hope soon to be able to establish the relative value of the two descriptions of the drug, on terms more moderate than those that have hitherto been proposed to the dealers. Your Malwa is of little importance, consisting of five chests only per *Carron*, which is worth at the present moment 565 dollars per chest, but being insured up to delivery, we shall give them the chance of a rise in price which is very generally expected by the Chinese.

Respecting the ultimate result of the stock of Malwa now on hand, I confess myself far from sanguine, and should not be surprised at prices declining again about the China New Year, though they are now so low that we can scarcely expect the new drug to inferfere with the old. Everything will depend, however, on the supply for the approaching season. As for prices with you they ought to rule low after the very severe losses that have been recently sustained by the dealers.

I avail myself of this opportunity to acknowledge you favour of the 4th of July and 2nd of August, which have already been attended to.

This goes by the *Jamesina* bound to your port for a thorough repair, and I beg leave again to solicit your good offices and powerful interest in procuring her a good opium freight back to Lintin. We trust to the influence of you and your good friend Motichund,[63] added to that of our mutual friends *Remington & Co.*, for returning her to us with a full cargo.

Be pleased to present my kind regards to your son[64] and to all friends in Bombay, and believe me, my dear Sir,

Yours very sincerely,

[62] The reason for this prejudice was that the opium sold in Calcutta by the East India Company set the market standard and it was packed in poppy leaves. See above Letter **30**, notes 43.

[63] Motichund Armchund, a Bombay opium trader, had been introduced to *Magniac & Co.* by Jamsetjee Jejeebhoy. In 1830 he ran an active account with the firm, owing it 51,903 Spanish dollars at year-end. (*JMArch.*, A2/15).

[64] Cursetjee Jamsetjee was Jamsetjee Jejeebhoy's son and active trading partner.

35. *Magniac & Co.* in Canton to *Biny & Co.*[65] in Madras,

31 December 1830

Dear Sirs,

We have the pleasure to acknowledge the receipt of several of your letters which we have in course been favored with, the: – 1st June, hands us your account current which is found correct, and in which we also notice the retirement of Mr. Scott from your establishment; – 14th June, contains a request that we will purchase for you a tortoiseshell work box accompanied by a note from Mr. Scott to our Mr. Jardine, pointing out the wish to have this little commission particularly attended to by him, which he has been most happy to comply with, and exceeding, rather, your limits, we have the pleasure of forwarding it by this conveyance, agreeably to the enclosed memorandum and receipt, and debit your account with the cost in 145 dollars; – 6th August, is upon the subject of Tinnively[66] cotton, inquiring into the expediency of your friend engaging in an adventure of that staple, for this market, which can best be replied to by acquainting you with its present condition.

The stock of Madras cotton here now is large, containing more than half of last season and nearly the whole of the importation by the late ships of this year. Howqua, the senior Hong merchant, is the only holder and, having the market under his command, is realizing a profit on his recent purchases from the company, which were made at 8.8 Taels per picul. Good Tinnively cotton would always be safe if purchased on terms that would not exceed 9 Taels per picul, but should not be bought if the cost and charges exceed 10 Taels. But the quality must be good, and this is a point greatly to be attended to, if any success from an adventure is expected.

Saltpetre is an article always in demand here, and might be availed of for dead weight,—if to be purchased at reasonable rates, when brought into the port of Canton, is from 5 to 6 dollars per picul, and when delivered from any of the ships at Lintin, generally one or two dollars higher, but it is an article much under the influence of extent of importation.

A vessel of the size you point out, would come under the 3rd class of measurement duty, and with the present, would amount to about 3,000 dollars, and to which the linguist and the comprador fees of 223 dollars, and with pilotage

[65] The firm's name was more often spelt '*Binny & Co.*'. It was one of the Agency Houses active in Madras at the time. Other mercantile firms listed in Madras by the East India Company were: *Arbuthnot & Co*, Joseph Barrow, Edward Gordon, *Hall & Bainbridge*, *Parry, Dare & Co.*, William Rutter, *Seth & Gregory*. (*EIRD*, 1831—Fort St George – Houses of Agency).

[66] Tinnevely: a district of the Madras Presidency which occupies the eastern half of the extreme south end of the Indian peninsula. It has an area of 5,389 square miles, with an extreme length of 120 miles north to south and a maximum width of 75 miles near the Madras frontier. (*Imperial Gazetteer of India*, 2 vols. Calcutta, Superintendent of Government Printing, 1908).

inwards and outwards of 60 dollars each, would constitute the Port expenses, independent of crews subsistence. We subjoin a list of the different rates at which vessels entering this Port are chargeable.[67]

– 29th September, 8th October, 6th, 9th, 14th August, severally hand us commissions which you will find attended to in our letter by this conveyance, where we give you the advice of our shipments per *Hercules*;[68] and your letter of the 11th August establishing credit in favor of Mr. Burn of the *HCS George the Fourth*[69] for 200 Rupees, has been complied with in receiving his draft upon you for that sum.

The subject of your favour of the 19th May and 6th August we should take into consideration and hereafter remark thereon. We beg leave to enclose Price Current for your information relative to our market, and remain, etc.

Your Most Obedient Servant

1831

36. James Matheson in Canton to W. R. Paton[1] in Glasgow,

17 January 1831

My dear Sir,

I have much pleasure in availing myself of Mr. Macvicar's[2] return to acknowledge receipt of your esteemed favor of 11th December 1829 introducing that gentleman to my acquaintance. Your kind remembrance of me, after so long an interval as has elapsed since we last met, is very gratifying, and I have to offer you my best thanks for the acquisition of so estimable a friend as you rightly described Mr. Macvicar.

He will inform you that he relinquishes his intention of establishing a House of Agency in China, and that he has consequently made overtures to us for conducting such business as he may be able to influence,[3] to which we have readily acceded. And I trust our intercourse is likely to become mutually beneficial.

[67] The list was not found.

[68] The *Hercules* was Captain Alexander Grant's ship and, after 1832, one of the firm's opium receiving ship.

[69] The *George IV* was a 1329 ton ship belonging to the East India Company. It sailed to Canton in the 1829–1830 season under the command of Captain T. W. Barrow. (*EIRD*, 1831, pp. viii–ix). Mr. Burn was a passenger on board the *George IV*. He later established a partnership with Framjee Pestonjee (Letter **165**).

[1] W. P. Paton of Glasgow was a regular correspondent of the firm from the early 1830s until well into the 1840s. (Over 200 letters are listed in the *BI*).

[2] For John Macvicar, see above, Letter **29**, note 35.

[3] For the kind of 'business as he may be able to influence', see below, Letter **46**.

You are no doubt aware that we are the correspondents here of our mutual friend Mr. Purvis[4] of Singapore, and in the early part of the Season we addressed him in detail on the subject of our market for British manufacturers; since when there has been no alteration of any importance. As he has of course made you acquainted with the substance of that communication, I shall not enlarge on the subject here.

The enclosed copy of a Petition to Parliament from British subjects in China may perhaps be interesting to you.[5] It relates to a subject of great importance and I trust it will receive due attention from the legislature and people of Great Britain.

I shall always be happy to hear from you and to attend to your wishes in this quarter, and remain, My dear Sir,

Yours very faithfully,

37. William Jardine in Canton to Hollingworth Magniac in London,

17 January 1831[6]

My dear Magniac,

I am quite ashamed of my neglect, in not having addressed you on the business of the House, or your own private affairs, since the 16th of November; and I am afraid the excuse I have to offer, though strictly in accordance with truth, will scarcely, by you, be considered sufficient. Business, in all its branches, has been going on most satisfactorily; but I have so often apologized for not forwarding closed accounts of the operations of the two last years, that my aversion to doing so again, and a hope that Chay would, long ere now, have closed his set of Books, has kept me silent. You may judge of my mortification, therefore, at being obliged to inform you, that there is little prospect of his closing his set in time to have the

[4] John Purvis, a friend of James Matheson, and partner of *Purvis & Co.*, Singapore. (See Letters **92** and **229**).

[5] This 'Humble Petition of the Undersigned British Subjects in China to the Honourable the Commons of the United Kingdom of Great Britain and Ireland in Parliament Assembled', was directed against the East India Company monopoly. For its text, see **Appendix IV.** The Petition as sent to Parliament was dated 24th December 1830. A full version of the Petition appeared in the *Canton Register* a few days before, on 18th December 1830. Greenberg asserts that the Petition was written by James Matheson (Greenberg, *British Trade*, p. 178). Although we have not found formal proof of this, it is highly likely that James Matheson was its most important contributor. It should be noted, however, that John Macvicar was one of the 47 signatories of the documents. John Macvicar's presence in Canton at the time, his connection with free trade associations of manufacturers and exporters back in Manchester, Liverpool and Glasgow, and the many conversations he had with William Jardine and James Matheson on the topical question of British exports, reinforced the radical convictions they all shared regarding the need to abolish the East India Company's monopoly on tea purchases, and to 'throw the China trade open' to all the private merchants.

[6] This copy in William Jardine's hand of an interesting private letter about Francis Hollingworth was found in the In-correspondence, although it was written from Canton.

balance sheet transmitted to you by the last ships of the Season; and, after Matheson and myself had adjusted the opium account of the previous year, the result, though according with my original view of the transactions, varied so widely from that come to by Mr. Ullman, that we feel desirous of proving its correctness by comparing the opium accounts of the two seasons which Mr. Ullman had mixed up together, previous to transmitting the corrected accounts of these years to you.

It is now nearly two months since Chay commenced his set of Books, Mr. Ullman having charge of the previous set, and Alexander Matheson of the set for the current year; but still, with Mr. Hollingworth assistance whenever he might think fit to employ him, Chay's set are far from being closed. I have no doubt you will be surprised at this statement knowing, as you do, that our young friend has plenty of talent; but, I regret to say, it is too true; and his want of zeal has annoyed me more than you can fancy. At the same time it has prevented us from increasing his salary, which we have, for some time back, been desirous of doing. It is distressing to see such abilities, as he possesses, so completely thrown away, when opportunities were not wanting to turn them to good account. His father has, however, lately admonished him, and, I am happy to say, with apparent good effect; so that there is some prospect of yet, one day, seeing the Books closed by his own industry.

I must do Chay the justice to state, that he has received very little assistance from Mr. Hollingworth; for, though they are very intimate, and constantly together, whenever I have asked why Mr. Hollingworth was not employed on the Books, the reply has invariably been: 'He asks so many foolish questions, I can get on faster without him than with him.' But for the able assistance of Mr. Wright, who works very hard, we should never be able to get through the business of the House; for Alexander Matheson, though industrious, is not gifted with Chay's abilities; and Henry Robinson has, hitherto, been very little at his desk owing to bad health. He is now better, and very desirous of making himself useful.

There are various points in your favors of the 21st and 28th of May that require replying to; but most of them are so mixed up with the final settlement of the accounts already alluded to, that I shall defer entering fully into most of them till said accounts are finally adjusted.

We shall by the last ship of the Season and the *Scott*,[7] complete your remittances to the extent wished for, having provided the means of doing so. We have been anxiously expecting letters from you by the American ship, *Walter* that arrived from Liverpool in the end of December, and might have brought your answer to Mr. Matheson's letter dated Singapore on the 6th of January last; which

[7] The *Sir David Scott* was a 1,324 ton East India Company ship belonging to Joseph Hare and commanded at the time by Captain D. J. Ward. (*EIRD*, 1831, viii–ix).

we presumed, had not reached you when the *Ann* and *Amelia* left England; though she brought an account of the arrival of the ship by which the original was sent. Mr. Matheson mentioned to me his intention of writing that letter, which I approved of; and from Singapore he sent me a copy of it. His account of Mr. Hollingsworth's want of business habits is quite correct; and agrees with the opinion I had formed of his character before we had exchanged one word on the subject.

It afforded me much pleasure to see Mr. Matheson, on his return from Calcutta, attach himself a good deal to Mr. Hollingworth (after his first visit to Calcutta); and I immediately availed myself of the circumstance, to place the Books of the 8th *Canton [Insurance] Office*; and accounts of the Lintin ships, in charge of the latter superintended by the former; with the view of bringing them as much together, in business, as possible; in hopes of inducing habits of application and thinking in a mind where such habits, as far as I am capable of judging, I should say, never had been cultivated.

My hopes have been sadly disappointed. The friendly feelings between them still exists; but they are seldom seen together—the one being in the office late and early, the other seldom more than fours hours per day. Without one single vice, unless idleness be considered a vice; and with the very best temper and disposition, Mr. Hollingworth has less idea of assisting others, or making himself in anyway useful, than any man I ever met with.

When Mr. Henry Robinson was obliged to leave the office from bad health, the letter book devolved on Mr. Hollingworth; and very soon got in arrears. When this was pointed out to him some idle reply was made about want of time; and a few days after, being reminded that he had not been at his desk even four hours per day, for two or three days past, his reply was: 'I had no work to do.' Mr. Manson[8] was then called in, and on the letter Book, etc., found abundance of work from ten in the morning till ten at night; in bringing up the very arrears that had been brought to Mr. Hollingworth's notice in vain. I am afraid such indifference, about what ought to be to him of the first importance, leaves very little hope of his ever being qualified to conduct the business of the House.

So far as money goes, I feel perfectly indifferent about the emoluments that may be deemed necessary for Mr. Hollingworth's future comfort in life, or the provision for that part of the family that are dependent on his exertions, and I am confident Mr. Matheson participates largely in the same feeling; but to place him as a partner in the House is what I feel very reluctant to do—not on my own account; but on account of the inefficiency[9] of a House so constituted.

[8] Daniel Manson was a clerk in the firm from 1825 to 1843. (One full card of correspondence in the *BI*).

[9] 'Inefficiency' is recorded as having been introduced in the English language in 1750 and 'inefficient' in 1749. (*OED*).

I have it in contemplation to proceed to England next season;[10] and can not, with any satisfaction, think of such a contingency as Mr. Matheson being afflicted with bad health, and the management of affairs devolving on one so little calculated to conduct them.

I have written much more at length, on this subject, than I originally intended; which proceeds from my anxiety to make you thoroughly acquainted with the real state of affairs and feelings here.

I am aware the reading of this long letter will give you much annoyance; but not more than the writing of it has given me. Nothing short of a thorough conviction of his unfitness ever to become an efficient member of this or any other House in China, could have induced me to write on the subject, in the manner I have done—and, in the event of your disapproving of the plan proposed by Mr. Matheson, I should recommend your remaining in the Firm yourself for a year or two longer; which would be likely to enable you to provide for Mr. Hollingworth, and his family without lessening you own means.[11]

I shall have the pleasure of addressing you again soon.

etc.

38. William Jardine in Canton to James Stewart[12] in Gillienbierigg near Lockerby, 28 January, 1831[13]

A long letter on various subjects. Have reason to believe my letter, acknowledging your favor, of 23rd of October 1828, never reached; and should that by the *Bridgewater* have shared a similar fate, which is more than probable, you will have reason to accuse me of the sin of ingratitude. But I am almost certain my letter, of the 23rd March 1830, addressed to your Brother Charles, reached him in due time. Johnstone must have seen you, and explained all my sentiments and views respecting the Moorhousehead and Kirkburn families.

In consequence of what you said respecting Chipnowe's son, Frank, I have authorized Johnstone to make the necessary advance to set him agoing in a farm—consulting you on the subject.

I feel anxious about the Kirkburn family, they being less comfortably situated than the rest of their relations. Perhaps an annuity to the Mother would be the surest and easiest plan—educating the boys at the same time to enable them to

[10] William Jardine probably did contemplate such a voyage to England in 1832 (see the end of Letter **38**). However, the mention of this eventuality at this point in the letter lends serious weight to his argument. In fact, William Jardine was to remain in China until he finally retired in January 1839.

[11] It was this plan which was finally adopted, despite Hollingworth Magniac's disappointment. (See below, Letter **40**).

[12] For James Stewart, (as well as others mentioned in this letter), see above, Letter **23**, note 6.

[13] This letter was copied by William Jardine himself. Unusually, the copy was made in 'telegraphic' style.

get on in the world, either at home or abroad. Could provide for one nephew in one of our ships. One or two voyages in a Company's ship necessary in the first instance, to qualify him. Willing to incur the expense of said voyage, etc...

Are you in earnest about sending one or two of your sons to India or China?[14] Pointed out the disadvantages of such a life. If determined, shall most willingly do anything in my power to aid your views—by receiving one of them as a clerk, to work his way up in the House. Promotion a work of many years; but the outlay is little. Salary 200 to 750 pounds sterling per annum, and everything found. Described society here and the nature of our Establishment. H[enry] R[obinson] last admission—former and present prospects, etc... May possibly pay a visit next year.

39. James Matheson in Canton to H. P. Haddow[15] in Bombay

10 March 1831

My dear Haddow,

As I seldom keep copies of my private letters, I forget how long it is since I have had the pleasure of writing to you. But I am afraid I have reason to accuse myself of remissness in this respect, and regret that I have little time left me before the final despatch of the *Aurelia* that I can do little more than ask your forgiveness of my apparent neglect, trusting I may be excused on the grounds of the heavy pressure of business which I have always to attend to.

On business matters I can have but little to add to the communications of the House, and those from Jardine to de Vitre. The Chinese are again apprehensive of a scanty harvest and the price of rice is consequently on the advance, which will lead to a succession of importations from Manila. We are sending the *Dansborg* over for a cargo in which, we hope, we will not be disappointed. We find, however, the government will not grant a licence in anticipation, for the exportation of the article, and reserve to themselves the right of refusing it, till the vessel destined to receive the cargo is actually on the spot ready to take in on board. This must necessarily attach some degree of uncertainty to such speculation, as you projected last year for the *Carron*. As, however, we shall have a second harvest approaching to maturity by the month of October next, which is very unlikely to

[14] Letters **243** and **251** below show that one of James Stewart's sons, William Stewart, did make his way to China to serve in the firm. William Stewart was subsequently admitted a partner in 1842 and retired in 1846. (Keswick, *The Thistle and the Jade*, p. 264).

[15] For H. P Haddow, see above, Letter **11**, note 14. Apart from *Remington & Co.*, of which H. P. Haddow and M. T. D. Devitre, or 'de Vitre' were partners, the other Houses of Agency trading at Bombay at the time (many with Scottish names) were the following : *Adam, Skinner & Co.*; *Thomas Crawford & Co.*; *Sir Roger D'Faria & Co.*; *Dirom Carter & Co.*; *Forbes & Co.*; *Gilder & Co.*; *John Leckie & Co.*; *William Nicol & Co.*; *Saunders & Co.*; *Ritchie, Finlay & Co.*; *Shotton & Co.*; *Stewart, Patrick & Co.*; *Robert Taylor & Co.*, *Owen, Caldecott & Co.* (*EIRD, 1831*, 'List of Merchants and Agents' in the Bombay Presidency, pp. 65–66).

be as unfavourable as its immediate precursors, it is possible the price will by that time revert to the usual standard of about 1.75 to 2.10 dollars. At less than the first mentioned rate, I do not recollect having ever known it, whether at Lintin, Canton or Macao.

We have written to Manila with a standing order to buy such importation of American copper as may make their appearance there and have likewise opened a correspondence with our Batavia Agents, *Thompson Roberts & Co.*,[16] with a view to become possessed of Japan copper. We have in fact authorized them to purchase 2,000 dollars if to be got at 28 dollars per picul, but I fear there is not much chance of this being practicable. It would be very little out of the way of a Bombay ship returning against the monsoon to call for it at Batavia. You may give us a hint as to how far you would like us to be concerned in the operation in the event of our succeeding. We could easily put them in funds in Java by remitting bills on England or Calcutta and partly by a moderate shipment of Canton Raw Silk which generally sells at a profit. You are aware that Japan copper is a monopoly of the Java government. The annual supply has, I believe, been about 12,000 piculs which has usually been put up for sale by auction, in one lot, in order to favor the Netherlands Trading Society,[17] it being thought [far] too heavy a concern for any of the Java houses to attempt competing with them.

We have written for information on the subject but I hardly expect that we shall find there is any encouragement to induce our desiring to compete with the Company. The fact is, Java is [like] every other Country which has the misfortune to have a depreciated Currency and a deficiency of remittable means. Every article likely to pay is bought up at excessive rates without any view to profit.

Our friend, Mr. Cushing,[18] who has just left us on his return to America, has had several conversations with us on the subject of providing us with a fast sailing vessel such as cannot [fail] be at [par with] any other, to serve as a despatch packet for conveying and receiving exclusive intelligence between us and [also] to be employed as a Lintin depot vessel in the intervals between the voyages. Cushing has a great fancy that way and possesses much judgment and experience as to the most suitable construction and will not send out any vessel unless she is a *nonsuch*—size about 100 tons, to cost not more than 10,000 dollars.[19] Our idea in contemplating the plan is that the opium trade,

[16] *Thompson Roberts & Co.* was the firm's principal Batavia (Jakarta) correspondent. (Over 100 letters listed in the *BI*).

[17] The *Vereenigde Oostindische Compagnie* or United Dutch East India Company. Once a rival of the British East India Company, it kept its supremacy over the Moluccas and the Javanese islands and traded principally from Batavia.

[18] For John Pershing Cushing, see above, Letter **29**, note 32.

[19] The American shipbuilders had started building fast ships 'clippers' in Baltimore during the 1812 War. By the time John P. Cushing returned to America in 1831, American shipbuilders and designers were predominant. (Reid, Alan, 'The Shipping Interest', in Keswick, *The Thistle and the Jade*, p. 132).

after the expiry of the Company's charter,[20] is likely to be so much [engaged] upon by speculators of every description for the mere sake of a remittance without a view to profit, that it can hardly be worth pursuing on the old plan, unless by operating on a large scale and on the secure footing of being always beforehand with one's neighbours in point of intelligence.[21] Your long experience and unremitting attention to the state of the trade in India could afford us great advantages in this respect, and you might probably find it desirable to improve still further your sources of intelligence by taking care to have accurate information from the interior, as soon as the supply of the season is completed, as to how far it may exceed or fall short of the usual quantity. Whether the cultivation of the poppy is encouraging, etc. With these data provided to us by you, we can draw our own conclusions as to the probable extent of supply which may find its way to this market—since high prices here must rationally attract a larger portion, while low prices may be expected to have a contrary effect. The extent of production with reference to the prevailing price here seems to afford the only criterion for arriving at a probably conjecture as to the extent of the importation into China—a point which parties in the interior seem of late to have been determined to envelope in as much mystery as possible. The best way of conveying intelligence to you, many remarkable changes occurring here, will probably be by landing letters at Madras. I have thus thrown together my ideas on the subject in a loose and hurried manner, as they have occurred to my mind, while writing. I shall be glad to have your sentiment on the plan, should you think it worthy of attention. Should it suit you to afford us your cooperation in it, it will be so much the better. Indeed your taking a part in it seems quite essential to its success. It may be well also to let Jamsetjee Jejeebhoy have a participation in it.[22] You can mention it to him as you please.

I need scarcely add that it is not on account of the comparatively trifling consideration of the cost of the vessel that we consider your being concerned with us as desirable—but under the existing relations between us, I do not see how we could make such a separation of interests, as to render it practicable for us to pursue the plan for our exclusive benefit.

[20] James Matheson anticipates here events which were going to take place more than two years later with the vote of Parliament on 28th July 1833 and the non-renewal of the East India Company Charter. See below Letters **83, 84,** and **85**, for the effect in Canton on China trade in general and on the tea trade in particular.

[21] This is the first time in the correspondence that the far-reaching concept of large-scale coastal operations in the opium trade is articulated as the only realistic means of overcoming increased competition. The implementation of this plan was to involve the firm in the gradual constitution of its own fleet of fast ships which, until then, had never been necessary to the success of a House of Agency.

[22] Jamsetjee Jejeebhoy was the firm's largest and most active Bombay correspondent, whilst *Remington & Co.* was the Bombay correspondent to which it felt closest.

Must now conclude this hurried and unconnected letter. I beg you will offer my kindest remembrance to Mrs. Haddow and also to *Haddow & Co.* and to De Vitre and his wife, etc. Believe me,

40. Hollingworth Magniac in London to James Matheson in Canton, 25 May 1831[23]

My dear Matheson,

I feel myself guilty of great neglect in not yet having written to you by the direct ships of the season and am now at the latest moment about to do so in Town, where I have been suddenly called upon business, having left my letters and papers at Colworth[24]. I must trust to my recollection therefore for replying to your letters to me. But this is the subject which having fully on my mind and having touched upon it in writing to Jardine, I could wish to enlarge in a letter to you. I allude to my great disappointment in regards to the eligibility of my relation Francis Hollingworth in the estimation of Jardine and yourself to be admitted a member of the Firm at Canton upon my retirement according to what I had understood [was] the arrangement between us, and indeed as the condition of that event. Considering this (that is, his admission into the Firm) as a consequence of my secession. You may conceive how much I was disappointed in the communication you made to me upon the subject, amounting to a notification, that you considered him unfit for the situation, and by an allusion to some other arrangement for his benefit as barred from any future qualification for the same appointment. Certainly, however disappointed and surprised as I must feel at his incapacity and more particularly at his want of zeal and application as asserted in making himself fit for the duties which could have devolved on him, my first feeling was to explain to you and Jardine how remote it must be from my inclination or intention to press upon you the admission of a person who would not be qualified to bear his proportion of the labours that could devolve upon him as a partner in the establishment. And this feeling I now repeat to you: neither will nor do I {believe} for a moment every bit against my intimate knowledge, as I can conceive of Jardine's and your own feelings towards myself, the [various] representations—as I must believe—which have been sent to me from many quarter in Canton[25] that [Francis] Hollingworth has never had a chance given him from his

[23] Hollingworth Magniac minute hand, his somewhat convoluted style, and the virtual absence of punctuation signs, all contribute to the difficulty of establishing the text of his letters.

[24] Hollingworth Magniac's country residence. 'Colworth House and Farm: extra-parochial place. One and half miles north-west of Sharnbrook station in Bedfordshire. The estate was bought in 1948 by *Unilever*. (*Gazetteer of the British Isles*, p. 163).

[25] Probably Charles Millet and James Frederick Nugent Daniell, both old friends of Hollingworth Magniac, both supercargoes of the East India Company and still residents of Canton at the time. (See below Letter **51**).

first arrival, either in employment or in due estimation in the position in which he has been placed, of making himself master of the business (excepting in a most subordinate situation), [ ] and indeed that his treatment exhibited altogether anything but an apparent intention of his admission in due course. I must tell you however in fairness to him that these representations have come from any quarter but himself, as he has invariably professed himself grateful for great kindness on your part, although he candidly admits that he thinks Jardine had conceived a great prejudice and dislike to him from his first arrival, accompanied however by occasional [moments] of great kindness and friendship.

I have now explained to you exactly what I have heard from China quite unsolicited on my part, and evinced wholly unexpectedly, and can only add to my conviction (from, as I said before, any knowledge of Jardine and myself) that, however disappointed I may feel I must unwillingly believe [Francis] Hollingworth to be unsuited to the employment which upon my own retirement, I had considered him to be named as my successor. And should this be confirmed [finally] in the minds of Jardine and yourself I can only be acquiescing in what must be considered for the good of the concern, in which I feel the most intense interest that may be showed to preserve to your care and attention under the same influence which I might be supposed to possess.

My nephew Charles Sansom[26] who is a young man of such natural quickness and ability that I should not apprehend the danger of his being found (upon trial) wanting in the two points of qualification, after a little experience, which have been complained of in Hollingworth, *viz.*, an aptitude of getting a knowledge of Chinese characters, and of zeal and diligence in discharging the duties committed to him. In making this request (supposing always the other arrangement to be [unsuitable]) I trust that I am not trespassing beyond the limits which custom has assigned in similar cases, or the claims which I may be supposed to have acquired in a concern descending to the present possessors solely from myself, and in making this remark, my dear Matheson, I trust that you will believe me to be saying that only which might account to myself for my requests, and not as in the slightest your doubting or undesirably even giving the spurr to what I feel convinced are the kind and friendly feelings of Jardine and yourself towards me.

Having said so much upon this subject I shall now leave it for the consideration of your two selves merely looking to the communicating that I may receive from you both by the direct ships of next Season, and merely adding that through circumstances which I could not much influence contrarily I find myself so materially injured by the failure of Sansom's banking house[27] in which however Charles has nothing to do [save from his] having been employed there as a clerk, that an establishment for my young nephew becomes a matter of great importance

[26] The son of Hollingworth Magniac's sister-in-law. See Letter **11**, note 18.

[27] 'Sansom's banking house': see above, Letter **11**, note 18.

at this time. The diminution of my means—(having no less than thirty thousand pounds[28] involved in that unfortunate concern) rendering it more than ever difficult to advance his interest by pecuniary influence. In fact, my resources are as you may suppose materially reduced by this unfortunate event, I am obliged to curtail my establishment and diminish my expenses as much as possible under this heavy diminution of my means. This is a subject that, although I do not feel pecuniary losses, I believe, much more strongly than my neighbours, puts me so much out of sorts whenever I advert to its consideration, that I can now write no more, but shall in due course [hope] to snatch another moment to write upon other and more agreeable subjects before the ships go away.

I received two days ago only a letter from Baylis[29] upon the subject of the child Daniel Francis[30], who Jardine has had the kindness under your assistance to send to Scotland for education. I could rather have written him to have gone to Calcutta, because unwilling to take [up your relation's] kindness in the way that has now been done, and having myself no means of an acquaintance which might obviate the necessity of so doing. His unfortunate father is in the same wretched position that I have before described, nor, judging from his want of conduct and want of thought and consideration for anyone, do I see any possibility of improvement. He is a continual drain upon me, both in pecuniary and in a sense of mental suffering, which cost is of course the most heavy to be borne. For yourselves I can only rejoice that I resisted his return to you in China, though he how imputes my opposition as a matter of great hardship to him and asserts that none would have been opposed by Jardine or yourself, urging me continually to propose to you *now* his coming back as a measure to which he feels confident of your sanction. Of course I have always refused to make any communication to you on the subject but at last have mentioned it as he has made it to me. I must now, my dear Matheson, bring this to a conclusion. My nerves are a good deal unstrung,

[28] A considerable sum at a time when £500 was considered a reasonable annual income to support a country gentleman and his family.

[29] Captain Philip Baylis was the commander of *HCS Canning* in 1831. (*EIRD, 1831*, pp. viii–ix).

[30] 'The child Daniel Francis' was Daniel Magniac's son. From the factual elements mentioned in this Letter and in Letter **11** above, it is possible to reconstruct part of Daniel Magniac's personal history. He resigned from the firm after having a liaison with an unspecified (Canton or Macao?) lady. A child was born to the couple ('the child Daniel Francis'), whom William Jardine eventually sent over from Canton to Scotland 'for education'. To his friends' dismay, Daniel Magniac 'married' the lady, (Letter **11**), but he later had second thoughts and wanted to return alone to Canton. The plan was opposed by both his brother Hollingworth Magniac and by William Jardine. The conventions of the time did not allow partners of respectable British firms to marry below their station, or to enter into mixed marriages, as this may possibly have been the case. If so, the child born of that union, Daniel Francis Magniac, was one in a long line of Eurasians who, particularly during the late Victorian period, made a considerable contribution to the commercial and cultural development of Hong Kong. (On the subject of Victorian Eurasian families, see Hall, Peter, *In the Web*, Peter Hall Publishing, Heswall, Wirral, England, 1992).

and really what with one pressure and another I hardly know which way to turn or how to bear up in spirits against the many trials I have lately experienced.

Mrs. Magniac desires to be very kindly remembered to Jardine and yourself and with our united and most sincere good wishes for your continued health and [prosperity] believe me, my dear Matheson,

Yours most sincerely,

41. William Jardine in Canton to James Matheson in Macao, 23 June 1831

My dear Matheson,

Your favor, of the 22nd Instant, reached me this forenoon, and told me, what I fully expected to hear, that you had had a very miserable passage down. Albino intends leaving for Macao tomorrow, and by him I propose sending this. Framjee Pestonjee[31] has, at last, stirred up Dent and the other consignees of ships to petition the Viceroy respecting Linguists and Compradors;[32] and I have been engaged all the evening getting our petition turned in to Chinese by Ahong[33]—not an easy task, but, I hope, we have succeeded tolerably well. The [Hong] merchants have not yet had an audience from the Viceroy; but are to have one tomorrow morning I believe.[34]

The drug market continues dull as ever; but we have been granting a good many orders for old sales. Veiga still anxious to sell; but no purchasers of Malwa—and very little demand for Patna and Benares. He has applied for a Chop to proceed to Macao and hopes to dispose of 50 or 100 Chests of Malwa previous to embarking.

I have sent the plan of Hine's[35] Table as requested.

Success to your efforts to fill up the list. I have sold the Cotton per *Hannah* at seven Tales per pecul, payable in 45 days. Quality very inferior. We have now got up 40 Bales of the *Carron*'s, which is said to be good; and I may possibly be the first to open the market for new cotton. Framjee [Pestonjee], while I am writing, has come to say he has sold the *Hannah*'s Cotton. The best at 8.9 Tales or 9 Tales, the inferior a 7.5 Tales or 7.6 Tales per pecul.

[31] Framjee Pestonjee: a Parsee merchant established in Canton and a signatory of the 24th Decembre 1830 Canton Petition to Parliament. He subsequently established a partnership with Mr Burn. (See above, Letter **35**, note 69).

[32] For 'linguists', see Letter **12**, note 22. For 'compradors', see Letter **7**, note 34.

[33] *Magniac & Co.*'s in-house 'linguist'.

[34] The dispute about linguists and compradors has not been identified.

[35] Captain John Hine, a friend of William Jardine, was the commander of *HCS Marquis of Huntley*, a 1,348 ton ship belonging to Thomas Ward. (*EIRD*, 1831, viii–ix). For a portrait of John Hine by George Chinnery, see: Keswick, *The Thistle and the Jade*, p. 136. In 1840, on William Jardine's return to London, John Hine arranged a public dinner in his honour at the London Tavern. (*Ibid.*)

Have you Jamsetjee Jejeebhoy's letter of the 30th of April, to my address, with you ? If you have you will see he says buy between 4 and 4.2 dollars per pecul 15,000 pecul of Manila sugar to be delivered all in October. The quality must be very good, white, and better than that per *Conde*. No risque to be run by advancing money. We have also a discretionary power, to give a little more if necessary. On the 9th of June Kierulf quotes the article at 3¾ dollars per pecul; but this is probably not the best quality, such as Jamstjee Jejeebhoy wishes for. Price here 4 Tales.

I shall leave you to write by any ship going, how you please, and to whom you please. If you have not the letter I can send you the duplicate.

Yours sincerely,

June 24th. The [Hong] Merchants have seen the Viceroy. They say he told them the Tsoo Yuen[36] could not avoid acting as he did, having order from the Emperor to do so; and they must give the [Select] Committee a few sweet words; and [they are] to remain quiet. Howqua and Mowqua threat the affair very lightly; and consider it settled. So much for the last notice.

Yours sincerely,

42. William Jardine in Canton to James Matheson in Macao, 26 June 1831

My dear Matheson,

Mr. Keating[37] has applied to me to know whether William Baynes's letter,[38] which I gave you, shall appear in the next Register. I said no, but he says the printer has put the whole in type. Therefore I put the question to you. You can ask the party most interested, and answer him.

I understand you read Mr. Innes's letter[39] of the 23rd Instant, addressed to me, and shall therefore say nothing on the subject matter therein contained. You may fancy my feelings on reading—and contemplating the possibility of such an untrue statement being made in earnest. It is fortunate for the sake of justice, that too much has been said, and too much written, on the subject, to leave a chance of success.

[36] The 'Tsoo Yuen' was a local Chinese official responsible for grain and transport. (Hucker, *Dictionary of Official Titles*, No. 6936).

[37] Arthur Saunders Keating, a Canton merchant and a signatory of the 24 December 1830 Petition. He died in Macao on 21 November 1837 'in circumstances so embarrassed, as to afford no hope of recovering the smallest dividend from his estate'. (See Letter **150**).

[38] On William Baynes (1789–1866), later Sir William Baynes, see above, Letter **29**, note 30. In 1831 he was a member of the Select Committee.

[39] James Innes's letter was not traced.

Having heard nothing from Mr. Smith,[40] on the subject of Chunqua's debts,[41] and the Viceroy being about to leave Canton, I have, today, in my capacity of Trustee, or Manager, addressed a few lines to the old Gentleman,[42] requesting a settlement previous to his departure for Peking, and Ahong has undertaken the business of converting them in to Chinese; in which, I hope, he may succeed. If he fails it will not be for want of good will, but it costs us both a good deal of trouble. I believe the Merchants will settle the Comprador question without delivering the *Chop* to the Viceroy. This cause is too good to admit of reference to his Excellency. I would rather it had been submitted.

No news. Drug market dull. Report from Silk districts, in Nankin province, said to be favorable. It is past midnight, and I remain,

Yours sincerely,

43. *Magniac & Co.* in Canton to *Messrs. Carnegy & Co.*[43] in Penang,

30 July 1831

Dear Sirs,

In consequence of the unsettled aspect of political affairs, in Europe,[44] we are induced to bring to your notice, the subjoined extract of a letter addressed to the Committee of the East India Trade Association,[45] in London, on the 26th of January last, suggesting that, in the event of Great Britain becoming involved in

[40] Possibly Robert Smith, the addressee of Letter **152**.

[41] On the subject of Chunqua's debts, see above Letters **28** and **29**. When a Hong merchant failed, the foreign creditors appointed a steering committee headed by a trustee representing their interests. That role often devolved to William Jardine, as the most experienced British merchant in Canton.

[42] Chu Kuei-Chen was viceroy of Canton in 1831. Born in 1767, he was 64 at the time, and died in 1839). (Low, *Lights and Shadows*, p. 388, note 12).

[43] *Carnegy & Co.* was the firm's principal Penang correspondent. *Carnegy & Co.*'s senior partner was James Fairlie Carnegy, whose name suggests a family connection with the firm's principal London correspondants, *Fairlie, Bonham & Co.* (*BI*).

[44] William Jardine and James Matheson refer here to the current political crises in Europe, of which the most threatening to British interests was the crisis of Belgian independence. At the time when this letter was written, Leopold of Saxe-Cobourg had just been elected King of the Belgians (4 June 1830). Palmerston convened the London Conference a few months later (November 1831) and successfully managed to have the independence of Belgium ratified by the two powers most likely to object—France and the Netherlands. Subsequently King William I of the Netherlands broke the peace and invaded Belgium. The crisis continued until 1839 when King William finally recognized Belgian independence. On the other European crises (Portugal and Spain), see Letter **74**. What remains unclear is the link that Jardine and Matheson established between the Canton opium trade and the 'unsettled aspect of political affairs' in Belgium. The most probable answer is that Britain's potential enemies, Holland and France, were colonial powers with a presence, or at least ambitions, in the region.

[45] The *East India Trade Association* which lobbied in London for the non-renewal of the East India Company's charter prior to the July 1833 vote, subsequently changed its name to the *East India and China Association*. (See Letters **151** and **255**). Association members were mostly merchants and export manufacturers.

war, an application be made to the Lord of the Admiralty,[46] for a naval force to protect the Opium ships at Lintin.[47]

To provide for the possible contingency of hostilities commencing before the arrival of our letter in England, we have to request if such should prove to be the case, that you will make known the object of our solicitude, to the Naval Commander in Chief in India,[48] or to the Commander of any of His Majesty's ships, at your port, who will doubtless feel desirous of rendering every practicable assistance for the protection of such valuable property. We should consider a frigate and a 20 gun ship amply sufficient for the purpose. But unless hostilities should actually take place, we have no wish for the presence of such a force.

We shall feel obliged by your not suffering the subject of this letter to find its way to the public prints; as it would tend to attract the attention of foreigners which it is obvious desirable to avoid.

We are, dear Sirs,
Your most obedient Servants.

Extract of a letter to the Committee of the East India Trade association, London, dated Canton 26th January 1831.[49]

'There is another subject which we would wish to bring to your notice, as of great importance to the mercantile community of India. We allude to the large amount of property in Opium on board the ships at Lintin, chiefly on British account, and insured in the Indian Offices, which in the event of Great Britain becoming involved in war, would be exposed to great risk of capture.[50] Without a settlement in China, this property amounting to between two and three millions Sterling per annum,[51] can only be protected by a naval force despatched for the purpose of the first prospect of hostilities.

[46] Sir James Graham was First Lord of the Admiralty of the Earl Grey ministry from 22 November 1830 to 7 June 1834. He was a cousin of the Earl of Galloway. (*BHF, DPC 1843*, p. 158).

[47] As early as 1831, the few British Private traders who signed the enclosed document thus held the view that waters outside the Bogue and particularly waters around Lintin constituted a free zone, where the imperial trading rules did not apply and where their ships should be protected by the British government from potential Chinese exactions. More than ten years were to elapse before British sovereignty over the Hong Kong island obtained by the treaty of Nanking transformed this minority view into historical fact.

[48] Captain Sir C. Malcolm was the Superintendent of the Indian Navy (*EIRD*, 1831, p. 59). The Commander in Chief of the army was General the Right Hon. Earl of Dalhousie. He was also second after Lord William Bentinck in the Supreme Council of the Bengal Establishment. The Commander in Chief of the Navy was Admiral Owen. (See Letter **54**, first paragraph).

[49] This 'Extract of a letter, etc.' was enclosed with the manuscript of Letter **43**.

[50] The Committee of the East India Trade Association does not elaborate on which power (possibly Holland) which it sees as a potential threat to the opium ships.

[51] The above broad-brush calcutations by members of the Committee assume an average price of 625 Spanish dollars per chest of opium. This was the equivalent of £156, a figure which, multiplied by the number of chests imported in 1830, or 16,257, (this figure was public knowledge by the time the

We mention the subject, in the hope that by your representing the circumstances to the Lords of the Admiralty, such protection will not be wanting, when occasion may require it.

We are, etc.

(Signed) *Magniac & Co., R Turner & Co.,*[52] *Whiteman & Co.,*[53] *James Innes,*[54] *Ilbery, Fearon & Co.*[55]'

44. William Jardine in Canton to Hollingworth Magniac in London,

17 October 1831

My dear Magniac,

Since I had the pleasure of addressing you per *Hannah*, on the 21st of July last, I have been favored with you letter of the direct ships of the Season, dated in April but no day specified. I have also been favored with a reading of your two favors, of 25th of April and 25th May[56] addressed to Mr. Matheson; and avail myself of the despatch of the *Buckinghamshire* and *Waterloo* to say a few words in reply, though too much pressed for time to enter fully on the subjects of which they treat.

I regret very much the severe loss you have sustained by the failure of Samson's Banking House, and the trouble Mr. Ritchie[57] with his friends, has so unnecessarily given you respecting the affairs of the *James Scott*. I fully intended entering on the subject of your proposal in favor your nephew Charles Samson, by this conveyance, but in consequence of the observations in your letter of the 25th May, have thought it advisable to await the receipt of your reply to my letter per *Marquis Camden*; in which I have explained fully the impression made on my mind by the general conduct of Mr. Hollingworth, and I regret very much

---

Letter was written) yields approximately £2,500,000. In 1831, a total of 18,956 chests of opium were exported to China, of which 12,856 were chests of Malwa from Bombay, 5,672 chests of Bengal (Patna and Benares) from Calcutta, and 428 chests of "Turkey' from Turkey. Depending on provenance and quality, prices could fluctuate between 500 and 1,000 Spanish dollars per chest. The overall shipment of opium to China had never been so high. The annual shipments from India had averaged 4,532 chests between 1811 and 1821. It continued increasing year after year to reach 21,985 chests in 1833; 20,486 chests in 1834; 21,885 in 1835; 30,202 in 1836; 34,776 in 1837; 34,373 in 1838; and 40,200 in 1839. (Owen, *British Opium Policy*, p. 80; Cheong, Weng Eang, *Mandarins and Merchants: Jardine, Matheson & Co., a China Agency in the early nineteenth Century*, London, Curzon Press, 1979, p. 21). Only the year 1838 saw a marginal regression in opium exports owing to increased vigilance by the Chinese authorities which culminated in imprisonment and execution of Chinese opium traders (Letter **168**).

[52] Richard Turner was the senior partner of *R. Turner & Co.*, see above, Letter **32**, note 56.

[53] The firm of a 'Mr. Whiteman', a Canton resident described by Hunter as a 'ship agent'. (Hunter, *Bits of Old China*, p. 202).

[54] For James Innes, see above, Letter **9**, note 48.

[55] For *Ilbery Fearon & Co.*, see above, Letter **33**, note 60.

[56] See Letter **40** above.

[57] See the negotiations described in Letter **18** above.

having had no occasion to alter my opinion. Only last night, when Mr. Matheson and the Jardine Juniors, Mr. Robinson, and even a young gentleman belonging to the *Samarang*, in Canton with Captain Grant, were all at work in the office till past midnight, he left it about 5 p.m. and never returned though aware the ships were to be despatched this morning. If questioned, I have no doubt, the reply would be he had nothing to do. The others find plenty to do and are always engaged without any interference on the part of Mr. Matheson or myself, and so might he, were he very desirous of making himself useful. Your informants[58] may be more capable of judging of his treatment, and capabilities than I am. I can only say that, on the score of the former I have nothing to accuse myself of, and that I regret the latter as much as you can possibly do.

As your letter of the 25th of May was written in London, while your papers were in the country, I shall not notice the inaccuracies, or what appears to me inaccuracies, you have fallen into in stating the conditions on which Mr. Daniel[59] was sent out to China, as you will readily discover them, should you ever take the trouble of referring to the correspondence on the subject; which you may probably do previous to replying to my letter by the *Marquis Camden*.

I am happy to say Mr. [Chay] Beale has this forenoon closed the Books of 1829–1830, but too late to admit of the Balance Sheet being examined and forwarded by this despatch. I hope to send you that and the others not yet sent, by the next opportunity.

The season has been usually dull for opium and cotton as you will see by the *Prices current*, and circular from the House. The Packet is closed or about to be closed; but the immediate departure of the ship is very doubtful; as the Company's trade is likely to be interrupted in consequence of an affray on Danes Island,[60] two days ago, in which two or three Chinese have been severely wounded, one of them dangerously so. An officer, a surgeon, and a good many sailors have been rather roughly handled; but no one seriously hurt on our side.

The *Clive*[61] Company cruiser from Bombay arrived at Lintin yesterday in consequence of the despatches, by the *Austin*, requesting assistance. Report says the admiral[62] is likely to come on, but we know nothing for certain respecting his movements. In the event of the admiral coming on, the [Select] Committee will feel very much at a loss how to act, having already made up their minds to pursue a peaceable course, and submit quietly to every insult the Chinese may think fit to offer them. The more I see of the negotiations between the Company servants and the local Authorities, the more I am convinced of the necessity of a

[58] See above, Letter **40** note 25.

[59] Daniel Magniac, Hollingworth Magniac's younger brother (*Ibid.*, note 30)

[60] Danes Island: one of the islands in the close vicinity of Whampoa.

[61] The *Clive* was a 420 ton eighteen gun sloop. It was built for the East India Company by the Bombay Dockyard. (Wadia, *Bombay Dockyard*, p. 362).

[62] Admiral Owen, Commander in chief of the India Station. See above Letter **43**, note 48.

commercial treaty being obtained from the Chinese. Without one, the throwing open of the trade to China,[63] can do no good.

I shall have the pleasure of addressing you again soon. In the meanwhile, with kind regards to Mrs. Magniac, and best wishes for her health, and happiness of your family, I remain, my dear Magniac,

Yours very sincerely,

45. Jardine in Canton to Hollingworth Magniac in London,

17 October 1831

My dear Magniac,

When addressing you this forenoon, I intentionally omitted touching on a subject which has of late caused us a good deal of anxiety—namely a report that has reached from friends in Broad Street Buildings,[64] being much talked of, as in a bad way, not only on the London Exchange, but even in Glasgow. It is said that W[illiam] F[airlie] and H[enry] B[onham] have both died without money, and that D. C[lark] was probably obliged to join for the purpose of propping up his friends, the bulk of his fortune being already involved in their fate. This report, whether true or false (and we strongly incline to disbelieve it) has this bad effect, that the mere prevalence of it will tend to bring about the catastrophe apprehended; should difficult times return. Our London Exchange operations are therefore in a great measure paralysed and must continue so, till we have the pleasure of hearing from you on the subject. Allow me therefore to beg the favour of your making every possible enquiry as to the real state of affairs, and communicating the result thereof, by the earliest opportunity.

I remain, etc.

46. John Macvicar in Liverpool to *Magniac & Co.* in Canton,

20 October 1831[65]

Dear Sirs,

By the *Royal Charlotte*, Captain Robert Dudman,[66] now here and to sail as soon as the wind permits for Singapore, and [from] there to China, I have induced various of my friends to consign the following goods to you.

[63] Again, William Jardine seems to have little doubt as to the outcome of a parliamentary vote which was not to take place for another eighteen months.

[64] 'Friends in Broad Street Buildings': *Fairlie, Bonham & Co.*, the firm principal London correspondent until its reorganization in 1832 as *Fairlie, Clark, Innes & Co.*, (see Letter **62**), and its failure in 1833.

[65] This unusually long business letter may be one of the first written to a Canton Agency by an export syndicator of British manufactured goods. It is particularly interesting to note the change of tone compared with previous mercantile correspondence, as well as the zealous activity deployed by John Macvicar and his aggressive business style.

[66] The only reference to Captain Dudman in the Letters. One single letter by Captain Robert Dudman is listed in the *BI*.

Invoice N° 1, letters N° 8 and 9. *Messrs. Garnett & Horsefalls*,[67] Clitheroe, Lancashire. GH [68], N° 1 to 15. Fifteen cases Gold End shirtings. Amount of invoices 647.10/– pounds sterling. This is a very extensive and wealthy house, power loom cloth manufacturers. Are related to Rawson of *Fox & Co.*[69] house and have shipped occasionally to them since their first establishment at Canton—and lately, I believe 43 cases by the [ ] to Singapore. They are *keen* people, but highly honorable. They make this shipment to ascertain what can do best, and with the intention of following up the Trade. To yield them a fair profit you ought to get at least 5½ and 6 dollars for their goods free of duty. As to returns I refer you to their instructions. They never require any advance, and their goods must on no account be sacrificed. They are staple articles and never likely to be afforded so as to sell at Canton for less than 5 dollars. The real cash value of their goods in the market could not be less than 5 and 6 dollars exclusive of all charges of packing, etc.

Invoice N° 2. *W & R Turner*,[70] Manchester. FMVC N°1 and 2. Two Bales, containing 8 Trusses of Flannel Donalts amounting without charges to 238.12/– pounds sterling. Very respectable Manufacturer who never require any advance. This shipment is altogether experimental. I hope you will at least obtain from 25 to 30 cents, and 40 to 45 cent per yard for these according to quality. Report particularly as to what qualities are most suitable. The quantity you want recommend of each, and accompanying these to me which pattern and the width in inches. Report particularly as regards the Donalts (which are cotton warp and wollen weft). They are a much finer looking article for the money than the flannels are—either article will be supplied in any quantity you recommend if any profit can be obtained. These goods are likely to fall in value in the Country. They are now much dearer than the year back on account of the high prices of wool. The return for this small shipment, make by a Bill of Exchange.

Invoice N°3, letter N° 2. *Black & Windgate*,[71] Glasgow. Handkerchiefs printers. MW, 1 and 2. Two Boxes Printed Handkerchiefs amounting without charge to 83.7/11 pounds sterling. They are very respectable. Friends of Mr. Mathieson[72] of Glasgow. This is quite experimental. Do the best you can with this small parcel

[67] *Garnett & Horsefall*, 'Cotton spinners and manufacturers. Low Moor Mills', Clitheroe. (*PODL*). 21 letters from this firm are listed in the *BI*.

[68] Most initial designations in this letter are inscribed in diamond frames.

[69] *Montgomery, Fox & Co.*, 'Shipchandlers and Sail makers, 18 Regent Road, and South Castle Street', Liverpool. (*PODL*). Another firm, *Fox Rawson & Co.* was listed as 'merchants, Commercial Buildings, 17 Water Street', Liverpool. (*PODL*). From evidence in this Letter, the firm had a branch in Canton managed by 'Mr. Fox'.

[70] *R. Turner & Co.*, 'Cotton Spinners, 90 Carruthers Street', Manchester. (*PODL*).

[71] *Black & Windgate*, 'Manufacturers and Printers, 9 Royal Exchange Square', Glasgow, (*GPOAD*).

[72] William Mathieson, 'Merchant of *James Ewing & Co.*, 300 Sauchiehall Street', Glasgow. (*GPOAD*).

and remit them a Bill. Send me patterns of such things as are suitable, and also of such part as is unsuitable, with any remark that may occur to you, recommending such quantity as you think proper, and stating what price per dozen you expect to be able to realize. And of course you will neither underrate nor overstate either price or quantity, but as much the true expectation as you can come at.

Invoice N° 4, letter 6. *The Lancefield Spinning Co.*,[73] Glasgow, cotton spinners and Power loom manufacturers. CLY, 49 to 63. Fifteen Bales Mule Twist, amounting without charges to 465.18/5 pounds. They are very respectable and wealthy (Graham Brothers). I believe they are the most extensive Power Loom Weavers in Scotland. Gentlemanly tradesmen. The freight upon cotton yarn comes very heavy. A ton of 40 cubic feet weighs on an average 950 pounds of yarn, so that the freight on all the yarn by the *Royal Charlotte* (at 80 shillings per ton) is equal to 5 per cent Primage, or above 1 penny or nearly 1 penny and one-eighth plus. Keep this in view in making your calculations of the cost of the yarn. The prices of cotton yarn in this country never were so low as at this present moment. The spinners are actually suffering a severe loss upon such prices as are current in the market. This arises from the interruption of their Trade to Russia and Germany on account of the cholera and partly on account of the generally disrupted state of the Trade of this Country. I have recommended considerable shipments of yarn to you, knowing that we are starting with prices, lower than were current before, and in my opinion likely to continue for any length of time. And I look to your market for cotton yarn as an encouraging one, and [hope] that this will become an article of great magnitude and importance. I would on no account submit to sacrifices on a staple article such as Twists, and would not sell under current circumstances, at such low rates. If we sell yarn at a loss under the present state of things we need not look for anything else than to lose our connection. I would rather hold for a better market than sell at a loss. You will [rely] on, and attend to the wishes of the different parties who ship yarn, from their letters. The qualities of yarn are very different, both from the very different sorts of cotton from which it is spun as also from the superiority of the manufacturers, and if possible you must obtain prices according to the quality of this. Invoice from the *Lancefield [Spinning] Co.* I only know from their own report of it. The real price in the the market for this parcel of yarn (as the market now is) I suppose may be from 1½ to 2 pence below their invoice. I mean this the cash price. Insurance by the *Royal Charlotte* has been done at 3½ to 4 per cent. Other charges you can calculate. But if interest may be taken at 7½ per cent until remittances [arrive] from China, *Nathan & Co.*[74] have, I believe, about 70,000 pounds weight of cotton

[73] *The Lancefield Spinning Co.*, '70 Miller Street', Glasgow. (*GPOAD*).

[74] *Nathan & Co.* was not identified. Macvicar seems to suggest that this firm would consider borrowing at up to 7½ per cent interest in order to finance a shipment of cotton yarn to China, pending remittances from Canton.

yarn ready for ships direct to Canton by a Vessel called the *Addison*, daily expected to arrive here from New York and if not before the *Royal Charlotte* will very soon be after her. The *Jeanne* [which] sailed from hence the 16th Instant for Singapore, had a cargo intended for Fox[75] of Canton and has I believe about 60 to 80.000 pounds of yarn on board. I also think that more parcels of perhaps 50,000 pounds are gone via New York. I will draw up a Proforma Account Sales of yours at Canton, that you may be quite aware how heavy the charges fall upon it. Returns to the *Lancefield Co.* in Bills as directed. They receive no advances but prompt remittances I know are acceptable to them.

Invoice n° 5, letter N° 7. *William Baskell & Co.*,[76] Bamberbridge near Preston, Lancashire. Very extensive manufacturers of all kinds of plain cotton cloth. C, N° 1 to 11. Eleven Boxes of shirtings. Amount without charges 400.16/− pounds. Exceedingly respectable, pleasant people. Are wealthy and take no advances. These goods are honestly invoiced. They are worth cash, about 15/− per piece. The expense of Tin and Wood Cases is nearly 6 pence per piece of 40 yards. The freight from Liverpool to China about 6 pence per piece. Other charges you can calculate. Such plain staple articles must never be sacrificed. They may rise a full 5 to 10 per cent in this country, but they possess a standard value, and they are a staple article with you. I hope you may get 5½ to 6 dollars for these, but if you can remit the Invoice and Charges, I think they will be satisfied, if better cannot be done. As to returns, I beg you to do the best you possibly can for them. I will write you separately about returns.

Invoice N° 6, letter N° 3. *Walker & Co.*, Glasgow (formerly the *Lanark Twist Co.*,[77] Owen). W, 1 to 18. Eighteen Bales cotton yarn. Amounting without charges to 598.2/4. pounds sterling. Mr. Wright[78] is the sole manager of the concern and is a highly respectable man. The character of the *Lanark Twist Co.* stands high for good yarn. Their production is very extensive and they are disposed to do an extensive business with you, if they can get any Profit. They are steady people and do not shift about from one agent to another when they are well traded. They will never have returns but in Bills. Report particularly on the quality of their yarn, how they are liked, etc. I think their invoice is a bit high, but the quality is probably such as to authorize it. Indeed, from their character and respectability I should expect this. I hope you will do well for them. The extent of their future business may be very great. They possess very abundant means, but like prompt returns.

[75] See above note 69 to this Letter.

[76] Not identified under *William Baskell & Co.* in 'Bamber bridge' near Preston. The firm may have been listed under another address.

[77] *Walker & Co.*, also known as *The Lanark Twist Co.* and as *The Lanark Cotton Yarn Warehouse*, '105 Miller Street'. Glasgow. (*GPOAD*).

[78] Three letters by this 'Mr. Wright' are listed in the *BI*.

Invoice N° 7, letters N° 10 and 11. An invoice of RM, 1 to 10. Ten packages for Mr. Richard Markwick[79] amounting to 805.4/2. pounds sterling due in cash in London 1st December next. This is particularly alluded to in my separate letter of the 12th Instant. Returns to *Gregson Melville Knight*,[80] London, for my account.

Invoice N° 8, letter N° 22. An invoice of BM 1 to 3. Three Boxes of dyed Worsted yarn amounting to 102.13/– pounds sterling. Refer to my letter N° 22. Returns to *Gregson Melville Knight*, to my account.

Invoice N° 9, letter N° 23. An invoice of WJ, N° 1. JVM, N° 1, sundries for yourselves amounting to 57.11/0 pounds sterling. See my letter N° 20. Returns to *Gregson Melville Knight*. This letter alludes to two small boxes R1 and 2 for Mr. Reeves, which please hand to him free of any charges.

Invoice N° 10, letter N° 4. *Archibald MacIndoe & Co.*,[81] Glasgow, Calico and handkerchief printers. PP, N° 1 to 10. Ten Boxes printed handkerchiefs amounting without charges to 490.10/2 pounds sterling. Respectable people, but I suppose not wealthy. An advance of about 50 per cent will be given them by *Gregson Melville Knight*, for our account, and the returns for the whole you will please make to *Gregson & Co.*[82] Those patterns, (from the land of China !) I think are very suitable. The goods are Invoiced at [somewhat] more than the real values. When I was in Canton they would have fetched about 3 to 3¼ dollars per dozen, the buyer paying the duty. I hope you will do well with them. Patterns and information as to styles send to me and refer them to me on this point. Remit *Gregson & Co.* and refer *MacIndoe & Co.* to them, for the settlement of any Balance on the transaction.

Invoice N° 11, letter N°5. *Thom & Struthers*,[83] Glasgow, Cotton Spinners. TSCH, 1 to 9. Nine Bales Cotton yarn. Amount without charges 202.10/–. Their mills are extensive and they are respectable. they require no advances. Mr. Struthers is brother-in-law of Mr. James Finlay.[84] They underestimate the amount of charges which actually amount to (including 18 months interest) 52.7/– pounds. Let me know whether 5 pound- or 10 pound Bundles are preferred. Some

[79] John Macvicar had met Richard Markwick during his stay at Canton in 1830. 'In about 1825 Richard Markwick resigned his employment as stewart of the [East India] Company' factory at Canton, and from 1826 to 1833 is listed among the private merchants there, as a shopkeeper. In 1830 he was a partner in *Markwick & Lane Co.*, a company that advertised itself as agent for the schooner *Sylph*, which carried passengers between Canton and Macao [. . .] By 1833 he had his own firm, *Markwick & Co.*, through which he also ran the European bazaar and a hotel at Canton, and the European warehouse and a hotel, Markwick's Tavern, in Macao. Markwick died in Macao at 8 am on Saturday 30 January 1836, after a lingering illness'. (Ride, *East India Cemetery*, p. 186).

[80] On *Gregson Melville Knight*, see above Letter **2**, note 6.

[81] Six letters from *Archibald Macindoe & Co.* are listed in the *BI*.

[82] *Gregson & Co.*, 'East India Agents, 14 Austin Friars', London. (*TCLD*).

[83] *Thom & Struthers*, 'Cotton Spinners, 26 Glassford Street', Glasgow. (*GPOAD*).

[84] James Finlay, 'Merchant, 63 Queen's Street', Glasgow. (*GPOAD*). There was also a 'James Finlay, Wholesale tea dealer' trading in Liverpool (*PODL*).

of the China men said they preferred 10 pound Bundles, but I do not suppose this is of importance. Remit them in bills as directed. Please to give me a particular report of the estimation in which the China men held the different parcels of yarn sent you, and furnish us with every information in your power to guide us in future recommendations of yarn and the assortment of numbers most suitable as to the mode of packing—if Mule Twist or Water Twist are preferred, if handsome gilded tickets on the Bundles are liked, if the Bales are preferred with loose hoops or corded—if 1st, 2nd, or 3rd qualities are most desirable. Will the China men buy a higher price for a better article of yarn ? Do they prefer a whitish or a yellowish shade of colours ? Do they prefer hard or soft twisted ? Send little samples back home of the qualities they prefer, and with a note of prices they were given for the different qualities and assortment of numbers. How does the consumption go on ? Is it increasing ? What are the amounts of your imports ? How much may I send out annually, and how much at a time ? I can without difficulty supply you to any amount, if you will get a moderate profit.

Invoice N° 12, letter N° 1. William Falconer,[85] Glasgow. A merchant who pays cash for everything he ships. PVG, 1 to 12, and FVW. Fifty-eight packages of sundries. Amounting to 2,270 pounds sterling. A very pleasant and gentlemanly correspondent, possessed of a handsome capital. Wants no advances. My old and intimate friend. He will do business with you to some extent in any thing you may want out, if he finds it profitable.

N° 1 to 8 Embossed Cotton—of those I sold 50 pieces for him in China, averaging 8 dollars a piece, duty paid (the duty was moderate, say 15 Taels for 50 pieces. Some pieces of favourite colors, say Pink, sold for about 70 to 75 cents a yard. Some bad colors as low as 30 cents. But in this lot of the objectionable colors are left out, and only the most approved colors sent. The assortment of colors of the present parcel is I think good. I hope the quantity is not too large, and that you will be able to obtain a large profit upon them. If you find that any further supply is saleable at some profit make out the assortment of colors you would wish and any remarks as to Pattern, whether large or small, that may be worth attending to, any Pattern that are better than others, send me swatches of—as also [of any] as are objectionable.

N° 9 to 12, 6/4 dyed Cambrics. This is entirely experimental. I think it probable such things may sell and to some extent. They cost but little and as they are a new thing I think it probable you may get a large Profit from them. I am not aware that anything similar has previously been sent out, I sold a few packages of Muslins when I was out at various prices averaging 1 dollar 93 cents. But I missed

[85] William Falconer, 'Merchant, 30 Montrose Street', Glasgow. John Macvicar describes him as '[his] old intimate friend'. Eight letters from William Falconer to the firm are recorded in the *BI*. Such relatively thin correspondence with the Canton firm suggests that many of the initial business contacts effected through the good offices John Macvicar never developed into full business relationships.

my market—the Chin Chew[86] men were gone when I sold. They had previously offered me 2 dollars 25 cents, but I was too greedy and suffered for it. Those now sent are of the most approved patterns and I hope you may get a good price for them. You will observe that contrary to what is usual, many of these goods are in Pieces of long lengths. The usual length of a Piece of Muslin being 10 to 12 yards. I have had these made double pieces and longer on account of the duties being so much per piece, no matter how long—and this ought to have a favorable effect on the Sale.

N° 40 to 41 is intended as an imitation of Gauze Cloth. Let me know particularly how they sell and if any quantity of it may be sent. Patterns of all descriptions of Muslins—indeed of all sorts of goods—must accompany your remarks for without patterns you will be unintelligible—where you do not send a pattern of the full breadth of the cloth, always state what the width is in inches and also what length the pieces are. The [goods] are of a pattern I consider to be adapted to the market, and I anticipate a good profit upon them. I think the whole of this Invoice will turn out well, and it would not at all suprise me, if you got a very large profit upon it. It is a fancy thing—some things may not do so well but upon the whole I expect very favourably of it. The Invoice is I believe the actual cash cost of the goods and as low as money will buy them for. As to the returns for Falconer, he refers you continuously to me, and I will refer you to my last letters on this point. Let me confirm his remarks as to being particular in your remarks about this shipment, sending patterns, etc. Falconer has not objection to returns in Tea going to Hamburg,[87] so that if there is an opportunity for you to do so with advantage he may be satisfied by bartering some of his goods for Tea. I am very anxious that his account should turn out well. Do all you possibly can.

Invoice n° 13, letter N° 13. John Bartholomew,[88] Glasgow, merchants and Manufacturers. MVM, N° 1 to 26. Twenty-six Packages of long Cloths and Yarn. Amount of Invoice without charges 700.9/6 pounds sterling. An exceedingly respectable and wealthy House. Pleasant and gentlemanly people. I had a consignment of a few hundred pounds from them when in China, the result of which was a loss of about 20 per cent. I should like them to recover this. I have no remarks to make on these goods as they are similar to the goods I have already remarked upon. I have not seen any samples of them, but they appear to be invoiced at fair prices, perhaps about 10 per cent above the Cash cost. Though not having seen them I cannot actually say they are. They order returns in Bills which please allied to prompt remittances will be agreeable to them. And a Profit will induce them to [trade] to some extent with you.

[86] Chin Chew: a port in the Fukien province north of Amoy (Xiamen).

[87] Until 1834, private merchants were not allowed to ship tea to England.

[88] *John Bartholomew & Co.*, 'Merchant, 78 Ingram Street; lodgings: 11 Abercrombie Place', Glasgow. (*GPOAD*).

Invoice N° 14, letter N° 12. *Philips Wood & Co.*[89] Manchester, Merchants and Manufacturers. FNA. Four Cases {Gold End} Shirtings amounting to 202.1/8 Pounds sterling. One of the leading houses in this Country. This is a mere [trial], their means and capability are endless. They are very cautious, extremely particular and some people say very troublesome in their [correspondence]. But let this be how it may, they are very honorable and in many points of view a desirable connection, not only that where they consider themselves in good hands they do a very extensive business, but the knowledge by other people of their consigning goods to you will induce many to follow their example, as it is considered that they are so fastidious, that it is only to first rate hands they will intrust their property. I refer you to their letter of introduction. Mr. Mark Philips of this house is expected to be the Radical M.P. for Manchester. Mr. Wood is a man of great intelligence. Their favourable opinion of our market may have a very valuable influence for us with *Messrs. {Strutt} & Co.*[90] of Leeds, whose business *I am most anxious* to get hold of.

Invoices 15 and 16. See letter. *Horrocks, Miller & Co.*,[91] Preston or London, Spinners and Manufacturers. MEM, N° 1 to 19. Nineteen Bales Cotton yarn. Amount of Invoice 417.8/14 pounds sterling and n° 20 to 109, 89 Bales Cotton Cloths. Amount of Invoice 4,718.9 Pounds sterling. The reputation of this house you must be well acquainted with. They are among the most extensive and I believe the very best Manufacturers in the Kingdom. Wealthy and pleasant people to be connected with. Steady in their attachments, not shifting from one agent to another in very many markets where their goods are known. The mere name carries such a character for the goods along with it that there is really no difficulty in making sales. Any particular kind of their goods sent out at any future time under the same mark may be depended upon to be identically the same thing. This is an account of very great value, and I expect will become one of the utmost importance. The present shipment consists of beautiful goods—and if we can do no good for these, we may give up the trade as far as white piece good goes. Give them but a moderate profit and we want no other connection to supply us with such goods as they make. They will ship you to any extent you can desire. I can say no more to impress upon you the great value of their connection—it is one of paramount value. The Camlets 20 and 21 are in 24 yard lengths, and those 32

[89] Four letters from *Philips Wood & Co.* are listed in the *BI*. Mark Philip was to be elected to Parliament in 1832. He was 'the eldest son of Robert Philips, born in 1800. A merchant, manufacturer. Reformer in favour of free trade. Has sat for the borough [of Manchester] since 1832.' (*DPC*, p. 191).

[90] Edward Strutt was a Cotton manufacturer and a barrister. See his name in Letter **199** among the members of the 'Committee of the Commons'. He was related to the Richard Arkwright's sponsor and partner. (Fitton, R. S. and Wadsworth, A. T., *The Strutts and the Arkwrights*, Manchester, 1964).

[91] *Horrocks, Miller & Co.*, 'Cotton Spinner and Manufacturers, Canal Mill, Canal Street', Preston. (*PODL*). This was one of the most famous firms in industrial Lancashire. It integrated vertically and operated well into the twentieth century.

to 42 in 48 yard pieces. You are aware the usual length of Camlets is 12 yards. I have them made of the present length on Account of the Duties.[92] And I expect prices [will] be found [to] our advantage. As to this please report. Report also upon the qualities most suitable of those now sent. Also if any of a [higher] or of a lower quality, should in future be sent of Camlets or of shirtings; if the width and lengths of the pieces are right, or suggest any alterations, that you may ascertain to be necessary. Two packages of unbleached cloths are sent as sample. Report particularly upon them—any quantity will be sent you may recommend. Would you recommend any of the Shirtings of Camlets to be sent out dyed—Light of Sky Blue—or any other colour? As to the yarns I have but little to say. It will be found to be of a *very superior quality*, and although it may not be sufficiently appreciated till it is known, whoever buys it once will want it again. I am inclined to think it is the best Yarn in the *Royal Charlotte*, The 30 to 36 [material] is a yarn as never was seen in China (Bales 12 to 14). They are desirous of establishing a name of their yarn in your market. Nurse this [special] lot and let it go only where you are likely to hear of the good satisfaction it gives.

With regards to returns for *Horrocks Miller & Co.* I refer you to letter nº 24 of 8th October from Mr. Kirfoot to me to which you will please attend. I think that good Taysam and Tsatlee Silk at the prices stated in that letter and in my letter Nº 25 of 5th-6th October will be safe, but would be greatly regulated by your opinion, founded upon the transactions in your market. As to Silk Piece goods the only thing I would at present reflect upon would be Black Silk [ ] but with reference to my particular letter on this subject. Your correspondence will be directed to *Messrs, Horrocks, Miller & Co.*, London.

Invoice Nº 17, no letter. *Butterworth & Brooks*,[93] Manchester, Calico Printers. V, 1 to 13. Thirteen Bales containing 38 Trusses of Printed Calico. Amount without charges 1,147.4/– pounds sterling. These are very extensive Printers (300,000 pieces a year) and Shippers. Mr. John Brooks who is the only {surviving} partner, is a most worthy man, and a rich one (connected with *Cunliffe Brooks*[94] etc., Bankers). He is one of the kindest and best friends I have. He is fond of a little Profit, and if he can get this, he will go thousands where other people go hundreds. The patterns and recommendations for those goods were given me by Chungsh'ing, Ewsh'ing, China merchants, who informed me that Nathan D[unn][95] imported them in lots of 1,500 to 2,000 pieces at a time, and got for them duty paid about 7 dollars to 7 dollars and 50 cents. The Cloth on which these goods are printed is worth about 8 shillings and 6 pence before it is bleached, so

[92] The suggestion is that the Canton import duty on cotton piece goods was charged per item and not by the length of the cloth.

[93] *Butterworth & Brooks*, 'Calico printers, 76 Mosley Street', Manchester. (*PODL*).

[94] *Cunliffe Brooks & Co.*, Manchester Bankers. (*TLCD*, Section 3, p. 23).

[95] Nathan Dunn of *Nathan Dunn & Co.* (See above, Letter **31**, note 54).

that the Invoice prices of 12 shillings will leave no great profit. I calculated that at 4 dollars per piece, the buyer paying duty, would barely cover cost and charges. Now you must see and get something better than this. This house likes to keep moving and not have goods laying long on hand. They would be glad to send you Prints of any kind you could sell profitably to the extent of 50.000 pieces a year. You cannot get a better account in all England, nor more honourable. Excellent people to deal with. Returns they leave entirely to me, and I must refer you to my general letter at this head. Get patterns of all descriptions of Printed Goods that are saleable, and send them to me with marks as to Colourings, Quality, Price, etc., etc.

Invoice nº 18, letter Nº 14. *William Fielden & Co.,*[96] Blackburn, Lancashire, Merchants, Manufacturers and Spinners. FD, Nº 1 to 100. One hundred Bales Cotton Twist, amount 2,359.14/6 pounds sterling. This house is one of very great wealth and high respectability—none more is in this County. Their transactions with you may become very extensive. This yarn is now shipping to New York to be forwarded you from thence as they expect that it will get cheaper to you that way than by Singapore. FD Nº 101 is a sample Bale per *Royal Charlotte* of the yarn. I refer you to their letter, which in many subjects I beg to confirm. This yarn has been purchased with ready money, and may serve you as a good criterion of the present actual cash value of yarn in the Manchester market. This house has an establishment at Hamburg and the firm of *Fielden Jackson & Co.*, and I believe will be inclined to have their returns sent thither in Teas, if good opportunity of conveyance and apparent advantage offer, but upon this point I am to have some further conversation with them, and in my next will write you on the subject. Mr. Duckworth[97] formerly of {*Caldwell & Co.*}[98] of Manchester is I believe interested in this shipment. Fielden is intimate with the Bartons,[99] and applied to them as to respectability, etc. They are also considerable Manufacturers of Shirtings and I expect will make a shipment of them shortly. They occasionally go into very large mercantile operations and I hope to have something of that kind with them ere long. This is a first rate connection.

[96] *William Fielden & Co.*, and also *Fielden & Jackson*, (See below, same paragraph), 'Cotton spinners and manufacturers, and Shipping merchants, George Street West, and Phoenix Mills', Blackburn. (*PODL*). (William Fielden was a relation of John Fielden, 'Merchant and Manufacturer and a radical reformer in favour of the Ballot, short Parliaments and universal suffrage. He sat for the borough of Oldham in the Parliaments of 1832 and 1835'. (*DPC*, p. 152).

[97] Mr. Duckworth of *Edward Duckworth & Son*, Commission Agents (Cloths, etc.), 21 A, Pall Mall', Manchester. (*PODL*).

[98] Not identified. But possibly '*Calvert & Co.*', 'Cotton Spinners and Manufacturers, 29 Cooper Street; Works: Walton le Dale', Preston.

[99] There were several firms with the name 'Barton', *inter alia*: *H. I (or J) & R. Barton*, 'Merchants, Mulberry Street', Manchester (*PMSD*); *William Barton*, Cotton manufacturer, Poole's Building, near Bolton' (*PMSD*); *Thomas Barton & Sons*, 'Cotton manufacturers, Union Street. (*PODL*); and *Daniel Barton & Sons*, as per last paragraph of this Letter.

Invoices 19 and 20, letter N° 15. *John Dugdale & Brothers*,[100] Manchester. XW, N° 1 to 30. Thirty Bales Cotton yarn amount 770 pounds sterling, and MC, N° 1 to 3. Three Cans Printed Goods. Amount 170 pounds sterling. Very rich and very extensive Spinners, Manufacturers and Printers. They are very sharp and queer fellows, and you must obey their orders. They have invoiced their goods moderately. If you can [better] their invoice and charges, sell their goods. If not hold them. Remit them either in Bills or in Taysaam Silk of good quality costing in London all charges paid not above 10 shillings and 9 pence, or Tsatlee costing not above 13 shillings and 6 pence all charges paid. Attend to their instructions as to sending home patterns, etc., but send those to me, referring them to me for information. They do a very large business in Singapore, and feel inclined to do so too in Canton. But they are slippery chaps and not greatly to be relied upon.

Invoice n° 21, letter N° 16. *James Dunlop & Sons*,[101] Glasgow. DMgS, 1 to 61. Sixty-one Bales of Cotton yarn. Amount 1,855.–/9d pounds sterling. Very respectable Cotton Spinners. I believe wealthy. Pleasant gentlemanly correspondents. Refer to their letter as respects returns. Their yarns are Invoiced I think fully 10 per cent above what they are actually worth in the market for Cash. I hope you will do well for them. The chief part of their business is to India. They are very nice people.

Invoice N° 22, letter N° 17. *James Oswald & Co.*[102], Glasgow, Spinners. MC, 27 to 57. Thirty Bales of Cotton yarn. Amount 843.17.6 pounds sterling. Very respectable and wealthy and extensive. Have lately established a house at Calcutta. Mr. Oswald a great radical, expects to be M.P. for Glasgow, a great antimonopolist. Refer to their letter as regards remittances. I think they will be pleased with Silk at low prices. No advances wanted on this side.

Invoce N° 23, letter N° 20. *D. Buchanan & Co.*,[103] Glasgow, extensive Spinners, Manufacturers and Merchants. DS, N° 1 to 17. Seventeen Bales of Cotton yarn. Amount 377.8.8. pounds sterling. Very respectable and pleasant people—a desirable connection. I hope to advise them to do considerably more with you in goods as well as yarns. Refer to their letter respecting returns, etc.

Invoice N° 24, letter N° 18. William Dunn,[104] Glasgow, Spinner, Manufacturer and farmer of 800 acres of his own land. CE, N° 1 to 18. Eighteen Bales of Cotton yarn. Amount 674.15/2 pounds sterling. Mr. Dunn is an extraordinary man, who has raised himself from being a Millwright to a fortune of above half a million

[100] *John Dugdale & Brothers*, 'Calico printers and manufacturers, 26 Booth Street; Mosley Street; works: Lower House Mill, Burnley'. (*PODL*).

[101] *James Dunlop & Sons*, '86 Miller Street and 91 Virginia Street', Glasgow. (*GPOAD*).

[102] James Oswald and *James Oswald & Co.* were not identified.

[103] *D. Buchanan & Co.*, 'Merchants, 157 Buchanan Street', Glasgow. (*GPOAD*).

[104] William Dunn, 'Counting House and Cotton yarn warehouse, 62 George Square; Machine works: 110 High John Street; House: 42 St Vincent Place'. (*GPOAD*). Again an introduction which led nowhere: two letters from William Dunn are recorded in the *BI*.

Sterling. He is one of the largest Manufacturers and Spinners in the Kingdom and one of the richest. This is a mere trial. If it goes well he will go to a considerable length. He has however sent a very different assortment to what I recommended, and made his Invoice out at absurdly high prices, without reference to which you must do the best you can, following his instructions as in his letters. His yarn is perhaps of very good quality (I have not seen it). But even then 1 shilling and 6 pence per piece of N° 42 is 4 pence per piece too high.

Invoices N° 25 and 26, letter N° 19. George Horrocks, Preston, a partner of *Messrs. Horrocks Jackson & Co.*,[105] Manchester, Spinners and Manufacturers. Y, N° 10 to 35. Twenty-six Bales Cotton yarn. Amount 668.3/7 pounds Sterling, and Z N° 20 to 40—21 Packages of Gold End Shirtings. Amount 964.1/1 ¾ pounds Sterling. Very extensive, wealthy and pleasant correspondent—my staunch friend, to whom I am under many obligations, and for whom I am most anxious to do well. The Twist is bought with Cash on my recommendations and is a very cheap and prime parcel. It must pay him good Profit. He has added a little less than 10 per cent to the Cash cost in Manchester. It is of good quality, [ ] and much better than a great deal that goes out. The Gold End Shirtings are his own Manufacture and he will supply you with them or any other article, that will leave a little Profit to any extent. These Shirtings are in like manner Invoiced at about 7½ to 10 per cent above the Cash Cost in Manchester. I refer you to his letter of instructions—as respects returns I would recommend Silk at 10 shilling to 10 shillings and 9 pence for good Tysaam or 13 shillings and 6 pence for good Tsatlee in preference to Bills at 4 shillings, but hope you may get at lower rates. Black Silk pieces and Black nankeens as alluded to in my separate letter I would recommend to the extent of 500 pounds. Pray do all in your power that this adventure may turn out favourably.

Invoice N° 27, letter N° 21. *William Grant & Brothers*, Manchester.[106] GBC, N° 1 to 12. Twelve cases of goods amounting to 575.2/11 pounds Sterling. I am afraid some part of these may be of difficult Sale. They are sent without my knowledge, as they said they knew the market perfectly well. I will be glad to find out it is so. They are very extensive, highly respectable and pleasant people, and it will give me great pleasure to do them good— and if so they will ship largely. As to returns do the best in your power for them. Report particularly upon these various things, and accompany your remarks with patterns, both of what is good and what is objectionable.

Messrs. Robert Thomson & Sons[107] of Glasgow have shipped by the *Royal Charlotte*, M, N° 1 to 20, twenty Bales; and V, N° 1 to 20, twenty Bales of Cotton

[105] *Horrocks, Jackson & Co.*, 'Cotton spinners and manufacturers, 25 Bridgewater Place, High Street; and at Preston'. (*PODL*).

[106] *William Grant & Brothers*, Cotton spinners, calico and quilting manufacturers and printers, 15 Cannon Street', Manchester. (*PODL*).

[107] *Robert Thomson & Sons*, 'Adelphi Cotton Works, Hutchesontown', Glasgow. (*GPOAD*).

yarn to John Purvis , Singapore, desiring him to forward at all events 20 Bales to you, and also the other 20 unless he can realize a satisfactory price for it in Singapore. Their letter to you I have not seen, it is under cover to Purvis and I must refer you to the same. *Robert Thomson & Sons* are highly respectable. Their yarn is said to be of an inferior quality.

Messrs. Thomas Sheils & Co.[108] of Glasgow, very respectable and wealthy Calico Printers and who have a house in Singapore, *Paterson & Co.*, have shipped per *Diadnee* to *Paterson & Co.*[109] 26 cases of Goods to be forwarded to you. They are prepared according to instructions I gave them when in Glasgow, and if they have adhered to these I think they will do very well, but not having a copy of their Invoice I cannot say much about it. They have sent forward their letter to you and Invoice under cover to *Paterson & Co.*, Singapore. They advised me to instruct you as to returns. They are partial to produce in returns in preference to Bills, and leave you to do what you think most advantageous. Silk at the limits of 10 shillings and six pence to 10 shillings and 9 pence for Taysaam, and 13 shillings to 13 shillings and six pence for Tastlee I think certainly better than Bills. *Thomas Sheils and Co.* would have no objection to returns going *to Schurr, Wilson & Co.*,[110] Hamburg. Teas to them taken in Barter may facilitate a Sale. William Falconer also writes me that he hopes I will write you to mark his returns in produce and not in Bills as he thinks in the long run it pays best.

Messrs. Staunton & Co.,[111] of Kings Arms Yard and Glostershire[112] have shipped you 50 Bales of Woolens by the *Royal Charlotte* and 43 to *Dent & Co.* This is not through any intervention of mine—but I will call upon them when I go to London a few days hence.

Messrs. Barton's of Manchester made you a considerable shipment this spring per *Waterloo* and do not at present feel inclined to do more, till they learn of what is pending.

Messrs. James Finlay & Co. of Glasgow express doubts as to the legality of the voyage and on that account declined doing anything at present. Mr. Finlay has been some time very unwell but is much better again.

Messrs. Daniel Barton & Sons of Manchester are preparing 2,000 pieces of very beautiful Chintz—a few patterns of which are included. They are done on a cloth made on purpose about 2 to 2½ inches wider than usual to measure 28 inches wide, which no other ⅞ Chintz do. This was particularly recommended to me by the China men. I think those goods are beautiful and well suited to the market, and I hope that they will do well. They are expensive things, and unless they bring

[108] *Thomas Sheils & Co.*, 'Calico printers and manufacturers, 18 St Vincent Lane', Glasgow. (*GPOAD*).

[109] Fourteen letters from *Paterson & Co.*, Singapore, are listed in the *BI*.

[110] Not identified.

[111] Not identified.

[112] Original spelling.

7 dollars to 7 dollars and 50 cents per Piece, the buyer paying the duty, they won't answer. As soon as you can let me know that you think of these patterns, and make any remarks upon them that occurs to you.

Nothing further occurs to me at present regarding the goods by this vessel and in preparation. Trusting everything to your good management, I remain, etc.[113]

47. James Matheson in Canton to Hugh Matheson[114] in Calcutta,

4 November 1831

My dear Hugh,

Although as usual pressed for time, I must not allow the *Waterwitch* to depart without a few lines in reply to yours of th 18th August, on the subject of your proposed association with Mr. Charles Lyall.[115] With him I have very little acquaintance, and only recollect that *Mackintosh & Co.* were not much pleased with him, while in his office, chiefly on account of his devoting too much time to his own affairs. For my old friend, his cousin James Lyall, I have a great regard, and through him have learnt to esteem Robert Lyall, while a partner in *Shotton & Co.*,[116] although I suspect he drove rather a hard bargain with them on retiring from the firm. I consider them a thriving and united family. And on this ground, supposing you to be sufficiently well acquainted with Charles Lyall to be sure of your getting on well together, I have no hesitation in entirely approving of this connection. Mr. Jardine, knowing nothing of the parties, allows himself to be regulated by my own opinion, which I have given on the express understanding that the House is one of mere Agency and that above all you must abstain from speculation[117] for the sake of effecting remittances in that most treacherous of articles,

[113] The total of the 27 invoices detailed in this letter was just over £22,800. Only five invoices were in four figures. Most firms were sending relatively small shipments, as a way of testing this new export market.

[114] Hugh Mackay Matheson (1805–1875), was a nephew of James Matheson and a brother of (Sir) Alexander Matheson. He was a merchant in Calcutta from 1829 to 1834. He founded *Lyall Matheson & Co.* in Calcutta in circumstances described in this letter. Under the management of Charles Lyall, the firm was to develop an important and steady business flow with *Jardine, Matheson & Co.* By 1839, Hugh Matheson was back in London (Letter **188**). He eventually settled down in Liverpool, a co-founder of the merchant firm of *Matheson & Scott* (Letter **261**).

[115] *Lyall, Bothers & Co.* was a firm of East India merchants established in London. Several members of the Lyall family are mentioned in this collection of letters: Charles Lyall, (Hugh Matheson's partner in Calcutta); William Lyall (in Letters **97**, **149**, **151**, and **193**); Robert Lyall (Letters **58**, **149**, **193**); John Lyall (Letter **207**) and James Lyall (**58**).

[116] A Bombay Agency House. See above, Letter **39**, note 15.

[117] A House of Agency was, in theory, a 'mere Agency' as James Matheson puts it in this Letter, that is, a brokerage where the 'Agent' took no risk and simply executed buy and sell orders on commission. In practice, however, many agents were tempted by speculation.

indigo,[118] which has entailed ruin on so many while a fortunate few have made money by it. Having premised this much, I shall proceed to add a few lines for your guidance.

I think you should avoid engaging for a long term of years, as you did in joining *E. M[ackintosh] & Co.*[119] A short partnership, with liberty to separate after a notice of a six or a twelve month, will be the most likely to keep all parties contented. So long as you get on well, the chances are none of you will wish to separate. As it appears possible Mr. William Lyall may have formed other arrangements at home, I would not consent to be advertised until it is ascertained that he has done nothing to interfere with you. This will effectually guard against a collision of interests, and subsequent discontent. I think you should have an equal share with Mr. Charles Lyall, if not now, certainly in the course of a year or two. Your business this season will not be a fair criterion of what you may expect to influence to the firm after your joining it. First because on account of the unfavourable prospects of the drug, and the probability of unreasonably high prices in India, our remittances and those of our friends will probably be on a more limited scale than usual. And secondly, the great confidence resulting from not having to rely on a single life will, it is fair to presume, gradually induce your friends to increase their business. In saying this, however, let me warn you that the greater part of *Magniac & Co.*'s business must necessarily go to *Fergusson & Co.*[120] You can only have a small share and the less this is known to *Fergusson & Co.*, the better.

It will probably benefit the firm to have your name appear in it as a Partner. One of the Lyalls (James or Robert) contemplates it as desirable that you or Charles Lyall should go home in a year or two. But the utility of this I do not

[118] Speculation in indigo was responsible for the failures of all the large Calcutta Agencies from 1828 to 1833. (See Singh, S. B. *European Agency Houses in Bengal*, Calcutta, 1966, pp. 244. The most prestigious Calcutta Agency House, *Palmer & Co.*, often called 'The Queen of Indigo', was the first to fail, on 4 Dec. 1829).

Following the failure of *Palmer & Co.*, the remaining Agency Houses listed in *EIRD* for 1831—most of them awaiting a similar fate because of indigo speculations—were the following : *Allport & Co.*, *Bagshaw & Co.*, *Barretto & Sons*, Charles Bernard, *Blaney & Co.*, *Bonnaffe & Co.*, *Boyd, Beeby & Co.*, *Bruce Allen & Co.*, *Buchanan, Mann & Co.*, *Carroll & Co.*, George Chisholm, *Colvin & Co.*, *Cruttenden Mackillop & Co.*, *Cumming & Co.*, *Davidson & Co.*, *De Souza & Co.*, Robert Eglinton, *Fergusson & Co.*, *Gillander, Ogilvy & Co.*, *Gilmore & Co.*, *Gisborne & Co.*, *Graham & Brewer*, Duncan Ingraham, *Lacherstein & Co.*, *Laprimaundy & Co.*, *J. Mackenzie & Co.*, *Mackintosh & Co.*, *E. Mackintosh & Co.*, *Daniel MacDonald & Co.*, *Henry Mathew & Co.*, *Mendieta Uriarte & Co.*, *Reddall & Co.*, *Rennie & Co.*, *Rustumjee, Turner & Co.*, *James Scott & Co.*, *Shedden & Co.*, *F. B. Smith & Co.*, *Smithson, Holdsworth & Co.*, *Sutton & Co.*, Francis Vrigon, *Walker, Roussac & Co.*, *Wilkinson & Petrie*, *Willis & Earle*. (*EIRD*, 1831, Houses of Agency, Bengal, p. 152)

[119] For 'E. Mackintosh & Co.' (in initials in the manuscript), and for 'Bagshaw' (three lines before the end of this Letter), see note 118 immediately above.

[120] The firm's principal Calcutta correspondent until its failure, two years later.

perceive, seeing that William Lyall is always there to look after your interests, and the absence of either of you would receive the objection of reliance on a single life which now exists.

And now, my dear Hugh, if this arrangement takes effect, I trust it will be final and that we shall hear of no more changes. Just reflect how many there have been since the spring of 1829, little more than two years ago! You first proposed to me to become an indigo planter. Then came the hastily patched up partnership with *E. M[ackintosh] & Co.*, then the consultation with lawyers, and forced separation. Then nothing is so good as doing business alone. And now comes the partnership with Charles Lyall, which, I readily admit, is an improvement on all other plans. You must recollect that when in one of my letters I hinted at a connection with Bagshaw, I lost no time in retracting it, in the very next letter, and not being then aware that so good a connection as Lyall would be attainable, I intimated a preference of you doing business alone, etc., etc.

Yours affectionately,

48. James Matheson in Canton to Hugh Matheson in Calcutta,

4 November 1831[121]

My dear Hugh,

I remit to you, enclosed, the following bills on London which, please, negotiate and credit, on negotiation, to an account you will open under the head of James Matheson Trust Fund.

3 bills n°4–6	each 500 pounds sterling	1,500
2 ditto n°14–15	each 250 pounds sterling	500
Drawn on Mr. Bannerman of the Factory and N.J. Chauncy Esq., of the well-known firm of *Chauncy Lucas & Lang*,[122] payable 3rd March 1833.		
1 bill n°10		200
Drawn by Andrew Johnston on *Gledstanes Drysdale* at six month, all endorsed in blank by *Magniac & Co.*		
		2,200 pounds sterling

This is a sum which I set apart some time ago to accumulate at interest as a fund for the support of my mother and sisters. But it being difficult to obtain interest with security I have latterly resolved to employ it in opium,[123] in doing

[121] This Letter is of even date with Letter **47**.

[122] Nathaniel Chauncy, 'Merchant, 39 Wilson Street, Finsbury'; and James Lang, 'Merchant, 55 Old Broad Street', London. (*TLCD*).

[123] Few statements of James Matheson's can suggest better that these two sentences how clear his conscience was when it came to dealing in opium.

which I must trust to your judgment in effecting purchases and to Alexander for disposing of it here, to whom you will therefore consign it. I refer you to the House's circular letter. Unless you hear of an enlarged supply of Malwa, and likely to come on soon, I should be disposed to go somewhat beyond the rate of 1,400 Rupees at the first sale, provided you take care to send on the opium in the ship that will, in all probability, arrive here first. And if the *Sylph* is one of those sailing, I think she will bid fair to beat the rest. It is not improbable too that we shall take a small interest in her. But on this subject I shall write to you again. You are aware that we have already a small interest in the *Falcon*.

Mr. Bannerman's bills on London being payable on a fixed date will, of course, become more valuable the longer the are kept. You will therefore be in no hurry to negotiate them, if the price of opium should be too high, in which case it must, I think, fall at the subsequent sale.

Benares will be equally eligible with Patna at 20 or 30 Rupees less. The amount will be insured here by ship or ships. Charge your commission on this business.

Yours affectionately,

P.S. You must exercise your discretion in the business as if the money were your own. And if prices are high at Calcutta and low at Bombay, you may invest the amount at the other Presidency; in which case you might employ Cursetjee Jamsetjee[124] as your agent, representing it as an affair of your own.

1832

49. William Jardine in Canton to James Matheson in Macao,

28 January 1832

My dear Matheson,

Your favor of the 25th reached me last night and soon after the letters per *[Bombay] Merchant* were delivered. Many private letters for you which I send herewith, and hope they may be in time. Mr. Keating[1] is sending newspapers to Mr. [James] Innes. I send none to you, as you can read his on the way up.

I have a long letter from [Jamsetjee] Jejeebhoy dated October 25th, in which he speaks of sending 1,500 chests of Malwa in the *Good Success* very early—passes already applied for; and the parties anxious for the *Success* to return. On this subject silence will be prudent. And I hope our subsequent letters may prevent them from sending on any ship so early as they then contemplated. Our letters are satisfactory on the whole, and Jejeebhoy's remittance has turned out well.

[124] Cursetjee Jamsetjee : see above, Letter **34**, note 64.

[1] Arthur Saunders Keating. See above, Letter **42**, note 37.

Mr. Low[2] volunteered to forward the protest etc., to Mr. Shillaber[3] by the *Nederlander*, and to write to him. If you have time, and inclination, you may as well favour him with a few hints how to proceed against Webb.[4] What would you think of his requesting the Consul to examine you and me on oath in the affair?—forwarding our examinations and depositions to America. [William H.] Low informs me *Messrs. R[ussell] & Co.* had allowed S[hillaber] three years to settle, in Java, [for a sum] not [to] exceed two thousand or three thousand dollars. Not knowing what had passed between you and Mr. Shillaber, respecting the Bags, I preferred leaving you to consign them in the manner agreed on; and I have no doubt my letter to you reached in ample time. Webb has acted like a vagabond; but I hope we may yet get out of the scrap without a loss, and Shillaber with some profit.

Mr. Gernaert[5] leaves this afternoon for Macao, and embarks from thence to Java.

I had made up my mind to Mr. Gutzlaff[6] being engaged for the *Clive*, from a variety of circumstances; and [James] Innes was of nearly the same opinion. So far so good. He may collect useful information for future purposes, but I shall be very much pleased when I hear of the safe return of the vessel. The voyage

[2] William H. Low. See above, Letter **31**, notes 46 and 47. William H. Low arrived in Canton from Salem in 1829. He was the third partner in *Russell & Co.* after Samuel Russell and Philip Ammidon. He 'left Canton for ill-health in 1833, he was landed and died at the Cape of Good Hope'. (Hunter, *The Fan Kwae at Canton*, p. 96). For a moving account of his death by his niece, see: Low, *Lights & Shadows*, II, pp. 723–727.

[3] John Shillaber was at the time American Consul in Batavia. In 1833 'he became the brother-in-law of Dr Thomas Richardson Colledge through his sister Caroline'. (Ride, *East India Cemetery*, p. 168). When he arrived in Canton he started an active business career and was an active correspondent of William Jardine and James Matheson. See Letters **70, 139, 141, 145, 188, 213, 215,** and **243**. The dispute referred to in this paragraph has not been identified. The reference to 'bags' points to a dispute about a sugar cargo.

[4] 'Webb' was not identified.

[5] One of the few references to Mr Gernaert is to be found in Hunter, *Bits of Old China*, p. 186 : 'For thirty years, from 1802 to 1832, the French flag had not been hoisted [at the Canton factories], and even the staff had been taken away. On December 1832, the French Consul (appointed in 1828), Monsieur Gernaert, rehoisted the flag, but lived almost entirely at Macao'.

[6] The Reverend Karl (or Carl) Friedrich August Gutzlaff (1803–1851) was a Pomeranian missionary. One of a handful of Europeans in Canton who could speak Chinese fluently, he also had a command of several Chinese dialects. As a missionary he saw it as his main task to convert the Chinese to Christianity. William Jardine, who needed an interpreter on board one of the three opium ships sent on secret missions up the China coast in 1832, struck a deal with Gutzlaff: the missionary would be free to spread the gospel and distribute his tracts among the Chinese people so long as he did not object to the opium being sold from the ships. (See in particular letter **76**). Gutzlaff accepted the deal gratefully. In 1834, he published an account of these voyages under the title: *Journal of Three Voyages Along the Coast of China, etc.*, London, Federick Westley and A. H. Davis, Stationers' Hall Court. Later, Gutzlaff was one of the joint interpreters to the British Superintendents of Trade and to the British Plenipotentiary. In this capacity he helped Sir Henry Pottinger during the Treaty negotiations at Nanking. He then became involved in the early administration of Hong Kong as Chinese secretary, when he trained some of the first consular interpreters, including schoolboy Harry Parkes, later British

required much management and great attention. The youngsters say young Morrison[7] feels disappointed at this affair; but he has not mentioned it to me.

When do you propose returning or rather when shall we despatch the *Jamesina?* I have secured the *Negrohead* from Mr. Latimer and Mr. Talbot,[8] [ ]. I should like the *Jamesina*[9] to have the Ladrone[10] astern on the 3rd or 4th at the latest.

Believe me, yours very sincerely,

50. *Baring Brothers & Co.*[11] in London to *Magniac & Co.* in Canton,
24 February 1832[12]

Gentlemen,

We have the pleasure to own receipt of your esteemed favor of 23 August forwarding the original of a letter of Credit upon us for 50,000 dollars granted to

---

Minister to China. He was buried in the Hong Kong colonial cemetery. (Keswick, *The Thistle and the Jade*, pp. 134–135; Fay, *Opium War*, pp. 60–61; Fairbank, *Trade and Diplomacy*, p.98; Le Pichon, *Origines de Hong Kong*, pp. 100–103).

[7] 'The youngsters': the clerks and bookkeepers like Alexander Matheson, Chay Beale, Henry Robinson, etc. 'Young Morrison' refers to John Robert Morrison, the son of the Rev. Dr Robert Morrison (Letter **8,** note 44). John Robert Morrison (1814–1843) was eighteen at the time. He was a fluent Cantonese speaker and Chinese Scholar. He would no doubt have liked to have been selected as interpreter for these secret up-coast missions. In 1834, upon the death of his father, he was appointed to succeed him as secretary to H. M.'s Commission in China, and in that capacity served under Lord Napier for a few weeks before the latter's own death (Letter **95**). He later became a close associate of Captain Charles Elliot. In 1841, he was appointed Treasurer and Secretary on the retirement of Edward Elmslie. In his *Trade and Diplomacy*, (pp.121–122), Fairbank shows that his early death whilst in the process of negotiating the *Supplementary Treaty of 1843* with China deprived Britain of one of her most promising servants in the East at the time.

[8] For John R. Latimer, see above Letter **5**, note 21. Charles N Talbot was another American merchant working in Canton at the time (Two letters listed in the *BI*; Hunter, *Fan Kwae at Canton*, p. 10).

[9] The *Jamesina*, 'a 382–ton brig' (Blake, *Jardine, Matheson*, p. 49) was the second of four ships which William Jardine and James Matheson chartered to mount new types of expeditions up the China coast. The aim of these expeditions was to open up new markets for opium and other products away from Lintin, in anticipation of greater competition (see Letter **39**, note 21). The first ship, the *Sylph*, (Captain Wallace), left Lintin waters on 20 October 1832 and returned on 29 April 1833. The second ship was the *Jamesina,* commanded by James Innes. The Jamesina left Lintin on 8 November 1832 and returned in early spring 1833. The next two ships sailed north on similar expeditions also in the autumn of 1832. They were the *John Biggar*, commanded by James Matheson's cousin, Captain William Mackay, and the *Colonel Young*, commanded by Captain John Rees. (Fay, *Opium War*, pp. 60–61; Blake, *Jardine, Matheson*, pp.49–53; Le Pichon, *Origines de Hong Kong*, pp. 100–104).

[10] The Ladrones: a group of small islands situated in the mouth of the Pearl River Delta.

[11] The London firm *Baring Brothers & C.* was not regular a correspondent of *Jardine,Matheson & Co.* It was best known at the time for financing American exporters to Britain. See : Hidy, Ralph, W., *The House of Baring in American Trade and Finance*, New York, (1949), 1970.

[12] At the foot of the letter, the page bears the signature of J. W. Ward written immediately under the phrase '*for Baring Brothers & Co.*' On the folded cover of the letter, James Matheson wrote the comment : 'Holding to a part of the Bills drawn by Captain DeKonen being unaccepted. Annexing the signature of their american Agent, J. W. Ward'. (The practice of spelling adjectives of nationality with a capital letter was not yet generally accepted).

Captain Walter Crocker[13] of the ship *Israel* by Mr. Israel Thorndike of Boston and stating that Captain Crocker had drawn upon us for 10,000 pounds Sterling and that you had entered into an arrangement with Mr. H. T. DeKonen, Supercargo of the American Ship *Clematis* for negotiating his drafts upon us to the extent of 25,000 to 30,000 pounds.

Captain Crocker's drafts are in order but Mr. DeKonen having exceeded his credit we have been obliged to leave part of his drafts in sufferance but we expect to hear shortly from a party concerned in them from Paris who may give us authority to accept them.

You will probably ere this be acquainted with the signature of our Agent in the United States, Mr. J. W. Ward[14], who is in the habit of approving bills drawn upon us by our American friends—in annecsing[15] it therefore at foot for your government. We have only to add that his sanction is deserving of every confidence. We enclose our Price Current.

Your obedient Servants.

51. Charles Millet[16] in Canton to William Jardine in Canton,

29 February 1832

Dear Jardine,

I am greatly obliged by your communication of this evening; and by a perusal of the papers which accompanied your note.[17] They have opened to my view the liberal feelings and excellent understanding constantly prevailing in your intercourse with Hollingworth Magniac on the subject of his Cousin; feelings alike honorable to the parties, and such as preclude the danger of disappointment, or misunderstanding in the course proposed regarding [Francis] Hollingworth.[18]

From him I learnt the offer which had been made by Matheson: and at once I advised its acceptance, with expressions of gratitude to you. Much I regret that my interview with him did not proceed and consequently prevent those expressions of disappointment, which seem to have forced on you a course necessarily productive to him of much anxious uncertainty.

[13] No letters to the firm by Captain Walter Crocker are listed in the *BI*. The same remark applies to Israel Thorndike and to H. T. DeKonen.

[14] Another reference to J. W. Ward as Baring's credit agent in America is found in Letter **58** below.

[15] Original spelling.

[16] Charles Millet and James Frederick Nugent Daniell, both East India Company supercargoes, had been close friends of Hollingworth Magniac in Canton before the latter's retirement to England. A similar letter was addressed to William Jardine by James Daniell. By keeping Hollingworth Magniac's old friends informed of the settlement regarding Francis Hollingworth, William Jardine was reducing the risk of further gossip being reported to London.

[17] Neither the 'papers' nor the accompanying 'note' were found with this Letter.

[18] As both Letters **52** and **53** make up in some measure for the missing papers referred to immediately above, they could usefully be read before this letter **51** which was written earlier.

The papers are returned with this and I remain,
Very truly yours,

52. James Matheson in Canton to Hollingworth Magniac in London

[ ] March 1832[19]

[ ] I was duly favored with your letters of 29th April and 12th May last, but have been unable to reply to them sooner, as well on account of the great pressure of business during the Season, as from the uncertainty attending the subjects to which they chiefly related, on which it was impossible to arrive at any decision before receiving your reply to Jardine's letter of 17th January 1831 per *Camden*.[20]

Jardine was induced to write that letter in consequence of our receiving no answer to mine from Singapore of January 1830, per *City of Aberdeen*, which vessel appears to have arrived at home in sufficient time for an acknowledgment to have reached us. In it he proposed, (as an alternative to the plan suggested by me) in regard to [Francis] Hollingworth, that you should 'remain in the firm yourself, for a year or two longer, to enable your providing for him and his family without lessening your own means', in the event of this proving more in unison with your feelings than that a provision should be made for him by us; and, having given you the option, we in consequence abstained from publishing your retirement from the Firm on the 30th June 1830, leaving it to be regulated by your reply.

Some months ago before Jardine received your answer of 17th June 1831 to his above-mentioned letter of 17th January 1831, Hollingworth accosted me to state that he regretted to have heard from you that I had written to you in terms of dissatisfaction respecting him, and hinting at the plan which I had suggested to you. I replied, it was certainly true that I had written, and touched, lightly, on the causes of our dissatisfaction, though naturally restrained, in no small degree from saying as much as the case admitted, by my unwillingness to hurt the feelings of one with whom I everyday sat at the same board and was in hourly converse, as a member of the same family. I added to tranquillize his mind, that he need be under no apprehension as to a provision for his family, who, with himself, would be sufficiently provided for, though not opulently, but that until an answer arrived to Jardine's letter of 1831 I could say nothing further, on the subject, a

[19] This copy or draft of an out-letter was found among the in-correspondence. It is dated 'March', with the day left blank. James Matheson's draft seems to have been written sometime between the date of Letter **51**, (February 29, 1832) which returned to the partners the supporting evidence which they had sent to show Magniac's friends the fairness of the settlement, and the date of Letter **53**, which actually sent the details the settlement to Hollingworth Magniac (2 March, 1832). Indeed, the efforts made by the writer at piecing together the exact chronology of letters exchanged between Hollingworth Magniac and William Jardine and at quoting exactly from letters received, suggests that it is likely to have been prepared in anticipation of the partner's final decision on the settlement.

[20] The letter was not traced.

new proposal for your remaining longer in the Firm, with a view to his (Hollingworth's) benefit, being made. The conversation ended by his saying he would prefer going home with a provision made for him, rather than remain here without the prospect of ulterior advancement.

Your letter to Jardine of 17th June 1831 we received on the 6th December, and I apprised Hollingworth some days afterwards, that Jardine could now explain to him the proposed arrangement, whenever he pleased to communicate with him, so as to enable his making the requisite preparations for going home.

Thus affairs remained till a few days before the sailing of the three last Company ships then here, the *Scaleby Castle*, *Huntly* and *York*, when I again spoke to him to say that, if he had any desire to take his passage in one of them, Jardine could explain everything, on whom, as the Senior Partner, the conclusion of the arrangement naturally devolved. He answered that he would prefer waiting for the *Winchelsea* or *Larkins*.

A further interval elapsed till a few days ago, when, as Hollingworth still avoided a conversation with Jardine, I thought it was high time to relieve him from the suspense and enable him to make up his mind as to going home or otherwise, before the departure of the last opportunities for the Season.

We had previously made up our minds to the original plan, which you considered settled, in terminating your Interest on 30th June 1830. But in place of appropriating to ourselves the vacant third share for the two succeeding Years, till June 1832, we resolved to consider it applicable towards making up a fund of £8,000 or £10,000 for Hollingworth in the first place; and the Balance to be at your disposal for your Brother Daniel. As Hollingworth's fund was to be bestowed, in great measure, for the sake of his family, we intended to stipulate, that a part of it should be placed under your control, for their security, to prevent that becoming again chargeable to you.

This I accordingly communicated to Hollingworth, after premising that we acknowledged no claims, on his part, but were actuated, merely, by friendly feelings. To my great surprise, he expressed himself disappointed, said that 10,000 pounds sterling at 3 per cent English interest, would give him only 300 pounds a year, whereas himself and family would require 500 pounds; that this was inconsistent with what I had before said as to their being provided for; he would in fact be worse off than on his present salary of 2,500 dollars per annum. He dwelt on the inadequacy of the sum proposed, to compensate what he had a right to expect as a future member of the Firm. I quoted in reply, your letter to Jardine of 20th June 1827, in which he is first proposed, where, after speaking of character, you state : '*His ideas being very moderate, nor aspiring to an admission, until you should find him essential enough to wish it yourself, etc.*', these words being scored by you. He rejoined that this was very different from his understanding with you and from your ideas on the subject; as a proof of which you intended sending out another to succeed to the Firm in his stead. I thought it necessary to deny any such right of succession; and, as I had nothing more to say, concluded by referring him to Jardine, if he wished for further explanation.

Having deliberated on what had passed, in reference to Hollingworth reliance on an understanding with you, we resolved as the best mode of meeting every view of the case, to resort to the alternative exposed in Jardine's letter of January 1831, to continue your interest for two years longer till June 1832, and thus afford you the means of remunerating Hollingworth, as you might deem proper. An advertisement to this effect was prepared and, after a few day's delay, was sent to the Canton Newspaper and *Price Current* for publication.

Before it was issued, I mentioned the purport of it to Hollingworth; when I was again surprised by his expressing a preference for the arrangement which he had before slighted, rather than that he should have to rely upon you—said it was liberal, and endeavoured to explain away, and even to deny, much of what I had understood him to say. I succeeded in recalling a good deal of it to his recollection, particularly the reference to his claims upon the House, your sending a successor in his stead, etc., etc. And as for the [misunderstanding] I am not very curious to have it decided, whether the fact be that I misunderstood him, or that he, in the flurry of the moment, said what he afterwards did not recollect.

53. William Jardine in Canton to Hollingworth Magniac in London, 2 March 1832

My dear Magniac

We have been so much pressed for time lately, that I have allowed the packets for the *Winchelsea*[21] and *Larkins*[22] to be closed without a single line to you; but Mr. [Francis] Hollingworth, who proceeds to England in the latter ship is still here; and by him I intend sending this.[23]

Your favour, of 17th June was received on the 6th December last, and we have nothing from you of a later date. Mr. Matheson is addressing you on the subject of Mr. Hollingworth's return to England, and the provision made for him, and his

[21] The *Winchelsea* was a 1,300-ton ship chartered to the East India Company. The ship owner was William Moffat, the London tea broker. (*EIRD*, 1831, pp. viii–ix).

[22] The ownership and particulars of the *Larkins* were not identified.

[23] The final departure of Francis Hollingworth, the settlement described in this Letter, and the final squaring of Hollingworth Magniac's accounts all mark an important date in the history of the firm. On 27 Feb., just days before this Letter was written, William Jardine and James Matheson had sent to most of the firms' constituents a circular announcing that 'the name of the firm [*Magniac & Co.*] is to be changed to *Jardine, Matheson & Co.*, on 30 June next.' To a few close acquaintances and friends, like Charles Marjoribanks or F. P. Alleyn, a paragraph was added to the effect that '[Francis] Hollingworth proceeded to England in the *Larkins* on a provision we have made for him, out of the profits of the last two years, during which period we kept Magniac's name in the firm, for the purpose of reconciling him to the measure, he having scruple about allowing us to provide for his relation.[. . .]'(*JMArch*, C4–1, Letter of William Jardine to F. P Alleyn dated 27 Feb. 1832).

family, on the occasion; which precludes the necessity of my entering on the affair further than to inform you, the terms proposed by Mr. Matheson, were proposed at my request, under an impression that it would be more agreeable to Mr. Hollingworth to confer with him than with me. And I regret very much he, Mr. Hollingworth, did not at once accept the terms offered, without entering into a discussion about promises made by you to him and various other topics, that might irritate and do harm; but could not have any good effect, while his assertions were in direct opposition to the contents of your letters in my possession.

When addressing you on the 17th October last, I mentioned Mr. [Chay] Beale having closed the Books of 1829–1830, but too late to admit of the Balance Sheet being examined and forwarded to you by the ships then under dispatch.

On examining Chay's set of Books, a few days after, we found *F[airlie] B[onham] &Co's* accounts had not been adjusted; nor had that of Shipments to Europe. Chay is now in Macao, where he has not been for two years before, having been ashamed, I believe, to go down while the Books were so much in arrears; but he appears now to have given them up; and Mr. Matheson will have to close them the moment a few days can be spared for that purpose; which will, I hope, soon be the case now. The Books of 1830–31 are in an advanced state, but cannot be closed till those of the previous year have been closed. In this year the Opium Account is a good one and the Commission Account the best I have seen, being nearly 150,000 dollars; but there are very unfortunately, considerable bad, or doubtful debt, which have arisen in a great measure, from the Books being in arrears. The profits will, however, be upwards of 100,000 dollars under any circumstances.

The Books for 1828–29 were first closed erroneously by Mr. Ullman, with a profit of 38,000 dollars : [they have] since [been] closed and will probably prove correct with a profit of 150,000 dollars odd. The Books of 1829–30 [were] closed by Chay with about 48,000 dollars [profit].

In this year there appears a loss on opium of about 30,000 dollars; though taken from original sources the purchases and sales show a profit particularly on the opium from India and *Jamesina* when towed by the steamer.[24] It is difficult to imag-

[24] This event is narrated by Robert Blake as follows (*Jardine Matheson*, pp. 54–55): 'Steam was, of course, destined to displace sail, and as early as 1829 James Matheson was interested in the idea. The firm of *Mackintosh & Co.* had ordered a special steam tug, the *Forbes,* for Calcutta Harbour. She displaced 302 tons and was powered by two 60-horsepower engines. She was launched at Calcutta in January 1829. On a visit to that city, Matheson conceived the idea of chartening her to tow the *Jamesina* from Calcutta to China. He backed her for 1,000 dollars to reach Lintin from Sandheads in a month. The *Forbes* got off to a bad start, running aground on a sandbank in the Hooghly On 14th March 1829 a second attempt was made. The *Forbes* could carry only 130 tons of coal and so the *Jamesina* was laden with another 52 tons in addition to her 840 chests of opium. The coal was not enough, and on 12th April, with only four days' supply remaining, the two parted company. The *Forbes*

ine whence the loss arises. It may be partly accounted for by our having carried all forfeited Bargain money to next year's account perhaps erroneously. Under such circumstances, we have decided on keeping back the accounts for the three years, till we have had time to examine the whole, and satisfy ourselves that they are correct. I am sending you, at the same time, copies of your private account, short the profits of each year; of which plan, I trust, you will approve for the present.

I shall now take leave of the affairs of the firm, to say a few words respecting the Factories, in which you are deeply interested. The demand for Factories, or rather the rent of Factories, have decreased very much; and every one of the tenants in the Creek complains of paying too much. Add to this the circumstance of Howqua's having declined the Company's contracts for tea [in] preparation to withdrawing from business entirely, if possible, and you will see how desirable it was to get quit of the whole concern. In conformity with this view of the case, I have disposed of the whole range of the Creek for 65,000 dollars, we renting them from the Cohong. With this arrangement I feel perfectly satisfied; and shall be happy to find you do the same. The Imperial must be left on its present footing, for a time—Howqua never having alluded to it.[25]

Enclosed you have copies of your private accounts for the last three years; and it will afford me pleasure [if you] find they are correct. I also enclose an open account for the current year, and an estimate of our account with *Fairlie Bonham & Co.*, which, for the reasons assigned in my private note to you of the 17th October last, is on a very contracted scale; and we have put ourselves to much inconvenience to keep it so, fearing, if the rumours that have reached us are correct, our numerous drafts might have tended very much to [inconvenience] them. Under this embarrassing feeling we have consigned to and drawn on Mr. Weeding to an extent far beyond our wishes or intentions at the commencement of the season. Not knowing what steps you have taken in consequence of my private note, we are naturally anxious to prevent the consignments to Mr. Weeding becoming a source of annoyance to our regular correspondents. To ensure this, it is necessary they should be acquainted with our motives which were of the most friendly description towards them; and were they acquainted with the tenth of the whole truth, they would give us credit for them. The first intimation we had came from too respectable a source to be disregarded—the party being engaged in business of a totally different nature, could not be actuated by feelings of jealousy, and, I believe, their motive was a feeling of friendship for the members of our firm. Having now fully explained this delicate affair to you, we trust to your friendship

---

proceeded by sail arriving at Lintin on 19th April and the *Jamesina* followed two days later. Matheson lost his bet, but despite these setbacks the *Jamesina* was the first brig of the year to arrive with the new opium'.

[25] See above, Letter **31**, note 53 on factory rents. This allusive paragraph suggests that Howqua was largely in control of what foreign merchants could or could not do in the factories in terms of holding master-leases and sub-letting. The detail of the transactions alluded to remains uncertain.

to render *F[airlie] B[onham] & Co.* such explanation as may be found necessary or desirable.

I cannot close this long letter written amidst many interruptions without saying a few words on the subject of Mr. Charles Sansom[26] coming to Canton with a view of one day joining this establishment; but never in the whole course of my life, did I feel more at a loss what to say or how to act. Mr. Hollingworth's conduct, from first to last, has caused me so much annoyance, and turned out so completely opposite to what you or I both wished and expected, that I feel great hesitation in encouraging a repetition of a similar experiment which may turn out equally unsuccessful. Under any circumstances, even the most favourable, he would have to fag for many years, and that most diligently or he never could give satisfaction. Such life would prove to him extremely irksome, if not disgusting; and I should gladly hope some appointment may turn up for him at home, or in India, more congenial to his habits and feelings. With every desire to meet your wishes, and promote your views, I have written thus far with great reluctance, but feeling as I do at present, I could not conscientiously have acted differently.

I have the pleasure of handing your receipts for four packages of tea, by the *Winchelsea* and *Larkins*, which I beg your acceptance of. Three of them contain my mixture—one is said by Sinqua to contain tea of a very superior quality. Mr. Hollingworth has taken charge of a box of lacquered ware for Mrs. Magniac—a present from Hipqua[27] to be manifested to Mrs. Magniac, and believe me,

Yours very sincerely,

54. James Matheson in Macao to H. P. Haddow in Bombay, 10 March 1832

My dear Haddow,

I have come down here for some three or four days to settle some Portuguese affairs; and find that the *Camoens* is at last on the point of being despatched for you Presidency, after keeping us in suspense as to the day of her departure for the last two or three weeks; I suspect, however, we shall have a better opportunity of writing to you, about a week hence by *H. M. S. Cruizer* which takes her departure about that time. She has just arrived with despatches from Admiral Owen,[28] recalling Captain Freemantle and the *Challenger*.[29]

[26] On Charles Sansom, see above, Letter **40**, note 26. Given Jardine's reaction, Magniac dropped the plan of sending him to Canton.

[27] Sinqua and Hipqua were Hong merchants known to Hollingworth Magniac during his time of residence at Canton.

[28] Admiral Owen: Sir Edward Campbell Richard Owen (1771–1869) was commander in chief of the Royal Navy in the East Indies. (*NL* 1841, p. 89). The *BI* lists a full card of his correspondence with the firm from Calcutta.

[29] Probably a misspelling for Captain Fremantle, (later Admiral Sir Charles Howe Fremantle), one of the sons of Sir Thomas Francis Fremantle (1765–1819). (*DNB*).

My latest news from Canton is of the 7th Instant when the drug market is represented as very dull. Malwa 700 demanded, but no buyers. Patna old 960; new no price offered. Benares 970.

I owe you many apologies for not having yet answered your long and friendly letter of last season; but beg you to be assured that nothing but a constant pressure of business could have induced me to be so tardy in doing so. Not having it by me at this place, I am unable to advert to the different subjects to which it related; but I believe the principal of them was that we should use our influence with Mr. Veiga,[30] and others at Macao, to induce their concentrating, as far as possible, their orders for the drug, in our hand, at your Presidency. You are aware, however, how inappropriately Mr. Veiga's impressions of the events of last season, frustrated anything that we could have hoped to effect in this way. I sincerely trust, and indeed have every expectation that you will be able to satisfy him as to the groundlessness of his complaints; and when this is done you may rely on our sparing no endeavours to promote an object of so much interest to all of us.

I am happy to tell you that we have got out of our Japan copper speculation without loss, as far as regards the sale of that portion which has not gone on to you. I am of opinion that money is to be made by this article, as soon as it may begin to rally with you; and if you will give us early intimation when this is likely to be the case, we shall be on the look out to see what can be done here, on a moderate scale.

I anticipated the resolution which you and Jamsetjee [Jejeebhoy] have come to respecting our proposal to navigate a fast sailing vessel for the purpose of conveying despatches on occasions of interest.[31] In fact, my principal motive, in submitting the plan to you was that we might not appear to have any exclusive views in it, for our own benefit separately from yours, without giving you the option of participating. We are as yet ignorant whether Mr. Cushing is to send us any vessel or not; but if he should do so, I have no doubt we shall be able to employ her without loss.

Lancelot Dent was to have gone a passenger in the *Camoens*, but has, it is said, changed his mind, and now goes to Calcutta in the *Waterwitch*. For nearly two years back he has been very active in uttering complaints to his friends both far and near, against Jardine, for the non delivery of his letters on the arrival of the Steamer *Forbes* in April 1830; and thinking it possible the subject might be resumed on this arrival at Bombay, I had the accompanying copies of correspondence respecting it made out for transmission to you, that you may be acquainted with the state of the case, should you hear it talked of.

[30] On Joaquim José Ferreira Veiga, see above, Letter **7**, note 37.
[31] On this proposal, see above, Letter **39**.

The circumstances as these.[32] The *Jamesina* took no letters except on condition of being delivered at pleasure, excepting those for consignees of opium shipped in her, which were to be delivered in due course. In the China Sea the steamer was obliged for want of coal to abandon the tow of the *Jamesina*, and by arrangement betweent the Commanders of the two vessels, neither authorized nor anticipated by me, the *Forbes* made her way to China singly, and arrived two or three days before the *Jamesina*. Dent complains because being a consignee of opium per *Jamesina* he did not receive his letters by the steamer, whereas the fact is, that his Agent in Calcutta neither applied for, nor had any right to such privilege. In fact noone contemplated such a contingency as the two vessels arriving separately in China. You will see the argument on either side set forth in the correspondence; if you have time and patience to read it. The remarkable point is, that Dent made no complaint till the day of the despatches for the steamers's return voyage leaving Canton. And even then he did not state what now appears to be his principal grievance—viz., Mr Jardine's want of friendly consideration in not acquainting him with *Palmer & Co.*'s failure;[33] when a knowledge of the event might have enabled him to recall Thomas Dent from Manila while in progress to New South Wales. It is only from other quarters that Jardine has learnt this is the greatest of Dent's grievances for the latter has never yet called for explanation in the only proper quarter where he ought to have applied if he thought himself aggrieved.

Before I conclude, it occurs to me as due to the friendly feelings subsisting between our respective establishments to add a word or two of explanation respecting Mr. Magniac's approaching retirement from our firm. This was in the first instance to have taken place on 30th June 1827, but was prolonged by Jardine till 1830: that he might earn enough to compensate for his loss by Manhop,[34] besides making up, in some measure, for the disappointment arising from the circumstances which led to his brother Daniel being advertised out of the firm. When we made up our minds that his cousin [Francis] Hollingworth did not possess the requisite qualifications to justify his admission as a partner we subsequently prolonged Mr. Magniac's interest for two years longer, for the purpose of forming a fund to make a provision for Hollingworth and other family purposes. Hollingworth now retires with 10.000 pounds sterling, which ought to enable him to get on comfortably at home. We submitted some correspondence on the subject to Mr. Magniac chief friends here, Millet and Daniell,[35] and enclose and send copies of their replies for your confidential perusal. If you feel Jamsetjee

[32] For the background to this episode which crystallized the enmity between *Dent & Co* and *Jardine, Matheson & Co.*, see above, Letter **53**, note 24.

[33] *Palmer & Co.* was *Dent & Co.*'s principal correspondent in Calcutta.

[34] On Manhop, see Letter **12**, note 21.

[35] On Millet and Daniell, see Letter **51** above.

[Jejeebhoy] will feel any interest in either one subject of the other, the enclosures are open for his inspection.

Excuse the inaccuracies of this too long letter which is written in haste, and away from my usual writing conveniences. I shall only add to it by expressing my hope that this may find Mrs. Haddow and yourself in the enjoyment of the best possible health. Make my best remembrance to her, to Mr. and Mrs. De Vitre, and Mr. Forbes, and believe me,

Sincerely yours,

55. James Matheson in Macao to John White in Calcutta 11 March 1832

My dear Sir,

Want of time prevented my writing to you by the last despatch in acknowledgement of your favor of 7th of November, communicating the truly mournful intelligence of the death of your brother William.[36] Few events could have afflicted me more deeply than this most unexpected dispensation of Providence—for, as you well know, I had the happiness of reckoning your brother among the most esteemed of my friends. His untimely fate is mourned by not a few in this part of the world.

Our House's letter enclosing his account current will make you acquainted with the state of his affairs in China and will apprize you that, in order to stop the accumulation of heavy China interest, we have drawn on you for the balance in favour of our friends *Messrs. Fergusson & Co.*, which I trust you will find it convenient to pay. Since closing the account, we have discovered an omission of a bill for Factory rent not charged, amounting to 800 dollars or 1,648 Sicca Rupees, which we are now sending to *Messrs. Fergusson & Co.* for recovery. It is for the Factory which he occupied during the last season of his stay in China, and, being a transfer in our books, was overlooked by Mr. Hollingworth in whose department it was.

Owing to the delay in the sailing of the *Challenger*, her packets were transferred to the *Penang Merchant*, so that the original and duplicate of our account have gone in the latter vessel, but it is to be hoped she will make a safe passage to Calcutta.

I am in possession of a standing desk and Almira[37] belonging to the deceased left in charge of his female pensioner,[38] but which she has deposited with me for

[36] Probably Captain William White, mentioned in Letters **7** and **29**.

[37] Almirah, or Almyra : 'Anglo-Indian for a cupboard or chest of drawers' (*OED*). James Matheson spells the word differently in the body of the letter and in its Post-Scriptum.

[38] This is the first mention in the correspondence of a 'female pensioner'. Much later, in colonial Hong Kong, Chinese or Eurasian Common Law wives of European merchants or sea captains were recognized and known to the authorities as 'protected women'. They remained unmarried, but were

safer custody. I propose opening it, and shall let you know the nature of its contents.

From your making no mention of a testamentary provision for his Pensioner, I am induced to bring her case to your notice with some earnestness in the hope that even if she should be omitted in the will you will see fit under the circumstances to continue some allowance to her, the want of which would reduce her to a state of misery that would be extremely distressing to the deceased's friends who respect his memory. She is of a superior class to women in her situation, being educated and able to read and write Chinese, to which, since coming to Macao, has been added a knowledge of Portuguese. She was brought from Canton, and, having become a Christian at Macao, she is of course an *outcast* from her own relations. When your brother last went to India, he left his house, furniture, servants, etc., *under her charge*. On my return to China, when your brother resolved to give up his Macao house, I was commissioned, in conjunction with Mr. [Thomas] Beale, to make arrangements for her living in a house hired for herself, which arrangements were approved of, and I shall continue them in force till I hear further from you. I have not seen the woman since the melancholy news reached me, and I believe she is still ignorant of her loss.

Repeating my condolence on the melancholy occasion that gives rise to our correspondence. I remain, my dear Sir,

Yours very sincerely,

P.S. Since writing the above I have looked over the papers in the Almirah. They are books of accounts up to 1825 and some loose letters up to 1829—apparently of no importance.

56. James Matheson in Canton to Dr Pearson[39] in Canton 15 March 1832

Dear Pearson,

I now take up your favours of the 31st ultimo on the subject of the Ullman fund[40] for the purpose of replying to it. As already stated verbally to you, I have procured the signatures of several subscribers to your paper, setting forth the conditions on which the fund is held; and I think it will be a good plan bye and bye to have a copy made of all the papers for the purpose of being deposited with the young ladies themselves.

---

not infrequently generously provided for by their 'husbands', whether the latter still lived locally or had returned home, and their children were sent to the new public schools provided by the colonial government. (See Hall, Peter, *In the Web*, Heswall, Wirral, 1992, pp. 118–119).

[39] On Dr Alexander Pearson, see above Letter **31**, note 48.

[40] William Jardine and James Matheson enrolled the good offices of Dr Pearson to raise money designed to provide for J. G. Ullman in his retirement. The largest single contributor to the fund (with 24 % of the total) was Hollingworth Magniac who had recruited Ullman in the first place.

The principal sum contributed being	8,800 dollars
besides Mr. Magniac's	2,800 dollars
together	11,600 dollars

This amount may be assumed as the capital of the fund, while the interest earned, say 816 [dollars], may be considered a sinking fund to be [drawn upon] in case of need. The entire sum of 12,416 dollars has interest in our hands and so far, the sinking fund, while suffered to accumulate, serves the purpose of capital.

There can be no inconvenience to us in paying monthly the whole or any portion of the interest that may be required. It only remains, therefore, for you and Sir Andrew Lyungstedt[41] to determine how much they are to draw. Ullman draws at present 80 dollars a month for the current expenses of the family.[42] If we suppose 50 dollars thereof to be his pension and the remaining 30 dollars to be on account of the young ladies' interest, it will perhaps answer every purpose.

Excuse my giving you so much trouble about an affair which is already so much endebted to your exertions, and believe me,

Very sincerely yours,

P.S. We shall endeavour to carve out some mode of assisting Mr. Ullman to [benefit] by some useful employment.

57. James Matheson in Canton to Claudio Da Costa[43] in Lisbon,
18 March 1832

My dear Da Costa,

Your concerns per *Novo Paquete* are so fully explained in my letter to you of 28th Ultimo in triplicate by this conveyance and in *Magniac's & Co.*, of 15th Instant, that nothing remains for me to say here on the subject, except to express my hope that they will turn out very much to your advantage.

[41] Anders Lyungstedt (or Ljungstedt) known as Sir Andrew Lyungstedt (1759–1835). He arrived in Canton in 1798 and took up his post as resident in charge of the Swedish factory. On his return to Sweden, he endowed an industrial school in his home town. He became a knight of Wasa for his benefactions. He returned to Canton as Swedish consul in 1815. In 1821 he retired to Macao where he died in 1835. (Ride, *East India Cemetery*, pp. 142–143). His portrait, painted by Chinnery, is exhibited in the Peabody Essex Museum in Salem, Massachusetts. He was the author of *An Historical Sketch of Portuguese Settlements in China, etc.* republished from the *Chinese Repository* by James Munroe, Boston, 1836. He also published *Contribution to An Historical Sketch of the Roman Catholic Church at Macao, etc.*, Canton, China, 1834. (Lust, *Western Books on China*, p. 34).

[42] In Macao a European family of five could thus live on the equivalent of £240 a year.

[43] Claudio Andriano Da Costa: only a few of his letter from this Lisbon merchant are listed in the *BI*.

I have mentioned to our Agents *Lucas [ ] Gribble & Co.*,[44] that there is nothing that you desire more than that your friends 'should remain perfectly at ease and tranquil in any transactions they may have with you', and that you will consequently be prepared to afford them all the usual mercantile securities on the occasion. As far as you and I are concerned, my dear Da Costa, securities and precautions would be superfluous and useless, if you would only be sure that you are immortal and unassailable by any of those mischances which are spreading their devastation over the land. We must of course always hope for the best, as I do very sincerely, that this may find you in the enjoyment of health and every prosperity, yet without forgetting the possible contingency of your no being present to protect our interest.

We have advanced to Captain Martin[45] 6,262 dollars on a Bottomry Bond[46] for the ship's expenses, and 3,134 dollars on the security of various goods shipped on account of Joao Gonsalves Marques.[47] Further more we have advanced to your protegé, G. Gonzaga,[48] 3,226 dollars for his bills on you against 5,000 pieces of brown Nankeens, 1st chop, consigned to you per *Paquete*. And you must allow me to hope that you will accept his draft, and do the best for his interest in the disposal of the Nankeens. He has been very useful in your concern here, which required his assistance, in consequence of your employing no Agent, and trusting entirely to Saoqua,[49] who would have sacrificed you in declining to ship the full quantity of 1,000 packages, had not Gonzaga brought the circumstance to my notice, and induced me to interefere. Perhaps therefore you might feel disposed to make him some return by exempting his Nankeens from Commission.

In consequence of your recommendation, I have done all I could to promote his interest. But I must candidly tell you that I question much if he has sufficient acuteness to get on in the world. He is so incorrigibly vain as not to be in the least aware of his shallowness of intellect. Thus he has not the same chance of improvement which a more modest man would have, nor the same facility of making up for his own deficiencies by resorting to the advice or assistance of a friend. He had a fair situation with Mr. Veiga but was so impatient of reproof as to give in his resignation, which, to his great surprise and regret, was accepted.

[44] The ship agents were not identified.

[45] Probably Captain Alexander Martin. (Two letters listed in the *BI*).

[46] Bottomry : '1622. A species of contract of the nature of a mortgage, whereby the owner or the master of a ship borrows money at a stipulated interest or premium to enable him to carry on or complete a voyage, and pledges the ship a security for repayment'. (*OED*). Lending on bottomry bonds was seen as risky by *Jardine, Matheson & Co.* Few examples of similar transactions are recorded in the firm's books.

[47] Joao Gonsalvez Marques was not identified.

[48] G. Gonzaga was not identified.

[49] Soaqua: one of the hong merchant.

He afterwards begged of me to intercede with Mr. Veiga to restore him to his place. I did so, but without success.

May I request your kind care for a matted package containing 2 chests of black tea, which Captain Martin has taken charge of, for my brother Captain Matheson,[50] H.M. 23rd Foot, Gibraltar. I enclose an order requesting that it may be delivered to you. Any of my countrymen at Lisbon will tell you whether the Regiment is at Gibraltar. If it be there, forward the tea at once. Should it have gone from your neighbourhood, pray, keep it for yourself.

I congratulate you most sincerely on your favourable prospect as a contractor.[51] And, hoping it may not be many years before I have the pleasure of passing some time with you in a magnificent [house] on the banks of the Tagus.

I remain, my dear Da Costa, Yours sincerely,

P.S. Jardine sends his best remembrances .

58. James Matheson in Canton to Hugh Matheson in Calcutta

7 April 1832

My dear Hugh,

As your letter of 19th January relates purely to business, I am now going to reply to it separately. The sum obtained for the London bills, on account of my Trust fund, 23,207.7.6 Sicca Rupees, is, as you say, a miserable result giving an exchange of less than 203 Sicca Rupees per 100 dollars, whereas I could easily have managed to obtain 206. I gave a preference to Mr. Bannerman's bills[52] at 4 Shillings and 3 pence per dollar, thinking they would turn out better than any other medium of remittance. Being, as you know, near the top of the list of the Company's Factory and returning this season with his fortune, his agent, Mr. Chauncey, being at the head of one of the oldest and best established Houses in London, and the bills being endorsed by that House, whose Agents, *Fairlie, Bonham & Co.*, never fail to take up for our honour any bills which we may endorse (which bye the bye they have never been called upon to do but once), I could never imagine that any sort of objection would be made to them, and far less that any person would be so absurd as to pay a commission of 2½ per cent to any of the tottering Calcutta Houses[53] for endorsing them. I shall be obliged by your letting me know who the person is.

[50] Several of James Matheson's siblings are mentioned in the Letters: 'my brother Duncan' (Letter **154**); 'your brother' (Letters **204**, **216**, **238**); and several sisters, including 'Elizabeth' Matheson (Letters **126**, **216**, **229**, **234**, and **237**).

[51] The term is used here with its meaning of supplier to the army and navy.

[52] See above, Letter **48** for bills drawn on Mr. Bannerman and Chauncey (spelt 'Chauncy' in Letter **48**) and note 122 for *Chauncy, Lucas & Lang.*

[53] Since the failure of *Palmer & Co.* in December 1829, no Agency Houses in Calcutta had been left unscathed. Credit was tight and trading conditions remained difficult until 1834.

As you say it took place after the bills were disposed of I conclude you cannot have been a consenting party to it. And rather than you should sanction any such expedient, or in any way press our bills on the market, we shall always prefer your keeping them in your desk, or even returning them to China. I do not think, however, that after the experience of this year we shall trouble you with many London bills till credit resumes a healthier aspect at Calcutta, for to the generally feverish state of credit do I attribute the objections that have been made, more than to any real occasion for them.

I do not think we shall feel disposed to adopt the plan you suggest of making a reference to *Fairlie Bonham & Co.* in case of need on bills endorsed by us. Because this would be in fact suggesting a doubt as to the probability or possibility of such a reference becoming necessary. Whereas we never endorse bills[54] except such as we are morally certain will be duly honoured.

I enable you to answer any comments which you may hear in the mouths of others, regarding the amount of bills in the market bearing our endorsement. I may observe that we seldom or never remit such bills, except when called for by our constituents; and as the demand for them has, latterly, been very great, especially for Bombay[55] (whence some would appear to have found their way to Calcutta) their amount has been considerable in proportion. So much so that I think it likely three fourth of all Exchange business of Canton have passed through our hands this season. Bills drawn by ourselves are sought after by Parsee agents here, at a penny or a half penny lower than those we endorse; but this we attribute to their ignorance, or to the nature of their orders from Bombay; because if there is any difference, those which we endorse should properly be considered preferable, having the security of the drawer in addition to ours. It would be easy for us in place of endorsing bills, to remit them all to *Fairlie, Bonham & Co.*, and then draw against them; but this, it appears to us, would be weakening the security of all parties, besides the possible injury that might result to *Fairlie, Bonham & Co.* from an enlarged amount of their acceptances being afloat in the home

[54] The endorsement of other parties' bills of exchange as a generalized practice was new in Canton at the time. Until recently, *Jardine, Matheson & Co.* and its predecessor firm, *Magniac & Co.* had tended to buy bills of exchange outright in the Canton market, ship them to *Fairlie, Bonham & Co.* and other London houses as means of remittance, and then draw new bills against their existing assets and deposits. The period 1830–1832 which coincided with a great increase in opium exports from India to China called for ways to accelerate credit-formation and increase liquidity in the market. This was largely provided by the practice of endorsing bills as a matter of routine when it had been much rarer before.

[55] The demand was greater from Bombay, because it was Bombay which was the main engine of growth for opium shipment, Calcutta being bogged down in its indigo problems. Bombay had shipped 6000 to 8000 chests of Malwa until 1830 on average. In 1831 it shipped 12,856 chests and, in 1833, 14,007 chests. (Cheong, *Mandarins and Merchants*, p. 21). For the overall picture of opium shipments in the period, see Letter **43**, note 51. See also in the Introduction above, Section 2: 'The Balance of trade'.

market. In this remark I am far from meaning any disparagement to our London friends; but as all security in commerce is relative, we think that we afford a stronger guarantee, against the hazards incident to all human affairs, by distributing the risk which is inseparable from doing business among a number of good Houses, whose bills we purchase and pay for, rather than relying on any single House, however strong—this strong House, be it remembered, being always prepared to pay in case of need, in protection of our endorsement.

Of the bills which we endorse, those on *Baring Brothers & Co.* are always drawn under credits either from themselves or their attorney at New York, Mr. J. W. Ward,[56] who has authority for the purpose. Other bills are drawn under credits from a known capitalist, John Jacob Astor of New York, who owns land almost equal to a principality in the United States. Bills of *Gledstanes, Drysdale & Co.*[57] are either drawn under credits from them, or on the security of Bills of Lading for goods. They are a House of known property. Mr. Thomas Weeding on whom we draw, is a merchant possessed of at least a lakh of pounds sterling. Thomas Wyatt,[58] on whom we also pass bills, is a still greater capitalist, though only an oilman. Then there are *Messrs. Spode and Copeland*,[59] Chinaware men, of solid wealth—you may have seen some of our bills on them also. On the whole, we feel that we are committing ourselves with people of far greater solidity than those whose bills are vaunted forth at 1/10 1/2 at Calcutta. And if any disappointment should occur to us, divided as our risk is among various parties, it cannot but prove comparatively insignificant.

It may probably prove a useful precaution on future occasions of sending you bills with our endorsement, to state who the drawers are, and the nature of the security on which we rely; authorizing you at the same time to assure parties taking them that *Fairlie Bonham & Co.* will be prepared to take them up in case of need for our honour. But as I have said before, it is not likely that we shall trouble you with any till we hear that credit is reestablished in the mercantile world at Calcutta.

Tell me how the bills of the United States Bank[60] are valued at your place, whether they would sell equally well with those of the first Calcutta Houses. They ought in fact to sell as well as the company's. The security to my mind is better.

[56] On J. W. Ward, Baring's agent in America, see above, Letter **50**.
[57] For *Gledstanes, Drysdale & Co.* see above, Letter **4**, note 12.
[58] Thomas Wyatt: an occasional correspondent with the firm. Only three letters from London are listed in the BI.
[59] For *Spode & Copeland*, see Letter **19**.
[60] The *Bank of the United States*, the largest American bank at the time. Its decision to stop supporting overextended American banks financing exports to Britain in April 1837 led to the resounding bank failures on both sides of the Atlantic. (See below, Letter **145**).

You are at liberty to show this letter of course to your Partner[61] and to James and Robert Lyall, but you must not let the *whole* of it be seen by any other, for I should not wish it to be known that I have spoken so disrespectfully of the Calcutta Houses. In doing so I merely re-echo what is in the mouth of all the world. Yet it will seem unkind on my part to do so, connected as I am with some of them.

Tell Robert Lyall I shall not be surprised if we get 17 Taels per picul for his [ ]. I am afraid I shall not be able to overtake the *Mercury* with a letter for your partner. Pray remember me kindly to him, and say I will answer his letter by the next ship.

You will of course invest all our funds either in opium, or in doing the needful with [chartering a] vessels rather than keep back anything, using your discretion as to price. I wish you had sent [up] opium by the *Red Rover* for the 23,208.7.6 Rupees. I could have sold it at 900 or 890 dollars and sent you the money by the *Mercury* for a second operation. This must be your plan next year. I rather think I made a mistake in mentioning 1,400 Rupees as the safe price in my letter of instruction—as I see in the House's letter, we authorized purchases even at 1,500 Rupees. You know, however, that these limits are never *positive*, and you should never scruple to exceed to the extent of 2 or 3, or even 5 per cent when you see no good to be gained by waiting.

I remain, etc . . .

59. William Jardine in Canton to Captain Grant[62] on board the *Samarang*, 9 April 1832

Dear Sir,

Our friend Allum,[63] the opium broker, has come to represent to us that a friend of his is building a smuggling boat somewhere in your neighbourhood, and requests that we will ask the favour of you to endeavour to afford him any protection which may be in your power, in the event of his being molested by the Mandarins. You must not of course go to the length of committing any acts of violence against the Mandarins; but he thinks the Mandarins will be deterred from giving annoyance by a mere show on your part of a disposition to protect the boat building operation.

Yours faithfully,

[61] Charles Lyall, Hugh Matheson's partner in *Lyall Matheson & Co.* Calcutta. (See above, Letter **47**).

[62] On Captain Alexander Grant and the *Samarang*, see Letter **14**, note 28.

[63] Allum was one of the twenty Canton brokers who bought opium from the firm in 1832. His was by far the largest account, 1,522,428 dollars worth of opium having been sold to him during that year, out of a total 3,687,020 to the twenty brokers. (*JMArch.*, A7/76).

60. *Smith Elder & Co.* in London to *Magniac & Co.* in Canton,
17 April 1832[64]

Dear Sirs,

In your order handed to us by *Messrs. Magniac & Co.* under date of 10th December last there are six Copies of *Stevens on Average*[65] mentioned which is at present so entirely out of print that we cannot procure any to supply your wants. When the new edition appears however we will take care to send you the required number.

Ellis's *British Tariff*[66] is also so scarce that of the 12 ordered we can only procure 9 Copies, which is less to be regretted as it is probable that a new edition will appear in the course of 6 months hence.

We have of our own accord sent in addition to your order 2 Copies of a new Work entitled *MacCullocks Commercial Dictionary*[67] which is in such high estimation here that we doubt not it will be extremely acceptable to you and therefore hope to find we have not exceeded our discretion on this point in vain.

Although we have no further interest in this Work than in any other of the same kind, yet if we felt warranted we would not have hesitated to send you 12 instead of 2, believing it will tend to your advantage, but nor having any such discretionary power vested in us we can only hope that in sending these 2 we have not committed ourselves in any way likely to prove injurious to either of us.

We should mention that *Martin on Averages*[68] being a Country Book, done up there, and delivered by the Publisher in boards, cannot be had in a better state or appearance than what those copies sent now present.

We are Dear Sirs, your obedient Servants.

[64] This letter was written to *Marwick & Lane* in Canton, acting in this instance as a letterbox or supplier to *Magniac & Co.*

[65] Stevens, Robert, (of Lloyds), An *Essay on Average and on other Subjects connected with the Contract of Marine Insurance*, London, 1813.

In maritime insurance, the concept of 'average' is based on the principle that 'no one ought to be enriched by another's loss' (*nemo debet locupletari aliena jactura*). Average: 'A term used in commerce and navigation to signify a contribution made by the individuals, when they happen to be more than one, to whom a ship, or the goods on board it, belong, or by whom it or they are insured [. . .] so the loss may be equal on all. (McCulloch, *Dictionary of Commerce*).

[66] Ellis, Robert, (of the Customs House, London), *The British Tariff for 1829–1830*, London, Longman, Orme, Brown, & Green, 1829.

[67] McCulloch, J. R., *Dictionary, Practical, Theoretical, and Historical, of Commerce and Commercial Navigation*, London, Longman, rees, Orme, Brown, Green, & Longman, 1832.

[68] Martin, M., *A Compendium of the Practice of Averages*, Liverpool, 1823.

61. William Jardine in Canton to de Vitre[69] in Bombay, 10 August 1832

My dear de Vitre,

I have been so much annoyed and disappointed with the result of the drug market here during the last season; and the miserable prospects our friends have now before them, as to the result of the operations of this season arising chiefly from erroneous reports from Bombay respecting the probable supply of Malwa opium, that various plans have at different times suggested themselves to me, as calculated to render the present depressed state of the market useful to those who may have sufficient nerve to venture upon the crop of the coming season.

By every report from your quarter yet received the ensuing crop is likely to be bountiful, and there being now no restrictions as to quantity beyond that which [exposure] to a non remunerating price would produce, unless the drug is bought very low, say 600 to 800 Rupees on board, I see no safety for the holders of it.

Take 800 Rupees or 400 dollars laid down here as the price, and suppose the supply to be 14,000 chests and sold at an average of 500 dollars per chest. The money expended by the Chinese in this species of the drug, would be nearly as much as has been expended in any one year, and considerably more than the average expenditure of the three last years, while the whole supply, after deducting the charges of keeping, would yield a very moderate profit to the purchasers on that portion kept till {July} or May [and] would stand them, on the most moderate calculations, 450–460 dollars per chest at the former and 470–480 dollars at the latter date, from which must be deducted the Commission of selling and remitting proceeds. This rough calculation is made on an interest of ¾ per cent per month.

Suppose on the other hand 8,000 chests only are sent on, and sold at an average of 875 dollars per chest, the same sum would be realized with a reduced expense of freight and demurrage, while the purchasers would have 6,000 chests for nothing; on the other hand, suppose 8,000 chests sold at 700 dollars clear of charges and the proceeds remitted back at 220 Rupees per 100 dollars, which is not very exorbitant, and the purchasers would have a profit of 11,200,000 Rupees to meet charges of shipping, freight and interest, with 6,000 chests of Malwa costing nothing but warehousing rent, which stock would render them very independent of the crop of the following season, and if shipped so as to reach [here] in March of April, would come into a bare market rather high priced,—and follow the matter a little further, the proceeds might be invested here in the new drug at very very low prices indeed—and, as low prices would check cultivation, the

[69] Mathias Theosodius Denis de Vitre was H. P. Haddow's partner in *Remington & Co.* Bombay. Some 100 letters from his pen are listed in the *BI.* He was an old friend of William Jardine, hence the free and easy tone of the letter. No letter written by William Jardine comes closer to a spontaneous note on how best to corner the Malwa market. Particularly noticeable is his belief in the inelasticity of demand, and in the monopolistic control of supply as the only means of lifting prices.

supply of the next season would probably be small and admit of prices rising again to 500 to 600 dollars per chest.

Even if the 8,000 chests realized only to 650 dollars (which they must do if that kept back can be rendered a dead letter), the purchasers would have their own money returned, say at 220 Rupees—11,440,000 Rupees for 11,200,000, and 6,000 chests for charges.

Had this plan been pursued this season and 8,000 or even 9,000 chests only been sent on, they would readily have yielded 750 to 800 dollars per chest, or say 8,500 chests to have come on netted 765 dollars per chest, or 6,502,500 dollars at 220 Rupees per 100 would be 14,305,500 Rupees—and supposing the whole 13,000 chests to have cost 1,100 Rupees per chest, the amount would have been 14,300,000 Rupees, leaving purchasers 4,500 chests to pay interest, freight [and charges] (while those holding the old opium in China would have been [spared] from heavy losses.

Had I been on the spot, with cash at command, I would not have hesitated one moment about purchasing the whole 13,000 at 1,100 or 1,000 Rupees and made 4,500 of them disappear for a time by some means or other.

I through[70] out these crude hints and calculations for your guidance, not doubting that they may have occurred to you before, but they can do no harm, further than probably exposing the wildness and folly of my plans.

Under this feeling, I send them to you and remain, My dear de Vitre,

Yours sincerely,

62. John Macvicar in Glasgow to William Jardine and James Matheson in Canton, 2 September 1832

Dear Sirs,

I avail of the departure of the *Norman* for Manila, to write you. I wrote you very fully from London, and of July, by the *Pauline* and *Elizabeth.* It is about three weeks since I left London, but nothing very material has occurred there since then. A statement of the affairs of *Fairly, Clark, Innes & Co.*[71] has been made. Their debts are about 800,000 pounds sterling, exclusive of acceptances to their Calcutta correspondents of 260,000 pounds, which the Calcutta Houses should provide for, but which it is feared they will not. They show a list of bad debts. Worthless—480,000 pounds, and they etimate their available assets at 530,000. If this item is not overestimated they would in any case be able to pay a dividend of 10 shillings per pound, but perhaps it may be safer to calculate on one

[70] An unusual slip of the pen.

[71] In spite of the capital reorganization and the arrival of Messrs. D. Clark and Innes as new partners, the firm did not survive.

of 5 shillings to 5 shillings and 8 pence.[72] It has been proposed that they wind up their affairs [following the] inspection, which will I think be probably carried into effect. Our last dates from India and from Bombay 17th April, with dates for Calcutta being only 6th March.

Timothy Wiggin[73] is paying all your drafts on *Fairlie, Clark, Innes & Co.* as they become due. And accepting all your drafts on them as they appear. A good [number of them] lately came in from Bombay, all of which are regularly honoured as they appear. Such Bills as are not at maturity, and which have been previously accepted by *Fairlie, Clark, Innes & Co.*, he does not accept, but without positively binding himself says they will be paid by him when due.[74] One or two Bills under these circumstances I have thought it as well to discount for the holders, giving them a letter [of indemnity], but will present them for payment when due to Wiggins.[75] With one or two timid persons in the Country, I thought this would do no harm. It gives me great pleasure to hear from Mr. Matheson that happen what may at Calcutta, you would not be seriously involved. We look forward to this fate if that house in unviable, and it is greatly apprehended that one, if not both of the houses will go.

I do not know of any change in the Credit of [ ] I wrote you about by the *Elizabeth.* At present Credit appears good in London. The advance in prices of goods impedes shipments to you very much. I have some goods preparing, but do not know if I can get a sufficient quantity to gather to take up a ship. If I can I will dispatch her early in November.

I remain dear Sirs, yours very faithfully.

[72] In a liquidation the inference was that the creditors might recover between a quarter and a half of their assets.

[73] Timothy Wiggin, of *Timothy Wiggin & Co.*, 'Merchant, 16, King's Yard, Coleman Street', London. (*RLB*), and subsequently of '7, Tokenhouse Yard', London. (*TLCD*). In 1832, *Timothy Wiggin & Co.* was an established bank financing American exports to England. It was fortunate for *Jardine, Matheson & Co.*, in the first few months of its existence under its new name, that Timothy Wiggin 'honoured' the drafts the Canton partners had drawn on *Fairlie, Bonham & Co.*, or *Fairlie, Clark Innes*, but which the London firm was no longer in a position to pay. The theoretical possibility of *Fairlie, Bonham & Co's* collapse had been anticipated by James Matheson and William Jardine, (See above, Letter **58**), but they were now faced with the reality of their London friends' bankruptcy.

[74] The uncertainty regarding eventual payment to holders of bills drawn by partners of financially sound Houses of Agency and bearing their signatures was always a source of anxiety. Given the time lag for the news to reach Canton, Letters **68**, **69**, and **70** below, which were written once the news was known in Canton, bear testimony to that anxiety.

[75] John Macvicar, for one, seems to have had entire confidence in Timothy Wiggin's honouring the bills at maturity, since he was prepared, on these two occasions to discount the paper, and hold it to maturity after paying the previous holder.

63. James Innes on board the *Jamesina*[76] [in Dansburg Bay] to James Matheson in Canton 7 December 1832[77]

Dear M[atheson],

I write Chinese Letters in duplicate, yet if this arrives pay no attention to them. On the 25th of November Humbug and his Partner landed *here* for Amoy. I had also communicated and made engagements *here direct* with two smuggling boats and their merchants but both these events left fourteen *free* days. I resolved to employ that time in a visit to my old friends at 'Seven-Chu-Fu' where the *Jamesina* got the 28 November. The courier went on there with a list of 28 names and asked them to come off and buy, since then, directly, without the intervention of a Broker, sales are made as under:

Quality	Price	Chests	Dollars
Benares	870	151	131,370
Heavy old Patna	870	2	1,740
Light old Patna	800	23	18,400
New Patna	870	29	25,230
Malwa	700	1	700
Chests sold		206	177,440

On these there is no brokerage; and cumshew[78] of 5% is paid to Captain Hector by the 6 Chinese to your order.

The result almost entirely in Dollars, about a score of Gold bars, and some Doubloons, hardly any Sycee. Notwithstanding what I wrote you from Namho, I have as yet only sold 14 Piculs of Rice, and that at 3 Dollars per 100 catties.

Founded on the information of my friends on shore confidence is great in nearly an entire delivery in *all January*: but *no other event* except being nearly cleaned out *will* induce me to return to Canton without endeavouring to carry your wishes into effect as to *Sylph*.

The *Sylph* was seen in Tat-ho-po Roads, trying to sell Opium about last of October, or 1st November. On the 7 November she passed through Chin Chew bay without anchoring. I have in compliance with your instructions sent notes for *Sylph*[79] in Chinese, and English by several good [couriers] as far as

[76] See above, Letter **49**, note 9, on the *Jamesina* 1832 expedition. 'Dansburg Bay' was not identified, but the Jamesina must have anchored in a bay close to Amoy.

[77] Remarkably, the letter was sent not by ship, but 'per courier over-land'. The actual form of address is: 'Dear M'. At the back, William Jardine wrote: 'Received December 22nd, Answered December 27th by James Matheson'. No copy of James Matheson's reply, however, was found in the relevant Out-letter book. For the price of an overland courier in China at the time, see the last sentence of this letter.

[78] Cumshew or cumshaw; '1839. In the Chinese ports: a gratuity; a baksheesh'. (*OED*). The word was used by Europeans and Americans resident in Canton long before 1839.

[79] For the *Sylph*, see also above Letter **49**, note 9. By the time James Innes was writing this letter, no news of the *Sylph* had been received by the firm and the partners were concerned about the whereabouts and safety of the ship and its crew. The Reverend Carl Gutzlaff was on board the *Sylph*, serving as interpreter, then transferred to the *Jamesina*.

Ningpo.[80] I contemplate returning to 'Seven-chu-fu' to keep engagements already made, in 14 days. Then *certainly* to Fu-chu-fu, and the *Sylph* once spoken probably to Kie-lau-tou.[81]

Sugar[82] is very high and large quantities going North to Ningpo and Pekin.

We are in excellent health and barring a few stormy days the weather is delightful. *All well together* ! and a sincere desire for your interests from the Captain down to the [petty] officer. Larkins men are well-behaved and very useful. Please write Captain Innes[83] in duplicate to inform my Mother of my welfare of this date.

I recommend the return of the courier to me in Chin Chew bay (failing that, Fou chu fu) with your instructions. If he delivers this in 12 free days he is worth thirty dollars.

Affectionately,

64. *10th Canton Insurance Company*[84] in Canton to *Lyall Matheson & Co.* in Calcutta.

10 December 1832

Dear Sirs,

We beg leave to inform you that at a general meeting held in Canton for the purpose of establishing a continuation of the long existing Insurance Company at this place it is resolved to form another copartnership under the denomination of 'the Tenth Canton Insurance Company' to be divided into 110 shares, commencing business of the 1st January 1833, and terminating on 31st December 1835. The members of the copartnership will be, for the most part, the same as those of the preceding company, the Ninth, which will expire on the 31st instant.

Having been appointed to act as the general Agents, we propose that you should be nominated the Agents in Calcutta; and we are instructed to wait upon

[80] Near the mouth of the Yangtze river.

[81] Seven-chu-fu, Fu-chu-fu and Kie-lau-tou: stations or anchorage points off the China coast which, like 'Dansburg Bay' above, were commonly known to *Jardine, Matheson & Co.'s* captains and partners, but have not been identified.

[82] The ships' captains and interpreters were asked to find out and report on anything that could sell up the China coast, not just opium.

[83] The commander of the *Jamesina* in this 1832 expedition (i.e. the James Innes who wrote this letter) was *the* notorious Captain James Innes who traded opium at Macao and Canton and was on friendly terms with William Jardine and James Matheson. (See Letter **9**, note 48) The mention here of a different 'Captain Innes' who was in a position to 'inform [the writer's] mother of [his] welfare to his date', does, however, raise a question of identity. The 'Captain Innes' referred to here by James Innes is probably Captain John Innes, a commander of East India Company ships (see Letter **29**, note 38), who later retired in Hendon (Letter **77**). On the evidence of this letter, the two captains Innes were at least friends, and probably brothers.

[84] The *10th Canton Insurance Company* was the last to be set up in association with *Dent & Co.* See above Letter **16**, note 2.

you accordingly in the enclosed Power of Attorney requesting at your hands the exercise of the utmost zeal and circumspection, in order to secure a continuance of the same degree of prosperity by which the Association has been generally distinguished.

We are likewise directed to acquaint you that 24 shares are appropriated for distribution among shareholders at Calcutta,[85] in selecting whom you will of course give a preference to those parties who may be most likely to benefit the Office, by the extent of their business. You will request them to send an authority to someone in China to sign the Deed of Partnership for them, which we shall willingly undertake should they have no other agents.

The Agents in Bombay will be *Messrs. Remington & Co.*, and in London *Messrs. Fairlie Clark Innes & Co.*[86]

We are instructed to authorize your taking risks upon any unexceptionable vessels *from Calcutta only* to such ports of the world as you may deem expedient, payable in case of loss either in Calcutta, by *Messrs. Fairlie Clark Innes & Co.* in London, *Messrs. Remington & Co.* in Bombay, or by us in Canton; not exceeding on one vessel eighty five thousand dollars, or Sicca Rupees one hundred and seventy thousand (170,000), being regulated in regard to rates of premium by the other insurance offices at your Presidency, where not otherwise instructed by us, and by your own judgment, to which we also beg to refer for any minor points not here provided against. We beg leave forcibly to call your attention to the necessity of confining your insurances to the most unexceptionable risks; those of doubtful character answering generally no other purpose than to absorb the premiums received by the others. We particularly request that you will avoid insurances on Blocks,[87] unless of the very first class. After a vessel has run three or four voyages without a general repair, she is almost sure to require some considerable outlay; and the underwriter is lucky if he escapes being called on to pay for them. In this view, time policies on Blocks, renewable for an indefinite period are particularly objectionable.

[85] To be the manager of an Insurance syndicate, as *Jardine, Matheson & Co.* was for this *10th Canton Insurance Company*, was not only useful for the management fees which accrued to the syndicate manager. The other two principal benefits were patronage in the allocation of shares, and the investment of the premium funds which was collected over a three-year period. Usually the dividend was paid in one lump sum at the liquidation of the syndicate, five years after inception. On the practice of maritime insurance under *Jardine, Matheson & Co.'s* management, see: Le Pichon, *Origines de Hong Kong*, pp. 261–277).

[86] By referring to *Fairlie, Clark, Innes & Co.* as the London agents for the *10th Canton Insurance Company*, (and indeed by actually appointing them as such through a similar letter of even date), William Jardine and James Matheson still thought in mid-December 1832 that their long-standing London correspondents were credit-worthy.

[87] 'Blocks' were encumbered ships. (See Letter **122** below). Insurance companies were often reluctant to underwrite this risk.

Indeed time policies of any description are far from desirable; unless there be some limitation of the voyage to be underwritten, there being some voyages which every prudent underwriter would wish to avoid, such as the neighbourhood of the Isle of France,[88] during the hurricane months, Torres Strait,[89] small vessels trading among the many islands, etc., etc. . .

Although not hitherto the case, we submit to your consideration whether it may not be advisable that the Calcutta shareholders should nominate a committee to aid you in the management, and to arrange the safe investment, at interest, of the accumulating premiums, which should be either in Government Securities, or in some other mode satisfactory to all parties, whenever your current realization shares amount to any considerable sums.

We request you will appoint as surveyor to the office Mr. J. J. James,[90] formally Chief Mate in the Honorable Company's service.

We are, etc. . .

1833

65. *10th Canton Insurance Company* in Canton to *Fairlie, Clark, Innes & Co.* in London, 4 January 1833

Gentlemen,

The *10th Canton Insurance Company* having commenced operations under our management for three years from 1st instant, in the usual alternative successing to the 9th which was conducted by our neighbours, *Messrs. Thomas Dent & Co.*, we have taken the liberty to recommend your highly respectable firm as Agents in London for the Association, venturing to anticipate your obliging readiness to undertake the charge, which we are accordingly instructed to confide to you.

The *10th Company* consists of 110 shares, an augmentation having been made to enable its embracing the leading American merchants at Canton.[1] We annex a

[88] Today's Mauritius.

[89] Torres Strait: between Cape York in Australia and the Island of New Guinea.

[90] J. J. James was not identified. The Mr. James mentioned at the end of Letter **72** below is probably a different person.

[1] Until the year 1833, the number of shares divided among the insurance syndicate participants was usually 60. Receiving shares was a lucrative privilege, as the annual yield to each recipient could be 'three to four thousand dollars' (Greenberg, *British Trade*, p. 171). The appended list of Canton shareholders of the *10th Canton Insurance Company* shows that the share pool was increased in order to accommodate four American firms which increasingly contributed to the insurance business: *Russell & Co., N. Dunn & Co. Olyphant and Co.*, and J. P. Sturgis. This was one of the first instances in the East of Americans being invited to participate in an otherwise all-British shareholding structure. The exclusion had not affected the Indian community in the same way. In commercial and financial transactions, the Indians and particularly the Bombay Parsees had been considered British and had long been members of insurance syndicates. The British attitude towards Parsee merchants started changing in 1834, following the so-called 'Napier Fizzle'. (See Letter **97**)

list of the principal shareholders here and in Bombay; those at Calcutta remaining to be arranged for by the Agents at that Presidency will be communicated to you hereafter.

The maximum insurable on any vessel is eighty five thousand (85,000) Spanish Dollars. The Agents at Bombay are *Messrs. Remington & Co.*, and at Calcutta *Messrs. Lyall Matheson & Co.*, both of whom are authorized to grant policies on approved risks payable by you in case of loss or average to which we request your attention.

The premiums on such risks will be remitted to you, for accumulation at the most favourable rate of interest which you may be able to afford, subject to our control, after answering such calls as may unfortunately be made upon you.

Messrs. Cockerell & Co.'s[2] compensation as former Agents to the Association appears to have consisted of a commission of 5 per cent on the net amount of all premiums on policies payable in London, the returns being previously deducted. And we trust the same will be satisfactory to you.

We enclose a register of Policies granted and payable eventually by you, and remain, Gentlemen, your most obedient servants.

P.S. *Messrs. Charles Thomas & Co.* will be appointed Agents for the Company at Singapore, with a view to protecting its interest in the transshipments made there, but it has not yet been determined to authorize their granting policies.

Members of the 10th insurance Company:

In Canton : *Thomas Dent & Co., Jardine, Matheson & Co., R. Turner & Co., Whiteman & Co., {Roy Rawson} & Co.*, James Innes, Framjee Pestonjee, *Russel & Co., J.R. Latimer & Co., Olyphant & Co.*,[3] *N. Dunn & Co., Blight & Co.*, J.P. Sturgis,[4] J.J.F. Veiga, Antonio Pereira, Oliver H. [ ], Thomas Beale, John Templeton, Joseph Cragg.

At Singapore : *Charles Thomas & Co.*

In Bombay : *Remington & Co., Forbes & Co.*, Jamsetjee Jejeebhoy, Cursetjee Jamsetsee, Hormasjee Bhicajee, Bomanjee Hormasjee,[5] with others to be arranged by the Agent there.

[2] *Cockerell & Co.* (spelt '*Cockerill & Co.*' in Letter **182**): 'Merchants, 8 Austin Frianrs, Old Broad Street', London. (*TLCD*).

[3] *Olyphant & Co.* An American firm founded in Canton in 1826 by David W. C. Olyphant. By 1837, the firm had admitted two more partners, C. N. Talbot, and C. W. King. 'Olyphant was a man of high moral principles, and his Company was one of only two foreign firms in China, both of them American, which appear not to have been trading in opium because of the strict Quaker tenets of their founders. (The other firm was *Nathan Dunn & Co.*). Olyphant died in Cairo on 10 June 1851 during his voyage home' (Bard, *Traders of Hong Kong*, p. 81).

[4] James Perkins Sturgis. A private American merchant from Boston. He had arrived in Canton in 1809. (Hunter, *The Fan Kwae at Canton*, p. 10; *Bits of Old China*, pp. 157, 276).

[5] Bomanjee Hormasjee (sometimes spelt 'Hormusjee') is recorded as a customer in the firm's accounts from 1830–1836. (*JMArch.*, A2–15, A2–16). Hormasjee Bhicajee was not identified.

Shares number :			
In all:	At Bombay		25
	China		63
	Calcutta		21
	Singapore		1
		Total	110

66. *10th Canton Insurance Company* in Canton to Charles Thomas in Singapore, 24 January 1833

Dear Sirs,

We have the pleasure to acquaint you that on the recent establishment of the *10th Canton Insurance Company*, under our management, it was resolved to nominate your respectable firm as Agents for the Association at Singapore, and in recommending its interest to your best attention, we feel assured of its being cared for with your usual efficiency and zeal.

Adverting to the limited extent of good risks originating at Singapore, the impossibility of realizing premiums except in produce,[6] and the unfavourable experiences of some of the Bengal offices having branches there, it has not been considered advisable for the present to authorize your granting policies. You will be pleased to consider your functions as limited in general watchfulness over the interests of the Canton [office] whenever they may come under your notice as requiring protection. More especially in regards to risks from China to Singapore and thence by ship or ships to England.

We will endeavour to give you notice of all such risks by the vessels conveying the property insured, and to place you in communication with the consignees thereof.

We will thank you to consider it your duty in the first place: to take care that the office shall not have a greater risk than the regulated maximum of eighty thousand dollars (85,000) or about 19,000 to 21,000 pounds sterling transshipped to anyone vessel; secondly, you will endeavour to prevent transshipments being made at the risk of the Office to vessels having any palpable defects or inferiority which may afford room for questioning their seaworthiness; and to prevent vessels in which the Office has a risks from sailing imperfectly, manned inefficiently, or at greater draft of water than in the general opinion of maritime men may be considered compatible with the safe conveyance home of their cargoes, more particularly where rounding the Cape of Good Hope in winter.

[6] The *Canton Insurance Office* agent in Singapore was allowed to underwrite only transshipping risks, and not general shipping risks. This was the consequence of Singapore being principally a place for transhipping goods in transit from China to Britain or to India. It had no exports of its own except 'produce', i.e. fruit and perishable goods.

You will of course make your interference as little felt as possible and never thwart the arrangements of individuals without a clear necessity for so doing.[7] In these cases gentle counsel with the parties concerned will in general be more efficacious than argumentative discussions which we trust you will avoid. Parties disregarding your wishes will do so at their peril and it appears to us that every purpose will be answered by your serving them with a simple intimation thereof, which should also be made known to *Messrs. Fairlie Clark, Innes*, the Agents in London, and to us here.

Be pleased to keep a register of all transshipments which you may know of at the risk of the Office, and forward copies to these gentlemen as well as to us here. The premium on risks from China to Singapore and thence to London in A1 vessels, or vessels with between decks of the East India [Company] is 3½ per cent; on inferior vessels, 4 per cent. You will therefore distinguish to which of these classes each risk belongs.

Messrs. Remington & Co. are the Agents in Bombay and *Messrs. Lyall Matheson & Co.* at Calcutta; and you will of course correspond with those Houses when occasion may require it.

In your remuneration as Agents, it has been resolved to offer you a share in the Office.[8] But should you prefer in lieu of this a fixed sum such as your commission of 5 per cent would probably amount to, had you been given authority to underwrite, we shall have no objection to arrange it and we await the expression of your wishes on this head.

We are, dear Sirs, etc. . .

67. Jamsetjee Jejeebhoy in Bombay to William Jardine in Canton,

27 March 1833

My dear Sir,

The *Golconda* being under dispatch for your place tomorrow I avail myself of the opportunity to acknowledge your esteemed favors of the 10th, 24th and 29th December and 27th January last, and note the contents thereof and return you my thanks for all the valuable information respecting the market of Drug and Cotton, etc.

The *Charlotte* and *Bombay Castle* are quite ready to start at moment's notice, but we think given dispatch now and a week hence will make no difference in the

[7] A rule of management generally followed by the partners themselves in their dealings with their own employees, and in particular with their ship captains, in order to develop virtues of entrepreneurship and resourcefulness.

[8] Insurance agents were normally remunerated through a percentage of the business they wrote. As Charles Thomas was not allowed to write business, a special provision had to be made for his remuneration.

passage. One reason for detaining is to know the Europe views by steamer expected every day, but we resolved to give leave by first week of next month. Framjee have sold half of this ship to Captain Boucher[9] who is to be expected from England to take command on her return from China and directing his agent to dispatch her in all June from China.[10] She carrie 230 chests of Opium which we undertake to provide her merely to prevent him from taking the Freight at low rate then 20 Rupees. She carry the whole Cargo of old cotton.

Our first dispatch from Malwa is not yet reached here but hope to expect by next week. The price of Drug, now ruling at 1,050 to 1060 Rupees per Chest, small sale effecting for want of cash, but if any person wished to purchase few hundred chests the price immediately rose up 100 Rupees more. Mr. McLeod[11] says in his *price current* 14,500 Chests of Opium will likely to go to China and as you have so much confidence in his statement I refrained to remark any thing on the subject, but only to say that passes obtained here from interior until now from Government are about 5,500 Chests and you must have had of correspon-ding date of last year the quantity obtained. However the time is so far advanced now if any merchant wished to send commission to buy the Opium at Malwa, it is doubtful to say whether arrive in time or not, you will hear from me on the subject by the *Fort William*.

She now got 2,300 Bales on Board. We hope to give dispatch about 20th of next month with full cargoes of new and superior Cotton except 1,200 Bales of past year's of same description. We have made two marks[12] merely for convenient to Land in two Hongs to insure early and advantageous sale. This year Company's have 7 ships and you may expect same quantity as last year from this quarter, unless war and Country ships employed in Transport service, but I don't think the case although the owners of several ships deferred to wait the news.

Our *Good Success* arrived at Madras on the 1st instant and discharged the Freight Goods on the 9th instant and on the 11th still there were directed to start immediately, but very careless on the part of Captain, which annoyed us very

[9] Captain Boucher was not identified. 'Framjee', the seller of half the shares in the ship, refers to Framjee Cowasjee, one of William Jardine's early business partners. Very few private ships until the 1830s were owned outright by single private merchants. A ship's shares were usually spread among a small syndicate of owners, each individual ownership being expressed as a fraction of 32 or even 64, e.g., 16/32nd or half an interest. As the anticipated end of the East India Company's charter approached in 1833, private merchants increasingly saw the need of owning ships outright so long as they controlled a sufficiently large flow of goods to ensure that the ships were in constant use.

[10] The likely meaning of the sentence is that Captain Boucher will await the return of the *Galconda* in Bombay.

[11] Probably the 'Mr. Crawford McLeod' mentioned in Letter **5**.

[12] Sent to the consignees were detailed lists of the goods shipped. The goods listed referred very precisely to 'marks' written on the consignments. Often these marks were initials, and numbers, often framed in rectangular or diamond shapes, and either carved or stamped in the wood of the chests, or otherwise clearly written on the bales or packages of goods dispatched.

much. As soon as she arrives we shall dispatch her, immediately with our cargo and I thank you for having obtained so handsome Freight for her, and hope you had, before this reaches you, sold the Rice and rendered us the Account of the owner.

We have received all the accounts and account of the last year, from your respectable Firm, and I delighted to observe you have given so active and so prompt attention to my wishes. Accept my acknowledgment for the kindness you have shewn to our interest, in all occasion and I am sensible your sincerity towards our Interest, and extremely regret for our n° 27 letter[13] to your Firm and hope you forget.

This season the Europe Bills so much received by almost all the merchants that they unable to dispose at any rate, and consequently total stoppage all the commercial dealings for want of means, and the merchants now discover the errors, in authorizing their agents to send Europe Bills and very likely every body will instruct for Sycee[14] and I beg you will buy for us the former at cheapest rate before hands any quantity you may deem proper. We have large fund at home unable to sell our Bill in face of present Exchange, beside no buyer. The Liverpool friends attended to buy the cotton and the holder oblige the send the Bills to England for recovery. If you can make any arrangement for Court of Directors[15] I presume will do well to all purposes.

You shall hear from me, by the *Bombay Castle*. She will follow her after a week, and remain with much regard and Esteem, My dear Jardine,

Your most Sincerely,

68. William Jardine in Canton to Thomas Weeding in London,

4 April 1833[16]

Dear Weeding,

I am not aware whether Mr. Matheson has written to you from Singapore, but think it more than probable he has, and that you are aware of his having sent a power of attorney to Hollingworth Magniac Esq., and, should he be absent or

[13] Not identified.

[14] The credit difficulty in the Calcutta houses affected the East India agencies in London as well, with the result that most London commercial bills sent to Bombay as means of remittance were tainted. Jamsetjee Jejeebhoy, like other Bombay traders, wanted remittances in sycee silver instead.

[15] Remittances in bills drawn on the Court of directors of the East India Company were equally acceptable.

[16] This is the first of three Letters (with Letters **69** and **70**) which illustrate the acute difficulty affecting the London bill markets in the spring of 1833, owing to the failure of yet more Calcutta houses. As soon as the news reached James Matheson, he sailed to Calcutta to assess the situation. Meanwhile William Jardine was left in Canton to send remittances to his most trusted London friends, Thomas Weeding and Hollingworth Magniac, in the hope that all the bills which the firm had drawn on *Fairlie, Clark Innes & Co.* would eventually be honoured.

decline acting, to your good self to enable you to protect our interests in these troubled times, should the failures in Calcutta produce a run on the East India houses of Agency at home. Mr. Matheson was at Singapore on his way to Bombay, when he heard of the failure of *Alexander & Co., MacIntosh and Co.*, and of *Fergusson & Co.*[17] having appealed to their creditors.

By precaution [ ], since the accounts reached us, we have secured ourselves against serious loss even should our friends *Fergusson & Co.* fail, and Mr. Matheson having proceeded to Calcutta in place of Bombay I have not the least apprehension from that quarter. The balance is very small indeed, not exceeding 30,000 Rupees.[18]

Mr. Matheson has explained fully, in a letter addressed to Mr. Hollingworth Magniac, absent to your good self, the view he takes of the probable consequence to *Fairlie, Clark, Innes & Co.* of the failure of *F[ergusson] & Co.*, request[ing] your assistance in protecting our interests[19] should there be any necessity of interfering. He has also spelled out the manner in which he thinks you can protect us from harm, and has forwarded a power made in conformity with the view he takes.

I forward by this conveyance a similar power to Hollingworth Magniac, absent to your good self, and have to beg you will do everything in your power to protect the interests of the firm of *Jardine, Matheson & Co.* I shall continue remitting to you in bills when they offer, Sycee and Raw Silk, and shall be particularly obliged by your assisting Mr. Magniac, should he require your assistance, which I sincerely hope he will not, as all we have to guard against is that our remittances may not be appropriated to their purposes, them meeting our drafts against them.

If *Fairlie, Clark, Innes & Co.* are in difficulty, and we protected, I should wish our account with them to be balanced, so that we may not add to their difficulties, and should Magniac require any funds for that purpose, I have to beg you may assist him what he may apply for.

By the *Falcon*, to be dispatched this afternoon, we are sending you some Sycee and Raw Silk, but I cannot forward the bills of lading, not having yet received them from Lintin where the ship is loading.

[17] *Alexander & Co.* failed on 12 December 1832. A few days later, in the New Year 1833, it was *Mackintosh & Co.*'s turn to fail, the agency house to whose partners James Matheson was related. *Fergusson & Co.* was the firm's principal Calcutta correspondent, until the foundation of *Lyall Matheson & Co.* (Letter **58**). The fact that it had appealed to its creditors left some hope that it might be reorganized. Eventually these hopes were dashed. (See Letter **80**).

[18] Approximately 12,300 dollars, or 3,000 pounds sterling.

[19] The difficulty of remitting goods or financial instruments directly to a house on the verge of collapse was that, if the failure occurred prior to bills coming due for payment, the assets sent would be pooled for the benefit of *all* the creditors. The 'necessity of interfering' would arise precisely in a bankruptcy situation. The holder of the Canton firm's power of attorney could then ensure that the remittances sent be segregated and the proceeds used towards the payment of bills coming due.

We send you some bills on *Messrs Baring & Co.* by this conveyance via New York. I shall have occasion to draw on you for about 8,000 pounds sterling through India. The bills are to go to Calcutta per *Falcon*, from thence to Bombay where they will be negotiated, and cannot reach you for many months. We shall have ample time to provide for them, as Bills offer here, or by Raw Silk, of which there is still a little in the market. The shipments of silk have been moderate this season, and will reach England much later than usual. Prices should improve with it.

I am sorry to hear so bad an account of camphor and musk, having sent you a large supply of each; but they have been purchased at low prices with the expectation of about a pecul of musk, and must make a fair remittance even at your quotations: manage them as you think best, and believe me, My dear Weeding,

Yours sincerely,

N.B.: *Messrs. Fergusson & Co.* have applied to their creditors for a letter of licence, which may tend to involve our friends in Broad Street.

69. William Jardine in Canton to Hollingworth Magniac in London,

4 April 1833

My dear Magniac,

You must, ere this can reach you, be in possession of Mr. Matheson's letter from Singapore dated February 3rd, 1833, giving cover for a power of attorney to enable you to protect our interests in case of need, and though I sincerely hope you may have no occasion to use it, I should never forgive myself were I to allow the property of ourselves and others to suffer from any neglect of mine in not furnishing you with a similar power.

I have therefore made a very short visit to Macao for the puposc of obtaining Mr. Plowden's[20] signature; and herewith forward a similar power to that forwarded by Mr. Matheson; and have only to confirm in every particular the instructions he has given you, adding my earnest entreaty to his that you will do everything in your power to protect us from harm should there be occasion for your interference.

Mr. Matheson has explained fully what we wish you to do, and I have nothing to add to what he has said on the subject. We are both most anxious not to give offence to *Messrs. Fairlie, Clark, Innes & Co.* But we should consider ourselves unworthy of being entrusted with the property of our constituents were we to hesitate about doing everything that can be done with propriety to protect that property from harm.

[20] William Henry Chicheley Plowden: East India Company supercargo. He was head of the Select Committee in Canton in 1833.

I am satisfied the parties themselves have too much liberality and good sense to disapprove your conduct, more particularly as the plan we have adopted will, in case of need, relieve them from being in advance on our account.[21]

I have been remitting and consigning to Mr. Weeding, and shall continue to remit funds to him, to be used for that purpose. I shall write to him, begging he will aid you in every way he can, should you require aid, in protecting our interest.

We had directed *Messrs. Goodhue & Co.*[22] of New York to remit about 6,500 pounds sterling—proceeds of [ ] – to *Messrs. Fairlie, Clark, Innes & Co.*, and Messrs. *Ralston & Co.*[23] of Philadelphia to remit 7,000 dollars to the same parties: but, by subsequent letters dated March 29th we have requested these funds to be remitted to you, assigning satisfactory reasons for the changes without referring to the true one. In the event of everything going right, you can have the bills over to the parties for whom they were originally intended, assigning any reason you please for their having been sent to you.

We had ordered a quantity of Sycee to be sent to the House in Broad Street for account of the Calcutta House; but it did not reach Lintin till after the sailing of [the *Sir David Scott*] for [Calcutta].

Before an opportunity offered of sending Bills via America we found that the opium purchased on our account at the first sale had not been shipped by any of the three first vessels; which induced me to wait the result of the proposed letter of licence; and I shall now write to Mr. Matheson and to the Calcutta Houses, explaining the circumstances and requesting the former to square our account in case there should be any small balances against us, which is possible if they have paid all the bills we drew upon them; and the usual deposit on the drug purchased on our account at the first sale.

I regret very much being under the necessity of giving you all this trouble; and shall be too happy to hear that there is no cause for alarm or interference.

If bills offer I shall continue to remit to Mr. Weeding, and should the funds not be required they will form a remittance for your private account. Our exchange is not likely to be favourable next season.

Believe me, My dear Magniac,

Yours very sincerely,

[21] In their situation as debtors to *Fairlie, Clark, Innes & Co.* through bills drawn on them and still outstanding in the market, *Jardine, Matheson & Co.* needed to handle the situation delicately. It needed to achieve two contradictory aims—to ease its burden on its creditor by remitting funds, and yet to keep control of the remittances for as long a possible in case the correspondent failed before the bills were due.

[22] *Goodhue & Co.*: a New York merchant firm. One of its partners was Mr. Perit. (See Letter **145** below).

[23] Matthew C. Ralston, a Philadelphia merchant, (mentioned in Letter **5** above. Several letters by M. C. Ralston are listed in the *BI*).

70. William Jardine in Canton to James Matheson in Calcutta,
6 April 1833

My dear Matheson,

The return of the *Falcon* affords me an opportunity of replying to your long letter from Singapore[24] and of explaining to you what I have done in consequence.

I have today forwarded by the *Roman* bound for New York a power similar to the one you sent to Hollingworth Magniac having made a run to Macao for the purpose of signing the same in presence of the Chief of the Factory. I have written to Magniac and to Mr. Weeding on the subject, begging them to attend to your request, in case of need.

To Mr. Weeding we have made considerable remittance since you left: we have more than balanced his account and have informed him of our wishes respecting *Fairlie, Clark, Innes & Co.*, and of our intention to continue remitting to him in bills when procurable, Sycee silver and Raw Silk, so as to make up a balance in his hands, to be used by Mr. Magniac or himself, or the two united, for the purpose of protecting our interests in case of need.

To *Fairlie, Clark, Innes & Co.* we have remitted, as nearly as possible enough to square our account.

We had arranged a remittance in Sycee per *Sir David Scott* to the extent of our drafts on *Fergusson & Co.* But the ship sailed before the Sycee reached Lintin.

We then determined on remitting in Bills; but before we had been able to arrange this, accounts from Calcutta reached which rendered carrying the plan into execution hazardous. And we, in consequence, in the absence of advising from *Fergusson & Co.* deferred going further into the business. This is better than having to write to stop the bills in transit in England, as proposed in your letter.

I have also written to America requesting two sums of 6,500 and 7,500 pounds sterling[25] to be remitted to Magniac in place of *Fairlie, Clark, Innes & Co.* as first directed, assigning such reasons for the change as cannot by any possibility injure the credit of *Fairlie, Clarke, Innes & Co.*

I have requested Magniac and Weeding, our interests being protected, in the first instance to balance our account with *Fairlie, Clark, Innes & Co.*, so as to prevent these from suffering inconveniences on our account, should they wish for such a balance. We have as nearly as possible balanced our account with *Gregson, Melville & Knight*.

We have, I believe, remitted enough to *Remington & Co.* in Bombay, independent of {Mr. Doveton's}[26] 10,000 pounds sterling placed at your disposal, and

[24] The letter was not traced.

[25] The amounts and currencies are somewhat different to those mentioned in the previous Letter.

[26] Probably Bazett Doveton, (one letter from Bombay listed in the *BI*). The other 'Doveton' listed, writing from London, was Major General Sir John Doveton (1783–1857).

have provided for the 13,000 sterling Bills which you took with you or rather, left by mistake, and sent after you by Captain Grant.

We have remitted to *Lyall Matheson & Co.* 14,000 pecul of Sycee on account of James Innes with orders to invest on his deal, subject to your instructions, or a limit of 1,150 Rupees per chest. We sent an additional quantity of Sycee to *Lyall Matheson & Co.* on our account.

You must arrange *Fergusson & Co.*'s Account with us; in which, I trust, you will meet with no difficulties. A transfer of 10,969 Rupees has been made by *Fergusson & Co.* from the Account of Angel de la Fuente[27] to our account at a very suspicious moment—what say you to this? We shall endeavour to carry your wishes in to effect in every way in our power as regards remittances to England making them to {*F. & Co.*}[28] in place of [ ] for the sake of convenience, Magniac being out of town.

I have requested Weeding to aid Magniac in every possible way in case of need. I sincerely hope everything will go right, if not we can do no more. Write by every opportunity that may offer.

We are sending 100 chests of Shillaber's[29] camphor to *Thomas & Co.*, Singapore.

The *Biggar* sailed for the Coast on 30th. No *Sylph*,[30] and no further accounts of her. This makes me a little anxious.

Trusting this may find you in Calcutta, I remain, My Dear Matheson,

Yours very sincerely,

71. William James Thompson[31] in London to *Jardine, Matheson & Co.* in Canton, 8 April 1833

Gentlemen,

You will learn from the Public Papers, as well as from private sources, that Government have resolved not to continue to the Company the exclusive Trade with China. Indeed, it is generally inferred from the paragraph in the 'Paper of Hints' of the President of the Board of Control,[32] that the Company will not be permitted to Trade at all, after the expiration of the Charter, in May 1834: if so,

[27] A customer of James Matheson's previous firm, *Yrisarri & Co.*

[28] The use of initials, and possibly of abbreviated initials, obscures the meaning.

[29] For John Shillaber, see Letter **49** above, note 3.

[30] For the *John Biggar*, the *Sylph* and the secret expeditions mounted in 1832–1833, see Letter **49** above, note 9.

[31] William James Thompson: Tea broker, '30 Mincing Lane', London (*TLCD*). Some 50 letters are listed in the *BI*.

[32] The Right Honourable Charles Grant, MP was president of the Board of Control. (*EIRD*, 1833). Charles Grant was the mover of the 1833 bill for the non-renewal of the East India Company charter. See below, Letters **74** and **75**.

their Ships of the Season will be the last employed on Company's Account, and their home Cargoes will be taken charge of by the Government, who takes also, the unsold Stock here; and who are expected to supply the Public according to the practice of the Company; at least till a sufficient quantity is brought by Private Merchants: and if so, the Private Trade Tea will be sold as heretofore.

At the March Sale, just finished, Company's Campois,[33] which were taxed in December at 2 shillings and 4 pence and refused have been sold at 1 shilling and 11 pence to 2 shillings and 1 penny. Some Company's Souchong has been sold at 2 shillings and 2¾ pence and the good Common Congou which the Company import under the denomination of Bohea, has sold at 1 shilling and 9½ pence to 1 shilling and 10 pence. Weak, though fine flavored Black Teas will not sell so well as sound coarse Common Congou. One or two of the Chops of Orange Pekoe and of Caper have been found to have Iron dust in some of the Boxes, and all found to contain any have been withheld from Sale.

You will observe from the annexed List of Prices, that Teas are cheaper than they were last year. The fall in prices last year, was in consequence of the Company having put up to Sale a greater quantity than was required for consumption, and the further decline this Sale is attributable to the reduction of the Taxed Prices,[34] and the very large quantity offered; viz—8,500,000 pounds.

[33] The market commonly recognized nine different varieties of teas in the category of black teas, and six of green teas. Black teas comprised Congou (or Congo), Campoi, Ankoi, Souchong, Pouchong, Pekoe (spelt in a variety of ways), Orange Pekoe, Hong Moi, and Flowery Pekoe. Green teas offered the following varieties: Singlo, Hyson, Hyson skin, Young Hyson, Imperial and Gunpowder. (See: William James Thompson's Prices current at the end of this letter; Mui, Ho-Cheung and Mui, Lorna H., (eds), *William Melrose in China, (1845–1855), The Letters of a Scottish Tea Merchant*, Edinburgh, T. & A. Constable, 1973, Annex III, p. 268; see also *JMArch.* A7–231, which provides a table of the varieties of teas purchached and shipped by *Jardine, Matheson & Co.* after a few years' trading in the article. The table lists the following fifteen varieties. Black teas: Canton Bohea, Fokien Bohea, Congo, Caper, Souchong, Campoi, Ankoi, Hongmuey, Pekoe, Orange pekoe. Green teas: Hyson, Hyson skin, Twankey, Gunpowder, Imperial).

An important shift in British consumer taste occurred in the eighteenth century. Green teas, which were originally preferred, lost ground to black teas. By the time the East India Company charter was revoked, between 75 and 80 % of all the tea exported from China and consumed in Britain was black tea. (*JMArch.* A7–231). For an account of this shift in consumer taste, see: Le Pichon, Alain, 'L'emploi dans les metiers du thé en Angleterre (1734–1834)', in Azuelos, Martine (ed.), *Travail et Emploi, L'expérience anglo-saxonne, Aspects historiques*, Paris, Presses de la Sorbonne nouvelle, pp. 97–135).

[34] The overall tax on tea, (excise and duty) which had been substantially reduced by the Commutation Act of 1784 (from over 100% of cost price to 12%) was still charged *ad valorem*, and was dependent on the variety of tea concerned. The yield to H.M.'s treasury was substantial, amounting to between 3 and 4 million pounds sterling during the period of the Napoleonic Wars. (Dermigny, *La Chine et l'Occident*, p. 1018, note 3). The tea trade was thus of great importance to the government. From the figures provided by Webber and Wildavsky, it can be estimated that the tax on tea amounted on average to some 6% of Britain's military budget, or 60% of her civil government budget. (Webber, Carolyn, & Wildavsky, (eds.) *A History of Taxation and Expenditure in the Western World*, New York, Simon Schuster, 1986, p. 289). This tax on tea was again reformed and simplified soon after the

Bohea being taxed at 1 shilling and 4 pence, Common Congou at 1 shilling and 7 pence, Contract Congou at 1 shilling and 11 pence, Twankay at 2 shillings, Hyson at 3 shillings, leaves ample scope for further reduction; and, should the Company do as they did last year, this must take place. I name this, while I cannot see anything that should lead them to pursue a course alike injurious to themselves and the Revenue; yet it is impossible to form an opinion, unsettled as their arrangements are with the Government;—and the best general recommendation that I can give is, to avoid purchasing weak Teas of every sort.

Our Market for Spices is generally improved, particularly as regards Nutmeg and Mace.

I remain, Gentlemen, your humble Servant.

9 April 1833. The Company have this day given their declaration for the June Sale—8,300,000 pounds.

19 April 1833. The frequently adjourned debate at the India House, on the Resolution proposed on the 15th of April—and in which the continuance of the Company's trade is not claimed—has terminated in the affirmative, and a Ballot, expected to coincide with this, is fixed for the 3rd of May.

Company's Teas		[in pounds and shillings]		
Bohea		1.9¼	to	1. 9½
Congou,	common	1.11		2.0
	good & fine	2.0		2.3
	Pekoe kind	2.4		2.6
Campoi		1.11		2.0
Souchong		2.2		2.7
	very fine	3.0		4.2
Twankay		2.0		2.3
Hyson		3.0, 3.1, 3.4, 3.6, 3.10, 4.4		–

Private Trade Teas[35]		Chests	Boxes
Congou	common	1.10	1.11
	good & fine	1.11	2.1
Sonchi	common	1.10	–
	fine	2.0	–
Fetsong		2.0	2.6
Pouchong		1.11	2.0
Caper	in 10 catty boxes	2.2	2.6
	in large ditto	2.2	2.4
Orange Pekoe		2.3	2.6

abolition of the East India Company charter in 1834. (Letters **75**, **83**, **114**, and **129**). For a complete summary of the rates of duty charges on tea imports into Britain from 1740 to 1840, see: *PP*. 1845, (191), XLVI, pp. 593 and following.

[35] 'Private Trade teas' were the teas imported by the East India Company Supercargoes in the ships they commanded, as a special privilege granted by their employer. No other individuals, prior to 1834 were entitled to ship teas for their own account and for resale. Total private trade teas could, however, reach as much as 16% of total teas imported. (Sutton, *Lords of the East*, p. 72).

Private Trade Teas[35]		Chests [in pounds and shillings]	Boxes
Ankoi Pekoe		2.1	2.3
Pekoe	good	2.8	3.4
	fine and flowery	3.4	3.10
Twankay	common	2.0	–
	good & fine	2.0½	2.3
Hyson Skin		1.11	2.1
Hyson	common	3.0	3.1
	good & fine	3.2, 3.4, 3.6	–
Young Hyson		2.10	3.4
Gunpowder		3.10	5.0

72. John Macvicar in London to William Jardine and James Matheson in Canton, 29 April 1833

Dear Sirs,

The last letter I had the pleasure of writing to any of you was to Mr. Jardine and dated the 9th Ultimo. I then acknowledge letters of the 22nd October and since then I have received all your letters up to those of the 11 December per *Dunira.*[36]

The Vessel building at Liverpool[37] will be launched on the 4th May and I know of nothing to prevent her being dispatched on the 20th to 25th. Templeton[38] takes her out. Johnstone[39] goes out in her. I have got a nice young man from Ely for Chief mate—Ovenstone,[40] a nephew of the Commander of the *Falcon.* Several of the Crew come from the same place, and I expect they will turn out to be steady and useful hands. The Vessel has every appearance of being what we wish her to be. She is said to be a perfect model. The builder says she will carry her tonnage but I doubt this. Templeton does not trust her to be overloaded with Cargo and in this respect, I think it best to grant his wishes. Her cargo will probably consist of 2,000 pieces of Chintz, the musters as selected by Mr. Jardine, Cash cost about 36 shillings per piece; 40 small Bales Woolens, cost about 6 shillings per yard; 1,000 pounds Sterling value of the most approved description of Handkerchiefs; and from 4,000 to 4,000 of 80 yard length of the bleached and unbleached Long Cloths. No advance is required on any part of this consignment. I will write you very fully regarding each particular shipment by the *Nepal.*

[36] The *Dunira*: a 1,325-ton ship whose managing owner was George Palmer. The ship was chartered to the East India Company and commanded by Captain J. P. Wilson in the early 1830s. (*EIRD*).

[37] Not identified.

[38] Templeton: possibly a relative of the John Templeton mentioned in Letter **65** as a shareholder in the *10th Canton Insurance Company.*

[39] Andrew Johnstone. See above Letter **23**, note 1.

[40] Captain David Ovenstone commanded the *Falcon* in the early 1830s and the *Lady Hayes* in 1836. (*BI*).

I have engaged a Mr. Thom[41] (a cousin of William Falconer[42] of Glasgow) to go out to Canton: Salary 300 pounds Sterling a year, for five years. His manners are rather against him, being very Scotch. But he appears to possess good sense and can correspond about Manufactured Goods in a very satisfactory manner, and in this department I look principally to his being useful. He is very industrious and obliging. As a salesman I think he will require your constant assistance for some time. You will find him awkward at first, but I beg you to make allowances and doubt not that he will ultimately [prove a worthwhile] an acquisition. If I had thought of Johnstone going out I would probably not have engaged Mr. Thom, but until a week ago I had no idea of this.

Mr. Thom will sail from Bordeaux to Canton. I have induced Mr. George Jones[43] of Manchester to go with an operation to Canton. I have just ordered a French Vessel of 350 Tons to be chartered at Bordeaux to sail about 15th July. [I estimate at] 25,000 the value of goods to go out in her, which will probably consist of about: 5,000 pieces 80 yards each Long Cloth Cotton; 100,000 Cotton yarn pieces Nº 18 to 30; 2,000 pieces scarlett Long Ells;[44] 1,500 Woolen cloths.

The Vessel will probably load part of her return Cargo in Manila and at your port. 20,000 pounds Hyson Tea; 10,000 pounds Imperial; 10,000 pounds Gunpowder; 10,000 Young Hyson; 10,000 pounds common Hyson; 20,000 pounds Hyson Skin; 5,000 pounds Pecco; 30,000 pounds Souchong;[45] 25 Peculs Gamboye; 200 to 400 Peculas Cassia *Lignea*; 50 Chests Vermillion; 60 Peculs Rhubarb.

But as our information as to Returns is not yet certain—the scheme of Cargo may be greatly altered. The Teas required for the French market you are aware are

[41] Robert Thom: during his several years in the piece goods department of *Jardine, Matheson & Co.* in Canton, Robert Thom developed a knowledge of the Chinese language. He acted as one of a few official 'linguists' during the Opium War and took over as interpreter from Robert Morrison after the latter's untimely death during the negotiations of the Supplementary Treaty in 1843 (Fairbank, *Trade and Diplomacy*, p. 126). In the 1840s he was appointed H. M. consul at Ningpo. During his consular years at Ningpo, 'his commercial sense of values involved him in [actions resulting in the] lowering of the flag'. (*Ibid.*, pp. 331–332, where Fairbank gives two examples). Robert Thom published an English translation of a Chinese Ming story (*The Lasting resentment of Miss Keaou Lwan Wang, A Chinese Tale*, Canton Press Office, 1839). He also published two readers for learners of Chinese: *Esop's Fables Written in Chinese by the Learned Mun Mooy Seen-Shang by his pupil Sloth*, Canton Press Office, 1840; and *The Chinese Speaker, etc. The Mandaring Language, as spoken at Peking, Compiled for the Use of Students*, Ningpo, Presbyterian Mission Press, 1846. (Lust, *Western Books on China*, pp. 241, 250 and 259). For references to Robert Thom in this collection, see Letters **87**, **91**, **108**, **109**, **127**, **132**, **170**, **171**, **211**, and **241**.

[42] William Falconer: see above, Letter **46**, note 85.

[43] Possibly Captain Charles George Jones, who commanded the *Marquis Camden* in 1838 and the *William Jardine* in 1843. (*BI*).

[44] Long ells: a variety of long cloths. The ell was originally, 'a measure of length varying in different countries. The English ell was 45 inches'. (*OED*).

[45] John Macvicar had made plans for being among the first to import a large assortment of 'free' teas.

of very good quality. Full particulars to guide you in the purchase of the Cargo will be transmitted to you. It would be well in the meantime if you kept yourselves acquainted with the prices at Manila of Rice, Sugar, Tortoise Shell, Cotton, Indigo, Coffee, Mother of Pearl Shells, that you may decide on the propriety of sending her there or not, as a condition of the Charter will allow of your doing so.

I have sent you no consignments by any of the Company's ships this Season. Your last quotations of prices are so very low that the shipments from Liverpool and via Bordeaux will be as large as I think should at present be sent. I wish I could have got off a shipment in February, but until I received your advice of October last, I had no information to act upon. The most important period for advices of the State of your market for European articles to arrive here is about the end of December or beginning of January, so that if Accounts are encouraging a Vessel may be sent off in February to get to Canton before the usual time of the arrival of supplies. To get to England about that period of the year I find that advices via America are often first—but better if an American or other Ship touches at St Helena, letter put under cover to Saul Solomon[46] there, to be forwarded to Liverpool or London by the first good Ship. Advices via San Blas[47] are sometimes out latest from you. This last Season the last advice from Canton of July and August was by way of Bombay, and I think it will be worth your while in same July and August to write to England via Bombay if your correspondent there selects a *direct* and fast Vessel—your letter will probably reach England quickly and would arrive here at a very desirable time.

I am afraid the adventure to Hamburg prepared per *Syden*[48] will do little good—from the high prices of Tea with you. I have letters from Hamburg 19th July, from which I extract competition has arrived in larger quantity than the market will bear and divided in many hands. Sales cannot be effected above 2 shillings per pound all charges deducted. Cassia *Lignea* 800 Chests arrived direct from Manila, sold on arrival at between 9 and 8 shillings per pound. Cassia buds, between 7½ and 5 shillings. Sifted ditto, at 9 shillings. Surat Cotton in demand at between 5 to 6 and 4¾ to 5⅝ shillings. Preserved ginger: 12 pence per pound. Rhubarb peeled 3½ to 4 shillings per pound, half peeled: 11 to 22 pence. Vermillion: 2 shillings and 9 pence per pound. Gamboye: 1 shilling and eight pence to 2 shillings and 9 pence.

Teas. Boheas: no Stock. Supplies will consequently come to a good market and find immediate purchasers at 10 to 12 shillings per pound. Congo: Stocks 1,700 quarter Chests—a favourite quality in season, and would command sales at 13 to

[46] A few letters from 'Saul Solomon' in 'Africa' are listed in the *BI*.

[47] Cape Saint Blaise in South Africa, half way between Port Elizabeth and Cape Town.

[48] In 1833, probably in partnership with undisclosed constituents, *Jardine, Matheson & Co.* mounted a speculative operation and sent a cargo of Chinese goods to Hamburg, in order to test the German market. (*JMArch*, account books for 1833 and 1834). *The Norden*, (Captain Bart), mentioned below was sent on a similar expedition.

16. Kampoi: Stocks 150 quarter Chests. Is not a quality of Current Sales. Prices 12 to 20 shillings a pound. Souchong: Stocks 900 quarter Chests. Ready buyers at 13 to 15 shillings. Middling, etc., 16 to 24 for fine qualities. Pouchong: no Stocks and in demand at from 18 to 28 shillings. Pecco: Stocks 1,450 quarter Chests, 1,350 eighth Chests, 2,200 sixteenth and thirty second chests. This description is flat and only fine middling quality has buyers. Ordinary to middling of difficult Sale. Present prices rule from 24 to 88 shillings. In this quotation, all sorts of Pecco such as Orange Pecco, Pecco Hang Chuey, Pecco Tae, Pecco Congo Lye, are not included and all shipment of such are unadvisable. Hyson Skin Stocks: 2,300 quarter Chests. In demand at 15 to 24 shillings. Young Hyson; Stocks 70 quarter chests. Much demand. Inferior 12 to 16 shillings, fine 18 to 28. Hyson: Stocks 400 quarter chests. Very current and of prompt Sale at 32 to 40 shillings. {Chulan} Hyson: Stocks 450 eighth Chests. Only saleable at the price of Hyson. Imperial: Stocks 150 quarter chests, 150 eighth Chests, 300 sixteenth chests. 48 shillings. Middling, 42 shillings. Gunpowder: Stocks 40 quarter Chests, 70 eighth Chests, 100 sixteenth Chests, price 10 to 48 shillings—Imperial and Gunpowder having been sold lately very low in Holland by public Sale, the prices in Hamburg are flat in consequence.

I am told that Captain Bart's arrival in Hamburg will be very acceptable as many persons are anxious for a settlement of consignments he had on a previous voyage. The *Norden*, a fine old ship, has been attached for sterling 3.000, a small sum, but no one to pay it, and people don't know how things stand. This information *entre nous*. There are twelve American Vessels at St Helena, last account. I apprehend they will convey more China produce to Europe this Season than the markets will support. I think the Americans this last Season, will have overtraded to China. There is a talk that *Baring Brothers* are to establish the Firm of *Labouchère* at Canton.[49] But I trace the rumour to no source.

Baring Brothers are extending themselves greatly as a commercial house. Their credit is beyond any question of doubt, but some people say they don't like their extending their business to such a great length as they are doing. The amount of their management of one kind or another must be enormous in the money market here. Their Bills are as current as Bank of England paper, and you might get them guaranteed at one shilling for 100 pounds Sterling. The Credit of *Fairlie Clark Innes & Co.* is as before. Not considered bad and not considered first rate. I think you are pursuing a proper and cautious course in that quarter. The failure of *Alexander and Co.* of Calcutta has produced no evil mercantile effect here. *J. Alexander & Co.*[50] are creditors to a large amount, but their credit is not in the

[49] The firm was never established in Canton.

[50] The firm became *Fletcher Alexander & Co.*, 29, Austin Friars, and was one of the best established East India agencies in London. The Calcutta agency of the same name had just failed (See above, letter **68**, note 17).

least affected. It is said that the loss they sustain [cannot] cause a dissolution or breaking up of the house. A circular which was issued by *MacIntosh & Co.* of Calcutta shortly after the failure of *Alexander & Co.* is a good deal animadverted upon here, and does not add to their Credit. *R[ickards] M[ackintosh] &Co.*[51] here are said to be very good. But the public don't understand why they should sell their Bills on India at the prices they have lately come down, say 1 shilling 7 and a quarter pence on Bombay and 1 shilling 8 and a half pence on Calcutta (at 2 Rupees to 1 Dollar when the dollar was equal to 4 shillings, the Rupee was equal to 2 shillings). The Credit of the houses in the East India generally speaking is not improving in the estimation of the money Dealers in London who say there are not 18 English Houses to the East of the Cape of Good Hope worth 50,000 pounds Sterling each—and I dare say this is true. The Credit of my friends Jardine and Matheson of Canton stands quite in an enviable position. There is not a whisper current to their disadvantage that I have ever heard. The amount of paper in the circle bearing their names, I have not heard named as being large or in any way objectionable, in short you need not desire to stand better than you do. I only allude to this in consequence of what Mr. Matheson said in one of his private communications to me, and it gives me sincere pleasure to congratulate you on this subject and on the great prosperity of your business, and so long as it is conducted on the sound principles and with the business like activity that now regulates it, there is no fear of any extent leading to the injury of your name. Should I at any time hear any thing to your disadvantage I will not be backward to let you know as I am certain you will set down my doing so to the proper and true motive.

I have had a confidential conversation with my friends *Gell & Co.*[52] respecting your operations with them, as alluded to in your letter accompanying the quadruplicate of yours to *Gell & Co.* of the —. They are very desirous of increasing their connection with you and would only wish to put such a limit upon the extent of it as could in no case inconvenience them or interfere with their other

[51] The sister agency to *Mackintosh & Co.* of Calcutta, which had just failed. (*Ibid.*)

Ultimately, in spite of the Calcutta failures, most of the London East India agency houses eventually weathered the storm. *Fairlie Clark Innes & Co.* is one of the rare houses which failed. The list of East India Agencies operating in London in 1841 (containing a remarkable number of Scottish names) was almost exactly the same as in 1831. (The sign (N) denotes the firms which were new in 1841. In alphabetical order, they were as follows : Henry Blanshard; *Briggs, Thurnburn, Acraman & Co.* (N); *William Burnie & Co.; Chalmers & Guthrie; J. Cockburn & Co.; Cockerell & Co.; Crawford, Colvin & Co; Dallas & Coles* (N); *Fletcher Alexander & Co.; Forbes, Forbes & Co.; Gregson, Melville & Co.; Haviside & Co.* (N); *Hunter & Co.; Sir James Lubbock & Co.; Lyall Brothers & Co.; Mangles & Co.* (N); *Marjoribanks, Ferrers; John Masson & Co.; Palmer Mackillop & Co.; Rickards Mackintosh & Co.*; James Rundall (N); Thomas Saunders; *Scott, Robert, Fairlie & Co.*; *Small Colquhoun & Co.*; Thomas Weeding; and *Wigram & Co.* (*EIRB*, 1831; *EIRD*, 1841)

[52] Probably the firm of William Gell: 'Tea dealer, Charles Place, East Street, Walworth road', London. (*TLCD*).

connections, several of whom look to them and require of them at times pretty heavy Cash advances. Your drafts upon them, I imagine, would be most serviceable to yourselves, if made in the early part of the year, say May, June, July or August, and for remittance to India. 20,000 to 25,000 pounds Sterling drawn at that time on them, you may rely on it, will meet with prompt honour, to be covered between November and January followed by consignments of Silk, Specie, or Bills of Exchange as may suit you best. You should guard their convenience as much as you can by arranging your remittances in such manner that they may relieve themselves from any heavy cash advances if they choose—as *you* must be aware that for any house on a business of this kind, an actual advance of the whole, or great part, or indeed any part, of the Capital should render that particular business undesirable. In the remittance of Specie, it is best to divide the amounts by different Vessels not only because if an accident kept a Vessel having a large amount long out that would be an inconvenience, but also because of the difficulty of employing at interest any very large amount arriving at one time. On this account it appears desirable that a part of the remittances should be in Bills of exchange which can be negotiated, when convenient and which cause no loss of interest. Perhaps on this (which I would call the anticipation) account it would be best to divide the covering with equal part Goods, Specie and Bills, or Specie and Bills only. Besides this twenty to twenty five thousand Sterling, to be covered by the January Ships at the latest, *Gell & Co.* are open to any other and to any amount of business you may find it convenient to do with them, such as drawing upon them against transmission of Specie, Bills or Silk or other Goods, their drafts being covered at the same time. In short there is a clear for uncovered Credit for 20,000 to 25,000 Sterling, anything beyond this amount to be covered upon.

These operations are distinct from my credit of 15,000 Sterling with them on your Account. But I don't see that the Credit is likely to be brought into play to any extent as I can find abundant supplies of Cotton goods without an advance, when a Profit is to be had. If you could get any Hong or other Merchant, on whom you can rely to give you a Positive order for 15,000 pounds Sterling of good, this Credit would then come in as *Gell & Co.* would not object to give me the use of this Capital to buy the goods with, and you to reimburse them after arrival of the goods, say in two months after arrival. By this means Capital would be placed in Canton if desirable, and I would gain a Commission, which would be very acceptable to me.[53] If you can work out any operation of this Kind you will oblige me.

[53] By this stratagem, John Macvicar would effectively transform a credit 'with [*Gell & Co.*] on [*Jardine, Matheson & Co.'s*] account' which could not yield him a commission, into one which could. The subsequent correspondence between John Macvicar and *Jardine, Matheson & Co.* shows the former's tendency to overtrade for the sake of making commission income. (See Letters **161**, **163**, **166**, **182**, and **216**).

I could buy the goods as cheap as any body—and particularly in Woolens where I have as yet a weak connection, it might be useful for opening up a consigning connection.

I will be glad should the prices of Silk decline with you before the close of the Season, so far as to enable you to execute some portion of the orders I sent you last Season—in which case I think the parties here would send out orders of greater magnitude for your next Season's Silk [as it] is rather advancing in price here. The Stock of Italian Silk in this Country is greatly reduced, which has a favourable influence on the value of Tsatlee. For the Prime parcel of Tsatlee Silk N° 1 and 2 I think the value in the market this day may be from 14/3 to 14/6 per pound. Taysaam is very high, in proportion in consequence of the short supply expected. I think we may look forward to the prices of Silk being pretty steadily maintained for some time—and if you can buy low next season the article will be safe, but beware of a high cost. The price here is regulated by the supply and consumption. The consumption goes on steadily. Good Tsatlee is very safe to Import to cost 13 shillings to 13 shillings and six pence, laid down in London, but I would not import at greater cost. At this price, 6 pence to 1 shilling per pound may be gained by it.

Camphore is not safe when at the present reduced prices. I think it will go lower. *Cassia Lignea* is on the decline. I think supplies will be heavy and in which case we may see the price down to 60 shillings. I think you should hardly continue your arrangement with *Cockerell & Co.*—it does not look well that you should charge them a different rate of commission from your usual charges. It would not be agreeable to me, that any part of my business, or that of my connections, should in any way pass through the hands of Mr. James James.[54] But as Mr. Thom will relieve you of part of the trouble, I will say nothing further on that subject.

With Kind regards to all friends, believe me, My dear Sir, Yours most faithfully.

73. William MacKay on board the *John Biggar*[55] to William Jardine and James Matheson in Canton, 28 May 1833

Dear Sirs,

I have the pleasure to announce the return of the *John Biggar*.

Having only 30 chests of Opium left I did not think it worth while remaining longer on the Coast, more especially as I saw no immediate prospect of their being cleaned out; the merchants having almost entirely deserted us since the new drug was finished.

[54] Not identified.

[55] On Captain William MacKay and the *John Biggar* expedition, see above, Letter **49**, note 9.

We have sold two hundred and sixty seven chests, viz—70 of new Patna at 720 dollars; 90 of new Benares at 720 dollars; 17 chests of old Patna and 77¾ chests of old Benares at something better than 800 dollars; and 12 chests Malwa at better [than] 675 dollars. Fees received in addition to the above. Our treasure consists of more than 200,000 dollars,[56] viz—about 33,000 dollars in large Sycee received at par; 25,000 dollars in small Sycee, average at 1½ per cent discount; 7,400 dollars in Gold at 224 dollars per bar and 15 dollars per Doubloon;[57] 30,000 in smooth dollars; and the remainder in chopped dollars.[58] The Mexican dollars are so very few (not amounting to more than one or two thousand) that I have not separated them. They were received however at 2 per cent discount.

The Chin-choo[59] merchants complained much of a scarcity of cash saying the returns had not yet been received for the large purchases made per *Jamesina* and *Sylph* which has been shipped for Tysam[60] and other distant ports.

I am of opinion that a temporary absence will have a good effect on the markets and enable those who purchased largely from us to realize more advantageously and have their friends in readiness for our return.

The enclosed statement will show particulars. In a box marked 'JM&Co.' are about 50 dollars in small quarter and half dollars, also 9 Tysam dollars. The former you will probably find useful, the latter curious.

According to Instructions I remain outside until I hear from you. We are at anchor on the North side of Lama,[61] between it and HongKong. No accidents.

As the money for the Piece Goods, etc., was received by number and not weighed I have packed it separately in a box marked 'AG' and shall deliver it over to [Alexander] Grant to whom I believe most of these goods belong.

I remain

Yours obediently,

[56] The 1832–1833 *John Biggar* operation and other similarly successful operations up the China coast convinced Jardine and Matheson that the Chinese demand for opium was far from being restricted to the Canton area or even southern China.

[57] Doubloon: '1622. Spanish gold coin = 2 pistoles'. (*OED*).

[58] Dollars which were worn, or actually broken. As no standard coin of exchange existed, shroffs (Chinese professional money counters) were taken along on all trading expedition. Their function was to assay gold and silver with their touchstones in order to ascribe a proper value to any and all precious metal offered as a means of exchange.

[59] More usually spelt 'Chin Chew'. See Letter **46**, note 86.

[60] This 'distant port' was not identified.

[61] The *John Biggar* must have been at anchor between Lama Island and Aberdeen, once a fishing village and now a large town on the south side of Hong Kong Island.

74. Horatio Hardy[62] in London to *Jardine, Matheson & Co.* in Canton, 7 June 1833[63]

Gentlemen,

I forwarded my last letter per *Waterloo* the 15th March with a Box of parcels. The letters were sent distinct from them in order to ensure early delivery at China. The *Elizabeth* will be detained a few days and all the subsequent letters, etc., will be transmitted by her, being the last ship this Season, and probably the very last in the Company's Service. The *Fairy*, Brig, Captain Templeton,[64] is to sail on 16th Instant to China via Singapore from Liverpool.

The Government plan for the renewal of the Charter, will be brought before the House of Commons the 11th Instant in the shape of resolutions by the Right Honorable Charles Grant;[65] two bills are prepared and Copies were sent to the Court of Directors yesterday. The particular sections are not to transpire until the Ministers publish them. The one Bill is to regulate the affairs of India under the Board of Control and Court of Directors. The second Bill to regulate the Trade with India and China, making the whole World free to the enterprize of the British Merchants. The Port of London it is expected will feel the change, for the Ports of Liverpool, Bristol, Hull, Leith, Glasgow, Dublin, and Cork are to have bonded warehouses for Teas.[66] It will be promulgated during next week to the proprietors on the 11th or 13th Instant.

[62] Horatio, Charles, Anthony, Hardy: 'Coffee House keeper, Cowper's Court, Cornhill', London. (*TLCD*). Horatio Hardy's establishment, the *Jerusalem Coffee House* was a popular and busy spot in the City, mostly patronized by merchants, ship owners, and ship captains with East India connections. See: Lillywhite, Bryant, *London Coffee Houses*, London, G. Allen & Unwin, 1963.

[63] This editor discovered the Horatio Hardy Letters by chance, in 1995. The letters were not listed as part of the In-Correspondence. They were found amidst sundry bundles of loose accounting papers, ('the A7 series'), which have since then been catalogued by John Wells, the Keeper of Manuscripts at the Cambridge University Library. Horatio Hardy sent the firm 25 letters in all, or about one a month, from January 1833 to February 1835. The partners of *Jardine, Matheson & Co.* were thus kept well informed of all political developments in this crucial period which was to 'throw open the tea trade' to all private merchants, and which was to see the dismantling of the East India Company's operations not only in China, but also in London, at least in all aspects of its enormous tea trade. This special intelligence enabled William Jardine and James Matheson to make appropriate preparations for the brave new world of post-1834 China trade.

[64] See above, Letter **72**, note 38.

[65] For the Hon. Charles Grant, see above, Letter **71**, note 32.

[66] Prior to 1834, all the tea shipped to Britain was imported by the East India Company. Before it was sold the tea was warehoused in the Company's vast tea warehouses located in the City. This single location made it easy for H.M. Excise and Duty to control the stock and collect the duty. After 1834, the need suddenly arose to have 'bonded warehouses' for tea in several locations throughout the country. A 'bonded warehouse' is under the control of H. M. Excise and Duty, and the imported goods can only leave bond after duty has been paid.

Political. The question of Portugal as to the propriety of this country declaring herself for Donna Maria Queen of Portugal,[67] was decided in the House of Lords by a majority of 12 against Ministers in addressing the King; but in the House of Commons last night on the same question, there were 263 in favor of Ministers. The embargo has been taken off from the Dutch Ships by proclamation and Peace restored between Holland and Belgium.[68] The Russian Troops remain at Constantinople, though Turkey and Egypt have made peace.[69] There are still disturbances in Italy, Germany, etc., occasionally, and there appears nothing in France to disturb or counteract the plans of the existing Government.[70]

The price of the Funds have improved during the last week. Consols.: 91¼; 3½ per cent: 96⅞; 4 per cent: 103½; Bank: 205; East India Company: 236; the price of Silk is improving now from 14 shillings to 16 shillings and 6 pence. The names you will perceive in the *Price current* enclosed.[71] Fine Teas have lowered 12 pence per pound and common Teas have increased half a penny per pound and the sale very brisk. Expecting to write per *Elizabeth* the 13th Instant.

I am, Gentlemen,

Yours most Obediently.

75. Horatio Hardy in London to *Jardine, Matheson & Co.* in Canton, 26 June 1833

Gentlemen,

The detention of the Ship *Elizabeth* so long beyond her time, has put all the Correspondents with China to a great inconvenience because it is not known one hour before the other when she will be dispatched. My absence from London I postponed until I was fearful if I waited for the ship I should be prevented going. Therefore a week has now elapsed, and the dispatching appears to be in the same

[67] Donna Maria, or Maria da Gloria, (1819–1853). She became Queen of Portugal in 1826, following the renunciation by her father (Dom Pedro of Brazil) of his rights on the death of her grand-father, King John IV. She was overthrown in 1828 by her uncle, Dom Miguel, and fled to England. Dom Pedro then abdicated the Brazilian throne (1831) and returned to Europe to fight for the restoration of his daughter. At the time when this Letter was written, the British Parliament was in the process of deciding which claimant to support. (*CBD, EWH*).

[68] On the crisis of Belgian independence, see above, Letter **43**, note 44. On 21 May 1833, shortly before this Letter was written, the Dutch were finally obliged by the British and the French to conclude an armistice of indefinite length. The armistice lasted until 19 April 1839, when King William at last recognized Belgian independence. (*EWH*).

[69] A reference to a stage in the long running crisis ensuing from the Greek revolt against Turkish suzerainty, and the ambitions of the Pasha of Egypt, Muhammed Ali, to force the Sultan to make territorial concessions.

[70] Louis Philippe I (1773–1850) was proclaimed 'King of the French' in 1830, following the 1830 Revolution. France prospered under his reign, until the agricultural and industrial depression of 1846. Two years later, the 1848 Revolution forced him to abdicate.

[71] The *Price Current* was not traced.

state. I have no advice of the next ship for China, whether it will be from Havre, Bordeaux or Liverpool. There is none likely to sail before the middle of July. The *Reliance* (10 February) last arrived brought very few Letters, and the *Sir David Scott* (the last ship) expected in ten days, if she brings no more, will disappoint a great many people, particularly under *Messrs. Rickards Macintosh & Co.* suspending their payments. We were in hopes of knowing by this time what effects it would produce upon the non-acceptance of *Messrs. Dent & Co.*'s Bills from China.[72] If any decision is made I shall add a postscript.

The state of the Company's Service in regard to the Commanders and officers becomes very serious, they are in a lamentable suspense as to future employment; the Petition to the Court of Directors for compensation for their expected losses and to know the state of the Poplar Fund[73] remains unanswered: all their Petitions for the last five years shared the same fate.[74]

The Court of Directors and Proprietors abandoned the China Trade without any appeal or resistance; it is true the voice of the country, and the views of Government demanded it, but the maritime Service are not prepared for so sudden a change, another Season was expected, and the sacrifice of so large a Property as the value of Fifty 1,300 Ton Ships is considered a desperate reform.[75]

The Directors' salaries are to be 1,000 pounds sterling per annum instead of 300 pounds. The Proprietors of East India Stock is to be secured at 10½ per cent

[72] The failure of *Mackintosh & Co.* in Calcutta temporarily affected the London firm of *Rickards Macintosh. Dent & Co.* was known to use the services of both firms. The fate of their bills in the London market was therefore a concern for the *Dent & Co.* partners. This private concern about the state of their respective credit in the London market was about all the two principal Canton firms had in common at the time.

[73] The 'Poplar Fund' was a relief fund set up by the East India Company and its commanders to 'compensate impecunious commanders for the loss of voyages'. (Sutton, *Lords of the East*, pp. 60, 63).

[74] The officers and commanders in the employ of the East India Company remained ignorant of their fate until redundancy proposals were adopted by the Courts of Directors and of Proprietors of the East India Company in May 1834. The compensation on offer was thought inadequate by those losing their jobs, and several meetings were held throughout the year 1834. The final meeting of the officers and commanders of the maritime service was held at the Jerusalem Coffee House on December 1834, with Captain John Hine in the Chair. (*JMArch.*, A7/214). For details of the resolutions, see below, Letter **98**).

[75] Most of the 'East India Company ships' were in fact not owned outright by the East India Company, but by syndicates of merchants. For each syndicate of owners there was a 'managing owner' (commonly known as the ship's 'husband') who was responsible for all aspects of building, fitting, manning and chartering the ship. (For details of Company ships and their 'husbands' see: Farrington, Anthony, (ed.), *Catalogue of East India Company Ships, Journals and logs, 1600–1834*, London, the British Library, 1999).

The 'sacrifice' mentioned here by Hardy refers to the fact that the ships would no longer be chartered by the East India Company. The fear was that no private merchant would be strong enough to charter such large ships, and in consequence that most of them would be sold, and not only the few ships belonging outright to the Company. For a list of HCS ships affected by the measure, see **Appendix IX**: 'East India Company Ships, managing owners and commanders'.

for 20 years from the revenues of the India Territory amounting to 630,000 pounds Sterling per annum.[76] Their principal of 6 Millions Sterling to be secured by a sinking Fund of 2 Millions, and at 40 years prospective they are to receive 100 pounds Sterling for each annuity of 5 pounds and 5 shillings—by which plan the territory, however immense or extensive its proceeds may be, will belong entirely to Great Britain. The whole of the commercial property is to be immediately given up to the Government when the Charter expires in April 1834, viz.—Warehouses, Wharf, Docks, East India House, and the Buildings with all Commercial property in India.[77] The Directors will retain their patronage but it is imagined they will only be as commissioners under the Government. As only three or four departments will be required in the Home establishments, and it is thought will be removed to the West End of the Town; what will be done with the East India House? cannot be conjectured, it is rated for taxes at 2,300 pounds Sterling per annum rental. The official departments retained will only be the Examiners of Correspondence Secretarys, Accountants, Auditors, civil and military, and extra clerks for such officers; the Treasury business conducted at the Bank of England. The number of Clerks and common men thrown out of employ will be almost 4,000.

The Plans of Government have been developed to the House of Commons in four Resolutions which were carried unanimously on the 19th Instant and Bills founded on them are to be brought up by the Right Honorable Charles Grant and five other members, after these resolutions have been submitted to the House of Lords on the 28th Instant. I fear the Copy of the Bill cannot be conveyed by this ship.

The Copy of the Bills were supplied it is supposed to the Chairman on the 22nd Instant, therefore they are doubtless before the Court, in profound secresy.[78]

You will regret that postages will be heavily charged in India, and the Government are disposed to extend it to China to increase that portion of the revenue: whether China in regard to the Trade, is to be managed by a Commission, Council or Consulate has not yet been divulged. The Trade cannot be opened until April 1834 under certain regulations, but it is absolutely certain *not one ship* is to be sent out by the Company. The Teas in stock and what is coming home in 1834, will be sufficient to supply Great Britain until 1836, consequently no Teas can be imported into Great Britain before that year. In respect to the Sales it is not yet made known whether for the sake of the Tax or Duty of 100 per cent whether all

[76] The owners of East India Company stock had to be compensated since the measure, which effectively altered the nature of the Company from a commercial to an administrative establishment, precluded it from making profits in future and therefore from paying dividends.

[77] The changes announced here altered the commercial, financial and social life of Britain in a radical way. This was a prime example of what the 'war against monopolies', which was so strong a feature of the period, was able to achieve.

[78] (sic).

is to be sold in london, or disposed of at Liverpool, Bristol, Hull, Glasgow, Leith, Dublin and Cork, but instead of *ad valorem* duty it is to be graduated according to the Value of the Tea, so as to bring the maximum of revenue between the fine and common Teas to produce the revenue as if the whole were at 100 per cent.[79]

When all the points are investigated in the Committee of the legislature, many alterations will of course be made. I can only furnish you with these items as at present known.

The Maritime Service had Petitions ready for both Houses and they have strong hopes to obtain some relief from Parliament or throw themselves upon what employment the Free Trade may open to them; one or two deputations have been to the President of the Board of Control, but neither of them gained any information. In respect to the other proceedings in Parliament, they are more preoccupied with business than the Session will enable them to go through.

The West India Compensation of 20 Millions to remunerate for the emancipation[80] will occupy much time and produce a struggle, as an addition to the National Debt.

The revision of the Laws and to have local judges has made its progress to the Lords. In fact, there is so much business that the Tories are stirring and many means are [being used] by them to overthrow the Ministry, if possible, and they are watching for some of these innumerable measures to produce a change in the government.

It is evident that the Reform Bill would accomplish changes in a variety of ways, and among the old established system, but none of its friends ever considered, it would produce so extensive a change.

The constitution being so wrought upon, the fabric of aristocracy begins to shake, they are making a cry against the House of Lords, and the Bishops as useless with no right to a seat there. You will form your own conclusions that since the days of Alfred, if a principle and a constitution has worked well, can a march of Intellect in the 19th century, has become so very wise that to work a new system will not possess, a revolutionary spirit, which time or talent cannot repress.[81]

The Funds continue. Bank: 203½; East India Stock: 247; Consols.: 89⅞; 3½ per cent: 95¾; 4 per cent: 102½.

The Silk keeps advancing a little: 14 pounds and 6 shillings to 16 pounds and 6 shillings. Teas as per last, the Brokers will write to the last moment.

[79] A rather doubtful clarification.

[80] West Indian slavery was ended by statute in 1833, against £20 million compensation paid to the owners of West Indian estates. (The slave *trade* had been forbidden to British subjects in 1807).

[81] An awkward sentence, which probably means: 'Can our modern reformers be so wise that they can introduce such changes without revolutionary consequences?' In spite of the 1832 Reform, there was still a general fear that a French-style revolution would come and destroy aristocratic government.

In regard to Foreign affairs I have little to remark upon. The impolitic warfare between Don Pedro and Don Miguel[82] continue without any advantage on either side. It is wished by almost all Europe it is ended: no Portugal Wine has been shipped from Oporto for eight months. I observe no appearance of a decided operation to settle the unnatural dispute between the two Brothers.

The embargo being taken off from Holland have revived Trade here.[83] Belgium appears to be in better progress and may prosper, as King Leopold is popular. France and Spain have nothing to notice; the Duchess of Berri[84] has gone to Italy, *Palermo*, and also Don Carlos[85] with his Sister have followed, to remain in the papal dominions.

The war is said to be terminated in Turkey where the Crescent has begun to wane. It appears extraordinary that the Russian Troops, remain at Constantinople, there is a great deal of policy in the Emperor Nicholas,[86] he is shewing some amelioration towards the Poles and our Government in England have too much to attend to at home, to notice at present Foreign affairs.

I cannot but observe still there exists a refractory spirit in Germany, and other parts of Europe, which would be too much for me to convey in detail. We have Peace it is true, but not universal harmony and concord.

I am Gentlemen

Yours most Obediently,

76. The Reverend Carl Gutzlaff on board the *John Biggar* to William Jardine in Canton, 6 August 1833[87]

My Dear Sir,

With a brisk gale we passed the first place of our destination, Namoa[88] Considering the loss of time to work up against wind and tide we judged it more conducive to the intent of our voyage to steer directly for Chin Chew Bay. Here

[82] Don Pedro and Don Miguel: see above, Letter **74**, note 67.

[83] The embargo was taken off following the armistice of 21 May 1833. See above, Letter **74**, note 68.

[84] Caroline of Bourbon Sicilies (1798–1870), married Charles, Duke of Berry and son of King Charles X of France. The Duke of Berry, presumed to be the last heir of the Bourbon line, was murdered in 1820. The duchess, however, later gave birth to his posthumous son, the Duke of Bordeaux. She subsequently attempted to organize an uprising in ultra-conservative Vendée in favour of her son. The attempt failed, and she fled to Italy.

[85] Don Carlos (1788–1855), second son of Charles IV of Spain. On the accession of his niece, Isabella II (1833) he asserted his claim to the throne. He was supported by the church, but was defeated by the liberals in the first Carlist War (1834–1839). (*CBD*).

[86] Tsar Nicholas I (1796–1855) became Emperor of Russia in 1825. His policies towards the Sultan and towards 'Congress Poland' (created in 1815) which had revolted in 1831, were objects of suspicion in England.

[87] This letter was written in 'Zoa Tuy'.

[88] Namoa: and island off Swatow, some 300 miles north of Canton.

we were very soon greeted by our old customer of the year before, when he had sailed in the *Sylph*, see below and the first sale made was a bale of calicoes. If it had not been for the Mandarins who have taken possession of all the fast sailing boats and manned them with their own people, we might perhaps by this time have cleaned the ship, the rice exempted. There have been large importations from Formosa and the harvest, which is just brought in, is middling, so that 180 catties (120 catties being equal to 1 picul) sell for 4 dollars. But the rice is superior to ours. Yet you ought not to despair, for we hope still to make a successful trip to Namoa, where the price is at least two mace more than the market price at Chinchew.

Calicoes sell well, but not above the Canton prices; yet as it is your grand object to introduce British manufactures, smile at our pigmy efforts to dispose of a few bales. If you dispatch a ship before the middle of September and can send the cheapest assortment possible (we sold in the *Sylph* long cloth of inferior quality for 4 dollars, and this suited the moment best) this long cloth will be a saleable article. Even now I might have sold for 1,000 dollars more if our stock, which was very small, had not been too soon exhausted, and so we are obliged to send the people away with their money. Chintzes do not sell at all. Camlets[89] at the low rate of 31 to 32 dollars; longells[90] for 9 dollars. We have however drawn the attention of the cloth merchants of whom several have been on board and therefore we expect better success in our future operations.

We have seen the Mandarins. The few boats which came near us, we attacked with many strong words without spilling blood; and terrified beyond measure they withdrew. However the harbour is in a state of blockade, and we ought therefore to make a diversion of a few days on behalf of the beleaguered merchants; who agree with us upon this point.[91]

We are now sending letters of invitation to the principal Hongs,[92] in order to come with them to an understanding. It is our wish to make them duly acquainted with the extensive connections of the house and to inform them that they can get every article for both the home, Formosa and Northern markets from our [constituents]. We shall in due time acquaint you with the result.

On the whole, I believe you will not be the loosers[93] in this voyage. I am very anxious to proceed up to the North as far as 31° Latitude, the Latitude assigned as a demarcation. Two tours which we made on the main [land] convinced us of

[89] Camlets: 'A name originally for a costly eastern fabric, subsequently for substitutes, made of various combinations of wool, silk, hair, and latterly cotton or linen'. (*OED*).

[90] 'Longells', or more usually 'long ells'. See above, Letter **72**, note 44.

[91] Although the local Chinese authorities seemed uncertain how to act when faced in their districts with foreign merchants who were supposed to trade exclusively at Canton, the local merchants had no such misgivings.

[92] By definition, they were not 'hong' merchants in the strict sense.

[93] (sic).

the friendly feelings of the natives who take a great interest in our commercial operations. Though my lack of medecine is very large, my practice is hitherto confined to heartache and itch; books are in demand, but we have little opportunity to get to the shore. Things remain at Formosa as they have been for many months. We saw several Mandarin junks return but the grand army is still on the island. I forgot to mention, that a great many calicoes were so damaged, that we were forced to sell them at a reduced price. Handkerchiefs are now in demand at a low price, and we have a great stock on hand.

Please to give my compliments to Messrs. Matheson, Jardine, Morrison, etc., etc.,

May the Almighty preserve you. I am, Dear Sir,

Your humble servant,

77. John Innes in Hendon to *Jardine, Matheson & Co.* in Canton,
6 September 1833

Dear Gentlemen,

Yours of 16th March last via *Philadelphia* reached me yesterday advising having shipped on my Account per *Jamesina* 22 Bales Raw Silk via Singapore for transshipment for London. I beg leave to express my best thanks for your kind attention to my investment throughout both the former shipment of Raw Silk per *Mermaid* lately arrived and these twenty two Bales of which you now advise me and which I daily expect are likely to pay me uncommonly well. Today's quotations are good Tsatlee 21 shillings and Tysaam 17 shillings per pound.

I observe what you say relative to the inferior quality of Silk on hand when you wrote which prevented Mr. Jardine interesting me in a further purchase. I feel equally obliged for his kind consideration as if the purchase had been affected.

As my Brother[94] pays the Balance of 330.20 dollars in your favor it closes the account. I confess I feel a little mortified that friend Jardine has caused [to] credit me for the trifling quantity of beer and wine which I was in hopes he would have accepted (not in any way as a set off for the essential services your House has rendered me both on this and former voyages) as a remembrance from an old friend for our acquaintance is not of yesterday.

You both with me Gentlemen will lament the heavy calamity which has befallen our mutual friends in Broadstreet Buildings,[95] our last account from Calcutta and Bombay are equally disastrous, which of course you have known, long before they reached us.

[94] This reference to 'my brother' (here and at the end of this Letter) is the clearest indication that Captain James Innes, of Canton, and Captain John Innes, of Hendon, were indeed siblings. See above, Letter **63**, note 83.

[95] The writer refers to the failure of *Fairlie, Clark, Innes & Co.*

Whether I am ever again to thank you in Person for all your kindness appears to me very problematical unless indeed I should bring out my Good Ship[96] as a purchase for you to make an Opium Depot, only she is too Good to make a hulk of. She must no doubt however come on Sale and really if you had not already bought the *Hercules* I should be almost tempted to buy her on your account. She will I expect go for an old Song, so many magnificient Ships thrown on the Market all at once will tend to depreciate the price exceedingly, I suspect one fourth of them will not find purchasers. So much for the East India Bill.

Officers as well as Ships are thrown adrift and we hear little talk of compensation as yet, though no doubt they will be compelled to do something towards remunerating the Officers of their Service now completely out of employ.

How will your Chinese authorities take to the new Superintendency[97] about to be appointed with their Judges, Courts of Justice, etc., etc., about to be established in Canton? I have not heard to a certainty of any of the appointments having filled up, though there is talk of a Mr. Stewart MacKenzie, M.P.[98] and member of the Board of Control being first Superintendent. I believe there is also to be a Naval Character among them to keep the Jacks in some Order.

I should think the duty they are by the China Trade Bill authorized to levy on Tonnage as well as Goods for the Support of the Establishment both on Country as well as Europe Ships will not be very palatable. I sent copies of the India and China Trade Bills to my Brother by an American that sailed from hence a few days ago which will explain to what I allude.

I remain, dear Gentlemen, very sincerely yours.

78. Horatio Hardy in London to *Jardine, Matheson & Co.* in Canton,

10 October 1833

Gentlemen,

I forwarded my last packet per *Philip the Ist* and letter N° 37. She sailed from Liverpool the 30th Ultimo. I now send this per *Albion* from the same Port.

The Government have not yet appointed the three Superintendents for China, the leading members of the Indian Board are on the Continent. A partial survey has been taken of the companys warehouses, wharfs and assets, no official report has yet been made, it is only preliminary for their disposal.

[96] John Innes probably refers to *HCS Abercrombie Robinson*, a ship he affectionately calls 'mine' for having commanded her, and which was going to be put up for sale, as all ships belonging to the Company.

[97] The East India Bill of 19 June 1833 provided that a Superintendency of British Trade comprising three officials was to be appointed. The First Superintendent of trade and his colleagues were to replace the Select Committee of the East India Company as the highest British authority in Canton.

[98] The Right Honourable J. A. S. Stewart MacKenzie, MP, later became governor of Ceylon. (*AL*, 1839, p. 68).

There are propositions for a new Company, either for Shipping or Tea. The one, 'S.T.' is merely a feeler from an accountant, and no names issued; the second from *John Nicholson and Co.* for Tea, editor of a Public Company, Capital two Millions, 20,000 Shares at 100 pounds Sterling each, *Messrs Smith, Payne & Co.* Bankers.[99] The third, a plan is formed by Stewart Marjoribanks,[100] Horsley Palmer,[101] William E. Ferrers Esq.,[102] two Millions Capital, Shares 4,000 in 500 pounds sterling shares, nine Directors only in the Company to be elected by Ballot, but none of them began with shareholders. The later Company if matured will only purchase the large ships.

The price of Silk continues at 21 shillings and 6 pence per pound and indigo has fallen 4 pence per pound. Teas as per page 6 sent by last conveyance.

The King of Spain[103] after a lingering illness died on the 29th September at 3 o'clock; the widowed Queen had the young Infanta, three years old, proclaimed the Queen Isabella II[104] immediately, assuming the Regency, without changing the administration. France and England have acknowledged this measure. Bilbao has declared for Don Carlos, this is the state of Spain, probably ripe for a civil war. The latest news from Portugal is the Battle of the 14th Ultimo. Don Miguel's General Bourmont[105] resigned and McDonald[106] placed in his room, it appears to be a *defeat*, as Don Miguel went to Madrid.

It is rather too premature to anticipate what will be the changes and effects with these countries, Spain and Portugal. The young Queen Donna Maria[107] had arrived

[99] A one page prospectus entitled *The India and China Company* was inserted in the letter. See immediately below, Document **79**.

[100] Stewart Marjoribanks: a former head of the Canton Select Committee. He was the 'husband' or managing owner of several East India Company ships, (the *Duke of Sussex*, the *Duke of York*, the *Thomas Coutts*, the *Hythe* and the *Berwickshire*). See **Appendix IX**.

[101] Horsley Palmer, conservative MP for Essex and governor of the Bank of England. (*DPC*). His brother, George Palmer, was also an important managing owner of HCS ships: the *Dunira* and the *Minerva*. (*Ibid.*)

[102] William E. Ferrers, 'Merchant, 25 Bucklersbury', London. (*TLCD*). He was managing owner of *HCS Duchess of Atholl*, and was a partner of Stewart Marjoribanks in *Marjoribanks, Ferrers & Co.* (*Ibid.*)

[103] Ferdinand VII (1784–1833) reigned from 1814, after a treaty signed with Napoleon restoring him to his throne. Only four months before this Letter was written Ferdinand VII had set aside the Salic Law to assure the succession of his infant daughter, Isabella. (*EWH*).

[104] Queen Isabella II (1830–1904). Her mother, Queen Maria Cristina acted as regent until the new queen attained her majority in 1843. In 1868 she was deposed and exiled to France and in 1870 she abdicated in favour of her son, Alfonso XII. (*CBD*).

[105] Louis, Count of Bourmont (1773–1864), French general. He later received the marshall's baton for his success in the Algiers expedition in 1830. (*CBC*).

[106] Macdonald: Jacques Etienne Joseph Alexandre Macdonald, Duke of Taranto (1765–1840). He was born in Sedan the son of a Scottish Jacobite schoolmaster. After fighting in the revolutionary armies, he was elevated to the rank of marshall and duke of Taranto by Napoleon. (*CBC*).

[107] Queen Donna Maria: see above, Letter **74**, note 67. Queen Maria was restored in September 1833, but Don Miguel was finally defeated only on 26 May 1834. (*EWH*).

and [been] proclaimed with great eclat; how changeable are states and nations subject to the caprice of factions, opinions, and speculative Political economy.

I am, Gentlemen,

Yours respectfully,

79. *John Nicholson & Co.*[108] in London to the Investing public

EAST INDIA AND CHINA COMPANY[109]

Capital two Millions Sterling
In twenty thousand shares of £100 each
Bankers: Messrs. Smith, Payne and Smiths

The first and main object of this 'COMPANY'[110] is to 'IMPORT TEA' upon the same system as has been hitherto acted upon by the 'EAST INDIA COMPANY,' in order to *secure* a *sufficient supply* of the article that can be *warranted* of *such quality* as shall be circulated to meet the immense consumption of this kingdom.

The paramount necessity of this 'COMPANY' is self-evident, in order to *supply* a commodity which is now deemed a necessary article of daily sustenance.

The Capital required to carry this undertaking into *full effect* will not exceed TWO MILLIONS STERLING.

The 'East India Company's' Charter will expire in April next, when the 'TEA MONOPOLY' will cease.

The Consumption of Tea in this Kingdom is about 'THIRTY-TWO MILLIONS OF POUNDS ANNUALLY,' and the price paid for it to the 'East India Company' has been about THREE MILLIONS THREE HUNDRED THOUSAND POUNDS STERLING *per annum.*[111]

[108] *John Nicholson & Co.*. 'Tea agents, 15 Fenchur ch Street', London. (*TLCD*). Only three letters are listed in the *BI*. Horatio Hardy's letter of 27 November 1834 mentions that 'the East India Company wharf was bought by Mr. John Nicholson, Tea Dealer, on 31 ult. for £25,600'. In 1818 John Nicholson introduced a new way of distributing tea. He attempted to bypass the wholesale trade by buying tea at the East India Company's auctions and then selling directly to retail customers throughout Britain. His *London Genuine Tea Company* became very successful, using no fewer than 1,200 agents in 1826. In 1823 he started publishing the *Nicholson's Tea List*, which informed local grocers about the latest tea auction prices. Such methods were thought revolutionary at the time, and Nicholson made many enemies. (See : Mui, Hoh-Cheung & Mui, Lorna, H., *The management of Monopoly, A Study of the East India Company's Conduct of its Tea Trade, 1784–1833*, Vancouver, University of British Columbia Press, 1984, pp. 20–22). By 1835, John Nicholson seems to have overextended himself, and his businesses failed. (See below, Letters **112** and **143**).

[109] This printed prospectus was found inside Letter **78** immediately above. The document is in poor condition, with some parts torn or missing.

[110] Most items between inverted commas are also capitalized in the printed text which is reproduced here with all its idiosyncrasies.

[111] Tea consumption increased rapidly in the 1830s. In 1832, 33.4 millions lbs were consumed; in 1833: 33.7 million lbs; in 1834: 38.0 million pounds. (Cheong, *Mandarins and Merchants*, p. 182). By 1838 exports from Canton had reached over 42.1 million lbs. (*JMArch*, 7–231).

It now becomes a matter of the first consideration, to devise the means by which this article of GREAT NATIONAL IMPORTANCE shall in future be supplied; and whether it be possible, that private individuals will venture to embark their capital to such an extent as to be able to 'import a sufficient supply of Tea' to meet the demand.

It is well known to all who have been connected with the 'tea Trade in China,' that it is utterly impracticable for 'Private Traders' to deal with the 'China Merchants' upon EQUITABLE TERMS; and that if the *supply* of THIRTY-TWO MILLIONS OF POUNDS OF TEA is to depend on '*Private traders*,' there can be no doubt but that this country will be INUNDATED WITH ALL SORTS OF STUFF, under the *name* of TEA, which will not only rapidly *reduce* the *consumption*, but be *deeply injurious* to the health of the people and fatal to the Revenue.

This has been the *result in America*, where they have carried on a 'FREE TRADE IN TEA' with CHINA; and in consequence of its *perniciousness*, has almost placed the article of TEA OUT OF USE.

It is well known to all who are connected with the *Tea Trade in China*, that the 'East India Company' possessed *singular* and *exclusive advantages* at CANTON over all other Nations, in their *selections*, and *management* of the '*Tea Trade*', and it may safely be attributed to *this cause* that the consumption of Tea in this Kingdom has so *rapidly increased*, whilst it has *rapidly decreased* in every other part of the world.

It will be a principle with the 'DIRECTORS' of this 'COMPANY' to conduct it with the greatest possible *economy*, precisely in the same way as should be adopted by every prudent '*Private Trader*'.

It has *not* been *deemed fit* to introduce this 'COMPANY' WITH A SET OF SELF-CONSTITUTED DIRECTORS; *this* must be the *act* of the '*Shareholders*,' who, no doubt, *will select men who, having each* embarked *a very large capital*, will offer the best *guarantee* for its correct, prudent, and faithful management, so that *every holder of a single Share will have equal security for its* SAFETY *as those who have invested from* TWENTY *to* FIFTY THOUSAND POUNDS.

The 'DIRECTORS' of this 'COMPANY' *will not have any 'fixed salary.'* Whatever *remuneration* may be given, will be the *act* of the *'Shareholders,' and should be regulated on the principle of the benefit received.*

This 'COMPANY' will differ essentially from many others; it has not been concocted in the '*usual way*,' namely, by an artist, an engineer, a surveyor, a lawyer, or any *Speculator*.

It is the act of persons of *real Capital*, who mean to embark *their own money* in the undertaking, and who must consequently be most deeply interested in the careful management of *it*.

It is not like the *erecting* of a new *bridge*, which, after the expense of 'half a million of money', is *discovered* not to be wanted; and when it often turns out that very few are to be found who will *pay* the *toll* to meet the interest for the money sunk.

It is not like the great project of the '*Thames Tunnel*,' which, after the expenditure of half a million of money, sunk at the bottom of the Thames, required another half million to dig it up again.

It is not like the '*Mines in Mexico*,' or elsewhere; the mere name of some is all that has ever been known, except that *immense sums of gold* have been sent out to work these Mines, when, *after years of labour*, it has been discovered that the *Mines had been exhausted of all their treasure by the 'old Spaniards !'*

It is not like a 'Rail Road Company,' that requires twenty-four Directors, Engineers, Surveyors, Canvassers, Travelers, Parliamentary Agents, Parliamentary Fees, Counsel's Fees, etc., etc., etc., without end, who may spend from SEVENTY TO ONE HUNDRED THOUSAND POUNDS BEFORE THEY DIG A SINGLE YARD OF GROUND, and at the end of three or four years may peradventure discover AFTER THE EXPENDITURE OF TWO MILLIONS OF MONEY, *that it is not wanted, one new discovery having been made to render it useless and from which it is impossible to derive any interest for many years.*

The money embarked in this undertaking will not be subject to any *risk*. The CAPITAL AND PROFIT MUST BE REALISED WITHIN EIGHTEEN MONTHS.

As a full and *perfect security against all risk*, every means will be taken which would be adopted by the most prudent individual. [ ] the most AMPLE INSURANCE effected, a proceeding which cannot fail to merit the attention of the great 'INSURANCE COMPANIES.'

In every *Department* of the *Management*, both at CANTON and in LONDON, persons will be employed who are highly qualified by *long experience* and a *perfect knowledge* of the 'TEA TRADE' in all its branches.

The CAPITAL which has been *employed* in LONDON in the 'TEA TRADE' during the last fifty years may be estimated from THREE TO FOUR MILLION STERLING.

It is a matter of deep interest with the 'LONDON CAPITALISTS,' whether this shall be taken out of employment, and the immense trade consequence thereon TRANSFERRED TO THE OUTPORTS. Should this be the case, thousands of persons must quit London, the effect of which will be felt to an extent not to be described.

The SHIP-OWNERS will be the first who will feel the loss of this trade; and next to them, thousands downwards to the carmen, who are employed in the various departments in this hitherto MOST IMPORTANT BRANCH OF TRADE to the City of London.

If therefore, at the last hour, it be not promptly and zealously taken up, the '*Tea Trade*' *must be inevitably lost* to the '*Port of London*.'

A DEPOSIT OF FIVE POUNDS *per Share to be paid to*
MESSRS. SMITH, PAYNE, AND SMITHS,[112]

[112] *Smith Payne & Smith*: 'Bankers, Lombard Street'. (TLCD). The banking firm of *Smith, Payne & Smith* was highly respected, and its name at the foot of this prospectus was meant to lend credibility to the venture. In fact, the projected 'East India and China Company' was never actually set up.

Applications for Shares and 'Prospectuses' may be made (if by letter, post paid) to

JOHN NICHOLSON AND COMPANY
FENCHURCH STREET, LONDON

80. *Fergusson & Co.* in Calcutta to *Jardine, Matheson & Co.* in Canton, 26 November 1833[113]

Dear Sirs,

It is with feelings of deep regret and disappointment we inform you that we have this day been obliged finally to suspend our payments.

It is not necessary for us to enter into a long explanation of the circumstances which have forced this painful alternative upon us, as the recent calamitous events in the Commercial Community of this City must be well known to you, and the extent to which we have been affected by them we have not attempted to conceal. It is enough to state that the unlooked for failure of our correspondents in London, involving the return of Bills to a considerable amount and causing a fresh paroxysm of alarm and distrust from the intimate connection that was known to have subsisted between the two Houses for a long series of years, superadded to the measures pursued by some parties with a view of enforcing a preferential adjustment of their claims by legal proceedings, and combined with the discovery of an extensive system of transfer which we had not other means of preventing, has crushed the hopes we entertained of a better issue to our exertions, and imposed on us the duty of taking steps for the equal protection of all by resigning the control of our affairs—a result we the more deeply deplore after the kind and generous support we have experienced from so many of our friends.

After mature deliberation we have considered it the best course for all to place our concerns under the management of the Insolvent Court.[114] We shall be prepared on an early day to lay before our Creditors a statement of our affairs, and it is some satisfaction to us to know that they will be found to be improved by the enhanced value of Indigo and Indigo Concerns, as well as by our general transactions since the beginning of the present year.

We are, Dear Sirs, Your most obedient Servants.

Neither did the competing projects mentioned in the Letter immediately above ever come to fruition. The John Nicholson prospectus is a good illustration of how some the most enterprising private merchants of the day, no matter how radical their ideology, had no sooner succeeded in bringing down the hateful tea monopoly of the East India Company than they hatched their own private schemes to rebuild large tea-buying companies. None of them succeeded, however, and the 1834 India Bill introduced a new era of freedom in the British tea trade, with radical consequences on the Canton market.

[113] This is a printed circular letter, with only the name of the addressee and the signature for the firm in ink.

[114] The loss incurred by *Jardine, Matheson & Co.* as a result of this bankruptcy was minimal. See above, Letter **68**, note 18.

1834

81. William Jardine in Canton to Carl Gutzlaff on board the *Colonel Young*, 13 January 1834

My dear Doctor,

Your favor of the 3rd ultimo, to Captain Grant and myself, was received on the 4th Instant, and your messenger Mr. Innes[1] handed me your letter of the 2nd Instant at 10 a.m. on the 8th—so much for the *Fairy*.

I note your wish to proceed to the straits of Malacca for a few weeks; and shall have much pleasure in assisting you in carrying your intended trip into effect.

We expected the *Colonel Young* to have returned from the Coast before the China New Year, but from what Captain Rees[2] writes, and Mr. Innes says, I deem it advisable to send the *Fairy* back; so as to enable her to bring back all the funds you may have realized on her return to you, and reach us three days before the China New Year. Leaving you to continue until the idle days interrupt business,[3] or even a little longer, should you wish it.

I am glad you have been going on so quietly, and doing so well; but regret one of our friends[4] has been suspected by government and I shall be glad to hear that confidence has been restore between him and his Mandarin Friends. I am clearly of opinion you should all leave the Coast for a month or two; and allow your Chinese dealers to reap the full benefit of their purchases; and with this view, we send you very little by the *Fairy*. No piece goods, the *Pauline* not having arrived yet.

The Company's small ships have not been heard of, nor have we any late advices from England.

Your Friend Plowden[5] is off in the *Sussex*, Captain Whitehead.[6] Grant's publication, (which I send you a copy of) will meet him everywhere—at the Cape, St Helena and in England. Copies have been sent on to the Governors of each place; and to the East India Company Directors. It opened the eyes of the Canton

[1] Mr. Innes: Captain James Innes

[2] Captain John Rees, one the firm's best captains. He became the head of the opium fleet. (Over 150 letters from Captain Rees are listed in the *BI*).

[3] The Chinese New Year, coinciding with the first full moon of the year in early February or late January was then—and remains today—the biggest Chinese festival. Commercial activity stopped for a whole week, as does business today.

[4] One of the Chinese go-betweens who gave a lead to develop the coastal market in piece-goods. He was not identified.

[5] The head of the Factory. See above, Letter **69**, note 20. He was Gutzlaff's 'friend' as a manner of speaking only. William Jardine was partial to this expression.

[6] W. H. Whitehead was the Captain of *HCS Duke of Sussex*, a ship whose managing owner was Stewart Marjoribanks. (**Appendix IX**).

Community. The Keiou affair still pending.[7] Chinese made a grand mistake in only listening to one side of the question. They wish to purchase a man, etc. I refused to put a Lascar[8] in their power, but offered to attend the meeting, and submit to be examined myself. This offer was declined.

Davis[9] is now Chief, and hitherto things have gone on quietly. On your return, bring with you a memo of such descriptions of piece goods—cottons and woolens—as are required with prices attached. Take the prices even of such articles as are very low and not in demand. We may possibly make a clean sweep, and sell them for whatever they will fetch.[10]

Your friends here are all well. No news. In hopes of seeing you here soon by the *Fairy* or *Young* as you may prefer.

I remain, My dear Doctor,[11]

Yours very sincerely,

[7] The Keiou affair is given a three page treatment in Fay, *Opium War*, pp. 62–64. The principal facts accounting for the otherwise obscure references in this paragraph occurred over a six month period and are the following. Keiou is a small island off Macao. Close to it, the anchorage of Cumsingmoon was supposed to be safe during the typhoon season. In August 1833, Captain Alexander Grant took his two opium receiving ships there for safety. The *Hercules* withstood the typhoon, but the *Samarang* ran aground. Grant decided to break it up. Some of the islanders stole items from the wreckage. Grant's party, led by Captain Parry, his chief mate, recovered what they could. In October, during a scuffle between the islanders and the British, a lascar was stabbed to death. Much armed agitation ensued, including the retaliatory kidnapping of a Chinese field labourer, and the wounding by gunshot—and subsequent death—of a Chinese coming to his rescue. The governor-general of Canton took matters in hand. He secured the release of the kidnapped labourer, asked for the handover of the murderer, and severely reprimanded the Select Committee for not controlling the British Community. The Select asked to hear Grant's version of the affair. Grant gave an unabashed defense of the kidnapping, adding that he would only be guided in what he did by the defense of his own property (meaning opium) and of the property entrusted to him. From the second sentence of this paragraph it is also clear (a fact so far unknown) that Captain Grant ensured that a printed version of his defense was publicized as widely as possible, in order to further embarrass the members of the Select Committee.

[8] Lascar : 'East Indian sailor'. (*OED*).

[9] John Francis Davis (1795–1890). The last president of the Select Committee of the East India Company in Canton, and one of the few who knew Chinese. He was appointed Second Superintendent to Lord Napier in July 1834. When Lord Napier died, her rose to First Superintendent of British Trade. He later succeeded Sir Henry Pottinger as second Governor of Hong Kong. He was rewarded for his work by a baronetcy in 1845. He wrote several books on China and various translations, including: *The Chinese: A General Description of the Empire of China and its Inhabitants*, two volumes, London, Charles Knight, 1836; *Chinese Moral Maxims, with a Free and Verbal Translation, etc..*, London, John Murray, 1823; *On the Poetry of the Chinese, etc.*, Macao, East India Company Press, 1834; *Chinese Novels, Translated from the Originals; The Shadow in the Water. The Twin Sisters. The Three Dedicated Chambers*. Etc., London, John Murray, 1843; *The Sorrows of Han*, Translated from the Original, with Notes, etc., London, John Murray, Parbury, Allen & Co., 1829. (Lust, *Western Books on China*, pp. 2, 32, 169, 256, 257, 261).

[10] An early sign that the piece goods from British manufactures shipped from England by John Macvicar were not selling well.

[11] A courtesy title.

82. Cursetjee Jamsetjee in Bombay to William Jardine in Canton

11 March 1834

My dear Sir,

In the absence of my worthy father[12] and in accordance with the wish expressed by him in a letter received yesterday, I take up my pen to address you in his name to thank you for your kind letter of the 1st January per *Hermazjee Bomanjee* especially for the information it contained, and also to inform you the soft sugar has experienced a considerable decline in price and will not at all answer for this market and that should you deem it advisable and a safe investment you may purchase Teas of different sorts suitable to the English Market to the extent of from 300 to 350 Tons shipping the same by the *Success* to this Port.

This suggestion has originated in the remark made by you that Teas of all description were much reduced in price consequent upon the withdrawal of the Select Committee from the Market. But upon this subject he wishes you to act at your discretion. The *Success* he is anxious that you should dispatch not later than the end of May or very early in June. If however any desirable object can be obtained by your detaining her for a few days you are at perfect liberty to do so. [The goods] he desires me to say he wishes you to forward by the *Success* are to the extent of One Lac of Dollars, to be invested as follows, viz—in Teas as above mentioned, Cassia as low as possible, with a little Sugar Candy, and in the event of any or either of these not being procurable at what you may consider a fair price, the remittance to be completed to the ful extent of One Lac of Dollars in either Silver or Gold. Should you have purchased Sugar on our account he begs that you will resell it on the spot as he is decidedly of opinion that it will not answer. Messrs. Charles Thomas and Co.[13] of Singapore inform us that no sugar was to be had and we have since advised them not to purchase but to remit all our available funds to Calcutta.

The *Bombay Castle* is on the eve of coming into Dock, and the *Charlotte* is back just out having undergone a thorough repair. The *Lord William* will be the first ship from the House to your Consignment. From all appearance it is surmised that there will be but a limited supply of Cotton to your place this Season. The first ships for China will be the *Lowjee Family* and *Cornwallis* which will be followed by the *Charles Forbes* and *Charlotte*.[14]

Our Exchange Market continues much in the same state as before. Some private Bills have been sold as high as 2 shillings and three pence per Rupee.

[12] Jamsetjee Jejeebhoy.

[13] For Charles Thomas: see above, Letter **33**, note 58 and **66**, note 6.

[14] Most of the ships mentioned in this paragraph were built by the Bombay Dockyard. *HCS Bombay Castle*, a 1,228-ton ship, in 1808; the *Royal Charlotte*, (672 tons), in 1803; the *Lowjee Family*, (926 tons), in 1790; The *Lord William* (393 tons), in 1800. (Wadia, *Bombay Dockyard*, pp. 355–358).

I remain with regards, My Dear Sir,
Yours very faithfully,

83. William Jardine in Canton to Thomas Weeding in London,
20 April 1834

Dear Sir,

I have just finished reading your own correspondence from 6th of June to the 23rd of October with a view of replying thereto by the ships about to be dispatched for the different parts of England and Scotland with cargoes of Tea.

Most of your letters have been already noticed; and little remains to be said on the most important subject treated therein; viz. the failure of our friends in Broad Street, and the settlement of our account with them, and our friend Hollingworth Magniac. Mr. Matheson has addressed the latter at great length, putting the affair of the transfer of 20,000 pounds sterling fairly before him with copies of letters, proving the state of the accounts at the time the transfer was ordered by us; and left it for adjustment, on equitable terms, between him and ourselves.[15]

This being the case, and our information being yet very limited on the subject of what has been done in consequence of our power of attorney having reached Magniac and your good self, I shall for the present refrain from troubling you on this head further than repeating our most sincere thanks for the friendly feeling and determined zeal with which you have attended to our interests. Believe me, I feel truly grateful.

The opening of the Trade between Great Britain and China is the next matter of importance treated in your letters; and, for the information communicated, as well as for the Acts of Parliament transmitted, I feel particularly obliged, but cannot, at the same time, conceal from you my disappointment, at not having been provided with your opinion as to the time when a ship, now in China, with the usual licence[16] of coming here, may *legally*[17] leave this port for England direct with a Tea cargo.

[15] For the settlement between Hollingworth Magniac and *Jardine, Matheson & Co.* following the failure of *Fairlie Clark Innes & Co.*, see below, Letter **113**.

[16] Since the India Act of 1813, private ships had been allowed to trade at Canton in all goods except tea, but they still needed a licence from the East India Company.

[17] As British citizens, William Jardine and James Matheson were scrupulous in the observance of English law. This is one of the reasons why they had great objection in being called 'smugglers'. In selling opium to the Chinese, they were not breaking any English laws. Their strongly-held view was that it was the Chinese who were smugglers, not the British merchants. 'We are not smugglers, Gentlemen !' declared Jardine in a speech at his leaving party in 1839, 'It is the Chinese government, it is the Chinese officers, who smuggle, and who connive at and encourage smuggling, not we !'(Fay, *Opium war*, p. 138, quoting from the *Chinese Repository*, V, p. 412).

A difference of opinion exists here, though we can see no reason why a doubt should be entertained on the subject. The restrictions have been removed. Liberty of direct trade has been granted, after the 22nd Instant, unconditionally, and we have determined on sending the ships, already alluded to, off without further delay, Superintendents or no Superintendents.[18] They should have been here a month ago—if their presence is absolutely necessary to legalize our proceedings. Were any accidents to befall the ships in which the Superintendents are coming out, they might not reach China in many months to come, and were their presence necessary to legalize this voyage, the trade between this and England would be suspended for a very inconvenient length of time. At the same time I reason in this way, I feel convinced the Government would have acted wisely had they prohibited the importation and sale of Teas in England on the new duties, till March or April 1835 which would have kept [unaltered] the regular routine here, and given the Company time to reduce their stock of Teas to one year's consumption or probably something under one year without injuring anyone.

I have asked Mr. Davis[19] his opinion as to the legality of the voyage; and whether he has received any instructions to act in case of need. I enclose copy of his reply. His opinion agrees with mine.

April 23rd, 1834.

We intend dispatching the *Camden Francis*, *Charlotte*, and *Georgian*, tomorrow, for Glasgow, Hull and Liverpool;[20] loaded with Tea, partly on our account, and partly on account of our friends, Europeans and Chinese.[21] Mr. Innes is a [party interested in the cargo], and addresses you on the subject.

The cargoes consist chiefly of Company's Congos which, had their monopoly continued, would have been sent home by the ships leaving this port in November next. The quality is very fair, and prices moderate. If we get 18 pence per pound, we shall realize a fair profit, even at 15 pence we should not complain; and if the prayer of our petition to Parliament[22] is listened to, the old ladies will drink good tea at about 3 shillings per pound. It would be very hard if our Congo sold at 1 shilling and 6 pence per pound to have to pay a duty of 2 shillings and 2 pence per pound.

Allow me to beg your best attention to the subject in case of need. Ministers will surely listen to reason; and not subject us to a higher duty than the *ad*

[18] The India Act had freed the tea trade as from 22 April 1834. The Superintendent of British Trade, Lord Napier, arrived in Macao only in July 1834.

[19] John Francis Davis was still head of the Select Committee. His change of status to Superintendent came three months after this letter was written. See above, Letter **81**, note 9.

[20] Three of the seven new ports allowed by the new India Bill to have bonded warehousing facilities. See above, Letter **74**, note 66.

[21] It was then a novelty for *Jardine, Matheson & Co.*'s Chinese business friends to become partners in investment transactions and to have a share in these first 'free tea' cargoes shipped to Britain.

[22] It is unclear which 'petition to Parliament' William Jardine is referring to.

valorem duty hitherto paid; as they have declared their intention of reducing, rather than increasing, the rates of duty on all teas.

The *Pyramus* is nearly loaded, and will be dispatched two or three days hence, for Falmouth, there to await your orders as to her port of discharge. We shall send you by this conveyance a copy of her manifest, or list of her cargo, as far as is in our power; and we have to request you will at your earliest convenience send orders to Falmouth to await Captain Weller's arrival.[23] We leave the port of discharge entirely to you and have no doubt you will select the one where you are likely to meet with the best prices and quickest sale, with the exception of the three ports already supplied, you have your choice of England, Ireland and Scotland.

The quality of the teas per *Pyramus* is the same as of those by the other ships; and I have no doubt about their realizing equally high prices. I am far from feeling sanguine on the subject of profit, but at the prices we have purchased we can scarcely suffer a loss.

Our market is very much overstocked with piece goods of all kinds, and prices have declined very much. You must be very careful not to ship large amounts by the *Sarah*, on your own account, particularly if the efforts have been extensive by the early ships. You must not expect a great increase in consumption in this country for several years, and our American friends have commenced, already, to supply the deficiency of goods consequent on the death of the Company. They have, I think, been premature and are scarcely realizing costs and charges.

The Winter Congos[24] have now been nearly all purchased by the different Houses, and individuals here, at various prices from 16 Tales to 18 Tales per

[23] Captain Weller was not identified.

[24] 'Congo' is a transliteration of the Chinese for a particular quality of black tea. Early in the Letter, William Jardine had referred to 'Company's congos'; now he mentions 'Winter congos'. In Letter **85** below, paragraph 4, he provides his reader with a succinct explanation of the difference between the two types of congos. The difference was not so much in the quality of the tea, as in the manner in which it used to be purchased by the East India Company, and in the timing of the purchase. 'Company Congo' was also called 'Contract congo'. This referred to the oral contract with the Select Committee members made with each of the Hong merchants for delivery of teas each year in November and December. These contracts were binding contracts in the sense that each hong merchant knew that he would be paid a pre-determined amount of silver in exchange for a certain weight of tea of a certain quality. But they were also unusually flexible contracts in the sense that the quantity stipulated in the contract with each supplier was left quite vague and was mentioned only as an order of magnitude. When the Congo arrived in Canton from the tea gardens in the Fukien province and other tea producing areas of China, the actual supply available reflected not so much the demand contracted for by the East India Company as the overall agricultural production offered for export. It was often the case that this exceeded the contractual demand. In such a situation, the Company's tendency had been to buy a little more than it had contracted for and to ship the tea immediately to London. This tea was known as 'Company' of 'Contract' congo. What congo was not bought was then warehoused by the hong merchants and left over until the following year, when it served as buffer against the next crop. This stock of tea was known as 'Winter' congo. The Company always bought

picul, and contracts have been made for new Congos at two and three Tales per picul less than the Company's contract prices. We commenced purchasing the Congo on account of orders from England and we were quickly followed by a host of speculators who soon raised the prices from 16 and 17 Tales per picul without much reference to quality.

I have omitted to say the quality of the Boheas per *Pyramus*, is exactly the same as the Company's Fokien Bohea, being in fact one of their chops which they had not room for. I shall have the pleasure of addressing you again soon.

In the meantime, I remain, Dear Weeding,

Yours sincerely,

84. William Jardine in Canton to John Thacker[25] in Scotland

23 April 1834

Dear Thacker,

I have before my eyes your favours of 17th June, 17th July and 13th September last, received on the 29th of January and 25th of February. I have to apologize for not having acknowledged earlier these letters, which arose from a wish on my part, to be able to reply satisfactorily to your inquiry respecting the necessity of a ship proceeding to this port for a cargo of Tea bringing with her funds sufficient to purchase one.

This is a question to be settled in England, not here, and I have refrained from addressing you, in hopes of receiving such information as would enable me to form an opinion on the subject, but we are still in the dark as to the views of the parties at home and the success or failure of the many proposed joint stock companies.

My own view of the case is this. The funds to load the ships sent here should be furnished from home, in dollars—Bills on the Supreme Government of India, credits on England, or an investment of goods from England according to circumstances. The interest of money is too high in this country to admit of advances on interest on cargoes shipped, and we have few speculators here to distant markets. The funds have hitherto been supplied from England and India by the Company, and generally speaking, they must be provided from similar sources in time to come.[26] Opportunities may offer when we can load one or two ships

---

Winter congo at a discount of 5 or 6 taels per picul, and it served as a means of balancing demand and supply in a 'market' where the East India Company was only buyer. (Le Pichon, *Origines de Hong Kong*, pp. 363–370).

[25] John Thacker: probably Captain Thacker, mentioned in Letters **197** and **206**, and nicknamed 'Jawing Jack' in Letter **245**.

[26] The message sent here by William Jardine to tea speculators was that they should not expect to borrow locally in Canton on the security of their tea purchases. The rump of the East India Company left in China to wind down its affairs (which became known as the 'Finance Committee') had very

without difficulty. We have this day completed the loading of three ships to Great Britain and could without difficulty load a fourth. But this may not occur again for years.

We shall have much pleasure in doing everything in our power to assist any ship you may entrust to our care. But I should be dealing unfairly by you, were I to hold out prospects that, in my opinion, might not be realized.

We enclose our latest *Price Current* and a copy of [a circular] for those about to engage in the China trade which may, even to an old stager like you, prove useful, and with ever good wish for your success.

I remain, dear Thacker,

Yours sincerely,

85. William Jardine in Canton to W. T. Copeland[27] in London,

26 April 1834

My dear Sir,

I have to apologize for not having earlier acknowledged your favours of the 20th May and 20th of July last and shall now endeavour to make up for my neglect by giving you a brief account of what has been done here under the new system of a free Trade between Great Britain and China, though we are still ignorant of the measures contemplated by the Superintendents daily expected from England. We are not even aware of the names of the parties who are nominated to rule over us with unlimited power.[28]

Three ships have been dispatched with cargoes of Tea. One for Liverpool, one for Hull, and one for Glasgow, and a fourth will be dispatched in two or three days for Falmouth there to await orders as to the port of discharge.

You are aware that the Company have been in the habit of contracting with the Hong Merchants about this time of the season for their annual supply of Congo Teas; which generally arrive in November and December, and were shipped off immediately they arrived, prices 28, 27, 26 Tales per picul according to quality; for such Teas as were selected and shipped by the ships of that Season. At the close of the Season musters of the remaining Congos were called for; and the best Chops selected, weighed and warehoused, ready for boarding the early ships of the following Season. Prices, generally speaking 22, 21, and 20 Tales per picul, but they have been purchased as low as 20, 19, and 18 Tales per picul.

---

different ideas on the subject and was soon to lend large amounts to tea speculators. (See Letters **93** and **96**).

[27] William Taylor Copeland: a partner in the firm of *Spode and Copeland* (see above, Letter **19**). Some 50 letters from W.T. Copeland are listed in the *BI*. By 1838, he was a Member of Parliament (see Letter **151**).

[28] There are relatively few letters where William Jardine's sense of humour shows through his usually guarded seriousness.

The Teas shipped by the vessels already alluded to, are of the latter description and would, had the monopoly continued, have been sent away in October and November next under the name 'Winter Teas' or 'Company Winter Congos'.[29] The whole of these Winter Teas have now been purchased by the Houses, and by individuals, at various prices from 16 Tales to 19 Tales per picul, free on board. Contracts have also been made for new Congos[30] deliverable in November next at 25, 24 and 23 Tales per picul, quality to be equal to those supplied to the Company in years passed at 28, 27 and 26. Similar contracts have been made for Boheas and Twankey teas, but I have not much faith in these contracts, and expect to have some trouble in fixing the qualities.

If the market is dull and Teas are abundant we shall have very little trouble; but if teas are scarce, and prices high, the Tea men[31] who are generally men of indifferent character, will insist on the contract Teas being equal to the Company's first quality when they are scarcely equal to the second, and if we do not yield the point, will sell their Tea in the market. In such a case we should have much trouble in obtaining redress; and may in some instance, be unable to succeed. The Company had a great advantage from being almost the only purchaser of Congo Tea; but in green Teas, where they had a rival in the demand for the American market, many tricks were practiced against them, such as keeping back a third or a half of the best Chops and selling them to the Americans at a higher price, taking care to change the chops, or characters, on the chests, which is easily done.[32]

We shall now have so many purchasers, and so much competition, that it will be difficult to keep them totally honest. I mean the Tea merchants, who bring the article to Canton, the Hong Merchants being the only intermediate party between them and us.

Had you been more decided about the Tea speculation, I should have been anxious to have interested you in the Winter Congo, and to a moderate extent in contracts for new Teas, as many of the most respectable of the black tea merchants

[29] On 'Company congos' and 'Winter congos', see above, Letter **83**, note 24.

[30] The private merchants and the private firms continued the East India Company tradition of contracting for teas a year in advance, in the belief that their orders were secure.

[31] This 'short supply' scenario envisaged by William Jardine shows that he had serious misgivings as to the honesty of the 'Tea men'. The Tea men supplied tea wholesale to the Hong merchants for resale to the East India Company. Contrary to the Hong merchants, whose reputation for honesty and fair dealing was recognized by all foreigners, and who shared with British merchants the motto: 'my word is my bond', the Tea men were untested. Although he had never previously dealt directly with them, William Jardine suspected that their 'indifferent character' would not resist the temptation of reneging on tea contracts if better deals could be had elsewhere. His misgivings proved entirely correct. (See below, Letters **132, 134**).

[32] The Americans in Canton did not fall under the jurisdiction of the East India Company. Their experience in buying tea was therefore long established and they had an expertise in this area which the private British merchants were lacking. The Americans, however, purchased mostly green teas, reflecting the different taste of their home market.

have applied to us to enter into such arrangements; which we have done to the extent of the orders we have received from England.

The quantity of Raw Silk exported this Season to England direct and via Bombay does not fall short of ten thousand (10,000) bales. Of this quantity about 2,000 bales, chiefly Taysaam, have been sent to Bombay; partly as a speculation for England and partly on account of the allure of the best Canton silk, which is consumed largely in Bombay every year.

The exchange with England has been fluctuating lately, between 4 shillings and 9 pence, and 5 shillings per dollar, according to the character of the Bills and the want of the parties negotiating them. Money is usually scarce among the Chinese; and an importation of dollars is required to keep up a sufficient supply of the circulating medium.

Be pleased to accept my best thanks for the parliamentary documents you have kindly furnished me with, and believe, My dear Sir,

Yours very sincerely,

86. *Lyall Matheson & Co.* in Calcutta to *Jardine, Matheson & Co.* in Canton, 2 May 1834[33]

Dear Sirs,

We have now the pleasure to wait on you with Invoices, and a Bill of Lading of [232] Chests of Opium shipped to your address on the *Red Rover*[34] now taking her departure again for your place. Of the above quantity 166 Chests are on your own account per Invoice amounting to 97,660 Rupees. 46 Chests are on account of {T.H.}[35] per Invoice amounting to 46,163 Rupees, and 20 Chests are on account of Mr. W. S. Boyd[36] per Invoice amounting to 19,363 Rupees—all which we trust will arrive to a good market. We shall prepare an Account Current for T.H. crediting him with Bills on England for 5,000 pounds Sterling, and debiting him with the shipment of Opium, but fear it will not be ready to go per *Rover*.

The following are the particulars of our last Opium Sale:

[33] It seems curious that few, if any, letters from *Lyall Matheson & Co.* in Calcutta were written personally by partners addressing partners. It is possible that the personal letters were set aside or placed elsewhere in *JMArch*. The writer of this particular letter appears relatively junior and somewhat lacking in business fluency.

[34] The *Red Rover*: a 254-ton clipper and one of the fastest. Year after year, in the 1830s, it beat the competition on the route from Cacutta to Lintin. It was built, owned and commanded by Captain Clifton. In 1832, *Jardine, Matheson & Co.* bought a third share in the ship, and subsequently owned an equal share with Captain Clitfon. (*Origines de Hong Kong*, p. 435–436; Lubbock, *The Opium Clippers*, Glasgow, Brown, Son & Ferguson Ltd. , 1933, p. 382.)

[35] T.H. was not identified.

[36] William Sprott Boyd, an employee of *Jardine, Matheson & Co.* He worked with Henry Wright in the opium department. See Letters **184, 207, 218** and **243**.

	Chests	Highest	Lowest	Average
Patna:	1401	960	935	944.11.2
Benares:	592	925	915	919.6.11

Prices have since then advanced, Patna to 985 Rupees and Benares to 955 Rupees, and are likely to advance still more.

The *Rover* was reported on the day of the Sale but no one expect ourselves received their letters till the day following. The Opium now going on account of yourselves and T.H., as also a further quantity we are sending you on our own account was purchased at our second Sale when we thought prices at their lowest, and we have not now to advise having made any purchases on your account, nor have we at present a single Chest remaining on hand.

We have not effected Insurance on your Opium, considering this done by yourselves in China. T.H.'s Opium is insured in the *Alliance Insurance Society*[37] and continues covered as usual for thirty days after arrival.

At Captain Clifton's request we continue to keep the *Red Rover's* block insured[38] in the Tenth Canton Insurance office for 50,000 Rupees.

We enclose a letter for Mr. Boyd and are, Dear Sirs,

Yours faithfully,

87. William Jardine in Canton to John Macvicar in Manchester,

9 May 1834

My dear Macvicar,

I cannot allow the *Pauline* to sail without a few lines for you though I have nothing of importance to communicate. The letters of Mr. Thom[39] and the Firm being sufficiently full of all important points.

I cannot conceal from you how much this speculation to Bordeaux[40] has annoyed me, and I am sadly afraid you will have reason to regret ever having entered into it. Had you steered clear of chartering her, and engaged or even purchased a smart English vessel to bring your piece goods [here] only via Singapore, the result would have been most satisfactory; but it is difficult to form an opinion as to the probable loss or gain on the Teas and cassia now sent per *Pauline*, so many shipments having been made to the same market early in the bygone season.

Mr. Thom has formed so poor an opinion of the Bordeaux market for Teas and the charter party has been drawn up in such a clumsy manner, that we have deemed it advisable to fill her up with cassia, as the article on which your loss is

[37] *Alliance Insurance Society*: a Calcutta insurance company.

[38] On 'insurance on blocks' or 'block insurance', see above Letter **64**, note 87.

[39] For Robert Thom, see above, Letter **72**, note 41.

[40] See Letter **72**, 3rd paragraph.

likely to be smallest. Mr. Brown[41] has allowed himself to be overreached by the owner, I am afraid, and it would not surprise me if they quarreled about the settlement of the account. It would afford me great pleasure to hear that you realized a remittance of even 4 shillings and 6 pence and closed the transaction.

The white goods[42] by the *Pauline* are still uncleared, the purchaser objecting to part of the goods as not equal to musters, and demanding an allowance of one or two dollars per piece or part of them, but this is all nonsense. He has paid only 3,000 dollars as bargain money, which he threatens to forfeit; but this, the Hong Merchant Hengtai[43] refuses to consent to, as we are waiting the man's return from the country to come to a settlement. We shall be obliged to make some allowance. I have compared the musters with the goods, and in one or two instances the difference is considerable. Cottons and woolens have fallen very much and are in fact unsaleable for cash on any terms.

Raw silk may be purchased at 340 dollars per picul, but there is none of good quality in the market. The quantity shipped to England direct and circuitously, exceeds ten thousand bales. We pick up every lot, of tolerably good quality that is offered, and we expect fresh supplies in a few days. Teas have advanced a little, the Winter Congos of good quality are now worth 18 Tales per picul. Middling and inferior quality 17.5 and 17 Tales per picul.

We shall have an opportunity of addressing you again soon.

Yours very sincerely,

88. Carl Gutzlaff in Canton to William Jardine in Canton, 20 June 1834

My dear Sir,

You have greatly assisted in the promotion of a free intercourse with the Chinese Empire, of which we may expect the greatest results both for religion, science and commerce. When I therefore proposed to dedicate a work to you entitled *A General Description of the Chinese Empire*, it was with a view of giving a public testimony of my esteem towards you and of expressing my gratitude for your kind aid in my paltry endeavours to promote the good cause[44] in China. You have accepted my offer and I avail myself of this opportunity to lay before you a plan of the work, that you may forward the substance to Mr. Weeding.[45]

[41] Mr. Brown: possibly Robert Brown, 'Dealer in marine stores, 8 Lombard Street, Chelsea'. (*TLCD*). A brother of Robert Brown, Richard Brown, was also a partner in the firm of *R. & R. Brown & Co.* (See Letters **151** and **182**).

[42] 'White goods': white cotton piece goods.

[43] The hong merchant Hengtai made a habit of obliging *Jardine, Matheson & Co.* by warehousing piece goods consigned to them, and taking delivery pending sale or barter. The consequence would soon prove dire. (See below, Letters **109, 125, 140, 141,** and **143**).

[44] To 'promote the good cause': to preach the gospel.

[45] In return for Gutzlaff's assistance on the opium ships, William Jardine was ready to help with the publication of this planned book and to enlist the help of his friend Thomas Weeding in London. A

It will consist of three parts. The Country, Nation and Government, will fill two or three moderate octavo volumes, be written in a style as concise as I am able to adopt, and be accompanied by maps and plates, so as to render it more interesting to the Reader. I shall consult native authorities for which the best libraries in the possession of Europeans are open to me in Canton. I have read most of the works written by Europeans upon China and shall avail myself of their remarks. To this I hope to add my own observations, made in the course of several years, which I spent exclusively amongst this nation. I therefore trust to add a great deal of what is novel to the European Reader, to the accounts which other writers have furnished. To expunge all expressions foreign to the English language, the manuscript will be submitted to my partner,[46] who is a competent scholar in that vernacular tongue.

The *Journal of the Amherst*[47] published by me in America and now republished in England, has met so rapid a sale in the former country, that I doubt not, but the bookseller, who undertakes to print this work, will be the gainer and be enabled to pay such a remuneration as to defray the expenses necessarily incurred in composing the work and to make good the toil and labour bestowed upon it.

The First Part will commence with a geographical description of China Proper and its Dependencies, its natural History, and resources. the Second Part a condensed History of the Empire. The Chinese Nation, manners, customs, rites, religion, characters, language and literature, (to the two latter parts many pages may be dedicated in order to elucidate a subject, which is so highly interesting).

The Third Part—Character of the Government, its origin, progress through the different ages of Chinese writings, present state, resources, stability, etc.

I shall study to be both amusing and instructive, commence the work, *Deo volente*, before the end of this month and entrust the manuscript in parts to your care, that it may be forwarded to England.

Conscious of my own inabilities, I ought to ask pardon for my presumption. I promise to be impartial and if I succeed it will afford me the highest pleasure of having removed the errors to which the pompous descriptions of Du Hald[48] and the Jesuits have led.

I remain, dear Sir, your most obliged Servant.

---

work of somewhat reduced scope appeared in London under the title: *A Sketch of Chinese History, Ancient and Modern, Composing A Retrospect of the Foreign Intercourse and Trade with China*, two volumes, London, *Smith Elder & Co.*, 1834.

[46] The 'partner' was not identified.

[47] The date of the American version was not traced. The English version was published under the title : *Report of Proceedings on a Voyage to the Northern Ports of China, in the Ship Lord Amherst*, London, B. Fellowes, 1833. The 'Reports' were by both Carl Gutzlaff and the commander of the *Amherst*, Hugh Hamilton Lindsay. (Lust, *Western Books on China*, p. 146).

[48] Gutzlaff refers to Jean-Baptiste Du Halde's *Description géographique, historique, chronologique, politique, et physique de l'empire de Chine et de la Tartarie chinoise, enrichie de cartes générales et particulières, etc.*, Paris, Lemercier, 1735. This standard, early work on China by a French Jesuit was

89. Carl Gutzlaff in Canton to William Jardine in Canton, 2 July 1834

My dear Sir,

I suppose you have written or will write very soon to Mr. Weeding on account of the *General Description of China.* I send him the images {belonging to the work}, with directions for the engraver, which you will have the kindness to forward. I have arranged the matters thus, that the first part of the Geographical Treatise will reach England simultaneously with the maps. It is my earnest wish that the work should be published at [the time of my] arrival in England. Having therefore arranged the materials thus, as to facilitate the object, I trust [ ] Mr. Weeding will do his part.

The first part of the description of England in Chinese, containing the history is now in the press. I have delivered the work to my best printers, that is may be done with the greatest neatness and elegance and have strictly followed your advice, that of expressing myself with conciseness. As soon as the work is printed, you will receive 40 copies, whilst I shall endeavour to furnish the other volumes, which still must be worked out. You will receive the whole amount of expenses when the business is finished.

I remain, dear Sir, Your humble servant.

90. H. P. Hadow in Bombay to James Matheson in Canton, 8 August 1834

My dear Matheson,

An attack of fever which I had last week, and the remedies applied, laid me up for nearly six days, and have very inconveniently abridged my time for writing to you and other friends at this busy moment, when the last ships are starting for China as well as two or three moving off to England.

The letters from the firm will I trust be found to contain all that is requisite regarding our own affairs, and I confidently rely on your and Jardine's supplying any deficiencies. I will only repeat what I said in my letter by the *Carron*, that her sale will be most agreable to us, and that I am sure you will do all you can to promote that object.

Our letters from London are to 17th April when 42 out of 50 Bales of Silk per *Salem* had arrived per *Guardian* and were valued at 17 shillings per pound only.[49] The extravagant expectations of some that prices could remain as last year will be

---

translated into English by R. Brooks and published under the title: *The General History of China, etc.* London, J. Watts, 1741. As a protestant missionary, it was not unnatural that Carl Gutzlaff should find many 'errors to be removed' from Du Halde's work.

[49] At 17 shillings a pound 'only', buyers were still making a profit, though a relatively small profit, as the purchase price in Canton was the equivalent of approximately 12 shillings. See above, Letter **87**, where silk is said to be priced at '340 dollars per picul'. (Conversion rates assumed : 1£ = 4.28$; 1 picul = 133,3 lbs.)

disappointed but I am not the less desirous of having our stake in the article to 50,000 dollars at last year's prices, or to 100,000 dollars if, as you thought likely, prices go below that mark.

In regard to that, however, as well as the 200,000 dollars ordered home direct, have the goodness to understand that it is our wish that 300,000 of our means should thus be sent to Broad Street,[50] and on receipt of this, be so good as to intimate to these friends. The balance of our funds we also wish invested in Bills on England if possible against consignments to Broad Street, but the Bills to be sent here, that we may negotiate or forward them as we find most convenient. Of these latter, we should like to have 10,000 to 15,000 pounds Sterling here, as soon as your arrangements will admit, so as not to inconvenience yourselves, or to injure us in the rate of Exchange.

Regarding your own concerns I need only refer to my last as matters remain exactly as they did. These ships have taken away 400 chests more of the Drug than I reckoned on; a great part or all of which is advanced against by parties sending money on to China to Tea purchases. Amongst others who have so ventured are the Ardaseers[51] and Cursetjee Cowasjee,[52] who have taken upwards of two lacs from the *Charles Grant's* people at 214 Rupees and paid from 1,150 to 1,200 Rupees for their opium. Cursetjee's son goes on with some other natives to form another branch of your numerous native agencies, and I shall be surprised if the result of this year's opium speculations realize the expectations with which they are entered upon. I hope we small Holders may creep out at a good price whilst others are holding, but I confess I look for a crash at some time or other during the Season.

Of course the scheme of buying opium on joint account for one of your clippers is at an end for the present, as in the first place the then expected quantity will not remain on hand and secondly, there is no chance of prices shortly falling to the limit. If however as I fully expect this season proves a bad one for speculators, the [speculators] will be unable to play the same game next year, and opportunities will offer in such case of picking up lots occasionally at moderate prices, to which alone we must look. When therefore you have leisure, let me hear your and Jardine's opinion upon what you consider safe prices for next year looking to a supply of 11,000 Chests which I think may be taken as about the mark, bearing in mind however that there is every reason to believe that the produce of

[50] The principal London correspondent of *Remington & Co.* was the firm of *Bazett, Colvin, Crawford & Co.*, later called *Crawford, Colvin & Co.*, 71 Broad Street. (*EIRD*. East India Houses of Agency in London; see also Letters **151, 182, 222**).

[51] Several 'Ardaseers' were opium shippers from Bombay to China at the time: Ardaseer Bysurjee, Ardaseer Cursetjee, Ardaseer Hormanjee and Ardaseer Jamsetjee (*BI*).

[52] There were also several Parsee customers from Bombay called both 'Cursetjee' and 'Cowasjee'. One of the 'Ardaseers' was also a 'Cursetjee'. He was Ardaseer Cursetjee, a member of the Wadia family, who owned and managed the Bombay Dockyard. (*Origines de Hong Kong*, p. 154).

the following year will be greater than ever, and consequently that holding will be proportionably dangerous.

Jamsetjee[53] is so busy with the furniture for his new House, and writing his China dispatches, that I have not seen him for a week, but when I last spoke to him he professed his intention of returning the *Good Success* immediately after arrival and with that view he had bought Cotton, not to be delayed for the arrival of what was detained to the Northward. The *Isabella* and *Anna Robertson* will however offer shippers of opium the means of sending on the Drug until the end of this month, but, I should think the funds of parties advancing against such shipments must be nearly exhausted. I shall look anxiously for letters from you and Jardine after your return, in regard to your views as to home arrangements,[54] and pray say to Jardine, with my kind regards, that he must excuse my not writing by these ships to himself, but that I will by the next departures. Remember me to all friends and with Forbes' and Crawford's[55] best wishes in which Mrs. Hadow joins with me.

Believe me,
Yours very sincerely,

91. William Jardine in Canton to John Macvicar in Manchester,
20 August 1834

My dear Macvicar,

The *Mangles* is to be despatched at noon today, and I have only a few minutes to write. Mr. Matheson has reached Macao in the *Berwickshire*, but I am not aware whether he writes to you by this conveyance.

The letters from the Firm and Mr. Thom informed you of the glutted and depreciated state of this market with piece goods of every description, woollens as well as cottons; and I have little to add on the subject. Chintzes and Handkerchiefes are unsaleable for cash on any terms, and when the stock in hand is to be worked off it is impossible to say. Many of them are not worth the duty. We have lately been trying the Manila Market, but many of the goods, we have on hand, are not

[53] Jamsetjee Jejeebhoy.

[54] 'Your views as to home arrangement' refers to the fact that since *Fairlie Clark Innes & Co.*'s failure, *Jardine, Matheson & Co.* no longer had a steady principal correspondent firm in London. It still used the services of *Thomas Weeding & Co.*, but Thomas Weeding had the drawback of operating on his own as a one-man firm, and merchants always tried to avoid too much exposure on what they called the 'risk of single life'. This situation had a restricting effect on the amount of bills the firm could draw on London, and therefore the amount of business the partners could transact. William Jardine and James Matheson were actively seeking to establish new relationships in London. New arrangements were not finalized until James Matheson's stay in England in 1835 and 1836.

[55] James Henry Crawford was a partner in *Remington & Co.* (*BI*). So probably was (or had been) 'Mr. Forbes', whom James Matheson asks H. P. Hadow to greet for him in Letter **120**.

fitted for it; while on the coast of China they offer little more than the Canton prices.

The purchases of the *Pauline*'s cargo have suffered severely; and many of the dealers, in piece goods, have failed lately. We have not realized the whole of the proceeds but have no apprehension on the subject, beyond a little delay.

A very small part of the Goods per *City of Aberdeen* has yet reached Whampoa; and it is not possible to procure a fair offer for them, while we have not the power of putting the purchasers in immediate possession of his property.

Part of the cotton twist has been sold at saving prices, and is now on its way up; but the offers made for the Long cloths are low indeed—scarcely equal to prime cost and charges—while for the woolens it is difficult to get an answer of any kind, as to their value.

The Americans have certainly overdone the business and must meet with severe disappointment.[56]

We have made an arrangement for returning part of Mr. Jones's[57] funds in Raw Silk purchased on reasonable terms, but the quality did not equal that of the muster, and the article was in consequence refused and we must now wait the arrival of the new crop.

About two months ago, contracts might have been made at, or [been] possible [at] five dollars per pecul under the prices of last years; but latterly a report has been circulating of a deficiency in the second crop; and higher prices have been asked. There are, however, no purchasers, and the first crop being abundant—say 8,000 Bales for Canton—with a large stock and [a] falling market in England, we have little to fear. In the meanwhile we have remitted in Bills to a greater extent than we have realized.

You will find from the Canton Register transmitted by this Conveyance, that the British Trade with China is everything but suspended. Cargo Boats have been refused, but no official Edict has yet proclaimed the stoppage. The question at issue, divested of all nonsense, is simply this, shall Lord Napier[58] address letters

[56] A polite way of saying to John Macvicar that he was bound to meet with the same severe disappointment.

[57] George Jones, a client of John Macvicar's. See above, Letter **72**.

[58] William John, ninth Lord Napier of Merchistoun was a Scottish peer and a naval officer. He received his commission as Superintendent of British Trade in China in December 1833 and arrived in Macao on board the frigate *Andromache* on 15 July 1834. He was accompanied by his wife and two daughters. On 16th July, he called a meeting at the Macao British factory (an elegant eighteenth century building used today as a museum and situated next to the Camoens Gardens). He appointed John Francis Davis, the former head of the Select Committee, as Second Superintendent and Sir George Robinson as Third Superintendent. Another supercargo, J. H Astell, was appointed Secretary and Treasurer. Alexander Johnston, a young gentleman who had come out with Napier, became his private secretary. Dr. Colledge was confirmed as official surgeon. And Captain Charles Elliot, R.N., was appointed master attendant responsible for supervising the English ships and crews in the river.

to the viceroy, or shall they be petitions addressed to his Excellency the viceroy through the Hong Merchants as the Company's Select Committee did?

His Lordship is firm in his refusal, and the viceroy threatens to convince him of his error by stopping the Trade for ever. We wait the result, in fear and trembling, as ordered by the Authorities to do.[59]

Matters have been badly managed at home, and I am afraid Lord Napier has not sufficient authority. A reference to Pekin might do good. We can scarcely expect the parties here to give up power, peculations, etc., etc., without a struggle.

We are much surprised here at the Company's finance operations;[60] and sadly at a loss to discover what induced all you merchants and agents to be silent. It is likely to turn out a vile job; as might have been expected. Is it not contrary to the Act of Parliament? Let the Company keep their Treasury in Leadenhall street open, grant Bills on Bengal and Bombay, and shut the Treasury in China. They will then do right. The Out ports have surely great cause of complaint as they are not to participate in the advances made here; and the manufacturers still greater, for who will barter his Teas for unsaleable piece goods, when he can get two thirds of the said Teas in cash, and the chance of the English market with the Honourable East India Company for their agents?

I have omitted to notice your letter respecting Quicksilver, but shall now explain. Had your letter reached us a little earlier we might have been able to purchase a small quantity at Lintin at your limits; but this was entirely accidental, the Quicksilver having been saved from a week in the China Sea and deposited at Lintin till an opportunity of sending it to Whampoa should offer.

Lord Napier arrived at the Canton factories on 25 July. From that date, he tried in vain to execute the instructions he had received from Lord Palmerston ('Your Lordship will announce your arrival at Canton by letter to the Viceroy'). The Canton viceroy, Lu K'un, was not prepared to receive letters directly from a foreigner, however high-ranking an official, and he insisted on Lord Napier using the customary etiquette of forwarding the letter through the hong merchants, in the same way as the Select Committee had always done. Lord Napier, meanwhile, stuck to his instructions. In retaliation, the viceroy ordered to trade to stop. (For a detailed account of the 'Napier Fizzle', see: Fay, *Opium War*, pp. 67–79).

59 'We await the result, in fear and trembling, as ordered by the Authorities to do': another example of William Jardine's humour. When translated into English, the official Chinese edicts appeared laughable to the Europeans, from their imperative use of threatening language. 'Fear and tremble heareat!—intensely tremble !' was the most common phrase ending the vice-regal or imperial edicts. The returned letters sent by the viceroy to Lord Napier were equally full of similar language. Lord Napier was variously characterized as the 'Barbarian eye' or as 'Labouriously vile'. In one of his letters to the viceroy, a letter equally unopened and returned to the sender—Lord Napier himself wrote: 'Tremble, Governor Lu, intensely tremble!' (*Ibid*., p. 75).

60 This is the first mention of the 'Company's Finance Committee' set up in Canton in the summer 1834 to make loans to merchants on the security of their tea purchases. See above, Letter **84**, note 26. The controversy about this possibly illegal Treasury function of the East India Company in Canton following the 1833 India Act remained a sensitive topic among merchants until the abolition of the Finance Committee, seven years later. The objections of the merchants are forcefully set out in Document **93** below.

You are aware that the Chinese levy a duty on goods exported again nearly equal to that paid on importation; so that it rarely happens, that you can purchase from exportation at the prices quoted in the *Register Price Current*—these being the prices at which an importer could sell, the purchasers paying the duty.

I shall have any opportunity of addressing you again soon. In the Meanwhile, I remain,

Yours very sincerely,

P.S. 28 August. Since writing the above a thing of importance has occurred. Lord Napier has had an interview with three mandarins of considerable rank who left him without receiving his *letters* addressed to the viceroy.[61] No trade. No official document stopping it. Only a threat to the Hong Merchants who are all obeisant.

[61] On 26 August 1834, Lord Napier gave a dinner in the Canton factory in honour of the King's birthday, an occasion which gave the British community an opportunity to show its confidence in its new leader and its approval of his action. The meeting with the mandarins on 28 August referred to here did nothing to break the four-week deadlock. An important change in the method used to try and force a dialogue occurred on 30 August, when Lord Napier resorted to posting a broadsheet at several places in the factory square. The viceroy was so incensed at the procedure which enabled Lord Napier to communicate to ordinary Chinese above his head, that he sent soldiers to surround the factories. All the Chinese servants vanished, leaving Lord Napier concerned for his safety. He then ordered his two frigates, the *Andromache* and the *Imogen* to sail up to Whampoa. On the 7 September, the frigates left the Bogue to obey the Superintendents orders. They were immediately fired upon by the Chinese from the Bogue forts, and they fired back. This was the first exchange of fire between the British and the Chinese. (The scene, *HMS Ships Imogen and Andromache passing the Batteries at Bocca Tigris* was sketched on the spot by Lieutenant White of the Royal Marines, and was subsequently drawn by T. Allom and engraved in London by W. Floyd). Two days later, on 11 September, the frigates arrived in Whampoa. The viceroy had blocked the river from Whampoa to Canton, and neither the frigates nor their smaller craft could go any further. On 14 September, cut off from his officers and suffering from a fever, Lord Napier decided to return to Macao. The viceroy, however, refused to allow him to return to his ships and to sail down the river. Lord Napier had to use the slow way back to Macao through the 'inner passage' of the delta. The permission he needed to leave the Canton factories with his retenue reached him on 21 September. The slow journey took five days and he arrived in Macao on 26 September, a very sick man. His fever grew worse, possibly aggravated by a feeling that his mission had failed. He died on 11 October. (*Opium War, Ibid.*)

There appears to be no letter or document in Lord Napier's hand in the *JMArch*. There exists, however, an undated, unplaced note to B. Barretto, probably written on 14 July 1834 by Lord Napier's private secretary, Alexander Johnston. The text of the note is as follows: 'Lord Napier presents his Compliments to Mr. Barretto and begs to thank him for his kind attention. Lord Napier received Mr. Innes's note this morning from a Pilot Boat and has thankfully accepted of the kind offer contained therein by a note to Mr. Innes sent on here in Mr. Davis's Boat. Lord and Lady Napier hope to land in the morning.' (*JMArch.*, 'Unplaced, undated, Letter 4929).

92. James Matheson in Canton to John Purvis in Singapore,
25 September 1834

My dear Purvis,[62]

I have been duly favored with your letter of 19th Ultimo, which would afford me great pleasure were it not for the account it contains of Mrs. Purvis's continued indisposition. I trust however she will by this time, have recovered her accustomed strength. But even in this case I cannot but approve of your resolution to take a trip home early next year. Such a remedy is always best when resorted to in good time and you are fortunate in being able to leave your business in good hands. I shall be most happy to recommend your interests to Macvicar, though I should fear he is pre-engaged with your neighbours *H.G.&Co.*[63] I regret we have no other connections likely to be useful to you.

I would afford me great pleasure, as you may believe, to be of your homeward party. But alas I see no prospect of this being within the bounds of possibility.[64]

I dare say the attention of you Singaporians has of late been intensely fixed on events in China; which in as far as Lord Napier has been unable to accomplish the wished for object of opening a communication with the Viceroy, must be admitted to have terminated in disappointment.[65] But in every other view, we cannot but think that in shelling the Chinese forts, he has placed us in a better position than if he had quietly yielded to them in the first instance. They have had a lesson, which they will not easily forget. It were too much to expect that they will not require a further demonstration of force on a larger scale before being brought to their senses. But the point of *direct* communications with the Government

[62] For John Purvis, see above, Letter **36**, note 4.

[63] Probably *Hunter, Gouger & Co.*, the Singapore branch of London East India firm of the same name, which had offices at 6, Great Winchester Street, Old Broad Street. (*TLCD*).

[64] The situation changed rapidly after Lord Napier's death, however, and James Matheson was able to leave Canton for England in March 1835. See below, Letters **103**, **108** and **111**.

[65] James Matheson puts a brave face on his disappointment, which was shared by most of the British trading community. Gideon Nye, the American missionary, dubbed the whole episode as the 'Napier Fizzle', an expression which found its way into history books. There is little doubt that Palmerston had misjudged the situation or been misinformed about the Chinese situation and that the instructions he had given Lord Napier stood little chance of being fulfilled. Meanwhile, Lord Napier was buried with full military honours in the East India protestant Cemetery in Macao. Lady Napier wished her husband to be re-buried in Scotland in due course. She left Macao on 10 December 1834. The interval between Lord Napier's burial and her departure was too short for her to obtain the necessary permission for disinterment. James Matheson completed the administrative process on her behalf. Lord Napier's remains eventually left for Scotland in March 1835 under the supervision of James Matheson on board the *Orwell*, a former East India Company ship commanded by Captain Dalrymple. A testimonial fund was opened for the erection of a memorial at Canton, with *Fox, Rawson & Co.* of Canton as treasurer. William Jardine and James Matheson contributed 100 dollars, John Morrison 50 dollars, James Innes 25 dollars, and Daniell (see 4th paragraph of this Letter) nothing at all. James Matheson made arrangements for the monument to be designed and sculptured in England. (Ride, *East India Company Cemetery*, p-. 259–262; Fay, *Opium War*, p. 79).

without the corrupt intervention of Hong Merchants is of such vital importance to the well being of the trade that the British government cannot rest until it is obtained.

A small party consisting of Daniell (of the Company) Dent and Whiteman[66] have used all their influence with the Hong Merchants to thwart Lord Napier's measures. And as long as the British representative has to do with the Cohong, so long will he be exposed to the baneful consequences of similar opposition. Party spirit has, as usual, been very high, and it is likely the *Singapore Chronicle* will be made use of, as a medium of disseminating all manner of unfounded assertions which the authors are afraid to give to the world here.[67] I am desirous of furnishing you with a few facts which I shall feel obliged by your bringing to the Editor's notice in case of need, in order to correct any misstatements that may appear. It is a favorite topic of declamation with the other party that they represent the sentiments of Canton society, and that we are a small faction who mislead Lord Napier. Now the fact is Lord Napier is not a man to be led by any one's advice. He would be better if he were open to counsel but he prefers thinking for himself.[68] And as to members, a reference to the signatures applied to a letter of the Chamber of Commerce to Lord Napier, in the *Canton Register* of the 23rd Instant will show that *we* are the *many*, the dissentients but few. Of Europeans I believe only Dent and Whiteman can be named in addition to Daniell who does not properly belong to the Commercial Community. Of the Europeans, Mr. Fox[69] who is sick at Macao, had no opportunity of making known his sentiment, and Mr. Cragg[70] is I believe neuter. If transient Europeans are spoken of, I have no reason to doubt the majority would coincide with the letter of the Chamber of commerce. Natives of India are not to be mentioned for they have not enough courage for such a crisis.[71]

[66] For Nugent Daniell, see above, Letter **40**, note 25; For Dent, Letter **8**, note 45 and Letter **20**, note 31; for Whiteman, Letter **43**, note 53. These three gentlemen, and a few others mentioned below by James Matheson, disapproved of the 1833 India Bill and of the dismantling of the East India Company establishment in Canton. They may well have used what influence they had to dissuade Lord Napier from following a course which they thought was doomed to fail. They were certainly accused of cowardice and treachery by John Slade, the editor of the *Canton Register* for pressing the chief superintendent to surrender. (Fay, *Opium War*, p. 77).

[67] James Matheson always proved sensitive to the power of the press in forming the readers' opinion. He therefore relied on his friends in the various Eastern ports to report whichever side of the stories he felt was the correct one. See, for instance, the last sentence of Letter **97**.

[68] When this Letter was written Lord Napier was very ill and had only two weeks to live.

[69] Mr. Fox: see below, Letter **97**.

[70] Joseph Cragg: a Canton merchant. See shareholders in the *10th Canton Insurance Company*, Letter **65** above.

[71] Fearing ruin, the Parsees—the only 'natives of India' present in Canton during the Napier crisis—were particularly anxious to resume trade and they had begged Lord Napier not to cross the viceroy. This prompted a remark printed in the *Canton Register* of 7 October 1834 to the effect that 'On the field of Waterloo, for instance, it is doubtful how far the Parsees, however well mounted or accoutred,

The formation of the Chamber of Commerce, will not I dare say, among other subjects escape the animadversions, of your good friends. It was formed at Lord Napier's recommendation,[72] with the general concurrence of the Commercial body some of whom had a secret expectation that it would tend to counteract the influence in society of *Jardine, Matheson & Co.* But when they began to see that this expectation would not be realized, they wished to quash it, and on the night previous to the day of the meeting a motion was made by a few to postpone it. We considered this irregular, being of opinion that those who had objections to propose would bring them forward at the meeting, where everything should be decided by a majority of those present. We accordingly attended the meeting and established the Chamber to the great disappointment of the absentees, who however, of Europeans at Canton were very few. Only Mr. Dent and Mr.Whiteman. Mr. Fry being absent at Macao and Mr. Cragg neuter—transient Europeans not counted, and natives of India not admissible except conditionally, for the reason mentioned in the last page.

I am particular in mentioning these circumstances in order that you may be able to answer by a reference to real names, any criticism which may be cast on the Chamber of Commerce, on the *false* ground of its containing only a *few* of the Mercantile body. It contains as you will see a great majority of the Europeans.

In case you should not be on communicative terms with the Editor, you can show this letter to George,[73] who, I have no doubt from his connection with the paper, will be able to do the needful, viz., to contradict the false assertions which I have no doubt, parties will attempt to push on the public through the *Singapore Chronicle*. If it should be possible by any means to prevent their publication, it would be still better than having to contradict them afterwards.

Excuse this trouble and I shall be happy to do as much for you some other time. Kindest regards to Mrs. Purvis, and believe me,

Yours sincerely,

P.S. Your friend Captain Jennice[74] of the *Ann* has been the first to break through the blockade[75] and make his appearance in Canton today.

---

would have been allowed to take the place of the 42nd, the Blues, or the Scots Greys'. (Quoted by Fay, *Opium War*, p. 77). As a result, the Parsees were excluded from the Canton British Chamber of Commerce. It was the first time that they were not counted as British.

[72] James Matheson makes it clear that it was Lord Napier's wish that the Canton Chamber of Commerce should be formed. Chambers of commerce had been in existence in England in the large commercial and industrial cities since the early 1820s.

[73] Not identified.

[74] Captain Jennice was not identified.

[75] The 'blockade' put in place on the river by Viceroy Lu K'un in the early days of September 1834 in order to stop reinforcements reaching Lord Napier from Whampoa to the Canton factories.

93. ***Jardine, Matheson & Co.*** **and other members of the British Chamber of Commerce in Canton, to H. M. Government in England,** 9 October 1834[76]

STATEMENT OF OBJECTIONS TO THE CONTINUANCE IN CHINA OF A PART OF THE EAST INDIA COMPANY'S FACTORY, FOR THE PURPOSE OF SELLING BILLS ON INDIA, AND PURCHASING BILLS ON ENGLAND, BY MAKING ADVANCES ON THE GOODS AND MERCHANDISE OF INDIVIDUALS INTENDED FOR CONSIGNMENT TO ENGLAND.

The British Chamber of Commerce of Canton, being strongly impressed with a conviction of the injurious consequences to the mercantile interests of their country, that must accrue from the East India Company continuing to maintain a part of their factory in China, for the purpose of carrying on dealings in the sale and purchase of bills of exchange, feel called on to make a public declaration of their sentiments on the subject.

It is with deference submitted that this procedure of the East India Company, is an infraction of the Act 3rd and 4th William IV, cap. 85, which declares that they 'consented to their rights to trade for their own profit, in common with other His Majesty's subjects, be suspended,' and enacts accordingly that they shall 'abstain from all commercial business, which shall not be incident to the closing of their actual concerns, etc., or which shall not be carried on for the purpose of the said government', which concluding exception, it may be inferred, was designed to legalise their trading in those cases where it may be necessary for realising India revenue, but not their applying that revenue to commercial purposes after being realised. It may, undoubtedly, be argued that the purposes of the company are promoted by the ultimate object of their dealing here, in transferring to London their surplus revenue: yet, as ample facilities exist for the direct accomplishment of this, by the Court of Directors drawing on the India governments, as well as by these latter remitting bills drawn on London against shipment of Indian produce; it is presumed that the Legislature cannot have intended to sanction so wide a departure from the principle of the act as the traficcing, *without necessity*, in the *sale* and *purchase* of bills, in a foreign country; the true object of which is, not merely to remit, but to make a profit in excess of the direct and natural rate of exchange; a latitude of action, which, if allowed, would authorize any species of trading, equally with that in exchanges, for the sake of a better remittance.

The two-fold operation, carried on by the Company's Factory here, of selling one description of bills in order to buy others (which falls under the legal definition of trading) is so opposite in its nature to the single and allowable object of

[76] *JMArch.*, Reel 251, Letter 498. This document (which retains its spelling inconsistencies—e.g., 'Company' sometimes spelt with a capital and sometimes not) was written two days before Lord Napier's death. The fluency of language and the cogency of the arguments make it likely it was written by James Matheson himself, as chairman of the new Chamber of commerce. See also Letters **96**, **105**, and **110**. The 'Statement of objection' was signed by: *Jardine, Matheson & Co.*, James Innes, Arthur S. Keating, N. Crooke (not identified), *John Templeton & Co.*, *R. Tuner & Co.*, J. Mc. A. Gladstone (not identified), J. Watson (not identified), William Boyd, and Andrew Johnstone.

drawing in London upon India, or buying bills for remittance from India to London, as to merit particular advertence.

In India the facility of obtaining money on shipments to London, arising from the company's extensive purchase of bills, tends to increase the demand for, and support the prices of, the productions of British territories.

But a similar facility resulting from their dealings here by acting as a powerful incentive to improvident speculation,[77] tends to raise the prices of chinese produce, and thus to benefit a foreign country, at the expense of the British consumer, while in an equal degree the productions of our India territories are deprived of that stimulus which they would receive from the same operation carried on there. On the other hand, the Court of Director's bills on India offered for sale in London, afford a means for the employement of individual capital, in place of counteracting it by the competition of India revenue; and may therefore be considered a still more appropriate mode of transferring this revenue to England.

In throwing open the China trade to the whole English nation, the legislature cannot surely have intended to abridge this right, by permitting the East India Company to shut out the British mercantile capital which must necessarily be excluded from it to the extent that they may occupy the field with the revenues of India; and should the Company's dealings here, with the immense revenues of India at their command, be sanctioned by our legislature, there is nothing to prevent the amount from being, in future, almost indefinitely increased beyond the £600,000, which they propose employing in the present year.[78]

But the mere circumstance of the rulers of India having any participation whatever in the supply of funds to the China trade, is, of itself, calculated to deter the British capitalist from adventuring in a competition where his rivals are sovereigns, whose situation exempts them from subjection to those principles by which purely mercantile operations are universally guided, and which experience has shown to be so indispensible to the well-being of every trade, that wide-spread ruin is, sooner or later, the certain result whenever they are disregarded.

The rulers of India, thus deterring by their overwhelming competition, and to the extent of their dealings here, entirely excluding the British capitalist from embarking in the trade, it is rendered in a great measure dependent on the company, who, regulating the annual amount of their commercial business by their

[77] 'Improvident speculation': James Matheson makes a revealing distinction between 'normal speculation', i.e. the commercial action of an established firm buying tea outright whilst not knowing the resale price, and 'improvident speculation' which describes exactly the same commercial action, though undertaken by individual traders or firms of little or no financial substance. The latter were naturally encouraged to trade by the borrowing facilities offered to them by the East India Company 'Finance Committee', since they had not enough capital of their own to risk in such ventures.

[78] This was a substantial amount of liquidity released in the Canton market. On the assumption of a picul of tea costing some 18 taels (the market rate in Canton at the time), £600,000 represented approximately 38% of the total amount of liquidities needed to buy 38 million lbs. of tea (the British consumption of tea for the year 1834).

convenience or caprice, become in a certain degree the arbiters of the merchant's proceedings at every stage, from the price he has to pay for his tea, its qualities and quantities, to the rate of exchange of the dollar, and even the rate of freight, all contingent on the amount of capital supplied by the company; which, being previously unknown to the free trader, he is effectually precluded from any satisfactory calculation respecting his future plans. By permitting the revenues of India to be employed in the purchase of China produce, not only are its prices enhanced, but a most serious barrier is interposed to the extension of the trade in British manufactures, which is always greatly promoted by transactions in barter;[79] the necessities of the Chinese seller often forcing him to seek relief by taking in exchange British goods, which are otherwise unsaleable, and for which a market is thus as it were created. How much is the inducement of this description of business lessened when the Chinese merchants has the means of obtaining from the Company's factory two-thirds of the value of his goods,[80] and the chance of the English market through the East India Company and its agents!

It does not appear whether the Company's factory are authorized to make advances on consignments to the British outports,[81] but if not, the circumtance will form an additional strong ground of objection to a plan, which in such cases, will exclude the great majority of the British Nation, who are out of the verge of the metropolis, from a due participation in the China trade.

To the Merchants and agents of Great Britain, it may be left to express their sentiments respecting the proposal of the Court of Directors to act as consignees in London, for parties receiving their advances; a proposal which, liberally seconded here, may, if permitted, attract to the honourable court no small portion of the agency of the China trade.

Finally, it is submitted, that in this very peculiar country, where the bulk of foreign trade is restricted to eleven Hong Merchants, who are also the only medium of our intercourse with the government, so large a command of capital in the hands of the Company's factory is susceptible of becoming a most powerful engine of influence, both commercial and political, in the former view, bringing with it, through an understanding with the Hongs, as close a monopoly of the

[79] The barter argument is cogent. The Letters sent to John Macvicar consistently show that selling British manufactured goods to the Chinese was a difficult and unprofitable business. For a hong merchant, the inducement to take manufactured goods in order to sell tea must have been greatly weakened when tea could be sold for cash.

[80] The Company's Finance Committee was advancing cash on a loan-to-value ratio of 66% based on the market price for tea. The loan was secured on the cargo, and the Company controlled the selling process through its London agents. Its risk was therefore minimal. In spite of the India Act on 1833, the abolition of the Company's tea buying monopoly, and the dismantling of the Canton official establishment, there were still therefore powerful forces at play to counteract the influence of the free-traders.

[81] The ports recently entitled to import tea from China by the new legislation. See above, Letter **74**, note 66.

most desirable teas as ever before existed; a monopoly less pure, because occult and not controlled by act of Parliament in a political view,[82] continuing the existence of an influential body, whom the Chinese have been accustomed to regard as paramount here, and whose readier access to the Hong Merchant from habit and old acquaintance, may at any time afford the means of counteracting His Majesty's representative.[83]

94. James Matheson in Canton to James Scott , *Messrs. Binny & Co.* in Madras, 10 October 1834

My dear Scott,

H.M.S. Andromache is on the point of starting, bound it is said for your Presidency, and though a good deal hurried I cannot omit the opportunity of writing you a line, were it merely to say that I still have a lively recollection of all your kind attentions and hospitality to which I was so much indebted during my recent wanderings.[84]

Since my return to China about the middle of August, business has been almost entirely at a stand still, owing to the discussions, between Lord Napier and the Governor.[85] And though it is now nearly a fortnight since they have been brought to a close so few of the Chinese dealers have yet returned from their Country residences to which they had retired at the commencement of the troubles, that they are still in a very inactive state; and the operations of the Season more backwards than I ever knew them at this period.

Owing to the East India Company being allowed to continue a part of their Factory here with instructions to make advances on Consignment to London, to the extent of 600,000 pounds sterling the aspect of our market is completely changed from what I contemplated when I thought it possible we might be able to influence shipments to your London firm.[86] And I now see little or no chance of our being able to do so: you had better therefore consider our proposed arrangement respecting Bills on England (per your memorandum of 19th April in reply to mine) as at an end, and take measures accordingly in supplying funds to your London account from other sources. Be assured, however, that we are impressed with the highest opinion of the respectability of your London friends;[87]

[82] Another expression of powerful sentiment in the 'war against monopolies'. See above, Letter **75**, note 77.

[83] The Superintendent of Trade, Lord Napier.

[84] James Matheson was away in India visiting constituents from March to August 1834.

[85] The Governor of the Canton province, usually referred to as the viceroy: Lu K'un. See above, Letter **91**, note 58.

[86] See previous Letter **93**. The competition indirectly fostered by the Company's loans reduced the margin for action of the established agency houses.

[87] *Scott & Bell* was *Binny & Co.*'s main correspondent in London. *Scott & Bell*: 'East India Agents and Merchants, 2, Alderman's Walk, Bishopsgate Churchyard. (*TLCD*).

and if a change in circumstances should hereafter enable our complying with your wishes, it will afford us pleasure to do so.

I have not time to advert to public affairs but, for your complete information on the subject, sent under the Firm's address [is] a series of *Canton Register* since the first of August. Lord Napiers actions on the whole have done good, though not to the extent that could have been wished. It is to be hoped that, though his illness is of a dangerous nature, he may yet be spared to complete the good work of improving our relations with China.[88]

I beg to be kindly remembered to Mr. Key[89] and remain,

Sincerely yours,

95. William Jardine in Canton to John Macvicar in Manchester,

23 October 1834

Dear Macvicar,

When the *Hellas* left for Ireland I was on my way up from Macao, from attending the funeral of the late Lord Napier;[90] whose death, under any circumstances would have been severely felt by most of the Members of our small Society; and has been doubly so from the peculiar nature of the treatment he experienced from the Chinese Government, when too much reduced by disease, to be any longer capable of carrying on negotiations, or of seeing any one but his Medical Attendents. The *Canton Register* will give you every information on the subject, and you may place implicit Credit in what is there stated, respecting his Lordship's proceedings.

He had a very difficult task assigned to him and, in my humble opinion, too little power granted to enable him to accomplish the object Ministers had in view. Those who are best acquainted with the Chinese character are of opinion, that a reference to Pekin would have settled the point without much difficulty. But this his instructions did not admit of.

Many idle reports will, of course, reach England, respecting his Lordship's views and proceedings—most of them originating from parties not in the slightest degree in his confidence. But, fortunately, he stated his own sentiments very fully to H. M. Ministers in a despatch by the *Mangles*,[91] in which he prepared

[88] Lord Napier died in Macao the day after this Letter was written.

[89] Mr Key: a partner in *Binny & Co.*

[90] On Lord Napier's funeral, see above, Letter **92**, note 65. For details of the funeral procession, etc., see: Ride, *East India Company Cemetery*, pp. 261–262.

[91] See above, Letter **91**, written on 20 August, in which William Jardine mentions that 'the *Mangles* is to be despatched at noon today'. This Letter makes it clear that the motives for Lord Napier leaving Canton when he did and giving up his demand to communicate directly with the viceroy were twofold: the proximate reason was his state of health, and the deeper motive was his wish not to hurt the trading season starting in November.

them for his being obliged to leave Canton, which was always his intention rather than allow the Trade to be suspended beyond the month of October, or an early day in November.

I saw a good deal of his Lordship during the time the Second and Third Superintendents were absent, and was aware of everything that was going on. The Frigates had orders on no account to fire upon the Junks or Forts, unless fired upon; and to act on the defensive only.[92] Had they not been detained by northerly winds and calms from reaching Whampoa, and sending their boats up to Canton, to keep open the communications and take Lord Napier on board, the result would have been very different.

You will see allusions made to a certain party here as inimical to His Lordship's measures;[93] and doing everything in their power to induce the Chinese to resist, by false representations; to Howqua, respecting the extent of his powers from home, his rank, etc., etc. These points can never be proved; but from many conversation with Howqua and Mowqua, I have every reason for believing that such was the case.

Business is now going on quietly, and the viceroy has been degraded; but we are not yet aware of the accusations against him.

I shall have an opportunity of addressing you again soon.

In the meanwhile, I remain,

Yours very sincerely,

96. James Matheson in Canton, as Chairman of the British Chamber of Commerce, to John F. Davis, Sir G.B. Robinson, Bart., and J. H. Astell, H.M. Superintendents of Trade in Canton,[94] 24 October 1834[95]

Gentlemen,

His most gracious Majesty having recommended the British Trade at the Port of Canton to your protection, and this trade being likely, in our opinion, to suffer

[92] For the *HMS Andromache* and *HMS Imogen* episode, see above, Letter **91**, note 58.

[93] The reference is to Daniell, Dent, Whiteman, etc. and to merchants opposed to the setting up of the Canton Chamber of Commerce. (See Letter **92**).

[94] When Lord Napier died, John Francis Davis, whom he had appointed Second Superintendent, became First Superintendent of British Trade. Sir George Robinson moved up to Second Superintendent, and J. H. Astell was appointed Third Superintendent. Alexander Johnston was appointed Secretary and Treasurer. Captain Charles Elliot kept his rank and appointment among the British officials, waiting his turn for promotion. For the original appointments, see above, Letter **91**, note 58.

[95] This letter, enclosing Document **93**, was sent to John Macvicar and to the Manchester Chamber of Commerce. The material was subsequently reworked and expanded by the Manchester Chamber of Commerce as presented in Letter **105**. This Letter **96** was duly acknowledged from Macao by John F. Davis, the Superintendent of Trade, on 3 November 1834. He wrote: 'Gentlemen, I have the honor to acknowledge the receipt of your letter to the superintendents of 24th October, with its inclosure, which

injury from the operations of a part of the East India Company's Factory left here, for the declared purpose of selling bills on India, and buying bills on London, secured by consignments of goods, under the Honourable Company's controul; we venture to ask the favour of your laying before His Majesty's government in England, and the Right Hon. the Governor General of India,[96] the enclosed statement of our sentiments on this important subject.

We are, Gentlemen, your most obedient servants, for the British Chamber of Commerce, of Canton.

97. James Matheson in Canton to [Charles] Lyall in Calcutta,
1 November 1834

My dear Lyall,

I beg to recommend to your attention the enclosures—viz:—Copy of an official letter to the Bengal Chamber of Commerce from the British Chamber of Commerce of Canton;—Printed paper therein referred to;—A list of members of the Chamber.

This is sent to enable you to defend us in the event of its being alleged (which it possibly may be) that we are but a *small* part of the Canton community, whereas, the fact is, that of white faces we only want Dent, who must be always singular, [and] Whiteman, who will not show his face, where James Innes is.[97]

Thomas Cragg, who is scarcely ever seen or heard of in business, *Daniell & Co*, who were not here, when the Chamber was established – but who would not, of course, join in our opposition, to the Finance Committee; because it is in fact a job got up to promote their interests, and give them a standing here. Mr. Fox was at Macao and there was no partner of his House on the spot.

Natives of India we do not want in our Chamber,[98] wishing it to be essentially British, and not Indo-British. In cases of negotiations with the Chinese, requiring nerve on the part of the foreigners, (and in such cases it is that the Chamber is

---

you request may be laid before his Majesty's government in England, and the Right Honourable the Governor General of India; and in reply I beg to say, that the same will be forwarded according to your wish. I am, Gentlemen, your most obedient servant.'

[96] Lord William Bentinck was Governor-General of India 1828–35.

[97] The argument and the names are the same as in Letter **92**. James Matheson and William Jardine want to be seen as expressing the views of the majority of the British merchants in China. The new Canton Chamber of Commerce was potentially a powerful platform to continue promoting commercial freedom and the dismantling of Chinese restrictions, provided that the views it expressed were not seen as those of a small, though active, minority.

[98] The argument used in this paragraph shows that the discrimination was not essentially racial discrimination at this stage. It was discrimination based on different appreciations in the two communities as to what the guiding commercial principles were. The Parsees had no political objective beyond trading and they were therefore happy to trade under the restrictions imposed by the 'Canton system'. William Jardine, James Matheson and the other members of the Canton Chamber of Commerce

likely to be useful), natives of India are sure to fail; and if they had an equal voice with Europeans, their greater number of heads would be sure to control us. They may of course have a Chamber of their own, if they please, but the mixture of elements so incompatible with each other, however commendable in India, would never do here.

To return to the subject matter of the printed paper,[99] although not signed by Dent, he concurs in the principal objective of it, as you will see by copy of his letter enclosed. And we had a still more important ally in the late Lord Napier whose opinion I also hand you.

It is a subject on which men's interests will naturally lead them to entertain a diversity of opinions; as there are many (perhaps the more numerous class) who, being unable to obtain money elsewhere for their speculations will be glad of the undue facilities afforded by the Company's advances; while on the other hand the capitalists will dread and lament the certain ruin which must sooner or later ensue from the stimulus afforded to improvident speculation. Hence it is that some effort may be required to secure the *right* side carrying the day, and it is important that we do not give time to the other party to gain strength.

Should doubt be entertained respecting the *legal* argument, pray go to the expense of obtaining counsel's opinion by submitting to him the printed papers. Under a separate cover I shall send you some spare copies, in order that they be sent to the Governor General, to each member of Council[100] and to whomsoever etc, you think useful in the cause.

Enlist the assistance of the Press.

I remain sincerely yours,

98. Horatio Hardy in London to *Jardine, Matheson & Co.* in Canton, 27 November 1834

Gentlemen,

I wrote on the 12th Instant and forwarded packets per American Ship *Regulus*; this proceeds per *Coeur de Lion* via Singapore and next per *Troughton* direct from London. The last date from China is the 12th May via Singapore, the *Pyramus* passed St Helena 26 September and not arrived yet in England.

believed in reforming the commercial *status quo* with China. In this desire for reform, they felt they had the British people behind them and the forces of progress which prompted the Whig Parliament to vote the 1833 India Act.

[99] The East India Company's newly set up Finance Committee.

[100] The Supreme Council of Bengal was the Governor General's executive Council. Its members were William Butterworth Bailey, Sir Charles T. Metcalf, and General Sir Edward Barnes. (*EIRD*).

The compensation to the Maritime Service is agreed to by the India Board, reducing one fifth from the Proprietors plan of the 13th August last.[101]

A very great excitement exists throughout the country, at the dismissal of Lord Melbourne's administration[102] and the Whigs on the 15th Instant. The King had commanded the Duke of Wellington to conduct the Government, and the new arrangement of Ministry awaits the arrival or Sir Robert Peel from the Continent. Lord Lyndhurst has been sworn in Lord Chancellor, therefore a few days will make known whether a Conservative Ministry can govern the Country, and the dissolution of the present House of Commons.

The Court of Directors have arranged for the late China Factory to receive 500 pounds Sterling per annum. The Supercargoes in the second list 750 pounds, and the writers 250 pounds per annum, allowing the latter to join the Civil Service[103] in India, according to their rank.

Teas, Silk and China produce continue the price as last conveyance.

The East India Company wharf was bought by Mr. John Nicholson,[104] Tea Dealer on the 31 Ultimo for 25,600 pounds Sterling situate in Thames Street.

I am Gentlemen

Yours respectfully.

[101] The 'plan of the 13th August last (1834)' was encapsulated in the resolutions adopted on that day by a general meeting of the Court of Proprietors. The measures recommended to the Board of Control can be summarized as follows. Pensions would be granted to HCS commanders and officers of at least ten years' service at the rates per annum of £250 for a Commander, £160 for a Chief Officer, £140 for a Second Officer and Surgeon, etc. down to £30 for Midshipmen and £25 for Boatswains, Gunmen and Carpenters. One-time gratuities would be given to such officers of less than ten years' service 'to be computed to their ranks and time of service, in proportion to the value of the Pension granted to those who have served ten years'. For five complete voyages, a Commander would receive £5,000; for four voyages, £4,500, etc., and for one voyage, £2,000.

The Board of Control agreed to endorse these resolutions, subject to certain modifications and reductions, e.g. that pensions be reduced by one fifth, and that widows be granted half of the pensions. A Court of Proprietors' meeting held the day before Horatio Hardy wrote this Letter agreed to the reductions suggested by the Board of Control. The Maritime Officers were unhappy at the outcome of a year's negotiation and called a meeting of protest on 2 December 1834. This meeting was held at the Jerusalem Coffee House. (*JMArch*., Miscellaneous documents in box A7–214).

[102] Viscount Melbourne was dismissed on 14 November 1834. The Duke of Wellington was appointed on 17 November and held his post until Sir Robert Peel's appointment, on 10 December. Lord Lyndhurst was appointed Lord Chancellor on 21 November. (*BHF*)

[103] Civil service: '1785. Originally, that part of the service of the East India Company carried on by the covenanted servants who did not belong to the Army or Navy'. (*OED*).

[104] See above, Letter **79**, note 108.

99. *10th Canton Insurance Company* in Canton to Timothy Wiggin[105] in London, 18 December 1834

Dear Sirs,

We have the pleasure to remit you the following bills, on account of premiums which at maturity please carry to the credit of the Company:

– C.R. Read,[106] [drawn] on	*Scott Bell & Co.*	213.15.0	pounds sterling
– ditto	*James Vere & Co.*[107]	207.16.3	pounds sterling
– C.S. Compton[108]	*Daniell & Dickinson*[109]	187.10.0	pounds sterling
– ditto	ditto	268.15.0	pounds sterling
– ditto	ditto	70.0.0	pounds sterling
– *Whiteman & Co.*	*Palmer McKillop & Co.*	1,143.15.0	pounds sterling
– *Fox Rawson & Co.*	*Rawson Holdsworth & Co.*[110]	249.13.4	pounds sterling
		2,341.4.7	pounds sterling

We are not without apprehension on your being subjected to an unusual number of claims for damage on the various free traders going home, who are not used to the stowage of so delicate an article as Tea. To guard as much as possible against such contingencies, we have engaged the permanent services of a surveyor to make a minute examination of the vessels covered by this office, and to report to us whether the mode of stowage is satisfactory as regards dunnage,[111] etc . . . But on this very important point it is obvious that no precautions adopted here can adequately protect us, and we earnestly request your direct and particular attention to be given to it, when the vessels are unloaded.

We wish particularly that you should have an eye to the dunnage of the ship *Carnatic*, Captain {Giles}, should you hear there is a prospect of a claim against us.

We are, dear Sirs, Your most obedient servants.

[P. S.] In the above observations we beg you to understand that it is not our wish you should depart from those principles of liberality by which we are generally

[105] See above, Letter **62**, note 73. By paying the holders of *Jardine, Matheson & Co.*'s bills as they came due in the London market in the summer of 1833, Timothy Wiggin had been acting as an alternative banker to the Canton firm, thus replacing *Fairlie, Clark, Innes & Co.* which had failed. Not surprisingly, Timothy Wiggin became the London Agent of the *10th Insurance Company*, in succession to the failed house.

[106] Possibly Christopher Read, a Singapore resident, previously William Hunter's landlord. (Hunter, *Bits of Old China*, p. 234).

[107] *James Vere & Co.*, 'Silkmen, 164, Bishopsgate Street'. (*RLD*).

[108] Charles Spencer Compton, a merchant resident in America (several letters listed in the *BI*).

[109] *Daniell & Dickinson*, 'East India Merchants, 9 Great Winchester Street, Old Broad Street'. (*TLDC*).

[110] *Rawson Holdsworth* ; 'Merchants, Corbets Court'. (*RLD*).

[111] Dunnage: loose wood of any kind laid on the bottom of a ship's hold to keep the cargo out of bilge water, or wedged between parts of the cargo to keep them steady.

actuated in business. The practice of Lloyds is, we presume, the best to follow. Etc . . .

1835

100. F. P. Alleyn[1] in the Macao Roads to William Jardine in Canton,

27 January 1835

My dear Jardine,

It may appear flattery to some persons, but I must relate to you Nan[2] was not aware of your late Picture,[3] till she saw it in the cabin coming on board today—when she exclaimed what a likeness, how delighted I am to see, such a treasure, the kind, benevolent, warm-hearted man. Never did any person, regret more than she did not seeing you more of you at Macao, and that she had no opportunity of saying to you personally what she felt for all your kindness. I wish I could sincerely say as much for her companion, however I pass this over in silence. Andrew [Johnstone] could say much on this subject.

Be pleased to recollect what I have written concerning Teas. And I know you will not forget what I have written you in my letter of yesterday.[4] If you can serve you will. One thing, any course you point out I will follow.

God bless you.

My dear Jardine,

Yours faithfully,

[1] Dr F. P. Alleyn was an old friend of William Jardine. Like him, Alleyn had trained as a surgeon and had been employed by the East India Company between 1810 and 1829; first as a surgeon's mate on the *Dover Castle*, and then as a surgeon on the *General Kyd*. (Farrington, Anthony, (ed.), *A Biographical Index of the East India Company Maritime Service Officers, 1600–1834*, London, The British Library, 1999, p. 14). In 1834, when *Jardine, Matheson & Co.* needed a tea-taster, F. P. Alleyn, who had lost his East India Company job, applied for the post and William Jardine took him on. He died in Macao on 3 October 1837. (Ride, *East India Cemetery*, pp. 136–137).The loss of this old friend caused William Jardine much distress. (See Letters **145**, note 58, and **208**, note 102).

[2] F. P. Alleyn had married Anne Roggett in St James's, Westminster, on 11 Sept. 1828. He had brought his wife to China and the couple resided in Macao. (Farrington, *A biographical Index*, etc. p. 14).

[3] Possibly the portrait painted by Chinnery, now part of the firm's collection. (Keswick, *The Thistle and the Jade*, p. 13). See PLATE I.

[4] The letter was not traced.

101. James Matheson in Canton to [Lancelot] Dent in Canton,

31 January 1835

Dear Dent,

In reply to your note of the day respecting averages[5] I may repeat what I think I must have before told you that my aim has always been to assimilate our practice as far as possible to that of Lloyds,[6] the grand Emporium of Insurance, and having seen Lloyds Policies with average payable on each bag of sugar I felt no difficulty in extending the same principle to a chest of Tea, a package of which the lower grade is twice as valuable as a bag of sugar and far less liable to damage. In regard to fraud the impression on my mind has always been that when underwriters are very particular in not acknowledging small claims it holds out an inducement to the assured to use every artifice to magnify their loss, in order that it may not fall short of the stipulated average. And [in] this I have had occasion myself to notice what peculiar openings to fraud may be afforded by the condition 'average on each package'[7] [whether] hinted at by you I am not aware. Your idea of admitting no average on a value under 50 pounds sterling will have the advantage of rendering shippers more careful of the character of the vessels in which they entrust their property and also as to the mode of dunnage[8] that may be adopted; and from recent experience of the difficulty of enforcing attention to these important points, in consequence also of the less favourable nature of the ships we are now [assuring] we shall in all probability in most cases adopt small measures of averages as you suggest, at all events till next season when we shall have more experience to guide us.

In reference to our form of notes respecting the duration of risk on Portuguese vessels after arrival in Macao Roads, I think some limitation of time desirable. But the Portuguese seem now so well aware of the danger of making a long stay in the Macao Roads, during the typhoon months, that they scarcely ever venture to do so, and it appears to me that we run no great risk in leaving the point to the discretion of the assured on which [party] we must place our chief reliance on almost all matters connected with Policy.

While on this subjet I may add that in my opinion a point of far greater importance in underwriting than any we have touched on above is, the *selection* of *good*

[5] Average: 'The expense or loss to owners, arising from damage at sea to the ship or cargo (1622)'. By, 1835, as the paragraph shows, the term had acquired a more precise meaning in marine insurance. An average clause stated that 'the sum paid on a loss should bear the same proportion to the value of the property [. . .] destroyed as the sum insured did to the real value of the property'. (Dickson, P. G. M., *The Sun Insurance Office, 1710–1960: The History of two and a half Centuries of British Insurance*, London, 1960).

[6] James Matheson was an ardent supporter of Lloyds practice. (See his final remark in Letter **99**).

[7] The context does not fully clarify the concept of 'average on each package'. It does suggest, however, that the practice increased the number of small claims.

[8] For 'dunnage', see above Letter **99**, note 111.

risks, and the adoption of rates of premium graduated according to the character of the vessel insured. A facility in insuring indifferent vessels at the lowest premium fixed for the first class leads to hold out a *bonus* to the former, and proportionate discouragement to the latter, and I will venture to say, you will find very few men of business who if the case is brought practically home to their own pocket, will approve of the system by which a vessel like the *Robarts* is expected to be covered at the same rate as the *Ann*,[9] or even the *Layton* and *Sarah*. To decline receiving risks is not likely to be the worst sin of an agent for an Insurance office—it is very easy to err on the opposite side, but requires some self-denial or at all events a conscientious feeling of duty to the shareholders when a risk is refused.

A further point susceptible of improvement is to avoid placing obstructions in the way of ships being surveyed. This has been done. But I am mistaken if you will not find on enquiring that you have advanced an opinion on this head which is not borne out by the practice observed elsewhere.

Yours truly,

102. William Jardine in Canton to Hollingworth Magniac in London,

25 February 1835

My dear Magniac,

I have to apologize for not having long since addressed you in reply to your favors of 15th January, 9th, 22nd of June, and 21st July last, more particularly those of June and July, referring to the establishment of a House of Agency under the management of your good self and Messrs. Abel and Oswald Smith,[10] under the designation of *Magniac Smith & Co.*,[11] which designation was only made

[9] The *Ann* was a 788-ton ship built in 1812 by the Bombay Dockyard. It belonged to Pestonjee Bomanjee. (Wadia, *Bombay Dockyard*, p. 359). The *Sarah* was built by the same dockyard in 1792, (ibid., p. 335). The *Robarts* and the *Layton* were not identified.

[10] This is the first mention of 'the Smiths, an eminent moneyed family' (Letter **117**). John Abel Smith became one of the *Jardine, Matheson & Co.*'s most important London relationships during the decade 1836–1846. He was born in 1801, the son of John Smith, MP for Buckinghamshire, and brother of the first Lord Carrington. His grandfather, Abel Smith, was the founder of the Nottingham banking firm *Smith, Payne & Smith*. John Abel Smith was an East India stock proprietor. He was a Whig and from 1830 he represented Midhurst and later Chichester in the House of Commons. His principal residence was Dale Park in Sussex, and his London address 43, Belgrave Square. (*DPC*). Oswald Smith, a relation of John Abel Smith, was a director of the Alliance Insurance Company (*RLD*, Section 3, p. 33). Thomas Charles Smith, was unrelated to John Abel Smith. He had been a supercargo of the East India Company and was an old friend of Hollingworth Magniac. He became a partner of *Magniac Smith & Co.* in 1837. See Letters **117**, **119**, and **150**.

[11] In founding the firm of *Magniac Smith & Co.*, Hollingworth Magniac was entering into a partnership with members of a family which had distinguished itself for three generations in the banking business and had connections at the highest political level. John Abel Smith's uncle, Robert Smith, had been made first baron Carrington by Pitt the younger. And John Abel Smith himself was on

known on the 19th Instant, by a copy of your circular, though hinted at in your favor of 22nd of June.

My reason for not writing to you immediately on receipt of your first letter was this: I had fully made up my mind to proceed to England in one of the ships of this Season when we could have entered more fully into the subject in conversation, than we can possibly do by letter; but Mr. Matheson having for some time past suffered a good deal from an attack of inflammation in his eyes, we have determined on his proceeding home in the *Orwell*;[12] and to him I must refer you for an explanation of our views as to the management of the business of the Firm in England.

Any arrangement that may be entered into, between your highly respected Firm, and Mr. Matheson, will of course be fully sanctioned by his partners here; and I shall be happy to learn that your views and his coincide on a subject of so much importance to both.

We are fully aware of the wealth, respectability and high character of the parties with whom you have associated yourself, and much will depend upon yourselves in the formation of an arrangement between the two firms. We are equally aware of the respectability and integrity of Mr. Timothy Wiggin and Mr. Thomas Weeding,[13] as well as the inconvenience inseparable from their situation as individuals only, unconnected with any other parties in the management of affairs entrusted to them; but, on this subject, it is unnecessary to say more at present.

Be pleased to accept my grateful acknowledgment for the kind consideration in bearing in mind the probability of my wishing at some future period to become a member of the Firm *Magniac Smith & Co.*[14] It is impossible to foresee what my wishes may be on my return to England; but I should certainly prefer having the option of joining an establishment of so much promise, should I live to return home in a state of health equal to my undertaking a share of the labours of the firm.

Mr. Matheson is so much better acquainted with parties in Calcutta,[15] to whom your letter alludes, that I must beg leave to refer you to him at this point as well as many others connected with Calcutta and Bombay.

---

friendly terms with Lord Palmerston who, at the time when this letter was written, had just been replaced as Foreign Office Secretary by the Duke of Wellington during the short-lived conservative government of 1834–1835.

[12] On the circumstances of James Matheson proceeding to England on the *Orwell*, see above, Letter **92**, note 64.

[13] Since the failure of *Fairlie, Clark Innes & Co.*, *Jardine, Matheson & Co.* had been in a dilemma about how to arrange its 'home management'. See above, Letter **90**, note 54.

[14] A flattering offer for William Jardine, and yet the motives he gives for postponing his answer may have forced his reader's admiration more than a prompt acceptance.

[15] This reference to the special knowledge which James Matheson had of the 'parties in Calcutta', and the suggestion in the following paragraph that William Jardine had similar intimate knowledge of the parties in Bombay point to the fact that the partners' combined knowledge of the two main opium-exporting Indian presidencies—a knowledge unequalled in any other Canton firm—was one of the reasons of *Jardine Matheson & Co.*'s early success.

De Vitre's claim, in favour of the Bombay House, is well founded; and will most likely be favourably thought of by Mr. Matheson, who is now well acquainted with the merits of all the Bombay establishments. The House in Bombay is naturally very anxious to do everything in their power to support their friends in London;[16] but as your business would, in general, arise from, or be in some way connected with, your own advances, I can see no reason why they should not be able to give perfect satisfaction to both parties. Returns from Bombay are very generally made through China; and advantageous operations have frequently been made by purchasing Company's Bills in London, and sending them to Bombay, or Calcutta, to be realized—the proceeds to be sent on to China, and from thence to England in Bills of Exchange or advanced in goods, according to circumstances. Such operations would, I presume, be in your way.

The *Waterwitch* and *Red Rover* arrived from Calcutta a few days ago; and by them on their return, I shall have the pleasure of addressing Mr. {Hamley}.[17] Your circulars have been distributed here, and we shall send a few of them to Bombay by the first opportunity. The name of the Firm was announced too late to admit of much being done, in the way of consignments from hence this season; but on the event of having to load the *Scaleby Castle* on 'owners' account', we may have occasion to have recourse to your services.

Captain Templer,[18] in a letter of 23rd of July, mentions the new Firm in very flattering terms and appears to look forward to its representing our firm in England.

This will be handed to you by Mr. Matheson who is perfectly acquainted with my sentiment, on every point connected with the management of our affairs in England; and being likely to continue a member of the Firm after I have resigned, he is probably the party best calculated to complete the proposed arrangement.[19]

Your old friend, Mr. T.C. Smith,[20] has paid us a visit in conformity with his brothers' request; and as far as his prospects here are concerned, I should say he will bear up for a seat in the firm of *Magniac Smith*.[21]

[16] The reference is to *Remington & Co.*'s special connection with its principal agents in London, *Crawford, Colvin & Co.* (See Letter **90**, note 50). While in the process of setting his new firm of *Magniac Smith & Co.*, Hollingworth Magniac had been asking William Jardine for hints about the best potential correspondent agents in Bombay and in Calcutta.

[17] William Hamley was a captain in the Royal Navy. In 1831 he had commanded *HMS Wolf*. (*BI*).

[18] Captain Henry Templer was a commander of the East India Company ships until 1834. He then became a merchant, speculated in tea, and amassed a considerable fortune. (See Letter **111**: 'Templer is worth a plum').

[19] The 'proposed arrangement' was that *Magniac Smith & Co.* would become *Jardine, Matheson & Co.*'s London agents, in place of Thomas Weeding and Timothy Wiggin.

[20] T. C. Smith: Thomas Charles Smith, mentioned in note 10 above. T. C. Smith was travelling to Canton and India at the time, while Oswald Smith was working with Hollignworth Magniac and John Abel Smith towards finalizing the partners' arrangements in the firm. (See Letter **119**).

[21] William Jardine may be obliquely referring to the episode of Hollingworth Magniac's cousin, Francis Hollingworth, being refused a partnership in *Jardine, Matheson & Co.*

I have much pleasure in informing you of an arrangement made by Chay Beale to join the house of *Alexander Johnston & Co.*[22] of Singapore. Mr. Read[23] is to retire from the firm and act for it in England; while Chay and Mr. Whitehead[24] are to join Johnston, after the affairs of the old firm have been compromised, and having offered to advance one half of the funds necessary to carry this compromise in to effect, I hope to see the new firm in full force in a few months with a fair prospect of doing well. Chay is, I believe, ignorant of the part I have taken in this arrangement; and I am willing his friend, Dent, should have all the credit for it. Whatever his uncle[25] may fancy, Chay has himself and himself only, to blame, for being placed in the situation he has been for some time.[26] Had he been my brother, I could not conscientiously have advanced one argument in his favor. It will, however, afford me much pleasure to see him succeed; and I believe I may safely say Matheson is actuated by a similar feeling.

On the subject of the Imperial Hong,[27] I shall write to you by the next opportunity.

I fully intended to have sent you supply of Teas by the *Orwell*; but have been prevented by a miscalculation as to the quantity she could carry, the last Chops having been shut out, they shall be sent by the *Upton Castle* now loading.

Excuse this long, unconnected letter, which has been written amidst many interruptions, and completed at 2 a.m. on 27th February.

Believe me, My dear Magniac,

Yours very sincerely,

103. William Jardine in Canton to Thomas Weeding in London,

27 February 1835

Dear Weeding,

I have for some time refrained from writing to you, in reply to your letters on various important points from a conviction, in my own mind, that one of us should proceed to England in the course of the Season; and Mr. Matheson is now at Macao ready to embark on board the *Orwell*, having suffered a good deal lately from inflammation in his eyes.[28]

[22] *Alexander L. Johnston & Co.* a Singapore Agency. (Several letters listed in the *BI*).

[23] C. A. Read was still the London agent of *Alexander L. Johnston & Co.* in 1839. See the list of signatories of document appended to Letter **182**.

[24] Mr. Whitehead: possibly a relation of Captain Whitehead mentioned in Letter **110** below.

[25] Thomas Beale. (See Letter **25**, note 12).

[26] The episode referred to here remains obscure.

[27] On factories and Imperial Hong rents accruing to Hollingworth Magniac, see above, Letter **31**, note 53.

[28] On James Matheson voyage home on the *Orwell*, see above, Letter **92**, note 64. James Matheson's portrait reproduced on PLATE II was probably painted around this time.

By the late arrivals we have received very few letters from you; and not one with the most distant allusion to the new firm of *Magniac Smith & Co.*[29] though several of our correspondents make mention of it; and Mr. Magniac has sent us a number of their circulars dated on the 1st of July.

Your 'Private and confidential' letter of 28th April last is the one that I felt the most anxious to reply to;[30] and the hope of being able to discuss the subject therein alluded to in conversation, and that only, prevented me from doing so on paper.

Allow me, in the first instance, to thank you most sincerely, for the frank manner in which you have stated your views; and the good wishes with which they were combined. As Mr. Matheson and I are in the habit of communicating most freely, on all subjects, public and private, connected with our interests and feelings, I at once laid your letter before him; and must now leave you and him to discuss the subject on which it treats: as well as various other points intimately connected with our interests in England.

I must not conceal from you, however, that the impression on my mind, produced in some degree by your own correspondence, is, that you would have less anxiety, and more peace and ease of mind, situated as you have hitherto been, than you could possible have as the sole manager of our affairs in England.

The principal advantage, which we look to, from our home connection, is the certainty of our Bills being protected to whatever extent (in moderation) we may have occasion to draw, in the course of any one season, without reference to immediately available assets to meet them; and this may occasionally involve our friends in much heavier acceptances; and, for a time, in much heavier advances, than you might feel comfortable under, or than might suit your convenience.[31] There are, of course, other points to be looked to, such as connections and influence with parties embarked, or likely to embark in the China trade; but, having said so much, I shall leave these to your and Mr. Matheson's serious consideration, he being as fully and deeply interested in the affair as I am.

[29] Thomas Weeding felt that his business with *Jardine, Matheson & Co.* was threatened by the setting up of *Magniac Smith & Co.* He was to be proved right.

[30] The letter was not traced. However, it can be inferred that Thomas Weeding had written to ask for a larger share of *Jardine, Matheson and Co.*'s London business, particularly after the assistance he had rendered them at the time of *Fairlie, Clark Innes & Co.*'s failure.

[31] This paragraph expresses clearly what had increasingly become a fact of business life in the China trade, particularly for the larger operators like *Jardine, Matheson & Co.* It was no longer possible for London agency houses to remain purely 'agencies'. They had to become bankers as well, and had often to accept bills drawn on them in excess of immediate asset coverage. The timing differences between shipping of goods from Canton and their realization in London, could involve William Jardine's London correspondents in 'much heavier advances' than Thomas Weeding was prepared to grant.

It afforded me much satisfaction to see the able manner in which you had advocated the cause of the Company's Commanders and Officers; for which they might, and, I have no doubt, they do feel highly grateful.[32]

We are looking forward with some anxiety for accounts from England subsequent to the arrival of Lord Napier's dispatches,[33] and I shall be thankful for any information you can give me respecting the intentions of the Government.

Believe me, My Dear Weeding,

Yours very sincerely,

104. William Jardine in Canton to Captain Rees[34] on the Coast (Barque *Colonel Young*), 9 March 1835

My dear Sir,

Your letters of the 4th, and 5th Instant have been received, and the *Fairy* has by this time delivered her Treasure to the{*Hawke*}, and is preparing to return to you with a fresh supply of the Bengal drug.[35]

If you have been fortunate since the *Fairy* left she and the *Findlay* may possibly cross each other; but this is of no importance, as you cannot be long without drug, under any circumstances, unless some accident befall the *Fairy*, which God forbid.

[32] Thomas Weeding had played an important part in the negotiations which led to compensation of the officers and other employees, following the dismantling of the East India Company maritime service. The Committee of the Maritime Officers which met on 2 December 1834 at the *Jerusalem Coffee House* made a point of thanking 'Sir Charles Forbes, Bart., Thomas Weeding Esq., Richard Twining, Esq., etc. [. . .] and other Proprietors, for their disinterested and valuable support in advocating the claim of the Service. (Extract from the Report of the Committee of the East India Company's Maritime Officers, 2 December 1834, *JMArch.* A7/214. For the background to this document, see above, Letter **98**, note 101.

[33] The way the British government was to respond to Lord Napier's failing to even make contact with the Chinese authorities was a matter of considerable interest among the members of the British community in Canton. Part of James Matheson's purpose in going home was to find out how the government proposed to move forward in its China trade policy following the disappointment of Lord Napier's failure.

[34] For Captain Rees, see above, Letter **81**, note 2.

[35] By 1835, *Jardine, Matheson & Co.* had already put in place an effective system of semi-permanent selling stations at various anchorages along the coast of China. When the ships were running out of opium, they quickly sailed back to Lintin for fresh supplies. Within two years the system was further perfected: the firm's larger ships, the *Colonel Young* and the *Austin* served as intermediary opium stores up the coast, while lighter ships were constantly bringing them new supplies from Lintin. In order to carry out the opium trade in this new way and to keep out competition as much as possible, the firm had to buy its ships outright, a departure from previous practice. At the time, its principal opium ships were ten in number: The *Hercules,* the *Austin*, the *Colonel Young* (often referred to as the *Young*), the *Lady Hayes,* the *Red Rover* (partly owned with Captain Clifton), the *Governor Findlay* (often referred to as the *Findlay*), the *Hellas*, the *Omega*, and later the *Jardine* (a small steam ship—see Letter **110**) and the *Harriet*). (*JMArch.*, 7/231). A number of these ships are mentioned in this Letter.

The *Amelia* started for the Coast a few days ago and reports say the *Syed Khan* is about to start for the same destination so that there will be no want of competition and you will require all your knowledge and activity to hold your own among them.[36] I am not however in the least degree afraid of the result. They may do us harm, but in doing this they must suffer still more themselves.

The Parsees are desirous of sending a vessel along the Coast, but have not yet determined what vessel to send. If you could manage matters so as to make the Mandarins attack every one but your own party, it would have a good effect; and Mr. Gutzlaff having agreed to accompany Mr. Gordon[37] to the Bohea hills embarking in a few days in the Austin you will have his aid in communicating with them. My principal fear is that numbers may bring down the displeasure of the government Authorities on the Dealers and Boat men while competition among the sellers will reduce the price very much.

You will however have every advantage from your knowledge of the Coast and number of vessels placed at your disposal while the quickness of our return will enable us to sell cheaper than any of them. It would be a great object to discover a station where Malwa could be run off at 40 or 50 dollars per chest higher than the Canton price.[38] Make enquiries respecting such a station and try all you can to find one. Tienshun[39] takes off a considerable annual supply from the Junks at high prices.

Your muster of Silk is not true nankin Tsatlee—nor is it Taysaam, the circle of the hank is smaller, and the quality as well as the Color is inferior—none like the Canton Silk, but if cheap, say, 250–270 dollars per pecul, it may answer for India or even for England.

In the event of your failing in an arrangement with the Mandarins another plan has occurred to me—viz, to place one of your vessels alongside of, or on the same station with, each of the strangers and by taking the first of the sales, following prices down to the lowest rate that would pay the other craft, say 40, 30 or even 20 per chest beyond the Lintin prices, you might possibly sicken them of the trade as you would, barring accidents to our carrying vessels, always have the

[36] This Letter shows as well as any the firm's various muscular tactics used to discourage competition in the coastal market which it had pioneered.

[37] George James Gordon was a member of the *Mackintosh & Co.* agency house in Calcutta. He was then appointed a member of the Tea Committee set up in 1834 by the Governor General of India, Lord Bentinck, to promote the culture of the tea tree in India. The Tea Committee sent G. J. Gordon on two successive missions to China (1834–1835 and 1836–1837) in order to bring back tea seeds for transplant on India soil. (Antrobus, H. A., *A History of the Assam Company, 1839–1953*, Edinburgh, T. & A. Constable, Ltd. 1957, pp. 30–55; Le Pichon, Alain, «Le premier thé de l'Inde britannique: du rêve à la réalité», *Cahiers victoriens et édouardiens*, No. 55, Montpellier, Avril 2002, pp. 183–203). See also Letters **108**, **116**, **121**, **151**, and **169**).

[38] Competition in the opium trade had virtually eliminated margins for those dealers involved in the Canton, Macao and Lintin markets.

[39] The station was not identified.

latest intelligence from hence.[40] In this however much must be left to you own good sense and much must depend on circumstances.

The *Governor Findlay* will be sent back immediately if required, and by her you shall have further instructions.

Your own affairs have our attention.[41] In haste, I remain, My dear sir,

Yours sincerely.

105. The directors of the Manchester Chamber of Commerce in Manchester, to the public, 18 March 1835[42]

OBSERVATIONS RESPECTING THE FINANCE OPERATIONS
OF THE HONOURABLE THE EAST INDIA COMPANY IN INDIA AND CHINA

Competition on the part of a sovereign power is incompatible with the general interest of trade, and hurtful to those of individuals who may be brought into contact with such power.

The principle has been ackowledged by the legislature of the country, and is responded to by the unanimous voice of the trading public.

The operations of the Honourable East India Company in advancing money in India and China, on the security of goods consigned to them in this country, are considered to be, not only highly prejudicial to the mercantile and manufacturing community of Great Britain, but hurtful to the interests of the company itself, and contrary to the spirit of the late act of Parliament, which stipulated, that the trading capacity of the company shall be in abeyance during the continuance of the present charter; this restriction being considered essential to the interests of the private merchants.

Trading in money by a sovereign body is as hurtful to the beneficial enterprise of individuals as trading in anything.

The honourable company have made advances on the security of eastern produce at Calcutta, consigned to Leadenhall-street,[43] at a rate of exchange disproportionate to the existing rates in London, and to the rates which the cost of

[40] William Jardine was confident of the firm's dominant position in the opium coast market and of its superior price-intelligence due to its fleet of ships, two of the prerequisites to win a price war.

[41] This reference remains obscure. Captain Rees may have ordered a purchase of opium from Bombay or Calcutta on his own account.

[42] This is a printed document on the back of which Letter **110** was written. It is based on the Statement of Objection, etc. . . (Document **93** above) written by James Matheson and sent to the Manchester Chamber of Commerce of which John Macvicar was an active member. One of the typographical peculiarities of this document is that, contrary to previous practice, most words which tended to be capitalized (*Act* of Parliament, East India *Company*, etc. . .) are spelt here with small letters.

[43] The East India Company's head office, the East India House, was situated in Leadenhall Street. An imposing classical building with its six-column portico had replaced the 1726 India House. For pictures of the East India Houses, see Sutton, *Lords of the East*, pp. 10, 19, and the colour plate betwe pp. 72 and 73).

transmission of bullion would justify; and they have recently established a finance committee at Canton, for the purpose of effecting exchange operations there, thus extending (most unnecessarily and improperly it is conceived) an interference with the natural course of mercantile affairs in a manner they have no right to do.

With equal right might they establish agencies in Batavia, Manila, or in other foreign countries, and take up the position of bankers for the whole of the eastern world. The controlling power which they would thus acquire over the exchanges, and consequently over the value of all imports and exports from the east, cannot be contemplated without the most serious apprehension.

The nature of the trade between this country and China is essentially one of barter.[44]

The advances advertised to be made by the company at Canton, causing the expectation of a superabundance of money for investment in tea, silk, and other produce of China, have already had the effect of enhancing the prices of those articles here, to the benefit of the Chinese, and to the disadvantage of the British merchant, whilst on the other hand (the Chinese trader being enabled to obtain cash for his produce, which, under other circumstances, he would gladly have exchanged for the produce of our manufacturing industry,) the value of our manufactures has been greatly depreciated.

The rates of exchange have been also most seriously and injuriously affected.

Previously to the operations of the honourable company at Canton towards the end of August last, the exchange on London was at from 4s. 10d to 5s. for a Spanish dollar, and that on Bengal at 204 Sicca rupees for 100 dollars. The company's finance committee advertised on the 18th of October last, that they would make advances on homeward cargoes at 4s. 7d. per dollar and altered the rate of exchange on Bengal to 208 rupees for 100 dollars, causing the enormous and destructive fluctuation in the value of the money[45] of from $5\frac{45}{100}$ to $9\frac{9}{100}$ per cent in the exchange on London and about 2 per cent in that on Calcutta.

Tea has been affected in a similar manner, and to fully as great an extent.

British manufactured goods have been depreciated 25 per cent in value, taking into consideration the rate of exchange at which they can be remitted for.

[44] This statement is a convenient shortcut to express a far less simple reality. In fact, the bulk of the funds used by the East India Company to purchase its teas until 1834 came indirectly from the private merchants' sale of opium. Up till the middle of the 1830s (though not always after that time) all opium sales were cash sales. Most goods that were neither tea nor opium were bartered to a certain extent, especially British manufactured goods.

[45] As William Jardine himself was quick to point out, however, (Letter **125**, paragraph 2), this 'destructive' devaluation of the dollar versus the English pound was very useful when seen from the point of view of Chinese remittances to England. 'It is very convenient for us to be able to obtain funds at 4 shillings and 4 pence in lieu of 4 shillings and 10 pence per Dollar, whenever we may feel disposed for an extensive operation in Silks or Teas'.

It is not the amount of the operations of the company which has, in the mean time, caused these great fluctuations, but the apprehension of the random procedure that may be adopted.

The history of the former trade of the company has shewn, that, except when protected by a monopoly, they have constantly lost their own money, and have caused severe losses to individuals ; and it is not a probable inference, from the facts above stated, that there will now be any improvement.

The expense of the company's finance establishment in China will be heavy. Two tea tasters are said to be engaged to ascertain the value of the tea advanced upon. If the company makes advances on silk, they must appoint an agent to value that also. There are several members of the finance committee (some, if not all, directors' sons) probably with a secretary and assistants, and with the usual profusion of the company, these individuals will, no doubt, derive large emoluments, which, added to the expenses of office and other incidents, will amount to a large per centage on a small banking business. If the business transacted be large, so much the more will the mercantile and manufacturing interest of their country suffer.

The general trade to India and China should not be subjected to the capricious dealings of a sovereign body, whose finance operations are thus regulating and controlling, or at least greatly interfering with the exchanges over all India and China, and thus disturbing the value of all commodities exported from and imported into Great Britain from thence; nor should it be subjected to the management of a finance committee composed of individuals closely connected with mercantile establishment at the same place, thereby exciting suspicion and distrust in the body of merchants.

The system of advancing a large portion of the value of a shipment to London, will have a tendency to bring adventurers into the trade, who will be enabled by the advances of the company, to enter recklessly into operations on more favourable terms than capitalists in this country, who would willingly employ a sufficient amount of capital in the trade, were they divested of the apprehension of interference on the part of the company.

There can be no doubt that the superabundance of unemployed capital in Great Britain,[46] would flow into any channel which presented a safe and profitable prospect of employment; but the uncertainty attending the course of operation of the Honourable East India Company, (who do not appear to be guided and influenced, and who do not act upon the same motives and rules which guide individ-

[46] This was one of the themes of Gibbon Wakefield's *The Art of Colonization*. (Wakefield, Edward, Gibbon, *A view of the Art of Colonization with Present Reference to the British Empire, etc. in Letters between a Statesman and the Colonist, etc*. London, E. G. Wakefield, 1849.

uals[47]) deters capitalists from investing money freely in the trade to the east, which of itself would be of great benefit to India.

From the peculiar situation of the honourable Company, a cause unfortunately exists for a certain degree of interference with the trade to the country over which it presides. It is, however, the paramount duty of the rulers of that country, not only to guard the interests of India, but to combine them with those of this country, by adopting the best means which can be devised for effecting these ends.

The removal of all unequal and excessive duties in this country, on the production of *our* possessions in the east, would greatly benefit both countries; but leaving this point out of consideration for the present, and in order to meet the necessity which exists for the transmission to this country of a large portion of the Company's revenue under the present state of things, it would appear, that, by opening the treasury in Leadenhall-street, at a fair and proper rate of exchange, and by shutting the treasuries in India and China, there would be paid into their hands at Leadenhall-street, an amount adequate to the necessities of the Company, whilst by this mode of operation much of the existing evil would be removed.

When the company's treasury in London grants bills on Bengal they are drawn at two months' sight, for which money is immediately paid into the treasury here: these bills reach Calcutta about 4½ months after they are drawn, and are paid by the company in India in about 6½ months after they receive the money in London. When the company advance money at Calcutta, they are repaid in this country about 12 months after date, which (making an allowance of ½ month for the opportunity of investment and negotiation at Calcutta) makes a difference of 19 months in the time when the amount is received into the treasury in London, which at 5 per cent per annum (the rate of interest at which the larger portion of the company's debt has been contracted) amounts to about 8 per cent; to which should be added the expense of agency in India and China, say 2 per cent. The equivalent to a rate of exchange at Calcutta on London at 12 months' date of 2s. 1d. per Sicca rupee, would therefore be in London a rate of 1s. 10½d. per Sicca rupee.

In December, 1833, the company opened their treasury at Calcutta, to advance money on the security of produce legally consigned to Leadenhall-street at the rate of 2s. 1d per Sicca rupee, which was known in London early in may last, at which time the treasury in London granted bills on Calcutta at 2s. per Sicca rupee. The company should then have *reduced* the rate here to a corresponding price, say to 1s. 10½ d.; instead of doing which they shortly afterwards *advanced* it to 2s. 1d., being about 10 per cent higher than it ought to have been, to be on par with

[47] Free-traders tended to see themselves in terms of courageous individuals fighting occult monopolistic or indeed hidden 'sovereign' interests.

the known existing rate of the company's own treasury at Calcutta; the natural consequence must be, to prevent money being paid into the treasury at home, which would otherwise have flowed into it.

When the treasury in London is open to grant bills, *at a fair and proper rate of exchange*, on the presidencies in India, and when it is known that the treasuries in India and China *discontinue to advance money* on bills on London, money will then freely flow into the treasury in London.[48]

When the treasury in China is shut, the company will be applied to in London for a large amount of bills on Bengal and Bombay, which will afford a means to merchants in this country of placing funds in China for the purchase of tea, silk, etc.; the value of our imports of which, at present, greatly exceeds that of our exports of manufactured goods and metals; and these bills will be anxiously sought for in China as a means of remittance thence to India of the large balance drawn annually by India from China in payment for cotton and opium supplied by India. But so long as the treasury on China is open, and the exchanges subjected to the capricious fluctuations incidental to the management of the honourable company, no sufficient confidence can exist with private individuals to induce persons of capital to trade to China with the degree of spirit which is necessary to its welfare; and the boon conferred on the public by the act of parliament, prohibiting the company from trading, is rendered in a great degree nugatory and valueless.

The company would be relieved from every risk, and from all the charges of expensive finance establishments in India and China, without any disadvantage to themselves, and divesting them (under proper regulations here) of the hurtful effects of a controlling and disturbing interference.

By order of the Board of Directors of the Chamber of Commerce and Manufacture of Manchester,

Signed THOMAS BOOTHMAN,[49] Junior Secretary.

[48] The East India Company's aim was to repatriate funds to England: it therefore benefited most when it got more pounds sterling for its dollars. The British manufacturers' aim was exactly the opposite: they benefited most when they got more dollars for their goods sold abroad (i.e. more dollars for their pounds). By 'opening the exchanges' in India and in Canton at rates which they could more easily dictate than in London and which lowered the dollar against the pound, the East India Company was pursuing a policy directly opposed to the exporters' interests. In the post-1834, post-India Act environment, this was interpreted in Manchester as in blatant opposition to Parliament's will.

[49] One letter by Thomas Boothman is recorded in the *BI*.

106. Henry Wright in Canton to William Jardine in Macao,[50]

10 April 1835

My dear Sir,

I addressed a note to you this morning by the return boat, giving it a chance of reaching you at Lintin. It was merely to say that I had seen Achun and Ahong[51] who both declare that Cash has left Canton, but from their manner I do not give the least credit to their assertions. And I also informed you that the *Austin* is insured for 22,500 dollars the *10th Canton Office* having been reserved on the 1st instant

Last night I sold five chests of Patna at 600 dollars, and this morning five chests of last year's Benares at 680 dollars. I have been told that Malwa has been offered at 585 dollars.

I received a letter from Otadui[52] this morning dated the 22nd March enclosing an Invoice and Bill of Lading of the [sugar] cargo consisting of 14,747 Peculs costing with charges 1.40 dollar per Pecul. To this is to be added the shipment at Manila of 715 Peculs Rice and 861 Peculs Paddy besides about 109 Peculs Paddy in the [ ]. Mackenzie[53] is on his way to Lintin in the *Mormon* American vessel. The *Nestor*, *Tourville* and [ ] are to be despatched tomorrow. The *Syra* is headed either for London or Liverpool.

Goddard[54] has just informed me that Messrs. Wetmore and Green[55] are elected members of the Social Club !

Mr. Smith[56] understands your instructions, respecting Teas, and shipments are going on. The *Captain Cook* has had two Chops of Bohea and one of Congo. Aho is at the Tomb of his Father and no clearances thought of.

[50] With James Matheson having recently left for England per *Orwell* and William Jardine away in Macao, Henry Wright, the most senior employee, was left to hold the fort. Henry Wright became a junior partner in the firm at about this time, together with Alexander Matheson and Andrew Johnston. (Keswick, *The Thistle and the Jade*, p. 264).

[51] Opium brokers.

[52] Eugenio de Otadui: a Manila merchant and senior partner in *E. de Otadui & Co*. The firm was *Jardine, Matheson & Co*.'s principal Manila correspondent.

[53] 'Mackenzie' was not identified.

[54] James Goddard, a British private merchant, and an occasional writer in the Chinese Repository. (Fay, *Opium War*, pp. 39–40). For subsequent references to James Goddard after his return to London, see Letter **151**, **249**, and **250**.

[55] William Samuel Wetmore: an American merchant and senior partner in *Wetmore & Co*., a firm with offices in the 'Imperial' Hong of the factories (Bard, *Traders of Hong Kong*, p. 84). John C. Green was the Canton agent of the New York firm of *Messrs. N. L. and G. Griswold*. In 1834, he was admitted a partner in *Russell & Co*. 'consequent upon the death of Mr. William H. Low'. (Hunter, *The Fan Kwae at Canton*, p. 96).

[56] James Warly Smith was *Jardine, Matheson & Co*.'s tea taster.

It is reported today that Old Atom[57] the Linguist is to suffer a temporary banishment of three years and his partner to be transported for life with some other connected with the offence with which they are charged.

Opium is the only business occupying much attention, and of this there is very little at present. I sent the Touchstoner to Captain Parry.[58]

Yours truly.

[P. S.] I have this moment opened a letter from Mr. Johnston[59] ordering the Balance in his favour (as treasurer) of 3,285.60 dollars to be held at the credit of Mr. Elmslie, and he returns his thanks for the manner in which you have performed past services.

107. William Mackay on the Coast (Brigg *Fairy*) to William Jardine in Canton, 11 April 1835[60]

My dear Sir,

The *Findlay* has arrived and delivered to me your favor of the 20th ultimo.

I arrived up here on the 24th and anchored first in [Lo Loo] Bay[61] where I found the *Aurelia*[62] only in a couple of days. Without communicating with her I proceeded to Chin Choo Bay and there found the *Colonel Young* clear of her Patna but with her large portion of her Benares remaining.

I transshipped to her fifty (50) chests Patna and then proceeded to Cheemoo Bay where Rees thought something was to be done. After waiting four days without boats coming off, I proceeded to this anchorage which is between the *Aurelia* and Amoy—passing well down outside to prevent Hadley's[63] seeing us. Yesterday four boats from Amoy and on their way to Hadley came alongside and having each a chit from Hadley saying he would sell for 690 dollars. I gave the opium at the same price. They cleared out among them eighteen chests which,

[57] One of the factories official linguists. His offence remains obscure.

[58] Captain Parry needed the touchstoner to authenticate the gold received in payment for the opium.

[59] Alexander Johnston. For his appointment as treasurer to the Superintendence of British Trade, see above Letter **91**, note 58. Edward Elsmlie was senior clerk to the Superintendence. He was promoted to secretary from April 1835 until he was invalided home in April 1841. (Hoe, *The Taking of Hong Kong*, p. 262).

[60] This letter is not dated. At the back, William Jardine wrote the following: 'No date. Received April 11th 1835. Answer: none required. Acknowledging my letter of 20th March. He arrived in Lo Loo Bay on the 24th of March, and found the *Aurelia* there. Reports progress. Intercepting boats, etc., etc.'

[61] The various anchorages mentioned by the captains of the opium ships were not exactly located. In 1835, many were situated in the vicinity of Amoy and also along the Chinese coast between Amoy and Canton. Later, from 1836 on, several anchorages were situated further north, between Amoy and Ningpo (900 miles north of Canton).

[62] The *Aurelia* belonged to the competition, probably to *Dent & Co.*

[63] Captain Hadley commanded the *Aurelia*.

with what we had before delivered, in the small way, makes a total sold by us of twenty two chests and three balls,[64] of which four chests are Benares and the remainder Patna. There is a demand here, now that the boats have commenced to come. I hope they will make a run upon us.

When I parted with Rees we agreed that the vessel clearing her Patna first should run down to the other. Rees, being the fortunate one, came here yesterday about noon and we decided that, as the amount of Treasure was large, and it being of consequence to inform you that the Benares is both inferior and shorter of weight than the Patna, the *Fairy* should start forthwith for Lintin. We transshipped all the opium to the *Colonel Young*, received all her Treasure, and I was in the act of taking leave of Rees when the *Findlay* [was] in sight. The Treasure now goes to her and I receive a portion of her cargo. Rees and I agree that less Benares and more Patna should now be sent. You will judge of this by the position of each sold. There are some inquiries for Malwa again, but perhaps we have enough of that description of the drug for the present.

Kennedy[65] tells me that a fleet of smugglers attempted to come off to him about the Cape of Good Hope[66] but having no shroff he did not [want to] heave to[67] for them. In case you think of stationing her there for a short time on her next trip up I have pointed out to Kennedy our former station in that neighborhood.

We had rough weather on the way up and carried away another jib-boom but are now all to rights again. When close reefing the main Topsail on one occasion, we unfortunately lost a poor fellow overboard. He fell from the yard, and we could not pick him up.

I have reason to think which almost amounts to a certainty that Hadley wrote to his employers on his last cruize *clandestinely* by my late chief mate, Mr. Haudley. This may account for the report of my refusing to take his letters being so carefully circulated in Canton. When I meet Hadley I shall tell him of it and shall take good care he has not another chance.

I forward to you the *Fairy*'s accounts made up to the end of February. You will perceive that the Brigg has credit of the amount of fees received on the opium sold on the Coast in last July and January. As Rees has given up receiving fees so have I, so that now the account Sale shows the whole sum received.

I remain, my dear Sir,

Yours sincerely,

[64] Opium balls: see above, Letter **30**, note 43.

[65] Captain George Kennedy commanded the *Governor Findlay* and the *Fairy* in 1835. (*BI*).

[66] A nickname for an unidentified local Chinese cape.

[67] Heave to: 'to bring the ship to a standstill by setting the sails so as to counteract each other'. (*OED*). Without a shroff on board, Captain Kennedy had no means of checking whether metal given in payment for the opium, was genuine gold or sycee silver.

108. William Jardine in Canton to James Matheson traveling to London, 10 May 1835[68]

My dear Matheson,

I cannot allow the *Captain Cook* to leave China without a few lines for you, though I have really little to say; in addition to my long letter of the 23rd ultimo, and the Firm's circular of the 7th Instant by this conveyance.

The most important event since the date of my last is the death of our friend Bardolph[69] after a few hours illness. His disease appears to have been cholera. Howqua and Demosthenes are very much at a loss for someone to assist them in their negotiations with the Mandarins in which art he is said to have excelled.

We have at last had two or three days heavy rain, which has set the husbandmen to work but the weather being now cold and cloudy, the wind north, the Barometer high and Thermometer 67°, they are very doubtful about being able to raise even an indifferent crop. Rice must rule high during the Season, say 2 to 2.50 dollars per pecul, probably higher. Keating[70] is still a large holder. The *Colon*'s Rice was sold at 2.20 and 2.40 per pecul. The *Lyden's* Rice pays very little, having been purchased at high prices in Manila.

Our coast trade has been going on tolerably well, the only competition having been the *Aurelia*.[71] The *Volunteer* started a few days ago chartered by Framjee Pestonjee[72] and carrying Malwa only. This is likely to be a failure, the demand for Malwa having fallen off very much of late.

Our friends have been doing a little good by their Patna and Benares this Season, on account of the *Sylph*'s misfortune, prices having ruled rather higher than they have done for some time past.[73] At present there is no Patna in the market, the second crop of Opium not having yet come on.

In a conversation with Mr. Wetmore[74] yesterday, I found that in the Brazils, they restamp the South American Dollars by pressure only, putting one of them only into the die and by one smart blow giving it the character of a Ferdinand or

[68] *JMArch. C4-4.* This letter was addressed to London, 'care of Thomas Weeding'.

[69] The reference is obscure. 'Bardolph' was probably the nickname of a 'linguist'. The nickname may have been inspired by Shakespeare's 'Bardolph' in *Henry IV*. (The only other 'Bardolph' referred to in the correspondence is later, in Letter **126**). As a skilled negotiator with the mandarins, he is unlikely to have been a European, in spite of the name. Equally the reference to 'Demosthenes', whilst clearly humorous, is obscure. He must have been one of the linguists working closely with Howqua, the principal hong merchant.

[70] For Arthur Saunders Keating, see above, Letter **42**, note 37

[71] See Letter **107** immediately above.

[72] Framjee Pestonjee had established his own opium agency in Canton, in the hope of attracting much of the Parsee business from Bombay.

[73] With the *Sylph* was temporarily out of action on the Calcutta-Lintin route, the supply of Patna was reduced in the market. The *Sylph*, loaded with treasure bound for Calcutta, disappeared for good much later, in 1849, the result of an attack by pirates. (Keswick, *The Thistle and the Jade*, p. 198).

[74] Samuel Wetmore, the American merchant: see above, Letter **106**, note 55.

Carolus dollar. You might easily get this tried in the Mint or at Birmingham, and if you find that one dollar can be converted into the other so easily and effectually, you have only to purchase a few dies and the cheapest mechanical power for giving the necessary impetus (no matter whether the latest invention) and send them out. We can then convert our Mexicans and Peruvians into Ferdinands at very little expense.[75] Even if five or six men should be required, it is of little importance. To make Spanish dollars out of sycee is a much more difficult task and would require extensive machinery, I fear, as well as a man to manage the alloying etc . . .

We are all going on very quietly. Mr. Thom and Andrew Jardine at Macao recruiting,[76] as is Innes.

Mr. Gordon[77] has joined Rees on the 30th ultimo. The *Findlay* had fallen in with the *Fairy* on the Coast, and given her a fair beating, so says Gordon. Mackay says the *Fairy* was out of trim. Kennedy returned in the *Fairy* and Mackay went on with the Tea seed Party in the *Findlay*.

Austin repairing in Macao back harbour; and we have made up our minds to give Captain Allen[78] six month pay and put Jauncey[79] in charge of the *Austin*. I could never have confidence in him after what has occurred.

Kind regards to all friends.

Yours very sincerely,

109. William Jardine in Canton to John Macvicar in Manchester,

22 May 1835

My Dear Macvicar,

I had the pleasure of addressing a few formal lines to you on 13th Instant per *Gulnare*, explanatory of the superintendance bestowed by me on the sale of piece goods consigned to the House. Since then we have been favoured with letters, invoices, samples, etc., per *Universe*; and Mr. Thom being still at Macao, it

[75] The desire to 'convert' Mexican and Peruvian dollars into Ferdinands arose from the fact that some of the opium sold up coast was partly paid for in these rare coins. (See above, Letter **73**).

[76] The principal book-keeper, Chay Beale, was leaving to become a partner in *A. L. Johnston & Co.* in Singapore. See above, Letter **102**, note 22. Andrew Jardine, a future partner in the firm (1839–1843), had recently arrived from London to help in the tea department. He was the eldest son of William Jardine's brother, David Jardine (of Muirhousehead).

[77] For G. J. Gordon, see above, Letter **104**, note 37. William Jardine humorously refers to him and his attendants as the 'Tea seed Party'.

[78] Captain William Allen had commanded the *Ann*. Three letters from Lintin are listed in the *BI*. Whatever error or mistake Captain Allen was guilty of cost him his job. At the time, the ship commanders were usually paid by *Jardine, Matheson & Co.* a fixed annual salary of 250 dollars. (*JMArch.* A7/231). They were expected to make much more money through their own private transactions.

[79] Captain Francis Jauncey took charge of the *Austin* as soon as the ship was repaired. In 1838 he became the commander of the *governor Findlay*. (*Ibid.*)

becomes my duty to let you know what project we have of realizing these valuable consignments.

It would be highly gratifying to me to be able to assure you that our friends would all benefit handsomely by these shipments, but I regret to say there is little prospect of this at present.[80] As far as I can judge from present appearances and the inquiries that have been made, the shippers of cotton Twists, Camlets, long Ells, and tin plate, will do tolerably well. For the Twist 56 or 58 dollars per pecul will be obtained, purchasers paying duty. For the Camlets we have been offered 28 dollars per piece. I want to get 30 and hope to do so. For long Ells assorted as your shipments are, we hope to get 9 dollars, which will pay, and be preferable, I think, to holding on, as a fall in the Exchange would be as injurious to the proprietors as a fall in the price—present rate 4 shillings and 9 pence per dollar. For the tin plates we are offered 11 dollars and expect to get 11½ per [lot]. So far we have no reason to complain. But the embossed long Ells, Spanish Stripes and ladies cloths, if sold at present, must leave very heavy losses, not being worth more than one dollar to one dollar ten cents per yard.

The Chinese attribute this to a falling off in demand from the Northern provinces and a scarcity of cash among speculators here, not to increased importation. On the contrary, it is generally admitted, that the annual supply has been smaller than usual. Selling at present is out of the question; but I may be inclined to make an arrangement, through one of the Hong merchants, to send a part of our stripes to the silk country and have the proceeds returned in Raw Silk. A proposal of this kind has been made to me; but there are difficulties in the way; and, unless we can fix prices to both articles, the plan will most likely be abandoned. Of the long cloth we have given out musters but have had very few offers. Some of them will yield a small profit, while others are not worth prime cost and charges.

The first musters sent out were those of invoice 122 marked 'GH/CM' and we have received offers as follows: for the white N° 206–272: 8 dollars per piece, with the exception of 322 and 328 for which they offer only 5¾ dollars per piece. In all these offers the purchasers pay the duty.

The white goods are not saleable, the market being overstocked with grey.[81] The Manila market is nearly equal to this. Should prices improve there we shall have plenty of opportunities of sending goods over as the rice ships are constantly running between that island and Macao.

While writing, Hengtai has come to inform me that Minqua the Hong merchant[82] has sold 2,000 pieces of scarlet long Ells at 8½ dollars per piece or 10½

[80] Hardly one Letter in the correspondence suggests that the sales of British manufactured goods were realizing good prices in China.

[81] This curiously suggests that unbleached linen was more in demand than bleached linen.

[82] Both Hengtai and Minqua were Hong merchants. Hengtai had bought his official Hong licence in 1830 (Morse, *The Chronicles of the EIC*, IV, p. 224). At first, *Jardine, Matheson & Co* had only an

dollars duty paid. If ours had been up yesterday we might have sold them at 9 dollars per piece. We must still try for it. I shall here explain for the satisfaction of your friends—for you know the facts already—that the charge of 3 dollars per bale on Silk privilege is so regular that every ship, if Silk is procurable, goes away with her privilege filled up and it is occasionally advertised for sale—the silk deliverable at Lintin—every one has to pay it who ships silk, and therefore, being money actually paid, must appear either in the price or as a charge.[83]

Etc . . .

110. John Macvicar in Manchester to William Jardine in Canton,
23 May 1835[84]

My dear Jardine,

I have to thank you for your letter of the 15th January via Bombay received about ten days ago. The proceedings of your finance Committee has proved what you justly predicted, a vile job and all together very injurious to the Canton Trade. Before the Receipt of the 'Objection of your Chamber of Commerce' in this Country, I had got our Chamber of Commerce to send forward to our Members the announced 'Observations' on the same subject which they transmitted to Lord Ellenbourgh[85] with whom I had also had an interview on the subject. Our 'Observations' have also been adopted by Liverpool and Glasgow East India Associations.[86] I send you a copy of a reply to them received from the India House through the Board of Control. The changes in the administration,[87] as also my not having had a moment to spare to make an agenda, has prevented anything further being done. But as soon as I get the pressure of business out of the way I mean to have another fly at them, I hope with some prospect of success. I hope at all events to shut the Treasury in China, as for India it seems more doubtful. The

occasional relationship with him. In 1834 and 1835, however, the firm increasingly dealt with Hengtai as he proved helpful in absorbing many consignments of British manufactured goods from John Macvicar, and he also regularly brought in supplies of teas and silks.

[83] For 'silk privilege', see Letter **5**, note 25

[84] This letter is written on the back of a printed document which is to be found as Document **105**. For the background to the discussion of the 'Finance Committee', see also Letter **93** and a further incidental letter, (**96**).

[85] (Sic). Lord Ellenborough was the head of the Board of Control from December 1834 to April 1835 in the Peel administration. He was then replaced by Sir J. C. Hobhouse. (*BHF*).

[86] The Glasgow, Liverpool and Manchester branches of the East India Association worked hand in hand with their respective Chambers of Commerce. (See **Appendices VI, VII and VIII**).

[87] Viscount Melbourne replaced Sir Robert Peel as Prime Minister on 18 April 1835. His administration, in which Viscount Palmerston was again Foreign Office Secretary, lasted until 30 August 1841. William Jardine was elected M.P. in the succeeding parliament and sat from September 1841 until his death in 1843.

sentiments of our Member, [C. P.] Thomson[88] who is now President of the Board of Trade, I know to be favourable to our views as relates to China. And with his influence in our favour I am rather sanguine, that a stop will be put to the operations of the Company at Canton. With Lord Ellenbourgh we should have had a harder battle to fight. The India House people will not believe it possible that they can get their revenue home without resorting to Canton.[89] All the arguments they use to show that they cannot, go [to] prove in my mind the opposite of what they desire to prove. If no other way is left to us than an appeal to Parliament, we must try that course. We are not supported by the London Houses. The reasons are obvious. The Company's advances they hope to use for ever larger consignments to them than the *actual* means of themselves and their correspondents can otherwise command.[90] At Liverpool one or two parties are adverse to us as might be expected. Daniell, partner Dickinson,[91] Nicol and Captain Whitehead[92] are firmly siding with *Dent & Co*. Kirman and Finlay[93] with his usual setback—caution—hung fire at first until he had seen that his people at Canton were pledged to our view of the case, and now the worthy man gives us his support, against the opinion I think of his friend James Ritchie.[94] I hear through Gledstanes in London that Matheson has taken his passage in the *Orwell* for London. I am very glad of it. It will give a spur to us all. I don't like to see business going past the house which I am sure they could get, if I had a little explanation with you or Matheson.

I have chartered the Ship *Cor[o]mandel*, 650 tons, her second voyage, to sail from Liverpool. I have only taken her up outwards. By her I shall send 300 Tons coals for the *Jardine*[95] and a pretty valuable cargo, say 25,000 to 30,000 value of Habit Cloths, stripes, 2,000 Long Ells, a few Camblets and a supply of long Cloths —perhaps some further yarn. The owners of the *Cormandel*, John and Thomas Ridgeway[96] of Liverpool (formerly Partners of *C. {Sayer} & Co*., are wealthy people. They propose sending you out 5,000 to 10,000 pounds to convert to Tea, and I propose that you will draw upon them in similar amount. Their orders will

[88] C. P. Thomson was President of the Board of Trade from April 1835 to August 1839, when he was replaced by H. Labouchere. (*BHF*).

[89] See the arguments put forward in Document **105**.

[90] An interesting shift in the argument. Previously, one of the reasons put forward against the Finance Committee was that 'improvident speculators' were going to be the borrowers. Now it transpires that respectable London firms will also be heavy borrowers.

[91] For *Daniell & Dickinson*, see above, Letter **99**, note 109.

[92] For Captain Whitehead, See above, Letter **81**, note 6. 'Nicol' was not identified,

[93] Kirman Finlay: Lord provost of Glasgow. (*DNB*).

[94] For James Ritchie, see above, Letter **44**, note 57.

[95] The *Jardine* was later added to firm's fleet of ships. See Letter **104** and the P. S. of Letter **137**.

[96] John and Thomas Ridgeway, Liverpool merchants and shipowners were not further identified, nor was the firm of *C. {Sayer} & Co*. (A few letters from the Ridgeways are listed in the *BI*).

be at fixed limits and Sir John Forbes's Ship[97], the *Gipsy*, will sail the 3rd June for Account of Sir John. I have bought 60,000 pounds cloth, Numbers 20 to 50, and 3,000 double pieces of Shirtings. By the *Gipsy* you will also have 60,000 pounds long cloth, 2,400 shirtings from the *Garnett Sons & Co.*[98] and some other supplies. Sir John is a fine old fellow, and I am very anxious to do well for him. He is very wealthy. He is sending you a present of cheese from his own dairy. We got nearly over the line the other night drinking [their health] to Jardine, Matheson and all hands.

My supplies to you this season will be about 200,000 pounds, and I am laying plans for next year's operations on a larger Scale. The per cent over this business will amount to something and will, I hope, convince you that the Rug dealers are not to be utterly despised.[99]

Cotton Goods are *monstrously* high. Sales at the late prices will lose money. Cotton yarn is 60 per cent higher than two years ago per *Pauline—and prices will be maintained.* Cotton keeps steadily advancing in price. Stocks of Cotton will be low to January next, and prices at Bombay and all over India will be high next Season. It seems by the ships list that the *Jardin*e only sailed from Aberdine the 20th May. I send this per *Gipsy*.

Yours very truly.

111. James Matheson in London to William Jardine in Canton,

8 July 1835[100]

My dear Jardine,

We arrived off the [coast] on the 5th (exactly four months from China); on the 6th I landed at Portsmouth, came up on the outside of the stage and reached London yesterday morning without having slept a wink during the night, so that I had but little hope of being able to undergo the fatigue of paying many visits. I hired a Hackney Coach, however, and started off for Weeding's, thence to Magniac's, whom I did not see being out of Town for a day or two. There I met John Innes[101] who took me to Lloyd, [ ] and Wiggins[102]. Hence I went to

[97] Sir John Forbes. Probably not directly related to the better known London Forbes, long-time East India agents. Sir Charles Forbes was the head of *Forbes, Forbes & Co* in London. See Letters **182** and **216**.

[98] *Garnett Sons & Co.*, a firm related to *Garnett & Horsefall* through their principal partner, Robert Garnett. (see also Letter **46**, note 67).

[99] A telling remark about the way some East India agents regarded the piecegoods exporters from the manufacturing districts.

[100] James Matheson was staying at the 'Burlington Hotel', from which this letter was written.

[101] For John Innes, the supercargo living in Hendon, see Letter **29**, note 38.

[102] The banker Timothy Wiggin was listed as 'Wiggin' in the London directories. 'Wiggins' was, however, how his name was often spelt.

Larkins[103] and after paying two or three more visits, came home to dress and finally went out to dinner, making it on the whole a most active day for me.

Weeding tells me he has been ailing and is much thinner than he used to be, but he is now in a fair way to recovery. His wife too is ailing. He was so kind as to offer me a room in his house, but this of course I could not accept of. It is satisfactory to find that he gives a good account of all our business concerns. Our letters to Able Gower[104] reached only the day before me, so that he was not able to take any steps about getting us a Bookkeeper, but this will engage the early attention of all of us.

I cannot of course say much about Markets on so short an acquaintance. The Tea Market is in an unsettled state owing to uncertainty as to the intentions of Government respecting a new rate of duty, and a dispute with the Customs House respecting [last year's] Boheas on which they wish to charge the Congo duty, among which is some of ours to Moffat.[105] Mr. Heath[106] who puts himself forward as a *leading* man tells me *there is no doubt* the customs House will be ordered to charge the same duty; that the future permanent duty, uniform on all kinds of Tea will be 2 shillings and 1 penny or 2 shillings and 2 pence, or thereabouts, with two year privilege however in favour of Boheas at 1 shilling and 6 pence (the old rate), to give time for winding up existing engagements. This is very equitable and considerate, and you may safely operate on the certainty of Bohea continuing for the time at 1 shilling and 6 pence. Tomorrow a deputation of about 40 is about to have a final interview on these subjects with the Premier[107] and by Mr. Heath's request I am to be of the number. The Government seems to act on the wise policy of conciliating public feeling.

Good Teas still pay well but not the inferior. Holders are however sanguine, the more as it is hoped Government will be induced to restrict the Company's sales to ten millions in place of sixteen as heretofore. This is one of the propositions to be discussed tomorrow. You will think me very vain when I declare my belief that holders are lulling themselves in a false security, and that many, at least the holders of inferior Teas will be disappointed. The knowledge of the fact of the impor-

[103] Captain Thomas Larkins had been a commander of *HCS Marquis of Camden*. He owned the *Orwell*. (Letter **136**). With Thomas Horsley, he then established the firm of *Larkins & Co*., 'East India Agents, 80 Old Broad Street'. (*TLCD*). See also Letters **151**, **152**, **182**, and **222**.

[104] Abel Gower, a partner in *A. A. Gower, Nephews & Co*. (Ten letters are listed in the *BI*).

[105] Probably George Moffat, one of *Jardine Matheson & Co*.'s best tea customers since the opening of the tea trade in 1834. There were two 'Moffat' firms in the tea business. One was *Moffat & Co*. (Later *Moffat & Sons*), was 'Tea Agents, 28 Fenchurch Street'; the other was *Thomas and Robert Moffat*, 'Tea Brokers, 38 Mincing Lane'. (*TLCD*).

[106] Mr. Heath: probably Thomas Heath, listed among the signatories of the letter appended to Letter **182**. From the context he was a tea broker or a tea agent. It is probable that he was the same person as the 'Heath' mentioned in Letter **208**, a partner in the firm where F. P. Alleyn learned his tea skills before joining William Jardine in Canton. (See above, Letter **100**).

[107] Viscount Melbourne.

tation so much exceeding the Company's is far from general and confined perhaps to those who possess our Circular. In that the business retains much of the mysticism[108] belonging to the Company's Monopoly.

Bye the bye, Mr. Nicholson[109] is supposed to be utterly ruined. Be cautious therefore in your transactions with him, and advance nothing without security. Weeding thinks Templer[110] is worth a plum. I have not seen him. Mr. Heather (his Supercargo) tells me: 'Mr. Templer will talk a great deal to you about the losses on his Teas. But don't believe him. I know him very well. It is his custom to talk so.' On asking Moffat how he liked our Teas, he answered: 'They are only *too good*. You have done us more than justice.' This must be gratifying to Smith.[111]

Not only has our shot against the finance Committee utterly failed but you will have them operating this season on a far larger scale than last. This is provoking. I have requested Weeding to take Mr. John Campbell's,[112] the Attorney General's opinion as to the law of the case. If he gives it against the Company, we may fight [on] but otherwise I have scarcely any hopes of doing good in the conflict. The fact is, [most] people appear to be so comfortable in this magnificent country, so entirely satisfied in all their desires, that so long as domestic affairs, including Markets go right, they cannot be brought to think of us *outlanders*. Until therefore there is a stoppage of trade or something to touch the pockets of the merchants and ship business, expect no sympathy here. The more successful you are in China in keeping things quiet and getting Tea, no matter at what sacrifices or in what manner, the less sympathy you will have here. Lord Palmerston[113] means to do nothing, but to leave Sir George [Robinson][114] in quiet possession of his

[108] 'Mysticism': often used 'as a term of reproach. Sometimes applied to philosophical or scientific theories which assume occult qualities or mysterious agencies of which no rational account can be given. (1763)', (*OED*). As several Letters show, (e.g. Letters **150**, **159**, etc.,) many irrational aspects of the tea trade continued to irritate both James Matheson and William Jardine long after this Letter was written.

[109] For John Nicholson, See above, Letter **79**, note 108.

[110] Captain Henry Templer, See above, Letter **102**, note 18.

[111] James Warly Smith, the firm's tea taster (first mentioned in Letter **106**).

[112] Sir John Campbell was Attorney General from April 1835 to July 1841. (*BHF*).

[113] When James Matheson wrote this Letter, Lord Palmerston had been back as Foreign Office Secretary for barely three months.

[114] In January 1835, John Francis Davis resigned as First Superintendent of British Trade in Canton. He was replaced by Sir George Best Robinson, a former East India Company Supercargo resident in Canton since 1819. Sir George Robinson lived in Lintin, the centre of opium smuggling, and was happy to return to the quiescent policy towards China which Lord Napier had opposed. John Harvey Astell, who had been Third Superintendent, moved to Second Superintendent upon John Francis Davis's resignation. However, Astell himself resigned in April 1835. Following these two resignations, Captain Charles Elliot was promoted to Third Superintendent in January 1835, and to Second Superintendent in April 1835. When Sir George Robinson was eventually recalled by Palmerston in June 1836, Charles Elliot became the First Superintendent and Chief of the British trade mission in China. (Hoe, *The Taking of Hong Hong*, pp. 260, 261, 267).

dignity. The quieter he (Sir George) is, the more resolute in doing nothing, the more surely he will be to retain his place.[115]

Larkins has been doing a very foolish thing—ordering Tea through Reeves[116] to be shipped and paid for by us. I told him of the bother we had from a similar involvement with Layton[117] last year, and he seems sensible of his folly. But it is too late to retract, and our only hope is that your good nature will kindly excuse him and manage matters with Reeves so as to avoid injury to Larkins. It will be a famous opportunity for Smith to show off the superior means which, with your influence, I am sure, we have of getting good Teas moderately, and from whispers I have heard but have not yet [checked] [James Warly] Smith shares the fate of his neighbours in having detractors who try to disparage his knowledge of Tea. You may try to outdo Reeves in quality etc. Timothy Smith[118] and Kiernan[119] are much disappointed not to have got their tea. Tell them to have patience and that really Silk was not to be got. It is favorably thought of. What a splendid [piece of news] for our friend A. L. Johnston,[120] and what magnificent new friend Andrew Johnstone has made.

I must conclude with kindest regards to all in your House and to all out of it who think of me, not forgetting Grant, to whom say that I will make a point of going to see his little ones.[121]

P. S. In a package for Robertson[122] which I am trying to get on board the *Camden*, I am sending you two bottles of the shaving liquid which you [so] admire.

In great haste, I remain

Yours very sincerely,

[115] It took eleven months for this untypically cynical judgment by James Matheson to be proved wrong.

[116] Mr. Reeves was the Inspector of teas for the East India Company in Canton until 1834 'and a clever naturalist'. (Hunter, *The Fan Kwae at Canton*, p. 17; *Bits of Old China*, p. 18). After the closing down of the Company's establishment, he became one of two public tea tasters in Canton.

[117] 'Layton' was the other public tea taster—i.e. a tea taster who operated on his own, unattached to any agency house (as opposed, for instance, to James Warly Smith, who was *Jardine, Matheson & Co.*, tea-taster). For other references to Layton, see Letters **125**, **156**, and **159**.

[118] Captain Timothy Smith was commander of *HCS London* before 1834. (**Appendix IX**)

[119] 'Kiernan' was not identified.

[120] This refers to the setting up by A. L. Johnston of a new Agency house in Singapore. (Letter **102**, note 22).

[121] On Alexander Grant's children, see also Letter **234**, 10th paragraph. In 1835, his son would have been about 14.

[122] Until 1839 Patrick Francis Robertson of Dundee was a partner of A. P. Boyd and Richard Turner in the Canton firm of *Turner & Co.* (Ride, *East India Cemetery*, p. 135).

112. James Matheson in London to William Jardine in Canton,

11 July 1835

My dear Jardine,

I avail of the opportunity of the *Coromandel* to give you a hasty glance of what has been happening since I wrote on the 9th per *Camden*.

The deputation who waited on the Premier obtained no definite reply on the subject of their application. They were asked for a written statement of their case which, in my opinion, they ought to have taken with them. As soon as they send it Government will reply. Horsley Palmer[123] was Spokesman assisted with good effect, by the worthy quaker, Mr. Sanderton.[124] The Chancellor of the Exchequer[125] [looked] runty and was rather snappish. Lord Melbourne was more complaisant and seemed clearly to comprehend the hardship and injustice of subjecting Fokien Boheas to the Congo duty. But in regard to the future uniform duty on all Teas, no satisfaction was afforded. That there will be a *uniform duty* you may be quite certain, but how long Bohea shall remain privileged, at 1 shilling and 6 pence, whether for one or two years seems uncertain. On the other point of restriction of Company's Sales in Teas in place of sixteen millions per annum, no satisfaction was afforded, and it is very doubtful whether it will be carried. General reasoning is against it; the Merchants knew they had sixteen millions per annum to compete with: they should put up with the consequences. My deliberate opinion is, Jardine, that the Tea Market cannot succeed, but it is more likely to decline. I grant you I have had very insufficient experience for arriving at such a notion. But when I see the business still in the hands of only the few brokers who are wedded to the old Company's system and who are seeking to bolster up prices by perpetual recurrence to artificial arrangements, I cannot help having misgivings. Leave the Markets to take care of themselves is my motto.

I wrote to you per *Camden* and now repeat that Mr. Nicholson is supposed to be a ruined man. You will of course be cautious in dealing with him. I have seen Templer who speaks very favorably of our Tea management. He is looking very ill. I have also seen Magniac and his wife looking remarkably well. He professes himself willing to abandon all his arrangements, if not agreeable to us, and indeed our good was his principal motive.[126] And if we do not like his plans, he is determined to relinquish them. This is so like the little man!

[123] For Horsley Palmer, see above, Letter **78**, note 101.

[124] Mr. Sanderson of *Sanderson, Fry, Fox & Co* : 'Tea dealers, 9 New Broad Street Mews'. (*RDL*).

[125] T. Spring-Rice was Chancellor of the Exchequer from April 1835 to August 1839, when he was replaced by F. T. Baring.

[126] For a discussion of the pros and cons of Hollingworth Magniac joining the Smiths in partnership, see below, Letters **117** and **119**.

I have a very growling and disagreeable letter from Macvicar[127] complaining of his having no silk, and you not paying more attention to his business. On this latter point I mean to try to convince him that we have paid attention to it, and having tried our powers to the utmost, really cannot do more. Should he be incapable of conviction on this head, I really fear we must be content to his separating from us. But I shall be temperate and mean to put myself in the hands of my old friend Mr. Anderson,[128] my adviser and moderator with Macvicar.

Yours very sincerely in haste,

113. Hollingworth Magniac in London to James Matheson in London,

12 July 1835

My dear Matheson,

Enclosed you have a copy from my letter Book giving, I am sorry to say, a very severely abridged summary of the contents of my letter to you, dated 20th February last, which has crossed you on your way home.

You will there see the kind of proposal I made of sharing between the three parties concerned (should it meet your ideas of the equity of the case, by your views of which case I wish this matter to be settled between us) the loss occasioned by Fairlie's failure under the non-payment of the transfer.[129] And as I should much prefer arranging this matter with you, under our present feelings, and without any other interference, upon this principle of your being entirely satisfied. Should this not be the case under the present proposal, I should really be much relieved if you would candidly state your opinions to me, depending that I should be perfectly contented with the present or any other principle of arrangement which you might propose, and delighted to have this principal business [taken] off my mind without further trouble of statement, correspondence, etc.

You will not be aware, my letter to the firm in China having crossed you, that I have received here on your behalf two dividends upon the whole claim against *Fairlie & Co.*[130] (less my balance of 2,000 pounds sterling recovered), making 25 per cent or one fourth of the sum at issue.

[127] John Macvicar's complaints were fuelled by the general lack of financial success of his export shipments over the previous couple of years. Being paid on commission, he did not personally suffer, but his manufacturing and exporting friends did.

[128] John Anderson was described by James Matheson in Letter **163** as 'a friend of 20 years standing'. He was a 'Merchant' and had offices at '65 Old Broad Street'. (*TLCD*).

[129] Hollingworth Magniac had transferred funds to *Fairlie Clarke Innes & Co.* shortly before the firm's failure, in order to protect *Jardine. Matheson & Co.*'s bills coming to maturity. (See above, Letter **68**). When the firm failed, Magniac lost most of the money transferred.

[130] Hollingworth Magniac uses the short version of the firm.

The transfer question would therefore stand thus in round numbers, supposing my principle[131] of settlement adopted by you.

Transfer amount, say,	20,000 pounds sterling
less dividends ¼, say,	5,000 pounds sterling
Balance	15,000 pounds sterling

And if, (as I suppose) the balance due on my account claimed as a set off and tacitly admitted be finally allowed by the Inspectors,

the balance would be lessened by	2,000 pounds sterling
Leaving at risk then	13,000 pounds sterling
or, to each of the three parties	4,333 pounds 6 shillings and 8 pence

to be further lessened by future dividends from *Fairlie & Co's* estate (one and 12/2nd percent being further expected on arranging my same disputed accounts).[132]

Yours ever sincerely,

114. John Macvicar in Liverpool to *Jardine, Matheson & Co.* in Canton,

15 July 1835

I have this moment learnt, that Government have declared that from the 1st day of July 1836 the Duties on all descriptions of Tea are to be equalized and charged with a fixed duty of 2 shillings and 1 penny per pound, on all classes without exception. Up to that day Boheas will pay the Customs at 1 shilling and six pence per pound. After that day they will pay 2 shillings and 1penny. Souchong and all other 3 shillings duty Teas will pay 2 shillings and 1 penny after the 1st July 1836.[133]

The consequence will be that Bohea Teas arriving here in time to pass the Custom before 1st July 1836 will be given a very large profit. After they are subjected to the 2 shillings and 1 penny duty, they will be *unsaleable*, excepting for exportation.

[131] The principle of settlement adopted by Hollingworth Magniac seems quite fair, since he is offering to take a third of the loss to himself and asking James Matheson and William Jardine to share the remaining two-thirds as equal partners in *Jardine, Matheson & Co.*, the firm on behalf of which the funds were transferred.

[132] The phrase 'to be lessened' refers to the risk of not being paid in full. The more dividends were paid, the less the risk of creditors being out of pocket.

[133] Tea was still a relatively expensive beverage in 1835. The cost price of a pound of 'Company Congo' bought in Canton a year before this Letter was written was well under 1 shilling. (Hence William Jardine's remark in Letter **83** above, that if they sell the tea in London at 18 pence per pound 'or even 15 pence per pound' they would make a reasonable profit. A duty of 2 shillings and 1 penny per pound therefore represented a 200% charge over the value of the tea actually landed in London. By the time the wholesalers and retailers had added their margin, the 1835 consumer was buying a pound of tea for well over three shillings. The daily disposable income of labourers and their families was about 1 shilling (or £20 a year).

Such Teas as now pay the 3 shilling duty, if very good of their kinds, will sell very readily and at a good profit as soon as they can come under the 2 shillings and 1 penny duty. Prompt purchases of good Boheas and of excellent Teas of such description as are now subject to the 3 shilling duty, and quickly dispatched from China, so as to insure the arrival here before the 1st July, will in all likelihood be attended with excellent results.

I have promised Captain Chapel[134] a present of twenty guineas if he delivers this letter at Lintin 48 hours sooner than any other ship sailing from this Country subsequent to the 12th Instant, and should you have the earliest information of this alteration of duty I hope you will be able to avail yourselves of it to the advantage of many of my constituents, among whom I would particularly mention *Butterworth & Brooks*, *R & J Barrow*, George Horrocks, *Garnett & Horsfalls*, *Messrs. Garnett & Sons*, William Falconer, George Armstrong, etc., etc.[135]

This alteration of duty will not be attended with any bad consequences to excellent Congou and Twankay Teas such as I have formerly recommended, but will be greatly in favour of very good Boheas and very good Souchong, Picco, Hyson, Gunpowder, etc. I am very glad to find that my views respecting Teas have proved correct, and I do hope that you will have acted upon my recommendations with spirit.

The Silk market continues improving. Tsatlee have advanced 1 shilling per pound. A middling parcel of Tsatlee would at the moment command 20 shillings and 6 pence and it does not appear probable that the price will decline this season or until the influence of the next crop in China and Italy are known and felt. In this prospect I may send you a cargo of goods again to sail in November, but this is uncertain, and it may be a few months later before I do.

I am, Dear Sirs, yours very truly.

115. Lady E. Napier in Castle Craig, Noble House, to *Jardine, Matheson & Co.* in Canton, 17 July 1835[136]

Dear Sir,

I beg to acknowledge your letter of the 27th February enclosing a statement of my account with your house and informing me that there is a Balance in my favour of 1,996 dollars and 2 cents. Mr. Jardine had previously mentioned that H. M. Superintendents claimed 432 dollars and a half cent. If you consider this claim as just and one which I ought to pay, I beg you will have the goodness to deduct it and to arrange the matter for me. If you think that claim doubtful, you will perhaps advise me how to act.

[134] Captain Chapel was not identified.

[135] For details on the John Macvicar's principal 'constituents', see above the various notes to Letter **46**.

[136] At the time when she wrote this letter, Lady Napier was still using black-rimmed letter paper.

I will thank you to pay the Balance into *Messrs. Smith, Payne and Smith's* Banking House, London, on my account.

Yours truly.

116. William Jardine in Canton to Captain Jauncey[137] aboard the *Austin*,
21 July 1835

Dear Sir,

With reference to your letter of the 18th Instant which came to hand last night per *Hawk* and our letter of the 15th we have now to request you to receive on board Malwa enough to complete the quantity of 200 chests, also the articles already mentioned, to be selected by Captain Mackay. Having done this, you will proceed along the Coast endeavouring to effect sales of your Malwa, and any other articles you may have on board. The most likely place for you to succeed is somewhere near Ningpo,[138] on the Buffalo's nose or, say, between 30° and 32° North Latitude,[139] but this is left very much to yourself and Captain Rees to decide. Our object is to find a Market for Malwa similar to that we have for Patna, on the Coast.[140]

We have no wish to name a limit: but trust you will have no occasion to lower than 600 dollars a chest. Of course, the further north, the higher the prices you should obtain. But sooner than not sell you may reduce the price to 580 dollars per chest. Much must of necessity be left to your own good sense and management.[141] Sell by retail or wholesale, and endeavour by patience and perseverance to find out what we so anxiously wish for—a steady market for Malwa from 50 to 100 dollars per chest beyond the Lintin price.

It may be some guide for you to know that Long Ells are worth here 9 to 9½ dollars per piece. Camlets: 27 32 dollars per piece according to quality. [Long cloths]: 23 to 24 dollars. Spanish stripes: 1.68 to 1.80 dollars per yard net prices, purchasers paying the duty. Your {rice} may prove useful.

We should send one of the small crafts up occasionally to communicate with you. Be pleased therefore to arrange with Captain Parry and Captain Mackay where a vessel can fall in with you.

When Patna and Benares arrive you shall have a small supply sent to you.

137 Captain Francis Jauncey : see above, Letter **108**, note 79.

138 Ningpo: see above, Letter **63**, note 80.

139 'Buffalo's nose': a small island south of Chusan off the Chekiang coast.

140 Opium consumers were particular about their favourite brands. The Malwa opium from Bombay had not yet found favour with the northerners.

141 As Captain Jauncey was new to this type of mission as a ship commander, William Jardine stresses here one of his key management principles: never constrain senior employees with narrow directions, but on the contrary encourage them to take initiatives best calculated to achieve clearly-stated targets.

Collect information regarding such articles as are saleable and send reports. If prices are higher than here a supply shall be sent. Try if you can purchase Nankin Raw Silk for Cash or in barter. Gold of 86 to 90 or 92 Touch should not be taken higher than 200 to 202 dollars per bar of nearly ten Tales. Be careful to cut the bars and examine the quality very minutely.

Enclosed is a note from Mr. Gordon[142] wishing you a pleasant and prosperous trip.

We remain, dear Sir, Your most Obedient Servant.

117. James Matheson in London to William Jardine in Canton,

31 July 1835

My dear Jardine,

I intend this as a letter of explanation respecting *Magniac Smith & Co.*

I wrote to you per *Camden* that Magniac has said one of his strongest motives for engaging in the plan was a desire to promote our views, and that he was determined to withdraw from it unless it should be concurred in by us. I of course made the acknowledgement for the friendly feeling, but remarked that it was not necessary he should let a regard for us have any weight in his deliberations, as however gratifying to us would be a connection with parties of such first-rate importance as *Magniac Smith & Co.*, we could yet manage to go on with our London business with the same Agents whom we have employed for the last two or three years.[143]

[Then] I said (in confirmation of your letter) that *Magniac Smith & Co.* might of course rely on being our principal Agents[144], and that he (Magniac) might always count on our cordial concurrence in whatever plans he should adopt. In regard to which [plan] we both agreed that his being a partner of *Magniac Smith & Co.* would be inexpedient;[145] but that there would not be the same objection to his being an assistant or manager of the concern.

As Magniac writes that we should have some transactions with the Calcutta House of *R. C. Jenkins & Co.*,[146] to whom Mr. Dunlop has attached himself, I agreed that a portion of our Calcutta business might go to them, provided they

[142] On George James Gordon, head of the 'Tea seed party', see Letter **104** above, note 37.

[143] Thomas Weeding and Timothy Wiggin.

[144] By becoming *Jardine, Matheson & Co.*'s principal London agents, *Magniac Smith & Co.* was to displace its current agents to a large extent.

[145] The reasons for this 'inexpediency' are not clear. On the face of it, the statement is quite contradictory. Perhaps Hollingworth Magniac feared potential conflicts of interest.

[146] *R. C. Jenkins and Co.*: a Calcutta agency in the process of formation. As Letter **119** and Letter **140** (3rd paragraph) make clear, this new Calcutta firm eventually adopted the name of *Jenkins, Fergusson & Co.*, and it was founded with capital belonging to 'Mr. Fergusson' and 'Mr. Innes'. Mr. Innes was the 'Innes' of the failed *Fairlie Clark Innes & Co.*; and Mr. Fergusson was (or was closely related to)

gave us a reciprocity. Reflecting further on this latter part of the arrangement and the ticklish nature of the sort of business engaged in by *Jenkins & Co.* as well as of Calcutta business generally,[147] as far as connected with Europe, I wrote to Magniac to suggest a pause about the Calcutta part of the arrangements, until we could meet totally over the matter, unless he was already committed.

When I next saw him, he stated that my misgivings on the subject were very much participated in by himself, that he had been furthermore reflecting on the circumstance of London business not being now conducted on so safe and satisfactory a plan as formerly, while its emoluments are comparatively trifling. The result of all which is, that on the return of Mr. Abel Smith from the continent a few days ago, it was finally resolved to recede from their whole plan, and suffer the firm of *Magniac Smith & Co.* gradually to be discontinued.

They will of course keep up an Establishment sufficient to attend the consignments that may in the meanwhile come from us, or from Calcutta. And the previously existing Firm of *Oswald Smith & Co.*, to be joined by T. C. Smith, will continue its operations, which it was otherwise intended should merge in those of *Magniac Smith & Co.*[148]

Should you not have sent home a Power of Attorney[149] from our new [London] Office, it may be as well to let *T. Wiggin & Co.* be the Agents. Should you have sent the Power to *Magniac Smith &Co.*, I scarcely know what to recommend. Better perhaps let it so remain until there is a little [time] to deliberate.

I have told Magniac that I think *Jardine, Matheson & Co.*'s best plan for the present will be to avoid entering into engagements for our London business, as there is no saying but the Smiths who are one the first moneyed connections in London may not feel disposed at some future period to revive an Agency plan on a better footing than the present. But this is a mere surmise of my own. The Smiths have not said so to me. You had better not, just yet, announce the firm of

---

the 'Fergusson' of the failed Calcutta firm of *Fergusson & Co.* Following these two failures, *Jardine, Matheson & Co.* had helped set up *Lyall Matheson & Co.* in Calcutta, which had become their principal Bengal correspondent. This explains the reluctance of James Matheson to doing business with '*Jenkins & Co*'.

Mr. A. Vaux Dunlop was not identified. He is listed in the *BI* as having written *Jardine, Matheson & Co.* 5 letters from Calcutta.

[147] The non-opium business of Calcutta was flourishing, but general business had not fully recovered from the recent bout of bankruptcies.

[148] After a further series of discussions between the parties concerned, *Magniac Smith and Co.*, (with John Abel Smith as one of its partners), remained in existence and did become *Jardine, Matheson & Co.*'s principal London agent from 1835 until 1842. Upon William Jardine joining Magniac Smith in 1842, the firm briefly became known as *Magniac Jardine & Co.* (see Letters **159** and **253**). After William Jardine's death in 1843 it was reorganized by James Matheson and eventually became *Matheson & Co.* This firm still operates today in London under the same name and at the same address.

[149] Unaware of all the foregoing discussion and initial uncertainty regarding the future of *Magniac Smith & Co.*, William Jardine had already sent the new firm *Jardine, Matheson & Co.*'s power of attorney.

Magniac Smith & Co. as discontinued. I believe the determination to this effect is final, but am not quite sure.

Yours ever sincerely,

118. James Matheson in London to William Jardine in Canton,

1 August 1835

My dear Jardine,

I have but a few minutes to write by the *Louisa Campbell* and must therefore be very brief in alluding to a few leading topics.

Lord Palmerston. I have had an audience with him. He has not had time to look into Chinese affairs, but the bent of his mind is not to interfere at present but give time to see how the China trade will work on its present footing.

Finance Committee. A very long case has been submitted to the Attorney General[150] by me and he has given it as his opinion that the Company's China Bill operations are not illegal. In a day or two we shall have an opinion from Sir W. Follett, the [previous] Attorney General.[151] The only resource now is to petition Parliament for relief; which shall be done.

Teas. All our shipments have given satisfaction, except the Orange Pekos which are generally complained of. I have some idea of getting our broker to examine Hope court[152] Orange Pekos. When good Teas are not to be got, it will be better to abstain from shipping inferior. Good Teas should be always branded[153] with our Firm. Respecting the state of the market I refer you to the brokers' report. They deserve much credit for maintaining prices. Howqua's Teas, through *Russell & Co.*[154] has given most satisfaction. *Russell & Co.'s* consignment per *Abel Gower* to *Inglis, Forbes & Co.*[155] are supposed to be on account of Howqua.

Book-Keeper. I have not yet succeeded in getting one.

I have been in a perpetual hurry since my arrival, paying and receiving business visits, etc., and still there are several I have to see. But I hope to get through everything by this day week, when I am to set out by steam to Scotland.

150 Sir John Campbell. See above, Letter **111**, note 112.

151 Sir W. Follet was in fact briefly Solicitor General in the previous administration, between December 1834 and May 1835 when Sir. R. Rolfe succeeded him. (*BHF*).

152 'Hope court' was not identified.

153 'Brand': the meaning of 'trade-mark' is recorded as early as 1827; and as 1854 for 'a class of goods'. (*OED*).

154 *Russell & Co.*, the main American firm in Canton had a special relationship with Howqua who had supplied them with tea since the early 1820s.

155 *Inglis, Forbes & Co.*, an established East India agency with offices at 2 Mansion House place. It is interesting to observe that Howqua who, in 1835 was one of the richest men in the world with a fortune estimated at 26 million dollars (over £6,000,000) was investing in teas for his own account and for resale in London. (On his fortune, see: Hunter, *The Fan Kwae at Canton*, p. 29).

Macvicar is here and goes to Bristol tonight with a view to secure for us the Tea business of that part, last year's management of which has given great dissatisfaction, as has the *Charles Grant's*. Macvicar is much dissatisfied to have got no Silk, and I strongly recommend it to your notice to endeavour to meet his views by securing [bills] so as to have proceeds at command to buy Silk when it is procurable, and not allow lose the chance of procuring it owing to the remittance of proceeds being done. Macvicar was a little rough when we first met, but has been smoothed down and is again cordial.

Thacker sends the *Neptune* to *Wetmore & Co.* in consequence of their growing a certain portion of outward and homeward freight, I having assured him you will not take amiss her not going to you. [. . .] With kind regards to all our circle.

Ever Yours very sincerely,

119. James Matheson in Inverness to William Jardine in Canton,

24 August 1835[156]

My dear Jardine,

I left London by steam on the 8th after a month's stay there, remained a week at Edinburgh and am soon [again] to see my mother and family with whom I hope to arrive this afternoon. By invitation I went to see the Lady Napier at [Castle Craig] and was grieved to see [what changes] grief has made in her.

[. . .] Mr. Reed[157] urges her to be quiet for the present, till Government have settled some allowance on herself and family, which has not yet been done. [. . .] I hope, however, she will be prevailed on to remain quiet for the present. She is certainly a very noble woman in all her feelings and seems to be the idol of all who know her [and were acquainted with] a couple so universally popular as she and the late Lord.

The present Lord who has come from Germany to spend a few days with his mother, is a dark lanky youth of sixteen, and without being showy seems steady and tractable to her. The second son I have not seen. He is studying for the Artillery at Woolwich. Miss Napier looked pale and thin, but perhaps she always did so. She is working a pocketbook for you. But *this is a secret*, and I promised not to tell you. The second Miss looked as red as ever, and both chatted [happily] about China and the folks they knew there. They begged I would remember them very kindly to you. [Also] they spoke a great deal about Innes[158] who, they say,

[156] Many passages in this Letter were not decipherable due the poor condition of the manuscript.
[157] Mr. Reed: Lady Napier's lawyer.
[158] 'When Lord Napier fell sick at Canton in September 1834, it was James Innes who took him from the superintendent's house to his own, which was far more airy, to be looked after until he left on his last journey to Macao'. (Ride, *East India Cemetery*, p. 224).

[has of] the Cochrane family[159] so much in spirit and even in looks that they cannot help liking him. Tell him to be kind when they go to London for the winter, next month. [. . .]

Copy of Hollingworth Magniac's note to James Matheson.

'What you have said [to me] is exactly what we had understood, and our determination is *final* to {all in the Firm} of *Magniac Smith & Co.* to do away with its precedent arrangement.

By keeping open to any arrangement, on your part, regarding your London Agents, it would at any time when [Jardine] is coming home, or previouly, should that event be delayed, be easy to make a House formed upon *Oswald Smith & Co.*, with T. C. Smith who will join his brother directly he returns from China, and should the business appear sufficiently considerable to admit further extension in the number of Partners, John Abel Smith and I could, its being agreeable to all parties be [then] joined in interest. But we can again talk these matters over more fully before the next opportunity of writing to Jardine. I have communicated our intention to retire, to Mr Fergusson and to Mr. Innes,[160] the former is now engaged in providing for the future Agency of *R. C. Jenkins & Co.* in England.

Signed: Hollingworth Magniac'.

I thought it right to send Magniac a copy of my letter to you, announcing the discontinuance of *Magniac Smith & Co.*, and the foregoing is his reply—which is, I may add, essentially in conformity with my feelings and wishes. But it will rest with you to decide on ulterior proceedings. No opportunity has occurred of again talking over the matter with Magniac. Many thanks for your letter by the *Upton*, and please [give my kind regards to all our circle], [etc.]

120. William Jardine in Canton to H. P. Haddow in Bombay,

5 September 1835

My dear Haddow,

The *Sir Herbert Taylor* being still at Macao, I avail myself of the opportunity to address a few lines to you via Calcutta, in hopes they may reach you sooner than letters by the direct ships now under despatch.

The Letters by the *Fort William*, *Hormanjee Bomanjee* and *Pestonjee Bomanjee* have come to hand, but having been delivered along with the letters from England, by the *Eliza Stewart*, I have not had time to maturely consider those you have favored me with.

[159] Like Lord Napier's, a Scottish naval family related to the Inglises. Sir Thomas James Cochrane (1789–1872) was to be second commander of the East India Station in the period 1842–1845. (*MEB*)

[160] See above, Letter **117**, note 146.

My object in addressing this to you, is to call your particular attention to the state of the Drug Market, in this quarter, which has been and is a matter of astonishment to every one, who has paid any attention to the subject.

The quality of Patna and Benares sent to the Coast in various Vessels, and the large quantity still in Calcutta, have kept this market bare; and prices have in consequence, advanced far beyond the expectations of the most sanguine. Our Calcutta friends, aided by Mr. Johnstone[161] have been too timid, and kept the *Red Rover*, with all our funds waiting for what is not likely to occur this Season, namely a reduction of prices in Calcutta; but if they buy at last at 1,200 Rupees per chest we shall do well with the article.

The rise in Malwa has been produced by a wild spurt of speculation among the Chinese Brokers and Dealers, aided by some purchases of our own, and a determination on the part of Framjee Pestonjee[162] to hold on for high prices. A good deal of Malwa has been returned from the Coast and the distant markets are by no means very favorable.

The operations here (as opposed to the Coast) have been on time entirely, with only fifty dollars per chest Bargain money. We have sold five or six hundred chest of Malwa on time, and only two chests for cash.[163] We have sold two-thirds to three-quarters of our whole stock, and if present prices continue, we shall get clear of the balance as early as possible; but money is so scarce among the speculators that they require three or four days to pay the bargain money. Some of our Parsee friends who sold early at low prices have lately been purchasing at 630 or 650 dollars per chest for cash and on time.

I fully expect to see the price decline again; but prices must, I think, be maintained above 600 dollars per chest. Framjee Pestonjee, who is a large holder, must use every exertion to prevent prices falling lower than 600 dollars; and if you can purchase the new drug at moderate prices, and have it here in February or March—the earlier the better—a moderate profit would be pretty certain. Buy therefore, if under 900 or 1000 Rupees per chest, and interest us to the extent of one hundred or two hundred chests. Were we certain of our being able to purchase, we should send on a clipper to bring them here, and funds to pay for our proportion.

I wish Grant would take it into his head to purchase. We shall most likely send funds and take our chance. If Framjee [Pestonjee] succeeds in supporting the market, the operation must prove a beneficial one.

[161] It is possible that William Jardine's displeasure with his Calcutta agents' usual excesses in buying opium may have prompted the formal assistance of Andrew Johnstone. His presence, however, proved of no avail, as the agents erred this time on the side of timidity.

[162] For Framjee Pestonjee, see above, Letter **108**, note 72.

[163] The remark by William Jardine is an unambiguous disproof that all opium sales were cash sales, as had often been written. During and after the year 1835, more and more opium sales were time sales, even though they were ultimately paid for in sycee or bullion.

You will oblige me by communicating this to Jamsetjee Jejeebhoy, to whom I shall write by some other conveyance.

With kind regards to Mr. Forbes[164] and all friends, I remain, My Dear Hadow [one d here], yours very sincerely.

121. William Jardine in Canton to G. J. Gordon[165] in Calcutta, 5 September 1835[166]

A hurried letter acknowledging his favors since the left Canton, and thanking him for his exertions at Singapore—his purchases are highly satisfactory. Captain Henderson[167] is anything but an honest man. Truth is not in him. He refunded a half per cent to us on a former occasion. What funds had he to purchase with? Cash or Bills ? If the latter you had an advantage, and any Boat from the Shore would have taken you on shore as readily as it would him. We have sold the Benares at 720 and 740 dollars per chest. Your money in our hands is at your disposal. And if anything befalls you Mr. Matheson will know your wishes, and to him I shall leave it.[168]

Yours sincerely,

122. William Jardine in Canton to Captain Ovenstone [in Canton], 7 September 1835

My dear Sir,

With reference to my note of this afternoon I shall now have the pleasure of addressing you on the subject of the exchange of vessels *Falcon* and *Lady Hayes* which should have been attended long ago. This subject has been rendered more complicated by the operation in Calcutta than it ought to have been, and from all I can learn you are likely to be deprived of the command of the *Falcon* whether we purchase her or not, so that unless we part with the *Lady Hayes* you will soon be adrift.

[164] Perhaps a relative of the senior partner of the Bombay firm of the same name: see above, Letter **22**, note 44.

[165] After collecting 80,000 tea seeds in China, G. J. returned to Calcutta via Singapore. The tea seeds were delivered to the Calcutta botanical gardens and they were planted under the supervision of Dr Nathaniel Wallich (see Letter **169**) for future transplants in the Madras, Kuman and Assam districts. (Alain Le Pichon, «Le premier thé de l'Inde britanique: du rêve à la réalité», *Cahiers victoriens et édouardiens*, No 55, Montpellier, 2002, p. 192).

[166] One of the hurried copies made by William Jardine in telegraphic style.

[167] Captain Andrew Henderson commanded the steamer *Forbes* in 1830 and the *Waterwitch* in 1835. Nine Letters are listed in the *BI*.

[168] Public servants like G. J. Gordon were not averse to a little opium speculation now and again, as occasions permitted. Like all sea travellers they were also deeply aware of their mortality and would not infrequently leave their wills with the partners of agency houses who had kindly looked after them.

I make the following proposals very reluctantly, actuated by no other motive than that of preventing you from being thrown out of employ, while I feel you are encumbering yourself with a Block[169] without having funds to pay for it, or the means of finding employment. In fact we must either find employment for the vessel or you must lose money by her; so that we increase, in place of diminishing, our shipping by this arrangement, which, as you are aware, is far from our wish.

Mr. Wright and I, the only partners now in Canton, have made up our minds to fulfill our part of the engagement by taking over the *Falcon* at the sum named of 7,500 dollars and handing over to you the *Lady Hayes* about the sum named of 17,500 dollars. Each vessel to be received as they are; we paying the wages of the commander, officers and crew of the *Lady Hayes* up to the 10th or 12th Instant.

In the event of your taking charge of the *Lady Hayes* we shall endeavour to find employ for her, and put you on the same footing as Captain Burd[170] and others who are similarly situated. They pay twelve per cent per annum for the funds advanced and the usual commissions on cargoes sold or provided by us here, but no other charges are made. Nothing for arranging or effecting insurance, and no charge on ship's disbursements.

The employment we recommend at present is a trip to Lombock[171] for rice, starting immediately or as soon as the equinox is over, as you may prefer. You will require copper cash and bags. Very little else. I shall write to Captain Parry[172] by this conveyance, and waiting a reply, I remain, etc.

123. Hollingworth Magniac in London to James Matheson in London, 29 October 1835

My dear Matheson,

Your letter of the 6th was forwarded to me by Oswald Smith to the country (where I was detained in forwarding the repairs and painting of my house)

[169] A 'Block' was an encumbered or mortgaged ship. Unless such ships had to be of the highest quality, they were more difficult to insure than ships owned outright. The transaction described here is reasonably clear, even though its background remains obscure. The transaction is similar to a 'leveraged buy-out'. Usually ship captains were depositors in the books of the firm, and very few of them were borrowers. Captain David Ovenstone was one of the few borrowers. The firm's account for the year showed that he had borrowed 28,905 dollars. This included the price of the *Lady Hayes* (17,500 dollars). By working the ship, Captain Ovenstone hoped to repay seller the principal of the loan and the 12% per annum interest. If he could do so, he would in due course become himself the owner of an unencumbered ship. (*JMArch. A2/16*).

[170] Captain Burd had commanded the *Norden* in 1830 and the *Syden* in 1832. (*BI*). He had borrowed the large sum of 122,771 dollars from *Jardine, Matheson & Co.* for similar transactions. (*ibid.*).

[171] The island of Lombock in the Bali Sea.

[172] Captain Parry took over the command of the *Hercules*, the firm's principal opium receiving ship, a few months after this letter was written.

accompanied by the information that it had been left in Mansion House Street by your brother whose stay (having seen him) was limited to a few days.

[I regret] exceedingly having been absent just at that moment, as I should have been glad to have made his acquaintance. Now, Oswald, who called upon him directly desires me to say how sorry he was, that owing to his wife's being in bad health, his family was all in the country, which prevented his introducing your brother and showing him that attention he should otherwise have had much pleasure in doing. I was thinking of writing to you otherwise to mention the new concern [which] Morrison[173] is concocting with great activity and upon an immense scale. [. . .] I suppose that Morrison is an immensely rich man. He married the daughter of Old Todd[174] who is said to have had [one] million and whose fortune centres principally in his son-in-law's. Morrison, we have heard is concocting his past India concern so as to ramify with all the pieces of any consequence in India and America, but principally in China, where he is about placing, our information says, an immense capital, and is determined to make and obtain business at all sacrifices and carry all before him. It has been intimated to us from such informed quarters that you might like to know this and perhaps at convenience be here upon the spot to know how matters are going on regarding this next establishment.

We have, that is, the Smiths have, likewise received overtures from the confidential agent here, for the purchase of British goods, of [a very] considerable American house in Philadelphia for Agency of that establishment in London which the members wish to remove from Barings where it has existed for forty years. And Oswald thinks from what passed that it would not be impossible to obtain their Agency in China (about 200,000 pounds sterling a year) for *Jardine, Matheson & Co.* after a little personal discussion and arrangements. This concern is most weighty and respectable as we have ascertained from the best authority in London, and perhaps you may think it quite worthwhile when you come up to make personal inquiries which Oswald Smith will aid in.

In the mean time prices being what we consider very favourable, and under every advice and consideration, we have sold 42 Bales of your Raw Silk per *David Scott* , viz—20 Bales Taysaam at 19 shillings and six pence; 22 Bales Tzat-lee 22 shillings, which must [pay] well, and I was decidedly against declining the opportunity. The remaining 47 Bales valued at 21 shillings and 6 pence

[173] James Morrison (1789–1857) was one of the richest London developers at the time. He left over £4 million pounds at his death. (See: Fox, Celina, (ed.), *London, World City, 1800–1840*, New Haven, London, Yale University Press and the Museum of London, 1992, pp. 51–76; See also: Rubinstein, W. D., *Elites and the Wealthy in Modern British History, Essays in Social and Economic History*, Sussex, The Harvester Press, p. 26, note 14. Finally, see the rare volume by Gatty, Richard, *Portrait of a Merchant Prince: James Morrison, 1789–1857*, (edition limited to 250 copies), North Allerton, 1977).

[174] 'James Morrison married Mary Anne (1795/6–1887), daughter of John Todd, a London haberdasher (*Oxford DNB*).

and 22 shillings were declined. But Captain B.[175] having since sold [ ], we expect strongly to realize the above transaction. We have likewise sold 200 Quarter chests Bohea Tea for Malcom at about 10 shillings,[176] very low, but [this was the best course] especially [as] no improvement appears likely. The residue was necessarily bought in at 10 shillings.

I have likewise finally settled the question with *Fairlie & Co.*'s inspectors that the balance of my account is as shown in the account I gave you, and shall be deducted from your claim; and in order to induce them to make out my account with *Fairlie & Co.* thus balanced, it only requires that you should authorize me to sign the Trust Deed on behalf of *Jardine, Matheson & Co.* without reservation, as acting for you {and Jardine}. You have now merely to write me a few formal lines, authorizing me to withdraw that reservation, or rather to sign without any reservation, and that point of difficulty will be arranged by the attorney.

I hope that you enjoy, as you must do indeed, your visit home after so long an absence.

Yours sincerely,

124. William Jardine in Canton to Captain Cilfton [in Lintin],
10 November 1835

Dear Clifton,[177]

This is to accompany your final dispatches, which will be sent off about 10 p.m. and the wind being northerly, may reach you by noon tomorrow.

We have sent you a Bill for 105,000 Rupees on the Supreme Government; and should have added 50,000 Rupees, had we been able to get our Bills of Lading up from the Whampoa ships, but we were unwilling to detain the *Rover* longer. *Messrs. Lyall Matheson & Co.* will have about 400,000 to 500,000 Rupees to invest at the first sale and ship on board the *Rover* as quickly after the sale as possible.

Our own portion of the funds is to be invested without limit of price; and should the limit of our friends be too low for the first sale, we have authorized *Messrs. Lyall Matheson & Co.* to employ these funds on our account, trusting to their being replaced by us before the second sale. In addition to this, we authorize you to take up funds on fair terms, and purchase on joint account with ourselves to enable you to fill the vessel in the proportion of one third for you and two thirds for the other owners of the *Red-Rover*. This purchase we leave to you

[175] Captain B. was not identified.
[176] Malcolm was not identified. A quarter chest was usually the equivalent of 15 lbs. This makes this lot of Bohea very cheap, at just over 8 pence a pound.
[177] Captain Clifton (see above, Letter **86**, note 34) was one of William Jardine's favourite captains. He sailed the *Red Rover* to Calcutta the next day in one of her regular opium shuttles.

to manage, and have requested *Lyall Matheson & Co.* to render you any aid you may require.

This drug bought and sold free of commission can scarcely turn out badly. Should Benares go off at 60 to 80 Rupee per chest less than Patna let a quarter of your purchase be of that description, particularly if the chests weigh the same.

Our first object is to have the *Red Rover* back the earliest ship, and we do not wish you to overload her or to wait for a few chests of the drug after she is nearly full. On your return we wish you to make 'Ty Tam Bay'[178] where you will, we hope, find a vessel or boat, waiting your arrival.

We have every confidence on your doing the utmost you possible can to carry our wishes unto effect and with best wishes for a pleasant and prosperous voyage, I remain, Dear Clifton,

Yours sincerely.

125. William Jardine in Canton to James Matheson in London,

24 November 1835

My dear Matheson,

The *Jumna* is under despatch for Cork and Liverpool and I cannot allow her to depart without a few lines for you in acknowledgment of your favour of the 8th July last[179] for which I feel obliged.

Your disappointment at the continuation of the Finance Committee made me smile. Our friends at home treat the affair as if they fancied *we* had a deep interest in the suppression of said committee; but this, you know, is not the case. On the contrary, it is very convenient for us to be able to obtain funds at 4 shillings and 8 pence in lieu of 4 shillings and 10 pence per Dollar, whenever we may feel disposed for an extensive operation in Silk or Teas. But to the manufacturers it is decidedly very injurious as to the prudent Trader possessed of property.[180] I never expected it to be abandoned this Season. It may be done away with next.[181]

The advances are now made one quarter in cash and three quarters in Bills on the Supreme Government, which is very inconvenient to many of those taking them.[182]

You will of course hear of Mowqua's troubles.[183] He has been in confinement about a week, contrary to law and custom with a view of inducing him and his nephew or his third brother, to carry on the business of the Hong as before. He has managed badly. We expect to see him at liberty in a few days. His debts are

[178] Tai Tam Bay, on the south side of Hong Kong island

[179] The first letter James Matheson wrote from London. See above, Letter **111**.

[180] The 'as' after 'injurious' should be understood as 'as also'.

[181] See above, Document **105**, note 48.

[182] They had to negotiate the bills before they could purchase the teas.

[183] Mowqua had been until then one of the more respectable hong merchants.

about 600,000 dollars to Europeans, and the brothers have among them property to a larger amount.

We were much gratified by your report of the Teas to Moffat and *Sanderson & Co.*[184] We have done with friend Layton.[185]

Hengtai has been fortunate in his Tea arrangements this season and has already supplied us with many good Chops, as well as with a large quantity of Raw Silk at comparatively moderate prices.

Alexander [Matheson] and Barretto have got their books well up; and after writing off every bad and doubtful debt, we shall divide upwards of uee,eee dollars.[186] I believe Alexander [Matheson] is sending you some particulars on the drug yie,eee dollars from which deduct je,eee or ae,eee dollars for the ships employed and the amount will still be a good one.

We are all going on quietly and have issued invitations for a party on St. Andrew's day. Mr. Gordon is here, and most likely writes to you by this conveyance.

I have got a severe cold and, being past midnight, must go to bed and if possible sweat it off.

[25 November 1835]

I left off last night without saying a word about a very extensive fire[187] inside the city, which commenced about 8 p.m. on the night of 22nd and continued burning with great fury till about 10 a.m. of the 23rd. (Stated particulars about the fire). We have not been able to ascertain the extent of property lost, but there were upwards of 1,000 houses destroyed. Nearly all the dealers in woolen have been burnt out, and a good many long Ells, etc. lost in the flames. The quantity destroyed might have tended to improve prices, had the dealers not suffered so severely in property of other description. But I am afraid the distress produced will injure markets generally, and probably even in woolens do more harm than good.

[184] For Mr. Sanderson, the 'worthy Quaker', and *Sanderson Fox & Co.*, See above Letter **112**. There was also a John Sanderson and a firm *Sanderson & Co.*, 'Discount brokers and merchants, 83 King William Street, and 4 St Helen's Place, Bishopsgate'. (*TLCD*).

[185] 'Layton': one of the two official Canton tea tasters. See above, Letter **111**, notes 116 and 117.

[186] Replacing actual figures by letters preserved the confidentiality of the information vis-à-vis the copyists and other employees.

[187] Periodic fires were most destructive. This fire destroyed '1,000 houses' and a great many warehouses, but it left the foreign factories unscathed. In contrast, the 1822 fire which had started on 1 November a mile and a half away reached the factories on the morning of November 2. 'By nine o'clock the British factories were in flames at five or six points and the line of fire embraced the whole of the foreign factories from the creek to Mowqua's Hong on the far side of Old China Street'. (Morse, *The Chronicles of the EIC*, IV, pp. 64–66). For the iconography of the 1822 fire, see 'Canton Factories—Start of the Fire', Hong Kong Museum of Art, Hong Kong, No. *AH64.31*; and 'The Canton Fire of 1822', Peabody Essex Museum, Salem, No. *M22,764*.

We have had a letter from Henry Shackell,[188] Token House Yard, Solicitor to the Assignee of Ladd & Rickett,[189] calling for accounts, etc., etc. Not being aware how far the Assignees of a Bankrupt Estate can claim property in China when held for a debt due, as the *Austin* was, and is, we shall not take any notice of his first letter; but I think it right to mention the circumstance to you.

Be pleased to present my kind regards to all friends and Believe me, My Dear Matheson,

Yours sincerely,

126. John Macvicar in Manchester to James Matheson in London,

30 December 1835

My dear Matheson,

I wrote to you on the 28th and have now the pleasure to acknowledge the receipt of yours of the same day which need only be very short as I expect to see you so soon. In case however you should see the Messrs. Smiths[190] before you have gone I merely write to say that I am gratified you have made an arrangement with a house of such character and respectability. This cannot be otherwise than advantageous and creditable and may possibly tend to an increase of my business with *Gell & Co.*[191] I do not mean that the facilities they are willing to afford shall be a dead letter, but will be glad to avail myself of them, when proper occasions may present themselves and it may not be long before I may see fit to make an application to them. It will be proper to go into some details and explanations with them before commencing operations. I will however defer doing so until I have seen you. My operations may at times be large. I presume they are prepared to consider that the account *may* rise up to a very considerable amount.

Wishing you many Happy Returns of the season. With best regards to your Sister in which Mrs. Macvicar desires to join me.

Yours very truly.

P.S. Bardolph[192] went to London this morning. I hope he would see you. If you can render him any service, you will greatly oblige me.

[188] Henry Shackell: 'Solicitor, 23 Tokenhouse Yard, Lothbury'. (*TLCD*). Only one letter is listed in the *BI*, which may suggest that William Jardine's policy of sitting on the letter may have worked in this instance. The reference is obscure.

[189] William Henry Ladd, of *Ladd & Rickett* is listed in the *BI* as a correspondent from Calcutta.

[190] The final decision of the partners to go ahead with *Magniac Smth & Co.* rather than discontinue the new firm was therefore taken in December 1835, some four months after the discussions mentioned in Letters **117** and **119** above.

[191] *Gell & Co.*: see Letter **72**, note 52.

[192] 'Bardolph' was not identified.

127. William Jardine in Canton to John Macvicar in Manchester,
30 December 1835

My Dear Macvicar,

Since I had the pleasure of addressing you in the 14th Instant your favor of 16th July last, has come to hand, and the contents have had my particular attention.

Unwilling as I am to carry on an useless controversy, I cannot refrain from remarking on your observation, on the spirit in which your letter of 20th may 1834,[193] had been received here. You must have fancied us to be callous indeed, and extremely wanting in due regard for our own characters as honest men, had we not felt, and expressed, our indignation at being falsely charged with acts, that must have been at variance with every principle of common honesty. Having said so much I shall drop the subject, I trust, forever.

I shall send this to Lintin, after the *Gipsy* which vessel we despatched today ; and hope to despatch the *Belhaven* three days hence; the *Edinburgh* in eight days hence, or thereabouts. By the *Gipsy* we have sent your friend Sir John Tobin,[194] 40 Bales of very good Tsatlee, and twenty of Tysaam, filling up the balance of the silk privilege with 45 bales on account of *B&B*[195] and your goodself, and 25 on account of William Thompson.[196]

The teas for Sir John will, we trust, give satisfaction. We consider the prices of both Silk and Teas high; but such is the state of the market, that we could have readily sold the Silk at 5 and 10 dollars per pecul and the Teas at 2 and 3 Tales per pecul profit.

Without a previous understanding with the Tea Dealers through the Hong Merchants, it is impossible to pick up any quantity of good Congos. The first chop of good Congo of the Pako kind purchased this Season was at 29 Tales by one of the Company's Tea Tasters—the quality by no means superior.

We have filled up the Silk privilege of the *Belhaven* as directed, giving the owners an interest in the article. The scramble for silk has been beyond anything you can fancy. The Market had not been opened more than a week or ten days, when Silk of middling quality was sold at 435 dollars per pecul; and good chops contracted for at 445 and 450 dollars per pecul, deliverable in the month of January. We have been in advance for this article nearly 500,000 dollars for the last four Months; and are still 600 to 800 Bales short of our expected supply. About 280 Bales arrived to day for which they ask 465 dollars per pecul. Taysaam 385 dollars per pecul; but these prices are ridiculously high.

[193] The 'letter of 20th May 1834' and the accusations which prompted this irate retort were not traced.

[194] Sir John Tobin: Liverpool merchant and ship builder. His firm was *Tobin, Thomas & Son*. (*PODL*). See also Letter **138**.

[195] Probably the Bartons of Manchester, who were good clients of John Macvicar.

[196] For William James Thompson, see above Letter **71**, note 31.

We have secured a good supply of fine green Teas on comparatively moderate terms; and have engaged a few tolerably good Canton Boheas; but not many and not an additional chest of Fokien Bohea.

The *Edinburgh* will, I believe, have Mr. Burn's Raw Silk[197] and some other parcels.

For piece Goods I must refer you to Mr. Thom's letters, it being past 2 A.M. of the 31st.[198]

Believe me, my dear Macvicar,

Yours sincerely,

1836

128. William Jardine in Canton to J. H. Gledstanes in London,

16 February 1836

My dear Gledstanes,

The *Bombay* and *Sarah* are under despatch, and the *Camden*, with the *George the fourth* will be off about the end of the Month, being detained by the China New Year Holidays.

My last letter would prepare you for the worst as regarded the fate of poor Markwick,[1] who sunk under his wasting disease, on the 30th ultimo. I have seen his partner, Mr. Edwards[2] since, and he expressed himself satisfied, that he would be able in a very short time to make good this Season's remittances on your account. Dr. Colledge[3] in announcing the death to me writes as follows: 'Poor Man, he very frequently spoke of your continued patronage and kindness to him, and regretted much that he was *not* to live to fulfill those worldly engagements which he considered to be within his compass; and which he felt he could have fulfilled in the course of a year or two more, had his life been spared; he was sensible and collected to the very last, and had no unusual dread of the change which awaited him.'

[197] Probably the Mr. Burn mentioned in Letter **35**, note 69.

[198] No New Year's eve celebrations for William Jardine in Canton.

[1] For Richard Markwick and his death on 30 January 1838, see above, Letter **46**, note 79.

[2] Little is known about 'Mr. Edwards' who continued Richard Markwick's business for some eighteen months after the latter's death. In 1838, Mr and Mrs Edwards retired to England. (See Letters **143**, **167**, and **245**).

[3] Dr Thomas Richardson Colledge (1797–1879) was an East India Company surgeon. He was so moved by the number of blind people in the streets of Macao when he arrived there in the 1820s that he decided to open an ophthalmic hospital in 1827. In 1838, he was the co-founder and first president of the Medical Missionary Society in China, although he was himself not a missionary. The first vice-presidents of the Society were Peter Parker, the Rev. Elijah Bridgman and William Jardine. (Choa, *Heal the Sick.*, pp. 8, 14–15). See also Letters **223** and **245.**

His papers were sealed up in the presence of the second Superintendent; and I received notice that they would so remain till we appointed some one to attend to your account. We immediately named Mr. A. Robertson[4] in the event of no one belonging to the House being at Macao.

The season is now nearly over and it has proved as unsatisfactory a one, as ever I saw in China. Teas in the face of the gloomy accounts received early in the Season were run up and have been kept up to prices quite out of all character, while Raw Silk was enhanced in value by every arrival from England and may now be quoted at 480 dollars per pecul for Tsatlee and 400 dollars for Taysaam. It is difficult to account for the high price of Tea; the first chop of Congo of the Pako flavor purchased this season, was of a fair, middling quality, and the price 29 Tales per pecul. The purchasers are the Company's Tea Tasters.[5] These gentlemen are in the habit of contracting with the Hong Merchants for a certain number of chops of Tea which they dispose of in the course of the Season, and the higher they can fix the Market prices, the greater their profit, so that it is evidently their interest to make prices rule high, even as Brokers, the higher the price, the more their commission. Add to this the wild speculators who take advances from the finance Committee, and if these causes do not appear to you sufficient you must search for others, but I think you will agree with me in thinking that the causes mentioned must tend to keep prices higher than they would be had we no Finance Committee and no Company's Tea Tasters.[6]

I was at one time of opinon that the high prices of, and the brisk demand for, Raw Silk early in the Season would have produced a large supply about this time, but this has not been the case. The competition among the purchasers in the Nankin province was carried to a great extent, prices increased, and when the last accounts left, the only purchaser was a man employed to buy on our account. The article was scarce and good Tsatlee will cost between 450 and 460 dollars per pecul on board. We have received a good deal of so so Silk that we could not ship on account of our constituents and have therefore shipped it on our own account.

I sincerely hope our friends {Stickley and Kieffer}[7] will make a little profit by their silk. I was unwell when they left, but am now nearly well having dined at the Table today for the first time,[8] the last three weeks—an unusual occurrence with me.

[4] Possibly a relative of the 'Robertson' mentioned at the end of Letter **111**, and a friend of James Matheson.

[5] Mr. Reeves and Mr. Layton. See above, Letters **111** and **125**.

[6] At 29 taels a picul, Congo prices had risen by 61% in two years. (Congos were obtained at 18 taels a picul in April 1834). William Jardine blames individuals and practices inspired by the East India Company for this unwelcome increase in prices.

[7] The firm was not identified.

[8] In imitation of the supercargoes at the East India Company factory, members of private firms tended to gather in the evening for a formal communal dinner.

Be pleased to present my kind regards to all friends, and believe me, my dear Gledstanes,

Yours very sincerely,

129. William Jardine in Canton to George Moffat[9] in London,
16 April 1836

My dear Sir,

I have to apologize for having so long neglected to acknowledge receipt of, and thank you for, your valuable present of a portable shower bath,[10] for which for the handsome manner in which it has been presented, be pleased to accept my grateful acknowledgment. On the receipt of this *life prolonger* I was, unfortunately, in the doctor's hands for a very severe attack of cold and fever, which prevented me from using the bath; and I deferred writing till it should be in full play. It is now in use, highly approved of, and not likely to be left off.

Many thanks for you letters of 1st and 26th of August last. I note what is said about Bohea Teas; and am of opinion you will have no cause for regretting the countermand of the order for such Teas—a large quantity has been shipped, since the alteration of the duty was known here[11]—many of them of inferior quality, and some of our neighbours got up a petition, praying the Home Government to extend the period, for arrival in England, till the 1st October; or, in other words, allow us three additional months, to convert inferior Congos and Souchongs into Boheas, at the expense of seven pence per pound to the said Government. Some of these Gentlemen had previously paid a forfeit of one Tale percent on their Boheas contracted for; under an apprehension that the Bohea duty would be raised to an equality with that on Congo.

We have now been endeavouring of late to induce the Hong Merchants to act with more unanimity; and resist the unreasonable remands of the Tea merchants;[12] who have for the two last years been reaping large profits while the Hong Merchants have not made enough out of the Teas to pay for the expenses of their Hong Establishments. This must appear to you almost impossible when you look at the relative position of the parties—the ten Hong Merchants having the power to levy any duty they please (in moderation, that is,) while the Tea merchants cannot ship a single chest of Tea unless through one of the ten Hong Merchants. In the Company's time the duty charged by the Hong Merchants to

[9] For George Moffat and the Moffat tea firms, see above, Letter **111**, note 105.

[10] Shower-bath: '1803. A bath in which water from above is poured in a shower upon a person. Also an apparatus for producing such a bath'. (*OED*).

[11] For the 'alteration of duty', see above Letter **114**. As the Letter from John Macvicar imparting the news was written in mid-july 1835, it must have reached Canton around the end of November 1835.

[12] William Jardine usually refers to the merchants supplying teas to Canton as the 'Tea men'.

the Tea merchants was 6 and frequently 7 Tales per pecul; which duty in the case of the bankrupt Hong Merchants nursed by the Company when Mr. Elphinstone[13] was chief of the Factory was deducted by him from the price of Tea paid to the Tea merchants and carried to the credit of the bankrupt in the Company's books.[14]

The Tea merchants are numerous—much above 100—, their interest and those of the ten Hong Merchants are opposed to each other; and the latter possess the power just mentioned. Still the foreign trade in Tea is more likely, at the present moment, to suffer from a combination[15] of the former than of the latter Body. This we have been endeavouring to prevent by establishing Company's prices, out of which the Hong Merchants are to receive five Tales per pecul duty.

As far as our contracts go they have been made on their terms, the quality to be the same as the Company's Congos in former days, half of the Paho kind and half the superior Souchong flavoured Congo. Though our contracts are with the most respectable of the Hong Merchants beginning with Howqua, we shall consider ourselves fortunate if we get one third of good and fine Paho Congos; for the very superior qualities of which we have agreed to pay one, two or even three Tales per pecul extra. The parties have latterly declined further contracts.

[13] J. F. Elphinstone was an East India Company supercargo. He became head of the Select Committee in 1813. (Ride, *East India Cemetery*, p. 198).

[14] Two Canton trade practices are mentioned in this paragraph. The first relates to the mode of remuneration of the 'tea men' before the end of the East India Company tea monopoly. The tea men were then paid a fee based on the quantity of tea they supplied ('6 or 7 Tales per pecul'). In 1832, for instance, the fee pool paid to the tea men was some £ 562,000. (Calculations based on 33 million lbs of tea exported ; 1Tael = 1,388 dollars; £1 = 4,28 dollars). Each tea man (if there were 100 of them as William Jardine believes) would have received an average of £ 5,620, a large income, out of which he had to pay his own suppliers. After the end of the E.I.C. monopoly, the nature of their income changed rapidly, as many tea men started selling their teas *directly* to the private British merchants, thus dispensing with the intermediation of the hong merchants. This change in the practice of the Canton tea trade had the most serious consequence upon the business of the hong merchants, most of whom, being suddenly deprived of the generous margin they had so far pocketed as compulsory intermediaries between the tea men and the foreign buyers, became insolvent within a few years. In fact, the liberalisation of the British trading system as implementing the India Act of 1833 had the indirect effect of destroying the 'Canton trading system'—and this, it achieved a few years before the Opium War itself.

The second practice is partly related to the monopolistic position of the hong merchants before 1834. The foreign merchants were always eventually repaid the debts owed to them by bankrupt Hong merchants. Usually, full repayment took a number of years. In order to repay the foreigners, it was left to the hong merchants to find means of raising new money. This they did either by raising import duties and accumulating the surplus in the 'Consoo fund' as a debt repayment pool or, as was here suggested by J. F. Elphinstone, they lowered their fixed fees paid to the tea men, with similar result.

[15] The Combination Acts which outlawed any 'combination' designed to restrain trade had been voted in the period 1800–1810. The repeal of the Combinations Acts of 1824 (June 21) allowed workers to organize but not to strike. (*EWH*). The debate about how far the tea men could go in the defence of their interests was interpreted in Canton against the background of the British debates about workers' combinations.

Excuse this unconnected letter written amid many interruptions, and Believe me, My dear Sir,

Yours sincerely,

130. William Jardine in Canton to John Macvicar in Manchester,
26 April 1836

My Dear Macvicar,

I am unwilling to allow the *Ellen* to sail without a few lines for you, though without anything of importance to communicate since the date of my last advices on the 14th instant.

A very considerable decline, in the price of Lead and Iron has lately taken place; owing to a superabundant supply of both articles. You will learn this from the Price Current, but may prefer having it noticed in a letter.

In the Woolens you must watch the Exports from, and prices prevailing with, you. Our Market holds out no temptation for the speculator at present, and in Spanish Stripes money must have been lost last season.

We have made some small consignments of Nankin Raw Silk by this vessel, but prices rule so very high for even the inferior qualitites (and there is none good in the place) that we despair of making a saving remittance in this article. The Nankin District is so completely drained of good Silk, that our last importations are of too inferior a quality to be shipped to any of our [constituents] for good Silk.

The evil consequence of the Company's Advances are becoming more and more apparent to every individual in this place; even our friends *Dent & Co.* have been obliged to admit their injurious influence.[16]

It is now evident to every one in Canton that the Chinese keep their Teas back, with the view of enhancing prices, knowing that they can, if left on hand, pledge them to the Company for two third of their value; and receive the amount at once, in Cash or Bills on the Supreme Government. The *Vansittart* and *Thomas Lowry* have been loaded in this way; and the *Aurora* is now commencing to load, on the same terms. And we expect to get her away by the 10th proximo.

By the last accounts from India, the *Castle Huntly*, *Lord Lowther*, and *Earl Balcarras* are likely to do well. In Bombay Cotton was cheap, and likely to be cheaper, while freight to China was up to 30 Rupees. I sincerely hope that they may all take cotton on freight, prices here having fallen very much.

Should we be unable to lay out the funds of your speculating friends, when realized, we may, if practicable, be induced to advance them on Tea Contracts, the Teas to be shipped by the *Castle Huntly*.

[16] *Dent & Co* rarely agreed on anything with *Jardine, Matheson & Co.*

We have done every thing in our power to have good Congos down early; and trust we may succeed.

Believe me, My Dear Macvicar,

Yours sincerely,

131. William Jardine in Canton to J. C. Green and W. S. Wetmore[17] in Canton, 13 August 1836

Gentlemen,

After having maturely weighed the arguments advanced on both sides, and consulted with the authorities within my reach—English and American—I now hand you the following opinion on the case your referred to me a few days ago, respecting the legality of detaining freight.

The goods being received the freight should be paid; and an action may be brought for any claim the receiver may think he has for damage, or any improper act of the Master of Owner of the Vessel. This appears to be the general principle laid down; and I see nothing in the case referred to make it an exception. See Abbot (Lord Tenterden)[18] on the *Law of Shipping*, Part III, cap. 7, p. 293. The Master may legally detain the Goods till the freight is paid or arranged for. See *Dictionary of Commerce* by J. R. McCulloch,[19] article 'freight', p. 543.

[Etc.]

132. William Jardine in Canton to John Macvicar in Manchester, 10 October 1836

My dear Macvicar,

I have before me your favors of the 7th, 9th, 29th January, 2nd February and 4th April, which I shall now have the pleasure of replying to per *Imogen*, and *Martha*, the former to be despatched tomorrow for London, the latter in six or eight days hence, for Liverpool.

Yours advices relative to, and orders for, Silk have our particular attention; and our Circular[20] will afford you every information, regarding the state of our market for that article, to which I have little to add. When the advices via Bombay, up to the 1st June last, arrived, there were only two parcels of Raw silk in the market; for which 500 and 510 dollars per pecul were asked; but we might have

[17] On John C. Green and William Samuel Wetmore, see above Letter **106**, note 55.

[18] John Henry Abbot was born in 1796. He was Lord Chief Justice of England under Lord Eldon as Lord Chancellor, and in 1827 he was created Lord Tenderden. (*DPC*; Campbell, John Lord, *Lives of the Lord Chancellors and Keepers of the Great Seal of England*, London John Murray, 1856, IX, pp. 385–386).

[19] On McCulloch, see above Letter **60**, note 67

[20] The circular was not traced.

purchased both at 480 to 485 dollars per pecul had we deemed it prudent to do so; but, having a few days before sent extensive orders to the Nankin district, with funds to purchase, if procurable at, or under, 480 dollars per pecul for fair cargo of silk, and 500 dollars for the finer qualities, per pecul, free on board here, we were unwilling to open this market at so high a rate; fearful that an express from hence, might have reached Nankin before our friends had been able to make their purchases.

Immediately after the receipt of said overland letters, the Silk in this market was purchased at 490 to 500 dollars; and several small lots, that arrived about the same time, were secured at 500 dollars per pecul, but the next arrivals were run up to 530, 540, 543 dollars per pecul for ordinary qualities; while the finer chops were run up to 560 dollars and 580 dollars,[21] till the Finance Committee, in consequence of orders, from the Supreme Government, suddenly declined further advances on Teas and Silk; since which few purchases have been made; and prices have declined to 520, 510, and 500 dollars per pecul, according to quality; but there are few fine chops in the market. The Silk of the Season is very inferior to that of last year, and the quality likely to reach Canton not yet known.

The musters of Tea were submitted for general inspection yesterday and today with the view of fixing equitable prices between the Teamen and the Hong Merchants, the former demanding 36 and 38 Tales per pecul[22] for fine Congos, which is 6 and 8 Tales higher than has ever been paid before. Nothing has been settled today and it is difficult to say when or how the matter may be arranged. This places the Hong Merchants in a very unpleasant position, they having in many instances bound themselves to ship off at from 26 and 30 to 32 Tales per pecul. We are the most extensive contractors,[23] but I despair of ever seeing our contracts fulfilled on the terms agreed on. The Teamen are a lawless set and much too powerful for the CoHong, a circumstance not easily understood when we call to mind the monopoly of the latter body, who, if unanimous and true to each other, can prevent the former from shipping off a single chest.

[21] In May 1834, silk could be purchased in the Canton market at 340 per picul (see Letter **87**). In Two and a half year, prices had risen by 70%. The increased number of participants in the Canton silk and tea markets since 1834 had an important effect on price levels. The credit facilities afforded by the Finance Committee were also a contributory factor.

[22] At 38 Taels per picul the asking price for Congo had more than doubled since 1834.

[23] *Jardine, Matheson & Co.* had contracted for their teas with various hong merchants, thus paradoxically continuing the East India Company practice. The problem was that the tea men refused to supply the hong merchants in the hope of making prices rise even higher and of selling directly to private merchants who offered the best prices. This had the effect of preventing the hong merchants from fulfilling their 'contracts'. What infuriated the established British merchants, and William Jardine in particular, was that in Canton they had no legal redress against the tea men for breach of contract or unlawfully withholding tea supplies.

If the tea men do not come to terms I shall recommend Howqua to appeal to the Authorities,[24] many of them having received heavy advances under a vague promise to let the Hong Merchants, who made the advances, have their Teas on the usual terms. So much for contracts in China, which are rarely fulfilled by the Chinese unless they can derive profit from them. On the contracts you allude to, few, if any, have been strictly complied with; and some of them led to long unpleasant disputes, particularly those in the hands of our friends *Messrs. Turner & Co.*

Your joint order for Raw Silk, has our best attention; and the fulfilment of it will depend much on the success of our Nankin orders, Canton prices being too high for your limit.

Your observations regarding your orders of last Season appear to me to have been made with reference to the result and without the smallest attention to the cautious wording of your letters;[25] but more of this by the *Martha*. Mr. Thom has addressed a long letter to you, on the subject of your complaints, in the name of the Firm.

You made a grand mistake in not having the permission to export dollars expressed in the body of the Bills on the Manila Government; or in the letter of advice. Our friends, fearful of a change of Ministry in Spain, and also of farther Bills being presented before those in your favor came due, submitted to a discount of a half per cent, and received the Cash. We trust this prudent step may be approved of. They are collecting Carolus dollars by our advice, and waiting Mr. Mendizabel's[26] promised letter to enable them to send them over. They are at a handsome premium here, and it is impossible to draw on Manila. The Bills drawn last year contained a permission to export the proceeds in dollars. We have desired our friends to petition the Governor[27] for leave to export the proceeds of your Bills.

Mr. Burn is at Macao, and the *Castle Huntly* at Whampoa. The *Imogen* carries old Teas and Raw Silk; the *Martha* new Teas and Silk—of the latter about six hundred Bales, almost entirely for you and your friends. The *Heywood* will have Silk for Liverpool; and the *Asia*, Stead, will have Silk for London. and we hope to get them away soon, that is, if the Tea question is settled.

You shall hear from me again soon, referring to Mr. Thom's letters regarding Piece Goods, and Woolens.

[24] For William Jardine, one of the most ardent British free-traders, to take such a step in the defence of the hong monopoly was one of the ironies of history in the post-1834 trading world in Canton.

[25] William Jardine was not one to mince his words in the face of evidence which he meticulously collected before putting pen to paper.

[26] Mr. Mendizabel was not identified.

[27] Pedro Salazar was governor of Manila between Sept. 1835 and Aug. 1837. (Burniol, *A History of the Philippines*, Manila, 1912, p. 128).

I remain, my dear Sir,
Yours sincerely.

133. William Jardine in Canton to Howqua, Senior Hong Merchant. and other Members of the Cohong, 4 November 1836

Gentlemen,

Your note accompanying a Chop from His Excellency the Viceroy, dated October 28th, was handed to me by a Linguist three days ago.[28] These documents have been translated and I lose no time in sending you the following reply for His Excellency's information.

I am a British Subject, have resided in the Creek Factory upwards of ten years, transacting Agency business, on the course of which we have been in the habit of selling Cotton, Sandalwood, and other articles the produce of India; Woolens, cotton piece Goods, Metals etc. from Europe, on which we have paid duties to a large amount every year. We have also for several years imported upwards of 100,000 peculs of Rice annually and exported Teas and Silk to a large extent.

We have now at Whampoa nineteen Vessels, not one of which has any Opium on board;[29] and we never heard of the Hong Merchants dealing in that article, nor have we any means of ascertaining exactly the quantity imported.

I remain, Gentlemen,
Your most Obedient Servant.

[28] The note was not traced. Canton officials had long been aware of the presence of the British and other free merchants trading opium in general, and of William Jardine in particular. In an official Chinese document quoted by Morse, William Jardine is referred to as 'Manyick (Magniac). [He is] the head of the business. He is always at the thirteen factories with Sampaling: a stationary demon, who receives money for the opium'. Howqua's own son was described in the same document as: 'Woo Showchang is the principal of the merchants who are securities for foreigners; defends and protects murderous foreigners; a traitorous merchant who monopolizes the fees derived from the sale of opium'. (Morse, *The Chronicles of the EIC*, IV, p. 268). N.B. The reference to 'murderous foreigners' is to an episode similar to the Keiou affair (Letter **81**, note 7) when a Chinese had died in an affray.

The fact that the new viceroy (Teng T'ing-chen, who had replaced Lu K'un after the latter's death in office late in 1835) was having a close look at the current opium situation and was asking for reports from members of the foreign community suggests that the great debate about opium had started at the imperial court in Pekin. 'In mid-1836, just as the advocates of [opium] legalization seemed on the verge of success, a vigorous resistance suddenly blossomed forth from the censorate, spearheaded by the Spring Purification circle, and backed by considerable informational resources that this network of literati politicians possessed'. (Polachek, *The Inner Opium War*, p. 113).

[29] The opium trade being segregated in and around Lintin and increasingly up the China coast, Jardine's statement is strictly correct, though of course misleading. He evidently felt that, since the authorities were perfectly aware of his activities and that of the other opium traders, their need for statements of this nature was a form of 'humbug' designed to placate the senior mandarin hierarchy in Peking. When dealing with Chinese officialdom, dispensing with the truth was thus felt to be compatible with keeping a clear conscience.

134. William Jardine in Canton to [Captain] Henry Templer in London, 22 November 1836

My dear Templer,

The *Asia* being under despatch, I address a few lines to you, though unable to add anything of importance to the information contained in the letters from the Firm.

We have commenced purchasing Silk, on your account, and shall continue to pick up chops, of good quality, whenever we can fall in with them, on fair terms, though we are instructed to ship the whole by your own vessel. Prices continue nearly the same as when I addressed you last, on the 23rd ultimo, and there is little chance of good Silk declining, the quantity now in the market being very limited; and some of it held for 550 dollars per pecul.

The dealers in Black Tea continue obstinate, though the want of warehouse room and fear of fire are beginning to produce dissensions among them; and I sincerely hope that they will, ere long, yield and listen to reason. Our countrymen are becoming very impatient and have been offering extravagantly high prices to the Hong Merchants for such chops as have reached Canton and are ready for shipping: 34 Tales per pecul have been offered for Congos of middling qualities, such as were purchased last season at 25 and 26 Tales, and valued in England at 1 shilling and three pence to 1 shilling and 4 pence per pound. The Hong Merchants have offered to fix the rate of Company's Congos at 25 Tales, China price; which would cost on board 29 or 30, and for the superior chops with the Paho flavour they are willing to pay three or even four Tales per pecul more.

I state these particulars that you may be able to form an opinion as to the probable issue of this struggle; on which the existence of the Hong Merchants as a public body depends.[30] If the tea dealers carry their point this season they will try it again next at still higher prices. They are a lawless set, and difficult to deal with.

The Teas of the Season are, as far as we have yet seen, of indifferent quality, and we anticipate much difficulty in executing the orders we have received. Every one wishes to have Teas of the finest description, while the quantity brought down is very limited—of Congos, say, 40 or 50 chops.

We shall have two or three Vessels for London, in the course of a few days, loaded chiefly with Hungmoy, Orange Pako, Souchong, and small chops of green Teas; with a few chops of Congos brought down by the Hong Merchants themselves.[31] By these Vessels we hope to be able to communicate more satisfactory

[30] Despite the difficulty of interpreting correctly the long-term significance of events in which one is a daily participant, William Jardine's remark shows unerring judgment. (See above, Letter **129**, note 12).

[31] To counter the unexpected competition from the tea men, their previously compliant suppliers, some of the hong merchants had themselves to resorted to securing supplies directly from the producing provinces.

information; and to state what price your cotton is likely to realize. Hitherto we have had no offer—the dealers talked of 9 Tales 5 mace per pecul, but made no offer. The quality is not very good, and the market being dull we have refrained from pressing it at a time when there are none of the dealers from the country, in Canton, this being the month in which the rice is gathered in.

Believe me, my dear Templer,
Yours sincerely.

135. James Matheson in Canton[32] to John Macvicar in Manchester

7 December 1836

My dear Macvicar,

Owing to the want of a boat, the *Susan*, dispatches have been unexpectedly detained till today, which enables me to communicate the important intelligence of the discussion between the Tea men and the Hong Merchants having been brought to a close in a manner unfavourable to the exporters.

[32] James Matheson returned to Canton on 16 November 1836, having left England in mid-August. (See letter to Jamsetjee Jejeebhoy dated 18 November 1836, *JMArch.*, C5-2). He had been away from Canton a total of 21 months, of which eight had been spent at sea and thirteen in London, the Midlands and Scotland. Some time between January and August 1836, he published an important pamphlet about China and the trading conditions in Canton : *The Present Position and Prospects of the British Trade with China; together with An Outline of some Leading Occurrences in its Past History*, by James Matheson, Esq. of the firm of *Jardine, Matheson & Co.*, of Canton, *Smith Elder & Co.*, Cornhill, Booksellers to their Majesties, 1836.

In his *Descriptive Catalogue*, Lust summarizes the pamphlet as follows : 'Furious and libellous attack on the Chinese. The case for an aggressive policy on behalf of free trade and against the East India Company. Also for the break-up of the Hong system, and the use of naval force to take advantage of Chinese pusillanimity'. (Lust, *Western Books on China*, p. 152).

This editor has spent some time analysing the content and presentation of *The Present position*, etc. The result of his inquiry can be found in *Origines de Hong Kong*, pp. 457–465. He does not subscribe to the view that the pamphlet is a 'furious and libellous attack on the Chinese'. On the contrary, whilst the intention is polemical and the views presented are biased, the pamphlet itself is written in a highly rational and argumentative style, with the assistance of a critical apparatus and learned (though highly selective) footnotes. Any reader familiar with James Matheson's letters can easily recognize his ideas, but fails to recognize his style. The reason for this is that in all likelihood James Matheson did not write the pamphlet himself. He used a ghost writer who must have had some training as a lawyer, and he provided him with material on which to build the arguments. This theory based on stylistic evidence became closer to reality when this editor came across the Hong Kong University copy of *The Present Position*. (Hong Kong University Library, Special Collection Section, No [U] 382 095 1042 M42). The back of the hard cover bears the following inscription : 'Presentation copy from James Warren who wrote this book. See opposite page'. And on the 'opposite page', in a different hand, another inscription reads: 'This book was written by Mr Warren from materials supplied by Mr Matheson'.

A reasonable amount of time was then spent in the *JMArch.* in a specific attempt to trace any correspondence between James Matheson and 'Mr Warren', or indeed between James Matheson and his publisher, *Smith Elder & Co.* However, none was found. This is not surprising given the fact that, if such correspondence has been preserved at all, it is likely to have been archived in London where it originated and where its recipients lived, rather than in Canton.

The finest teas which the Company used to ship at 28 Taels have been settled at 30.5, China price, or 35.5 shipping price.[33] The second quality which the Company shipped off at 27 Taels is now settled at 29½ Taels, China price, or shipping price, 34.5. The third, 26 Taels Company shipping off price, now 28½ China, or shipping price, 33½. The fourth, 25 Taels Company shipping off price, now 27½ China price.

You will at once see that the above prices are so extravagantly high for low qualities of Congo as to preclude their being thought of for the present, and the greater bulk of the season's supply thus locked up till the Tea men shall become tired of holding, the difficulty of filling the ships awaiting cargoes seems alarmingly increased.

The silk exports of the season are said to be: in the *Imogen*, 789 bales; in the *Martha*, 801; in the *Asia*, 2,197; in the *Baring*, 839; in the *Eliza Stewart*, 935; in the [ ], 273; in the *Suzanne*: 963. Total: 6, 797 bales.

[Etc.]

136. James Matheson in Canton to Captain Larkins in London

12 December 1836

My dear Larkins,[34]

It is not unlikely that among the idle talkers at the *Jerusalem*[35] you may hear Hengtai's credit called in question on the authority of letters from Canton. There has been a good deal of talk on the subject here and, among the initiated, even some degree of alarm. Should this extent itself to you, I have only to say that we are quite ready to guarantee the sale advised in the House's letter of the day,[36] on your writing by the first ship that you wish us to do so. The rumour takes its rise from a dispute with the Tea men who, to force him to compliance with their terms, refused to deliver his teas and this put a partial stop to his shipping operations for some days. Meanwhile, however, he is going on shipping other goods to a considerable extent. And we have no apprehension as to his weathering the present storm at least.

I am sadly puzzled how to floor your good ship the *Orwell*.[37] But trust Jardine's wisdom will discover some mode of getting over the difficulty.

Etc.

[33] China price is the cost price. Shipping price includes the freight cost.

[34] For Captain Larkins, see above, Letter **111**, note 103.

[35] The *Jerusalem Coffee House*, Horatio Hardy's establishment in the City and the hub of all East India business gossip. See Letter **74**, note 62

[36] *Jardine, Matheson & Co*. had just sold to Hengtai a consignment of goods shipped by Captain Larkins. James Matheson, still hopeful that the firm's favourite hong merchant is going to 'weather the storm' offers to make the seller whole in the event of Hengtai's failure. In the event, another three months elapsed before Hengtai was finally declared bankrupt. (See below, Letter **140**).

[37] The *Orwell* was a former 1,335–ton East India Company ship. Her previous managing owner had been Matthew Isacke. (**Appendix IX**).

137. William Jardine in Canton to John Macvicar in Manchester,
24 december 1836

My Dear Macvicar,

The *Castle Huntly* has now in: 4,389 chests of Congo, 726 boxes Caper; 729 chests Hyson, 48 ditto Gunpowder—chiefly on owner's account—but partly on that of the owners of the *Edinburgh* and your other friends.

Our progress has been much retarded by the refractory conduct of the Teamen who adopted the novel course of refusing to deliver teas (though contracted for under advances) without previously receiving cash or security from the Hong Merchants, which had the effect of placing several of the latter in a situation of embarrassment seriously affecting their credit. This demur, on the other hand, alarmed their European creditors and created a general panic that prevented for a time our ascertaining which of our contract chops we could rely on receiving, the Teamen having a plausible excuse for delay by saying that only part of their chops are coming down and we must wait for the arrival of the whole according to custom. We have now however in a great degree overcome these obstacles by bringing ourselves into immediate communication with the Teamen themselves.[38] And I have hopes we shall be able to get on more expeditiously, particularly after the cessation of the Company's advances on 31st Instant which may be expected to have a favourable influence on our market for both Silk and Tea.

Our final despatches respecting your various complaints are in progress and shall be completed before Burn's departure in the *Balcarras*, at the end of this month. Captains Hine and Grant have each occupied their own Silk privilege and went home [with] their silk in the *Juliett*, an advantage derived from their position as owners. But we have every reason to believe the existing scarcity of privilege will not be felt next month.

We are doing all we can to get off the *Heywood* but are not yet able to fix a day for her despatch. I remain, with kind regards to Mrs. Macvicar,

Yours sincerely,

[P.S.] The *Mr. Jardine* will in all probability be our Cape[39] ship

[38] It was only be a matter of time before *Jardine, Matheson & Co.* came to terms with local market forces which had been unleashed by competition among the Chinese themselves. But William Jardine's low opinion of the moral 'character' of the tea men was at first his major objection for refusing to do business with them directly.

[39] Cape: '1650. [var. of cop]. Top—1812'. (*OED*). Cop: 'The top of anything'. (*Ibid.*). The steamer *Jardine* raised expectations which it failed to deliver.

1837

138. William Jardine in Canton to Sir John Tobin[1] in Liverpool,
21 January 1837

[Dear Sir,]

Although our firm has already expressed their gratification at the handsome compliment you have paid in conferring my name on one of the finest vessels belonging to Liverpool, I cannot allow the *Heywood* to depart without addressing a few lines to you expressive of my own feelings on the occasion.

Be assured, my dear Sir, your kindness is appreciated as it ought to be and grateful as I must have felt for such an honour proceeding from any quarter, I feel doubly so on reflecting that it proceeds from one holding so eminent a position in the commercial world and to whom I have not even the advantage of being personally known.

It is with liveliest pleasure I look forward to the prospect of one day enjoying the benefit of your personal acquaintance should it please Providence to return me to my native land. Meanwhile, I trust you will consider me sincerely desirous of evincing the sentiments of gratitude and friendship by which I am actuated.

Be pleased to accept our united thanks for a very superior Cheshire cheese presented to us by Captain [ ] in your name; which proved a great treat, and for which we feel obliged.

I have taken the liberty of sending you per *Heywood* three boxes of Tea – Peko, Souchong and Congo. The two first are said to be very superior, the last good— and, if mixed in nearly equal proportions, as used, will, I trust, be approved of.

Begging your acceptance of the same, I remain, etc. . .

139. William Jardine in Canton to John Shillaber[2] in Manila,
31 January 1837

Dear Shillaber,

Since I had the pleasure of addressing you on the 8th Ultimo we have been favored with your letters of the 19th Ultimo and 6th Instant, to which I shall now have the pleasure of replying.

19th Ultimo. States the views of the Government as to the creation of a Light House, the expense to be paid by a duty on vessels entering the port for ten years ; at the expiration of that period the Light House to become the property of

[1] On Sir John Tobin, Liverpool shipbuilder, see Letter **127**, note 194

[2] For John Shillaber, see above, Letter **49**, note 3. During the middle years of the 1830s he was attached to the agency firm of *Otadui & Co.* in Manila. Both William Jardine and James Matheson seem to have been his mentors in business and wrote much more freely to him than to ordinary correspondents.

Government. If your estimates are correct the parties contracting must do well but it involves a considerable outlay.

The Tobacco contract would most likely answer, but we are incapable of offering an opinion on the subject, not having a sufficient knowledge of the details of the business; but we may remark that you cannot be too cautious in entering on an affair involving so heavy an outlay in the first instance.

6th January. Refers to the remittances made in dollars; and the difficulty you experienced in procuring them—which we regret, as keeping back the remittances which should have been here in time for investment per *Castle Huntly*,[3] and bringing us under advances for the parties, who are interested in the speculation.

The 30,000 dollars, per *Henry Ewbank* have been received and turned out as follows: 24,800 good, worth 14 shillings and 3 pence premium; 5,156 marked, sold at 6 per cent premium; 40 copper dollars and deficient in number on counting them; and 4, making up the amount shipped: 30,000 dollars. We shall be glad to receive the balance as soon as you can conveniently pick them up; being desirous of closing the account with the parties in England.

On the subject of the *Trinidad* we shall address you in a separate letter, Captain Grant being at Lintin. I had a conversation with Captain Moller[4] on the subject.

The Rice market continues dull as ever, and we see no prospect of an immediate rise; but the weather has been so fine of late, without a drop of rain that we may possibly have a wet and unpropitious seed time; which period is now approaching. Prices must I think decline with you, ere long. Present price: 1.50 to 1.70 dollars per pecul, in little demand.

I am glad you have discovered the murderers of poor Mackay,[5] and shall be anxious to hear the result of the investigation. The *Fairy* had a good many gold

[3] The ship was ready for dispatch the month before this Letter was written. (See Letter **137**).

[4] Captain Moller was not identified. He was probably related to Edmond Moller, the editor of the *Canton Press*, and English language daily which started in 1835 and remained in circulation until 1844. (Fay, *Opium War*, pp. 126, 150).

[5] For Captain William Mackay, James Matheson's cousin, see above Letter **49**, note 9. Captain Mackay was one of the most trusted captains of the opium ships. He set off from Lintin in the spring of 1836 with a cargo of opium and other goods and sailed north as he had done many times before (e.g. Letter **73**). He regularly reported his sales progress and his receipts in treasure, which accounts for William Jardine's well-documented comments at the end of this Letter. In September 1836, four months before writing this Letter, William Jardine's concern turned to worry as he was no longer receiving news from Captain Mackay. On 5 September 1836, he wrote to Captain Rees: 'Many unpleasant reports still prevail at Macao [. . .] respecting the fate of the *Fairy*. If anything very serious had happened to her we should have had a report by now. But still the state of suspense in which we have been kept is far from being pleasant. We hope for the best, however, and wait patiently.' (*JMArch.*, C4-5). At the end of the year his hopes were dashed as news reached Canton that Captain Mackay had been murdered by pirates. The presence of treasure on board the opium ships (and indeed of opium itself which was easily saleable) made them favourite targets of pirates. The ships were armed and could defend themselves when attacked, but this was of little avail when pirates happened

Bars on board, in small lingots[6] of nearly ten tales each—about two inches long, one broad, and a half to three quarters of an inch thick with Chinese characters on them. Touch from 80 to 96 and 98, worth from 195 to 200 dollars each. We get very little Sycee Silver from Chinchew Bay or Amoy. Our returns are generally in gold Bars, broken coins and entire dollars.

We shall endeavour to furnish you with further particulars by this or the next opportunity. I believe we shall be able to identify the vagabonds.[7] The gold and silver on board, amounted to about seventy thousand (70,000) dollars.

Be pleased to present my kind regards to Mr. Otadui, and believe me,

Yours sincerely,

140. James Matheson in Canton to John Abel Smith in London,

3 March 1837

[My dear Sir,]

I have at length the satisfaction of addressing you by the good ship *Lord Lowther*, the despatch of which has been protracted much longer than anticipated, owing to the Teamen keeping back the middling and inferior Congos at higher prices than justified by the state of the Home market. Her despatch, with that of the *Asia*, will have a good effect in bringing those gentlemen to their senses and will, it is hoped, occasion our tea market to assume a healthier aspect than at any period for the last three years. This, it is to be feared however, will be of short duration should the East India Company be allowed to continue their Exchange operations next season, which, by the facilities they afford to overtrading,[8] disturb the equilibrium of our market, and by fostering a ruinous competition, completely disable us from doing the best for our constituents, being beneficial only to the Chinese.

The *Lord Lowther* is owned entirely by our friend Captain Grant,[9] who now retires from business, after having been for several years in the management of, and interested in, our Lintin shipping. He has been always very much in our confidence, and being aware of our views on most subjects, he may be safely

to mount their operations through members of the crew as seems to have been the case here. In this instance the pirates made off with the equivalent of £ 14,000.

[6] The old word for 'ingot', in use since the 15th century. (*OED*).

[7] Vagabond: 'a disreputable or worthless person; and idle good-for-nothing fellow; a rascal or rogue 1686'. (*OED*). But as used by William Jardine the term was meant as his worst possible insult and expressed his deepest disgust. He even applied it in 1841 to Captain Charles Elliot, calling the then British plenipotentiary an 'unprincipled vagabond'. (See Letter **229**).

[8] Overtrade: 'To trade in excess of one's capital, or the needs of the market'. (*OED*).

[9] Captain Alexander Grant had made a large fortune to be able to afford the *Lord Lowther*, a 1332-ton former East India Company ship. (Sutton, *Lords of the East*, p. 154). He subsequently lived in London and Scotland, speculating mostly in teas, though not always successfully. He died in 1841 in dramatic circumstances (Letter **225**).

consulted on points connected with our interests where his local knowledge may be useful. He has copies of our communications respecting the controversy with Mr. Macvicar. He will of course confide a portion of his Teas to your good management: his interests in this respect being necessarily divided, owing to family connections with *Messrs. Forbes & Co.*,[10] and previous business relations with *Messrs. Gledstanes & Co.* We shall feel much obliged by your kind and friendly attention to the promotion of his interests and wishes.

Mr. James Fergusson, of the House of *Jenkins, Fergusson & Co.*[11] Calcutta, has been lately here, and you will perceive from the enclosed copies of his correspondence with us, that in the event of your again entering into business relations with them (which he seems to expect) we have agreed to reciprocate to a certain extent whatever business they may influence to us here under the idea that our doing so would be acceptable to you. We shall no doubt hear in due time what your intentions are.

You will see from the House's letters that we have fared better than we expected in our first essay of American agency. I at one time looked forward to a loss of five dollars per Ton in our share of the *Commerce*'s tonnage, besides being obliged to run the risk of filling it up with Teas, on our own account, to a precarious market; but the opportune occurrence of Chinese shippers offering has relieved us from this dilemma. It is probable that we may have similar opportunities of obtaining American freight from our influence in being able to make advances in the Spring months[12] of most Seasons, if not earlier. But still we should be unwilling to incur again such a risk as in the case of the *Commerce*, from a feeling of its being irregular, and we are told too, not usual nowadays.

You will have perceived from one of the House's letters that while *Messrs Howland and Aspinwall*[13] are in high estimation with their countrymen here, we cannot say the same of the Gentleman[14] who acted as your go-between with them. I may mention in *confidence* that we have had a caution respecting him from an intelligent friend who refers to some of his transactions with the *House of Perkins & Co.*, Boston, (Mr. Cushing's)[15] as not being of a satisfactory character. They

[10] The family connection between Captain Alexander Grant and Sir Charles Forbes's firm, *Forbes & Co.* (later *Forbes, Forbes and Co.*) was not traced.

[11] On the formation of *Jenkins, Fergusson & Co.*, see above, Letter **117**, note 146.

[12] The firm's liquidity was at its highest after the low of the tea 'season' which lasted from November to February. Early spring was also the time when shipments of new opium arrived from Calcutta and Bombay. Within a few weeks the firm's treasury was flush with the proceeds from opium sales.

[13] *Howland and Aspinwall* was indirectly referred to in Hollingworth Magniac's Letter **123** as the firm which was seeking an alternative London agency to *Baring Brothers & Co. Howland and Aspinwall* soon became *Jardine, Matheson & Co.* principal agents in America. Over 700 letters are listed in the *BI*.

[14] The 'gentleman' was not identified.

[15] On John Pershing Cushing, and *Perkins & Co.* see above, Letter **29**, note 32.

were connected, I believe, with the *Gibraltar*. I mention this merely as an *on dit* for your consideration; as the party in question has no relations with us to induce our being solicitous on the subject.

As a means of extending your connection with America, should you be so desirous, it occurs to me to send you the enclosed form of letters of credit, which are annually granted to a large amount by the constituted Attornies in America of *Baring Brothers & Co.*, *Thomas Wilson & Co.*, *Timothy Wiggin & Co.*, *George Wildes & Co.*, and latterly *Morrison Cryder & Co.*[16] Like every other paper currency they are apt to become depreciated, when issued to excess, and this was the case some three years ago with the credits of *Baring Brothers & Co.,* of which, more recently, but very few have come in our way. At present those of our friends *Timothy Wiggin & Co.* are not much liked, though considered as strong as the Bank, owing to an idea whether true or not, I am unable to say, that they have dishonoured Bills which ought to have been paid. Were you to enter into this description of business I should think it desirable that your Attornies in America should be jointly concerned with you by way of check on their granting credits on insecure terms.You might safely commence to the extent of one to two hundred thousand pounds per annum, and gradually increase them, as your House become better known. We should of course be desirous of giving a preference to your credits, as far as practicable, but as we must generally be driven by those which may be procurable on the best terms, our influence in this way would not be so great as might, at first, be supposed.

You will perceive from our Newspaper that the long talked failure of the Hing Tae[17] Hong has at length taken place, his creditors having petitioned the Viceroy[18] for a settlement of their debts, who has replied, with unusual promptitude, that the Hong Merchants must forthwith arrange the business, and that the 'property of foreigners cannot be left without an ultimate guarantee for its safety.' This is so far very satisfactory. It is supposed the principal of his debts will be paid, without interest as usual, by annual instalments in five or six Years, some hope in less time. Owing to the considerable extent of our transactions, compared with those of other Houses, we shall appear as creditors for a very large amount,[19] on behalf

[16] *Morrison Cryder & Co.* was the firm recently formed by the London millionaire 'Mr. Morrison' referred to above in Letter **123**.

Thomas Wilson & Co., *Timothy Wiggin & Co.*, *George Wildes & Co.* were, with *Baring Brothers & Co.*, the principal London agencies financing American exports to Britain. At the time when James Matheson wrote this Letter, the first three firms were on the verge of collapse. For their failure, see below, Letters **145, 149**, and **150**.

[17] 'Hing Tae', the name of the hong Merchant who went bankrupt in 1837, is usually spelt 'Hengtai' in this correspondence (e.g. in Letter **136**, and the two main letters dealing with his bankruptcy—Letters **141** and **143** below).

[18] Viceroy Ten T'ing-chen.

[19] The 'very large amount' is only disclosed in Letter **141**. It was essential that John Abel Smith, *Jardine, Matheson & Co.*'s main support and banker in London, should continue his confidence in the

of ourselves and friends. But I am happy to say we are in no wise inconvenienced by the circumstance.

We shall wait with considerable anxiety till we receive your advices as to the course which our differences with Mr. Macvicar are likely to take. His conduct has been such as to make us look forward with perfect indifference to the dissolution of the connection, should such be the result.[20] As the excessive supply of Nankin Silk will no doubt occasion the usual effect of a disproportionate depreciation of the middling and lower qualities, we think it not unlikely that this article will furnish him with a ground of attack this season as Tea in the last. He gave us positive orders without any discretion to invest large sums in Tea and Silk; and to expect all of first quality seems just as absurd as to fancy that the produce of the dairy should be nothing but cream. On this head our Circular of 2nd Instant contains some remarks which may be worth attention. The more we reflect on the subject, the more indispensible do we think it that all such complaints should be referred to us, and that you should be entirely relieved from the trouble and annoyance of listening to or adjusting them. Accordingly so soon as you are clear of the discussion with Messrs. {Burrow}[21] and Mr. Macvicar, we shall feel obliged by your endeavouring to avoid any more, unless where indispensably necessary to take up our bills, or to ward off imminent loss. Or if Mr. Macvicar should be dissatisfied with our concessions, we think it will be better to refer the whole to China.

Mr. Baines[22] of the *Falcon* having informed me that you wished to have two of the largest China Bidets[23] I have purchased a pair for you, not so ornamental as he wished, (which were not to be had without waiting a year and paying three times the cost) which are shipped in the *Lowther* per enclosed receipt. Cost 26 dollars at 5 shillings per dollar—6 pounds sterling, 10 shillings, which please credit to *Jardine, Matheson & Co.*

I also send you	1 chest black tea,	Eulong
	½ ditto	Hyson
	2 ten catty Boxes	Hyson Peko, of which I request your

acceptance.

Canton firm. James Matheson provides here all the arguments which should reassure him, except for the loss of interest on the principal lent to Hengtai.

[20] The firm's connection with John Macvicar was unravelling fast. It had lasted some six years, and had had an important impact both in Canton and in the British manufacturing districts. The fact that many British manufacturers had lost money on their exports to China (even though they had sometimes made money on the returns) had widened the audience for James Matheson's pamphlet, *The present position, etc.* and had given credibility to those who thought that the British government should attempt to open the China trade by force if other avenues proved ineffectual.

[21] Messrs. {Burrow} were not identified.

[22] 'Mr Baines' was not identified.

[23] Bidet: 'A vessel on a low narrow stand which can be bestridden for bathing purposes'. (*OED*).

A receipt accompanies for a similar supply for Mr. Oswald Smith, which I beg the favor of your handing to him with our kind regards.

Jardine writes in kind regards to yourself, Magniac, and the other members of your firm, and I remain, my dear Sir,

Yours very sincerely.

141. William Jardine in Canton to John Shillaber in Manila,

11 August 1837

Dear Shillaber,

Since I had the pleasure of addressing you on 23rd June last, your favors of the 9th and 7th of July have come to hand, the former on the 4th, the latter on the 8th instant, I feel obliged for the trouble you take in explaining various operations in which you have been engaged during the last two years; but my object is not so much to investigagte what you have done, as to endeavour if possible to prevent your suffering from a repetition of such hazardous and extensive speculation. I hope most sincerely you will make up your mind to preserve that safe and steady course which is open to you, which under prudent, cautious management must ultimately lead to independence[24] if not to ample fortune. I shall be happy to hear of the safe arrival of the *Colon* and of her funds having reached our friends in England. In consequence of the embarrassed state of the American Houses in London and Liverpool our friends felt somewhat anxious about the remittance to be made on account of the proceeds of her cargo, but I trust they would not be put to any inconvenience on that score.

The times are, however, very trying, and many must be ruined before the commerce of England and America can be placed on a firm footing. Our friends have been wild beyond anything in their orders for Teas and Raw Silk, and much money must be lost. We are fortunate in having little interest in either article this Season, and still do not expect to escape a loss in some way or other. It would be too much good luck, and we are prepared to bear a fair proportion without grumbling, but unlike your neighbours in this particular we shall have no satisfaction in seeing our friends or even our enemies (and we appear to have some) suffer

[24] William Jardine writes to John Shillaber as though he were a younger member of his own family. The reason may be that John Shillaber, who used to be an American official, had no previous training in business. It is likely that when he decided to become a merchant, he went to William Jardine and James Matheson for advice. It must also have been through the partners' good offices that he obtained his position with *Otadui & Co., Jardine, Matheson & Co.*'s principal agents in Manila.

The advice given here is similar to that given by James Matheson to his nephew Hugh Matheson in Letter **47**. By avoiding speculation and cautiously attending to pure agency business, an industrious person could not fail to reach financial 'independence'.

with us. On the contrary we hope most sincerely that your liberal minded neighbour[25] may escape unhurt.

Your favor of 7th ultimo deserves my best thanks, and we feel obliged for the trouble you have taken. If your friends knew how little trouble Hengtai's failure has given us and the indifference we feel about the comments on the amount of our claim they would have little gratification in sporting their malignant wit on such a subject.[26] The statement is nearly correct as to the amount of our claim which for ourselves and friends is upwards of two millions of dollars. We have never attempted to conceal the amount and have no fear about recovering, but what is of much more importance we have never felt the slightest inconvenience from being deprived of this large sum, though we have completed all our remittances as if there had been not outstanding debts, and that, at a time when a number of our neighbours were complaining of the scarcity of cash—this between ourselves—we have not much inclination to boast, but your friends will not have an opportunity of failing in our company for some time to come, however *we* may have already failed in prudence, good sense, and good breeding, in your society. As for the Doctor,[27] poor man! he only repeats what he has heard, knowing little of the subject on which he is talking. Let this idle gossip give you no uneasiness: it gives us none, and we freely forgive the amiable gossipers.

[25] The reference is obscure.

[26] William Jardine's annoyance at the gossip following Hengtai's failure and the public disclosure of his firm's claims belies what he describes as his 'indifference' on the subject. The claim against Hengtai described here as 'upwards of two millions of dollars' was in fact 2,261,000 dollars, of which more than 60% was due to *Jardine, Matheson & Co.* and the rest to the firm's constituents. At the previous year-end date (30 June 1836), Hengtai already owed the firm 1,430,912 dollars. (*JMArch.* A2-16). This was the equivalent of £350,000 pounds, a very large sum indeed. At the time of his failure, the amount owed *Jardine, Matheson & Co.* must have been higher still.

When Hengtai's bankruptcy was declared (March 1837), there was every expectation that the Cohong would repay the principal of Hengtai's debt 'over five or six years', as James Matheson wrote in Letter **140** to John Abel Smith. Interest being excluded from repayment, the shortfall on the firm's claim would in any case amount to some £80,000 (say, 4% on £350,000 for six years). This was a loss which the firm could easily absorb out of profits over a six-year period. With the events of the Opium War, however, and the breakdown of the Cohong system from 1839, the principal was not fully repaid to Hengtai's creditors. Hence the special relevance of William Jardine's remark to Palmerston in February 1840 (mentioned in Letter **193**) : '[I] brought to his notice the debts due by the cohong to foreign merchants before their expedition for Canton, reminding him that they had been settled on the best terms we could obtain, and that settlement [had been] approved by the emperor. For years instalments had been paid, but the remaining instalments, together with some additional debt, incurred since I left China, must be taken into consideration when we come to treat, which we presume we will do, sooner or later, after having carried on the war for some time. His Lordship said no one had brought these claims to his notice, inquiring how they arose, from what source such claims had hitherto been paid, and requested I should favour him with a memo' on the subject, which I promised to do without loss of time'. Final payments to *Jardine, Matheson & Co.* and other creditors on the Hengtai claim thus eventually came out of the proceeds from the Treaty of Nanking.

[27] John Shillaber had received news of Hengtai's failure from Dr Colledge, his brother-in-law.

Be pleased to present my kind regards to Mr. Otadui, and believe me, my dear Shillaber,

Yours sincerely.

142. William Jardine in Canton to Captain Rees on the Coast on board the *Austin*, 19 August 1837

My dear Sir,

Since I had the pleasure of addressing you, on the 17th ultimo, by the *Jardine*, I have been favored with yours of the 16th ultimo per *Psyche*, 18th per *Jardine*, 3rd and 3rd instant, to which I shall now have the satisfaction of replying.

From these advices, and the memo' of proceedings on the Coast dated the 3rd instant it is evident that the Trade was still in a precarious state, and subject to constant interruptions; but we must hope for quieter times.

The drug trade here has been subjected to another interruption, and the whole of the new Boats destroyed by the Owners. Various reasons are assigned to this second conflagration of Boats: the most feasible of which is a panic produced by an Edict from the Emperor, published a few days ago, ordering the Viceroy to send all the receiving ships away from Lintin, and the two Moons;[28] making inquiries at the same time, as to what class of natives aided the foreigners in conducting the Opium Trade.

We shall probably have to request the Commanders to move the ships a little further on towards 'Lyee Moon' or 'Cowloon'[29] for a time.

You will be surprised to hear that the *Red Rover* has not yet returned from Calcutta: our friends on that side of India appear to have taken leave of their senses and are keeping our Opium back,[30] while we are obliged to buy for the Coast. Under these circumstances you will receive a short supply by the *Harriet* now under despatch for your quarters; but the *Rover* must be back in ten days or a fortnight, and we shall send her on to you with as little delay as possible. In the event of her having arrived before this reach the *Hercules*, you may have 100 chests of each description, Patna and Benares by the *Harriet*.

Prices here are nominal, the Brokers having taken themlseves off for a few days. Patna 670–665, Benares 660–665, and Malwa 520–510 dollars per chest. We send you five chests of Patna by this conveyance as requested, and your Account Current shall be sent by the next opportunity. Mr. Barretto is making a fair copy which is not quite finished.

[28] 'The two Moons': two reputedly safe anchorages near Lintin used by the opium ships during the typhoon season. One, east of Lintin, was 'Cumsingmun'; the other, west of Lintin, (facing today's Hong Kong International Airport) was 'Capsingmun'.

[29] 'Cowloon': today's Kowloon, the peninsula facing the north shore of Hong Kong island.

[30] See below, Letter **146**.

The accounts received are under examination, and I feel obliged for your memo' of proceedings.

The *Amherst*'s[31] shot striking a small Junk was an unfortunate occurrence, and must have tended to widen the breach between you and the Mandarins.

As we wish the *Harriet* to bring us back Treasure from the *Findlay* and *Jardine*, by 6th or 8th of September we trust you will have no occasion to detain her on the Coast. She will have about 40, or 45 chests of Patna, and a similar quantity of Benares.

I remain, my dear Sir,
Yours sincerely,

P.S. I note what you say respecting Mr. Davis;[32] from whom we have not a line, but this is of little importance. I regret you should have given him an opportunity of asking you a *second time* to fill up his berth. He sought the employ, we did not seek for him, and the sooner a discontented officer is discharged, the better.

I hope Mr. Forbes[33] may give you satisfaction. When I saw him last he appeared to want a little brushing up. His dress was too slovenly for a smart officer; but he was ailing at the time.

143. William Jardine in Canton to Hollingworth Magniac in London,

26 August 1837

My Dear Magniac,

When I had the pleasure of addressing you on the 15th of March last, it was under the impression that, long ere this I should have been enabled to have laid before you a memo' of the terms on which we had let the Imperial Hong to the parties occupying it; but Mr. Edwards[34] left Canton before anything was done, and has not been up since.

They are all going on steadily, however, and we anticipate no difficulty in the settlement of all the accounts connected with *Markwick & Edwards*. At present *Messrs. Wetmore & Co.*[35] pay 2,000 dollars per annum for Nos. 1 & 2 and Mr. Markwick, now *Markwick & Smith*, pay 5,800 dollars for the remaining

[31] The *Lord Amherst* was not one of *Jardine, Matheson & Co.*'s ship. She had been commanded by Captain Hugh Hamilton Lindsay in 1832 when the East India Company had chartered her to explore commercial possibilities on the China coast.

[32] Mr. Davis: possibly a young relation of J. F. Davis, the Superintendent of Trade who had resigned in January 1835.

[33] 'Mr Forbes' was not identified.

[34] On Mr. Edwards and *Markwick & Edwards*, see above Letter **128**, note 2.

[35] On *Wetmore & Co.*, see Letter **106**, note 55.

Factories. You are aware that we pay 4,600 dollars per annum on account of said Hong.[36]

Our Circular, to the Firm, will give you every information relating to Markets here; but it is difficult to describe the anxiety that prevails per advices from England; our latest dates being the 1st to the 3rd of April, when things in general looked alarming enough; though some of the letters spoke of the American Houses as if they had overcome all their difficulties, but this does not appear to me to be the case.

We must have later advices soon; and I hope of a more satisfactory nature than those we have had lately. We are anxious to make remittances to your firm; but at a loss how to proceed, there being no Bills procurable, but those of *Messrs. Thomas Wilson & Co.*, and other Houses similarly situated; which in the face of recent advices it would be imprudent to purchase. We shall lose no time, however, the moment an opportunity offers in putting you in funds equal to all your engagements and advances, on our account, without reference to the rate of Exchange.[37]

We have lately received back, and cancelled three sets of our Bills, Nos. 115, 116, and 117 for 3,000, 2,000 & 1,000 pounds sterling, together with 6,000 pounds sterling on your Firm; the party in whose favour they were drawn, Bernardo Lhuarte Dos Santos, having died, without endorsing them at Batavia, on his way to Europe.

In times like these, we must expect to suffer along with others;[38] but have no reason to apprehend anything that can materially inconvenience us; and we have every reason to believe that nearly all the bills we have drawn or endorsed will be ultimately made good, if not paid when due.

Much money must be lost in Silk and Tea, particularly the former; but fortunately we have a very trifling stake in that article. Many of the orders were without limit as to price, and no discretion, of any kind, given to the Agent. We now hold some of these orders for Silk that have never been cancelled. I mention these

[36] This paragraph clearly establishes that, in connection with the Imperial Hong, Hollingworth Magniac was in a position of head-tenant, subleasing to other parties. He received 7,800 dollars from the sub-tenants and paid the landlord 4,600 dollars, making an annual turn of 3,200 dollars. (See above, Letter **31**, note 53, and Letter **53**, note 25).

[37] Usually, the partners were reluctant to make a remittance 'for the mere sake of a remittance without a view to profit' (as James Matheson put it in Letter **39**). This meant that, in normal circumstances, they would have tried to increase their and their correspondents' profits by buying sterling at a profitable rate of exchange. In the critical trading conditions described here, however, where no safe means of remittance were to be found in the Canton market (bills drawn on London 'American' banks being unsafe, and teas and silks being too expensive), the Canton firm was acutely aware that it inconvenienced its London creditors by not covering the advances it had received. It was therefore prepared to do so when safe bills could be bought, regardless of the exchange rate.

[38] William Jardine was particularly concerned about the bills he had drawn on *Timothy Wiggin & Co.* See below, Letters **145** and **146**.

particulars to show you the wild speculative spirit that prevailed among the parties carrying on the trade with China; which, added to the Company's advances here not only raised the prices of Teas and Silk to an exorbitant rate; but made it a matter of favour to obtain the refusal of good chops at absurd prices. We are all very quiet now, and I hope to see purchases made at moderate rates. No contracting for or bespeaking favourite chops this season. If we can manage to keep the supply under 30 millions of pounds, this season's Teas must advance very much in price in England, and Nicholson[39] may yet have an opportunity of benefiting by purchasing the last of the *good Teas*,—Congos, I mean, in the Company's sale.

When silk is to improve again, I know not; the stock in England is equal to more than two years' consumption at the rate they have consumed for the last two years.

Hengtai's affairs are progressing slowly. The accounts are under examination and the Merchants intend to collect the Consoo fees[40] in Cash and divide them among the creditors every month, or every quarter. In the meanwhile we are endeavouring to bring about a system of cash payments for Cotton and other articles of import, by giving the purchaser the option of discounting at the rate of one per cent per month; and when the parties avail themselves of the time allowed we add ten days to the time specified and insist on immediate payment.[41] In case of failure, the parties to be petitioned against.

Nearly one half of the Cotton imported this Season has been in our hands; and we hope to bring the dealers who are a troublesome set, into a regular system of prompt payment. The respectable part of the Hong Merchants are as anxious as we are to establish this plan in view of that which has prevailed for some years of paying in goods at distant dates. Our rival editors[42] have written a great deal of nonsense about the responsibility of the Co-Hong and the payment of Hengtai's

[39] For John Nicholson, see above, Letter **79**, note 108 and Letter **111**, note 109.

[40] One of the most important functions of the Chinese Superintendency of Maritime Customs (the 'Hoppo') was to administer and collect port duties. His administration operated from the Consoo House in Canton, in the vicinity of the Factories. When additional funds had to be levied to repay bad debts left by bankrupt Hong merchants, and in the absence of occasional imaginative solutions (e.g. as described in Letter **129**, note 14), the traditional method was for the Consoo administration to raise port dues. Indirectly, therefore, the foreigners were partly paid back their claims on China out of their own contributions. This practice was summarized by William Jardine in a letter to Jamsetjee Jejeebhoy dated 4 February 1837: 'This is a gloomy picture but it is too true, and what is worse of all [is that] their fees to the Hoppo and debts due to foreigners must be paid by additional charges on the foreign trade'. (*JMArch.*, C4-5). See also: Van Dyke, Paul Arthur, *Port Canton and the Pearl River Delta, 1690–1834*, Ann Arbor, MI, ProQuest Microform Edition, 2002, pp. 66 and following.

[41] The foreign merchants were slow in realizing that the barter system itself, particularly in connection with Indian cotton and British piece goods, had contributed to the accumulation of debts by the Hong merchants well beyond prudential levels. There is no evidence suggesting that the resulting plan for cash payments described here was ever successfully implemented.

[42] The editors of the *Canton Press,* as opposed to those of the *Canton Register* (indirectly *Jardine, Matheson & Co.*'s daily paper). *The Chinese Courier and Canton Gazette* had stopped publishing in 1833.

debt, and must have caused much alarm amongst the parties unacquainted with China. The responsibility we never doubted; but the failure is, I am convinced, a dishonest one:[43] the money has not been lost in trade. The sum we have locked up is large, but we have not yet felt the least inconvenience from it, though we have completed all our remittances to our Constituents.

This letter has been written amidst many interruptions but, I trust, you will be able to make it out; and with kind regards to Mrs. Magniac, [I] remain, my Dear Magniac.

Yours sincerely,

144. James Matheson in Canton to John Abel Smith in London,

9 September 1837

My dear Sir,

In the absence of direct conveyance I am unwilling to omit the opportunity of the *Himmaleh* for New York, to acknowledge your favour of 1st May, which reached me via Suez along with your firm's letters, on the 30th Ultimo. And we feel much obliged not only for the punctuality of your advice, but for the liberal protection you were affording to our interests in this emergency arising from the unexampled difficulties of the times.[44] I need not say how much we regret being burdensome to you at such a moment, which, could we by any possibility, have foreseen the crisis, we should have been most anxious to avoid. All we can do now is to use the earliest practicable *safe* means for placing you in funds to meet your advance; and to this object our attention is particularly directed. As yet everything connected with our European trade, is in a complete state of inaction, and must remain so for some time to come.

The failure of *Messrs. Marjoribanks & Ferrers*[45] occasioned no less suprise than it did with you ; as it was generally imagined they had much more bottom than to be upset by their losses in the China trade, heavy though they were known

[43] Unfortunately, William Jardine does not explain why he thinks that the hong merchants were largely 'responsible' and why the Hengtai's failure was a dishonest one.

[44] James Matheson refers here to the fact that *Magniac Smith & Co.* were 'protecting' (i.e. accepting or paying at maturity) the bills of exchange they had drawn on *Timothy Wiggin & Co.* or other bills drawn on others 'American' houses on the verge of collapse which they had endorsed to finance their remittances from Canton. The situation was very similar to the crisis the firm had faced in 1832 when they asked Thomas Weeding and Hollingworth Magniac to 'protect' their bills. The big difference was that in 1837, instead of one single London agency (*Fairlie & Co.*) it was the whole of the Atlantic trade and the greater part of the banking houses financing it which were threatened. For the extent of the financial and commercial damage, see below, Letter **145**.

[45] For *Marjoribanks Ferrers & Co.*, see above, Letter **78**, notes 100 and 102. The surprise comes from the fact that the partners were, or had been, very wealthy East India Company ships' husbands. Like John Abel Smith's family, they represented 'old money' in a world where many new fortunes were being made and lost.

to be. It is said the Bills of their correspondents here, *Messrs. Daniell & Co.*[46] will be taken up by *Messrs. Daniell & Dickinson* of London and Liverpool ; and I hope this will prove to be the case. We have had no transactions with them nor with any of [their] neighbours, beyond the Bills we have taken under American credits, and a small account with the House of *L. Gemmell & Co.*,[47] a branch of a Glasgow House, who are about to withdraw from the China trade, which is likely to be the case with some more of the new establishments of Canton.

It is consolatory to reflect that ultimate good is likely to result from the present difficulty in the diminution of future competition and the adoption of a more secure and wholesome system of agency business, which it is our firm intention to adhere to in time to come.

Mr. Jardine wrote to Mr. Magniac on the 26th as did our firm to your's by the American ships, *Champlain* and *Duncan*. Referring to those communications and to a Price Current by this conveyance, I remain, My dear Sir,

Most sincerely yours,

145. James Matheson in Canton to John Shillaber in Manila,

12 October 1837

Dear Shillaber,

After a long suspension of arrivals the *Edinburgh* arrived yesterday from Bombay, bringing London news, via Suez to 5th June; and under a separate cover, I hand *Messrs. Otadui & Co.* the latest commercial and political intelligence. The former, I regret to say, continues very unfavorable. As regards the state of credit, the Bank of England, in consequence of the Bank of the United States rejecting certain proposals which had been made, were under the necessity of refusing further assistance to the American houses who were in difficulty, and between 1st and 5th June, the following houses consequently stopped payment: *George Wildes & Co., Timothy Wiggins & Co., Thomas Wilson & Co., Gowan & Marx, Bell and Grant*, and three others not named.[48]

[46] For Nugent Daniell, see above, Letter **92**, note 66.

[47] *L. Gemmell & Co.* was not identified. The *BI* only lists six letters from '*William & Thomas Gemmell & Co.*' William and Thomas Gemmell of Glasgow arrived in China in 1836 and started this firm in 1838 in Canton. (Bard, *Traders of Hong Kong*, p. 59).

[48] Since the middle of 1836 the general deterioration of credit in the London and American markets led to a collapse of confidence. Bills of exchange, particularly those drawn by American exporters on their London bankers lost their value. The demand for gold increased, particularly in the latter part of 1836, when the American *Land Office* decided to accept only payment in gold. Bills of exchange became more and more difficult to discount, with liquidity drying up in the London discount market. As a result, some of the affected banks could no longer face their obligations. In an attempt to avoid a series of bank failures, the Bank of England started extending liquidity to the banks in difficulty, particularly 'the three Ws', *George Wildes & Co., Timothy Wiggin & Co.* and *Thomas Wilson & Co.* At the beginning of 1837, commodity prices collapsed, particularly commodities imported from America

We have letter to 1st June from *Magniac Smith & Co.* who were protecting our signature whenever requisite. Mr. Weeding was under considerable apprehension lest the state of affairs in New York should prevent the remittance from the cargoes of the *Colon* and the *Tarquina* coming forward in time. Having been informed by Mr. [ ] Perit (then in London) that his firm *Goodhue & Co.*[49] would not be disposed under present circumstances even to advance the amount of freight on any India or China cargo that might be consigned to them, he adds: 'in the instance of the *Colon* it is true there is no freight payable, but nevertheless sales are next to impossible'.

Timothy Wiggins having issued a circular of which I enclose a copy showing:

– Their bill engagements since reduced:	674,700	(pounds sterling)
– Advanced by the Bank of England against notes of debtors:	200,000	
– Private creditors:	33,400	
Engagements:	908,100	
– Assets after deducting 103,800 pounds sterling for bad debts and which they deem extravagant:	1,392,800	
Balance:	484,700	
– Deduct subscribed fund:	200,000	
Leaving a surplus Capital of:	284,700	pounds sterling

Our concerns with them are very trifling: and owing to *Goodhue & Co.* having deferred remitting them, we are in their debt.

Talbot Olyphant & Co.[50] are mentioned among the New York failures.

I now proceed to reply to your favors of 6th and 17th September; from the former of which I regret to observe you had been attacked by influenza, which However, I hope was but of short duration. The view it gives of the general amelioration of your Colony likely to result from the firmness and intelligence of the new Governor[51] is very satisfactory, and still more so the favorable aspect of

(cotton, sugar and tobacco). The failure of all the New Orleans cotton wholesalers, and of most of their counterparts in London, Liverpool, Manchester and Glasgow deepened the general gloom. In April 1837, the Bank of the United States made an unsuccessful attempt at rescuing the financial market with an injection of liquidity. In May, the New York banks failed. On 1 June 1837, the Bank of England decided to suspend its life-lines to the banks it had helped. As a result, these banks stopped their payments the next day. The only 'American' bank to have survived this very severe storm (though not unscathed) was *Baring Brothers & Co.* (Hidy, Ralph, W. *The House of Baring in American Trade and Finance*, New York, (1949), 1970, Chapter VIII, 'The year of the Locust', pp. 205–234). See also: Matthews, R. C. O., *A Study in Trade-Cycle History. Economic Fluctuations in Great Britain, 1833–1842*, Cambridge University Press, 1954). *Jardine, Matheson & Co.* was left with an exposure of some £100,000 to *Timothy Wiggin & Co* and the other failed banks. (See Letter **147**).

[49] On *Goodhue & Co.* and its partner, Mr. Perit, see Letter **69**, note 22.

[50] For *Olyphant & Co.*, the sister firm in Canton, see above, Letter **65**, note 3.

[51] Andres Camba succeeded Pedro Salazar as governor of the Philippines in August 1837.

Messrs. C & Co's[52] affairs from your good standing with the *Messrs. Rothschild & Co.*[53] I sincerely hope a *cautious* and *prudential* use of your advantages will lead to every good result you can desire, while without caution the resources and opportunities at your command will be only so many additional sources of danger. With our recent experience of the evils of the Banking system in England, the greatest vigilance is necessary in managing your proposed Manila Bank, to prevent its being attended with more harm than good; more especially if created with the power of issuing notes, which are very apt to occasion a redundancy in the currency, unless care is taken never to let the issues exceed by more than a certain proportion the amount of bullion in the Bank Coffers.[54] Many thanks for the *confidential* information in yours of the 17th respecting your neighbours and their friends *Messrs. CB&Co.* We shall be anxious till we hear the bills on the latter are paid.

In our official letter we have dwelt but slightly on the regret occasioned to us by your having been (as we conceived) so precipitate in drawing in favour of *Messrs. {K} M&Co.* For us as agents it is quite immaterial whether the money in the hands of these gentlemen, or *Messrs Magniac Smith & Co.*'s funds were the first to come over to us. But we naturally supposed you would not draw till the sugar was in the course of delivery, and that, more especially, in the present state of our accounts, you would put off drawing as long as you possibly could. Your pursuing a different course is a source of regret in as much as (you must excuse my saying) it tends in a manner to weaken confidence, and to suggest a more wary wording in future instructions.[55]

Captain Morgan[56] of the *Scaleby Castle* is very much in the confidence ot *Messrs. Cursetjee Ardaseer & Co.*; and I would suggest your being very full in your communications with him as to the causes which occasion its being invoiced so much above the market price—in the first place, their own desire that we

[52] The firm of 'Messrs. C & Co.' was not identified. Nor were the other firms in this Letter mentioned by their initials alone: *CB&Co.* and *KM&Co.*

[53] *N. M. Rothschild & Co.* was a very infrequent correspondent of *Jardine, Matheson & Co.* (Only eight letters are listed in the BI, most of them dating from a later period).

[54] There is no evidence that this ambitious issuing bank project mentioned by Shillaber and commented on here by James Matheson was subsequently carried out.

[55] The question of how much latitude to give agents in instruction letters was particularly acute at the time when correspondents worked in distant ports and communications were slow. So much then depended on the agent's market intelligence, business acumen and experience. The golden rule was to instruct agents to act as though they were disbursing their own money. But it only truly applied when there was a complete meeting of minds between order-party and agent. Examples of this are relatively rare in these Letters, and would include the relationships of the firm with the *Remington & Co.* partners and, in the current period, with *Magniac Smith & Co.*

[56] Captain William Morgan had commanded the *Pascoa* in 1835. (*BI*).The *Scaleby Castle* was one of half a dozen ships belonging outright to the East India Company before 1834. (**Appendix IX**). The new owner of the *Scaleby Castle* in 1837 was not identified.

should contract without delay, rather than wait the chance of the market. And secondly its very superior quality compared with the general run usually provided by your neighbours. Captain Morgan dwells with satisfaction on the *good weight* of your last cargo—and as it costs but a small sacrifice to be liberal on this score, it will be for your interest to attend to it. The Parsees are gratified with attention in correspondence – and you cannot be too diffuse or minute to suit their taste.

We are much pleased that you had got insurance at Manila on the *Trinidad.* You will have seen that we anticipated your suggestion to have all the Manila vessels as they reach Macao, inspected by Captain Rickett.[57] They do not appear to be generally good risks.

Jardine has been unexpectedly called off for the purpose of conveying to Macao the remains of his intimate friend Mr. F. P. Alleyn,[58] who was attached to our Tea department, and died here unexpectedly on the 3rd Instant I expect him back tonight.

I beg my kind regards to Mr. Otadui and remain,

Sincerely yours,

146. James Matheson in Canton to Charles Lyall in Calcutta,

18 October 1837

My dear Lyall,

You may imagine the joy with which on awakening five mornings ago, I found my table covered with the despatches of the long expected *Rover*, bringing the interesting news of the July mail, and of the munificient bonus granted by the Company[59] besides a liberal supply of the drug for our Coast operations, and all in the remarkably short period of 34 days between the land's ends and the Grand Ladrone.[60] Be assured we give you full credit for your strenuous and successful exertions in obtaining the *bonus*, and are duly sensible of the arduous difficulties you had to contend with. If it were possible for any *merely* pecuniary consideration to compensate to us the annoyance occasioned by the long detention of the *Rover*, we might see reason to be now satisfied with what has passed. I cannot

[57] Captain Rickett commanded the *Austin* in 1834. He is mentioned here in his role as surveyor of the *Canton Insurance office*, an assignment he kept until 1850. He also became the Secretary of the Hong Kong Club at its formation in 1846. (*BI*).

[58] For Frederick P. Alleyn, see Letter **100**, note 1. After his death, his widow returned to England. When William Jardine himself retired to England he would occasionally visit her. (See Letter **208**).

[59] In Letter **149**, James Matheson again mentions 'the magnificent *bonus* granted by the Bengal Government, to relieve us from loss on some heavy purchases of opium rather incautiously made for us by *Lyall Matheson & Co.*' The circumstances of how this bonus came to be paid, or indeed what form the bonus took, have not been traced. The two parallel passages are a reminder that 'the Company' and 'the Bengal Government' were interchangeable terms.

[60] On the Ladrones islands, see Letter **49**, note 10.

say, however, that the recollection of it can be thus effaced; but I will not at present resume the disagreeable subject.

It is singular that the very evil I anticipated has actually occurred, viz—our remittances reaching you after the object for which they were intended has been fulfilled. This is exceedingly disagreeable as compelling us to be interested in the drug to a heavier extent, than we desire, and rendering it extremely difficult to adapt our instructions[61] to the various contingencies which it becomes necessary to provide for, more especially when writing under feelings of annoyance, and under a painful apprehension lest our instructions should not be understood in the sense we wish to convey. I trust however the investment of the 218,000 Rupees will be managed with such adroitness and success as to justify better hopes for the future.

You letter of the 16th August per *Ann*, via Singapore, reached on the 11th, two days before the *Rover*.

Alexander [Matheson] tells me that you are in the habit of realizing bills in your favour sent to you from England on the Government, under an old Power of Attorney from Jardine and me. Let me beg you will discontinue this practice (the existence of which we never contemplated) and hold all such bills, under acceptance, unrealized, at the disposal of our endorsement on the set sent from China. *In fact the power does not apply to our present firm.*

Alexander has returned in famous condition. I never saw him looking better. With love to Harriet,[62] I remain

Yours sincerely.

147. James Matheson on Canton to [Captain] Alexander Grant in London, 20 October 1837

My dear Grant,

The foregoing copy of our last Indian circular will inform you that no improvement has yet taken place in our opium market which continues in the same state of inaction as then described. The nominal price of Malwa is about 480 dollars a chest, but deliveries continue to be made at Namoa[63] at 540 dollars, though latterly on a very limited scale owing to the competition arising from so many vessels (about 15 in number) scattered on different parts of the Coast.

[61] On 'instructions' see above, Letter **145**, note 55. The relationship with *Lyall Matheson & Co.* in Calcutta remained always cordial, but it was also marred by repeated misunderstandings of instructions.

[62] 'Harriet': Charles Lyall's wife and one of James Matheson's nieces. (See the end of Letter **149** below).

[63] Namoa: see Letter **76**, note 88.

The legalization of the trade is no longer thought of; and government is evidently making a strong effort for the entire suppression.[64] In this course they will be unable to succeed, but some time may elapse before they will be convinced of this: and then perhaps the idea of legalizing may again come *on the tapis*.

The failure of the American houses Wiggins, Wilson and Wildes involve us in heavy liabilities for endorsing their bills, say about 100,000 pounds sterling; but to you who know our affairs so well I need hardly observe that the utmost loss resulting from this will fall lightly on us; and as *Magniac Smith & Co.* were kindly protecting our signature, our chief regret is on account of the temporary inconvenience to which this may subject them. If you can in any way contribute to their or our relief by placing at their disposal the unencumbered property which

[64] Opium came close to being legalized by the Chinese in 1836. (See above, Letter **133**, note 28). However, opponent of legalization successfully delayed and eventually reversed the emperor's decision.

William Jardine, well informed as ever, had written to Jamsetjee Jejeebhoy on 5 November 1836: 'There are two parties in Pekin—one in favour of admitting opium on the payment of a trifling duty; the other adverse to its admission, and advising the Emperor to put an end to all traffic in the article by making the laws more severe, and enforcing them more rigidly. One individual on this party advises [the punishment for] the smuggling or selling of opium to be made death by law, and urges the necessity of making a few examples among their own people, and in the event of foreigners persevering in the trade, to extend the punishment of death to them'. (*JMArch.*, C4-5). By late February 1837, William Jardine was still of opinion that opium would be 'allowed as physic for a small duty'. The Hoppo's head servant's nephew had reported the news to Mowqua, who had told William Jardine. (*Ibid.*)

The hong merchants themselves had been asked to write their views about the opium question. Their comments are set out in the Archives in an English translation entitled 'Report made to Government by the Hong Merchants in reference to the admission of opium as an article of legal commerce'. The relevant passages are the following: 'The Chinese rule says that, after striking the balance exports/imports, 3/10 of net exports can be exported in cash, i.e. Spanish dollars. Hence the exportation of three tenth has received the licence of Government. [But if] the surplus foreign money being greater than the exportable 3/10, whatever exceeds that sum is either left here to the purchase of either goods or is lent to other foreigners. This is a thing of common occurrence. [. . .] Now, in reference to the question at present under consideration, whether permission should be given to import opium, paying a legal duty thereon, we have, as a provision in case such [permission] should be given, enquired of the foreign merchants if they can export goods to the extent as to equal in value their importation of opium, so that they need not have any occasion for exporting money. Their answer was of the following tenor: 'that it is right and proper that they should comply with the arrangement to take cargo in exchange for the proceed of their opium, but that the ports to which they return are not all alike, and that our native commodities are not equally saleable everywhere; that, were the merchants who bring opium to Canton to make their returns in cargo purchased here, such cargo would be unsaleable and therefore the arrangement to purchase goods with the proceeds of opium cannot be universally adopted. [If they cannot use all the proceeds, they are willing to lend to other merchants; and they are willing for the rest to be bound by the 3/10 rule], but that to require each several ship to take export cargo in exchange for imports will, they apprehend, be found inapplicable, injurious, and impractical'. (*JMArch.*, A-8-91-6). Consultations with the hong merchants and, indirectly through them with the foreign merchants, finally led nowhere. The anti-legalization faction was in the ascendant in Peking throughout 1837.

you took home in the *Lowther* under advances from us, we feel assured you will not be wanting in doing all that friendship suggests. As soon as the operations of the season commence we shall make large remittances to *Magniac Smith & Co.* At present everyhing is at a stand, in consequence of prices demanded by the Chinese being far too high for the depressed state of the home market. Nankin silk is at 450 dollars, of course without buyers. In teas, nothing done. No ships loading. Exchange on England for Government bills at 30 days: 4 shillings and 4 pence. Good private at 6 months scarce at 4 shillings and 6 pence. The Company's Finance Committee have about one and a half million in their treasury, but have not declared their terms for advances. We have no arrivals from England later than April.

Poor Alleyn died here on 3rd. after being unwell all the summer. Jardine accompanied his remains for interment at Macao. Mrs. Elliot[65] has got a little boy. Everything else at Canton and Macao is much as [when] you left us. Etc. . .

148. William Jardine in Canton to Thomas Weeding in London

20 October 1837

Dear Weeding,

Since I had the pleasure of addressing you on the 26th of August last your favors of the 1st of May, and 1st June have been received: the former pointing out the state of the three American Houses, that had been aided by the Bank of England; and various other particulars connected with the money Market and the state of Credit in which various parties were held in England; for which accept my grateful acknowledgments.

The latter informed me of your having accepted a bill in favour of *Messrs. Gledstanes & Co.* for £210 and 'abstained from accepting numbers 245 and 246 and 248 and 250 for the present'; and begged my indulgent consideration of the circumstances which have led to this act.

You know best how you were situated as to money matters at the time you did us all the injury in your power. If you had not the means you are not to blame. If you had the means, and hesitated ever from prudential considerations or want of confidence, you acted in a manner which I certainly should not have done had our positions been reversed.

[65] Clara Genevieve Elliot (1806–1885), daughter of Robert Harley Windsor and Marie-Madeleine Jouve. She was born in Haiti, married Captain Charles Elliot in 1828, and accompanied him to his various foreign postings. She arrived in Macao in 1834 and left in 1841. The 'little boy' referred to here is the couple's youngest son, Frederick Eden Elliot, who was born in Macao. The Elliots had five children: two other sons and two daughters. At the time when this Letter was written, Charles Elliot had been First Superintendent of British Trade in China since December 1836. (Hoe, *The Taking of Hong Kong*, pp. 261, 262).

I have to thank you for the protection afforded to our signature beyond the extent of funds in your hands and to assure you that as soon as the business of the Season commences we shall make arrangements for our friends *Messrs. Magniac. Smith & Co.* paying you such balances as may be due on your account.[66]

With best wishes for your health and prosperity, I remain, Dear Weeding,

Yours sincerely,

149. James Matheson in Canton to William Lyall in London,
9 December 1837

My dear Lyall,

I have much pleasure in acknowledging the receipt of your favours of 6th and 26th June (the former via Suez), and feel greatly obliged for your considerate attention in communicating your views regarding the troubled state of affairs in the great Metropolis, a continuance of which kindness will be always extremely acceptable as often as you can spare a little leisure for dropping me a line by the overland despatch,[67] now decidedly the most expeditious route.

The crash in the commercial world has been truly awful, such as no previous experience could have led one to foresee or guard against. From the extent of our transactions we could not have expected to escape unscathed: but the amount of our losses, even in the *worst* event of the American bills in which we are interested, cannot under any circumstances give us serious concern, and their utmost possible extent would be easily met by our safe earnings of a single year.[68] Our expectation is, however, that so much will be recovered from the drawers of the bills in question and the parties in America on whose account they were drawn, as to render our ultimate loss comparatively light.

The uppermost feeling in our minds is regret that at such a Crisis we should be so heavily burdensome to our friends *Magniac Smith & Co.* who are so kindly protecting our signature. The assurance of your readiness to assist in this, if

[66] After this episode when Thomas Weeding showed a lack of confidence in his old Canton friends by refusing to accept their bills, the business relationship came to a virtual end and the friendship was left under a cloud. (See Letter **167**).

[67] The 'overland' route referred to the route from England to India via the Mediterranean and Suez, as opposed to the traditional, and now longer, route via the Cape of Good Hope.

[68] A verifiable statement. The worst possible loss was estimated at £100,000, or some 500,000 dollars at the then exchange rate. The firm's profits for the year 1835–1836 had been 645,584 dollars, and 711,299 dollars for the year 1836–1837. (*JMArch.*, Ledgers and Accounts Current, A1/36, A1/37). In 1833–1834 profits had reached only 141,545 dollars, and had increased to 327,479 dollars in 1834–1835. The firm's profits thus took off in 1835, at about the time when it relinquished its traditional 'pure agency' commission-based business in favour of a more risky but highly lucrative position-taking business in both teas and opium. These changes in the firm's business were made possible by the 1834 liberalization of the tea trade and by its investment in an opium fleet.

required at a further period, is highly gratifying. We should long ere now have placed them in funds to meet all our engagements, were it not for the impossibility of obtaining safe paper or purchasing produce unless (till within these few days) at ruinous prices. The market having at length opened at safe prices for the finer Congoes, we have loaded the brig *Richard Bell* and are rapidly filling the *George IV* with teas chiefly consigned to *Magniac Smith & Co.*, and as our export will no doubt fall greatly short of the last years while they are laid in considerably cheaper, we have every reason to hope they will turn out well.

Before I have done with our own affairs, it may not be amiss (as you take so lively an interest in our affairs) to explain the motives which induced our embarking so largely in American paper. Several of our constituents, and particularly the most considerable of them at Bombay, are not satisfied with any bills, unless drawn or endorsed by ourselves, our usual charge for which is (or rather was) a penny per dollar or about 2%. We were thus compelled in a manner by the nature and the extent of our business, to become either large drawers or endorsers of bills—and reflecting maturely on the least hazardous mode of meeting the circumstances of the case, most especially about the period of *Fairlie & Co's* credit being called into question, it occurred to us as advisable to divide our risk by trusting to the security of *several* leading houses (such as *Barings, Wiggins & Co.*) rather than risk all within one house *only* in the capacity of our exclusive agents. *Fairlie & Co.*'s failure occurring not long afterwards confirmed us in the expediency of the plan; and thus grew up a system which would not have been necessary, nor thought of, could we always have reposed the same unbounded confidence in our agents as we are now enabled to do.[69] But once established it was impossible to make a sudden change in it, on the formation of our connection with *Magniac Smith & Co.*, however much we may have desired it. The convulsions which have occurred will however now enable us to set on foot a plan for conducting our business generally on greatly improved principle of entire security; as a commencement of which you will see in the P. S. to our Circular of this date that we decline executing orders for Goods, unless when in funds to an extent not less than a third of the probable cost, and that the shipping documents, in every case of being drawn against, must pass through the hands of our own Agents. We wished to exempt from this rule some of our intimate friends, such as Walkinshaw[70] and a few others in whom we have entire confidence. But on reflection, it seemed impossible to draw a line of distinction, which could hardly fail to

[69] The financial strength of John Abel Smith and the 'unbounded confidence' the Canton partners 'reposed in him' now enabled them to omit diversifying their risk. This is clearly a statement of trust and gratitude, rather than one of financial prudence.

[70] Several 'Walkinshaws' are listed in the *BI*. In the absence of a first name, there is uncertainty as to which one James Matheson refers to. Possibly James Walkinshaw (a signatory of the appendix to Letter **151**), or Captain William Wilkinshaw who had commanded the *Scaleby Castle* in 1835. (*BI*).

be thought invidious by some; while the circumstances of its being general and invariable must prevent its being a subject of particular complaint with any.

We much regret the loss entailed by our shipments to you last season—but we were absolutely forced to adopt this mode of investment by the nature of Captain Young's instructions,[71] though he was strongly advised by us to qualify the urgency he expressed for Goods.

The long detention of Clifton's and General Carpenter's funds[72] is a source of great annoyance to us; but both they and you must feel convinced that in the absence of safe bills we have no option left us but wait. We have a confident expectation that a few weeks activity in shipments to England will make a great change in the aspect of our bill market, more especially on the commencement of operations for the United States, in which no progress whatever has yet been made.

I now have to advert etc. [. . .]

Charles[73] of course gives you notice of all that is interesting in Calcutta affairs, and has no doubt told you of the magnificent *bonus* granted by the Bengal Government, to relieve us from loss on some heavy purchases of opium rather incautiously made for us by *Lyall Matheson & Co.* I fear he has rather too much to do just at present, till the youngsters become more habituated to act and think for themselves. I shall hope to hear from Robert shortly, telling me how he likes home, as what his plans are as to returning to Bengal.

Pray remember me most kindly to him, to Mrs. Lyall, and to your good friends on the Surrey side, not forgetting a kiss to my God-daughter. Remember me also to our excellent friend 'the member', Walkinshaw and any other enquiring friends, and believe me always,

Yours very sincerely,

[P. S.] Alexander [Matheson] who is quite well desires his remembrances.

[71] Captain Young is referred to in several subsequent Letters (**164**, **205**, **206**, **237**, **239**).

[72] Major General George C. Carpenter, 10 January 1832, (*AL*, Bengal; *EIRD*).

[73] Charles Lyall was, after Robert Lyall (mentioned as 'Robert' in the same paragraph) the remaining partner in Lyall in *Lyall Matheson & Co.* in Calcutta since Hugh Matheson had left India for England. In a letter to William Lyall date 26 February 1837, Hugh Matheson was described by his uncle as 'enjoying rural recreations [in England]'; and in a letter dated 15 March 1837, James Matheson wrote to John Abel Smith: 'My nephew [Hugh Matheson] is also at home, but as his views are moderate he has some idea of retiring. One of the partners, however, having married my niece will still keep up the family connection'. The partner in question was Charles Lyall, and his niece was 'Harriett' Lyall, mentioned at the end of Letter **146**.

150. James Matheson in Canton to John Abel Smith in London,

11 December 1837

My dear Sir,

Since I had last the pleasure of addressing you, I have been favoured with your letters of 14th. April, 2nd, 5th/6th and 10th June; in proceeding to acknowledge which, I beg to repeat the assurance of the very grateful sense we entertain of your great kindness, as already expressed in the communications of our Firm.

14th April adverts to the threatening aspect of the affairs at home, and the announcement that our friend Mr. T. C. Smith[74] had become a member of your Firm, which is to us very satisfactory; and I beg to offer our congratulations and best wishes on the occasion.

2nd June communicated the failure of *Messrs. Wiggins, Wilson* and *Wildes'* Establishments, in consequence of the Bank being unable to continue granting them assistance; an event which occasioned us no small surprise, as we participated in the general conviction expressed in your letter of 14th April, that the Bank was too deeply interested to admit of any hesitation in carrying them through their difficulties. It is very pleasing to find that neither your Banking nor Agency house are likey to lose a shilling by these disasters. The correspondence of our Firm, or should I say my letter of 19th October to Mr. Magniac, explains the reason of our being unfortunately in a different predicament from yours, on this score, in consequence of our having deemed it advisable several years ago, to prefer dividing our risk of the large bill transactions necessarily devolving on us, rather than stake all on the security of our *then* Agents. A course which, though it has ended badly, proved at the time highly advantageous and prudent; and we ought in fairness, to balance the good against the evil consequence of the system.

Being now differently situated in the entire and unbounded confidence we are able to repose in our agents, we are glad of the opportunity afforded us by the late crisis, to revert to a more wholesome and safe mode of business, and you may feel sure of being troubled with no more of our endorsements for the present. Could we have anticipated even the remotest possibility of any such general calamity as has befallen the Houses in question, no consideration would have induced our running the risk of becoming so heavily burdensome to you, which, believe me, is a source of far deeper regret to us than even the losses themselves.

[74] For the Smiths of the banking family, (John Abel Smith and Oswald Smith), see, Letter **102**, note 10. Thomas Charles Smith, who had just joined *Magniac Smith & Co.*, was an old friend of Hollingworth Magniac, William Jardine and James Matheson. He was an East India Company Supercargo (1828), who had worked his way up from being a writer in Canton (1815). The Rev. Dr Robert Morrison had taught him some Chinese. In 1830, he was the fourth Member of the Canton Select Committee. 'He returned to England after some indiscretion in 1831, making his way back to China as a private merchant when the Company had ceased operating there in about 1834'. (Ride, *East India Company Cemetery*, p. 239).

If we could by any means have put you in funds at an earlier period, without running unwarrantable risks, we should, most gladly, have done so from the large deposit of cash we have had lying idle in our Treasury for months back. I hope however our means will after all arrive in time and that we have been enabled by the delay, to obtain produce at such rates as will, at all events, avoid loss. By the *Richard Bell* under despatch we are sending you teas invoiced at 48,000 dollars, the remainder of the cargo (about 24,000 dollars) being for *Messrs. Forbes and Forbes*, on account of our Bombay friends *Messrs. Jamsetjee Jejeebhoy Sons & Co.* whose engagements we consider it but right, to attend to, simultaneously with our own. The *George IV* will follow in about a fortnight wih teas for you to a far larger extent. We also contemplate making considerable shipments by the *Isabella* of Leith for Cork and a market subject to your control but with a strong recommendation to proceed to Leith to the consignment of our friends *James Duncan & Co.*,[75] should no other vessel take a similar destination this season, as we have reason to believe. These shipments will, we trust, go far to square our account. Good Bills are so scarce and Silk held so extravagantly high that we have, at present, no other resource than Tea for making remittances. But the Silk men having come down a little in their demands, 400 dollars being the rate now demanded for *ordinary* Tsatlee, it may be hoped this state of things will not long continue, though we must still await a farther considerable decline.

On Mr. Weeding's conduct I shall make no comment, further than that it greatly enhances our estimation, as it does the value, of your kind aid. It will of course prevent our having further recourse to his agency.[76]

The very unlooked for state of our account with *T. Wiggins & Co.* is owing to *Messrs. Goodhue & Co.* of New York having omitted to remit for, and delayed the sale of, a cargo of tea, sent in January 1836, on Chinese Account, which we valued at 27,000 dollars, but which it appears, is now estimated at only half that amount, in consequence of the panic in America. We cannot but hope, however, it will yield greatly better, if held till affairs become more settled. We are much obliged for the suggestions in your favor of the 10th as to the expediency of our adjusting Messrs. [ ] account through you in order that you may be able to make a set off of Bills under their Credits, in which we may be concerned.

We thank you very much for your other recommendation in the same letter that we should decline executing orders for goods unless furnished with funds for a

[75] *James Duncan & Co*, the firm of Leith agents is not listed in the *BI*. It was possibly related to *Duncan, Dunbar & Sons*, 'Wine and spirit merchants, 95 Fore street, Limehouse' for which the *BI* lists several entries. (*TLCD*).

[76] For a comparison of James Matheson's and William Jardine's respective response to what they felt as business betrayal, see also Letter **148**.

part of the cost, and you will perceive from the P. S. in our Circular of 9th Instant that your advice is literally complied with.[77]

The return of your Manila funds and *Messrs. Everett's*[78] is engaging our attention and shall have effect at the earliest possible moment, but while E. J. Coy's[79] Agents are making advances against shipments to the extent of two-thirds, it would be in vain to hope that any partner would accept advances from us of only a half to which you intimate you wish that we should limit them. I apprehend the only check we can apply is to be careful to avoid overvaluing, etc. at the low ebb to which prices have arrived and are likely to fall here, I should think there will be little or no risk.

We feel much obliged for the very handsome manner in which you agree to realize our bills against shipment for our constituents (passed through your hands as security) at any rate of commission we may deem reasonable. We readily, however, acquiesce in one per cent as you propose which will be charged on the amount we may draw for and not on the value of the goods pledged for our security, always supposing you are not called on to in any trouble or responsibility for the latter.[80]

Being so deeply interested, we naturally feel not a little solicitous as to the characters, which may be assigned to our Teas. In a pamphlet published by Mr. Travers[81] in 1834, it was it broadly stated that: 'in no precise opinion of quality have two of the trade ever yet agreed', and of this capriciousness we have had ample experience in common with our neighbours in no few instances of parts of the same chop being valued at the same sales at a difference of 30 or 40 per cent, while in many cases we saw a low charactered Tea fetch a higher price by a great deal than those classed as superior. It seems to be well ascertained that Tea is apt to go out of condition and change its appearance during the voyage. All these circumstances render the trade extremely precarious and it is out of the question that we should now be responsible for supposed mistakes in the selection of our taster. When in London I fancied I should trace a disposition in some of the Brokers to run down teas from our House, as a counteractive of which I came to an understanding (as you perhaps recollect) with *J. & R. Moffat*[82] that they would do all they could to prevent such a prejudice when it came under their notice. In this I

[77] Bankers' habit of tightening lending rules *after* financial crises rather than *before* is as old as the world of banking.

[78] Four letters from *Everett & Co.*, 'of New York and Boston' are listed in the *BI*.

[79] Neither E. J. Coy nor his agents were identified.

[80] The arrangement described in this paragraph is a virtual contract of exclusivity for *Jardine, Matheson & Co.'s* London agency business.

[81] Joseph Travers of *Joseph Travers & Sons*, one of the established London firms of tea brokers. (Six letters listed in the *BI*).

[82] On the Moffats, see above, Letter **111**, note 105.

have no doubt they will be well seconded through your influence[83] by the new firm of *Watkins, Smith & Hope*.[84]

I regret much to inform you that Mr. Saunders Keeting[85] died at Macao on the 21st Ultimo in circumstances so embarrassed, as to afford no hope of {recovering} the smallest dividend from his estate. His end was accelerated by the desperate state of his affairs, owing to reckless and injudicious speculation. It is a source of the sincerest concern to us that this loss should have occurred to you through our introduction. I was in hopes the hints I gave on the subject while in London would have prevented any bad Consequences, though at that time there was by no means such room for apprehension, as his subsequent {Career} gave rise to.

With kind regards to the members of your firm, I remain,

Yours very sincerely.

1838

151. Report of the East India and China Association in London to its members, January 2, 1838[1]

– China relations

'On the subject of our relations with China, Lord Palmerston gave an assurance that the 'suggestion of the Committee should have due attention in the consideration which His Majesty's Government were giving to the subject.' Amongst them was one for sending a Commercial Agent or Consul to Canton, to prevent, as far as practicable, the infraction, by British subjects, of the Chinese Laws.

Your Committee again took occasion to address his Lordship for information as to the appointment of Captain Elliot, R. N. to the situation of Deputy

[83] John Abel Smith's influence extended to all branches of business, not only banking, and both James Matheson and William Jardine were anxious to improve their knowledge of the tea trade and to establish their reputation as China's principal tea exporters.

[84] *Watkins, Smith & Hope*, 'Tea brokers, 133 Fenchurch Street'. (*TLCD*).

[85] On Mr. Saunders Keeting, see Letter **42**, note 37.

[1] This 28 page printed document, not counting two tables of 'Outward and Inward movements of ships from and to British ports, from and to Eastern destinations', contains paragraphs on the following topics, of which the above are extracts: 'Bohea tea-duty, Sugar Act, China relations, Cotton and Silk piece-goods, etc., Warehousing ports, Cotton, Roads, Madras, [Tea] Quarterly sales, Overland Mail, Remittances of the India Revenue.' The document was printed for the Association by Pelham Richardson, 23, Cornhill. The appended lists of Committee members of, and subscribers to, the Association are particularly interesting in that they comprise most British firms and individuals involved in the China trade a year before the start of the Opium War.

The same bundle of papers also contains a similar report for the year 1837. With only 20 pages plus two appendices, this earlier document is slightly thinner. Its title page reads: 'Report / of the / Committee of the London / EAST INDIA AND CHINA / ASSOCIATION / Presented to the General Meeting, / held at the *Jerusalem Coffee House* / January 3, 1837'. And at the bottom of the title page: 'London / Printed for the association by W. Marchant, / Ingram Court, Fenchurch Street.'

Superintendent, and were furnished a reply from Mr. Under-Secretary Backhouse,[2] of which the following is an extract:

'With reference to the suggestion made by the East-India and China Association, of the expedience of sending a Commercial Agent or Consul to Canton, I am desired by Lord Palmerston to observe to you, that the office of Chief Superintendent has been abolished, and that of the office of Third Superintendent has been changed into that of Deputy Superintendent, and that, by these changes in the establishment, the character of the Superintendent and of his Deputy have been placed more nearly upon the footing of those of a Consul and Vice-Consul.'[3]

A Bill was shortly after brought into the House of Commons authorizing Her Majesty to appoint a Consul-General, Consul, and Vice-Consul, or Officers, not exceeding three in number, or under any designation which Her Majesty may deem expedient, and with such powers and authorities as to her Majesty may seem meet, instead of or in addition to such Superintendents.' It was entitled 'A Bill to authorize the Establishing a Court or Courts, with Criminal, and Admiralty, and Civil Jurisdiction, in China; ' and was introduced into the House on the 27th June [1837], and passed to the Lords on the 3rd July, but it did not make further progress.

– Quarterly sales

'In compliance with a requisition from the Chairman of the Tea-Brokers, the propriety of Quarterly Sales, instead of eight in the year, was taken into consideration.

Among the reasons urged were, that the bringing of Teas at such short periods precluded the Dealers and Brokers from carefully examining them, and in most instances from making the requisite comparison as to quality and value; causing the rejection of great portions of each Sale, which were again brought forward, whereby the apparent magnitude was increased and prices depressed. And the Committee, after the fullest consideration, came to the Resolution, that it would be for the general benefit of the IMPORTERS, DEALERS, and all connected with the Tea Trade, that QUARTERLY SALES should be adopted.

– Overland Mail[4]

'The Association are aware of the disappointment that was felt at the delay which occurred in the receipt of the July, August, and September mails, and your Committee wrote in consequence to the Admiralty, Board of Control, and Lord

[2] *BHF* states that W. F. Strangeways was the Foreign Office Under Secretary at the time. There were in fact two Under Secretaries at the Foreign Office, though John Backhouse (1784–1845) was nominally an official in the excise department (*Oxford DNB*).

[3] These changes were more formal than substantial, and the bill mentioned in the next paragraph 'did not make further progress' than the House of Lords.

[4] For the 'overland' route, see above, Letter **149**, note 67.

Palmerston. His Lordship was asked, if, until the new regulations between this Government and the East-India Company had come into complete operation, a messenger might leave Malta with the mails through France on any occasion of their reaching that place after the steamer to Gibraltar had left; the reply was, that the establishment of Queen's messengers is too limited to permit the requisite number to be stationed at Malta for that purpose, and Sir John Barrow[5] stated that 'the Lords of the Admiralty were satisfied the regulations between the Government and the Company, when matured, would be found to answer in every respect ; and that the Government packets are to remain either at Alexandria or at Beyrouth fourteen out of every twenty-eight days, waiting the arrival of the mail from India.'

This will prevent similar delays in the future, and tend to that regularity without which the arrangement cannot be considered as complete.

Respecting letters *to* India, the Committee wrote to the Post-Master-General with reference to an order issued the 14th September, altering the day for making up the mails; 'the Earl of Lichfield[6] regretted the inconvenience that may result from the new arrangement, stating that as they had been decided upon by the Board of Admiralty and the East-India Company they could not now be altered.'

But the Committee are not without hopes of prevailing upon the Honourable Court and the Government to adopt further arrangements, so that the account of stocks and deliveries, so important in all mercantile operations, which are not made up till the end of each month, may be forwarded a few days afterwards.[7]

[5] Sir John Barrow: second secretary at the Admiralty. (Fay, *Opium War*, p. 215).

[6] The Earl of Lichfield had replaced the Marquis of Conyngham as Postmaster General in the Melbourne administration on 22 May 1835. (*BHF*).

[7] List of the East India and China Association Committee Members:

G. G. de H. Larpent , Esq., Chairman, Archibald Hastie, Esq., M.P., Deputy Chairman, Joshua Bates, Esq., Robert Brown, Esq., C. D. Bruce, Esq., W. T. Copeland, Esq., M.P., John Cryder, Esq., B. D. Colvin, Esq., R. Durant, Esq., W. E. Ferrers, Esq , J. H. Gledstanes, Esq., Samuel Gregson, Esq., John Hodgson, Esq., William Lyall, Esq., James Malcolmson, Esq., John Horsley Palmer, Esq., Robert Small, Esq., William Scott, Esq., John Sanderson, Esq., William James Thompson, Esq., Richard Twining, Esq., James Walkinshaw, Esq., Thomas Weeding, Esq.

The document also lists the 1837 subscribers to the Association:

A: *Arbuthnot & Latham, John Atkins & Son*, H. J. Albrecht, Esq., William Anderson, sen., Esq., Thomas Asmore, Esq.

B: *Barclay, Brothers & Co., Baring, Brothers & Co., Barber, Neate & Co.*, G. *and J. Brown & Co., R & B. Brown & Co*, John Bagshaw, Esq. M.P., Capt. James Barber, Henry Blanshard, Esq., W.Burnie, Esq.

C: *Cheape & Leslie, Clarence & Franks, Sir C. Cockerell, Bart & Co., J. Cockburn & Co., Copeland, Barnes & Co., Crawford, Colvin & Co., Curtis & Harvey*, Charles Compton, jun., Esq., Alexander Crowe, Esq.

D: *Dallas & Coles, Daniell & Dickenson, C. Devaux & Co., Douglas, Anderson & Co., D. Dunbard & Sons, Durant & Co.*

E: *Evans, Foster & Langton, Ewbank & Cordes*, Robert Eglinton, Esq., H. Elias, Esq.

152. James Matheson in Canton to Robert Smith[8] in Bombay,

9 January 1838

My dear Smith,

Though late, I hope you will not consider me the less sincere in taking this opportunity to thank you for your favour of 1st July which reached me in due course; giving cover to an extract from Mr. Macvicar's private correspondence which proved extremely interesting; as did the similar communications which Burn[9] was kind enough to send me from time to time. I trust we have now learned the worst of the sad crisis,[10] in which commercial affairs have become involved, and that future advices will have the more pleasing object of communicating the progress of the gradual amendment which may be looked for.

As Alexander [Matheson] has been tolerably punctual in writing to you by almost every conveyance, and has, I concluded, mentioned whatever of interest has been passing here, I have deferred addressing you from time to time, in the hope of being able to announce the opening of the Silk market. And great, I assure you, is our disappointment that your limits put it out of our power to carry into

---

F: *Finlay, Hodgson & Co., Fletcher, Alexander & Co., Forbes, Forbes & Co., Forman & Hadow, J. G & W. S. Fry & Co.*

G: *Gardner & Urquhart, Gledstanes & Co., Gregson, Melville & Co., Green, Wilson & Burton,* James Goddard, Esq., J. G. Gordon, Esq., R. M. Grindlay, Esq., John Groves, Esq.

H: *W. J. Hall & Co., W. Harper & Co., Hayter & Howell, Hodgson & Drake, J. P. Howard & Co., Hulbert, Layton & Co., Hunter, Gouger & Co.,* Archibald Hastie, Esq., M.P., Thomas Heath, Esq.

I—J: *Jamieson, Brothers & Co., Johnson & Renny,* W. Ireland, Esq.

K: Thomas Kilby, Esq., Henry Kirk, Esq.

L: *Larkins & Co., John Locke & Co., Lyall, Brothers & Co., Lindo & De Castro.*

M: *Magniac, Smith & Co., Marjoribanks & Ferrers, Moffatt & Sons, Charles Moss & Co., Morrison, Cryder & Co.,* John MacKenzie, Esq., Thomas Merry, Esq., George Moffat, Esq.

N: *Norton, Kilburn & Co.*

P—Q: *Palmer, Mackillop, Dent & Co., Patry & Pasteur, Phillipps & Tiplady, Jonas Phillips & Son, John Pirie & Co., Palmer, Delafosse & Co., J. & B. Pearse & Co.*

R: *Rawson, Norton & Co., Reid, Irving & Co., Rickards, Little & Co., Ripley, Brothers & Brown,* J. M. Richardson, Esq.

S: *Sanderson, Fox & Co., Scott, Bell & Co., Small, Colqhoun & Co., Smith, Hyde & Lennox, Smith, Goodhall & Reeves, T. W. Smith & Co.,* Simon Samuel, Esq., William Short, Esq., John Straith, Esq., C. Sutherland, Esq.

T: *Thorpe & Rogers, Trueman & Cook, Twining & Co.,* Capt. H. Templer, William J. Thompson, Esq., William Townend, Esq.

V: *Varnham & Delafosse.*

W: *Walkinshaw & Co., White & Batt,* William Watts, Esq., Thomas Weeding, Esq., Money Wigram, Esq.. R.C. Wyllie, Esq.

[8] Robert Smith was not identified. This is the only reference to him in this collection. He was not listed in the *EIRB* as doing business in Bombay, nor is he listed individually in the *BI*. The form of address used by James Matheson suggests the two correspondents were on friendly terms. The reference to 'two lacs of rupees' (200,000 dollars) makes him in any case a large operator.

[9] For Mr. Burn, see above Letter **35**, note 69.

[10] 'The sad crisis': the failure of the London banks in June 1837.

effect your views for being interested in the article. The calculations in our official letter will however show you this was impossible.

Being now free to return your funds to Bombay we shall spare no endeavours to do so, with as little delay as possible, in the most beneficial manner; and I hope with the interest we shall be able to credit, you will at least sustain no loss in the business.

Since we agreed with Burn to receive from you as far as 4 Lacs of Rupees per annum by payments to *Remington & Co.* in order to facilitate your remittances to China, circumstances are so entirely reversed, that in the contemplation of your possibly not desiring a continuance of the arrangement, we were induced some time ago to request *Remington & Co.* not to draw the amount unless you preferred paying it, for your own convenience, which alone it is our wish that you should study on the occasion; unless indeed the prices of the drug should rule too high to authorise their purchasing on your account, in which case they will not require any funds. On the whole as far as we can at present foresee it seems more than probable that circumstances will occasion our above named arrangement with Burn being in abeyance at least for the present season, and it will rest with you to say whether or not it will have effect in time to come.

Our drug market has undergone a complete revolution within the last twelve months.[11] There is no such thing now in operation as a regular smuggling boat; and the Mandarin boats paid to prevent smuggling which were formerly most accommodating on being paid for their services are now afraid to pursue such a course. The Viceroy having been threatened by the Emperor with personal punishment if detected in making false reports respecting the outside ships and the importation of the drug, he has issued such order to the commanders of said boats as render them of no use in the delivery of the drug from foreign vessels.

[11] This 'complete revolution' in the opium market stemmed from the fact that, as soon as he had received instructions from Emperor Tao-kung in the autumn of 1836 to 'cut off the opium trade at its Canton source', Viceroy Teng T'ing-chen starting sending offenders to prison. The effect of these repressive measures was to deter the Chinese 'fast crabs' (opium rowing boats) from taking delivery of the drug, and surveillance mandarin boats from turning a blind eye on offenders against suitable payment. (Polachek, *Inner Opium War*, p. 125).

The consequence was that the Chinese 'smugglers' (i.e. the intermediaries taking delivery of the drug from the receiving ships and taking it to Chinese wholesalers and consumers) virtually disappeared from Lintin and Whampoa waters. As a result, some private traders, British, European and Parsee, started doing what they had never done before: they replaced the Chinese 'smugglers' and delivered the drug to Whampoa themselves. This was highly disapproved of by both James Matheson and William Jardine who had until then reserved the term 'smuggling' for this delivery trade and now called it 'disgusting'. See Letter **160:** 'The expense and risk of bringing the drug to Whampoa is very considerable and the trade is a very disgusting one'. (William Jardine to Jamsetjee Jeejebhoy).

The paradox was that the year 1838 turned out to be the most lucrative in the decade for the operators rich and bold enough to continue it, in particular Jamsetjee Jeejebhoy and *Jardine, Matheson & Co.* Profit rose to a previously unheard-of record of 200 dollars per chest. (See in particular Letter **163**, second paragraph and Letter **166**, last paragraph).

The limited deliveries now effected here are entirely in decked European sailing boats which convey the drug to various points on the neighbouring coast and islands and as high up the river even as Canton, for which latter purpose several ships have brought supplies of it to Whampoa to the great alarm of the Hong Merchants. It is even said that some of the Parsees retail it from their factories. All this however is to a very [small extent] and is tolerated only on account of the Viceroy being afraid to interfere with the property of foreigners. Were it not for this we should not be able to get on half as well as we now do, though that is far from satisfactory. Such is the true state of affairs, and it is evident such a system cannot continue for any length of time, whatever the changes may be. A change must take place, but of what nature, it is impossible to say. One thing is self-evident: the drug must be purchased at very low prices in India to give the most distant chance of a profit in this country. While a continuance of violent and determined measure on the part of the Chinese authorities steadily persevered in, may lead to ruinous losses.

Malwa may now be freely purchased at 440 and 435 dollars a chest. The stock on hand is unprecedently large for the season of the year.[12] And we are forcing sales in every direction here and on the East Coast.

The only cotton sale we have for some time made of any importance is 4,414 Bales and 288 half Bales *ex Earl Clare*, at the miserably low price of eight Taels per picul; but low as the rate is, the purchaser has still about 3,000 Bales on hand for which he cannot obtain the price he bought at. Under these circumstances it is impossible to force sales, unless at prices still more ruinous than those already obtained; and it is questionable if sales to any extent, could be effected on any terms whatever, as we are now within 17 days of the Chinese New Year.

It must be superfluous to inculcate great caution in purchasing cotton on your side. The Chinese appear to be now suffering from the Commercial distress that has pervaded all the rest of the world; and prices are likely to rule low during the whole of the approaching season.

The Exchange with England is 4 shillings and 5 pence to 4 shillings and 6 pence per dollar and the East India's Company's Agents have reduced their rate for advances from 4 shillings and 7 pence to 4 shillings and 6 pence, at which they have hitherto advanced very little. Bills are so scarce that the smallest symptom of a demand for them is sufficient to induce the drawers to contemplate a further

[12] At the beginning of January 1838, the firm's stocks of opium stood at 1,182 chests. This compared with 536 chests at the same time in 1837 and a deficiency of 25 chests in 1836. But, remarkably, thanks to the new technique of selling opium in very large wholesale batches (see below, Letter **155**), the firm sold 1,657 chests in January 1838, against 42 chests in January 1837 and 308 in January 1838. When the sales of the months exceeded the stock at the beginning of the month plus the new consignments received, (as was the case in January 1838) this meant that the firm had to buy opium locally (usually from Parsee traders) to make up for the deficiency. The management of the opium stocks was under the efficient supervision of Henry Wright. (*JMArch.*, A7-78).

reduction to 4 shillings and 4 pence, so that in order to get them at any tolerable rate, we are obliged to remain very quiet, and avoid enquiries on the subject.

There are few orders for Teas or Silk unless at rates too low to admit of purchases being made at prevailing prices and we have every reason to believe the Season's shipments of both articles will prove moderate, say, of teas, not much more than 20 millions pounds, [of] Nankin Silk about 5,000 Bales. Both however would no doubt be increased were favourable accounts to reach us from England.

The general quality of the Silk is more mixed than in any previous Season, not excepting even the last; which makes the execution of orders extremely difficult, without the possibility of giving satisfaction to those who expect or require good qualities only. And of all our Correspondents I am sorry to say there are none whom we find it so *absolutely impossible* to satisfy in this respect as your Agents, my good friends in Austin Friars.[13]

Parts of Chops received without objections and sold at fair prices by others are sure in the hands of their brokers to be pronounced trash or something not much better. Why, we cannot devine, but such is the fact.

The *Edinburgh* has commenced loading and we hope to get her away full in about five weeks. The *Camden* belonging to our friend Captain Larkins despairing of a cargo for England is up for Madras.

With kind remembrances to Mr. {Sonnenkalb}[14], I remain, my dear Smith, sincerely yours.

153. James Matheson in Canton to John Abel Smith, MP, in London,

23 January 1838[15]

My dear Sir,

In reference to the accompanying communication from our Firm to yours respecting Mr. Macvicar's Commission account with us, I venture to write a few lines to your individual address as we find considerable difficulty in expressing ourselves, as we should wish, in the scope of a mere official letter.

In the first place we shall feel obliged by your submitting our accompanying letter with its enclosures to your legal adviser, that he may take care they do not commit us in any manner which may prove inconvenient. With his sanction, we request the favour of your delivering the letter to Mr. Macvicar; but if disapproved of by your legal adviser, its purport only should be communicated.

Our feelings towards Mr. Macvicar, as we have stated to your Firm, have been always of a friendly nature and it is with considerable regret that, in consequence of the line of conduct he has adopted, we find ourselves compelled, in self

[13] Probably *Dallas & Coles*, a London agency firm with offices at 29 Austin Friars, or possibly *Fletcher, Alexander & Co.* (*EIRD*).

[14] Mr. Sonnenkalb was not identified.

[15] The Letter is marked '*confidential*'.

defense, to set bounds to the liberality which our good will would otherwise have dictated.

It is impossible for us to foresee what turn the discussions in which he has involved us at home may be destined to assume; but should they result as favourably for us as we have a right to expect; should Mr. Macvicar have desisted from his unfriendly proceedings,[16] and conducted himself so as, in your opinion, to deserve any consideration on our part; should he also have accounted for our consignments and honoured our bills of last year, payable to your Firm for 5,008 pounds sterling, we request the favour of your exercising such measure of liberality towards him as you may deem right. Were it not for the reasons we have stated to your Firm, we should have appropriated to Mr Macvicar the 70 Bales Tsatlee Silk marked '*JM&Co.*' per *Lady Macnaughten*, for which we have sent you bills of Lading and Invoice amounting to Spanish dollars 25,000.

In any case, *unless you see strong reasons to the contrary*, we should wish you to hand over to Mr. Macvicar 14 Bales of this Silk, being about the amount of one per cent to which he is entitled on the Invoice value of consignments to us, from his friends, and which we feel disposed to give up to him, by way of maintenance, without reference to his share of liability for bad debts. If his necessities require further aid, and you consider him deserving of it, we authorize your appropriating to him such further portion of the above Silk, or a corresponding amount of money as you may consider advisable, acting for us, as you may think we should ourselves be inclined to do under the circumstances.[17]

We continue to receive consignments, on a limited scale, from three of Mr. Macvicar's friends, viz—Mr. George Jackson, Manchester; *Messrs. Garnett & Horsfalls*, Clitheroe; and Mr. Miles Rodgett, Preston;[18] besides the consignments of the ship *Edinburgh*. Mr. Macvicar share of Commission on this will be comparatively inconsiderable. It is right however you should be aware of his confidence being so far continued to us, in order that the circumstance may have all the weight in his favour to which you may consider it entitled.

If our intercourse with Mr. Macvicar is to go on, I think you will concur with us in opinion that it must be on a totally different footing from the past,[19] and with

[16] The term used here and the legal care with which *Jardine, Matheson & Co.* was now handling its communications with John Macvicar suggest that the latter was contemplating or threatening legal action. No direct evidence of legal action, however, was found in the correspondence.

[17] A good example of what James Matheson and Willian Jardine conceived of as the best kind of 'instructions' between a party and his agent.

[18] For *Garnett & Horsefall*, see above, Letter **46**, note 67. Only 2 letters by George Jackson are listed in the *BI*, and only 8 from Miles Rodgett (although there are several from *Rodgett Brothers*).

[19] The 'intercourse' with Mr Macvicar did not go on for much longer. By July 1838, six months after this letter was written, John Macvicar was replaced by 'Mr Anderson' as the firm's agent for British manufactured goods. See Letter **163**.

a stipulation for his abstaining from the extensive liabilities and speculations in which he has been hitherto concerned.

May I ask the favour of your telling him that want of time only prevents my writing to him, which I shall certainly do by the next ship.

I remain, my dear Sir,

Yours very sincerely,

154. James Matheson in Canton to John Macvicar in Manchester,
24 January 1838

My dear Macvicar,

The detention of the *Kyd* for an hour or two enables me to address a few lines to you, although from the business of the period allowed me and the multiplicity of other affairs claiming my attention, they will be scarcely more than an apology for a letter.

Since our official letter respecting the *Edinburgh*, I am happy to say 4 Chops more have been sent to her, making in all 20, while six are ready to follow immediately after the holidays.[20] So that we consider her early despatch as now secure.

I have to thank you for your various favors of 30th November received 24th May; 30th April received 29th August; 31st May received 11th October; 26th June received 21st November, the last accompanying 30 engravings of my portrait. And while I beg you to accept my grateful acknowledgements for this flattering though I fear unmerited mark of distinction and regard, I cannot but feel extremely sorry that under the circumstances of the case you should not have paused before giving effect to the plan. I remember you used to speak of it as a speculation that would pay its own expenses, but I fear it will be an addition to the other speculations which are now so rife. The engraving seems to convey a very accurate representation of the miserable looks and miserable health which characterized the latter half of my stay in England, but I cannot say the associations it suggests are on that account at all pleasing. I hope, however, you will consider me entitled to claim from you the purchase of the plate and copyright which pray put to my debit or rather that of the House.

I shall request our mutual friend Mr. John Abel Smith to arrange for the transfer of the Bank shares you have allotted me, which had better perhaps be placed in the name of my brother, Duncan Matheson, unless they involve any risk to which he would be averse; and should this be the case they had better perhaps be sold. We write very fully to Mr. Smith and to his Firm respecting business matters connected with you.

Much do I regret the tone which you have thought proper to assume in your correspondence with our House. You cannot feel surprised that it should

[20] 'The holiday': the Chinese New Year. (See above, Letter **81**, note 3).

occasion some abeyance of the feeling of cordiality which one and all of us desire to entertain for you and would still entertain did your line of procedure permit.[21]

Begging to be kindly remembered to Mrs. Macvicar, I remain,

Sincerely yours,

155. William Jardine in Canton to Captain Jauncey on the Coast,

24th January 1838

My dear Sir,

We have instructed Captain Parry to put on board the *Governor Findlay* on account of Manwa 250 chests of Malwa,[22] and 20 chests of Patna sold to him by the House and 4 chests of Malwa of his own. Of these he has paid for 70 chests of Malwa and 10 chests of Patna out of which he can deliver 75 chests without paying one dollar. The other 5 chests being left on board as security for the ship's expenses.

On clearing the balance of his Malwa, he must pay previous to delivery 325 dollars per chest; if in Sycee of 50 Taels per price, at a premium of three (3) per cent; if in gold bars of about 10 Taels each and 86–88 touch on the average at the

[21] The whole Letter is a model of how to combine frank criticism and quiet urbanity. In this, James Matheson showed himself to be not only a master businessman but a master communicator. Compare this with William Jardine's moral outrage and frontal attack on John Macvicar (Letter **127**, 2nd paragraph).

[22] The sale of 250 chests of Malwa to the Chinese opium dealer Manwa referred to here is an example of the important changes which occurred in the drug market at about that time. As a single sale, 250 chests, (not far from 100,000 dollars), was a very large sale indeed, and as such a novelty. In the absence of local Chinese 'smugglers' to transport the opium from the receiving ships to the consumers, the smallest European and Parsee merchants had taken the 'revolutionary' step of delivering the drug to Whampoa themselves. (See above, Letter **152**, note 11). The large dealers like *Jardine, Matheson & Co.* however, resorted to sales tactics much more in keeping with their sizeable stocks and existing opium fleet. In fact, they started chartering their vessels to their wholesale Chinese customers, like Manwa and Tonshing mentioned in this Letter. Instead of haphazardly sending their ships to semi-permanent stations along the coast where they hoped to finds customers, they waited for large orders to come through the Chinese brokers who requested the ships to be sent to specific destinations, taking on for their own account the ships' expenses, freighting and, increasingly, insurance. Very often, as in the transactions described in this Letter, the Chinese Broker came on board the ship for the duration of the delivery expedition. Thus the firm's opium fleet supplemented the Chinese 'smugglers' fleets which had often been destroyed for fear of the Viceroy's enforced repression.

These large new individual sales were all contracted for in Canton, and it was William Jardine who personally centralized and supervised all the movements of stocks and ships. As an aide-memoire for transactions which he agreed with the Chinese brokers and which were increasingly complex and tailor-made, he used a 150 page leather-bound note-book described in the Archive as 'William Jardine's Day Book', (*JMArch.*, A7-48). In this book, he entered all the sale contracts which he made from the the Spring of 1837 to his departure from Canton in January 1839. The contracts are detailed and meticulous, with important or unusual specifications underlined in red, although the hand is often hurried. The terms of the contract were then promptly sent on (with all its details, as in this Letter) to the opium fleet officers available and best suited to carry out the delivery missions.

rate of 195 dollars per bar. If you are detained more than one month, receive 10 dollars per chest extra to cover additional charges.

Tonshing has on board 200 chests of Malwa and 20 of Patna. He has deposited 10,000 dollars to cover charges and that sum is to remain till the last. You must receive previous to delivery 555 dollars per chest in Sycee or gold bars on the terms specified above. If detained longer than a month, charge ten (10) dollars per chest extra to cover the charges. The same party has charge of both lots of the drug. Treat them well and keep them in good humour.

You will of course do everything in your power to inform us what is going on and if you fancy a few chests of the drug and a few bags of saltpetre are likely to be disposed of, you can take them with you from the *Lady Hayes* and *Hercules*.

We shall send a vessel up with an additional supply of drug on account of the same party, you having only half their purchases on board. You may possibly have opportunities of sending letters to Captain Rees who will have opportunities of forwarding them to us.

With best wishes for a pleasant voyage, health and prosperity, I remain, my dear Sir,

Yours sincerely,

156. James Matheson in Canton to John Abel Smith, MP, in London,
12 February 1838

My dear Sir,

we have just received intimation from our Tea inspector, Mr. James Warly Smith,[23] of his wish to relinquish our employ and set up as a taster for the public on the conclusion of his engagement with us at the end of the present Season; it being rumoured that Mr. Layton, who is at present the only public taster intends giving up acting in that capacity. Knowing the warm interest which you and your partner take in the efficiency of our Firm, in all its departments, we lose no time in bringing this circumstance to your notice, and in laying before you our views for supplying Mr. Smith's place, in the assurance that you will kindly afford us your aid in carrying them into effect. I may premise that Mr. Smith will leave us with the kindliest feelings of good will, and with a strong desire to promote our interests, which he thinks he will have opportunities of doing to a considerable extent though no longer in our employ.

We always intended as his eventual successor, a nephew of Mr. Jardine[24] about 20 years old, who has been bringing up to the business since 1835 with *Messrs.*

[23] James Warly Smith: see above, Letter **106**, note 56.

[24] David Jardine, the second son of William Jardine's brother, David ('of Muirhousehead').

Styan & Son,[25] Broker, and we learn with tolerable success. But the vacancy is occurring so much sooner than we expected that we are doubtful whether he is not too young to undertake the office even with the assistance which Mr. Smith would afford him. With this feeling we shall be obliged if you will kindly send for the youngster and form your opinion as to his qualification from conversation with himself, as well as enquiring of Mr. Styan, determining accordingly whether to send him on to us immediately, or detaining him in London for the acquisition of further experience. Even in the event of his coming, however as it requires some local experience, to become habituated to this market, we should not be averse to have the co-operation of your young friend Mr. J. R. Nicholson[26] for one or two seasons, should you find him inclined to afford it, as he is likely to be coming, at all events, on his father's affairs, in which case we should cheerfully grant him a gratuity for his services equivalent to the salary which Mr. Smith received on first coming out, say five hundred pounds (500) per annum. In any event we trust that you will be able to arrange for letting us have the services of either the one or the other of the parties named. For so short a time as will elapse before young Jardine must be fully qualified (if not so already) we scarcely deem it necessary to authorize your engaging a stranger for us, more especially as the want of local experience would greatly impair his usefulness for the first season.

With this explanation we leave the affair in your hands, begging you to excuse the trouble. I enclose a letter for Mr. Jardine's nephew and remain, my dear Sir,

Yours very sincerely.

157. William Jardine in Canton to Captain Rees on the Coast aboard the *Austin*, 13 February 1838

My dear Sir,

Being in daily expectation of the *Red Rover* from Calcutta, and having determined on sending her up to you immediately, I avail myself of a spare moment to acknowledge your letter of the 6th February per *Aurelia*; and inform you what has been doing here, since the date of our last advices, the 24th ultimo.

The prices at which you were selling are sufficiently remunerating when compared with those that prevail here at the present moment; and if the old Patna and Benares could be sold in larger quantities by reducing the rates 20 or 30 dollars per chest, it would be desirable, as the large supply of old and new drug, about to arrive here, must, I think, reduce prices still lower.

[25] *T. W. and T Styan & Co.*, 'Tea brokers, 12 Little Tower Street, Eastsheap'. (*TLCD*). At a later date, A. G. H. Styan was active in Shanghai. (*BI*).

[26] Probably John Nicholson's son. See Letter **79**, note 108.

Our arrangements with the party for whom Captain Jauncey has been sent to the North Eastward[27] is of such a nature that very much depends on the success of their sales and we naturally feel a little anxious on the subject. We have sent on about one half of the quantity sold to them and do not intend sending on the other half or any part of it, till we hear of the sales, to a certain extent having been effected and the money received on board the *Governor Findlay*. At the same time we should wish [you] to have a supply of Malwa nearer at hand than Lintin, or even Namoa,[28] and I shall therefore send a supply of that article on the *Red Rover*, which we shall place at your disposal or at the disposal of Captain Jauncey, as circumstances may require. It is no doubt a very desirable object to open communications with the Chusan group[29] for the disposal of the drug and we would willingly make some sacrifice to accomplish this business in the way we wish; but to make the arrangement complete, we should be able to obtain Nankin Raw Silk in return for the drug. The Silk to be sent on board of one of your vessels in the vicinity of Poo-to.[30]

If the Season is a mild one the *Rover* will have little difficulty in beating up from your station to Poo-to; and should it prove unusually boisterous, she can make herself useful in your vicinity, till the winds moderate. We leave these details in your hands with perfect confidence that every thing will be done that can be done, for the general good; but we shall be anxious to hear that the drug sent out by Manwa and Tongshing[31] has been commenced upon; as I have not much confidence in their arrangements though they are very sanguine that every thing will be succeed according to their wishes, and expectations. The penalty on their part is small, and they may realize a very handsome profit.

Prices have declined here since the date of my last advices on the 24th ultimo. Malwa may be purchased at Macao or Lintin at 410–405 dollars, Patna at 520–510 dollars, and Benares at 425–415 dollars, per chest, without the most distant chance of improvement. The new Patna will open at a rate somewhat in conformity with the above quotations, particularly if prices ruled low at the first sale in Calcutta; which we suspect they have; but this we shall ascertain in a few days.

With this information before you we leave you to regulate prices according to your own views on the spot, and look forward to the result with perfect confidence.

Believe me, my dear Sir,

Yours sincerely.

[27] For Captain Jauncey mission to the 'North Eastward', see above, Letter **155**.

[28] Namoa: see Letter **76**, note 88.

[29] The 'Chusan group': probably a number of opium dealers operating in the Chusan islands (100 miles south of Shanghai and 900 miles north of Canton).

[30] Poo-to or Puto : one of the small islands west of Chusan.

[31] Sometimes spelt 'Tonshing'.

158. Warren Delano[32] in Canton to James Matheson in Canton,

16 February 1838[33]

My dear Sir,

Having communicated with Mr.Sturgis[34] at Macao I am now enabled to acknowledge receipt of your note of the 9th Instant respecting the expedition per *Griffon* to Mexico.

The Invoice proposed to be shipped will be made up of:

30 peculs Sewing Silk		
10 peculs of loose Silk		
15,000 Crape Sashes or Scarfs		
300 pieces Satin 1/1/4 [ ] wide, [ ]		
800 Crape Shawls embroided	at	6.
800 ditto	at	10.
400 ditto	at	20.
100 ditto	at	40.
a few camphor trunks		
[ ] 100 peculs		

The whole to cash about 100,000 dollars to go consigned to *Messrs. Rascon Castairos & Co.*,[35] {with} the sum of 8,000 dollars to be paid as freight thereon. Commission in Canton 2 per cent, and in Mexico 5 per cent on Sales. Freight on treasure from Mexico, as customary, 2 per cent.

It is intended if possible, that the transaction shall be closed and the proceeds of goods brought back by the *Griffon*; in case this cannot be accomplished, the balance of proceeds of your interest of 15,000 dollars may be paid on to your friends, *Messrs. Barron Forbes & Co.*,[36] or otherwise as you may order.

With reference to Mr. W. James Sturgis acceptance of Mr. J. P. Sturgis[37] bill for the 15,000 dollars, I will explain the wishes of the former to you in person tomorrow. The entire 30,000 dollars to be insured at your Office, and your advance not to be called for until after Shipment of your merchandise.

I remain,

Yours truly,

[32] Warren Delano: a partner of *Russell & Co.* in Canton. Warren Delano became the head of the firm in 1840. (Hunter, *The Fan Kwae at Canton*, p. 96). His daughter was the mother of US President, Franklin Delano Roosevelt.

[33] A related letter, (*JMArch.*, Reel 28, Canton, P. 127), written in James Matheson's hand, bears the annotation: 'Respecting our interest for JW (possibly 'James Walkinshaw') in the cargo of the *Griffon*'.

[34] For James Perkins Sturgis, see above, Letter **65**, note 4.

[35] *Rascon Castairos & Co.*: one letter only from Macao listed in the *BI*, and none from Mexico.

[36] Captain R. B. Forbes and John Forbes had been Canton partners of *Russell & Co.* In America, the Barrons and the Forbes formed an agency house together.

[37] W. James Sturgis: a non-identified relation of James Perkins Sturgis.

159. James Matheson in Canton to George Moffat in London,
28 February 1838

My dear Moffat,

I am ashamed that I should have allowed so long an interval to elapse before writing to you, especially when I look at your numerous, kind and interesting letters lying before me, the last dated from Hamburg, informing me of your having set out on a short continental tour and having admitted a partner in your concern, which I was sincerely rejoiced to learn, for I could not help fancying that you were more devoted to the desk than was advisable on the score of your health. I hope it will be only the prelude to your selection of another partner of a different gender, which I consider a very indispensable addition to the arrangements.

Be assured I should not have been so long without writing were it not that I was desirous of being able to make some return in kind for your valuable information. But time slipped on without finding myself in a position to satisfy my wishes on this head, and the more the delay, the greater was the difficulty I experienced in breaking the spell by which I had allowed our correspondence to be interrupted. In truth, I fear I cannot avoid pleading guilty to great remissness but I should be sorry indeed if you fancied this could arise from anything like indifference to your friendship; for the case is very much the reverse and there is none of my English friendships I look back to with livelier feeling of gratitude and satisfaction then your own.

The fact is your trade in tea dealing is the most complete mystery I ever had to do with,[38] and it seems quite in vain for an uninitiated person like me to attempt to master all its difficulties and incongruities. I regret therefore that I must despair of being able to write anything on the subject that would be likely to interest you, beyond what is contained in our official circular. It is fortunate for your market that the speculative rage received by the late intelligence from England and fostered by the Company's advances is kept within wholesome bounds by the impossibility of obtaining tonnage. This check can however be but of temporary operation, and I should think about May 1839 there is some risk that you may begin to experience the effect of an oversupply.

Now that the commercial difficulties are over one cannot but wonder what can have been the cause of the commercial body allowing themselves to be thrown into a state of such serious alarm, to the sacrifice of so vast an amount of property; while it would appear that the four leading American houses whose large dealings were the chief cause of the panic, are likely after all to turn solvent.[39] I am glad to say we shall have suffered comparatively little, as far as we can judge

[38] A theme often touched upon, when the partners were writing about the post-1834 Canton tea trade.
[39] This applied to at least *Timothy Wiggins & Co.* and *George Wildes & Co.* (See above, Letter **145**, note 48).

from present appearances. I am much obliged for your *private* hint about our Manchester friend. I hope he is quite safe and his strict honor may, I believe, be implicitly relied on, but our relations with him which are now likely to cease, were not of a nature to subject us to any harm from whatever may have happened to him.

I regret much your limits are too low to enable our doing anything at present under your instructions lately received. You may rely on their being attended to at the proper time. Mr. Layton is about to retire from the office of public inspector, when our Mr. Smith will set up for himself as his successor, still continuing on the most friendly footing with ourselves, though he will no longer be in our employ. We have taken measures for the continued efficiency of this department of our business, and I hope the experience we have had will go far to enable our avoiding past causes of complaint, as far as it is in the nature of things to do so.

Mr. Jardine and his nephew Andrew Jardine desire their kind remembrances. Pray offer mine to your mother and brother, and always believe me, my dear Moffat, yours very sincerely,

160. William Jardine in Canton, to Jamsetjee Jejeebhoy in Bombay,

13 March 1838

My dear Sir,

The *Anna Robertson* being under despatch for Madras I have much pleasure in availing myself of the conveyance to acknowledge your favor of the 31 December, thinking possible letters by her may reach Bombay before those per *Rob Roy* via Calcutta.

Many thanks for the enclosed letter from *Messrs. Forbes, Forbes & Co.*,[40] respecting Raw Silk, which is satisfactory as evincing a disposition on their part to hold on for improvement in prices, and I am fully persuaded they will not be disappointed, provided they hold out till the very short supply of this season is known in England. Parties there will become less scrupulous about quality [as] the stock on hand diminishes. When Tsatlee was at 25 and 26 shillings [per pound] advancing, the Brokers and Speculators purchased for arrival by the Bill of Lading, without Muster, and without Invoice! But the moment prices began to decline—the supply being large—much silk of very fair quality was pronounced to be trash. The Tea Brokers were equally inconsistent in the characters given to many of the Black Teas: we have many instances of Congo Tea valued at 11 pence and 1 shilling per pound selling at one shilling and ten pence and one shilling and eleven pence within two months of the time they were so valued, while the rise

[40] *Forbes, Forbes & Co.*: 'East India agents, 9 King William Street, City'. (*TLCD*). The firm was Jamsetjee Jeejebhoy's principal agent in London. Letter **163** below shows how *Magniac Smith & Co.* started competing with *Forbes, Forbes & Co.* for a piece of Jamsetjee Jeejebhoy's London business.

on the Market was only 4 to 6 pence per pound. I note what you say respecting remittances to England, and have only to express my extreme regret that the oversight should have occurred[41]—having on a former occasion explained the manner in which the misunderstanding originated.

Your remittances of this Season have had and still have our most anxious attention. I must refer you to the correspondence of the Firm for the progress made assuring you that the difficulties we have had to overcome have been formidable, and the source of much perplexity to us all.

I am aware you will feel disappointed at not receiving a large amount of Bills on England as desired for the proceeds of your Cotton per *Earl of Clare*, but such has been and still is the {scarcity} of Bills that there was no possibility of accomplishing this ; and at the same time making good our heavy engagements on your account to *Messrs. Forbes, Forbes and & Co.* It is true we might latterly have remitted to these gentlemen in Teas purchased at prices likely to pay, had freight been procurable ; but this was not the case. As out remittances to these gentlemen were then so much more backward than was agreeable to us, or contemplated by you, we naturally felt anxious to adopt every possible means for putting you in funds, and therefore shipped on your account by the *Water Witch* to Calcutta a portion of Sycee that arrived too late for the *Mangles*, in hopes that you can have no difficulty in drawing against it advantageously. But if you should not approve of this proceeding we shall of course hold ourselves responsible for what the Sycee would have realized had it been sent to Bombay.[42]

Our *Opium Market* has fluctuated very little since the date of last advices, the 28th ultimo, particularly at Whampoa ; while along the Coast prices have been better maintained, but the deliveries have been on a reduced scale.

In Macao Malwa fell to 345 dollars per chest, and several hundreds of chests were sent out to Lintin, when the prices, of all kinds, improved a little and may now be quoted as follows. Old Patna: 545; New: 430–420; Old Benares: 440–450; and Malwa: 400–410 per chest. New Benares is seldom inquired after, and the New Patna is in little demand.

At Whampoa prices rule from 20 to 50 dollars per chest higher, while at Lintin Old Patna is procurable at 480, Benares at 400, and Malwa at 380 to 390 dollars per chest.

The expense and risk of bringing the drug to Whampoa is very considerable, and the trade is a very disgusting one.[43] But we must persevere till some change of system is adopted by the Authorities.

[41] The nature of the 'oversight' was not traced.

[42] Given the 'formidable' difficulty of remitting to London, which Jamesetjee Jeejebhoy needed in order to be able to obtain advances from *Forbes, Forbes & Co.*, William Jardine shipped sycee to Calcutta for account of Jamsetjee. But the latter objected that he might have obtained a better price in Bombay. Jardine is therefore offering to make up any difference in the price.

[43] On the 'disgusting' aspect of the Whampoa trade, see above, Letter **152**, note 11.

In Cotton there has been very little alteration. The Market is firm, but prices do not advance. They are nearly the same as they were when I wrote last.

Raw Silk is scarce and most of the inferior Chops have been purchased for England. About 1,000 or 1,500 Bales are expected in a fortnight or three weeks. We shall look after them, if of good quality.

Referring you to the letters from the firm for more general information, I remain, My dear Sir,

Yours Sincerely,

161. James Matheson in Canton to Alexander Grant of Carnousie in London, 18 June 1838

My dear Grant,

Having been slightly ailing lately, I am not very well up on my correspondence, and you must therefore be content with a brief reply to your favors of 23rd December received 24th May, and 20th January received 10 instant. You may believe we are all delighted to learn that you are getting on so well and doubt not that you will be equally so to hear that we are going on as prosperously as could be wished. The opium season has opened splendidly.

The great bulk of the Malwa has come on as yet to our consignment[44] and is paying a profit of nearly 200 dollars per chest, while Patna is yielding about 150 dollars per chest. Though I was much pleased to observe that your speculative turn was so far sobered down as to have induced your giving direction for your funds being sent on from India in Bills, we cannot help regretting that you have not some interest at least in the drug, as we are not likely to have so profitable a season soon again and you may lay it down as a general rule that the best of all periods for speculation is in the midst or at the termination of such a panic as we have just escaped from, when the minds of most men are disheartened and many are disabled from competing with.

It is right that you should know of a great change that has taken place in the opium department in Bengal. Formerly purchasers at the sale were allowed by the government three months for clearing what they bought, and owing to abuse among the underlings, the payment of the deposit or bargain money was very generally evaded, so that men of straw possessed of no capital were enabled to speculate largely and maintain the article at high fictitious rates. The exposure of this last year has led to an entire change, which has had a most beneficient effect, as a heavy deposit must now be paid within three days after the sale or the drug will

[44] The total Malwa exports for 1837–1838 amounted to 14,773 chests, and the total Bengal exports to 19,600 chests, making it a total of 34,373 chests. The following year, which marked the start of the Opium War, total opium exports to China reached the still higher figure of 40,200 chests. Imports had multiplied by ten in twenty years. (Cheong, *Mandarins and Merchants*, p. 21).

be resold, and the whole must be cleared within a month.[45] In spite of these wholesome regulations, it is to be feared the successful results of this season's shipment will occasion disproportionately high prices at the next year's Bengal sales. Still you cannot go far wrong in authorizing purchases at such rates as we may consider safe. The early Bengal Sales offer a better chance than Bombay of your funds coming on soon enough to benefit by the favourable rate of exchange usually prevailing in February and March. We look for a considerable advance in our rate of Exchange next Season, but do not delay sending your funds at the present rate, low though it be, that you may have the amount in time to operate next year. Though tea and Silk are above your limit we will try whether we cannot send you a small interest in one or other for 8,600 pounds sterling at 4 shillings and 5 pence. We have not a word yet from *Forbes & Co.*[46] about Sir George Robinson's funds.[47]

Magniac Smith & Co. have sent us advice of Macvicar's final separation from us and proposed firm at Canton;[48] and you will readily believe that we feel it a relief to be quit with him. Your Turkey plan is bold but at so low a figure promises well. Who are the parties concerned with you ? [etc.]

162. William Jardine in Canton to Captain Parry on board the *Hercules*, 6 July 1838

My dear Sir,

I have been so much engaged of late that it has been out of my power to finally dispatch the *Hellas* or *Omega* with Tonshing's Drug though I announced to you my intention of doing so, some days ago.

We have not yet, however, heard of the arrival of his men at HongKong.[49] He has paid for *197* chests of Malwa and *15* chests of new Patna—together *212* chests.

[45] The new regulations had a beneficial effect on margins, since they discouraged competition among buyers and enabled the moneyed merchants to buy more cheaply. It remains that the Bombay opium market, which was less regulated than in Calcutta, achieved better margins still in 1838.

[46] *Forbes & Co.* was the Bombay sister agency of *Forbes, Forbes & Co.* in London.

[47] The former Chief Superintendent, Sir George Best Robinson, had left Canton with his family in December 1836 after being recalled by Palmerston. (Hoe, *The taking of Hong Kong*, p. 267).

[48] The firm of *Macvicar & Co.* was subsequently listed as active in Canton. In 1839 it was one of the firms ordered by Commissioner Lin to surrender its opium (1,146 chests). With *Jardine, Matheson & Co.* and a few other firms, it was one of the early purchasers of land in Hong Kong (1841). It continued operating in Hong Kong into the 1850s and was then reorganized to become *Neave & Co.* (Bard, *Traders of Hong Kong*, p. 73).

[49] Hong Kong had existed unofficially for the private merchants and the opium ships a good many years before it was recognized as having official and legal existence as a British colony. In particular, its harbour had been increasingly used by the *Jardine, Matheson & Co.*'s ships from 1837.

He sends two men with the Drug and hopes to be able to transship the whole to junks at Namo or How Tow Shan, within one month from the day the vessel leaves HongKong, but she may have to go as far as Tan Pan Shan or even Poo To;[50] if however, the Opium is on board more than a month the party should pay ship rent at the rate of 66 dollars per day before his drug is delivered to them. The drug is paid for here—fees, ship here, etc., etc.[51]

Enclosed is a letter for the Commanding Officer of the *Hercules* respecting eight (8) cases [ ] which the purchaser of the drug wishes to be sent to the Coast in charge of the party who attends to the drug.

Your letters of 3rd and 5th Instant have been received, also the treasure per *Castlereagh.*

We shall require another vessel for the Coast in a few days; but I am anxious the letters for Captains Rees and Jauncey should be conveyed to them without loss of time.

Manage this in any way you think best, or rather leave Baylis[52] to manage it on his becoming aware of your wishes.

Nothing new here. Malwa: 665 dollars. New Patna: 530 dollars per chest. New Benares: 500 dollars per chest. The old drug as last quoted.

The sooner the vessel is off, the better. The *Omega*, I presume.

Should Captain Wallace[53] wish to take a couple of chests of the drug with him, I should think new Patna or Benares the safest at the foregoing quotations.

Believe me, my dear Sir,

Yours sincerely,

[50] All the locations mentioned in this paragraph are in the vicinity of Chusan.

[51] For this new type of large-scale opium business and the chartering of opium ships to the Chinese brokers, see above, Letter **155**, note 22.

[52] 'Baylis': probably Captain Parry's assistant, mentioned in Letter **14**, and not Captain H. P. Baylis who commanded the *Colonel Young* at the time. As often, William Jardine suggests delegating as a useful management tool. For the firm's opium ships, see above, Letter **104**, note 35. By 1838 it was established practice that captains kept the command of the same ship for a number of years. The *Hercules* was commanded by Captain E. Parry (first officer : Porteus; second officer : Stewart); the *Austen*, by Captain J. Rees (Forbes, Smith); the *Colonel Young*, by H. P. Baylis (Thompson, Donaldson); the *Lady Hayes*, by A. Paterson (Hardy, Jauncey); the *Governor Findlay*, by F. Jauncey (St Amour, Holmes); the *Hellas*, by A. Scanlan (McMinnims, Rankin); the *Omega*, by W. Strachan (Martin, Denny); the *Jardine*, by T. Denham (Bellamy, Galb), and the *Harriet* by J. Hall (Bateman, Swan). (*JMArch.* A7/231, *'List of our vessels and Officers'*). The annual pay for commanders ranged from 400 to 200 dollars; for first officers, from 60 to 40 dollars; and for second officers, from 40 to 25 dollars. (*Ibid.*)

[53] Captain Gustavus, Alexander, William Wallace commanded the *Omega* in 1838 in place of Captain William Stracham. (*BI*).

163. James Matheson in Canton to John Abel Smith, MP, in London,
27 July 1838

My dear Sir,

Presuming that it would be acceptable to your Firm to have a portion of the agency of our intimate friends *Messrs. Jamsetjee Jejeebhoy Sons & Co.*, Bombay, we have for some time been desirous of bringing them into correspondence with you, but feelings of delicacy[54] have prevented our interfering with their established arrangements, till now that an opening has occurred, of which we have availed ourselves as I am about to explain. Their London business consists chiefly of the remittance to Bombay of funds arising from their consignments to us which are by us forwarded to *Messrs. Forbes, Forbes & Co.* who have hitherto acted as their Agents. The usual routine has been that on receipt of their consignments to us we write to *Messrs Forbes, Forbes & Co.* engaging them to remit to them in the course of the season such sums as we may be instructed. On receiving our engagements *Messrs. Forbes, Forbes & Co.* agree to advance a certain portion (I believe a third) of the same, and the remainder as soon as the Bills or produce reach their hands. Last year, in consideration of the difficulty of making remittances from hence, they relaxed from this rule and came under advance for more than a third, but they are too fond of making remarks tending to over-rate the value of their services, and are apt to [being] captious in reminding our friends that sometimes our letters of Engagements, sometimes our remittances (when bills happen to be secure here) are late in reaching, all which our friends remark in a late letter is very unpleasant to them. We have taken advantage of this to reply that you will furnish advances without unduly hurrying our operations here,[55] so as to give time for our picking up bills and produce at the most advantageous periods of their being procurable within the range of the season; and as a commencement we have sent them a letter of credit on you for 20,000 to 30,000 pounds sterling agreeably to the accompanying extract of our letter to them.[56] It will rest with you (if they adopt our plan) to encourage a continuance and extension of this business or the contrary.

They have for many years carried on a well managed and lucrative business through our predecessors and us, which has latterly exceeded a Million of Dollars per annum of which about 150,000 pounds sterling per annum pass through the hands of their London Agents. They also consign on a limited scale to several other Houses at Canton. Jamsetjee is Proprietor of numerous well let Houses, and

[54] Delicacy: ‘A refined feeling of what is becoming, modest, or proper; sensitiveness; delicate regard for the feelings of others 1712’. (*OED*).

[55] An example of the sense of anticipation and timing which a good agent needed if he was to fulfill instructions well beyond the order party’s expectations. There is something almost biblical about such a discerning use of one’s talents. (Mt 25, 14–30).

[56] The extract was not found.

of valuable property at Bombay. He has lately built the most spacious mansion in the Island for his own dwelling. He is owner of the *Fort William* and principal owner of the *Balcarras*, both of 1,200 Tons, besides having several smaller vessels in the China Trade. That his means are most extensive there cannot be a doubt, but what is of more importance is that his business is in general exceedingly well managed, the most so probably of any on this side {of} the Cape of Good Hope, so as to bring him in constant accession of fortune.[57] While opium has this year been neglected by most speculators in India, partly from want of means and partly owing to the unfavourable prospect, he availed of the depression to become possessed of some 1,500 chests, by the greater part of which he clears more than 200 dollars per chest.

I have insensibly allowed a longer time to elapse than I could have wished ere acknowledging your highly esteemed letters with which I have been favoured. This has arisen partly from a desire to avoid unnecessarily troubling you with letters in the absence of any thing particular to communicate and partly from the pressure of official correspondence leaving me no time to spare on the occasion of an English despatch. Your letters bear dates 6th September, 25th, 29th November, 5th February and 6th March, which I shall not be able to notice in detail at present; but I cannot avoid repeating how very grateful to you we are feeling not only for your unbounded confidence and all important protection of our signature last year, but for your unwearied kindness in seeking every opportunity that presents itself to promote our views even of the most minute description. We feel particularly obliged for the pains you were at to set our minds at ease by obtaining authentic information respecting the intentions of Government in sending the Admiral to China. His Excellency Sir F. Maitland arrived here a few days ago on which occasion Captain Elliot has returned to Canton, and again hoisted the Flag;[58] but he speaks of going back to Macao in a few days. His object

[57] This sentence contains an implicit philosophy about the nature of good management as a powerful adjuvant to good fortune.

[58] Rear Admiral Sir Frederick Maitland, commander of the East Indian Station, arrived in *HMS Wellesley*, a 74 gun ship-of-the-line. The *Wellesley* was accompanied by the Corvette *Larne* and the brig *Algerine*. Palmerston had finally agreed to Captain Elliot's suggestions to send a warship on the coast. By raising the flag at Canton, the Admiral fulfilled the principal instruction he had received from London. Taking the opportunity of the Admiral's visit, Captain Elliot endeavoured to open direct communications with the Viceroy, and again, as at the time of the Napier Fizzle, there was a fruitless exchange of unopened letters between the Chinese and the British. Later, outside the Chuenpi forts, a potential confrontation at sea between Admiral Maitland's war ships and Admiral Huan's war junks was eventually averted. In October, Admiral Maitland finally sailed back to India, having achieved nothing. He left behind the *Larne*, however, a ship which was to be much used by Elliot in the first year of the Opium War. Meanwhile Palmerston's general instructions remained unchanged, which meant that Captain Elliot had to remain neutral in his dealings with British opium merchants, taking care neither to protect nor to discipline them (Fay, *Opium War*, pp. 125–126; Blake, *Jardine, Matheson*, p.86). See also William Jardine's comment on Admiral Maitland's visit, ('What a mess they made of it!'), in Letter **167**.

is of course not known, but report says he is making one effort more to open a *direct* communication with the Viceroy without the intervention of the Hong Merchants. Failing in this as will probably be the case it is said the admiral will propose an interview with the Viceroy which if not granted recourse will be had to the Imperial Court in Peking. Such is the *on dit* of the day. But the latter part I do not believe.

Business goes on quietly and we do not apprehend any interruption. London Letters via Suez have been received to the end of April;[59] but ours from you appear to be coming in a slow craft from Bombay and have not yet reached. The check and retrograde action to which the prices of Tea and Silk were then subject will have a good effect on the opening of the Season's operations here; and is so far are a source rather of satisfaction than othewise. In regard to Silk indeed we think it is not unlikely that your market will have recovered as the Season advanced, and that the tendency to decline may have been the result of the manoeuvres usually put in place by Mr. Durant[60] to enable him buying up the expected importation on moderate terms. You will see from our official letters that we are likely to have this Season an unusual falling off in the supply of Nankin silk

We shall take an early opportunity of writing fully respecting the nomination of Mr. Anderson[61] as successor to Mr. Macvicar. Your promptitude on the occasion has our most grateful thanks, but we have some doubt whether the success of the two experimental years for which he is engaged will justify a continuance of the arrangement. We are, however, very willing to give it a trial, though from the working of our arrangement with Mr. Macvicar in inducing him to force consignments and encourage overtrading by recommending hazardous risks to his and our constituents for the sake of increasing his commissions, we think unfavourably of the system. Mr. Anderson is a friend of 20 years standing and I have the utmost confidence in his honour and perfectly good intentions, while he is of a far soberer turn of mind than Mr. Macvicar, but a system intrinsically bad[62] is apt to get the better of the best intentions. I have a letter from Mr. Anderson in which he speaks of sending out a piece good assistant under an idea that the gentleman in that department had resigned. This, however, is not the case as he is still

[59] The overland mail via Suez therefore took approximately three months, as opposed to four months for letters shipped via the Cape of Good Hope.

[60] Several 'Durants' are listed in the *BI*. The 'Durant' referred to here is possibly J. K. Durant who commanded the *Eugenia*.

[61] John Anderson: 'Merchant, 65 Old Broad Street'. (*TLCD*). John Anderson is further referred to in Letters **210** and **222**.

[62] The influence of systems, structure and strategy (the 'three hard Ss') in relation to controlling the behaviour of employees or agents is still a point hotly debated at the Harvard and other Business Schools.

with us and makes himself very useful as Chinese interpreter,[63] in which capacity we shall miss him far more than in the piece good line if he leaves us, the latter being now so simple that we shall not require a successor, having other gentlemen in the office competent to take charge of the department.

We hope therefore Mr. Anderson will not have carried into effect his intention of sending out an Assistant; and if this arrive in time to prevent it, we beg he will not take the trouble. I write confusedly amidst a thousand interruptions and with kindest regards to the members of your Firm, I remain, My dear Sir,

Yours most sincerely,

I add a P.S. to say that if Mr. Anderson should have actually sent out a Gentleman for us, I have no doubt we shall be able to employ him one way or other.

164. James Matheson in Hong Kong on board the *Hercules* to William Jardine in Canton

10 August 1838[64]

My dear Jardine,

There seems to be some mistake between Heerjeebhoy[65] and his broker about the place for which you destine the *Findlay*. Heerjeebhoy write 'Teen Pack or thereabouts'; but the China man here, a smart young man insists on going to a place called Lieu or Liew Chow,[66] in the Gulf on Tonquin, beyond Hainan. The man is very intelligent and points out on the chart Teen Pack, then 'Now Chow' further South, on the East side of a neck of land stretching towards Hainan. Between this neck of land and Hainan there is a narrow channel for junks, and then a considerable distance off, on the West side of the neck, is the {desired} place Leen Chow. In the North East Monsoon the narrow channel alluded to might be passed through by the *Findlay*, as I believe has been done by Captain Young. But in this Monsoon, in the face of the South West Monsoon, it would be highly dangerous and indeed impossibe, so that the *Findlay* would have to go round to the southward of Hainan.

[63] On Robert Thom, see above, Letter **72**, note 41.

[64] This is one of the first letters written from 'Hong Kong' in the *JMArch*. The very first, written five years earlier in 1833, had been sent by James Innes. On the back of this Letter **164** William Jardine wrote 'Received August 13th. Answer: None required. Referring to Heerjeebhoy's sale of Patna deliverable to the Westward. A failure'.

[65] Heerjeebhoy: a Parsee opium merchant resident in Canton. (See Letter **188, 194, 215, 224**, and **235**).

[66] The Chinese names are rendered phonetically by James Matheson. 'Lieu Chow' or 'Liew Chow' refers to the *Western side* of the Luichow Peninsula (Leizhou Bandao). Whereas instructions were given to sail to 'Now Chow' on the *Eastern side* of the Peninsula (today's Naozhou). The Letter proceeds to explain that in the summer months (a time when winds blow from the South-West), the Hainan straits are dangerous and the *Governor Findlay* should sail round the island rather than risk the straits shoals.

If you will look at the Chart you will see that the western entrance of the strait alluded to and the North West end of Hainan are studded with sand banks. I was surprised to learn from the China man that the broker employed was Hingqua,[67] the painter and Chart-maker; who could not be expected to manage such a negotiation well.

Yours sincerely,

165. James Matheson in Canton to Jamsetjee Jejeebhoy in Bombay,

6 October 1838

My dear Sir,

I have much pleasure in availing of the favourable opportunity of the *Sir Herbert Compton* to reply to your esteemed favours of the following dates.

1838 – July 23rd. Intimated your preference of bills as returns for your consignment per *Good Success*, on account of Mr. J. D'Faria,[68] which has been attended to; and we are only awaiting an improvement in our exchange to continue our remittances. Our american neighbours are at present demanding 4 shillings and 6 pence or 4 shillings 6 pence ½ for their bills; but we are in negotiation for some of the U. S. Bank at 4 shillings and 7 pence. As however Tea shipments to America will not probably take place to any extent for two or three months to come, most of the drawers, being in no immediate want of cash, seem disposed to hold their bills rather than submit to an advance in the exchange of which therefore we are not sanguine for some time yet, although not unlikely at a later period.

Many thanks for the early notice you gave us of the connection between our friend Framjee Pestonjee's Firm and Mr. Burn,[69] which seems to be now in full operation. Framjee had made overtures to Mr. Jardine for giving us their business here, but on terms which we could not accede to; and Mr. Jardine is only now answering his letter which reached us in May last. I sincerely hope for your friend's sake, that his plans may turn out better than public opinion seems to anticipate.

[67] Chinese portrait and landscape artists had started painting in the European style in the very early years of the nineteenth century. Spoilum (1774–1805) was a pioneer in this field. Many of the later artists were known to Europeans by a name ending in '—qua', not unlike the hong merchants, e.g. Piqua, Tingqua, Yeuqua, Tooneequa, etc. (Hong Kong Urban Council, (ed.), *Views of the Pearl River Delta*, Hong Kong, Hong Kong Museum of art, 1996, pp. 232–235).

James Matheson's surprise at finding out that the opium broker is 'a painter and chart-maker' largely reflects an early nineteenth century European attitude to artists. Cantonese mercantile versatility saw nothing unusual in the idea of monetizing one's artistic talent whenever the opium market happened to be sluggish.

[68] Of the firm *Sir Roger D'Faria & Co.* in Bombay.

[69] On Framjee Pestonjee, see Letter **41**, note 31. On Mr. Burn, Letter **35**, note 69. Framjee Pestonjee acquired the reputation of being a sharp operator. See Letter **215** for the cornelians episode.

1838—July 23rd. Approves of the suggestion I made that we should supply your countrymen here with London bills on a limited scale to prevent our neighbours having them entirely in their power, and thus dictating the rate of exchange which, I have not doubt, will have a beneficial effect.

Your wish for the early realization of your drug has our particular attention; and you may rely on its being complied with.

We have not seen the intimation you alluded to, of *Messrs. Russell & Co.*, that opium to their consignment shall be realized at a higher rates than their neighbours'. What is the nature of it, and to whom was it made? We should think their constituents must find that they are not able to act up to such an estimation.

1838—August 22nd. In conformity with your request, the clipper *Hellas*,[70] lately bought for us in London by Captain Grant will proceed to Bombay on the 15th or 20th instant to be at the joint disposal of your good self and *Messrs. Remington & Co.* She measures 208 tons but carries 300 tons, or say at least 1,500 chests of opium.

We have much pleasure in agreeing to your proposal of owning a clipper in the Bombay opium trade with your firm, *Messrs. R&Co.*, and any other friends whom you may desire to have an interest in her. But to secure her being superior to all others we think she should be built in England where it is probable there will be the additional advantage of her costing less than in India. And we are about to give the requisite instructions to *Messrs. Magniac Smith & Co.* with a request that they will engage the superintendance of Captain Grant or Captain Clifton formerly of the *Rover*. We think she should be about 300 to 350 tons and hope she may be out with you by January or February 1840. The clipper building[71] by *Lyall Matheson & Co.* is for a friend of ours and will cost probably not much less than a lac of Rupees to see through only 258 tons, nearly the size of the *Rover* which cost only about half the money. All the Calcutta docks being monopolized by a single company, they are now able to make any change they please at that place.

We are much obliged by the intention you express to make advances on consignment to us, if, as is probable, prices should prove too high, in the early part of the Season, to enable your speculating yourselves, with the prospect of advantage. On bills received from you on consignments which pay the usual commission of 4 per cent for sales and returns, we shall make no charge and shall use our best endeavours to remit their amount in whatever manner you may direct. When invested in Goods, the usual commission for the purchase of returns will be alone

[70] The *Hellas*: the latest addition to the opium fleet. See Letter **162**, note 52.

[71] This clipper being built in Calcutta was not traced. There were four principal dockyards in Calcutta (*John Gilmore & Co., Gillet & Co., Hamilton, Aberdeen & Co.*, and *Cruttenden MacKillop & Co.*) against one in Bombay (*The Bombay Dockyard*). The Calcutta dockyards tended to build smaller ships that the Bombay dockyard, and although there was local competition, their prices tended to be higher than in Bombay. (Singh, S. B., *European Agency Houses in Bengal*, Calcutta, 1966, p. 21).

charged. This arrangement will, I hope, prove satisfactory and evince the desire we always have to meet your wishes, as well as our gratitude for your unbounded confidence and friendship.

The Curtain Gauze for Mr. Anderson[72] is in preparation.

With kindest regards to Cursetjee, I am, my dear Sir,

Yours sincerely,

P. S. We have at length prevailed on our Committee[73] to discontinue the *increased* rates of premium during the South West Monsoon, and we shall be able in future to make your insurances at the same rate all the year round.

166. James Matheson in Canton to John Abel Smith in London,

19 November 1838

My dear Sir,

I cannot but feel that I have too long deferred expressing our grateful acknowledgments, so justly due for your highly valued favour of the 14th June received here 25th September. The delay has been owing mainly to the melancholy nature of family news[74] which reached me about the same time, on which ground I rely on your kindness making every indulgent allowance for me. While we greatly regret the boundless trouble occasioned to you by our concerns, from particular circumstances not likely, we hope, to recur, nothing affords us so much satisfaction as to observe how accurately all our wishes and feelings are not only understood by your Firm, but improved on in those cases when your position enables you seeing that they can be modified with advantage.[75] I am happy to say in one word that all your proceedings on the various important subjects embraced in your above letter are in the highest degree satisfactory. [. . .]

We are in daily expectation of the *Eliza Stewart* with Mr. Humpston and Mr. Jardine to superintend our Tea department,[76] which is in the meanwhile taken care of by Mr. James Warly Smith in addition to his duties as a public inspector. I feel particularly grateful to you for the liberal discretion with which you have improved upon our instructions in selecting a person so generally acceptable as Mr. Humpston to aid Mr. David Jardine; and in all such cases of your giving us the benefit of your judgment, in correction of our own, you may be assured of our thankful approval. It is a singular circumstance connected with Tea tasting, that

[72] John Macvicar's replacement. See above, Letter **163**, note 61.

[73] The risk 'Committee' of the *Canton Insurance office.*

[74] The death in James Matheson's family was not traced.

[75] The compliment and the way it is phrased bears witness to how much the partners were thinking about the meaning and responsibility of 'agency' business, and to how grateful they were when they noticed a similar frame of mind and reciprocal feelings in other merchants. See above, Letter **163**, note 55.

[76] See above, Letter **156**. For another reference on Gervas Humpston (*BI*), see Letter **262**.

though Mr. Macvicar's establishment have an experienced inspector recommended by *Sanderson Fry & Co.*,[77] he finds himself so much at fault in this market on first coming out that he has insisted on Mr. James Warly Smith being employed to revise his tastings, thus formally submitting his judgment to that of the individual so loudly vituperated as incapable by Mr. Macvicar and his friends.

After a careful and practical insight into the working of the Tea market both here and at home, I feel convinced that parties in this country and importers generally not belonging to what was called '*the Trade*' under the East India Company Monopoly, have been made and still are the victim of a system of *jockeying*[78] by which their interests are liable to be sacrificed unless they have capital to enable their holding over those periods of depression of which we must expect to see the constant recurrence while a vigilant look-out should be kept to avail of the favourable intervals which may be confidently anticipated for effecting sales. In this respect we have great pride and satisfaction in reflecting that our interests are in your hands, when we call to mind your unshrinking firmness in holding over the fearful panick of last year, while burdened on our account to an extent which I hope may never recur.

In general it will perhaps be better to avoid placing tea consignments on show, or permitting Brokers to value them, while prices are forced below the probable cost of production, from the state of the money market, or a superabundant supply.

Though we fear the increased depression at the date of our last house advices will subject you to a long suspension of sales, and a continuance of heavy advances, on our account, the turn the market has taken is in other respects far from unacceptable to us in as much as it enables purchases being made here on safer terms than would otherwise have been practicable. On the whole, with your powerful aid at home, and a good inspector here, I should hope the alternation of high and low prices in your market, will be found to suit our purpose extremely well. As yet nothing has been done towards the opening of the Tea Market, and the longer it is put off, the better pleased we shall be. We apprehend however it will not be deferred beyond the end of this month or the beginning of next.

Our silk market is equally at a stand. But I am happy to say we have secured the refusal of the best chops, and shall not be afraid of them if it is to be laid down in England at about 22 shillings per pound.

After a splendid opium season we have at last been overtaken by the usual alternation of stagnation and depression, increased by a recent Edict from the Emperor threatening with death all those who may be concerned in the sale, preparation, or use of the drug, after a lapse of three months. This is far too severe to be acted on, and the conduct of all the Mandarins, from the Viceroy down-

[77] *Sanderson Fry Fox & Co* : 'Tea dealer, 9 Broad Street Mews'. (*RLD*). 26 letters listed in the *BI*.

[78] Jockeying: 'Adroit management for the purpose of gaining an (unfair) advantage; trickery, cheating 1807'. (*OED*).

wards, clearly proves that they have no wish or intention to entirely suppress the trade;[79] all their threats being invariably accompanied with connivance at some means of evasion. The present state of affairs has come on very opportunely to have a beneficial effect on the next season's purchases in India; and we do not therefore regret it. [. . .]

167. William Jardine in Canton to Thomas Weeding in London,
3 December 1838

Dear Weeding,

My last letter to your address was dated April 30th and gave cover to a receipt for fine packages of Tea. I have now to acknowledge your favors of the 26th June, 1st July 1837, also January 29th, May 22nd, June 21st, 1838, with December 9th, 1837, all of which would have been replied to a long time ago but for two reasons: the one a feeling of aversion to writing pending the uncertainty of my own movements as to returning to England; the other a certain feeling of discontent, not to say disgust, at your conduct in dishonoring the Bills of *Jardine, Matheson & Co.*, which nothing but time can wear off.[80]

When I contemplate the position in which we now stand in comparison with that which one should have stood had you been our sole Agent in England, as you were desirous of being, I cannot but feel grateful to *Magniac Smith & Co.* who evinced such determined confidence in their protection of our drafts and endorsements when dishonoured by you and others, though John Abel Smith is a gentleman I never saw to my knowledge—the contrast I wish to forget for many reasons—the feeling of gratitude I should despise myself did I forget it. Enough of this, to me, a very disagreeable subject.

Yours letters of the 26th June, 1st July, and 9th December 1837 require no further notice than my thanks for your attention to present Teas; and the copy of a Bill for establishing a Court or Courts in China with Criminal, Admiralty, and Civil jurisdiction. Her Majesty's Ministers had better trouble themselves about home and European affairs, about which they may possibly know something (of this I do not pretend to judge), but about China they know nothing. What a mess they made of it by sending Admiral Maitland here to be insulted, refused provisions, and ordered away like an evil doer.[81]

Your favour of 20th January last announced to me your marriage; on which happy event I beg to congratulate you, and with much sincerity wish you and the

[79] In this instance, James Matheson's judgment was at fault, as the event of December 1838 showed. (See Letter **168** below).

[80] For this episode, see above, Letter **148**, note 66.

[81] On Admiral Maitland's visit to Canton, see above, Letter **163**, note 58. On the Admiral being 'refused provisions and ordered away', either William Jardine is puffing things up, or the historical sources used by Fay and Blake were incomplete, as neither mentions that he was 'ordered' away.

good Lady all the happiness you can wish yourselves. As my present intention is to leave China about the end of the month and proceed to Bombay on my way home,[82] I hope not long after this reaches you, to have the pleasure of being introduced.

Many thanks for the trouble you took on account of Mr. Edwards, who has left China for England; so that it is as well he did not get the appointment.

May 22nd. gave cover to Account sales of present Teas per *Inglis*, net proceeds 156 pounds, 10 shillings and 8 pence to credit of my private account. I addressed you very fully, now a year ago, respecting the accounts of the Owners of the *Sarah* in Bombay; but have never heard of your having sent out proper powers to any one there to settle on your part, a circumstance I regret extremely; as I must settle my account there previous to leaving, and should have preferred settling in conjunction with your Agent, which would tend to simplify the account very much.

On the subject of Markets I can say little that would be any guide [ ] to you in England. The Tea and Raw Silk Markets have not yet been opened, nor does there appear any anxiety on the part of the Europeans to open them, at the prices now asked, viz—two Tales per pecul beyond Company contracts for Congo, and 600 dollars per pecul for the best Tsatlee Silk, being for the latter 160 dollar per pecul higher than the opening price of last Season. The first crop proved very deficient, the second about an average one.

There are upwards of 3,000 Bales now in Canton, and an equal quantity may be expected before the end of the Season. Some of our neighbours are prepared

[82] William Jardine's intention to leave Canton and return home at the end of December 1838 was carried out with only a month's delay. He left Canton on 26 January 1839, and sailed on the *Bolton* a few days later. In a letter dated 29 Januray 1839 addressed to Thomas Charles Smith (then a partner of *Magniac Smith & Co.*), James Matheson wrote: 'Jardine left us three days ago, and will probably be tomorrow afloat in the *Bolton* for Bombay. You will see from the newspaper that he has been magnificently feted by the commercial community, and presented by the Parsees with a service of plate of the value of a thousand guineas. As he will probably have to pass some weeks at Bombay and contemplates visiting Constantinople, etc., there is every chance that your advice, on receipt of this, will be in time to overtake him in that part of the world; and we shall feel obliged by your writing him a few lines about what is going on addressed to Alexandria, with a credit for his expenses of the homeward route, though I have no doubt our Bombay friends *Remington & Co.* will sufficiently provide for him in this respect.' (*JMArch.*, C5-3).

On 22 of January, a farewell dinner was given by the commercial community in honour of William Jardine. The guest list included many recognizable names: 'Adam, Astell, Burn, Blenkin, Bell, J. Cragg, Cox, Compton, Dickenson, Drysdale, Elmslie, Gilman, Gemmell, Tray, How, Holliday, A. L. Johnston, Kennedy, Lindsay, Livingston, Leslie, MacClean, Morrison, Routh, Scott, Slade, Smith, Turner, Thompson, Templer, Bull, Delano, Forbes, Bridgman, Green, Hathaway, Morse, Nye, Parker, Rawle, Talbot, Tiers, Wetmore, Veiga, Jardine (3), Matheson (3), Boyd, Barretto, Thom, Webster, Hampston, McLeod, Markwick, Captains Scott, Young, Redman, Collard, Bolton, Hullock, Dunlop, Geoffrey; Roberts, Shillaber; Walkinshaw, Fallowfield, Rodgett, Dent apologies (*sic*), W. Cragg, Kerr'. (List given in the order found in *JMArch.* A7-231). The guest list comprises no Parsees.

The Parsees feted William Jardine separately. Their munificent gift mentioned above by James Matheson reflected their appreciation of a merchant who had significantly contributed to the enrichment of the Bombay commercial community for over twenty years.

to pay 540–550 dollars per pecul free on board; but they do not appear anxious to commence operations, being afraid that such high prices would induce a large supply before the close of the Season.

There are no old Teas in the market, the supply of new moderate. So far as we yet know. We hope to open one or two Tales per pecul below Company's prices for good and middling congos.

A few days ago I received a long letter from my young friend, Matilda Jane Ratcliff,[83] complaining of bad health; and a want of the comforts of life, Mr. Harris having been unfortunate in becoming security for his son and lost all his property[84]. I have no doubt she exaggerates their sufferings; but have sent her in the enclosed letter, an order on you for ten pounds (10), which sum be pleased to pay and place to the debit of my account.

I shall send them some Tea by the first vessel we despatch for London. Oblige me by sending the enclosed to Matilda.

On my arrival in England I shall be prepared to settle with you my own account and that of the firm. In the meanwhile I remain, dear Weeding,

Yours sincerely,

168. William Jardine in Canton to Jamsetjee Jejeebhoy in Bombay,

5 December 1838

My dear Sir,

An opportunity offering for HongKong, I give these few lines the chance of reaching the *Castle Huntly* there, though I have nothing but bad news to communicate.

The number of the Chinese now in the prisons of Canton amounts to upwards of two thousand, of whom three or four die daily. They have been arrested by orders from the Viceroy, some for smuggling Opium, some for selling it, and others for having shipped it off to Tienshun and ports at a distance.

One of the Hong Merchants, Poonhoyqua,[85] has been sent down to Whampoa today with the wooden collar round his neck in consequence of an American ship, which he secures, having been accused—I believe incorrectly—of having

[83] On 'Mrs. Ratcliff', see Letter **23**, note 4.

[84] The reference to 'Mr. Harris' and his loss of property is obscure.

[85] Poonhoyqua or Punhoyqua. This hong merchant was security for the *Thomas Perkins*, a ship consigned to Talbot, the American merchant. Two days before this letter was written, two coolies delivered opium in front of the Creek factories. When caught by the authorities they said they were acting on instructions from James Innes and mentioned the ship from which the opium came. The authorities mistakenly understood the ship to be the *Thomas Perkins*, and they gave Innes and Talbot three days to leave China. The 11 hong merchants were summoned by the viceroy, and Punhoyqua was paraded with the cangue around his neck in Whampoa. This, together with the two thousands Chinese opium dealers and addicts in prison, many of whom died every day for want of their daily doses, was the surest sign to date that opium offences were now punished severely.

Opium on board. The trade is neglected. No delivering or shipping of cargo, the merchants and Hoppo being engaged with inquiries after Opium seizures and seizures of Men, Compradores and others belonging to Europeans.

You will do well to refrain from purchases unless at very low prices—I had almost said at any price—but Mr. Matheson is bolder and thinks 600 or 700 Rupees per chest might be ventured. Buy cheap, if you buy at all.[86] We know similar storms have blown over, and so may this; but appearances are at present unfavorable, probably more so than ever we saw them. We have engaged some English Bills for you at 4 shillings 7½ pence per dollar, about 8,000 to 10,000 pounds sterling, which shall be sent by next ship.

Yours very sincerely,

1839

169. Nathaniel Wallich[1] in Calcutta to *Jardine, Matheson & Co.* in Canton, 15 February 1839

Sear Sirs,

I have the honor to address you in behalf of the Tea Committee appointed by the Supreme Government of India.

A few days after this Letter was written, on 12 December, much worse happened and a riot broke out in Factory Square. The Chinese authorities had prepared the centre of factory square for the public strangulation of a convicted opium dealer, Ho Lao-chin. A great many curious Cantonese gathered in the Square. Some Europeans, furious that the chosen venue for the excecution should be right in front of their windows, started 'laying about them with sticks'. The Chinese crowd replied by throwing stones. The disturbance soon grew into a full scale riot, forcing the foreign merchants to barricade themselves in their factories for safety. Although no one was badly injured, the tension did not subside. Captain Charles Elliot, who was constrained by his instructions neither to protect nor discipline the opium traders, simply asked them to remove their small craft out of the river. In pre-1834 fashion, he then used the hong merchants as traditional intermediaries and 'respectfully reported' to the viceroy that boats taken inside the Bogue would receive no help from him. (On the 12 December riot and its immediate cause, see Fay, *Opium War*, pp. 131–133). Hunter has three colourful pages on the same episode and the role he played in it. (Hunter, *The Fan Kwae at Canton*, pp. 47–49).

[86] William Jardine reversed his advice to Jamsetjee Jeejebhoy in his letter of 7 January 1839. 'Avoid purchasing even at low prices', he wrote, 'till you hear again'.

A week before this reverse order was written, the emperor had appointed Lin Tse-hu a special high commissioner with plenipotentiary powers to solve the opium problem. On the 8 January 1839, Commissioner Lin set off from Peking with a small retenue. He eventually arrived in Canton on 9 March. James Matheson was the senior partner in charge of the firm, and William Jardine was on his way back home.

[1] Dr Nathaniel Wallich (1786–1854) was born in Copenhagen. In 1807, he became surgeon to the colony at Serampore, India. In 1815, he was appointed Superintendent of the East India Company Botanical Garden in Calcutta and thus began a distinguished career as a botanist. Between 1830 and 1832 he published his most important work, *Plantae Asiaticae Rariores*. This Letter (the only one by Wallich listed in the *BI*) was written on behalf of the Calcutta Tea Committee, of which he was the

The committee having already benefited in several cases by your valuable and courteous assistance in procuring, at the instance of their late secretary Mr. G. J. Gordon,[2] manufacturing men from China,[3] they entertain a confident hope, that you will likewise grant your cordial cooperation on the present occasion, especially as is it one of great national interest and importance. I have accordingly been ordered by the Committee, under the sanction of the Government, to state that they will esteem it a great obligation if you would undertake the extensive importation into Bengal of the Chinese artisans and materials, which it is desired through your aid to obtain.

At this distance from China, and unacquainted with the peculiar usages of that country, the Committee are unable to offer you any practical instructions for guidance in the matter which they now take the liberty to recommend to your good management and execution. They have not the means even of specifying the rate at which the different artisans are to be engaged, nor to suggest the particulars of the different materials which are required. But they place entire reliance on your judgment and discretion ; they feel sure, that you will do all that is needful on the occasion and that they could not confide the contemplated measure to more able or more generous hands. It is their duty however, to urge on your especial attention, the necessity of exercising that strict economy in all your disbursements on this occasion, which may be compatible with the prompt and effectual attainment of the object in view. As far as they have been able to form an estimate of the charges likely to be incurred in procuring and shipping for Bengal the artisans and materials indented for (being guided principally by some data furnished in your own correspondence with the Committee) they conclude that a sum of Twelve Thousand Dollars (12,000) will amply suffice to defray all the expenses of engaging 60 Chinese artisans (as enumerated in the margin)[4] advancing them six

---

Secretary. He had been appointed to this post by Lord Bentinck who had set up the Tea Committee on 24 January 1834 with the pressing mission to transplant and grow tea in India in order to break away from the Chinese monopoly. (See Le Pichon, 'Premier thé de l'Inde britannique: du rêve à la réalité', *Cahiers victoriens et édouardiens*, N° 55, April 2002, p. 183–201).

[2] On G. J. Gordon who had been sent twice to China by the Calcutta Tea Committee to bring tea seeds back to India, see Letter **104**, note 37.

[3] The phrase 'manufacturing men' is used here in an agricultural, as distinct from an industrial, context; but it is explained by the need for experts in making boxes, lacquer and paper. See below.

[4] In the margin of the letter, Nathaniel Wallich had specified the following: '16 Green Tea Makers, 8 Black Tea Makers, 8 Canister Makers, 8 Box makers and Lackerers, 8 Tea paper Makers, 12 Tea cultivators, 1 Respectable Interpreter to act likewise as the responsible Foreman of the whole Chinese Establishment under the Superintendent of Tea cultures'. This list was drawn up at the request of the superintendent of Tea Cultures in Assam. A few months after this Letter was written, C. A. Bruce wrote a report on his experimental tea garden in Assam and on the progress made by the first group of Chinese tea cultivators and 'artificers' ever sent to British India through the good offices of G. J. Gordon and *Jardine, Matheson & Co.* (See Bruce, C. A. 'Report Dated 10th June 1839 of the Manufacture of Tea, and on the Extent and Produce of the Tea Plantations in Assam', *Transactions of the Agricultural and Horticultural Society of India*, Vol. VII, 1839, Calcutta). In this document, Bruce

months wages, and defraying their passage to Bengal; likewise of purchasing a large supply of paper and lackering materials, also a [pair] of each sort of tea boxes and canisters for patterns.

The Committee have accordingly solicited the Government to authorize their Agents in Canton to hold funds at your disposal to the above-mentioned amounts ; unless you should find it more economical drawing, as heretofore, on the Committee for the amount of your advances, but of course limiting yourselves to the sum specified; in which case your drafts will be duly honored.

On an occasion like the present, when a large number of artisans are to be engaged among a nation of such peculiar prejudices and difficulty of intercourse as the Chinese, it is not to be expected that you should be able to procure the men all at once, or of equal abilities in their respective callings. It is anticipated that the Tea manufacturers will have to be sent for from distant, as well as different provinces, and although they are amongst the men most urgently required in Assam, yet the Committee would wish you not to delay on their account sending such other artificers,[5] as you can by means of active exertions procure for a more speedy shipment. The Committee need not point out that importance that a proportion of each class of artisans should be selected amongst the cleverest and ablest procurable ; all the rest being engaged at a lower scale of wages as assistants to the former. The Committee have been informed that independent of the two grand classes of Tea-makers, each has such division of workmen for particular description of Teas, who are unskilful in the manipulation proper for other sorts. This circumstance, if correct, the Committee beg you will keep in view.

The Committee are extremely solicitous to obtain some experienced Tea-cultivators, who may be capable of conducting the management of the Assam plants. They cannot suggest the precise number of this description of men which it would be desirable to engage ; but they are of opinion that a few respectable cultivators of each class with a limited number of assistants would answer every purpose.

In the above detail of men required the Committee have specified 12 Tea-cultivators, but they beg to be understood that this number is to include likewise any other artisans not named in the list, whom you may consider as necessary for the perfect completion of the Chinese Tea Establishment in Assam; for instance a few experienced Packers of Tea, in case that occupation should form a distinct trade in China. But on this point the Committee wish to rely entirely on your local knowledge and experience. With respect to the Cultivators the Committee pro-

---

wrote: 'Should what I have written on this new and interesting subject [cultivating tea in Assam] be of any benefit to the country, and to the Community at large, and help a little to impel the Tea forward to enrich our own dominions, and pull down the pride of China, I shall feel myself richly repaid for all the dangers and fatigues, that I have undergone in the cause of British India tea'. (p. 14).

[5] Artificer: 'One who makes by art or skill; esp. a craftsman'. (*OED*).

pose soliciting the valuable cooperation of Captain Scott,[6] Master Attendant at Singapore, a gentleman who, to an extensive knowledge of most the eastern countries, unites an intimate acquaintance with many of the Traders coming from remote Ports of the Chinese Empire, and who may therefore be able to render important and essential service in this particular, as well as in other matters connected with the subject of this letter. With this view the Committee will request that officer to put himself in communication with you.

With respect to the 8 Box Makers and Lackerers, it may be possible, perhaps, to procure workmen who are expert in both professions; nevertheless it is very desirable that you should engage the services of some first rate lackerers; as mere carpenters or Box-makers may be easily procurable even in Calcutta, or at least from the Straits. Although the province of Assam and the adjoining countries are known to produce several kinds of Varnish, suitable probably for lackering Tea Boxes, yet it is highly expedient to provide a sufficient stock of the materials for lackering employed in China, in order that the Tea Boxes may to the free Trade in England appear to have all the attention and precautionary solicitude bestowed by the Chinese. The Committee therefore request that you will take measures for purchasing such a quantity of the ingredients as may suffice for lackering a couple of [hundred] boxes. The same observation is applicable also in regard to the different kinds of paper, coloured as well and uncoloured, used in China for the packing of Teas; and you are solicited likewise to forward an adequate supply of that article.

In regard to the 8 paper manufacturers the Committee are of opinion, that although it would certainly be advisable to have such artisans of each class who understand the particular sorts of manufacture required for Tea-Purposes, if indeed they form a separate branch of workmen, yet it is desirable also to procure some men who are thoroughly acquainted with the processes of manufacturing other, and especially the superior sorts of China paper.

It is of course indispensable that the men should be furnished with one complete set, and wherever you may think proper with spare sets of the Tools required in the exercise of their respective professions; the cultivators should bring with them the different implements in use among them; and like supplies should accompany the other artisans.

In your selection of an interpreter, the Committee beg to urge the importance of engaging a man of respectability and influence as he will have to exercise the authority of the responsible Headman over all the Chinese establishment in Assam ; subject of course to the control and orders of the Superintendent of Tea-Culture. It occurs to the Committee that it would be a good plan to enact from each individual a distinct engagement, that he is to consider the Interpreter as the

[6] Captain Scott was not further identified.

Foreman of all the artisans. This clause might very properly be inserted in the paper of agreement which you will of course require in duplicate from each man, according to your very judicious procedure on a former occasion. There is one point to which the Committee would beg your kind attention; namely the necessity of your distinctly explaining to the men that, as they receive an advance of six months wages, they are not to expect any additional or extra allowance whatsoever during that period. I can best explain the meaning and object of this precaution, by furnishing you with the annexed Copy of that part of the Committee's letter to the Government under date of the 29th march 1838, which relates to this very subject, as connected with the last importation of artificers from Canton through your Kind Agency. As to the specific time for which the men are to engage their services, you may perhaps be able to stipulate for a somewhat longer period than three years which was the limit of your agreement with the men now in Assam.[7]

The Committee have received such polite assurances from the Reverend Mr. Gutzlaff as to satisfy them that he will with the greatest readiness afford you his most valuable aid, should you have the occasion to consult the Reverend gentleman on any of the details contained in this letter.

In conclusion I have to apologize for the length of this intrusion and to repeat again on the part of the Tea Committee that your compliance with their wishes on this occasion as promptly as may be in your power, will place them under very high obligation to you.

In the hope of being favored with an early reply I have the honor to be, Dear Sir,

Yours most obediently,

[P. S.] Extract from a letter to the Revenue—Department from the Tea Committee dated 29th March 1838
Paragraph 3.
'It appears from a counterpart of the agreement originally made with the Chinamen, that each received on 20th November last an advance of 6 months. On the other hand it is evident from the repeated assurances of the men, that they took the said advance in the belief that they would not reach their final destination in much less than 6 months, during which period they would be at no expense whatever, it being expressly stipulated in the agreement, that the men were to have free

[7] This is one of the very early examples of expatriation for work purposes in the context of a transfer of technology from an ancient civilization to a modern colony. These expatriate craftsmen were sought after both for their expertise in the tea-making processes and for their ability to train others, particularly local Assam personnel. Few of the first group of Chinese tea cultivators and processors who moved to Assam in 1837 seem to have lasted the full three years of their contract. The massive expatriation of Chinese coolies to the West coast of America which started in the late 1840s and continued during the gold rush was a phenomenon of a different economic nature.

passage, food, etc., on shipboard. They accordingly left the whole amount of their advances with their families at Canton, and did not even provide themselves with a sufficiency of clothes. Under these circumstances, it was necessary to allow them a small monthly sum of 6 Rupees for each man, by way of subsistence money instead of insisting on any deduction from their regular wages when these should become due'.
/a true extract/
N. Wallich, [M.D.]

170. James Matheson in Canton to William Jardine in London, 1 May 1839

My dear Jardine,[8]

You will receive with this the outstanding intelligence of the Chief Superintendent and all foreigners at Canton, having been placed in durance by the Chinese government to extort the surrender, on pain of death, [of] all opium under their control for the purpose of being destroyed; and 20,283 chests of drug are accordingly in course of delivery, being the quantity given up by British subjects. The Chief Superintendent having issued a public notice requiring its surrender 'for the service of the British Government', on whose behalf he holds himself responsible for its value, in the most full and unreserved manner. To anticipate events, I may add there seems no chance of the surrendered drug being destroyed, it being carefully assorted according to quality, weighed, packed and stored partly in the Bogue forts,[9] and partly in a spacious house about two miles east of

[8] This long Letter gives a full account of the events which directly led to the Opium War. It was the first Letter which James Matheson could send to William Jardine since 18 March 1839, the day when Commissioner Lin ordered all opium aboard foreign vessels to be surrendered to him. In the few days which immediately followed the announcement of this edict, the members of the foreign community found themselves under house arrest, or at any rate confined to their factories and therefore unable to leave Canton. They were deserted by their servants and deprived of their usual comforts. Although Commissioner Lin insisted on keeping them in this enforced confinement until all the opium was delivered, their lives were never threatened.

The authoritative work in English on the principal events mentioned or alluded to from Letter **170** on is Peter Fay's *Opium War*. Fay used the *JMArch.* extensively for his source material alongside the principal Canton and London Newspapers, the Foreign Office records and Parliamentary Papers, the Missionary society papers and the two principal American commercial archives, the Forbes Papers and the Heard papers. The events alluded to in this Letter are set out in detail in *The Opium War*, pp. 142–161.

Hoe's *The Taking of Hong Kong* (a more recent work published in 1999) incorporates previously unknown Elliot papers. The work, however, deals only with the first part of the Opium War until Captain Elliot's recall in August 1841. The events are mostly seen from the point of view of Captain Elliot's wife, Clara Elliot.

[9] The opium was in fact meticulously destroyed, most of it during the four week period starting on 3rd April and the remnant in May. James Matheson did not know this at the time he was writing, which suggests the letter was first written as a diary over the period of a month.

Chuenpee, waiting instructions from Peking. The Chinese are evidently staggered with the largeness of the quantity, and with the circumstance of its being surrendered on account of the British Government; and Howqua has all but avowed to Captain Elliot the intention of granting a liberal compensation; (it is thought they will offer 100 dollars per chest) to furnish the means for which some think the Chinese will be ultimately induced to sell the surrendered drug as a government monopoly.[10] Should compensation be offered, however, neither Elliot nor the merchants can accept [any] of it till an answer comes out from the British Government.

To facilitate your understanding the whole bearings of this whole momentous case, you will receive herewith a brief narrative of events which I recommend your perusing first, together with the documents in the accompanying 'Press' of 20th April as a key to the more diffuse remarks which I am now to make.[11]

Your first reflection may possibly be, why we did not remove the drug beyond reach, on the first appearance of danger; to which I answer my mind was always strongly inclined to some measure of this description. In confidential conversation with Mowqua I told him our determination to make the ships go out of sight and begged him to let us know as soon as he might think it right for them to move. Our stock of drug had become so large[12] that we had contemplated stationing some of the depot vessels at Singapore and warehousing some of the drug on shore there. None of our neighbours were, however, disposed to concur with us in such a plan which naturally gave rise to hesitation, and some delay arose from Dent's usual dilatoriness in answering our application to the committee of the Canton Insurance office and the appropriate rate of premium for the voyage to Singapore and back. Meanwhile the danger became so imminent that we at last gave orders to Alexander Matheson at Macao, to send out ships away at all hazards; which orders were in course of execution when they were put a stop to by

---

The site chosen for the opium destruction was on the edge of the Bogue, five or six miles above Chuenpi (or Chuenpee). See PLATE VI. The scene was drawn by Lt. Walford Thomas Bellairs, R.N. on 7 January 1841, two years after the event. The opium balls fragments were pushed into man-made basins built next to a creek. Lime and salt were scattered into the basins, the stinking mixture was stirred by coolies and then flushed into the creek and out to the sea. The scene was described in detail by Elijah Coleman Bridgman and Charles King, two American missionaries who had been invited to attend by Commissioner Lin. They wrote their report in the *Repository*. The article was subsequently reprinted in *The Times* on 1 November 1839. (*Opium War*, p. 161).

[10] The granting of Chinese compensation was a rumour spread by the hong merchant which may have reflected their hopes, but not Commissioner Lin's intentions.

[11] John Slade, the publisher of the Canton Register, published a detailed article of the events narrated here up till the 20 April 1839. He subsequently gathered all his revised articles and published them in Macao in book form. (Slade, John, *Narrative of the late proceedings and Events in China*, Macao, 1840).

[12] *Jardine, Matheson & Co.* eventually surrendered its entire stock of 7,000 chests, of which 5,000 belonged to the firm's constituents (with only 97 to Jamsetjee Jeejebhoy), and 2,000 was its own property. (*Opium War*, p. 157, note *). The second largest stock holders were *Dent & Co.* and Heerjeebhoy Rustomjeee, with 1,7000 chests each. Fourth was *Macvicar & Co.* with 1,000 chests. (*Ibid*).

news of Elliot's unexpected surrender, a measure which, though for a long time highly repugnant to my feelings, I cannot but feel sanguine on mature reflection, will prove far more advantageous than if we had to work off so large a stock in an overburdened and persecuted market.[13]

It is right you should know the Opium Commissioner's office of Kinchae[14] (in the Canton dialect Yum chae) is one of extraordinary authority equal to that of the Emperor himself, and conferred only four times before since the accession of the present dynasty, the last occasion having been the suppression of the Chang Ki Ur's rebellion.[15] For several days before he arrived there were rumours of his being *incognito* in Macao, and at other times at Canton, which though then disbelieved is now supposed to have been really the case. He reached Canton on 10th March and commenced by ordering the arrest of Wung Cao Man and some other mandarins as well as the broker Chinam and A-Wung,[16] who had however taken themselves off. His first proceedings favoured the belief that he would follow up the usual Chinese system of *humbug*[17] and were evidently calculated to veil his ulterior designs. Presently there came an inquiry as to the arms and ammunitions in the possession of the foreigners, but this being attributed to circumstance of a cask of gunpowder having been sent up by mistake in one of the St Vincent chops did not awaken our suspicion. We next heard of several house compradors (but not ours) having been summoned to give information. On the following day the same process took place with the linguists and lastly with the Hong merchants.

The Kinchae's style of examination was new to the Chinese, in a tone of great familiarity and with a singular knowledge of his subject. When a witness hesitated or pretended ignorance, he warned them: 'I know all about it as well as you do. You had better therefore tell all the truth if you wish to escape punishment'. He asked one of the linguists: 'which is the largest opium dealer, Mr. Dent or Mr. Jardine ?', 'Is it true that Mr. Jardine is worth 3 millions of dollars?'. 'No,' said the linguist, 'perhaps one million more.'[18] 'And has he taken all away in money?'

[13] For James Matheson's further assessment of Captain Charles Elliot's opium surrender decision as 'a statesmanlike measure, see below, 3rd paragraph before the section entitled ARRANGEMENT FOR THIS SEASON'S BUISINESS.

[14] 'Ch'in-ch'ai': Chinese for 'by imperial decree'. The term 'Kinchae' describes the function of plenipotentiary, and is used in subsequent Letters to describe Commissioner Lin and his successors holding the same imperial commission.

[15] The last rebellion suppressed by the Ch'ing dynasty was the White Lotus Rebellion (1796–1804). (Fairbank, John King, *China, A New History*, Cambridge, MA, Harvard university Press, 1992, pp. 189–191). James Matheson may be referring to the Uighur invasion of Chinese Turkistan in 1826 by Jeehangir. (*Ibid.*, p.198).

[16] Chinam (or Chienam) and A-wung were wholesale customers of *Jardine, Matheson & Co*. Wung Cao Man was not identified.

[17] Humbug: a favourite term of both James Matheson and William Jardine to describe what they regarded as insincere, manipulative behaviour on the part of the Chinese.

[18] The information given by the linguist to the Kinchae was a guess and an overstatement. See The Introduction, **Table 7**, p. 34.

'No,' was the answer, 'he dealt largely in China produce.' Strange to say the Kinchae's had a vocabulary of foreign languages, and used to astonish the witness by the occasional use of an English or Portuguese word. At length, on the night of 18th Howqua sent for Thom to translate the Edict (document A)[19] requiring the surrender of our opium. None, however, not even the Chinese themselves contemplated its being literally enforced. Some portion of drug seemed to be all they wanted, a thousand chests being suggested by the Hong merchants themselves, and it was *privately* hinted to me that Howqua's Treasury might probably be put in requisition to make good its value. This is no part of the official case, and was told only to myself by one Hong merchant in great confidence. The Kinchae however appears to have suddenly adopted a severer tone. The Hong merchants evinced the deepest terror and all idea of compensation was abandoned, but they still seemed to think a thousand chests would be enough.[20]

I refer you to the '*Brief Narrative*' for the events of 20th and 21st March; on which latter date after two meetings of the Chamber of Commerce continued till past midnight, we agreed to surrender 1,037 chests made up by the subscription among us (our share being 275) with which the Hong merchants expressed themselves perfectly satisfied; and never throughout the whole subsequent proceedings have they evinced anything like the alarm from which they were then relieved. At the Chamber of Commerce Wetmore as Chairman[21] conducted himself with great propriety. A resolution was passed to the effect that we acted under fear of our lives. I explicitly declared to the meeting, however, that I was influenced by no such motive, but submitted to the sacrifice as a measure of expediency calculated to produce a compromise and accelerate the return of quiet to the traders. I viewed it in fact in the light of the compromises for smuggling made with collectors of Customs in South America.

About this time it was ascertained that the Kinchae had hired a comprador and two cooks accustomed to foreigners and we all amused ourselves with conjecture about his object. We spoke in jest of his wishing to see us in the City; but Dr Parker[22] and the wise ones remarked, how absurd to suppose that he would have so much foresight for our comfort if he really contemplated imprisoning any of us.

[19] 'Document A' (not traced) was a translation of Commissioner Lin's edict dated 18 March (eight days after he had reached Canton and conducted his interviews). The edict ordered the foreigners to surrender all the opium on board their ships and to undertake to bring no more opium to China.

[20] The hong merchants had been severely reprimanded, accused of treason and threatened with loss of property and even life by Lin on 18 March. In spite of this, they still continued to misunderstand his purpose and must have thought that the surrendering of a thousand odd chests would appease him.

[21] For the Canton Chamber of Commerce, see Letter **92**, note 72. Wetmore took the chair as the outgoing chairman, Hugh Hamilton Lindsay, had just left Canton and was sailing home. (*Opium War*, p. 145).

[22] Dr Peter Parker (1804–1888) was the American medical missionary.

On the 22nd March, the day following the surrender of 1,037 chests, rumours were afloat of its not being deemed satisfactory, but the Quang chow foo[23] had said that if 4,000 chests were offered they might perhaps be accepted. In the afternoon Thom came to tell me that the Quang chow foo wished to see Dent at the City gate, who had promised to go tomorrow and that he (Thom), at the resquest of the Hong merchants had gone to the gate to assure the Quang chow foo of this, who however would not receive him, and said he wanted Mr. Dent. I remonstrated with Thom as to the impropriety of what he had done and hastened to dissuade Dent; which of course was a matter of no great difficulty. The foreigners then intimated that on account of the treachery of the Government to Mr. Flint[24] and others on various occasion, Dent would not go unless his safe return were guaranteed by the Kinchae. The object of hiring the compradors and cooks was now but too apparent and the Chinese scarcely conceal that it was intended to detain Dent till he gave up every chest of his drug, and afterwards try the same experiment on some more of us.

The 23rd of March afforded the most complete exhibition of humbug ever witnessed in China. At an early hour Howqua and the younger Mowqua with chains round their necks and without their mandarin buttons, attended at Dent's with others of the Cohong alleging they were to be executed on account of his disobedience and that some of the Hong merchants were imprisoned on the same ground. It was now disclosed that it was the Kinchae himself who wished to see Dent to ask him some questions as head man of the foreigners and admonish him against dealing in the drug, and that the Quang chow foo had come to the Consoo house to receive and conduct him to the City giving an assurance that he would be permitted to return. We replied that nothing but the Kinchae's own safe conduct would be considered sufficient. At the Hong merchants' request a party (of whom I was one) went to the Consoo house to state this to the Quang chow foo; who thereupon sent the Nanhay [foo][25] and a higher mandarin to Dent's factory to try and persuade him; but of course in vain though they alleged they must remain overnight unless Dent went with them. It was replied he will not go unless under the required safe conduct, but if you force him we cannot resist. I raised my voice against the *volunteer of non-resistance* as being most uncalled for and urged that Dent should be placed in the Superintendent's Hall, guarded by the whole foreign community and that we should dare the Chinese to take him. But, will you believe it? There was scarcely one to second me! At dusk the mandarins and Hong

[23] 'Quang chow foo': 'Canton senior magistrate, or prefect'.

[24] Mr Flint: in the middle of the eighteenth century, James Flint had been a gunner on the *Lady Hughes*. The British community had kept the memory of his being arraigned in similar circumstances and kept in prison for two years. Hence James Matheson's insistence on Dent being issued a safe-conduct by Commissioner Lin himself.

[25] The Nanhai magistrate. Nanhai (or Nanhay) was a district of Canton. (Garrett, *Heaven is High*, p. 35, note 2).

merchants retired, having persuaded Inglis, with Thom, Fearon and Slade to go into the City and report Dent's answer to the Judge, Treasurer, etc., etc. , by whom they were well received and returned to the factories about 10 p.m. It was understood they would tomorrow take Dent by force, which however being Sunday was consistently granted us as a day of rest. In the midst of our troubles, it was almost amusing to witness the forced gravity which Howqua and the younger Mowqua tried to assume in their chains, which however did not prevent them from occasionally chatting about business or news with any friends who happened to be near. Not a whisper of chain, loss of rank, or threatened execution have we heard since.

THE FUNCTIONS OF THE FOREIGN MERCHANTS IN THE DELIBERATIONS HAD NOW CEASED.

Sunday 24th March. It was an animating sight about 6 p.m. to descry from our terrace a small foreign boat with a sitter in a cocked hat, pulling rapidly up, and crowds of Chinese boats in chase. It proved to be Captain Elliot[26] who managed to effect a landing just as a barrier of boats was closing in to intercept him. In a moment the flag was hoisted and we followed him to Dent's whom he persuaded to remove to the Superintendent's Hall whither we escorted him at a slow pace, followed by a multitude of Chinese a good deal excited.

He then read to the foreigners assembled in the Hall his proclamation dated Macao 23rd march (See document E)[27] couched in terms of defiance which but ill accorded with what three days after, he felt compelled to submit to. He was of course a good deal excited, and many expressed their fears of his adopting a too violent course. While reading his proclamation Howqua and Mowqua entered, whom he cordially welcomed on closing his address. Before we had done dinner, our Chinese establishment were ordered to leave and instantly decamped; nor, though formally promised to be restored on the delivery of a fourth of the opium, have we yet got back more than our cooks, coolies and 3 of the servants, who returned about the 19th instant,[28] there being a new regulation allowing one Chinese only for each foreigner, a palpable breach of faith! They also impose

[26] The Chief Superintendent, Captain Charles Elliot, had been in Macao. As soon as he learned about Commissioner Lin's 18 March edict (it was translated to him by Robert Morrison on 22 March), he sent the translation with a despatch to Palmerston to the effect that '[he] had no doubt that a firm tone and attitude [would] check the rash spirit of the provincial authorities'. He was facing the worst crisis of any British official since Lord Napier, five years earlier. He immediately left for Canton in the *Louisa*. He reached Whampoa on 23. There he found communications to Canton blocked. He changed to full military uniform, and charged ahead regardless of the blockade, transferring to his gig when he could not sail. (*Opium War*, p. 147).

[27] Neither Document E nor any other attachments mentioned in this Letter were traced.

[28] This part of the Letter was written on 19 May. The arrangement James Matheson refers to had been that upon delivery of ¼ of the opium (towards the middle of April) Lin would allow the foreigners' servants to return to the factories and some of the merchants to be released.

fresh responsibilities on the servants by which many are deterred from returning. By the kindness of Heerjeebhoy[29] in lending us his Indian servants, with the assistance of some sailors who happened to be up, we have not only lived comfortably all along but have entertained the remaining inmates of the hong[30] including Slade and his printers.

Monday 25th March. A special Committee of the Chamber of Commerce drafted a reply from foreigners to the Kinchae's Edict, in which we pledged ourselves to abstain from dealing in the drug; adding arguments calculated to deprecate his severity, such as the encouragement given to the trade by the contemplated plan of the Chinese Government to legalize it in 1836, and stating the impossibility of surrendering to be destroyed the opium stored in vessels off the Coast, in consequence of its belonging chiefly to parties in other countries, etc., the British subjects concerned being however of the opinion that as the Chief Superintendent had arrived in Canton, it would be impossible for them to act without previous consultation with him. It was resolved to submit to him the draft which had been prepared; he advised its being restricted to a simple pledge to abstain from dealing in opium, and that on other points the Kinchae should be referred to the consuls of our respective nations; which was accordingly done and generally concurred, etc.

I consider this an important feature of our case as shewing the course we proposed to have adopted but for the interference of the Chief Superintendent. As far as regards *Jardine, Matheson & Co.* we had resolutely determined to abide by the cession already made of which on the 22nd ultimo[31] we conveyed advice by a circular to Captain Parry and the other commanders of our depôt vessels, telling them also that [as] our firm had promised the Chinese government to abstain from the trade all future orders for delivery will be granted by Mr. Alexander Matheson at Macao. Should we have occasion to issue any orders here, they will have the signature 'Alexander' simply annexed to them and they were requested to attend to none others. We thus in a manner divested ourselves of control;[32] and in proof of this a certified copy of our circular shall be sent to *Magniac Smith & Co.* to be used in case of need.

On Wednesday 27th March soon after 6 a.m. Johnston[33] brought to us and read Elliot's public notice requiring the surrender before 6 p.m. the same day of all

[29] Heerjeebhjoy Rustomjee, like most Parsees, brought their own Indian servants to Canton.

[30] The 'hong' here refers to the Creek Factory, where *Jardine. Matheson & Co.* had its offices, and most of its employees and friends like Slade had their living quarters.

[31] The cession of 275 chests referred to above.

[32] A very transparent arrangement as Alexander Matheson was himself a partner in the firm.

[33] Alexander Johnston (1808–1888) was a relation of Lord Napier. He had been Deputy superintendent to Captain Charles Elliot since December 1836. He later became the first Administrator of Hong Kong. He retired to England in 1853. (Hoe, *The Taking of Hong Kong*, p. 264).

British-owned [opium] with a declaration that, if not surrendered, Her majesty's Government shall be wholly free of all manner of responsibility or liability.[34]

Before Elliot's arrival several parties had transferred orders for their opium to the deputy Superintendent by way of shielding it from the grasp of the Chinese. Never contemplating the possibility of surrendering all more especially after Elliot's war-like preparations, I could not help jumping to the conclusion that his requisition was with the object of getting all the opium under his control to protect, not to surrender it. At all events, be his objects what it might, the only safe course before us was that of implicit obedience, as we should otherwise have placed ourselves beyond the pale of the protection of the British Government; and though in the early stage of the proceedings it had occurred to me, it might be a good plan to surrender a part only on obtaining compensation, and retain the rest for the chance of effecting sales, this seemed inadmissible in dealing with the British Government, as Elliot's requisition being for the whole; should it be discovered we kept any back, it might be alleged we had not acted in good faith, and thus damaged our claim for what was given up. We therefore surrendered all both at Hong Kong and on the Coast, according to the last returns of stock we had received, and as I imagined it was merely a form to place the property at the risk of the British Government, we deemed it unnecessary to make any reserve for intermediate sales not yet advised. I was still further confirmed in this impression by the circumstance of Elliot having directed the quantities to be specified in separate sealed envelopes. We at the same time verbally stated to Elliot that our drug had been ordered to Singapore and elsewhere and might not be all forth coming.

[34] Elliot's public notice read as follows : 'Constrained by paramount motives affecting the safety of the lives and liberty of all the foreigners here present in Canton, and by other weighty causes, I, Charles Elliot, Chief Superintendent of the Trade of British Subjects in China. . . do hereby in the name and on behalf of her Britannic Majesty's government enjoin and require all Her Majesty's subjects now present in Canton forthwith to make a surrender to me for the service of Her said Majesty's government, to be delivered over to the government of China, of all the opium belonging to them, or British opium under their respective control; and to hold the British ships and vessels engaged in the trade of opium subject to my immediate direction'. (Fay, *Opium* War, p. 153, quoting *F.O. Correspondence Relating to China, 1840, 36 (223), 374, PP*).

Captain Charles Elliot's decision was highly controversial at the time and has remained so amongst historians since then. His subsequent recall by Palmerston for failing to secure a sufficiently advantageous treaty from the Chinese (See Letter **223** for details on the Convention of Chuenpee) sealed his fate as a historical failure, while other government officials (like his successor, Sir Henry Pottinger) have been feted as British heroes. Elliot could not take emergency instructions from London as the electric telegraph introduced in England in the 1830s was not yet extended to Asia. At the critical moment, he had to decide by himself what was best for his country. An examination of his opium surrender notice can easily convince a dispassionate reader that he had found the only solution to the unresolved problem of establishing a direct communication of equals between the British and the Chinese governments. He ordered the surrender of opium to himself '*in the name of HM's government*' in order for him to '*deliver it over to the government of China*'. By this radical measure he hastened the collision of two reluctant governments whilst securing the release and freedom of his countrymen.

To our surprise, however, he had no sooner received the returns than he summed up the quantity of each house and early next morning made himself responsible for the whole 20,283 chests, to the Chinese Government, our share being [blank] for ourselves and constituents;[35] accompanying you have a memorandum of what was given up by others. This is perhaps of no further consequence than that it may cost him some trouble to account to the Chinese for not being able to make up the full quantity at the last.[36] I suspect he had an expectation, that so large a quantity being tendered on account of *the British crown*, the Chinese would shrink from receiving it; and that he wished to take them aback by the largeness and promptitude of his offer. Certain it is the Hong merchants were most completely taken aback. Their remark was: 'what for he pay so large! No wanted so much! Six, seven thousand so would be enough!' As for the mandarins they could not believe we were in earnest; and at the moment of stepping into their boats to go and receive the drug at Chuenpee, the Viceroy is said to have remarked to the Kinchae, that he was sure we were playing false and that none would be forthcoming! All this, however, is for your private ear and must not be repeated to prevent possible injury to our cause.

Though [expressing doubt] at the time and long after much [dissatisfaction] with what Elliot had done, now that I have been able to review its progress and probable prospects more dispassionately, I am inclined to regard it as a large and statesmanlike measure, more especially as the Chinese have fallen into the snare of rendering themselves liable to the British crown.[37] Had the Chinese declined receiving it and said: 'We are satisfied with the reverential obedience you have shewn, but we do not wish to press too hard upon you. We restore the drug you offer on condition that you enter into a solemn engagement to take it back from whence it came and never more permit its coming back to China', had this been done our position would have been far less favourable.

Their still keeping us in durance ever since 22nd March is even fortunate as adding to the accounts for which we have to claim redress, and as proving to our

[35] See above, note 12.

[36] This action by Elliot inconvenienced the larger firms, particularly those which, like *Dent & Co* and *Jardine, Matheson & Co*., had coastal delivery capacity. Whilst the partners knew the amount of stock on the day they disclosed it to Elliot, they had no means of controlling what was being sold up the coast. Whatever was sold after their disclosure to Elliot had therefore to be re-purchased later, so that The Chief Superintendent could honour his pledge.

[37] This 'more dispassionate' judgment of Elliot's actions was arrived at a month after the event. It was a judgment which James Matheson never fundamentally revised, although he was more than occasionally critical of Elliot's subsequent individual actions, and in particular of his haste in negotiating with the Chinese. This was, however, not the judgment which 'History' chose to retain. Nor was it William Jardine's. As his subsequent Letters from London show, the firm's retired partner did not have strong enough words to condemn Elliot's actions. The founding partners who usually agreed on everything held two diverging views of H. M.'s Chief Superintendent.

own Government how inveterately lient[38] the Chinese are in following up their declared purposes. To you it will no doubt occur that if more spirit had been shewn on our side the Chinese would never have ventured to go the length they have done. But as Lord Napier was blamed by Lord Palmerston for having provoked the severity of the Chinese, it would appear as if Elliot had determined to steer clear of such an accusation by doing their will in all things. And before leaving Macao on 23rd March, he addressed the authorities to state that such was his wish. The inevitable tendency of such a course is to invite aggression and indignity. To a close observer it would seem as if the whole of Elliot's career was expressly designed to lead on the Chinese to commit themselves, and produce a collision. He now writes strongly to impress on Lord Palmerston that the act of spoliation which has been committed must for ever destroy confidence in Canton, and prevent our continuing to do business here, that therefore we must have a possession of our own to which the Chinese shall be bound to bring their produce. He has not said which possession he recommends, but it is probably Chusan. I recommend Formosa as the best, but that is thought too extensive.[39]

Whatever possession we take I do not think we can expect the Chinese will bring us their produce, if they can meet with purchasers at their own ports; and parties submitting to the risk and indignity incident to trading at Canton would consequently have the advantage of the English to prevent which it seems essential that the primary point insisted on in the new arrangements should be the liberty of trade and security at the principal marts of the Chinese Empire. That a powerful armament will be sent to China, we consider certain. Elliot thinks that before it arrives, the Chinese will have the Opium compensation ready to pay over,[40] still the armament will not be the less necessary to secure its being paid.

ARRANGEMENT FOR THIS SEASON'S BUSINESS

As soon as the communication is open Elliot will publish a proclamation (already written) strictly prohibiting British ships from entering the port, until an assurance is given that we shall never again be placed in durance or in other words that we shall always have liberty of egress from the country, and that if charged with any offence British subjects shall be given up for trial to the jurisdiction of our nation.[41] Elliot will not apply to the Chinese for these securities, but

[38] An interesting verbal invention on the pattern 'inveterate liar'.

[39] James Matheson made the recommendation to Elliot as he had made it before to the British public in his 1836 pamphlet, *The Present Position, etc.*, (See Letter **135**, note 32).

[40] Elliot showed here and in his subsequent negotiations with the Chinese officials a certain trusting naivety which, to William Jardine, was always a mark of weakness and a harbinger of failure.

[41] When all the British subjects were released from Canton at the end of May (Lancelot Dent and James Matheson were among the last to be allowed to leave), Captain Elliot gave strict orders for them not to return to Canton. As early as 4 April Commissioner Lin had insisted that a personal bond be signed by each individual merchant. (See Letter **171**). The signing of the bond (which most American

they are what he will accept for a temporary renewal of trade if offered. Ships in port will in all probability have time to complete their outward cargoes, which is fortunate for the *Orwell*, *George IV* and *David Scott*, under our management.

Elliot contemplates making an arrangement for ships arriving with cargoes, to unload at Macao, but I do not much like this for a variety of reasons; and in all cases of vessels with cargoes to our consignment not being obliged to return immediately, we shall probably detain them for a time at HongKong, in the expectation, which seems far from improbable, that the Chinese will patch up some plan to admit of their coming eventually to Whampoa. Parties will do well, however, not to consign to China, unless on a very limited scale. Captain Elliot says that when he leaves Canton, which he proposes doing as soon as released from durance, he will make the place 'too hot' for the foreigners of other nations to remain here; but I question if he can manage this till he has a squadron to blockade the port; and meanwhile most of our American friends contemplate remaining at Canton.

RATE OF OPIUM COMPENSATION OR INDEMNITY FROM BRITISH GOVERNMENT[42]

Elliot is desirous to make our documents for the opium given up as complete as they can possibly be rendered, to obviate doubt or cavil. His receipts will be accompanied with a declaration acknowledging the surrender of it to have been necessary as a ransom for the safety of the lives and liberty of the foreigners at Canton. His powers by the China Trade Act and the Order in Council of 9th December 1833 are of the most extensive nature and not those of an ordinary consul. The only point left for adjustment at home, is the rate of compensation. And there are anxious opinions in our community as to how this should be settled. Some (Wetmore among others) think each holder is entitled to the cost of his drug, but this would involve such a minuteness of detail and of proof, as it is to

---

merchants agreed to sign) committed the parties 'to suffer death at the hands of the Celestial Court' should opium be found on their boats or in the cargoes consigned to them. When pressed by the hong merchants to accept the bond, Captain Elliot 'tore it up and desired them to tell their officers that they might take [his life] as soon as they saw fit, but that it was a vain thing to trouble themselves or [him] any further upon the subject of the bond'. (Elliot's letter to Palmerston, *Correspondence Relating to China, PP 1840*, 2230, 392; quoted in Fay's *The Opium War*, p. 163).

[42] The Opium compensation question and the rate of indemnity were to occupy William Jardine in London and the whole of the *East India and China Association* for the better part of the following four years. (See in particular Letters **190, 193, 197, 200, 209, 216, 233, 249, 256, 260, 261,** and **263**. The Lords Commissioners of H. M. Treasury eventually announced the rate of compensation in a notice in the *London Gazette* dated 25 August 1843. The rate was fixed at 66 pounds, 7 shillings and 7½ pence for a chest of Patna; 61 pounds, 11 shillings and 3¼ pence for a chest of Benares; 64 pounds, 11 shillings and 2 pence for a chest o Malwa; and 43 pounds , 3 shillings and 5 pence for a chest of Turkey. (Keswick. *TheThistle and the Jade*, p. 73). The total amount paid by government to the opium receipt holders was just over £1.3 million, i.e., an average of £64 per chest. (See Letter **263**). This average compensation price was close to the average selling price of opium at the time of confiscation. Traders who had bought it higher that the then selling price realized a loss.

be feared would require years of delay before coming to a final settlement and payment to the great inconvenience of the claimants.

On the other hand there would be some awkwardness in adopting the market price here as a standard, small sales having been made during the height of the alarm at 200 dollars for malwa and about 300 dollars for patna. To any one acquainted with the trade it required no argument to prove that such insolated retail transactions cannot be quoted as a standard of the market because the great bulk of the holding had no intention of accepting these rates and were holding for remunerating prices. In a market so proverbially fluctuating as this (witness the rise of Patna from 300 dollars in April to 600 dollars in May last year) there surely can be no fairness in compelling a party to give his merchandize away during the height of a panic and telling him he must be satisfied with the lowest panic price. Moreover it may be said that for months back there has been no market at all here for the drug, the principal holders like ourselves looking exclusively to distant parts of the Coast for effecting their realizations, where up to the latest dates prices have not fallen below about 500 dollars,[43] ranging in some places still higher, though but on a very limited scale; of this and of the extent of business done upon the Coast, ample proofs shall be sent home. {Mr Brown} strongly insisted on our at once fixing the claim for Patna and Benares at the average of the last January sales with the charges say about 450 dollars per chest for Patna and that the same should be also claimed for the Malwa. But this seems so unjust to our Bombay friends, who had paid a much higher cost that I thought it necessary to give it the strongest opposition, so as to leave it an open question, that our Bombay friends may be at liberty to fight their own battle for prime cost, if they can, though I confess I am not sanguine in their succeeding.

Elliot's idea is, and I am disposed to agree with him, that the rate of indemnity should be fixed on the same principle and plane as when land is forced to be given up by Act of Parliament for a road or any other public purpose, in which case the damage is I believe assessed by a jury, on a combined consideration of cost and of the circumstance, affecting its permanent value. The average of the January sales with charges should be at least the minimum of claim for the new Bengal drug, in as much, as having been paid for in hard cash and remitted from the Company's godowns to China where it arrived early in March, on the 27th of that month before under any circumstances there could have been time for its realization [as] we were compelled to surrender it to Captain Elliot, an officer partly paid by the East India Company. We shall endeavour to send home documents calcu-

[43] After reaching a low of 250 dollars a chest in March, opium prices were up again in the 700 dollar range by the month of July, such was the pent-up demand for it, in spite of the risk taken by the Chinese dealers and consumers. The large firms like *Jardine, Matheson & Co.* were back in business along the coast, operating out of Manila where the receiving ships were now anchoring. (*Opium War*, p. 168).

lated to furnish *data* for a just settlement according to whatever principle the Government may adopt.

We have determined to send home Alexander Matheson to supply information on unforeseen points, should it be found at home that there are any such overlooked by us here. It has been resolved and generally concurred in by the claimants to nominate a deputation consisting of you or Alexander Matheson,[44] Hugh Hamilton Lindsay, and Robert Inglis, jointly with a members of *Messr. Magniac Smith & Co.*, and one of *Palmer Mackillop* and *Dent & Co.* for the purpose of pushing the recovery of the claims and to place at your disposal for expenses a contribution of one dollar per chest, say about 5,000 pounds sterling. You will not, however, be limited to this outlay as the magnitude of the object can well bear any amount of expense that may be considered necessary or desirable and it is even contemplated that you may find it expedient to secure, at a high price, the services of some leading newspaper to advocate the cause. The best legal advice will of course be engaged at the outset to make the most of the strong points of our case and we are told there are literary men who it is usual to employ [for] drawing up the requisite memorials in the most concise and clear shape. More than one long memorial to send to Palmerston has been drawn up here, for general signature, attempting to justify the opium trade from the anticipated vituperation of the High Church party and mixing up the question of opium compensation with complaints of the stoppage of the general trade. But we in this House resolutely set our faces against being parties to any such document considering it likely to do more harm than good, as affording our Government a pretext for delay, etc., and I sincerely hope the idea will be abandoned.[45]

The *Ariel* has been taken up for 7 months at 8,000 dollars and afterwards *pro rata* to take despatches to the Red Sea and wait there news from London.[46] It is singular that till within the last few days, sales on a small scale have been going on at Macao, some as high as 500 dollars per chest, but they have since entirely ceased and it is well ascertained that several of them were the spy of the Government. Elliot and the Community are greatly annoyed with them as tending to prolong our captivity. I recommended at the beginning his issuing a proclamation to prohibit such transactions, but was not attended to. The Portuguese on hearing of our dilemma at Canton promptly despatched the whole of their opium to Manila, having previously made a regulation to admit no more at the Custom House. It is said that the Kinchae has demanded their surrendering 3,000 chests,

[44] Alexander Matheson went home to London in June and gave a helping hand to William Jardine throughout the period 1840–1841 in the preparation of the various papers and meetings concerning the 'opium compensation' question.

[45] Acting in secrecy and with a minimum of public fuss was always the policy of both James Matheson and William Jardine.

[46] By this means the private merchants established their own courier using the overland route independently of the government service.

also possession of their forts, but whether the latter be true seems doubtful. His leaving Macao unmolested, as notoriously the focus of the opium trade is not very intelligible.[47]

The communication between Macao and Whampoa is still so rigidly interdicted, that we are able to send only chits of the smallest size, though it is several days since more than half of the promised drug was delivered, another breach of faith on the part of the Chinese, which they justify on the plea of the small sales from British shipping which I have just alluded to as going on in Macao; as if it were in our power to prevent them while we are kept here in durance. During the first days of our captivity so rigid were the restraints that we were obliged to restrict our correspondence to small slips of paper in the heart of a Chinese paper cigar.

Since writing the foregoing, I have had a conversation with Elliot who seems to think it not impossible that the Chinese may make no such favourable offers of compensation as to induce us to forego our claims on the British Government. I have replied to him that if this should be delayed till after our claims are sent home it will be impossible to listen to any overtures from the Chinese and that all claimants that I have conversed with would even now be disinclined to such a course.

Elliot has written very urgently to the Bengal and Bombay Governments, as well as Lord Palmerston begging they will lose no time in issuing a public declaration to the effect that all claims on the Government arising from recent events in China shall have prompt attention and adjustment, the object being to inspire general confidence and prevent the shock of commercial credit which might ensue were people left in doubt as to the granting of full indemnity for the vast amount of property as is at stake. We ourselves feel comparatively indifferent on this subject, but as the excitement of a general panic would prove more or less disastrous to every branch of commerce, as happened in regard to the American Houses in 1836–1837 we think it of the last importance that Elliot's wish should if possible be carried into effect.

171. James Matheson in Macao to William Jardine in London,

13 June 1839

My dear Jardine,

The *Horatio*, a fast sailing America vessel being under despatch, I am tempted to write to you a few lines to bring up our news to the latest date. The *George IV*,

[47] Commissioner Lin did leave Macao 'unmolested'. He was mostly interested in dislodging the British who had taken refuge there upon leaving the Canton Factories. His visit to Macao in September 1839 is described in Letter **175**.

Reliance, and *David Scott* are still at Hong Kong completing their transshipping[48] operations but will be dispatched in two or three days, the two former intending to keep company. Mr. and Mrs Daniell[49] are passengers per *Reliance* and Mr Pickwick Smith[50] per *George IV*.

The Americans have at length agreed to sign the Opium bond, by which any seaman smuggling opium at Whampoa, however small the quantity, is to suffer death, and if the Captain smuggles drug both he and the supercargoe are to be subjected to the same fate. The American ships are all therefore going up with a good deal of British property on board, contrary to Captain Elliot's injunctions, and it is said some British vessels contemplate following the example on the plea of Elliot's interdict of 22nd not being tantamount to a positive order against proceeding to Whampoa. A meeting of British merchants was held today to deliberate on what is best to be done, when it was resolved to ask Elliot whether his above-mentioned public notice was meant to have the effect of an embargo. What his answer will be remains to be seen, but I foresee much confusion is likely to ensue and shall not be surprised if some British ships venture up to which however our House will in no ways be parties. It seems Elliot has not adhered to his intention of discontinuing intercourse with the Chinese Government; but soon after reaching Macao applied to the Viceroy for permission for British ships to unload at Macao. It has been refused as a matter of course, and he has been ordered in conjunction with the Government of Macao to devise a plan for putting a stop to the outside drug trade!

Owing to a mistake of the linguist, the chop boat containing our office records could not start with the rest of the establishment, and we have been much inconvenienced for the want of them, but they have happily arrived this morning.[51] Meanwhile Thom was sent up to hurry them down, and in a letter received from him this morning he tells a curious story of the Kinchae (Yum Chae) [or] opium Commissioner having been so unwell as to have felt desirous of consulting Parker,[52] but, too proud to send for him, he sent the Hong merchants to say that

48 As the British merchants were asked by Captain Elliot not to sign the opium bond (for which, see Letter **170**, note 41, and the first sentence of next paragraph) they were barred from entering the Pearl River. Chinese goods ready for export had therefore first to be brought downriver by American and other ships to the Hong Kong anchorage, there to be transshipped to British ships.

49 For Nugent Daniell, see above, Letter **92**, note 66. Daniell was later examined by the Parliamentary commission on China, together with Inglis, Captain Thacker and a number of other former Canton residents. See Letter **206**.

50 Mr Pickwick Smith was not identified.

51 After two months of 'duress' in the Canton Factories, James Matheson was personally adamant he would not return there to work. The office files were first removed to Macao, where the firm worked from the house he rented there. On 24 August, when the Chinese authorities expelled the British Community from Macao, the most current office files were moved to the *Hercules* where James Matheson and the firm's employees worked and lived for a time. (See Letter **175**).

52 For Dr Parker, see above Letter **170**, note 22.

he understood Parker and Thom wished to see *him* the Yum chae. The Nanhay[53] was therefore sent to Howqua to ascertain from the parties if this was really the case. They of course answered they had not expressed a wish to see him, but would not object to wait upon him if he wished to see them. It will be curious to see how his Excellency will act. I hope Alexander Matheson will start in a week per *Mahommedie* for Bombay.

Yours in haste very sincerely,

P.S. The coast trade promises fair. Rees and his gang are at work again.[54]

172. James Matheson in Macao to Jamsetjee Jejeebhoy in Bombay,
23 June 1839

My dear Sir,

The *Mahommedee* for Bombay and *Red Rover* for Calcutta are at length under dispatch with full accounts, and I avail myself of the opportunity to acknowledge your much esteemed favors of 19th, 20th and 21st April per *Fort William* brought on from Singapore per *Hellas* which reached us on 15th instant; while the big ship herself made her appearance not long after, on 17th, with the *Bombay Castle* in company. Accept a repetition of our most grateful thanks for your continued confidence in consigning those vessels to us, with their valuable cargoes; and it is superfluous to assure you no exertion shall be spared to dispose of them to advantage under the difficult circumstances in which we are placed. Both vessels after entering protests before Captain Elliot have proceeded to HongKong and I am in great hopes we shall soon be able to advise some satisfactory progress in realizing their cargoes; for although Captain Elliot prohibits British property from going to Whampoa on British account it seems he is neither able nor desirous to prevent sales being made outside to foreigners who will take it to Whampoa in foreign vessels on their own account. We have had overtures from Americans for transactions of this nature; and to enable our making a commencement we have sent up per *Robert Fulton* musters of the *Bombay Castle's* cotton to ascertain their

[53] For Nanhay or Nanhai, see above, Letter **170**, note 25.

[54] Captain Rees and the other opium ship captains had sailed back to the coast after surrendering the opium pledged to Captain Elliot. The strength of Chinese demand for the drug, the continuous flow of supplies from India, and the determination of the principal British traders not to discontinue their participation in the trade, all combined to counteract the destruction of the very large stock which had just been completed by Commissioner Lin.

Andrew Jardine was now directing the opium sales from Manila. The word 'opium' disappeared from the partners' instructions to their captains. Instead the new vocabulary was borrowed from the piece-goods trade. Rees and 'his gang' now only sold 'whites' (Patna), 'greys' (Benares) and 'chintzes' (Malwa). (*Opium War*, p. 168). (The term 'gang' used here by James Matheson did not then have its modern derogatory connotation: 'Any company of persons who go about together or act in concert' (*OED*).

market value before striking a bargain. We have an American friend[55] residing in our factory at Canton introduced by our New York friends, who will be of some use to us ; and you may be assured we shall adopt every possible expedient to benefit your interest. I am not without hopes we shall have the *Bombay Castle* clear and ready to return to you, in almost a month, with the remittances [to] you direct. Of the state of the cotton market I cannot give you any very accurate idea. I annex our American friend's last quotations which are of the 5th Instant, but as he is wholly inexperienced in the market, I do not place much reliance on them, and since then prices have given way owing to the dealers having become alarmed on witnessing the unexpected importations in American ships. Latterly, however, they have again rallied and within the last few days we have been able to close for the *Good Success's* cotton on board the *Robert Fulton* at 10 Taels and 7 mace which could not have been attained within three or four mace a week earlier. On the whole I have a sanguine expectation that the shortness of the season's supply will enable us to command profitable sales. I notice the remark in your letter to my nephew, that we may hold till the Chinese are fully satisfied of the limited extent of the supply.

The existing state of affairs of course puts it entirely out of the question to send the *Fort William* to England, and the prospect is not very favourable for obtaining rice, its exportation being prohibited from Manila; Lombock,[56] where it is to be had cheapest being devastated by a renewal of civil war, while in Java the article is unusually scarce and dear. But circumstances may change between this and the month of October, the period for the return of your big ship.

I now revert to your letter of 11th April (acknowledged in mine of 10th instant) and you may be assured we shall have great pleasure in availing of the first opportunity to appropriate an interest in our Insurance offices for the benefit of our unfortunate friend Sir Roger's family.[57] I fear there is no prospect of an opening occurring for the employment in our office, of one of his sons-in-law which would have afforded us great satisfaction had it been practicable.

We shall endeavour bye and bye to send you some Bills on England at short sight of 30, 60 and 90 days. They are likely to be scarce, however. Our exchange with England has latterly been looking down, being now at 4 shillings and 10 pence for bills at 6 months' sight, some say even 4 shillings and 9 pence. The want of other means of remittance will probably occasion also a decline in our Bengal exchange, bills being now scarce at 218 [Rupees] per 100 [dollars].

55 'An American friend': James Matheson is referring here to James Ryan who was acting as their principal Canton agent for the duration of he Opium war. See Letters **177**, **188**, **201**, and **213**.

56 For Lombock, see Letter **122**, note 171.

57 Sir Roger D'Faria, the Bombay merchant and senior partner in the firm of the same name.

I am sorry to say I cannot at present obtain a copy of Manabhoy Framjee's account with Kingqua[58] as requested in your favour of 4th April, all I can learn being that Manabhoy's sales to Kingqua amounted to 277,483.77 dollars and his receipts from him to 211,691.05 dollars, leaving a balance due of 65,792.72 dollars, which the cohong have engaged to pay in ten years with interest at 6 per cent in the two following years—and this is confirmed in the books of the cohong, to which we have referred.

The curtain gauze was ordered in due course, but our records not having yet been placed in order, since their removal from Canton, I cannot ascertain by what ship it was sent. We shall look to the matter.

The *Mahommedee* is now returning to you with a fair freight which will, I hope, be some compensation to her owners for her long detention here which has very far exceeded our wishes and intentions. Had we not detained her, we should be now without the means of sending on the opium receipts[59] which I consider an object of great importance, nor could we have obtained any freight at all for her.

Our official correspondence explains the circumstances connected with the opium per *Charlotte* adverted to in your favour of 1st April which I have no doubt will ultimately wind up equal to our first expectations.

Many thanks for your private note of 11th April respecting F. P. and his new connection of *CC&Co.* which is ending in the way that all sensible people expected. I feel also greatly obliged for you hint respecting H. M.[60]

I take this opportunity of noticing that several account sales now going to you, of drug to my individual consignment and on account of office friends etc. have been made out according to office routine, with full charges of commissions which shall however be refunded as soon as we have leisure to look into them.

You will be surprised to hear that the old *Cambridge* has been taken up by Captain Elliot as a sort of man-of-war to supply the place of *H.M.S. Larne* for a time, at a rate corresponding to the usual Indian terms of 20 Rupees per month per ton. Her crew is to be made up to 100 men and she will mount 32 guns,

[58] Kingqua was another Hong merchant who failed during the breakdown of the 'Canton system' in the years immediately preceding the Opium War. As early as 1837, William Jardine had been writing to his correspondents about the difficulties facing the hong merchants. In a letter to Hollingworth Magniac dated 16 January 1837, he wrote: 'In the early part of this season [i.e. in the autumn of 1836, when James Matheson had just returned from home], I fully expected to have left China by the ships sailing in March next; but the combination among the black tea merchants has brought to light such serious embarrassment among the hong merchants, that I cannot think of leaving till some arrangement has been made for the settlement of their accounts, and placing the trade of the port on a more solid and safe basis than it is at present'. (*JMArch.*, C4–5).

[59] The 'opium receipts' issued to owners by Captain Charles Elliot against delivery of the opium stocks were precious financial instruments as proof of claims against the British government.

[60] 'F.P.' and 'H.M.' were not identified. '*CC&Co*' probably stands for *Colvin Cowie & Co.*, the Calcutta agency.

Captain Douglas[61] having brought on 20 purchased at Singapore; which with the circumstance of his belonging to the Royal Navy induced Captain Elliot to give him a preference without the usual formality of inviting tenders. For my own part I cannot see what good end is to be answered by the measure.

Enclosed you have a copy of a document circulated by the Chinese among the British shipping inviting them to proceed to Whampoa, also Captain Elliot's printed reply.

You will see from our printed circular that the application to trade at Macao met with a decided refusal from the Chinese, and most people regret that it ever was made.

The Yam Chae or Opium Commissioner has granted an audience to Mr. C. W. King,[62] and American merchant who went to see him, and assured him he would be glad to see without ceremony any other foreigner who may be desirous of waiting on him. This is a remarkable instance of condescension, and strongly indicative of the desire of the Chinese to re-inspire confidence and resume amicable relations. Mr. King witnessed the process of destroying the drug which is now nearly completed.

The American ships at Whampoa have not yet commenced unloading, and they are still in hopes of avoiding compliance with the obnoxious Opium Bond.

In conclusion, my dear Sir, permit me to offer my grateful acknowledgments for your munificent presents per Fort William, which have been safely received and are highly esteemed for the donor's sake.

With kindest regards to Cursetjee, I remain, my dear Sir, Most sincerely yours,

Our American friend's quotations of Cotton at Canton 5th June:

[61] Captain Elliot needed a few armed vessels to protect British interests in what promised to be a difficult summer. The *Larne*, left behind by Admiral Maitland in 1838 (see Letter **163**, note 58) needed refitting. He therefore hired two small opium craft, the *Pearl* and the *Psyche*. The *Cambridge* was an unexpected addition. She was a large Indiaman bringing cotton and opium from Bombay. Her owner and commander, Captain Douglas, had been a master in the Royal Navy. He heard in Malacca from the *Good Success* that the British were held prisoners in Canton. He then stopped over in Singapore and 'bought 26 eighteen pounders and four long twelves to add to the six carronades she already carried'. (Fay, *The Opium War*, p. 170–171).

[62] Charles W. King (1809–1845) was a partner in *Olyphant & Co.*, the American firm established in Canton. From the Canton Factories where he was held prisoner in March-April 1839, he wrote to Commissioner Lin protesting his innocence. He was an ardent anti-opium campaigner. (Hoe, *The Taking of Hong Kong*, p. 265).

After witnessing 'the process of destroying the drug', Charles King and Elijah Coleman Bridgman wrote an article in the American missionaries' paper, the *Repository* (Vol. 9, 70–77), in which the following (earnest, albeit rhetorical) question was asked: 'Have we any-where on record a finer rebuke administered by Pagan integrity to Christian degeneracy?' (Quoted by Fay, *Opium War*, p. 161).

[63] The quotations are expressed in taels and mace. For 'Tinnivelly', see Letter **35**, note 66.

	Bengal		Bombay	
B	n°1	12/5[63]	JFT	11/3
	n°2	12/-	B	11/–
J	n°1	11/5	S	10/5
	n°2	10/3	Dn°1	10/–
C	n°1	10/3	n°2	9/5
	n°2	10/–	Tinnivelly n°1	11/3
			n°2	11/–

173. James Matheson in Macao to Lady Napier in London 25 June 1839[64]

Dear Lady Napier,

Though extremely hurried with despatches for several vessels about to sail for India and England, I cannot omit the opportunity of my nephew proceeding by way of Bombay and Suez to acknowledge the honor of your Ladyship's letter of 3rd September which reached me in duplicate in February last.

Your wish to have the monument erected in the Macao burying ground in the absence of any better site, was entirely in unison with that of the resident subscribers; and we were about to take measures for carrying the plan into effect, when the commencement of the present discussions induced our pausing in the hope of their leading to such an amelioration of circumstances as may pave the way for a better arrangement.[65] And some are even sanguine enough to expect that we may ere long have a British settlement in this part of the world, in which the monument will be more appropriately placed than it could be anywhere else. This, time will tell. Meanwhile it remains in good keeping at the Macao Custom House, and your Ladyship may rest assured not a moment shall be lost in erecting it as soon as circumstances may permit.

My nephew will do himself the honour of paying his respects to your ladyship; and to him I beg to refer you for any particular connected with the state of affairs here, which is far from satisfactory.

It affords me always the greatest happiness to hear of the good health and welfare of your Ladyship and family; I beg to be respectfully and cordially remembered to one and all, and remain always

Most faithfully yours,

[64] The letter is addressed to 'the Rt. Honble. Lady Napier, Kew Green, London'.

[65] On the subscription for Lord Napier's monument, see above, Letter **92**, note 65. James Matheson's hope that 'we may ere long have a British settlement in this part of the world in which [Lord Napier's monument [would] be more appropriately placed than it could be anywhere else' was indeed fulfilled, but Lord Napier's monument had to wait close to 120 years before it was erected in the Hong Kong Colonial Cemetery. When James Matheson finally went home in 1842, few people in or outside the firm—if anyone at all—remembered his pledge to Lady Napier. The memorial column was eventually found by chance in 1953 by a ship's captain 'while rooting about in an old marble-grinding shop, lying next in line to be pulverized for construction work'. The inscription on the column proved it to be Napier's monument. The Hong Kong government bought it from the finder and eventually had it erected in the colonial cemetery. (Ride, *East India Company Cemetery*, p. 262).

174. Charles Elliot[66] in China to James Matheson in Canton, 5 September 1839

[. . .]

'I could not think it was a becoming task of H.M. Ship[67] to shoot to death three Chinese Junks, which {my} poor Cutter could {sink} under their batteries [ ]. Neither did it seem to me to be politic to take a step so inevitably driving the Commissioner to aggressive measures against the fleet. Perhaps I ought not to have fired at all but every man's patience has limits and mine has been sorely tried.

I am afraid I have disappointed the men's ardent spirits here but I believe I have done well to refrain'.

175. James Matheson on board the *Hercules* in Hong Kong to John Abel Smith in London, 9 September 1839

My dear Sir,

We have had an eventful time of it here since I had the pleasure of addressing you per [ ] on the 19th ultimo, and I have now to announce the expulsion from China of the whole British Community who have been obliged to take refuge on board the shipping at this anchorage,[68] where Captain Elliot

[66] Captain Charles Elliot wrote at least thirty notes or short letters to the firm or to the firm's partners between the beginning of the Opium War and his return Home in the summer of 1841. (*BI*). His Letters, including Letter **219**, show signs of having been written in a rush, which makes the small, rapid handwriting doubly difficult to decipher. This Letter **174**, however, is an extract copied in James Matheson's own hand.

[67] Letter **175** accounts for the episode alluded to here. H.M.S. *Volage* was the only frigate available to Captain Elliot at the time. It was a 28-gun ship. (Melson, *White Ensign, Red Dragon*, p. A2). It had arrived from India on Thursday 28 August with the news that the '18-gun *Hyacinth* was not far behind'. Four days earlier, Lin had expelled the British from Macao (in circumstances alluded to as 'the Hong Kong homicide' in Letter **177** —see accompanying note). While the British community were on board their ships in the Hong Kong anchorage, Lin attempted to cut off their food and water supplies. To this effect, he had ordered three war junks to block access to the mainland. It is in this context that Captain Elliot, in a fit of exasperation attacked them in the 75-ton cutter *Louisa*. The three war junks opened fire, and so did the nearby batteries. The *Louisa* and the *Pearl* withdrew, but the junks gave chase. The skirmish, sometimes known as 'the battle of the junks', ended without casualties. The next day, however, Captain Smith of *H.M.S. Volage* tried to persuade Captain Elliot to sink the three junks and blow up the Chinese battery. This, Elliot resisted as 'unbecoming'. This was the first, and by no means the last time that he preferred disappointing his men who were keen to fight the Chinese, rather than what he regarded as spilling blood unnecessarily. In time, Captain Elliot would be much criticized for his 'soft' attitude.

It is interesting that Captain Charles Elliot should have felt inclined to share this confidence with James Matheson, and it says something about the personal relationship which was developing between the two men.

[68] What had provoked Commissioner Lin into expelling the British from Macao on 24 August was the murder of a Chinese in 'Cowloon's Chien-sha-tsui' today's Tsim Sha Tsui in Kowloon) on Sunday 7

contemplates ordering a general removal to Manila as soon as the northerly winds set in next month.

He has still a lingering hope that the announcement of his intention to the authorities may induce their making such concessions as may preclude the necessity for the measure, but for our part we cannot indulge such expectation. Nor do we see any reason to regret the removal to Manila, as abundance of neutral shipping will no doubt follow us there to enable our still trading with China; and as goods can be landed in the entrepôt and again exported on payment of 2 per cent duty it will afford an economical mode of releasing the shipping, which have so long been detained with their inward cargoes. It is yet premature to decide what specific course our firm may adopt, but I think you may consider it certain that, happen what may, one of us will remain in the vicinity, and we shall have an American friend in our employ to operate for us at Canton. Mr. Andrew Jardine has already proceeded to Manila (per *Poppy* on the 3rd instant) and will be prepared to do the needful there.[69]

Captain Elliot had no sooner embarked from Macao on the 23rd ultimo, as advised in our circular of 24th, than the Chinese taking courage from the circumstance published a notice threatening to arrest and punish any of the English who should remain. On the 25th rumours were industriously circulated that all the English houses would be surrounded that night; this was no doubt a mere ruse to intimidate, but I suspect few were able to sleep quietly that night. Next day the 26th, all embarked in good order, without any casualty; but bad weather intervening prevented several (our establishment among the rest) from reaching HongKong for a week later. Enclosed you have a copy of the Chinese document ordering us from Macao.[70]

Here we had scarcely breathing time allowed us when the {fleet} was on the 4th instant thrown into the greatest alarm by a loud and protracted firing near Cowlung beyond a point of land to the eastward whither. Captain Elliot had proceeded in the morning in the *H.M.S. Cutter*, accompanied by Captain Smith of *H.M.S. Volage* in an armed boat and the schooner *Pearl*; to remonstrate on the stoppage of provisions with three mandarin junks, who intercepted supplies. Much negotiation of an evasive nature took place, both afloat and onshore, between the Chinese and Mr. Gutzlaff, as interpreter. At last some provisions

---

July 1839. British sailors had got drunk and fought with the villagers. One man was left dead. Captain Charles Elliot gave financial compensation to the villagers (2,000 dollars) and convened a special court which sat on 12 August, with himself as judge and merchants for a jury. Five sailors were charged with riot and assault. But Elliot would not turn them over to the Chinese, which angered Lin. On 15 August, Lin prohibited the sale of provisions to the British, and on 24 August, he directed Portuguese Governor Pinto of Macao to expel the entire British community. (Fay, *The Opium War*, p. 173). What followed is narrated here by James Matheson.

[69] The planned 'general removal' to Manila never took place.

[70] The document was not traced.

were procured, and on the point of being landed into the boat, when they were deliberately carried off by the Mandarins; which so excited captain Elliot that he could not refrain in the heat of the moment from opening a fire from his little vessel. This was returned from the junks and from the neighbouring fort, with some very heavy guns but without any decisive result, when night put an end to the conflict. Meanwhile Captain Smith had sent for his frigate to the scene of action which weighed with armed boats from the whole fleet but night prevented their doing anything; and next morning the junks having been evacuated, and the mandarins offering no molestation, Captain Elliot deemed it more becoming not to carry matters further. I hand you in strict confidence [an] extract from his *private* note on the subject.[71]

He is much blamed for having suffered himself to be betrayed into such an act of violence. It is most fortunate that reflection induced him to pause.[72] There is but a very limited supply of gun powder among the merchant shipping, and were the Chinese to attack us vigorously it would be difficult to hold our ground, while going to sea in the bad weather to be apprehended between this and the Equinox is much to be deprecated. What effect the conflict may have on the Chinese authorities remains to be seen. Here on the spot provisions have been procurable with rather less difficulty than they were before.

The High Commissioner visited Macao on the 3rd ultimo, merely traversing the streets without examining the Forts, as it was thought he would have done. The Portuguese procurador with some members of the senate waited on him, and were well received. He told them, however, he had a list of such inhabitants as had before dealt in the drug, and expressed his hope that their future conduct would be such as to relieve him from the necessity of punishing them for the past! He did not see the Portuguese Governor.

There is a report of a second High Commissioner being on his way from Peking to examine into Lin's doings,[73] if this be true his disgrace and degradation may not be far off, but of this I am not sanguine just yet, though of course it will ultimately happen.

With kind regards to your Partners, I remain, my dear Sir,

Sincerely yours,

P.S. I have no letters from you since last writing. Those of your firm extend to 15th May for which we are very much obliged. The Manila Bills they enclosed

[71] See Letter **174** immediately above.

[72] James Matheson therefore approved of Captain Elliot's restraint. This paragraph and similar paragraphs in other letters alarmed William Jardine in relation to the ability of the firm's smaller opium ships to defend themselves if attacked. (See Letter **199**).

[73] Lin's enemies were plotting against him at the Imperial Court and eventually brought about his disgrace for mishandling the opium problem. The new 'High Commissioner', Kishen arrived in Canton in December 1839, according to Letter **191**.

have been sent for acceptance per *Poppy*. The *Marmion* and {*Eucles*} sail in a few days will full cargoes for London . Kindly show this to Mr. Jardine and Mr. Alexander Matheson.

176. Lord Palmerston in Windsor to John Abel Smith in London,

14 September 1839[74]

My dear Sir,

I am sorry that I am prevented from going to Town today as I had intended, and I shall not be there till the latter end of next week. I have not, however, anything positive to tell you as yet, about the course which the Government may deem proper to pursue with respect to China. Our last Despatches from Captain Elliot were written at a time when he was still in duress:[75] we must wait to receive fuller accounts before we can finally make up our minds as to the steps which it may be fitting to take.

Yours sincerely,

177. James Matheson on board the *Hercules* in Hong Kong to John Abel Smith in London,

24 September 1839

My dear Sir,

Affairs have, I am sorry to say, been going on in a most unsatisfactory manner, since I had last the pleasure of addressing you on 9th Instant. We are now said to be on the eve of a settlement on the wished for basis of the English being allowed to trade outside of the Port, but I am assured on good authority, the Chief Superintendent is as usual oversanguine in his view of the circumstances on which he founds such expectations. I have also a strong conviction that even if liberty of outside trade should be granted, it will be clogged with so many impositions and restrictions as to be in effect valueless in the hope of still enticing British ships to Whampoa. Some of the commanders are actually threatening to go up, and will if they persevere be gladly welcomed by the Chinese, but although

[74] This letter is marked: 'Copy'. The original was obviously received and kept in London.

[75] In the last dispatch received by Palmerston Captain Elliot recommended that 'an ultimatum should be sent to Peking demanding full financial compensation and free entry for British ships and cargoes into Canton, Ningpo, Amoy and Nanking'. (Blake, *Jardine, Matheson*, p. 92). When the dispatch reached London, William Jardine had arrived in Genoa on his leisurely voyage back home. He now hurried back to London and went straight to see John Abel Smith, the senior partner of the firm's London agent, *Magniac Smith & Co*. John Abel Smith immediately asked Palmerston for an interview. Palmerston saw him a few days after this Letter was written. A further interview eventually took place on 27 September, when John Abel Smith introduced William Jardine and Alexander Grant to Palmerston. (See Letter **180**).

a legal opinion has been received, by Mr. Norton[76] Advocate General, at Madras, denying the legality of Captain Elliot's order to suspend the trade,[77] I question much if any commanders will have the courage to disobey in the face of all the trouble and inconvenience to be apprehended from the opposition of the Chief Superintendent, and the treachery of the Chinese. Under all these uncertainties, we still look to neutral shipping as the most satisfactory mode of conducting business, and have been fortunate in thus operating to a considerable extent.

I shall now proceed to a brief narrative of recent events. On the 11th Instant all were much surprised by two official notices; one ordering away from this *outer* anchorage all vessels having opium on board, at the most dangerous season, when equinoctal gales were almost sure to occur—enclosed you have a copy of the document.[78] The other declared the port and the river of Canton under blockade, at the end of six days. The chief ostensible motive of this measure was the disappearance of a boat belonging to the country ship *Mayaram Dyaram*, with her chief mate on board and Captain Macdonnel[79] of the *Psyche*, and our sapient Superintendent immediately jumped to the conclusion that they must have been cut off by the Chinese. The fact was the tide had carried them further from the shipping than they intended and, fearful of being intercepted by the Chinese on their return, they [sailed] away in their boat for Macao where they were picked up by the *Lady Nugent* and brought to this anchorage two or three days after the declaration of blockade. A Lascar who had belonged to the unfortunate *Black Joke*[80] was also brought to the anchorage about the same time by the Chinese; clearly proving that they were not so bloodthirsty as Captain Elliot had hastily assumed. Meanwhile, however, he had no sooner declared his blockade, than he proceeded in the *Volage* to Macao with pacific overtures to the Mandarins who

[76] George Norton was the senior Court officer in Madras in 1839. The other legal officer was the Court solicitor. The Madras Supreme Court was established in 1801. (*EIRD*).

[77] 'Suspending the trade' is a manner of speaking. The trade was not suspended and it operated successfully, thanks to the American transshipping system. Captain Elliot's purpose and intention had been to stop the British merchants from sailing their ships to Whampoa, which they could no longer do without signing the opium bond. In Whampoa they were in a situation where he could not easily protect them if they needed protection.

Whilst friendly ties developed between James Matheson and Charles Elliot, the former always maintained a pragmatic judgment over the latter's individual actions. This whole Letter is highly critical of Captain Elliot's excessive optimism in his powers to negotiate a settlement allowing the British to trade outside Whampoa, and insufficient distrust of the Chinese negotiating manoeuvres. As in many other instances, events proved James Matheson's judgment to be correct.

[78] The document was not traced.

[79] Captain Charles E. Macdonnel is listed in the *BI* as 'Captain of the *Lord Amherst* in 1839'.

[80] The *Black Joke* was a passage schooner which had been found by the *Harriet* (a *Jardine, Matheson & Co.* ship) off the island of Lantao on 23 August 1839. Its crew had been murdered and an English passenger named Moss, left for dead, eventually survived. James Matheson thought that this was the work of pirates. Many thought, however, that the murders had been commissioned by mandarins. (Fay, *The Opium War*, p. 173).

declined receiving them, till he was obliged to solicit the mediation of the Portuguese through whom they were presented and through whom (always hitherto more disposed to embroil than favour British relations with China) the negotiations have been since carried on. While he was away at Macao overtures from the Chinese strongly evincing their desire of an accommodation were brought me through an indirect but authentic channel, so that, had he been less impatient, he would have had the advantage (a most important one) of the application for terms coming from them rather than from him.[81]

The *Volage* returned from Macao on the 16th, the day before the blockade was to have commenced; when it was rescinded, most fortunately on many accounts, for which our insignificant force of a small 28 gun frigate, with the *Cambridge* merchantman, it could not have been effective, it would have provoked the Chinese into active measures of aggression, it might have embroiled our country with the Americans and other foreigners who deny its legality, and worst of all it would have stopped the realization of the large amount of British property now at this anchorage, to the incalculable injury of its owners. Yet strange as it may appear, a small party of our merchants wholly blind to these vital considerations, and looking to nothing but the support of the tea market in England, are exceedingly exasperated at Captain Elliot's return to reason in abandoning the blockade,[82] and are still striving all they can to prevent business being carried on. Unfortunately they have far too much of Captain Elliot's confidence and ear and we have much to do to counteract their selfish counsels.

The parties I allude to are the correspondents of *Palmers Mackillop*, *Cockerells*, *Gledstanes*, *Gregsons* Houses. Our own impression is that the tea market will take care of itself next year, if not this. At all events, be this as it may, we cannot in conscience sacrifice for it the extensive interests we have in hand consisting at this moment of 18,000 bales of Cotton at this anchorage, besides about 14,000 which we have been sent up and more to come, not to mention other goods.

The accommodation now under discussion is based on the following requirements of the Chinese:—first, the retirement from China of the proscribed foreigners, it having been announced to the Emperor that they had actually gone, but with a proviso that if they repent and abstain from dealing in the drug they may

[81] An interesting comment about the strategy of negotiation by someone who had lived in China twenty one years.

[82] Questions of interest were naturally important to merchants caught in the uncertainty of supplies in time of war. Market manipulation was, however, another matter. At about this time, Captain Elliot's wife, Clara, wrote in a letter : 'He [Captain Charles Elliot] has had a set of them [his own countrymen] to deal with whom it was morally impossible to satisfy—a rapacious and ravenous race of wolves each howling after his prey. Never was I so brought into contact with the mercantile world as of late and truly they have lowered the English character in *my* eyes. They sacrifice everything, every feeling, for *dollar making*'. (Quoted by Hoe, *The Taking of Hong Kong*, pp. 98–99).

return. Secondly, the retirement of the opium ships from the waters of China. These being agreed to by Captain Elliot, he requires from the Chinese: first, the withdrawal of the offensive proclamations against the English; secondly, a return to the state of affairs as they existed on 1st august,—viz., the restoration of Chinese servants, food, etc., at Macao; Thirdly, permission to English ships to trade outside. This, the Chinese have great difficulty in granting. Elliot is sanguine of obtaining it, but (as I have said) others with equal means of judging are not so. Fourthly, the Hong Kong homicide is to be considered as balanced by the unfortunate affair of the *Black Joke* and no more demand of life for life on that score.[83]

It is well ascertained that the High Commissioner is most desirous of preventing an outbreak, and feels himself to be in a most critical position. He sent for Mr. Bridgman, an American missionary, and though he did not admit him to an audience, he expressed through his officers his extreme anxiety to know when answers can be expected from the English Government to Captain Elliot's despatches, and his wish till then to let matters remain in their present footing.[84] His great object is to annihilate the opium trade, on which he has staked his official character, most probably his life, and he perhaps knows enough of what I must be excused for terming the senseless clamour of the High Church party,[85] against the traffic, to hope for the cooperation of our Government in his designs. You, I think, will not be led away by the misstatements, which are so industriously circulated on the subject and as you have access to accurate information from so many of your friends who have lately gone home, you will, I hope, give the benefit of your powerful influence to the right side. During 21 years that I have passed almost entirely in China, I can conscientiously declare that I have never seen a native in the least bestialized by opium smoking, nor any Chinese

[83] 'The Hong Kong homicide': the murder of the Chinese referred to in Letter **175**, note 68. The '*Black Joke*': see note 80 above.

[84] Elijah Coleman Bridgman (1801–1861) was one of the first two American missionaries to arrive in China. The other was the Rev. David Abeel. Both had sailed from New York to Canton with William Hunter in the *Roman* (Captain Lavender). (Hunter, *The Fan Kwae at Canton*, p. 12). Bridgman was the founder and principal contributor to the *Chinese Repository*. For details about the Repository, see Fay, *Opium War*, p. 83). Two Americans, Elijah Bridgeman and Charles King, were the only foreigners who were permitted to witness the destruction of the opium stock. (See Letter **172**, note 62).

[85] The 'clamour of the High Church party' was led in England by the Rev. Algernon Sydney Thelwall (1795–1863) who was a fellow of Trinity College, Cambridge. In 1839 he published a book against opium which supported the attitude of the Chinese authorities on moral ground: *The Iniquities of the Opium Trade with China; Being a Development of the Main Causes which Exclude the Merchants of Great Britain from the Advantages of an Unrestricted Commercial Intercourse with that Vast Empire*, etc. London, Allen & Co., 1839.

Instalment extracts from Thelwall's pamphlet appeared in *The Times*. In the margin of one of the instalments, Palmerston wrote: 'most probably the work of anti-slavery agitators whose occupation is in a great measure gone'. (Quoted by Fay, *The Opium War*, p. 192).

with his faculties more impaired from excessive indulgence in the habit, nor indeed so much so as gluttons and topers in our own country, while of this the influences are far from common, and much of the opium smoked, used to be on convivial occasions of the upper classes as in England Champagne and costly wines.[86] Forgive this little digression which I shall sum up satisfactorily by adding that our operations in that line go on well and our treasury well replenished from that source, possesses almost a monopoly of ready money in the fleet.

Captain Elliot thinks that to comply with the conditions of the Chinese, it will be necessary for me to make a voyage to Manila and back, which can be easily managed in three or four weeks, but will be exceedingly inconvenient.

In conclusion I cannot but think that the coming season's export of tea to England will be limited under any circumstances, so that you will be safe in holding out for good prices, but should these be obtainable, it is always satisfactory to realize.

The *Black Joke*[87] from Singapore brings accounts of the *Coutts*[88] being there with overland news to 25th June, but she has brought us no particulars except a *Times* of the 8th.

With kindest regards to your partners, I remain, my dear Sir, most sincerely yours,

P.S. Please communicate this to [Mr.] William Jardine and Mr. Alexander Matheson. The *Robert Fulton* sent out by *Howland & Aspinwall* sails today for New York. Her supercargo, Mr. James Ryan,[89] remains as our agent in Canton.

178. The same to the same, 24 September 1839

My dear Sir,

Since writing my letter of this date, I have received the enclosed communication[90] of 21st instant from my friend Mr.Veiga of Macao, confirming, on the authority of an influential Chinese, who is a go-between with the Mandarins, the hopes of a speedy accommodation of differences; on which I am therefore more disposed to rely than I was before. His letter gives so characteristic an account of

[86] The view that opium was an innocuous social habit was held sincerely by James Matheson. Like that of most other opium traders of the time, his investigations into Chinese addiction could only have been superficial, and the financial advantages derived from the trade (mentioned in the same breath at the end of the paragraph) were a powerful disincentive to investigating matters further.

[87] It is unclear whether the *Black Joke* referred to here is the same ship as the unfortunate *Black Joke* mentioned earlier in the Letter and in note 80 above.

[88] For the *Coutts* episode, see below, Letter **183**.

[89] For James Ryan, see above Letter **172**, note 55.

[90] The 'communication' was not traced. It suggests, however, that on some critical matters the firm's intelligence could be better that official intelligence.

the state of affairs, that it will be worth your while to have it translated and it may even be interesting at the foreign Office should you wish to give them good information; of course suppressing names.

I still think the permission to trade outside will be so clogged with conditions as to prove fallacious and nugatory.

Yours sincerely.

P.S. Captain Elliot proceeded yesterday to Macao, no doubt with the view of continuing his negotiations in accordance with the mandarins there. I have had the Portuguese letter translated and hand you a translation in lieu of the original.

179. William Jardine in London to James Matheson in China,
25 September 1839[91]

My dear Matheson,

I have this moment heard of one [ship sailing] for Singapore from Liverpool, and write these few lines to inform you that Mr. John Abel Smith begs you will not take any more American bills till you hear again from him, or me. His language is very strong. 'Tell him, not to be tempted by any rate of exchange'. He has his reasons for giving you this advice. Mr. {Jordan}[92] is supposed to be in a scrape, and is borrowing at a very high rate of interest.

We have heard nothing satisfactory from Lord Palmerston, nor have I seen him.[93] He is desirous of having an interview, and hopes to find time in the course of a few days.

There are three or four addresses prepared and now in circulation for signature. One here, one in Liverpool and Manchester, and one in Glasgow.

As [and] if an opportunity offers from hence tomorrow or next day, I shall write to you more fully by that conveyance. In the meanwhile we are all well, and with kind regards to all our establishment, I remain, yours sincerely,

[91] This is one of the first letters written by William Jardine to Canton following his return to London from the Orient via the Levant and Italy .

[92] Mr. Jordan was not identified.

[93] By the time William Jardine wrote this Letter, Palmerston had already seen John Abel Smith and George Gerard de Hochepied Larpent (the Chairman of the East India and China Association— See Letter **151**, note 7). He had also seen Sir Alexander Johnston, the father of Captain Elliot's deputy, Alexander Johnston. (Fay, *Opium War*, p. 192). Aside from requests for interviews, Palmerston was inundated by petitions to the Queen, to the Government, and to himself as Foreign Secretary. The Bombay Chamber of Commerce had petitioned for a cash advance against the Opium Receipts; the Calcutta Chamber of Commerce had sent a similar petition; and besides the 'addresses' mentioned here by William Jardine, from the East India and China Associations of London, Liverpool, Manchester and Glasgow, there were also petitions from Newcastle and Hull. All the petitions were asking for the China trade to be put 'on a more secure and permanent footing'. (*Ibid.*, p. 190).

180. William Jardine in London to James Matheson in China,

25–27 September 1839

My dear Matheson,

The [ ] being under despatch for China direct to our consignment, I avail myself of the opportunity of acknowledging and thanking you for your letter of the 24th of May with a few lines added on the 30th of the same month; from which it appears you were once more at liberty but ordered away from the celestial empire. On the recovery of your liberty I congratulate you most sincerely, and as for your expulsion it gave me uneasiness [. . .]

I notice particularly what you say respecting Elliot forbidding the ships to enter the river, and your apprehension that the Chinese may coax him out of his boasts; of this apprehension I partake but hope most sincerely he may act more consistently; for should he be induced to receive payment from the Hong merchants for the opium given up and then open the trade, H.M. ministers will take no notice of the insult, but leave you to carry on the business in the best way you can, while the Chinese will become more insolent and oppressive than ever they have been. Should an accident {or death} occur and the Englishman connected with it make his escape, Elliot would in all probability be {seized} upon and told unless you give up the murderer in ten days or in three days, we shall strangle you; and if the Viceroy of the day should, per chance, be as determined as your friend Lin, he might [act accordingly] though I cannot bring myself to believe that he would in the present occasion have put any of you [into harm's way]. [. . .] He has acted very differently from what was expected and might have gone still farther. Mr. John Abel Smith has, this instant, come to see me. It is his particular wish you should take no more American bills till you hear again from him. His language is very strong: 'Tell him not to be tempted by any exchange rate.'

You will be surprised to hear that we have heard nothing from H.M. ministers reporting their intention, nor have I seen Lord Palmerston. Mr. [John Abel] Smith had an interview with him three days ago when he told him I was anxious to leave town for Scotland, and would not be back for some time; his Lordship said he was desirous of having an interview; as he has many questions to ask and added: 'I suppose he can tell us what ought to be done'. He proposed a day in town in the end of the week and promised to let me know through Mr. Smith when it would [be convenient] to see me, and begged I would not leave Town till we had met. In his conversation with Mr. Smith he led him to believe that as far as his own sentiments went, he was convinced some measures ought to be taken of the gross insult and robbery; but would not commit himself further, even to him, with whom he is on intimate terms.

A deputation from Liverpool and Manchester has reached London, and one from Glasgow is on the way up, to present an address to H.M. Ministers, calling upon them to take measures for protecting our commerce, and our merchants in China, etc., etc.

I attended a meeting of the East India Association the other day when an address was drawn up for signature,[94] and is now in circulation among the mercantile houses. It is addressed to Lord Palmerston, and calls his attention to what has occurred in China, but says nothing about the opium given up. We prefer waiting till the receipts come to hand.

Mr. Crawford[95] and some others are anxious to have it presented immediately. We prefer waiting a few days, in hopes that Lord Palmerston may, of his own accord, make a satisfactory communication on the subject, but shall not wait more than three or four days. The question is very little understood here, and many people are for doing nothing; they, very foolishly, mix up the insult and violence with the illicit trade, and are for remaining quiet, pocketing the insult, and refusing to pay for the opium. I have, however, no fears about the payment either by this government or the Chinese.

September 27th. I was interrupted here and the vessel being detained I have waited quietly [for the] interview with Lord Palmerston which [is due] today—interrupted by a visit from Mr. Trot, a Quaker constituent of the firm[96] who detained me till it was time to go to Lord Palmerston. After waiting two hours, John Abel Smith, [Alexander] Grant and your humble servant were admitted, and, having taken charts with us, we commenced by spreading them out in order that his Lordship might have a clear idea of the country with which we must cope, should H.M. Ministers determine on demanding redress.

He began by asking [about the] difficulty in holding the numerous ports, being decidedly unacquainted with the power, or rather the want of power, of the Celestials—the probability of [a force] was also alluded to, the extent of armament, number of troops necessary, number of shipping, etc. were all described; but no direct avowal made of a determination to coerce [ ]. The conference ended in his Lordship retaining the charts and saying they were to hold a Cabinet counsel Monday next,[97] and he hoped to see us again, in the course of the ensuing week. All this is unsatisfactory enough but we must await silently.

[94] For this address and its signatories, see second attachment to Letter **182**.

[95] William Crawford was an East India agent and one of the two senior partners of *Crawford Colvin & Co.* of 71 Old Broad Street. (*TLCD*). The other partner was B. D. Colvin, who was a member of the executive Committee of the East India and China Association. (See Letter **151,** List of Committee members). William Crawford was also M. P. for Rochdale. 'He took the surname of Crawford in addition to that of Sharman, in pursuance of the will of John Crawford, Esq., to whose estates he succeeded'. (*DPC*). He was elected a member of the influential steering committee of the East India and China Association in charge of the relationship with the government and Parliament. (See Letter **182**).

[96] Mr. Trot was not identified. He was probably a constituent of *Magniac Smith & Co.* ('the firm').

[97] The Cabinet met on 30 September 1839. Sir J. C. Hobhouse, who was the head of the Board of Control and a member of the Cabinet kept a diary of the Cabinet meeting. Palmerston explained 'how

It is difficult to form an opinion as to the real views of the Government, though it is still more difficult to believe they can remain quiet, pocket the insult, and purchase the continuation of the legitimate trade at two million sterling.

We shall see by and by. In the meanwhile be pleased to remember me kindly to all around you, and believe me, my Dear Matheson, yours sincerely.

P. S. Midnight.

I have just returned from dining with Lady Napier who enquired very kindly after you, I have not yet seen Lord Napier.

Teas are firm, and have advanced about a penny per pound, since we received your last advices. We purchased 1,200 or 1,400 chests of Congo a week ago; they might be sold at a penny, or halfpenny per pound advance. Silk rather dull, though the stock is small. Your circular of the 29th of May had not yet come to hand. No complaints from our constituents. I have explained to all I have seen.

181. William Jardine in London to James Matheson in China,

25–28 September 1839[98]

My dear Matheson

[. . .] Since writing the foregoing I have seen Lord Palmerston [. . .] reaction of about one hour, but received no satisfaction about his intentions respecting China; he was civil; asked many questions; examined charts, maps, etc., etc. Many of his questions were to the point, but he did not appear to be aware of the want of power of their war junks.

On Monday the council[99] meet, and he wishes to see [Alexander] Grant, John Abel Smith and myself about the middle of the week. After this interruption I shall [write] again; when I hope to be able to say something more satisfactory. [. . .]

---

one line-of-battleship with two frigates and two or three steamers and some small armed vessels, might blockade the whole coast from the river of Peking down to Canton'. Macaulay, the Secretary at War, was 'eloquent against the Chinese'. And F. T. Baring, the Chancellor of the Exchequer, insisted on knowing 'what was to be done in regards to the two millions of money which the merchants had lost by giving up their opium'. With a small and fragile majority in Parliament and an existing budget deficit of already over a million pounds, Melbourne was quite clear that he would not ask Parliament for the two million pounds owing to the merchants. 'Macaulay was for seizing Chinese property. And so was Palmerston'. The cabinet thus embarked upon a course which meant that China would eventually pay for the opium. This meant that China had first to be defeated in battle and dictated terms. (On the Cabinet meeting of 30 September 1839, see: Fay, *The Opium War*, pp.193–194).

[98] This 5 page long letter is virtually illegible.

[99] 'The council': the Cabinet.

182. William Crawford in London to Robert Wigram Crawford[100] Bombay, 14 October 1839 [101]

My dear Robert,

By the last overland Packet, I wrote you all I could then say on the subject of China affair. I must, to the great disappointment perhaps of many of your friends, repeat that there is no probability of the question of indemnity under Captain Elliot's undertaking, being at the present time brought under discussion with the authorities here with any advantage to the true interests of the Parties. The Memorial from Calcutta was sent thence by the *Waterwitch* and is not yet arrived, but I have a printed copy of it together with the other official papers at that time received in Calcutta from China. I have no reason to doubt but all measures will be taken in perfect concert by those who may be called upon to look after the various interests involved and I cannot say more than that I hope Jamsetjee [Jejeebhoy] and your other friends who had given me their confidence will feel assured that my most unremitting endeavours will be directed for their benefit. It may be proper to observe to you that *Forbes, Forbes & Co.* take no part in the general proceedings on China matters; this is no doubt by the order of Sir Charles[102]. You will see Malcolmson's name[103] in the Committee of nine appointed at the General Meeting of the trade on the 19th September, but he has declined to act, and the signature of [his] House was not given to the letter to Lord Palmerston[104] founded on the Resolution of that day at which *Malcolmson was present* and in which he then concurred. In case there should be discrepancies between my information to you and what may be received from that quarter, you will now be better able to judge of the value of each.

The Committee appointed on the 19th September met on the 24th and appointed a Subcommittee consisting of Larpent,[105] John Abel Smith, and myself

[100] Robert Wigram Crawford was William Crawford's son. (See the ending of this Letter). He may have been a partner in *Thomas Crawford & Co.* in Bombay. (See list of Bombay Agencies in Letter **38**, note 15. The firm is no longer listed after 1841. (*EIRD*).

[101] This copy of the original letter was probably sent to James Matheson in Canton by John Abel Smith in London.

[102] Sir Charles Forbes, the head of *Forbes, Forbes & Co.*, which was Jamsetjee Jejeebhoy's principal London agent with *Magniac Smith & Co.*

[103] James Malcolmson was a member of the committee of the East India and China Association. (See list of committee members in Letter **151**, note 7).

[104] The 'letter to Lord Palmerston' and its list of signatories is quoted below in full.

[105] Sir George Gerard de Hochepied Larpent (1786–1855) was the chairman of the *East India and China Association*. (See above, Letter **151**, List of committee members). He was an MP in several parliaments, starting in 1840, and was created a baronet in 1841. He published a pamphlet in support of protection of West Indian sugar, and another on the pre-1833 negotiations between the Board of Control and the East India Company. He also edited the journals of his half brother, Francis Seymour Larpent and the *History of Turkey* of his grandfather. (*DNB*). Earlier in 1839 he had become one of the founding investors in the *Assam Company* which was created shortly after the first tea grown in

delegating to us the powers of the Committee particularly for the purpose of holding communication with Government. On the 27th this Subcommittee saw the deputation which was in Town from Liverpool, they have also entrusted to us, the care of the interests of the People there. It was understood the Manchester people would do the same, but it seems it did not comform with the self-importance of Mr. Macvicar to take that course.[106] He saw Lord Palmerston a few days ago and enclosed you will find an extract from the Manchester Guardian, being Mr. Macvicar's report of that interview. We have since seen Lord Palmerston, and I cannot better convey to you the knowledge of what past than by sending the enclosed Precis which Larpent committed to paper[107] immediately afterwards. Indeed part of it is Lord Palmerston's dictation made for the purpose of public communication to those interested in the Property which on the 30th May last was on its way to China and which is estimated at 1,000,000 Sterling from Liverpool and London. I do not think this packet will carry the Despatches from Government for which the *Ariel* is understood to wait in the Red Sea. The *Mor*[108] is now ordered to Falmouth, and Lord Palmerston said his despatches for her would be ready by the end of next week, and the *Mor* will wait at Falmouth for them. A very high opinion is entertained here of the judgment, discretion and firmness of Admiral Maitland,[109] he may very likely be [in] charge of the force that *is intended to visit* the shores of the Celestial Empire, putting all things together as well as we can. We are now enclined to believe that the Season 1839–1840 will be got through with the Chinese, and that English property will be withdrawn in good time in the coming year to prevent its being involved in the immediate consequence of the first measures of the Force that may appear *there in April next.*

Matters must assume a very different aspect to what I contemplate to warrant the hope that the Port of Canton will open to British Trade, I may say to any Trade, in the Season 1840. It does not appear likely that the object which will be insisted upon on our behalf, will be either acceded to on the part of the Chinese

British India was sold at auction in London in January 1839. (Le Pichon, Alain, 'Le premier thé des Indes britanniques: du rêve à la réalité », *Cahiers victoriens et édouardiens*, No 55, 2002, p. 198 ; Antrobus, H. *A History of the Assam Company, 1839–1953*, Edinburgh, T. & A. Constable Ltd., 1957, pp. 35–36).

[106] An interesting independent opinion about John Macvicar. Early Victorian cabinet ministers had apparently more time to make themselves available to a variety of petitioners than latter-day cabinet ministers.

[107] Larpent's précis is quoted in full below.

[108] The *Mor* was a new steamer owned jointly by *Jardine, Matheson & Co*. and Jamsetjee Jejeebhoy. It sailed on its maiden voyage from Falmouth to Bombay on 23 October 1839. Palmerston used the new ship to send his dispatches and alert Captain Charles Elliot that a force was being assembled and would reach him the Spring of 1840. (Fay, *Opium War*, p. 194).

[109] On Admiral Maitland previous involvement with China, see Letter **163**, note 58. Admiral Maitland died on 30 November 1839, six weeks after this Letter was written.

or abandoned by us without such struggle as will occupy much time. I do not see where you will find ground to sanction your going into the India market for cotton and other usual exports which will be in course of growth and preparation at the time when those advices reach you and if there should be no imports into China, the exports must be very limited indeed, even if matters should be accommodated in time for the latter operations, and if Tea, Raw Silk, etc., should be in readiness at Canton, what then will become of your next year crop of Cotton? This is the only other market known, and the price must fall till it tempts shipments to this country. I have expected that the price of American cotton here would have given way before this time. I still think that this is a result to be reckoned upon, not only in connection with the general state of our pending transactions with America, but because I believe the parties interested and active in upholding the market will not be able to do so long in the face of the present stock and the further supplies which the coming new crop must bring. I understand De Vitre's opinion[110] of prices to be reckoned upon your cotton ranges from 3½ to 3 according to quality, [which] I repeat here, because their rates express also my prospective view on their point; but to assist you in any dealings to their quarter, our advices by December mail will no doubt be in very good time to meet the requisite fall in price with you [ ].

We, (I mean Larpent, Smith and myself) have undertaken to give Lord Palmerston our opinion on the point which ought to be insisted upon to regulate our future Trade with China. This will engage our immediate very serious attention in conference first, with those now here more fully informed of localities than we can be. I consider that the information that the opium is ordered to be sent to [Chuenpee] is working with good effect on the public mind in respect to the indemnity. No one doubts but it will eventually be sold. Its removal at an expense of 300,000 Dollars would not be indulged in merely to make bonfire there.[111] This is the estimate cost of the proceeding as mentioned to us by Lord Palmerston, and which, we suppose, has been reported to him by Captain Elliot. I hope you will be able to satisfy Jamsetjee [Jejeebhoy] that the delay in sending in the Memorial being in accordance with the unanimous opinion of all his friends here with whom I am acting, there ought to be no misgivings on your side as to the prudence of the course we are taking. Government being in possession

[110] On Mathias, Theodosius, Denis DeVitre, see above, Letter **61**, note 69.

[111] It is curious that the writer, William Crawford, should have formed the view that the opium delivered to Commissioner Lin was not destined to be destroyed, but to be resold, particularly in view of the fact he mentions that 'despatches till 30 May 1839' had been received in London by the time this Letter was written. The only explanation can be that none of the despatches described the destruction of the opium stocks, and that the accounts of Elijah Bridgman and Charles King (the sole foreign witnesses of the opium destruction) had not yet reached London, not even orally. Their *Repository* Article was reproduced in the *Times* only on 1 November 1839, a couple of weeks after this Letter was written.

of Captain Elliot's despatches furnishes a sufficient ground for an instruction to require indemnity for the opium, a claim much strengthened by the more recently ascertained fact[112] of there being no intention on the part of the Chinese to destroy it. DeVitre has read this. I cannot add to it.

Ever your most affectionate father.

. . .

'At an interview between Messrs. Larpent, Crawford and Smith and Lord Palmerston on Thursday the 10th October 1839,[113] His Lordship made the following communication:

'By despatches received from Admiral Maitland, dated 13th July last, in the Bay of Bengal, it appeared that in consequence of the accounts received from China of the transactions there, the Admiral had sent the *Volage* Frigate 28 pieces to Macao for the protection of British interests, but that he had thought it better not to go there in the *Wellesley* 74, until he should know what course the Government in England intended to pursue, at the same time stating he should hold himself in readiness to go if subsequent accounts should lead him to think that his presence in the China Seas was necessary for the protection of British subjects. As far as is known the Governor General of India[114] thought the question of too great magnitude to be dealt with by his own authority and therefore it was probable he would want to receive communication from the Government at home.'

It then appears that measures have been taken to protect British property in China and with regard to the future Trade, the deputation were assured by Lord Palmerston that the question was under the serious consideration of Government. His Lordship did not of course give any information of what was intended to be done, but he repeated his caution that the Merchants connected with China should act with prudence in taking care of themselves and their properties. The deputation heard nothing to induce them to believe that the state of things would be altered at Macao or Canton from what there were in May last, by any measure on the part of the Superintendent.

The communication on the other side was the answer dictated by Lord Palmerston to the question put by the Deputation on the security of Property etc., at Macao, and on the intentions, as far as they were known by Government, of the Admiral in the India station, and of the Governor General of India, as regards to the recent events in Canton. In reply to the question of the Deputation as to what

[112] It was clearly not an 'ascertained fact'. *Ibid.*

[113] This is 'Larpent's précis' referred to in the second paragraph of this Letter.

[114] The Governor General of India: George Eden, Earl of Auckland (1784–1849). Auckland was a first cousin of Captain Charles Elliot. He was First Lord of the Admiralty in 1834 and again in 1846. His tenure as Governor General of India, from 1835 to 1841, coincided with the Afghan War and the beginning of the Opium War. (*DNB*).

should be written by the mail of the 14th instant to India and China, Lord Palmerston observed that he could only say the subject was under serious consideration of Government, and that in a few days the despatch would be sent to Captain Elliot to go by the *Ariel.* He repeated his former remark that the Merchants at Canton should act with prudence and caution for their own safety and that of their property; and he seemed to consider Captain Elliot's notice to them rather as proceeding from the wish to caution them than as ordering them to leave Canton, and that they might remain there upon their own responsibility.

In reply to the question as to future measures, Lord Palmerston left it to the Deputation to infer what the view of Government were from the general tone of the conversation. At the same time it was clear that nothing should be said or done to alarm the Chinese until the time for action came.[115]

The impression left in my mind was that during the season 1839 the Merchants at Canton must shift for themselves and do the best they can, until the armed Force should arrive about the time of South West monsoon, April or May 1840.[116] They should not let themselves or their properties [be] exposed to any hostile endeavour on the part of the Chinese, at the same time nothing fell from Lord Palmerston to commit him as to the intention of Government, nor were the words 'armed Force' used by him. He wished to have from the Merchants an exposition of their sentiments upon the subject generally, and also in some detail what should be the objects Government should endeavour to obtain from the Chinese Government.

. . .

The Right Honorable Viscount Palmerston, G.C.B. etc., etc., etc.[117]
My Lord,

The undersigned British Merchants and others engaged in the Trade with China on their own behalf and on the behalf of their friends and Correspondents in that Country beg to represent to H.M. Government the very great apprehension and alarm, with which they view the recent events at Canton.

In all former suspension of the Trade no personal violence of so general a trend was used against British Residents, but in the present instance measures have been adopted against the whole body of Foreigners of such a character as to render their continuance at Canton in the opinion of H.M. Superintendent incompatible with the security of their persons and property. By the latest accounts (30th May last) it appears that under the authority vested in him by H.M. Government

[115] It is difficult to imagine a more guarded and uncommitted response.

[116] The interpretation of the Palmerston's response is equally remarkable, showing George de H. Larpent to have been exceedingly adept at interpreting political oracles.

[117] This is the China 'address' mentioned in the first paragraph of this Letter. It was written by the *East India and China Association* on behalf of its members. Many members of the Association were signatories to this document.

the Chief Superintendent of the Trade of British Subjects in China had withdrawn [from] Canton and closed the British Factory, and that in compliance with his orders, the whole of the British residents at Canton had either followed him to Macao or was preparing to do so, whereby the British Trade with Canton may be considered as closed.

It is necessary for the undersigned to point out the magnitude and importance of the China trade, involving as it does so largely the Commercial and Manufacturing interests and the Revenue and personal Comforts of the whole British Empire. Nor is it desired to mix up in their address the question regarding the trade in opium, which they think should be reserved for a separate consideration; when the gentlemen deputed from China arrive,[118] and when the several Memorials from India and elsewhere are brought before H.M. Government by the parties to whom they are entrusted, but the undersigned respectfully submit that as by the 3rd and 4th William IV Chap 9.3.[119] and by the Orders in Council agreed in pursuance thereof, and by the Royal Commission and Instruction to the Chief Superintendent, the Regulation of the Canton trade was placed under H.M. Government and subjected to the Control of its representative, the Merchants engaged therein feel it indispensable to call upon H.M. Government to know what course is to be pursued in respect to the Property which may be unavoidably left at Canton, that which has been and may be detained at Macao by order of the Superintendent, and that which may now be afloat.

The undersigned would also most earnestly pray H.M. Government to give them as early an intimation as possible of its intention to guide them with respect to future prosecution of their most important Brands of commerce, in which their interests and that of their friends are so deeply involved, and they would the more strongly urge the necessity of an early decision from the apprehension that in the event of any protracted delay the trade would pass into the hands of the merchants of other nations[120] not subject to a control similar to that experienced on the subject of Great Britain.

And further the undersigned beg leave to state that they have approved a Committee of Gentlemen named on the margin connected with the London, East India, and China Association to represent them, and with that Committee the

[118] Alexander Matheson was among those 'deputed from China'. The other two were Robert Inglis (Lancelot Dent's partner) and Hugh Hamilton Lindsay. (*Opium War*, p. 190). When reaching London the three 'deputies' joined forces with William Jardine and Alexander Grant.

[119] '3rd and 4th William IV': statute previously referred to in the footnotes as the '1833 India Act'. The sense of the text should be to ignore the semi-colon after 'separate consideration' and to treat the comma after 'entrusted' as a full stop.

[120] A thinly veiled reference to the Americans, whose Canton merchants had signed the 'opium bond' and were virtually the only ones now allowed to trade at Whampoa. As the only transhipping agents for British exporters and importers to and from China, the Americans were minting money from the situation.

undersigned solicit the most unreserved communication from H.M. Government, and have the honour to be, my Lord, etc.
Committee: Messrs. Larpent, Crawford, MP, Gregson, Bates, Gledstanes, John Abel Smith, MP, Weeding, Malcolmson, J. H. Palmer.

Signatories {94}[121]: *Cockerill & Co.*, *Crawford Colvin & Co.*, Thomas Weeding, *Baring Brothers & Co.*, *Gledstanes & Co.*, *Palmer McKillop*, *Dent & Co.*, *Fletcher Alexander & Co.*, {*Rawson Norton & Co.*}, *Scott Bell & Co.*, *Jamieson Brothers & Co.*, *Daniell & Co.*, *Hunter Gouger & Co.*, *Truman Cook*, *Barclay Brothers & Co.*, *Gregson Melville & Co.*, *Wise Trubridge & Co.*, *Lyall Brothers & Co.*, *Findlay Hodgson & Co.*, Alexander Grant (of Canton), *Gardner Urquhart & Co.*, M. S. Thomson, *Magniac Smith & Co.*, *Small Colquhoun & Co.*, *Robert & Richard Brown & Co.*, R.G.S.A. & {E. Turning}, *Copeland & Gareth*, *Dallas & Coles*, *Walkinshaw & Co.*, *J & B. Pearse & Co.*, *William Burnie & Co.*, *Saunderson Fry Fox & Co.*, *Curtis & Harvey*, *Ewart McNaughty & Co.*, *Thomas Ashmore & Co.*, *Hyde Lenox & Co.*, *Hulbert Layton & Co.*, *Johnson & Renny & Co.*, *{Millman}*, *Larkins & Co.*, *Grew Wigram & Crew*, *John Pierce & Co.*, *R. Eglington & Co.*, *Copeland Barnes & Co.*, Alexander Crow, *Richards Little & Co.*, *Grindlay Christian & Matthew*, *Phillip & [ ]*, *A. W. Robertson*, {*J.*} *Cochran & Co.*, G. Lamsley, A. Lungley, *Reed Irving & Co.*, *Morrison Crydert & Co.*, W.G. *[ ]*, {*Jey*} *Brothers*, William Brylling, James Richardson, *William Harper & Co.*, Francis Chambers, *Williams & J. Wales*, Thomas Heath, *[ ]* {*Lerte*} *& Co.*, {*Broudribble*} *& Lloyd*, P. Herris, E. V. Thomas Green, John Hide, *Houghton & Howell*, *S. Wardell & Co.*, G. J. Bowring, Walter Joseph, *Pitman [ ] & Co.*, *Thomas Miller & Co.*, J . *[ ]* Lancaster, H. Thompson, C. J. Green, {*Maugher Pruit & Co.*}, {*Cothweith Paul & Pryer*}, *R. & R. J. Hornton & {Urst}*, J. R. Robertson, C.A. Read of the Firm of, *A. L. Johnston & Co.* Singapore, Alexander [ ], M. Elias, C. W. Furle, *Shaw & Maxwell*, *William Freeman*, *Buckler*, *Bagster & [ ]*, *J. Clegg & Co.*, *Guild [ ] & Co.*, Timothy Smith, *Macleod & Co.*, W. C. Crack, N. de Croix, *Durant & Co.*, *J. & R. Moffat*.

183. James Matheson in Hong Kong to J. W. Henderson[122] in Bombay.
16 October 1839

My dear Sir,

After a most anxious and unsatisfactory period of suspense since I had last the pleasure of writing to you (on 9th ultimo per *Hellas*) I am at length enabled to inform you of Captain Elliot having issued a Public Notice two days ago, that British ships pending the receipt of instructions from the home government will

[121] The number 94 refers to the actual number of signatures collected.
[122] J. W. Henderson: a partner in *Remington & Co.* in Bombay.

have provisional liberty of trading outside of the Bogue at Cheunpee paying the Whampoa port charges,[123] subject to the conditions of being searched, and to the penalty of confiscation, should opium be found on board. The punishment of death is also still persisted in by the Chinese; but Captain Elliot considers it important to have set aside their demand for our signing a bond voluntarily to submit to it.

The Portuguese made a strong effort to have the outside trade conducted through Macao, which would have been more convenient, but on this the Chinese set a decided veto. Chuenpee presents many serious difficulties, the most obvious of which is the want of warehouses. But Captain Elliot is sanguine that means will gradually be found to arrange all matters of detail to mutual satisfaction, with which view he yesterday proceeded, accompanied by some of our mercantile community as a council, to meet the Hong merchants at Macao. While such trade is going on he will engage that no hostile measures to jeopardize property shall be commenced by the British Government. Should the plan of outside trade be found feasible it will undoubtedly be a valuable boon, but sad experience renders most of us sceptical on this head; and transshipments to American vessels are accordingly still going on at the high freight of 5 dollars per Bombay bale; all, however under engagements previously contracted which could not be broken off. The High Commissioner is said to be extremely anxious to leave the province and take possession of the new Government to which he has been elevated by the Emperor. Hence his desire to make provisional terms of accommodation, including the remarkable concession of no longer holding Captain Elliot and the general trade responsible for the surrender of a man to atone for the Hong Kong homicide,[124] alleging that he knows the vessel to which the murderer belongs (meaning it is supposed the *Mangalore*) and unless he is delivered up, the vessel and crew will be assuredly exterminated!

To incline his Excellency to conciliation Captain Elliot has, however, volunteered some concessions which are in our opinion highly objectionable. Of these, the most remarkable is his proposing to the Commissioner that no British firm shall in future be allowed to reside in China till he, Captain Elliot, shall have forwarded to the authorities a declaration signed by each member of it, solemnly engaging in [having] no concern with opium, either direct or indirect, nor [permitting] anyone in their employ or under their control to have anything to do with the drug, on pain of the firm being expelled; furthermore the commander and consignee of every vessel must on the day of arrival hand to the Superintendent a

[123] The new Chuenpee trading arrangement negotiated by Captain Elliot and which James Matheson is so skeptical about, had hardly time to come into effect before the *Coutts* episode put it in jeopardy. (See the end of this Letter).

[124] On the Hong Kong homicide and the Black Joke, see above, Letter **175**, note 68, and Letter **177**, note 83.

solemn declaration in Chinese and English, that he has brought no opium to China, has none on board, neither will receive any. Captain Elliot had previously on the 11th ultimo ordered away from the *outer* anchorage all vessels having opium on board at the imminent hazard of their suffering from the equinoctal gales which were almost sure to occur. At a subsequent period he made a voluntary offer to the Chinese that they might search any suspect vessel at this anchorage and confiscate her with her cargo, if they found opium, a proposal which they were cautious enough not to act on. To so extreme a point did he carry his animosity against the drug that he persuaded Captain Smith[125] of the H.M.S. *Volage* to the unwarrantable step of seizing the Portuguese Barque *Ann* which had a few chests on board, on the plea of the papers not being regular, because they were dated two years back. A reference to the Portuguese governor of Macao set this right and she was released after a few days.

We shall modify the arrangement of our firm so as to prevent our drug operations at Manila being interfered with by Captain Elliot's views, should they be carried into effect, which, however, we much doubt; for we cannot believe that the British Government will adopt the novel and unheard of principle of acting against its own subjects to enforce the fiscal regulations of a foreign power; unless indeed far larger concessions can be got from the Chinese than have yet been thought of.

It is well-known the trade of Gibraltar is supported almost entirely by smuggling for the Spanish market. What would our Government say were that of Spain to call on the British to put a stop to this? The very idea would, I presume, be scouted as ridiculous and absurd.[126]

The *Coutts* which arrived only a few days ago, took a pilot at Macao without communicating here and has proceeded towards Whampoa. It is believed the supercargo has since sent an express to stop her, but if is doubtful whether it would be in time. Captain Elliot is fearful lest this example should be followed first by one, then by more and gradually by all;[127] chiefly under the influence of

[125] Captain Henry Smith was the commander of *H.M.S. Volage*. (*NL*). He was involved in the 'Battle of the junks' in September 1839. See Letter **175**.

Captain Charles Elliot's personal aversion to the opium trade had been well-known for a number of years. But the instructions which he had observed until March 1839 had been neither to condone not to hinder the opium trade. Since the opium confiscation, however, the situation had changed and he regarded the protection of the legitimate trade—his immediate duty—impossible to fulfill without curtailing the opium trade in the vicinity of Whampoa. James Matheson mentions that the *Ann* was a Portuguese ship, but he does not state who owned the opium on board.

[126] The argument in the parallel drawn here between the smuggling situation in China and that in Gibraltar acquired its full force only *after* the Treaty of Nanking, which totally failed to mention, let alone regulate, the opium trade. (Fairbank, *Trade and Diplomacy*, pp. 133–151).

[127] The full significance of this defiance of Captain Elliot's ban on British shipping sailing to Whampoa to trade appeared only a few days later. In order to sail to Whampoa, the *Coutts* captain had

two legal opinions by the advocate General of Madras[128] declaring Captain Elliot's interdiction of Whampoa as illegal and not binding. We will hope however for better things and shall ourselves be most reluctant to belie our past conduct by turning round at this late period to disobey the Chief Superintendent's injunction under the conviction that if you or *Messrs. Jamsetjee Jejeebhoy & Co.* had doubted the legality or expediency of obeying his interdict of 22nd May you would long since have informed us.

Amidst the weighty cares of the High Commissioner you will be surprised to learn that the only points on which he is unbendingly firm are the departure from China of the rest of the proscribed merchants and of the ships that surrendered opium in April last; with a proviso, however, that the proscribed may return on repenting and engaging to abstain from their former malpractices. Till these conditions are complied with, which it is believed they will be this week, the British community cannot resume their habitations at Macao. We have in consequence sold the *Hercules* to the Americans for $25,000[129] to take cotton to Whampoa, and shall reside on board the *General Wood* till permitted to land at Macao.

You will have seen from the blockade announced in our circular of the 23rd ultimo, as declared on the 11th, that Captain Elliot did not long hold to the plan of removal to Manila alluded to in mine of 9th. The chief ostensible motive of the blockade was the disappearance, etc.[130]

By an estimate we have just made of tonnage for England now here, I am sorry to perceive it amounts to 15,000 registered tons, besides about 10,000 ditto known to be on the way, and other which will no doubt come that we are not aware of. Some of the vessels, now here will no doubt go for cargoes to Manila; but making every allowance for this the quantity of tonnage is far too large for a healthy tea market either here or in England, which is calculated to throw a gloom over the prospect immediately before us unless war with China [occurs] to check supplies.

I remain, my dear Sir, sincerely yours.

---

to sign the opium bond. Commissioner Lin concluded that if one British captain could sign the bond, all could. He used this argument to go back over the Chuenpee trading arrangement so laboriously negotiated by Captain Elliot. This was the immediate cause of the 'Battle of Chuenpee' of 2 November 1839. See below, Letter **188**, note 142.

[128] On George Norton, Advocate General at Madras, see above, Letter **177**, note 76.

[129] The American houses were now busy buying ships to increase their tonnage, a precondition of coping with the growing British transshipping business between Hong Kong and Whampoa. Besides the *Hercules*, the Americans (Shillaber) bought the *Sir Charles Malcolm*, (see Letter **188**, 2nd paragraph), which now became known as the *Kosciusko* (after the Polish-American patriot). (For the '*Kosciusko* episode', see below, Letter **224**). They also bought the *Cambridge*, (see above, Letter **172**, note 61) which was no longer needed as an auxiliary warship and became the *Chesapeake*. (*Opium War*, p. 201).

[130] The text of the letter is interrupted here by the following bracketed remark: 'as in letter to J. A. Smith p. 138, of 24th September 1839 to 'sacrifice for it the extensive interest we have in hand here'.

P.S. I enclose an abstract[131] of Captain Elliot's negotiations with the Chinese, prepared by the Chamber of Commerce, which not being yet in general circulation, please reserve for the confidential perusal of your goodselves and *Messrs. Jamsetjee Jejeebhoy & Co*. It is not calculated to give a respectable idea of the consideration accorded by the Chinese to the representative of our country.

184. James Matheson on board the *Scaleby Castle* in Hong Kong to H. W. Hubble[132] in Canton, 17 October 1839

My dear Sir,

I avail myself of the opportunity of the ships starting for Canton to forward the enclosed copy of Captain Elliot's public notice of the 14th Instant announcing permission from the Chinese for carrying on British trade at Chuenpee, on condition of the ships being searched, and without signing any bond. He went to Macao the day before yesterday to arrange the details of the plan in which, however, so many difficulties seem to present themselves that considerable delay will probably occur before it can come into operation.

This will of course prevent the *Laconia* obtaining any outward freight for HongKong and render her coming down for a second cotton freight hence to Whampoa so much less advantageous than your reckoned on, that you will probably not be adverse to concur with us in canceling the proposed arrangement; which we shall much prefer under existing circumstances. And if as we hope, you are disposed to meet us, on this point, on a liberal and friendly footing, you may consider the contemplated arrangement as already cancelled and at once commence on your plans for loading the *Luconia* to America.

I must confess to a great looseness and incaution in my verbal understanding with you on this subject; which ought to have been on the implied condition of cancellation as a matter of course, in the event of British Trade re-opening. As it is we must in some measure trust to your indulgence on the occasion, which we shall be always desirous of reciprocating in the course of future transactions between us.[133]

I propose embarking in the *Good Success* at daylight on Saturday, but shall not be long absent.[134] You may continue to address me in reply, which will be answered by Mr. Wright or Mr. Boyd.

131 The 'abstract' was not traced.

132 Henry W. Hubble: an American agent in Canton. 26 of his letters are listed in the *BI*.

133 'My word is my bond' still applied here, and the contract—written in the present case—could only be modified by mutual consent.

134 James Matheson here misinformed his correspondent on purpose, in the knowledge the information would not fail to reach the Chinese authorities. At the request ot Captain Elliot, he wanted to be seen to comply for a time with Commissioner Lin's order which had expelled the established opium traders from China. In fact James Matheson did not sail to Manila as originally planned. He merely

Hoping you continue to improve in health, I remain, dear Sir,
Yours sincerely,

185. William Jardine in London to James Matheson in China,
21 October 1839[135]

[. . .] Andrew Johnstone and Alexander Grant are both in town. John Abel Smith is in the country and will not be here until tomorrow. Hollingworth Magniac is in the country. [ ]

We have employed W. P. Freshfield,[136] the solicitor, to look into the nature of our claims [against] H. M. government and to engage the *Times* newpaper to write in favour of them; but I have not heard what he has done.

Be pleased to present my kind regards to all around you, and believe me, my dear Matheson,

Yours sincerely,

186. James Matheson in Tytam Bay[137] to John Abel Smith in London,
31 October 1839

My dear Sir,

You will be much surprised to hear by this conveyance, that, after a Committee of British Merchants had gone to Macao, by Captain Elliot's request, and arranged with the Hong Merchants, on 22nd Instant, the mode of conducting trade at Chuenpee, Captain Elliot, on 25th Instant, announced in a public notice, that the Chinese authorities had broken faith, and required all ships to proceed to Whampoa, besides peremptorily demanding the surrender of a man to atone for the Hong Kong homicide. 'This shameless proceeding of the Government',

sailed to 'Ty Tam', on the other side of Hong Kong island, and did not disclose his whereabouts except to a few trusted friends.

[135] This letter is almost completely illegible.

[136] The firm of City solicitors which became Freshfields was founded in 1716 by Thomas Woodford. Later in the eighteenth century, the successor firm became solicitors to the Bank of England. The first Freshfield to join the firm was James William Freshfield who was a partner from 1801 to his retirement in 1840, when he was active mostly as an MP. His son, James William Freshfield Jr., was a partner from 1824 to his death in 1857. William Jardine is therefore probably referring here to the latter, mixing up his initials. Freshfield was one of the foremost firms of solicitors in London at the time, and the choice would have been a natural one. But the firm also had a long connection with the Smiths, the Carringtons and the Paynes of banking fame. There was also a connection with William Crawford (the writer of Letter **182** above), as James William Freshfield's brother, Henry Ray Freshfield, was about to marry Jane, William Crawford's daughter. (Slinn, Judy, *A History of Freshfields*, London, Freshfields, 1984, pp. 31, 68).

[137] Tai Tam Bay is situated on the south side of Hong Kong island.

Captain Elliot observed, 'is obviously attributable to the [disobedience] of the *Thomas Coutts*[138] etc., etc.'

I cannot say, however, that this satisfactorily accounts to my mind for so extraordinary a result, and private accounts attribute it to the sinister influence with Howqua, of Mr. [Nugent] Daniell[139]—naturally strong from his former position in the Company's Factory. The Hong Merchants, it is said, at their first interview with the British, were keen for the arrangement, and inclined to give way on many fronts that night, Mr. Daniell had a long consultation with Howqua, and next day the manner of the Chinese was completely changed to the most unaccomodative indifference. [By] what step they, at last, came to an open rupture with captain Elliot, I have not learnt. I am inclined to accuse him of an incautious haste in his negotiations, a disposition to take for granted that favourable concessions are made, without being at sufficient pains to obtain such a clear acknowledgment of them as may remove ambiguity and quibbles. He seems to be quite unaware, that with the Chinese, more than with other people, the appearance of being indifferent to the object sought is the surest road to its attainment. I observe the rupture of the negotiation is as yet only with two inferior officers, the Kuen-min-foo, and a Wei-Yuen[140]—which leaves the High commissioner an opening to disavow their acts.

The last accounts state that Captain Elliot had given up the negotiation to Captain Smith of the *Volage*, who, he thinks, will manage to bring on the Chuenpee scheme again. The *Alligator* man of war, had just arrived, which with the *Volage* and *Hyacinth*, had proceeded to the Bogue.

I still continue in the belief that a great portion of the season's teas will find their way home and would recommend your continuing to sell, if saving prices can be obtained for what you may have on hand of ours. At the same time we should not be afraid of your holding if saving prices are not attainable.

I wrote you in my last that I had agreed to absent myself, for a while, in obedience to the Chinese authorities, lest my presence should prove an obstacle to Captain Elliot's contemplated arrangement, and for the last ten days I have been

[138] On the *Thomas Coutts*, see above Letter **183**, note 127. See also the P.S. to this Letter.

[139] On Nugent Daniell, see Letter **92**, note 66. Mr. and Mrs Daniell were mentioned in Letter **116** as 'passengers' per *Reliance*', but on the evidence of this Letter Mr. Daniell had not yet left China. The *Thomas Coutts*, whose commander, Captain Warner (see Letter **188**), had disregarded Captain Elliot's order and signed the opium bond to sail to Whampoa, was consigned to Daniell. (*Opium War*, p. 178). As at the time of the Napier Fizzle, difficulties heightened the tensions between merchants like Daniell who were former Company servants and followed a policy of accommodation with the Chinese, and those who wanted the trade to be conducted on an entirely new basis. Although they criticized his negotiating skills, the free traders like James Matheson realized that Captain Elliot, like Lord Napier before him, was fighting in their camp.

[140] 'Kuen-min-foo': the prefect of Kuenmin. 'Wei-yuen': a deputy, or literally an 'expectant appointee'. (Hucker, *Dictionary of Official Titles*, entry No. 7688).

living in seclusion,[141] within a day's reach of communications with the shipping, where I am glad to think all our affairs seem to be going on favourable. The interruption of the Chuenpee arrangement suits us very well, as we had a large stock of cotton sent up, at a heavy expense, to Canton; which our American friends had not been sufficiently prompt in disposing of. With kind regards to your partners, I remain, my dear Sir,

Yours very truly,

P.S. Kindly show this letter to Mr. Jardine and Mr. Alexander Matheson.
Hong Kong, 4th November

I have today come here *unknown* and find the suspicion of the evil effects of Mr. Daniell's conduct on the existing state of affairs amply confirmed by Chinese official documents in the last numbers of the *Canton Register* and *Canton Press*, to which I refer you. *H.M.S. Alligator* has not arrived as was reported. The *Volage* and *Hyacinth* are still at the Bogue; but nothing is known of their proceedings. The Chinese are erecting a battery with heavy guns within a short distance of the shipping here and affairs have a highly menacing aspect.[142]

187. James Matheson in Toon Koo[143] to Mrs. Turner on board the *John O'Gaunt* in Toon Koo, 21 November 1839

My dear Mrs. Turner,[144]

Since I saw you I have been reflecting on the subject of our conversation, with more deliberation than was possible on the spur of the moment.

It appears to me that it will be expedient for you, as a preliminary step, to request Mr. Thomson[145] to deduct from his estimate of the ultimate outturn, the amount due by the Bankrupt Hongs, and any of the sums, (if any), not readily

[141] On James Matheson living in seclusion in 'Tytam', see also Letter **184**, note 134.

[142] The menace was real. The 'Battle of Chuenpee' took place three days after this Letter was written. Admiral Kuan was waiting for the British off the Chuenpee forts with sixteen war junks and a dozen fireboats. The two British ships, *H.M.S. Hyacinth* (Captain Elliot) and *H.M.S. Volage* (Captain Smith) went in to protect the *Royal Saxon* which, like the *Coutts,* was defying British orders and entering the river. After several attempt unsuccessful attempts at opening talks with the Chinese Admiral, Elliot gave the order to fire. The battle lasted only two hours. Losses and casualties were heavy on the Chinese side (5 war junks sunk and 24 boats put out of combat), but light on the British side, with only one sailor wounded. (For details on the Battle of Chuenpee, see: Fay, *Opium War*, p. 179; Hoe, *The Taking of Hong Kong*, p. 97).

[143] Toon Koo, or Toon Coo : see Letter **20**, note 34.

[144] Mrs. Mary Croft Turner was the wife of Richard Turner, an English opium merchant who died on 28 March 1838. She had returned to Macao six months before her husband's death, accompanied by two of their sons and their tutor, Vincent Stanton, a divinity student at Cambridge. (See: Letter **32**, note 56; Ride, *An East India Company Cemetery*, p. 24).

[145] Mr. Thomson must have been one of the trustees of Richard Turner's estate. He was not further identified.

realizable. The Balance will constitute the estimated sum, at present available; one third of which you will, of course, be free to dispose of, in any manner you deem fit,—in China, New South Wales, or elsewhere. Your Boys will require more precaution, in as much as the will directs their being invested in such 'public or private securities, as the Trustees may deem advisable either for the safety or advantage of the children' and I suspect the law is strict in requiring the Trustees to avoid, as far as possible, every sort of risk, so long as it is thought advisable they should reside with you. I think the Trustees will be justified in allowing you a liberal board, say about one hundred pounds a year for each, or perhaps more, as they grow older, besides expenses of tuition. In regard to your own share, you might perhaps venture to remit at once to New South Wales, the greatest part of which is realizable which, at the interest of that Colony, about 10 or 8 per cent, would, with the Boys' allowance, yield you a comfortable income. Your share of Hong Merchants' debts, etc., etc., might be afterwards invested in England, as realized; and you would thus avoid the, not very prudent, course of having the whole of your means deposited in a distant Colony beyond your control or care. Should it be necessary to exceed the interest of what is now realizable, there might be no great objection to such a course, to a limited extent; and I, for one, would not hesitate to sanction it, though your own good sense will at once see the less this is done the better.

The exchange with New South Wales is at present favourable say 4 shillings and 9 pence to 4 shillings and 10 pence per dollar; and should you think of remitting to that quarter, it would be very desirable if Mr. Thomson would be kind enough to permit its being done soon, as it is uncertain whether it could be accomplished with equal advantage at a later date.

I remain, My dear Mrs. Turner,

Yours very sincerely,

188. James Matheson in Toon Koo to William Jardine and Alexander Matheson in London, 24 November 1839

My dear Jardine and Alexander,

But little of interest has occurred during the week since I last wrote you per [ ] via Calcutta. We have conflicting reports in circulation from day to day. Sometimes of an accommodation being on the eve of taking place with the Chinese; but the latest rumour received yesterday is that the Chinese admiral, having died of his wounds,[146] the authorities are in the highest degree incensed with Captain Elliot, and are making extensive preparations, with renewed vigour,

[146] The rumour was incorrect. Admiral T'ian Pei Kuan recovered from his Battle of Chuenpee wounds. He later died in the 'Battle of the Bogue forts' which was fought in February 1841. (See Letter **228**; [?]oe, *The Taking of Hong Kong*, p. 263).

to attack and exterminate the shipping. At the same time pains are taken to assure the mercantile community that if they go to trade at Canton they will be nowise involved in the consequence of Captain Elliot's misdeeds; and Captain Warner of the *Coutts*, who came down the inner passage and is now here is said to have been urged by the authorities through Howqua, to take down invitations and warrantees of personal safety to all who may be inclined to go up. Warner, however declined ostensibly at least, being a go-between on the occasion, though it is natural to suppose he will privately use all his influence to induce others to follow his example. But his conduct is viewed in the fleet with universal disgust and reprobation; and the conviction is becoming more general than ever that the Chinese are actuated by treacherous motives in their good treatment of him, in the hope of decoying the Community within their clutches and re-enacting the captivity of March-April and May last. Meanwhile the Macao mandarins have again commenced making overtures through [Joaquim] Veiga, who has addressed them to us. These might have had a chance of coming to good had Elliot waited patiently till they had assumed some shape; but with his usual precipitation he went yesterday to Macao in the *Volage* to present himself, in all probability, as an applicant for terms, in place of waiting till they should apply to him. The Portuguese are pushing all their influence to have British Trade opened at Macao; and the tacit connivence at this in the same footing as before, seems certainly the [best] mode the Chinese could adopt of escaping temporarily from present difficulties till the determination of the British Government is known, which they look for with much anxiety.

Shipments of cotton in foreign bottoms to Whampoa are going on with great briskness. *Wetmore & Co.* have bought the '*Triumph*' for the purpose, at 8,000 pounds sterling. We have sold the *Sir C. Malcolm* to Shillaber (backed by Heerjeebhoy)[147] at 55,000 dollars, and the *Vansittart* to Burd[148] (backed by ourselves) at 68,000 dollars, with which and his former ship, the *Syden*, he will make great progress in wiping off his debt to us. Freights hence to Whampoa are about 6 dollars per bale of cotton and 10 dollars per ton of 40 feet back, which will almost clear the cost of a ship in a single voyage.[149] When done with, they could be resold and obtain British pass for the Company's Government to enable them trading in India. With these facilities we shall be enabled to send up almost all our cotton, so as to be clear handed pending further consignments on the way.

I am sorry to say the tea market has been opened by the Agents of *Turner & Co.* and by *Wetmore & Co.* at 32 Taels for the best chops of Congo which though it will no doubt pay handsomely in the *John O Gaunt* going home, *as a single*

[147] Heerjeebhoy Rustomjee. See Letter **170**, note 29.
[148] On Captain Burd, see Letter **122**, note 170.
[149] The new Canton transhipping operations were therefore a godsend for borrowers like Captain Burd who looked to repay their debts from freighting activity.

ship, we consider too high to venture on with the chance before us, of no war taking place with China; not to mention the uncertainty as to quality which must result from the improbability of their being inspected by our taster, and the freight of 10 dollars per 40 feet equal to 3 pounds sterling per ton of 50 feet which must be paid from Canton to Toon Koo. We have had musters sent down, for Humpston's inspection,[150] and have written up to secure on any terms his n° 1 character; but there are very few; and we have since heard of Samqua having shabbily given *Turner & Co.* two chops that were promised to us.

The fact is our [American] agent has not yet got into the way of doing business to our satisfaction, and for this reason, added to those before explained, we are keeping aloof from the tea market. This we shall perhaps have occasion to regret, should war break out before we are enabled to supply ourselves at lower prices; and of my whole policy, since you Jardine left us, there is no point which I am more doubtful of meeeting your approval than this. You can tell Armstrong[151] and Andrew Johnstone there is no chance your executing their point orders for Hull, unless times greatly change; and we propose sending home their funds, when realized, in bills. We hope we have been fortunate in receiving through young Tingqua, a considerable lot of scented Orange Pekos for Captain Pidding.[152]

Nankins, Raw silk [are] stationary, without transactions. To any inquiring constituent, who may ask you what we are doing, or intend doing for them, you can answer it is very doubtful if we shall be able to execute any tea orders to our own satisfaction. Nankins silk has less difficulties[153] connected with it, and as we have almost a monopoly of the ready money in circulation,[154] I hope we shall bye and bye be able to operate with advantage. We mean to send young Barretto up by an early opportunity to tutor our American agent and should indeed, in the first instance have employed Bartolomeu Antonio Barretto as our agent, in lieu of the American, were it not that his being known as our assistant might have endangered his person and perhaps our property under his care, in connection more especially with our Coast operations.

Andrew Jardine was well at Manila, by last account three weeks old, as was David Jardine at Chinchew on 6th instant. The unusual vigilance of the mandarins prevented his doing tea business which might otherwise have been practicable. In Rees's department things are going on well. He retires, and Jauncey having declined, is succeeded by Hall.[155] We purposely detain the *Rover* till after the first

[150] Gervas Humpston: the new tea employee who arrived in November 1838 with David Jardine. (See Letter **166**, note 78).
[151] For other references to George Armstrong, see Letters **205**, **220**, **222**, and **234**.
[152] On Captain Pidding, see Letter **213**, note 135.
[153] (Sic).
[154] The good liquidity of the firm was almost entirely due to its continuing coastal opium operations.
[155] Captain J, Hall had previously commanded the *Harriet*.

sale; sending on our orders by a previous conveyance. A. Johnston's Brother, David,[156] is well, in the ships, but wishes to go home.

My dear Alexander, say to Hugh[157] I am going to consign to his care per *John O' Gaunt* our friend Mrs. Morgan[158] who goes home to see her mother. Hugh's transactions here will answer well. Let all friends know that I am well as I [cannot] write to any by this conveyance.

189. James Matheson in Toon Koo to Charles Lyall in Calcutta,

1 December 1839

My dear Lyall,

On 25th august I wrote to you expressing a wish that you would send us, our old servant Ibrahim, and one or two others whom he could recommend as assistants, besides [a] water cooler, with the requisite apparatus. If Abrahim[159] cannot be spared, send another capable of acting as head of our establishment of servants.

I have now to request further you will endeavour to send us a *good cook*, as we wish to be entirely independent of the Chinese.[160] We should wish him to be a first rate artist, accustomed to cook for a large family; and to secure this I do not care how liberal his wages—so long as they are not large enough to raise him above his business. He may also bring an assistant, if he insists on it. I should think *Gunter & Hooper* or Spense[161] in the best position to recommend a suitable person. And I do not care if the expense be 50 Rupees per month or even double.

Yours very sincerely,

[156] Probably the Deputy Superintendent's (Alexander Johnston's) brother.

[157] Hugh Matheson, one of James Matheson's nephews, and co-founder with Charles Lyall of *Lyall Matheson & Co* in Calcutta. At the time this Letter was written, Hugh Matheson had not yet founded his Liverpool firm, *Matheson & Scott*. (See end of Letter **261**).

[158] Mrs. Morgan was the wife of Captain William Morgan, the commander of the *Pascoa*, and later of the *Scaleby Castle*. Captain Morgan worked for *Jardine, Matheson & Co.* from 1833. In June 1840 the firm appointed him its agent in Hong Kong, and he lived on the depot ship, *General Wood*. He died in Macao in June 1843. (Ride, *East India Company Cemetery*, pp. 201–202).

[159] The copyist of James Matheson' letter spelt 'Ibrahim' with an 'I' in one line, and with an 'A' in the next.

[160] James Matheson new insistence on 'independence of the Chinese' even down to the servants' quarters suggests less a change of culinary taste than a renewed desire to run his establishment without reference to, or interference by, any superior authority.

[161] Neither '*Gunter & Hooper*' nor '*Spense*' were identified. They were probably Calcutta provision merchants and caterers.

190. William Jardine in Scotland to James Matheson in China,
3 December 1839[162]

My Dear Matheson,

I have only time to say we are here and refer you to London letters for information. John Abel Smith will tell you what passed when we visited Lord Palmerston on 20th Ultimo. H. M. Ministers intend to make the Chinese pay for the drug;[163] and they will succeed if the force sent is sufficient.[164]

Magniac Smith & Co. have arranged with *Jamsetjee Jejeebhoy & Co.* for all our engagements; and they have, at Jejeebhoy's request, through me, sent him 10,000 pounds sterling in Company's bills to Calcutta and a credit for 20,000 pounds sterling. This was done nearly two months ago; and I mention the business now, that you may arrange matters accordingly. Any goods arriving on *Jamsetjee Jejeebhoy & Co.*'s account are to be handed over to *Magniac Smith & Co.*; but the profit or loss on them will be *Jamsetjee Jejeebhoy & Co.*'s unless they are otherwise instructed by you and them.

Winter has set in here with frost and snow. The cold I can stand. The rain and snow are not so agreeable, but I ride, and run about like a three year old.[165] I have not yet seen half the gentlemen around us. We dine with General Sharp[166] today. [I] have not yet been to Dumfries nor seen the Marquis of Queensberry[167] nor Sir William Jardine,[168] who is in Edinburgh. Tell Andrew [Jardine] his family here are all well. Excuse this hurried note and believe me in haste,

Yours sincerely,

162 This letter was sent from Halleaths, Andrew Johnstone's estate in Scotland.

163 See above, Letter **180**, note 97.

164 For a discussion of Jardine's role in advising the government, the timing of his written note to Palmerston in December 1839, and the use of the quoted letter dated 19 December 1839 found in Gerald Yorke's unpublished typescript *The Princely House* (c. 1937), see note 107 of the Introduction.

On 2 March 1840, as Parliamentary Papers on the China question were being printed, Jardine wrote to Matheson: '[. . .] Lord Palmerston is the only member of the administration, who knows anything about the China question; and, in my opinion, he is more in our favour than any of the others. / The force sent out is fully as large as was recommended, and if this business is properly managed, the result ought to be favourable. [. . .]' (*JMArch.*, J.42, unnumbered letter dated 2 March 1840, William Jardine in Blendon Hall, to James Matheson in China).

Gerald Yorke's unpublished typescript *The Princely House* (c. 1937) has been used by several historians as a shortcut to access the Jardine Archive. There exists few copies of Yorke's typescript, and they are all in private hands. For an analysis of how *The Princely House* came to be written, and for an account of why it was not published, see: Le Pichon, Alain, '*Jardine, Matheson & Co.* à la découverte de ses archives et de son identité historique', *Etudes anglaises*, t.50, No 2.

165 A rare admission by William Jardine that he enjoyed recreation.

166 General Sharp was not identified

167 John Douglas, Marquess of Queensberry (1779–1856). He was Lord Lieutenant and Sheriff Principal of Dumfriesshire. (*The Complete Peerage*, Vol. X, p. 705).

168 Sir William Jardine, seventh baronet of Applegirth. He was not related to William Jardine.

191. James Matheson in Toon Koo to Charles Lyall in Calcutta,

14 December 1839

My dear Lyall,

I have pleasure in availing of the opportunity of the *Rover* to inform you that affairs still grow quietly and, in a commercial view, as favourably as could be expected. Foreign vessels with goods transshipped here are admitted to entry as before, with only the difference of enabling the authorities to shut their eyes with a good grace, by the exclusion of deck loads, which would betray rather too glaringly what had been going on. From this grace the *Cambridge* (transferred to the Americans under the name of the *Ellen Douglas*)[169] is excluded on the ground of her recent employment as a man of war. It is, however, probable that in the accommodating spirit manifest on such points by the Chinese, the difficulty will in time be got over. The Hong Merchants have as yet declined securing the recent arrivals at Whampoa fearful of becoming implicated, were they to act without a more decided sanction than the mere tacit connivence of the High commissioner; and Howqua has accordingly suggested to the Americans to petition for His Excellency's formal approval, which will of course be granted. It is to be hoped the delay will in some measure benefit the languid conditions of the cotton market, which as was to be expected, is suffering from the large quantities lately poured in; only about 25,000 bales or less being now estimated as remaining outside. We have fortunately intelligence of all the vessels, laden by us, having passed within the Bogue.

The newly-appointed Commissioner, whom I before mentioned, as expected from Pekin, has reached Canton,[170] whither Lin preceded him from the Bogue to meet him. Whether this new functionary [will] have controlling authority is not well-ascertained. He is uncle of the reigning Emperor, and was third member of the Canton Government, in Lord Napier's time. Every circumstance combines to give credibility to the current reports of the Chinese authorities being in the highest degree disquieted and perplexed, and they would no doubt be too happy could they devise some mode of settlement that would merely save appearances. But matters have become so embroiled that I cannot think an early accommodation as, by any means, probable. And I now begin to form a more favourable opinion than before of operations for the home market, if we could only devise some mode of satisfying ourselves as to the quantities of teas before shipment; which is a point of some difficulty, as there are no American tasters.

[169] According to Fay, the *Cambridge* was transferred as the *Chesapeake*. (*The Opium War*, p. 201); see also Letter **183**, note 129.

[170] The appointment of Kishen was first mentioned in Letter **175** above. Neither Fay nor Hoe make any mention of Kishen being in Canton in December 1839. In both works, Kishen makes his first appearance in the summer of 1840 when he started negotiations witth Captain Elliot near Tientsin. (*Opium War*, p. 232; *The Taking of Hong Kong*, p. 133).

By far the most important event which occurred to influence our market for some time back is the withdrawal of the East India Company's finance agency. Mr. Astell,[171] the senior agent having proceeded to India in the *Fort William*, leaving in our hands what little matters the Company have still pending. Another favourable feature is the diminished quantity of tonnage available for the English market, in consequence of several vessels that have been sold to foreigners, which will make a material restriction from the estimate we at one time made of 25,000 registered tons.

The *Ann Griffiths* will be the first general freight ship for London about a fortnight hence. Our neighbours, *Gribble, Hughes & Co.*[172] had engaged 600 tons in her, which were in course of transshipment, when they discovered that about 2,000 chests of Congo sent them by *Wetmore & Co.* were so inferior as to make it necessary to reject them; an instructive warning as to the hopelessness of attempting to execute orders satisfactorily without a taster at Canton.

The *Coutts* is still at Whampoa and those concerned in her being without means to load her, she is offering to take freight to London, at 6 pounds sterling per ton—so strong and general, however, is the feeling against her that no shipper are offering.[173] There is also a strong feeling in our community against the shipments on Howqua's account, per [ ], *John Barton* and *Baring*; and several of our neighbours are urging their home agents to use their influence with the Government to prevent their being admitted; Captain Elliot refusing to sign their manifests on the ground of its being foreign property. It seems certainly very intolerable that one who like Howqua has the power of influencing the acts of the Chinese Government against the English should be also able to profit by his wrong doing in carrying on a trade under the English flag,[174] from which he is the means of the English themselves being excluded.

With kind regards, I remain,

Yours sincerely.

[171] John Harvey Astell resigned as Second Superintendent in April 1835. Since then he had been the East India Company Agent in Canton in charge of its treasury (the so-called 'Finance Committee') whose lending operations had so annoyed William Jardine and James Matheson from 1836 on. (See Letter **93**, note 78), etc. In August 1839, during the Hong Kong murder trial presided over by Captain Charles Elliot, Astell had been chairman of the Jury aboard the *Fort William*.

[172] Captain Henry Gribble commanded the *Marquis Camden* in 1838. He became British consul at Amoy in 1844.

[173] The free traders boycotted the *Coutts* on account of what they regarded as the additional difficulties it had brought upon the British community over the past two months. See above, Letter **188**, first paragraph.

[174] Since 1834, Howqua (who had probably amassed the largest mercantile fortune of the day), regularly speculated in large shipments of teas which he sold in the London market. His favourite London agents were *Baring Brothers and Co.* who also acted for his largest American customers, *Russell & Co.* He also speculated in the American market. (Dulles, Foster Rhea, *The Old China Trade*, Boston and New York, Mifflin Company, 1930, AMS Press, 1970).

192. James Matheson in Toon Koo to John Abel Smith in London,

14 December 1839

My dear Sir,

Just as we are dispatching the *Rover* to Calcutta a most important communication has reached me from Macao, stating on the authority of a respectable Chinese who has long acted as go-between in negotiations between the Portuguese and Chinese authorities, that Lin, the high commissioner, is to proceed to Pekin on 21st. Instant, when the Viceroy will resume his former chief authority in the Province, and 'great changes will take place'. Whether these will go to the extent of an accommodation for the renewal of British trade seems very doubtful, there being so many sore points that need healing. But at all events we may expect increased facilities and convenience and perhaps a rather greater export of tea than if Lin had remained here, though of course nothing approaching the full supply, which the withdrawal of the East India Company's finance Agency would tend to prevent were there no other cause.

We have engaged Mr. Varnham[175] (formerly *Wetmore & Co's* taster) to proceed to Whampoa [and] to inspect teas for us there, in the hope of its leading to some good.

Reverting to the intelligence above mentioned, it yet needs confirmation, but it comes from an informant whom we have hitherto found correct. Please show this to my partners to whom I have no time to write.

Yours most sincerely,

1840

193. William Jardine in London to James Matheson in Macao

6 February 1840[1]

My Dear Matheson,

I had the pleasure of addressing a long letter to you on the 4th Instant [ ] per overland mail, but having heard that the *Blonde* frigate is to carry through letters to China direct, touching at the Cape of Good Hope only, I avail myself of the opportunity to send you a few additional lines, but shall not trouble you with a duplicate of my letter of the 4th, being aware that *Magniac Smith & Co.* are sending duplicates of all their letters, per mail, public and private, and they containing nearly all the particulars mentioned in mine.

[175] Mr. Varnham: probably a relation of Charles Varnham, 'Tea dealer, 4 Crown Row, Walworth Road'. (*TLCD*). The *BI* also lists a firm *Varhnam & Ewart* as an episodic correspondent. Finally, *Varnham & Delafosse* is listed as a subscriber to the *East India and China Association* in Letter **151**.

[1] The letter of 4 February 1840 referred to in the first line is virtually illegible.

I had an interview with Lord Palmerston on the 4th Instant, and brought to his notice the debts due by the cohong to foreign merchants before their expedition for Canton;[2] reminding him that they had been settled on the best terms we could obtain, and that settlement [had been] approved by the emperor. For years installments had been paid, but the remaining installments, together with some additional debt, incurred since I left China, must be taken into consideration when we come to treat, which I presume we will do, sooner or later, after having carried on the war for some time. His Lordship said no one had brought these claims to his notice, inquired how they arose, from what source such claims had hitherto been paid, and requested I should favour him with a memo' on the subject, which I promised to do without loss of time.

I was amused by an observation he made respecting the petition got up by Inglis signed by many of the Canton merchants, but not by us and a few others. He pointed out the absurdity of petitioning the Government to settle claims for which they were themselves [responsible] and which they settled before receiving an answer to their petition. I understood the Government gave them a [rebuke] on the occasion, of which, I think, we never heard in China.[3]

Elliot, in his letter of 23rd September last, said he hoped, by the [later] despatch to be able to communicate a favourable result respecting trade—outside—with which Lord Palmerston appeared pleased. The ministers must be anxious for teas on any terms, as without an additional supply the revenue would suffer at the expiration of [   ] months. The *Marmion* has been permitted to discharge, I understand.

I should send some newspapers by this conveyance if practicable, addressed to Andrew Jardine, which you can read, and then forward.[4] I may report here that your friends in the North were well when I visited them. Alexander was to leave Liverpool, for London, this day.

I have seen both the Lyalls,[5] but neither of them offered me any explanation. The young one was waiting for Robert's return from Scotland when I was in Town first. I am to dine with Robert tomorrow; and should he avoid the subject, I shall, in a few days, send him a paragraph from your letter to me. The stout one, William I think is the name, spoke to Andrew Johnstone on the subject soon after my arrival. Kind regards to all around you.

[2] On the effect of William Jardine's bringing the failed hong merchants debts to Palmerston's notice, see above, letter **141**, note 26.

[3] The petition and the events referred to in this paragraph have not been identified.

[4] Andrew Jardine was in Manila at the time, managing the firm's opium business.

[5] John, William and Robert Lyall, of *Lyall Brothers & Co.*, 69 St Helen's Passage. (*TLCD*). George Lyall, M. P. was also listed as 'Merchant, Winchester House, 52, Old Broad Street. (*Ibid.*). The Lyalls were friends of James Matheson. The two references to 'the subject' are obscure. The frequent misunderstandings of orders by the Calcutta firm, *Lyall Matheson & Co.*, (e.g. Letter **207**), may possibly have been 'the subject'.

Teas are dull, in consequence of letter per *Marmion*. We expect the India Mail on the 8th or 10th Instant.

Believe me, my Dear Matheson,

Yours sincerely,

194. James Matheson in Macao to William Jardine in London

17 February 1840

My dear Jardine,

I have much pleasure in announcing the safe arrival of the *November* (mail) on 15th instant after a splendid passage of 114 days. Her general packet is not yet landed, but we have received most of our letters including your N° 2 of 21st October,[6] which is of course exceedingly acceptable, being the first of your letters coming to hand, since you left Constantinople. Your N° 1 is still missing, which will doubtless contain much of singular interest. Meanwhile it is most satisfactory to notice that you do not appear to be much cast down about the state of affairs here, and that you have engaged the able co-operation of Mr. Freshfield[7] in the affair of the surrendered drug.

Elliot is beyond measure delighted at his release from a state of inconceivable anxiety and suspense in receiving Lord Palmerston's approval of his measures which is conveyed in a short autograph letter; beyond which he appears to know nothing of the detail of intended measures.[8] He is now pretty well cured of the thraldom which he was held by certain parties here.[9] But he is not to be depended on and it requires all one's caution to be sufficiently guarded in intercourse with him.

The Chinese are exceedingly anxious, and in the course of yesterday, the local mandarins addressed no less than two letters to the Portuguese Procurador,[10] asking if it were true that the British[11] Government *dis*approved of Captain Elliot's

[6] The letter referred to is Letter **185**. At the time when he wrote this Letter, James Matheson had not received the earlier Letters **179** and **180** which William Jardine had sent from London shortly after his return to England.

[7] On Mr Freshfield, see Letter **185**, note 136.

[8] On 23 February, a few days after this Letter was written, Captain Elliot mentioned Palmerston's compliments in a letter he wrote to his wife, Clara. (Clara Elliot had left Macao with their children for the safety of Singapore). 'Your letter', he wrote, 'was accompanied by a private letter from Lord Palmerston announcing the determination of the government to support me, or at all events, to accept the transactions of last Spring. But his letter was most gratifying as it manifested great confidence both in my zeal and capacity. I hope he may have no reason to regret it'. (Quoted by Hoe, *The Taking of Hong Kong*, p. 109).

[9] An oblique reference to the two principal opponents of *Jardine, Matheson & Co.*'s policy: the anti-opium 'Church' party (sometimes referred to by William Jardine as 'the Saints'), and the *Dent & Co.* partners and their friends.

[10] 'Procurador': the chief of the Portuguese administration in Macao.

[11] James Matheson usually spelt the adjectives and even nouns of nationality with a small letter—e.g. british, and chinese. (see 'Editorial Method' under 'Capitalization').

measures, and if so why they longer hesitated to drive him away. The Chinese Government appears to be assisted to their ruin by Missionary Cant; of which I am heartily sick and tired, and I begin seriously to think of discarding our friend King whose business subsisting as it does exclusively by his extensive negotiations with us, would be extinguished were we to drop him.[12] Let him then try how he could get on without the aid of the drug, against which he is waging so unfair a crusade making a tool of Bridgman, to a far greater degree than consistent with Christian principles. As for the use they make of the press, it is better in the long run to treat it with silent contempt, though I am aware it places us temporarily at a disadvantage.

The last news from Canton of 15th instant mentions a chop having arrived from the Emperor inquiring of the local authorities as to the policy of excluding the foreign trade of all nations without exception with a view to its bearing on the opium trade and other difficulties and authorizing the Governor to carry the interdict into effect without referring to Pekin, if he deems it politic to do so. But the prevailing opinion among the Chinese, is that there are too many opposing interests to admit of such a course being adopted, which would in fact be playing the game of the English whose very first [action] will no doubt be a blockade.

On the day of our very last departure (the *Coutts*) Macao was in a state of extraordinary excitement from the *Hyacinth* having entered the inner harbour. She went out next morning after producing an admirable effect for the Chinese troops, immediately scudded off; and the Mandarins announced they would be satisfied if Captain Elliot and some others would make a pretence of going away in daylight and returning *incognito* in the evening; when their reciding[13] here would be connived at, as is now the case.

To Heerjeebhoy [Rustomjee]'s great disappointment the mandarins after having bought his ship *Norden*, formerly *Anithras* formerly *Trinidad*, for 45,000 dollars (she having cost him 6,000 dollars) have thrown up the bargain.[14] Allegedly she is rotten. I have a little doubt the *Danish King*, formerly

[12] For Charles William King, see Letter **172**, note 62. For Elijah Coleman Bridgman, see Letter **177**, note 84. King had been doing agency business for the firm in Canton. Except in missionary circles, he was generally unpopular among the merchants (both American and British). He had just published a long critique of the opium surrender crisis in the Repository which was 'decidedly hard on the English and the Americans' (Fay). Shortly after this Letter was written, James Matheson did 'drop' him by withdrawing business from his agency. King then left Canton with his wife by the overland route. (Fay, *Opium War*, p. 238).

The argument about King's unchristian 'use' of a fellow human being is in character. There is ample evidence in the Letters as a whole that James Matheson's was usually guided by 'Christian principles' in his relationships with fellow human beings.

[13] (Sic).

[14] The Chinese were starting buying European or Indian ships at this time. Although the purchase of the former *Norden* fell through, Lin (who had just lost his post as 'High Commissioner' and been appointed Viceroy of Canton—see first paragraph of Letter 195 below) managed to buy the

Vansittart will be released; so that we shall have abundant tonnage and means to exploit teas, and I begin to think the season's export will be nearer thirty than twenty five millions. Our consignments at Canton are now about equal to meet our engagements and we mean to get into debt with the Hong Merchants, as to enable our sending up more goods without risk, and be on the right side, should any unforeseen stoppage occur.

Affairs under the management of Rees, Jauncey, etc., continue to go on well. I wish the *Mor* had a full supply for them from our Friends in Western India for which destination we shall despatch her as soon as possible.

Many thanks for your promised kindness to my young nephews. I remain always,

Yours most sincerely,

195. James Matheson in Macao to John Abel Smith in London

29 February 1840

My dear Sir,

This goes per *Moor*[15] to Bombay, which will I hope have a favourable passage and establish her reputation as a clipper. Nothing of interest has occurred since I last wrote except a rise in cotton at Canton to about 14 Taels, of which our friends are awaiting to clear off the remains of our consignments. We are all quiet and likely to remain here, for the present, unmolested. Lin has evidently abated much of his violence since surrendering the seals of his [grand] office of high Commissioner, for those of Governor.

The *Charles Grant* is under despatch today and the *Falconer* will be so in a week. The two Danish ships that had been seized are released, and our Canton friends are busy bringing tea to load them. If no interruption occurs the season's export will considerably exceed 20 millions. We submit entirely to your kind considerations the effect which this is likely to have on your home market, and you will of course act either in selling or holding our consignments as you deem best.

It is worth of consideration whether, as tea is such a necessary of life in England, the British Government will not even in the event of hostilities with China, prefer to connive in the export of teas, as now with foreigners, rather than by establishing a blockade, and cut off the supplies to the distress and discontent of our turbulent home population.[16] You can no doubt easily ascertain the view of

---

Cambridge, temporarily owned by the Americans as the *Chesapeake*. Lin 'equipped her with a heterogeneous collection of cannon, some of them western, painted two great eyes upon her bows, and hoped he would keep the foreign devils from Canton'. (Fay, *Opium War*, p. 207).

[15] James Matheson's frequent spelling for the *Mor*.

[16] 'The turbulent home population': Francis Place and William Lovett had drafted the Charter in 1836, which provided impetus for the Chartist movement (1838–1848). Feargus O'Connor's *Northern Star* which advocated the use of force in the defence of the rights of labour had been started in November

Government on this head and regulate your proceedings accordingly. I incline to think the British Government will not, under any circumstances, consent to be long without supplies of tea.[17]

Yours most sincerely,

196. William Jardine in London to James Matheson in Macao, 4 March 1840

My dear Matheson,

I have already written a long letter to you, and shall confine myself in this one to one subject—namely—my being advertised out of the Canton firm.

When dining with John Abel Smith yesterday, I asked his opinion as to the propriety of doing so on the 30th of June next, under existing circumstances. I have some doubts about the propriety of your doing so; but shall leave you to act as you may think best when the time comes. Mr. Smith renewed the subject today, and told me he wished me out of the Canton house, that I might be able to join *Magniac Smith & Co.* here about the end of the year; which is the first time we have ever spoken about my joining them. This is all as it should be; but I am ready and willing to continue in the firm of *Jardine, Matheson & Co.*[18] till you think there is no necessity for me continuing longer. John Abel has given you his view of the matter, and you have only to decide as you may judge best, resting assured that I shall be satisfied whatever way you decide. Believe me in haste,

Yours sincerely,

197. William Jardine in London to James Matheson in Macao, 9 March 1840

My Dear Matheson,

I address these few lines to you at the request of Captain Thacker,[19] who has taken up a small vessel called the *Frances Yates* to carry provisions, etc., to

---

1837. At the time he wrote this Letter, James Matheson had just received news of the violent Newport uprising of 4 November 1839, following which several Chartists were sentenced to death, though the sentence was subsequently commuted to life in exile. (*EWH*).

[17] Future events showed that Captain Elliot was well aware of the problem. He did all he could to secure reasonable shipments of teas to Britain even during the blockade. On tea shipments during the blockade, see Letters **214**, **224**, **230**, **235**.

[18] James Matheson approved of William's Jardine proposal to join *Magniac Smith & Co.* and to be 'advertised out' of *Jardine, Matheson & Co.* Contrary to common practice, however, he suggested that the name of the retiring partner be retained in the name of the firm. It is therefore 'due to [James Matheson] that the firm is still called [*Jardine, Matheson & Co.*] today'. (Alan Reid, *in* Keswick, *The Thistle and the Jade*, p. 24).

[19] Captain John Thacker: see Letter **83**, note 25. After the Opium War he settled in Australia and joined the firm of *Hunter & Co.* (See Letter **245**; some 60 letters listed in the *BI*).

Manila and China, in hopes that the ships of war may require a supply;[20] and also the free traders, that have been so long detained at Hong Kong. You will see, from his instructions, that he leaves you to do as you may deem fit with the vessel and cargo, feeling it impossible to frame instructions to meet the urgencies that may occur under Lin and Elliot's modes of management.

He was at a loss for fifty tons of dead weight, and came to me to say Captain [ ] would ship fifty tons of iron provided he would take half of it with him; but after speaking to the Smiths, I preferred shipping that quantity on our own account, under an impression that there is little chance of loss, and you would prefer having the whole on our own account, to being connected with any one else, in such a trifling adventure. I trust you will do every thing in your power to make Thacker's voyage a profitable one, by getting the vessel a cargo home, and realizing a handsome profit on his provisions.

We have nothing new here. Tea market very quiet, every one being unwilling to sell, or buy, till the mail from February arrive, which is hourly expected, but it is not known whether it left Bombay on the 25th of January, or 1st February. I have sent newpapers by the *Frances Yates* for Andrew Jardine in Manila or China, which you can read of course, should the vessel come direct to China.

The China papers[21] were laid before the House of Commons on Friday night, but have not yet been sent to the members. We shall probably hear more about them tonight, Monday, as many of the members are very impatient. Believe me, my Dear Matheson, very sincerely yours.

198. James Matheson in Macao to Jamsetjee Jejeebhoy in Bombay,

21 March 1840

My dear Sir,

By the arrival of the *Rover* on the 8th Instant, I have been gratified by the receipt of your much esteemed favours of 21st December, 8th, 11th., 12th, 14th

[20] Some of the 'ships of war' being fitted out for the China campaign belonged to the India station : the *Wellesley*, Admiral Maitland's flagship, which was commanded after his death in November 1839 by Sir Gordon Bremer; the *Druid* (a 44-gun frigate); the *Alligator* (a 26-gun frigate); the Conway; the *Larne* (newly refitted); and four steamers: the *Atalanta*, the *Queen*, the *Enterprize* and the *Madagascar*. Some ships were being readied in Portsmouth and their crews recruited in Britain : The 74-gun *Blenheim*, the 42-gun *Blonde*, and two corvettes, the *Pylades* and the *Nimrod*. Finally, the 74-gun *Melville*, was to sail from the Cape where Admiral Sir George Elliot, the officer appointed to command the China force, had been in charge of the South Africa station. Admiral Elliot (1784–1863) was one of Captain Charles Elliot's cousins. He was the brother of the 2nd Earl of Minto. (Fay, *The Opium War*, pp. 207–208; Hoe, *The Taking of Hong Kong*, p. 262).

[21] At the end of January 1840, the government undertook to publish the China correspondence of the past six years in anticipation of a debate in Parliament. The documents were bulky and 'Palmerston complained that the weight of the type required for [their] printing broke through a floor of the Foreign Office'. (*Opium War*, p. 202). MPs acquainted themselves with the China documents and the

and 18th January; and I beg you to accept my most grateful thanks for the highly interesting information they convey, as well as for the additional marks of your kind confidence in the consignment which you announce per *Good Success*, *Red Rover*, etc.; all which shall have our most earnest attention, as shall be more particularly noticed when I have leisure to reply to your communication in detail. We are hourly looking with impatience for the arrival of the *Good Success*, and doubt not we shall be able to get her cotton to market, though the recent news from England has already created no small alarm among the residents at Canton—as much so that *Russell & Co.* have issued a circular declining to receive any further consignments or orders for goods, from their outside friends.[22] I also trust we shall be able to realize your drug to advantage; but the continued keeping out of the *Water Witch* increases the general apprehension of some disaster having happened on the Coast and throws a temporary gloom over our prospects. Nothing has yet been done with any of the late importations either from Calcutta or from Bombay.

We have instructed our agent at Canton to petition for the admission of your cotton now lying here; and as the Government are evidently desirous of increasing their duties, we are not without hopes of success.

We are in hourly expectation of the *Harriet* with the [cargo] of your cotton from Manila.

The refusal of Government to confirm Captain Elliot's guarantee for drug surrender and the dishonour of his bills to *Dent & Co.*, will, I fear, do much harm among the minor parties concerned.[23] To me it is a heavy and most unlooked for disappointment, on account of the distress it will occasion to so many of our friends. But I derive much consolation from what you state of the sanguine terms in which Mr. Jardine and Alexander Matheson write to you, and also from Mr. Crawford's letter to his son of which you are kind enough to send me a copy;[24] from which we come to the conclusion that Government have determined to demand full indemnity from the Chinese. Many thanks for the copies of Mr. Jardine's and Mr. Alexander Matheson's letters, as I have nothing from them of

---

Parliamentary debate eventually took place from 7 to 10 April (See Letters **200** and **204**). Meanwhile, two months *before* the House of Commons was given the chance to debate the China question, Palmerston had already sent orders to Lord Auckland and to the Admiralty to ready the force. (Blake, *Jardine Matheson*, p. 94).

22 With the expectation that a British force would soon be in China, concern grew among the Americans houses that they might be barred from trading by the Chinese authorities if they continued their transhipping operations.

23 James Matheson is echoing Jamsetjee Jejeehboy's opinion. The reference to Captain't Elliot's bills 'to *Dent & Co*.' suggests that the issuance of opium receipt may have been complemented by the drawing of a few individual bills in order to make up the total number of opium chests promised to Commissioner Lin. (See above, Letter **170**, note 36).

24 See above Letter **182**.

news by so late a date. The price of the drug continues as before. 400 dollars nominal. The *Rover* being required here will not for the present, return to India.

Yours most sincerely,

199. William Jardine in London to James Matheson in Macao,

27 March 1840

My Dear Matheson,

I have this moment received your letters of the 30th of December and 8th December, per *John O' Gaunt*; also a duplicate of the 24th of November,[25] but the original as well as your other letters, per overland mail, had reached me on the 13th instant.

I have also seen your letters to John Abel Smith, which are upon the whole satisfactory. One thing, however, produces in my mind, and in his, very uncomfortable feelings—namely the position of our small craft on the coast. A letter I had from James Innes gave such an account of proceedings there that I have been anxious about the *Harriet*, *Shannon*, etc., etc., ever since. For the large vessels I have no fears, they being more able to defend themselves if attacked; while I have full confidence in all the commanders doing nothing to provoke an attack—defence, not offence, has hitherto been our motto; and I trust they continue to bear it in mind, I do not understand why Jauncey has declined acting as Commodore, without resigning his command, as most men prefer being in power, to acting under orders, and he does not, in my mind, increase his risque or danger, by acting as senior officer. What I fear most is their being boarded in a calm, on the mariners going off, in disguise, as purchasers; and their carrying the vessel. I wish you had described the occurrence that you thought 'would cool down [their] violence'; as I presume you allude to some attack on the coast vessels, which had been repulsed with loss.

The rigidly righteous have been doing every thing to prejudice the public mind against us, and our court proceedings. They are extremely ignorant, and willing to listen to every absurd report. But, by the exertion of John Abel Smith, Crawford,[26] etc., we have, at last, got a Committee of the Commons to inquire into our claims, and report to the House.[27] Lord John

[25] See Letter **188** above.

[26] *The East India and China Association* Committee chairman and writer of Letter **182**.

[27] The government granted the request made by Crawford in the House of Commons on 24 March 'that the subject of grievances set forth in the [opium merchants' petitions] should be referred to a select committee of this House. He [Crawford] understood it was not the intention of government to oppose that committee'. Whereupon, 'Viscount Palmerston rose merely to state that his honourable friend who introduced the subject was right in saying that no objection would be urged to the appointment of this committee; because, undoubtedly, government must acknowledge that the subject was one into which it would be impossible with any appearance of fairness or justice to refuse inquiry

Russell,[28] and Lord Palmerston were for us. Melbourne, Hobhouse, and others against us. Lord John Russell saw that, by refusing to [form a] Committee, he would lose many of their firm supporters, and if the opposition joined the discontented the ministers would be left with a great majority against them. The names of the Committee, if not altered, will be: Crawford; J. A. Smith; Sir G. Staunton;[29] A. Bannerman;[30] Mr. W. Clay;[31] E. Harrison;[32] Strutt;[33] H.G. Ward;[34] Archibald Hastie;[35] Lord G. Somerset;[36] Lord Sandon;[37] Lord Palmerston;

---

before a committee of that House. [. . .] The superintendents had followed exactly the same course which had been pursued by the supercargoes. Like the supercargoes, they knew the existence of the [opium] trade, for it was a matter of public notoriety; but they had not even the same powers which the supercargoes had in order to put it down if ordered to do so, because the supercargoes had a certain authority; they could order any British subject who was pursuing a trade discreditable or injurious to quit the Chinese waters, but the superintendents had not such power. He had explained this in a dispatch [to Captain Elliot] which would be found at page 129 of these papers: 'As a misconception on this point (the want of powers) might give rise to much embarrassment both to H.M.'s government and to the superintendent personally, I have to state to you, for your guidance, that the clause of the Act 26 Geo. 3rd upon which you rest your opinion (namely that the superintendents had certain powers over the British subjects in China) was repealed by the 146th clause of the Act 33 Geo. 3rd, c. 52; and further, that the only power exercised by the supercargoes was that of removing unlicensed persons. But as no license from his Majesty is now necessary to trade or reside in China, such power of expulsion has altogether ceased to exist with respect to China'.

[. . .] All [the superintendents] could do was, not to encourage or protect [the opium traders], which he had given positive instructions that they should abstain from doing'. (*Hansard*, 1840, Vol. 53, 24 March, Palmerston's reply to Crawford, p. 11–12)

28 Lord John Russell was Home Secretary in the Melbourne government until 30 August 1839 and Secretary for War and the Colonies from that date to 1841.

29 Sir George Staunton (1781–1859): MP for Portsmouth. As a boy, he had accompanied his father and Lord Macartney in the latter's embassy to Peking; chief supercargo for the East India Company to China; founder of the Royal Asiatic Society (1823). He took part in the China debate in Parliament in April 1840. (*DPC*; Hoe, *The Taking of Hong Kong*, p. 167).

30 Alexander Bannerman: MP for Aberdeen; formerly supercargo of the East India Company; Commissioner of Greenwich Hospital. (*DPC*).

31 Sir William Clay: MP for Tower Hamlets; merchant and ship owner; Secretary of the Board of Control. (*DCP*).

32 'E. Harrison' was not traced.

33 Edward Strutt: MP for Derby; barrister and cotton manufacturer. (*DCP*).

34 Henry George Ward: MP for Sheffield; only son of Robert Plumer Ward, author of *The History of the Laws of Nations*; at various times Lord of the Admiralty, Clerk of the ordinance, Auditor of the Civil List, etc. (*DCP*).

35 Archibald Hastie: MP for Paisley; a London East India agent. (*DCP*).

36 Lord Granville Somerset: MP for Monmouthshire; second son of the Duke of Beaufort; he held various government posts : Lord of the Treasury ; Chief Commissioner of woods and forests; Chancellor of the Duchy of Lancaster, etc. (*Ibid.*)

37 Viscount Sandon: a Conservative MP for Liverpool; eldest son of the Earl of Harrowby; he was for a short while Secretary of the India Board. (*Ibid*).

D. Maclean;[38] Sir R. H. Inglis; [39] Honorable Sydney Herbert;[40] and Mr. Hogg.[41] There are other names mentioned, and there may be some changes made before the business is finally arranged.

Robert Garnett Sons & Co. have been bothering me about some orders of theirs, which, they say, were not properly executed by us in China. I understand from Alexander [Matheson], one of the partners has written to you on the subject, but has had no answer. I am not acquainted with the merits of the case, and averse to interfering; but shall see what can be done when Alexander returns to Town.

He has been absent attending the funeral of one of your brother's daughters, Elisabeth, who died in Edinburgh on the 15th Instant at 4 p.m. We expect him back tomorrow or next day. The poor girl had been ailing for some time. I did not see her when in Edinburgh.

Teas are flat and many purchasers have forfeited, and are forfeiting their bargain money, which is only 3 pence per pound. I see no cause for alarm ultimately; unless you send home upwards of twelve, or even fifteen, millions of pounds; but the dealers, and speculators, are strange people. Hold on in a rising market, and sell in a declining one, is the order of the day. Company's Congos are at 2 shillings; good Congos: 2 shillings and 2 pence and 2 shillings and 4 pence; best: 2 shillings and 6 pence and 2 shillings and 8 pence per pound. I hope you may succeed in getting sound teas, even if of ordinary quality.

Kind regards to all around you. Believe me, yours very sincerely,

200. William Jardine in London to James Matheson in Macao,

2 April 1840[42]

My Dear Matheson,

This now 1 a.m. I have just returned from dining with *your friend*, Mrs Hubbard,[43] and, finding Grant, who is living here, in bed half asleep, I shall, following up Canton custom,[44] address a few lines to you, per overland mail, to inform you how we are proceeding with our opium claims—and you may believe

[38] Donald Maclean: MP for Oxford; second son of General Sir FitzRoy Grafton Maclean, chief of the Macleans; a barrister. (*Ibid.*)

[39] Sir Robert Harry Inglis: MP for Oxford University since 1828; a conservative. (*Ibid*).The Inglises were close to the Dents.

[40] The Honourable Sydney Herbert: MP for Wiltshire; half brother of the Earl of Pembroke; Secretary of the Admiralty. (*Ibid.*).

[41] James Weir Hogg: MP for Hastings; a barrister with a Calcutta practice, and an East India Company director. (*Ibid.*).

[42] The first part of the letter was written at the Brunswick Hotel, the second part at *Magniac Smith & Co.*'s offices in 3, Lombard Street.

[43] Mrs Hubbard was not identified. Various oblique remarks in the correspondence point to her being in fact a friend of William Jardine's.

[44] In Canton, the partners usually expedited the firm's business during the day and attended to their private correspondence after dinner and into the early hours of the morning.

me, when I say they have caused John Abel Smith and your humble servant not a little anxiety. You have already been informed that H.M. Ministers had reluctantly granted us a Committee of the Commons to inquire into the merits of our claims. A list of names, 10, was handed me by Mr. Smith, and Lord John Russell pronounced it an unobjectionable fair list,[45] but, after mature consideration, some of the party took the alarm, and wished to add six more names to the Committee, at the same time changing some of those they thought of favourable to our views, which led to opposition on all hand and consequent delay.

Pending this discussion, Sir James Graham[46] postponed a notice he had given for the 2nd and the 7th Instant with the view of gaining further information, to enable him to word his motion in the manner most likely to injure the commercial cause. Up to the day he has declined informing the House as to the manner of his attack; but it is generally understood that his object is, to manage matters so as to get a majority in favour of a vote of [no confidence] on ministers for having mismanaged China affairs in general and, should he succeed, the feeling is ministers must resign.

Under these circumstances Lord Palmerston, who has all along been friendly to our cause, made John Abel Smith his confidential adviser, acknowledged the dilemma in which they had been placed, their fears of being beat on Sir James Graham's motion,[47] unless they could keep all their friends and supporters with

[45] The list of committee members mentioned in Letter **199** was only a provisional list.

[46] Sir James Robert George Graham, MP for Dorchester, was a cousin of the Earl of Galloway. He was first Lord of the Admiralty in 1830–1834 and then Secretary of State for the Home department. (*DPC*).

[47] This Letter **200** was written in the midst of the preparations for the Parliamentary debate on the China question. Letter **204** summarizes the outcome. The Parliamentary debate started on 7 April and ended three days later with a narrow win for the government by only nine votes.

Sir James Graham opened the debate with a long speech in which he tried to show that the government had neglected its duties in relation to the China question and that Palmerston's feeble instructions to Captain Elliot had left him to cope unaided with a critical situation. He reminded the House that Palmerston had taken no action in spite of Captain Elliot's repeated dispatches about the urgent necessity of government action. 'Was the noble Lord [Palmerston]', he said, 'ignorant of that change in [Chinese opium] policy ? On the 15th of May 1838, a despatch, alluding to this edict, was received by the Noble Lord. It was dated the 19th of November 1837, and was in page 241. This despatch stated to the noble Lord several facts which had followed the changes in the policy of the Chinese cabinet. [Captain Charles Elliot] states : 'Native boats have been burnt, and the native smugglers scattered, and the consequence is, as it was foreseen it would be, that a complete and very hazardous change had been worked in the whole manner of conducting the Canton portion of the trade. In fact, weighing the whole body of circumstance as carefully as I can, it seems to me that the moment has arrived for such active interposition upon the part of HM Government as can be properly afforded, and that it cannot be deferred without great hazard to the safety of the whole trade, and of the persons engaged in its pursuit". (*Hansard*, vol. 53, p. 691–692).

'These warnings'. Sir James Graham continued, 'were constantly repeated by Captain Elliot in a series of despatches, even in stronger and more forcible language down to the month of April 1839. To quote one passage in a despatch, dated 2nd of January 1839, to be found on page 327, Captain Elliot stated : 'It has been clear to me from the origin of this peculiar branch of the opium traffic, that it

them, and requested he would suggest some [way] of accommodating matters so that they, he thinks, and his immediate adherents might feel at liberty to support ministers to the very utmost of their powers. Mr. Smith acknowledged his willingness to meet ministers fairly and honestly, in their own ways, provided they enabled him and his friends to do their duty to their constituents; and suggested the plan of their arranging the Committee in such a manner as they should advise the House to grant a loan in Exchequer Bills for half the amount claimed, say, £1,200,000, on the security of Elliot's opium receipts. The suggestion was received most eagerly by Lords Palmerston and Russell; and even Melbourne appeared willing to entertain the question. On these terms they parted, on the evening of the 31st Ultimo; yesterday Mr. Smith consulted with William Freshfield and myself as to the propriety of agreeing to the above arrangement, should ministers make up their minds to adopt the plan proposed. After most mature deliberation, we were [still undecided] on the subject, and at 4 p.m. Mr. Smith left the office to the Common's House to settle the point—and being past 2 a.m. I shall go to sleep, in hopes of being able, before 2 p.m. to say the understanding has been agreed upon.

April 3rd. 1 a.m.

I met John Abel in disarray and found that after a long discussion with the ministers he has been unable to get a written or even an [oral agreement].

[. . .][48] The point was to be settled today; but not having been to the Houses this evening, I am ignorant of what passed.

---

might grow to be more and more mischievous to every branch of the trade, and to none more than to that of opium itself. As the danger and shame of its pursuit increased, it is obvious that it will fall by rapid degrees into the hands of more and more desperate men; that it would stain the foreign character with constantly aggravating disgrace in the sight of the whole of the better portion of this people; and, lastly, that it would connect itself more and more intimately with our lawful commercial intercourse, to the great peril of vast public and private interests". (*Ibid.*, p. 693).

There followed three days of debates when the main orators were Macaulay and Gladstone. Macaulay, the Secretary of war and the Colonies, praised Elliot's actions and announced that war with China was pending. Gladstone, then an opposition Tory, condemned both the opium trade and the government on moral grounds. (*Ibid.*).

Eventually the House divided on Sir James Graham's motion : 'It appears to this House, on consideration of the papers relating to China, presented to this House by command of her Majesty, that the interruption in our commercial and friendly intercourse with that country, and the hostilities which have since taken place, are mainly to be attributed to the want of foresight and precaution on the part of her Majesty's present advisers, in respect with out relations with China, and especially to their neglect to furnish the Superintendent at Canton with powers and instructions calculated to provide against the growing evils connected with the contraband traffic in opium, and adapted to the novel and difficult situation in which the Superintendent was placed'. (*Ibid.*, p. 704).

[48] There follows two illegible pages.

This affair is a very perplexing and annoying one;[49] and I feel anxious about the result. We must, however, have patience and manage matters as well as we possibly can.

Teas have improved a little yesterday, and today—say a penny to two pence per pound. We are naturally enough very anxious for further news from China. Mr. Magniac was in Town two days ago, and expressed a wish that you should have remitted a considerable portion of his funds when the exchange was high.

Poor old Major Heart of Castle Milk[50] died a few days ago; and the property will be for sale. This is one of the properties I spoke of purchasing when in China, and I may possible make an offer for it when the proper time comes, though at present not very flush of cash.[51]

April 4th 1840. [No 3] Lombard Street.[52] 2 p.m.

I may mention, for your gratification, that *Jamsetjee Jejeebhoy Sons & Co.* have written a severe letter, to *Forbes, Forbes & Co.* complaining of their want of confidence, and a subsequent short note requesting them to hand over bills, to the amount of 61,400 pounds sterling to *Magniac Smith & Co.* on his account as agreed upon some time ago. These are bills remitted by you to *Jamsetjee Jejeebhoy & Co.* on Jamsetjee Jejeebhoy's account. I should have been delighted, had this amount been remitted in teas, or silk, that they might have had the mortification of seeing the commission on goods slip through their fingers.

Alexander has not yet returned from Scotland, but has written to say he will be here positively on Monday the 6th Instant. Mr. John Abel Smith, who is with me in N° 3, begs to be kindly remembered to you, and being aware of what I have written, considers it unnecessary for him to address you on the present occasion.

The list of the Committee, as enclosed,[53] was finally arranged last night, and Mr. Smith is, on the whole, tolerably well satisfied with it; and prepared to vote with ministers on Sir James Graham's motion, though many of the conservatives think otherwise. He is of opinion ministers will have a considerable majority, and I hope they may, being of opinion that we shall fare better with them than with the conservatives in power. I believe [Hugh Hamilton] Lindsay thinks otherwise.

[49] The affair referred to here is the possibility—by then remote—of an advance being granted to the merchants against the security of Captain Elliot's opium receipts.

[50] Castle Milk: 'Seat, three miles south east of Lockerbie. The ancient possession of the Bruces, the royal stewarts, and the Maxwells. [Subsequently] the seat the Sir Robert Jardine'. (*Gazetteer of the British Isles*). The estate was subsequently purchased by one of William Jardine's nephews.

[51] William Jardine bought eventually the estate of Lanrick in Perthshire. (Keswick, *The Thistle and the Jade*, p. 24).

[52] No 3, Lombard Street was the address of *Magniac Smith & Co.*'s offices, and it has remained that of *Matheson & Co.* to this day.

[53] The enclosure was not traced.

It would be an important point gained, were the Committee to recommend Government to advance fifty per cent on Elliot's receipts, the drug being valued at 500 dollars per chest and 4 shillings and 10 pence exchange. This would be a relief to every one concerned, particularly to the natives of India.

Mr. Pickwick[54] has just come in, and begs to be kindly remembered to you and your [esteemed] family. His wife and family are well, but no new keel laid—so he says.

Be pleased to remember me very kindly to all your family, now much reduced in numbers. What does Mr. Wright say to all this annoying business of our friend Lin, who must, ere now, consider himself in some little danger. Believe me, my Dear Matheson,

Yours sincerely,

201. Santiago Thomasen[55] in Macao to James Ryan in Canton,

11 April 1840

My dear Sir,

Kindly let Dr. Parker have the enclosed after you have perused it and affirmed the signatures of the writer. You can also explain its import to the Chinese Gentlemen principally concerned.

I have no time for more.

Yours sincerely,

202. James Matheson in Macao to William Jardine and Alexander Matheson in London,

26 April 1840

My dear Jardine and Alexander,

I have the pleasure to inform you we are all well and quiet, and everything is going as well as could be wished. Towards the end of the week, we shall despatch the *Kyd*, and about the same time the *{Lyser}* for Glasgow, which I should feel obliged if Alexander will announce to *Samuel Ewing & Co.*[56] We shall afterwards load the [ ] for London and shall still require further tonnage (at present not procurable) for teas to come out per *Syden.* The Canton authorities seem still to look with unconcern at the prospect of hostilities, but Canton business is much obstructed by form and delays, so much so that the Americans have got up a petition to Lin, begging he will expedite matters to enable their finishing their

[54] Mr. Pickwick, (possibly a ship-builder from the reference), was not identified.

[55] Santiago Thomasen was the code name James Matheson used when he wrote to his American agents in Canton during the Opium war. 'Thomasen' is an anagram of 'Matheson'. The allusions in the note are obscure.

[56] William Mathieson, whom James Matheson describes as his 'namesake' was a partner of *James Ewing & Co.* 300, Sauchiehall Street, Glasgow. (*GPOAD*). Was '*Samuel*' a slip of the copyist's pen ? See Letter **27**, note 18.

business before a blockade and hostilities commence. The retirement from Canton of Snow,[57] American Consul, has created a great sensation among the authorities, who will not acknowledge Delano[58] as Vice, unless the Hong Merchants agree to secure him, which they decline as unusual.

I have requested Mr. John Abel Smith to send you a copy of my *private* letter to him of 19th Instant, if you should not be in Town. It [outlines] Elliot's ideas as to the nature of the object to be obtained by the proposed armament and the strong conviction he feels as to there being no *long* suspension of Trade; in which I agree with him in thinking there will not be a *total* suspension, though supplies of tea will no doubt fall short of the consumption for some time; but I have a strong predilection for realizing when a handsome profit is to be obtained, and I hope you will so manage matters at home as to leave us with little or no tea on hand at the period of Trade re-opening.

One of Elliot's hobbies is to penetrate up the Yantze Kiang with a part of the force, and we have agreed at his request to obtain information as to the practicability of the channel, soundings, etc., for which purpose and the prospect of favourable sales of Malwa Jauncey is about to start in the *Hellas* for Chusan.[59] By way of securing my cordial co-operation Elliot has read to me some of his most confidential despatches *to and from*, and it was some consolation to me after Lord Palmerston's denial of compensation, to ascertain from them that there is no doubt as to its ultimate payment, with the recovery of the Hong debt, will all be insisted on, in less time than the stipulated twenty instalments of the Cohong.[60]

The *Hellas* saw the *Sir Edward Ryan* on the north Coast, with Calcutta news to 1 March and a *precis* of news by the January overland mail but nothing of interest. The report of the H.M.S ships fitting out at home having accommodation for an ambassador is perhaps the most interesting item. There is much competition now on the Coast and the *golden* days of the Trade are gone by,[61] but prices

[57] Peter Snow, the American Consul in Canton is mentioned episodically in Fay, *Opium war*, e.g. pp. 133–134, 150, etc.

[58] For Warren Delano, see above, Letter **158**, note 32. The appointment of consuls and vice consuls in a context when there were no official diplomatic links between the countries naturally led to temporary uncertainty.

[59] This expedition of Jauncey's and the *Hellas* to Chusan was organized by James Matheson as a gesture to oblige Captain Elliot and enable him to obtain channel marks and soundings for the naval force. The expedition ended up badly. On 22 May, the *Hellas* was attacked by eight junks. In the calm, she could not bring her broadside to bear. For four hours she was exposed to musket fire and flaming pitch from the Chinese. She managed to escape when the wind came up. All the 25 officers and crews were injured, including Jauncey who sailed back to Macao on 28 May with a broken jaw and an eye nearly put out. (Fay, *Opium War*, p. 209).

[60] William Jardine's conversation with Palmerston on the subject of the hong merchants' debt proved particularly effective. (See Letter **193**, second paragraph).

[61] The 'golden days' of opium trade on the coast: James Matheson refers to the earlier period (1835–1837) when the firm's sole competitor was *Dent & Co.* (See Letters **104** and **107**).

having risen at Calcutta nearly 50 per cent above our first sale purchases, we cannot easily be undersold. Andrew Jardine was well a few days ago at Manila. I have suggested his returning to China.[62]

Yours most sincerely,

203. James Matheson in Macao to Carl Gutzlaff in Macao, 28 April 1840

My dear Gutzlaff,

In a letter from my namesake Mr. William Mathieson of Glasgow, he authorizes you to draw upon him 120 pounds sterling, amount subscribed at that place for your publication of a 'Library in the Chinese Language'. At the current exchange of 4 shillings and 9 pence per dollar, the amount will be equal to 505.50 dollars, which you can draw for, when you please, on

Yours sincerely.

P.S. Your letter for Mr. Jardine shall be duly forwarded. Accompanying is a note for Mrs. Gutzlaff,[63] omitted to be forwarded sooner.

204. William Jardine in London to James Matheson in Macao, 2 May 1840

My Dear Matheson,

I can not allow the overland mail to depart without a few lines for you, though I have really nothing of importance to communicate. When I had the pleasure of addressing you last we were anxious about Sir James Graham's motion on the China question;[64] from which we were relieved by ministers having a majority of nine—they should have had sixteen, or eighteen; but some of their supporters were absent from bad health, and some from other causes—Bannerman had paired, but the pairing was upset by the unavoidable absence of the other party. Ministers then sent for him; but, he having just landed from the steamer in Aberdeen, when he received the notice to return to London, his zeal was not sufficiently strong to induce him to put himself in to the mail and retrace his steps *chop chop*. The opposition have been busying themselves not a little, about a letter that was got up by the [merchants] interested in the China question, the last

[62] The approaching British naval force made James Matheson more confident that the firm's opium department could again be managed from the Macao roads and Hong Kong. Andrew Jardine subsequently sailed to occupied Chusan and temporarily directed the firm's opium traffic from there. (Fay, *The Opium war*, p. 251).

[63] Whilst the Rev. Carl Gutzlaff went on writing books and articles on China and preaching the gospel, his wife was busy teaching in the school for Chinese pupils she had founded in Macao. (Endacott, *History of Hong Kong*, p. 133).

[64] See above, Letter **200**.

day of the debate, and read by Lord Palmerston, to whom it was addressed, at the end of his speech, in the House of Commons, with great effect.[65]

You will see by the newspapers, that Mr. George Palmer[66] has been playing the fool, in a most extraordinary manner, by giving notice of a motion to the effect that a refusal, on the part of the Chinese government, to pay for the opium *seized*, is not a sufficient cause for declaring war against China. His brothers and other

[65] [Viscount Palmerston] held in his hand a letter from thirty respectable firms engaged in the China trade, and which he would beg leave to read to the House. The noble Lord then read the following letter.

'London, April 9, 1840—To the Viscount Palmerston—My Lord, We, the undersigned British merchants connected with China, cannot but view with the greatest alarm and apprehension the probable effect of the expression of any public opinions with respect to the justice and policy of the measures understood to be taken by Her Majesty's Government to obtain redress for the insults and injuries inflicted on British subjects by the Chinese Government, and the for future protection of the legal trade with that country. We disclaim all pretension of dictating to the Chinese the mode in which the British trade which China shall be carried on; but we cannot refrain from expressing our deliberate opinion, that unless measures of the Government be followed up with firmness and energy, the trade with China can no longer be conducted with security to life and property, or with credit or advantage to the British nation. // We have the honour to be your Lordship's most obedient humble servants, (signed: G. G. de Larpent, Chairman of the East India and China Association, J. Horsley Palmer, J. Mackillop, *Briggs, Thurnburn, Acraman, & Co., Gledstanes, Kerr & Co., Alexander George Milne & Co., Small, Colquhoun & Co.*, John S. Rigge of the firm *Sanderson, Fry, Fox, & Co.*, H. H. Lindsay, *Gregson & Co., Daniel Dickinson & Co., Crawford, Colvin & Co., Larkins and Co., Lyall Brothers and Co., Walkinshaw & Co., Gardner Urquhart & Co.*, John Hine, W. J. Hall & Co., Alexander Matheson, James W. Smith, *Walkinshaw, Skinner & Co., Magniac Smith & Co., Dallas & Coles*, William Drayner, *Hunter, Gouger & Co.*, C. S. Gover, *Robert Eglinton & Co., Scott Bell & Co.*, John Brightman, *C. R. Read & Co.*

The parties whose signatures he had read were these. These are the parties whose interests are at stake—these are the parties most interested, yet although I believe the majority of them are hostile to the Government generally, yet they come forward voluntarily, spontaneously, to say, that if the objects of the Government are not carried out, British commerce in China would be at an end. It was impossible, it was indeed preposterous to suppose, that if the same indignities which had been heaped upon British subjects in China, from the time of Lord Napier's expedition down to the present period, were to be persevered in, unresisted and unredressed, it would be impossible to suppose that, under such circumstances, any British merchant would, with any regard to his safety of his self-respect, continue his commercial operations in those parts. But the Right Hon. Baronet, in the motion which he has submitted to the House, evaded all the real and substantial merits of the question. His motion said not whether any measure should be taken by the Government to diminish the trade in opium, though he thought it doubtful whether the usual effect would not be produced upon the destruction of any monopoly, and the produce be increased. It was not likely that, supposing we were to diminish the supply in India, it would not immediately be transferred to Turkey, Persia, or some neighbouring country. The motion of the Righ Hon. Baronet, however, steering clear of all the difficulties in the case, evading all the real circumstances, attempted by a side wind, bearing upon an incidental part of these transactions, either to cripple the measures which Her Majesty's Government had adopted, for the accomplishment of the subject which they had in view, or else to take the matter out of their hands in order that the Right Hon. Baronet and his colleagues might themselves reap the harvest of which Her Majesty's Ministers had sown the seed. (Hear!). [. . .] (*Hansard*), 1840, vol, III, pp. 946–947).

[66] George Palmer, the brother of J. Horsley Palmer, who later became Governor of the Bank of England. George Palmer was a Conservative MP for Essex. (*DPC*). For his speech in the Parliamentary debate, see *Hansard*, vol. 53, p. 833.

partners are very much vexed and annoyed with him; but he is extremely obstinate and, though his motion has been postponed, it has not been withdrawn. The general opinion, however, is that he begins to see his folly, but has so far committed himself to his party, that he finds it difficult to back out. Such conduct is considered absurd and foolish in the extreme, on the part of the senior partner of a House of East India Agency.[67]

It is said, Sir Robert Peel has declared he will have nothing to say to Mr. George Palmer's motion. Our Committee has met once, John Abel Smith chairman, Mr. Crawford being at Brighton on account of his health. Most people consider this as fortunate; as Mr. Smith is much better liked, and has much more influence with the members of the Committee. Mr. Crawford is very persevering, but few persons like to work with him, he is so fond of having his own way in everything, and has a very disagreeable manner, and wretched address. He has, however, been very zealous in the cause, and has done good. His disappointment is great indeed, but his health is so very bad that he is quite unequal to the task.

Our hope is that the Committee[68] may be induced to recommend an advance in Exchequer Bills, to the extent of one half our claims, on the security of Elliot's opium receipts, valuing each chest at 500 dollars, exchange at 4 shillings and 10 pence per dollar.[69] If we could induce H.M. ministers to make such an advance in shape of a loan, till the Chinese shall be made to pay for the drug extorted from our representative, we should gain a very important point, in the acknowledgement of our claims.

Lord Palmerston has said, in private conversation, that the admission on their part, of its being their duty to recover for us from the Chinese, implied their being bound to make the claims good in the event of their failing to make the Chinese pay. John Abel[70] was well pleased with this good feeling the members of the Committee displayed at their first meeting. They permitted Freshfield to state our case, and consented to him, and Courtney[71] being permitted, as a matter of courtesy, to remain in the room pending the whole investigation, which is not customary. Sir Robert Peel was absent and Gladstone was the only member that

[67] *Palmer Mackillop & Co.*, known at the time this Letter was written as *Palmer, Mackillop, Dent & Co.*, of 11 King's Arms Yard. (*TLCD*).

[68] 'The Committee' refers to the House of Commons Committee looking into the China affairs. The Committee was mentioned in Letters **199** and **200**.

[69] After the 9 April House of Common's vote on Sir James Graham's motion, questions about the war and the work of the Commons Committee on China continued in Parliament well into June 1840. See Letter **208**.

[70] John Abel Smith. A rare instance in William Jardine's correspondence of the use of a Christian name not followed by a full surname to refer to a person who was no family relation.

[71] Courtney was the Parliamentary agent employed by the Committee of the *East India and China Association* (the merchants' representatives).

started a difficulty;[72] and he is quite wild about the pernicious effects of opium on mind, morals and body. He is anxious to have our government to interfere to prevent the East India Company from growing the poppy; and unwilling that any evidence should be taken that would tend to implicate the Chinese Authorities as encouragers of the importation of the drug. This is absurd enough. He ought to see, that by proving them encouragers, and active agents of the native opium dealers, to the extent of carrying the drug in their own boats from our ships at HongKong and Canton, we get clear of the charge of importing opium contrary to the laws of the empire.[73] The Viceroy being the only authority we had to look to for information respecting the Laws, and regulations by which foreigners were to be encouraged, or punished. You must not fancy, from this observation, that the absurd paragraphs in the papers give me the slightest uneasiness, quite the reverse, I laugh at them, and take no trouble to refute them. Silent contempt is all they deserve; though our friend, Lindsay, has been vindicating himself.[74]

Since I had the pleasure of addressing you on the 4th Ultimo, your favours of this 10th and 14th November last have come to hand; and by the 8th instant I hope to hear from you again.

May 4th.

The foregoing was written in the country though dated here, N° 3, and the first thing heard on my return to town this forenoon, was a report, of an express being in from Marseilles, but I have been unable (4 p.m.) to trace it to any authentic source.

The tea market has been fluctuating a penny or two pence per pound, during the last month, without any apparent cause; and is likely to continue doing so, till we have some more decided news from your quarter. The wild speculators are nearly all out of the market, and the heavy prompts being over, we shall have prices better supported than they have been lately. It is scarcely possible that we can receive anything like a full supply, of 38, or 40, millions of pounds annually for this, and the coming season. Indeed my own opinion is against our having more than 25 millions this year, and 30 or 35 next, and with such a supply prices should ride a little higher than they were in January and February last. With such views I shall be glad to hear that you have purchased freely, even at the prices that prevailed, in Canton, in November last. *Walkinshaw & Co.*[75] are very desirous

[72] Gladstone's line was the same as the one he adopted in the Parliamentary debate. See Letter **200**, note 47, 4th paragraph.

[73] This was the most frequent argument used by the British opium merchants to convince themselves and others that they were no smugglers. Gladstone thought the argument was pure sophistry. See Letter **83**, note 17.

[74] Presumably Hugh Hamilton Lindsay had been writing to newpapers editors, an action which William Jardine's habit of secrecy and sense of privacy would naturally shun.

[75] Probably the firm of James Walkinshaw, the 'intimate friend' referred to in Letter **149**.

of hearing that you have bought teas from them, and say they ordered teas of ordinary qualities—no fine, or expensive teas.

Raw silk continues nearly in the same state as it was when I arrived in England—prices keep up, but the consumption is very much reduced. I wish you would ascertain, as correctly as you possibly can, whether the consumption of Company's camlets has fallen off in China, and, if so, to what extent, and from what cause. I am aware that Howqua had a heavy stock at the time the Company ceased to import; and a good many have been received since. *Wetmore & Co.* wrote to Hall[76] and to Mr. Roberts,[77] saying the article was going out of use, and three or four days after sent them an Account-Sales of two or three thousand pieces, at favorable prices, 24 to 26 dollars per piece clear after paying the reduced rate of duty. Mr. Roberts is now almost the only maker of the article now solvent; and is naturally anxious to have correct information respecting them. He has a thousand pieces ready for shipping; on which he wishes us to make an advance. He will then keep a few of his best workmen employed, and make a very reduced quantity annually till your report comes to hand.

Your brother left London for Edinburgh on the 2nd instant. He is in high health. Waghorn[78] has arrived; but nothing has transpired. We shall have our letters tomorrow or next day.

Be pleased to make my chin chin to all friends, particularly to those of your own[79] establishment, and believe me, my Dear Matheson,

Yours very sincerely,

205. James Matheson in Macao to Andrew Johnstone in Scotland,
4 May 1840

My dear Johnstone,

I owe you many apologies for the irregularity of my correspondence with you, occasioned chiefly by the troubles and anxieties of the last eighteen months; which will, I hope, plead my excuse, while you have the less reason to regret my silence, as you will no doubt have had ample intelligence from your uncle and Alexander of all which has been passing here both before and since their departure.

[76] Both James and William Hall had been ship captains in the Jardine fleet.

[77] There were two 'Mr. Roberts': James Roberts and William Roberts, 'Cotton spinners, manufacturers and agents, 29, Cannon Street, Manchester. (*PODL*).

[78] 'Waghorn': short for 'the overland mail', from the creator of the Overland Route, Thomas Waghorn, R.N. The new route stretched 84 miles across the desert from Alexandria to the Red Sea port of El-Suweis. It had seven relay stations and became the standard route for sending mail between England and India. (*DNB*). Se also: Karabell, Zachary, *Parting the Desert*, New York, Alfred A. Knopf, 2003.

[79] 'Your own establishment': *Jardine, Matheson & Co.*, from which, as a retired partner, William Jardine was gradually withdrawing his capital.

I much regret the circumstances of the times have prevented our giving effect to your spirited plan of a speculation to Hull. The first obstacle arose from our exclusion from Canton, rendering it impossible to provide any assortment with the minute distinction of quality prescribed in Armstrong's[80] order; dire experience having convinced both ourselves and our tasters that in such cases we must be guided by business rules and not overstep them from a feeling, however strong, that a constituent is going thereby benefited. As it often happens, the most promising speculation turns out the reverse, and the greatest profits are frequently made when least expected. If indeed the order had come from yourself alone, and not from one who like Armstrong, had always badgered us on the grounds of deviation from instructions and transferred nearly all his business to other parties, the case might have been different. And when you operate again, I recommend your giving us your own instructions without reference to others. When after a time the course of events gave no greater confidence in the home tea market, we wished to charter a vessel for Hull; but not succeeding we have made such shipments to London on Armstrong's account and yours, to the extent of 30,629 dollars per *Balcarras*, 23,193 [dollars] per *Royal Saxon*. Your half now [very] considerably exceeds your funds in our hands, and we shall have to draw upon you for the difference; but our Book keeper B. A. Barretto, has been at Canton this greatest part of the season, our Books are rather in arrear and we cannot make up your account [accurately] at this moment. It is most provoking that Turner[81] has not remitted your funds from Calcutta. What was there to prevent him authorizing our drawing upon his firm if, as Mr. Stewart says,[82] his doubt as to the practicality of procuring teas prevented his sending us the money?

As David Jardine is now attached to *Lyall Matheson & Co.*, I hope you will no longer be disposed to go wondering after strange agents to bungle your business.

We are much obliged for your kind consideration in having agreed to relieve Captain W. O. Young[83] of his share in the *Moor*, your motives for which we fully appreciate, and knowing this we wrote to *Magniac Smith & Co.*, as soon as we knew of the arrangement, intending also to write you, though it was overlooked that we shall feel obliged if you relinquish your shares to us, the vessel having been expressly built as a joint concern with Jamsetee [Jejeebhoy], *Remington & Co.*, with other Bombay friends and ourselves. Captain Young got his share as a favour, to induce his building and commanding her, and being economical in the expenses. The admission of a new resident shareholder would interfere with the plans of the owners, who will probably wish to give your share, if you relinquish

[80] For George Armstrong, see Letter **188**, note 151, and Letter **222**.

[81] 'Turner': W. Turner, a partner in the Calcutta agency house *Alexander, Turner & Co.*

[82] 'Mr. Stewart' was not identified.

[83] Captain W. O. Young was the first commander of the *Mor*.

[it], to her present commander, as a stimulus to activity and economy.[84] I therefore propose, if you approve, that your purchase from Captain W. O. Young, shall be transferred to us, as if you had nothing to do with her. Her outward voyage is of course a losing one, and it depends entirely on the future of the opium trade whether she is to make money or not, as she is greatly too small for any other trade.

I ought long since to have answered your letter of 14th March 1838 enquiring for the information of Mr. John Irving[85] whether a Bank would answer in China. Under the old system of Canton trade, which it is to be hoped is now at a end, it would not have answered; as business [is] being conducted almost entirely between the Chinese on one side, and foreigners on the other, there can be no medium of circulation that will not be equally [valued] among the Chinese of the interior as among foreigners.[86] The Chinese are yet far too backwards in their notions, to understand the nature of a Bank; as will be obvious to Mr. Irving, when you tell him, what you well know, that Carolus dollars are considered 10 per cent more valuable than others merely because more modern dollars do not circulate in particular districts; and Republican dollars being less known will not circulate in any part of the Empire at even 4 and 5 per cent discount below Ferdinands, though of equal intrinsic value. Furthermore, *pure* silver bullion is often bought at par, or weight for weight for the broken dollars current here which are 9 per cent lower in touch or purity. The people with whom such absurdities find place are not ripe for the establishment of a Bank. Though it may be otherwise by and bye, if as is rumored, we are to have a settlement, under the British flag on the Coast. But I think for some time to come, we shall get on more securely and better without it. More especially *Jardine, Matheson & Co.* who, I hope, will always have as much capital as they can well use.

I refer you to Mr. John Abel Smith, with Mr. Jardine and Alexander Matheson for our views as to the probability of their being a long interruption of Trade, though supplies will probably for some time be on a limited scale, and give you a comparatively firm market. But we ourselves are not for holding long. Write me soon and believe me

Yours very sincerely.

[84] The financial arrangement described here links the employee's financial reward in the form of an allocation of shares to the efficiency of his performance. The stock-option system for today's executives and managers is thus a contemporary version of an early Victorian practice. The financial reward system in force at the East India Company before the abolition of its tea monopoly was that of perquisites ('perks'). 'Perks' were adjuncts to salary linked to a Company servant's rank or grade, not to his performance.

[85] John Irving: a Conservative MP, merchant and first president of the Alliance Insurance Company. (*DPC*).

[86] The meaning of the sentence appears clearly when the double negative is omitted.

206. William Jardine in London to Jamsetjee Jejeebhoy in Bombay,
4 May 1840

My dear Sir,

Since I had the pleasure of addressing you on the 3rd and 4th ultimo I have been favored with your esteemed letter of the 27th February with the enclosures for which receipt my best thanks.

Little has been done in the China affair since the above date but that little has been as satisfactory as we could possibly expect it to be. The Committee has met once and the result of the meeting was everything the chairman could have wished for or expected. The Members allowed Mr. Freshfield our solicitor to state our case and consented to him and our Parliamentary agent, Mr. Courtney remaining in the Committee room during their sittings.[87] This is not regular and only granted as a matter of courtesy.

You are a aware that Mr. Crawford was to have been chairman of the Committee but his health is so extremely delicate that he is unable to attend and has been at Brighton for some time past. In his absence [John] Abel Smith was elected chairman and has been taking a great deal of trouble to conciliate Ministers as well as the Members of the Committee in which task he has succeeded admirably.

Between ourselves I think the cause has benefited by the change of chairman. Mr. Crawford is able enough and has taken much interest in the business but his manners are not so conciliatory as those of Mr. Smith and he has not so much influence with Ministers or with Members of the Committee. On his (Mr. Smith's) applying to Lord Palmerston for permission to name another Member in lieu of Mr. Crawford he said immediately: 'You may not only name one but you may name any one you please.' Mr. Smith elected Mr. Brownrigg[88]. They meet again on Thursday when Mr. [Robert] Inglis, Captain [John] Thacker and Mr. [Nugent] Daniell will be examined as to the delivery of the opium to Elliot.

You will see from the newspapers what a quantity of nonsense was talked by Sir James Graham and his friends on the occasion of his motion respecting China and will no doubt be surprised at the notice given by Mr. George Palmer in opposition to the wishes of his brother and all his Partners. How he as the head of a house of East India Agency could give notice of such motion we are at a loss to comprehend, and hope his notice will yet be withdrawn. If we can succeed in getting the Committee to recommend an advance in Exchequer bills even to the extent of half our claim on the security of Elliot's receipts it will materially benefit our cause as it will be an acknowledgment of our claim.

[87] On this episode, see Letter **204**, note 71.

[88] John Studholm Brownrigg: a Conservative MP for Boston; a merchant and a partner in the firm of *Sir Charles Cockerell & Co.*, (*DPC*).

Mr. John Abel Smith gave a few lines of introduction to you to a young gentleman named Kishton who is on board of Captain Young's ship[89]. May I request you to pay him any attention in you power and promote his views should you have it in your power to do so.

Our Tea Market has been fluctuating a penny or two per pound during the last week or two without any apparent cause, but I feel no anxiety about it. We must have more favorable news from China before any permanent fall can take place.

Mr. Bowman[90] will reach Bombay about the time this letter does and by him I was anxious to have sent out my account with Framjee Cowasjee but he and Mr. Lindsay have refused to declare the principles on which they made their award until Framjee shall have signed the release. Consequently I cannot make up my account for they have taken the whole of the *Sarah*'s accounts into consideration. This is very annoying, as I could have settled with Framjee at any time had I not waited at Weeding's request till they settled their account at the same time. Oblige me by mentioning this to Framjee.[91]

Be pleased to present my kind regards to your Sons and believe me, my dear Sir,

Yours sincerely,

207. James Matheson in Macao to Charles Lyall in Calcutta, 11 May 1840

My dear Lyall,

I have the pleasure to acknowledge your several favours [ ] which arrived within the last few days; and while I am writing the arrival of the *Tartar* is announced, but she has not yet had any communication with the shore. As long ago as 24th Ultimo the *Hellas* brought news to nearly the same date, which she received from the *Sir Edward Ryan* on the Coast.

We were already so bountifully supplied with drug that we could well have spared the heavy importation now coming in, previously to which the price of Patna had been well maintained at about 400 dollars per chest, but is now looking down at 390 to 380 dollars. Malwa from being in smaller quantities and fewer hands is better supported and may be quoted at around 500 dollars to 480 dollars, though some of the *Arderseer*'s has been sold as low as 450 dollars. We have an alteration to suggest in my instructions of 29th ultimo which I now confirm.

[89] On Captain Young, see Letter **205**, note 83. 'Kishton' was not identified.

[90] 'Mr. Bowman' and 'Mr. Lindsay' may have been arbitrators in a dispute involving the *Sarah*. (See Letter **244** which again mentions the difficulty of closing the *Sarah* account). The *BI* lists three entries under the name 'Mr Bowman'.

[91] Being now retired, William Jardine wanted to repatriate his capital in the *Sarah*, the first ship he owned in partnership with Thomas Weeding and Framjee Cowasjee. Some unspecified commercial dispute followed by arbitration proceedings repeatedly delayed the settlement of the account.

I was in hopes you would not have found it necessary to buy for us at the 2nd sale, and cannot understand how it is that you did not invest, at the 1st, all the funds of which we gave you previous notice, as going in the *Rover*; our intention having been that you should have dealt with them exactly the same as if they had been in your possession. But you must excuse my hinting that it seems to be the singular fate of *Lyall Matheson & Co.* to act boldly in stretching instructions for purchases in the market when prices are high, and on the other hand stinting them in the most possible specific manner by buying as little as possible when prices are low—a remark I should perhaps have spared, were it not that I am going to suggest a solution and a remedy which will have a salutary effect for the future.[92] It seems to me to arise from the old fault, which I formerly noticed, of your being too apt to be led away [by], to take your tone from, the example of what others are doing in place of being guided solely by the *spirit* of your instructions, and by the common sense maxim that the great art of trading is to buy cheap as the surest prelude of being able to sell dear. Let me therefore earnestly impress upon you and beg you will inculcate on your youngsters, let it be written in letters of gold, that in the drug trade, when prices are high, or in other words, when competition is eager and *shipments briskly going on*, then is the time for caution, for thinking much, for shaking all feelings of confidence derived from the example of others, and substituting diffidence for leaning to the safe side, and giving the narrowest possible construction to your instructions. On the other hand when prices are low, with a want of competition, no activity in shipments and your neighbours generally disinclined to buy, then is the time to screw your courage to the utmost, to act on the most liberal construction which your order can be stretched to; when your mind is once made up, endeavour to shake off the feelings of diffidence which will more or less be inspired by others, take your measures totally and *promptly*, do not risk the counteraction of your object by putting off in the hope of doing better. Be content to do well, without risking the loss of your chances (as in your negotiations with Carr)[93] by trying to do too well.

You will think I am harping unnecessarily on a doctrine which is admitted to theory by all the world. You acted well on it last year—or rather last summer by way of corrective to the wild purchases of the winter. But I do not think it sufficiently impressed upon you to secure its being uniformally attended to. It would be an inconceivable comfort to me, if we could feel a tolerable assurance of our instructions being rightly apprehended and acted on by you. As it is, I must be

[92] James Matheson has difficulty containing his exasperation at *Lyall Matheson & Co.*'s persistent lack of real understanding of his instructions. (See Letter **146**). The whole Letter can be regarded as a lesson about how to buy and invest soundly.

[93] Possibly William Carr, a 'merchant of 65 Old Broad Street'. (*TLCD*). But the reference is more likely to be to the 'William Carr' who was at the time a partner in the Calcutta firm of *Carr Tagore & Co.* (*EIRD*, 1841).

candid enough to say, we feel directly the reverse and are afraid to let drop a sanguine word lest it should lead you into a reckless course of purchases. Hence it is that the tone of our instructions is perhaps generally tempered down rather below what circumstances might warrant, from a fear of their being misconstrued into a more sanguine hue than we intended. Never let this, however, induce you to stretch them in the least when prices are high and competition active.

The *Brigand* has been a most unfortunate concern, and it is a thousand pities you did not, in preference, secure the *Rob Roy* on almost any terms; (which Captain McKinnon[94] informs us would not have been difficult) seeing you were striving for the great object of getting ahead of the 1st sale; which I do not hesitate to say, would have made a difference of about 200 dollars per chest in the realization of her drug. Besides having been badly commanded and [managed], she is a tub that cannot sail, the *Rob Roy* having beat her about a fortnight from Singapore— though Mr Boyd inadvertently stated in our official letter that she performs well. Report says the Captain's sad fate might not unnaturally have been anticipated from his habitually violent contact to the crew.[95] His successor, the only one that Scott could get at Singapore, was formerly given to intemperate habits; but in the hopes of his having reformed, Captain Parry with too much facility was induced to let him take the vessel to the Coast; the consequence is that from want of a good water the *Brigand* got foul of the *Hayes* in the night, disabling both vessels, and rendering it necessary to transship 253 chests for safety to the *Cowasjee Family*, for which we have now a claim made against us of 25,000 dollars salvage.

Give my best thanks to John Lyall for his attention in sending a cook and servants,[96] the two last of whom have just arrived per *Tartar* from Singapore, where they were returned to give evidence on the trial for murder.[97] The [assistant] who arrived some time ago is a sad clumsy fellow. It is a pity the cook is not younger and of any other religion but Hindoo. He is old and infirm and declares he and his assistant would require no less than 4 mates to cook for one family of twelve.[98] I

[94] Captain MacKinnon was not identified.

[95] The (unnamed) captain appointed by *Lyall Matheson & Co.* to command the *Brigand* was murdered by his crew. An (unnamed) replacement captain was found by 'Scott', James Matheson's agent in Singapore. The *Brigand* made it to Hong Kong. Captain Parry, the commodore of the opium fleet allowed her to sail directly up coast to deliver its opium, when the accident occurred with the *Lady Hayes*.

[96] See above, Letter **189**.

[97] The murder of the *Brigand*'s captain.

[98] James Matheson had made a specific request for a cook who was 'a first rate artist'. This whole Letter is a tale of woes brought on by the carelessness and lack of intelligence of his Calcutta agents. James Matheson's self-control and matter-of-fact response in the face of life's reversals make this letter a fine example of unintentional humour.

should think a [Buddhist] would have been better suited for this part of the world.
I remain in haste
most sincerely yours,

208. William Jardine in London to James Matheson in Macao, 3 June 1840[99]

My Dear Matheson,

[. . .]

The tea sale came to a close yesterday, prices having declined as it advanced, and the report is as follows: Congo, the first day, went off at 1 shilling to 4 shillings per pound under the rates that prevailed on the 18th May. The second day prices ruled generally ½ to ¾ per pound lower than the first for Congo; and throughout the greatest depression was for the finer qualities, of which there was a large proportion in the sale—prices from 2 shillings and 2 pence to 2 shillings and 4 pence per pound. There were 9,702 packages: 795,564 pounds sold. Twankay fine to Hyson Skin bought in at 2 shillings and 2 pence; Hyson skin, common: 2 shillings to 2 shillings and a half-penny; good to fine: 2 shillings 4¼ pence to 2 shillings 7 pence for exportation only. Fine: 2 shillings 11pence and 3 shillings 1¾ pence for home consumption. Prices today a shade higher than yesterday; but little doing.

I saw Griffith[100] yesterday, who gives a good account of you all, particularly of those connected with the drug department. Mrs Morgan[101] went to her mother for a few days; but Lyall has taken lodgings for them, and they are both expected in Town shortly. I dined with Mrs. Alleyn,[102] in her father's house on Sunday last, for the first time. She was in high spirits, looking well, and drank your health in a [toast]. Alleyn's account with Heath[103] is not yet closed. He makes out a small balance of 400 or 500 pounds sterling in favour of the widow; the teas unsold being estimated at current prices.

I have a note from Elliot[104] today, in which he expresses discontent and says 'it is Timothy Wiggins's intention to ask you to take a look at them'. I regret this and hope we may be able to settle the business amicably. I have settled Captain Clark's affair[105] through Mr. Freshfield, by paying him the 1,400 dollars you

[99] This letter was written at the Oriental Club which William Jardine joined on his return to London. Its first three pages are illegible.
[100] Probably Captain John P. Griffith, who had commanded the *Ann* in 1836. (*BI*).
[101] On Mrs Morgan, see above, Letter **188**, note 158.
[102] F. P. Alleyn's widow. See Letter **100**, note 1 and 2; and Letter **145**, note 58.
[103] For Thomas Heath, see Letter **111**, note 106.
[104] Probably Gledstanes's friend, 'Bob Elliot', mentioned in Letter **4**.
[105] Two correspondents known as 'Captain Clark' are listed in the *BI*—one was 'J.' Clark, and the other 'Thomas' Clark.

offered to him in China, at 5 shillings per dollar; and he has now found out that his legal adviser has not acted correctly. When I saw him in his lawyer's office, I told him he should have come to me or written to me, without the intervention of his legal friend.[106]

Mr. John Abel Smith called on me this forenoon, and drove me into the City. He is extremely anxious about the report of the China Committee, and doubtful if he can get a majority to recommend compensation, though more than half of them are for compensation of some kind. They disagree on the amount. Captain Elliot's brother[107] is against us, and the Blue Book[108] will prove to you, that Elliot himself has done all he could to injure our cause. Horseman,[109] who was decidedly for compensation, is not connected with the government, and does not vote. Sir Robert Peel declines attending tomorrow, and offers no opinion. Gladstone proposed yesterday, that the Committee should not give in a report—which must be overruled if possible. Mr Smith thinks the bills, Elliot drew, will be paid;[110] whether the receipts are or not. But this would be the highest possible injustice to all those who hold receipts. If possible I shall let you know what is done in the committee tomorrow. Believe me, we are all anxious enough, John Abel most so, he feels the responsibility of his position as Chairman of the Committee, most severely.

Adieu for the present. Your letter of 15th January, per *Cordelia*, came to hand on the 16th of May. Mr. Alexander Matheson has just brought us the following report of the Committee at ½ past 5 p.m.

June 4th

'Your Committee to whom it was referred to inquire into the grievances complained of in the petition of Merchants interested in the trade with China presented 24th March, by reason of the surrender of opium to H.M. Superintendent there in the month of March 1839, feel that they best discharge their duty by laying before the House, without any observation on their own part, the evidence which they have taken on the subject'.[111]

[106] Aside from his new 'political' activity in relation of the opium receipts, William Jardine was spending a fair amount of his time settling unresolved minor commercial disputes with a number of *Jardine, Matheson & Co.*'s correspondents.

[107] Probably Captain Charles Elliot's younger brother, (Sir) Frederick Elliot (1808–1880). He entered the Colonial Office in 1825 and was some time Under-Secretary of State. (Hoe, *The Taking of Hong Kong*, p. 261).

[108] The book compiling the findings of the House China Committee.

[109] Edward Horseman, (1807–1876); member of the Scottish Bar. MP for Stroud and Lisheard. Lord of the Treasury June-Sept. 1841. (*MEB*).

[110] On the bills drawn by Captain Elliot, see above, Letter **198**, note 23.

[111] Contrary to William Jardine's expectation and that of all the opium merchants, a majority of Committee members refused to recommend to the House that an advance be paid to them on the security of their opium receipts. The merchants were to be equally unsuccessful in the House. They now

Damn them all—or at least the majority of them ! We must now hope for better luck in the House. I am disappointed at this report, but have not time to say more.

Yours very sincerely,

209. William Jardine in London to Jamsetjee Jejeebhoy in Bombay, 4 June 1840

My dear Sir,

Since I had the pleasure of addressing you in the 4th ultimo, we have been in great anxiety about the proceedings of the Committee of the House of Commons on the China question, for, though the evidence given has, upon the whole been satisfactory as proving our claims against the Government, still the members of the committee entertain such different views as to the extent of remuneration, and the mode of wording their resolution that up to this hour, when the Committee are sitting for the purpose of drawing up their report, the Chairman is doubtful of the result. Mr. Gladstone proposed [reporting] without making any [recommendation], but this will, I hope, be overruled, and a favorable set of resolutions agreed by a majority of the members of the Committee, if not by the whole. Sir Robert Peel has seldom attended their meeting and it is understood that he will decline offering an opinion on the subject.

Mr. Alexander Matheson is waiting in the House of Commons, and will bring us the particulars of what is done in Committee; so as to enable me to mention them previous to closing this, if possible.[112] The evidence taken is printed, but not yet in circulation. When it is we shall send you a copy. There are one or two answers, in the evidence given by Mr. Inglis, which have done harm, by creating a feeling, in the mind of many members that Commissioner Lin would, by threats, imprisonments, etc., etc., have forced the Merchants to give up the whole of their opium, whether Captain Elliot had interfered or not. I am of a different opinion, and so are many others. But as he was in Canton at the time it was given up, his evidence gives the opposers[113] of the claim a strong arguments against the compensation; which is unfortunate.

We are anxiously awaiting further accounts from China, the *Ann* having left on the 17th January without anything positive respecting the loading of the *Earl of Balcarras*, which makes me suspect Captain Morgan's report to you may prove incorrect;[114] though we know the House in Canton has purchased rather a large

---

had to wait three full years for payments from the government. The opium receipts were finally paid up in August 1843. See Letter **263**.

[112] The beginning of this Letter was written before the end of Letter **208**.

[113] 'Opposer': an old word recorded as early as 1483 with the meaning of 'one who 'opposes' the defender of a thesis in an academic disputation'. The newer term 'Opponent' is recorded as of 1601. (*OED*).

[114] Captain Morgan's report was not traced.

supply of Teas on account of the constituents, and themselves—and had also begun to purchase Raw Silk. No mention is made of any seizure, or confiscation of ships under the Danish flag, from which we are led to hope the report to that effect, circulated in the Ceylon Newspapers was incorrect.

Teas continue low and the demand for them very limited; which surprises me not a little, but the tea market will ultimately take care of itself. I have no fears on that score. Raw Silk is too high, in consequence of which, the consumption has fallen off very much; I speak of Tsatlee and Tysaam, the demand for which at present prices is very limited, and becoming more so. Our friends in China have been paying too much for the article, of late years, and must either buy cheaper, or the first time they land a large supply, there must be money lost by it, or it must be kept on hand for a long time.

Your friends *Forbes Forbes & Co.* have handed over to *Magniac Smith & Co.* [the bill of lading] and other documents, for a small shipment of Raw Silk and Silk Piece Goods, *per Ann*, on your account, respecting which the two firms have, no doubt, written to you.

Mr. Malcolmson[115] has, latterly, been very desirous of taking an active part in the China question, and applied to have their solicitor admitted into the Committee room; but this was impracticable, Mr. Freshfield and Mr. Courtney having been permitted to be present, as a matter of courtesy only, not as a matter of right. Mr. Malcolmson has been examined, however, and gave evidence from your correspondence, and other sources, as to the distress produced, in Bombay by the refusal on the part of the Government to pay for the Opium. I suppose you have been giving your friend a lecture on that, and other subjects.

It is now past five o'clock, and Mr. Matheson has not made his appearance. I shall wait till the last moment.

Mr. Matheson has this moment arrived, and the following is the report of the Committee, carried by a majority of one. 'Your Committee to whom it was referred to inquire into the grievances complained of in the Petitions of Merchants interested in the Opium Trade with China, presented 24th March, by reason of the surrender of Opium, to H.M. Superintendent there, on the Month of march 1839; feel that they best discharge their duty by laying before the House without any observation on their own part, the evidence which they have taken upon the Subject.'

I feel much disappointed at this report, and so does Mr. Smith. We must now hope for better luck in the House, but it will be a tedious process. I have not time to say more.

Believe me,
Yours very sincerely

[115] On James Malcolmson, see Letter **182**, note 103.

210. James Matheson in Macao to William Jardine and Alexander Matheson in London, 25 June 1840

My dear Jardine and Alexander,

Being very much taken up with the double despatch of the *Ann McKim* for New York and *Ardaseer* for Bombay, I find I must confine myself to a hurried [note] on two or three points, in place of answering deliberately the letters I have received from you to 4th March.

Firstly. Under all circumstances, I think it will be better to compromise by paying *Hyde Lennox & Co.*[116] the value of their 45 chests surrendered by *Cowasjee Family* and *Walkinshaw & Co.*,[117] their 30 by same vessel. The circumstances connected with them are described with sufficient accuracy in Alexander Matheson's letter of 4th March to *Jardine, Matheson & Co.*, to which I may add that in a long and painful interview which I had with [Captain] Elliot during our durance at Canton, in which I represented to him the absurdity of his having pledged a fixed quantity of the drug while it must be every day diminishing on the Coast, without any means of ascertaining the extent owing to the stoppage of the communication,[118] he wrote a minute (now under lock and key in Elmslie's possession)[119] stating that he had done so with the express object of embracing future arrivals, which he considered equally liable to be surrendered *during our imprisonment* with the drug previously on land. I replied that he being Chief Superintendent of the Trade, it only remained for us to obey his orders. This minute could be referred to in case of need, but it appears to me we are so certain of recovering compensation that it is not worth while contesting the point. They may be paid at invoice cost, which will not, I suppose, be 100 pounds sterling per chest. They may perhaps claim the profit they would have had on investing the amount in Teas, but to this they have not the shadow of a pretext, both their limits having been far too low as proved in open letters to them to *Magniac Smith & Co.* for their and your perusal, to which I entreat your particular and pointed attention.

Secondly. Mr. John Anderson.[120] You are the best judges as to the advisableness or otherwise of retaining him. I think we shall postpone any decision and have him on the present provisional footing till we learn Alexander Matheson's sentiment in person. You will see we are ordering a Manchester Investment on House Account from Magniac Smith & Co. which I hope you will approve of, on the

[116] The country firm was not identified. The *BI* lists ten letters from Thomas Hyde in England.
[117] For *Walkinshaw & Co.* see Letter **149**, note 70.
[118] On the commercial difficulty resulting from Captain Elliot's opium surrender order, see above, Letter **170**, note 36.
[119] Edward Elmslie was Captain Elliot's secretary. (See Letter **106**, note 59).
[120] On John Anderson, the 'successor to Macvicar', see Letter **163**, note 61.

grounds stated in the orders. But should there be any particular reason against it, you can of course exercise your discretion in suppressing [it].

Thirdly. Mr. Garnett of Manchester[121] has long since received our final reply. And it is of no use exchanging long controversial letters with him. He offered Mr. Anderson to renew business with us, if we admitted his claim, but I think we are better without such litigious constituents.

Yours sincerely,

211. James Matheson in Macao to Jamsetjee Jejeebhoy in Bombay,

1 July 1840

My dear Sir,

I have much pleasure in announcing the arrival of the long expected *Charlotte* from Manila last night, of the *Pearl* on the 29th, and of Admiral Elliot in the *Melville* with *H.M.S. Blonde* and *Pylades* on the 28th. Ultimo,[122] also the *Young Queen* on the same date with your highly interesting favours of the 6th, 7th, 7th & 9th May. I congratulate you most sincerely on the favourable prospects of compensation conveyed by the April mail, which I earnestly hope will be still more strongly confirmed by that of the succeeding month. The copies of letters which you enclose from Lord Clare,[123] Mr. Jardine and Mr. Wallace,[124] are most satisfactory, and I have the pleasure to state we have forwarded your Pekoe tea for his Lordship per [ ]. I regret to observe China goods are so low at your Presidency, and we shall not, as you desire, purchase any on your account unless compelled to do so, or unless tempted by very low prices.

We are making arrangements to load the *Charlotte*'s cotton here in the hopes of being entitled to forward it to Canton for advantageous sale; and we have every expectation of returning her immediately with a profitable freight to Bombay, calling at Manila for some of your sugar, as Captain Liebschwager[125] considers the season highly unfavourable for touching at Singapore. The [ ] is also

[121] Robert Garnett, of the Garnett family, see Letter **46**, note 67.

[122] Since the beginning of June 1840, the British force had started assembling around the islands close to Macao and Hong Kong. The first ship to arrive from Singapore on 1 June was the frigate *Alligator*. (See above, Letter **197**, note 20). Between 16 and 21 June, several other war ships arrived: the *Madagascar*, the *Atalanta*, the *Wellesley*, the *Larne*. A land force of some 5,000 men had been assembled comprising several regiments stationed in India, including the 26th (Cameronians), the 49th and the 18th (Royal Irish). Admiral Sir George Elliot was the last to arrive from the Cape in his flagship, the 74-gun *HMS Melville*, accompanied by the 42-gun frigate *Blonde* and the 18-gun *Pylades* .(Fay, *The Opium War*, pp. 208, 210, 214).

[123] John Firtzgibbon, second Earl of Clare, had been Governor of Bombay. The enclosures were not traced.

[124] Mr Wallace was not identified. James Matheson may be referring to Captain Wallace (see Letter **162**) who had commanded the *Omega* in 1838.

advertised for Bombay, but it is very doubtful if she will go, as her cargo will be transshipped to the *Mor* should she arrive within a reasonable period.

Admiral Elliot without landing at Macao proceeded to Chusan at daylight yesterday accompanied by Captain Elliot and his establishment,[126] also by Mr. Thom,[127] a gentleman from our office well acquainted with the Chinese language who is instructed to ascertain and communicate to us the fullest information on commercial subjects at the places he may visit. There is now no doubt that Chusan will be taken possession of, to which effect we expect a public notification some six weeks hence, but although it may be possible perhaps to find a vent there for some articles of British manufactures, such as long cloths, I fear we shall have no encouragement to send up cotton. To be prepared, however, for any opening that may occur we now write to Singapore requesting that your cotton ships may come on direct to China rather than Manila. But should they reach after September the north east monsoon will be so strong as to render the passage to Chusan impracticable for any vessels but clippers. We shall vigilantly watch the course of events, and shape our instructions from time to time as circumstances may render advisable. Captain Elliot's treasury was open for a few days for bills on Calcutta at 218 [Rupees] for 100 [dollars] but was unexpectedly closed; there is no doubt, however, he will have to open [it] again.[128]

125 Captain Liebschwager was not identified. (A few letters are listed in the *BI*).

126 Admiral Elliot having arrived a month later than planned, there was a need to move north immediately in order to take advantage of the favourable monsoon winds and avoid the typhoon season. Palmerston's instructions were that they should put in place a selective blockade of the Chinese ports, seize the island of Chusan as hostage, present their demands at the mouth of the Peiho river, a hundred miles from Peking, and there negotiate a treaty of which they had received a draft. Palmerston had left the joint plenipotentiaries little room for manoeuvre. (*The Opium War*, p. 215).

127 For Robert Thom, the firm's piece goods manager, and how the Opium War launched him on a new official career, see Letter **72**, note 41.

128 For all Captain Elliot's and his cousin's dislike of the opium trade and their banning it from Chusan waters in August 1840 after the British force occupied the island (the Tinghai forts controlling Chusan had fallen on 6 July following Sir Gordon Bremer's attack), the joint Plenipotentiaries still had the responsibility of financing the fleet. This they did by 'opening [their] treasury', i.e., by selling bills drawn on the East India Company in Calcutta. Only those firms which had cash could buy the bills, and that meant principally the firms most active in the opium trade. James Matheson was well aware of the Elliots' situation and on 4 August, just a month after this Letter was written, he wrote again to Jamsetjee Jejeebhoy: 'We look with some uneasiness to Admiral Elliot's prohibition of the drug trade at Chusan as indicating the same sort of disaffection which gave us so much alarm and trouble on the part of Captain Elliot. But as they have no mode of raising money for the expenses of the war unless from the drug sales in China, we think they cannot avoid giving it some toleration' (*JMArch.*, C5-5; also quoted by Fay, *The Opium war*, p. 239). The financial necessities of the war thus influenced Captain Elliot to adopt a realistic *modus vivendi* with the opium traders and with James Matheson in particular. The sale of India's opium which had led to the war in the first place was also an indirect source of its financing.

As a result James Matheson lost no time in sending Andrew Jardine from Manila to Chusan, where he continued managing the opium fleet, soon aided by David Jardine, Donald Matheson and others. (See the end of Letter **202**; Letter **218**; *The Opium War*, pp. 253, 259).

Some of the Portuguese cotton per *Marquis of Hastings* has been sold at 17 Taels per picul, and about 90 chests of her Malwa at 485 dollars per chest, which we were induced to give Dr. Oliveiro[129] to support the market. We have not received any further accounts from Canton but expect our agent down in a few days, when we shall be able to report sales. Everything was quiet there on the 29th. Two men of war went up yesterday to the Bogue to enforce the blockade,[130] but we have no intelligence of what passed there. We hope all will be quick.

With kind regards to Cursetjee, I remain,

Yours very sincerely.

212. William Jardine in London to James Matheson in Macao, 4 July 1840

My Dear Matheson,

I have deferred writing to you by this conveyance, till the last moment, in hopes of your letters, by the India mail of the 23th of May reaching us before the closing of the overland mail this evening; but of this I now despair.

You will, no doubt, feel much annoyed, and disappointed at our want of success—in making the government responsible for Elliot's Bills and receipts; the conservative members of the Committee threw us overboard in a very shameful way.[131] Sir Robert Peel attended very little, if any, after the first day, and you may collect, from certain questions put by him to Mr. Inglis and the answers to them, what must have been the impression on his mind, as to the giving up of the opium. The evidence given by Inglis is considered by most of us as much too vague and diffuse, and calculated to very much injure our cause. You will however judge for yourself. Alexander [Matheson] gave good evidence, which is generally satisfactory. We are now endeavouring to get Sir Robert Peel to support our claim in the Commons; and, if we succeed, we are likely to have a majority; but he is a sad slippery politician, and will endeavour to turn the question to the advantage of himself if possible. He seldom commits himself by a promise, and party feeling is now mixed up with everything; the goodness of our cause avails us nothing. The Reform Bill has done very little good so far as my weak judgment is capable of forming an opinion on the subject.

Alexander [Matheson] and I have been bothered by your friends *R. Garnett Sons & Co.*, about the losses they sustained in consequence of their friends being

[129] Dr Oliveiro was not identified.

[130] The blockade of the Canton River was applied by Captain Smith and his squadron. He directed operations from the 44-gun *Druid* with the *Hyacinth* and the *Larne*. (*The Opium War*, p. 244). The Chinese grain and salt junks were detained by the British and the Chinese authorities retaliated by offering rewards for the capture of British citizens. A few were captured and imprisoned for a number of months, including Vincent Stanton, the Turner children's tutor and later Hong Kong Colonial Chaplain (see Letter **187**, note 144; *Ride, East India Company Cemetery*, p. 24).

[131] See above, Letter **208**.

detained in China, etc., etc. the negotiation was carried on between Mr. R. Garnett and myself. He stated their loss at 3,881 pounds sterling 8 shillings and 8 pence, expressed an earnest desire for an amicable settlement, and requested we would make him an offer. I examined the correspondence, and feeling we were in the first instance wrong, I offered him half that sum, which he accepted. My agreement was—the greater part of the loss arises from your having sold the raw silk, on our account, at a time the market was very much depressed, without consulting our agents or asking them to interfere on our account. I am glad it is over; and hope you will approve of the plan pursued. I need scarcely say I consulted John Abel Smith and Alexander [Matheson], on the subject.

Mr. Starkey[132] has made an appeal to me, but I have declined interfering till we receive your promised statement of the case. It appears to me there was a lack of good temper on both sides; which he appeared to be extremely sorry for when too late. Poor man, he is badly off in money matters; and, I think, if you were here you would be disposed to assist him, and would try to forgive him; but it is impossible for me to relieve him without admitting the principle of our being responsible for the opium given up to Captain Elliot, which would not answer our purpose in the present state of things.

I have just seen John Abel Smith, who tells me I cannot write too generally about our claims, as everything is uncertain, and it is necessary to feel our way before the question is brought before Parliament.[133] It would do harm had we a large majority of the Commons against us.

I have since the 4th. Ultimo, received your letters of 17th and 25th of January, 2nd, 4th and 17th of February; for which accept my thanks—duplicated of the 17th February per [ ] received today. She has made rather a long passage, so that the *Balcarras* may come in any day. The *Times* Newspaper announced the arrival of the Indian mail at Marseilles on the 2nd Instant; but few letters have come to hand. We have not received one; nor shall we now till Monday.

The tea market keeps fluctuating a penny or two pence per pound every day; but prices must ultimately advance very considerably. I feel quite easy on this head; and should not object to your sending me my annual remittance entirely in teas.[134] By the way, you drew against the teas and silk last year, to the extent of

[132] Possibly Captain Starkey who had commanded the *Thistle* in 1839. (*BI*).

[133] This is the first intimation that the House of Commons would not volunteer to give advances to merchants on their opium receipts until the money was first recovered from the Chinese authorities.

[134] As Hollingworth Magniac had done before him, and as future retiring partners were to do after him, William Jardine was withdrawing his capital from the firm gradually. From the retired partner's point of view this had the advantage of having ready money to invest in China whenever local prices were low. And from the firm's point of view, it was useful to have a substantial amount of working capital in reserve. At the time this Letter was written, remittances in tea were a sound bet, on the reasonable assumption that trading difficulties during the hostilities were likely to reduce the supply to Britain and that prices would rise.

two thirds in favour of the Company; so that you only sent me about five or six thousand pounds; but with the profit up in them I shall have enough till Pidding's bills come in to play.[135] Magniac has no objection to his funds being remitted home.

With kind regards to all around you, I remain, my Dear Matheson,
yours very sincerely,

213. James Matheson in Macao to J. W. Henderson in Bombay.

19 July 1840

My dear Sir,

But little of interest has occurred since I had the pleasure of addressing you on the 1st. Several Junks, I believe seven or eight chiefly laden with salt, have been taken by the blockading squadron at the Bogue, and sent to Capsingmoon where they are anchored alongside of the *Druid* though report says some have been released.[136] Two more being deserted by the crews drifted on shore and went to pieces, which gave rise to a report that they had been sunk by the men of war and some lives lost; but for this there is no foundation. The orders are to seize only Government Grain and Salt Junks. The Viceroy[137] is highly incensed at the Junks being stopped, and has ordered a levy of 2,000 and 3,000 men to be paid by the Hong Merchants, but we learn recruits come in very slowly.

In the first transport of rage, Lin told the Hong Merchants to summon to his presence all the foreigners in Canton (for what purpose is not known) but next day he stated that [they] would not be wanted. The Hong Merchants alarmed by this violence recommended the foreigners to leave Canton as soon as possible; but in the face of this, Mr Delano[138] the American Vice Consul is returning there this evening, Mr Coolidge[139] went up four days ago, and Mr. Shillaber still remains there. The two latter Gentlemen are in our interest to take advantage of

[135] James Matheson had sent William Jardine's his previous year's remittance ⅔ in bills on the East India Company. The request for 1840 was that most should be sent in teas. Meanwhile William Jardine still had sufficient cash from the tea he had sold at a profit and from the bills on Captain Pidding soon coming due.

Captain J. R. Pidding was the founder of *Pidding & Co.*, 'Tea dealers, 2 Botolph Lane, Eastcheap'. (*TLCD*). In 1839, he had cornered the entire first crop of the *Assam Company* (the first 280 pounds of British India tea ever sold at auction in London) at the exorbitant average price of 26 shillings per pound. (Antrobus, H. A., *A History of the Assam Company, 1839–1953*, Edinburgh, T & A Constable Ltd, 1957, pp. 264–266).

[136] On the Canton river blockade, see above, Letter **211**, note 130.

[137] Lin, the former 'opium Commissioner', was still the Canton viceroy.

[138] On Warren Delano, (also mentioned in Letter **202**), see above, Letter **158**, note 32.

[139] This is the first mention in these Letters of Joseph Coolidge, a partner in *Russell & Co.* who had arrived in Canton in 1832. (Hunter, *The Fan Kwei at Canton*, p. 96. At the time, both Joseph Coolidge and James Ryan (as well as John Shillaber) were acting as the firm's agents in Canton. (*BI*).

any favourable opening for business. The Inner Passage[140] for native craft between Canton and Macao is still left open by the blockading squadron, nor is it intended to be interfered with. Lin however interdicted the passage of goods, but whether this will be enforced is doubtful. Our Agent Mr. Ryan writes us on the 1st that the Chinese Merchants themselves speak confidently of being able to send down goods, and even Teas in spite of the restrictions.

We expect Mr. Ryan here in two or three days which will, I hope, enable us to send your final accounts by the [ ] to sail for Calcutta in about a week.

With kind regards to your Partners, I remain,

Yours sincerely,

P.S. Patna has been sold at 380 dollars per chest. Malwa, 550 dollars. Here prices continue without variation. At Chinchew the Mandarins and Pirates are becoming alarmingly formidable. The *Black Joke*[141] (a clipper of *Messrs. D. & M. Rustomjee & Co.*)[142] was attacked by 16 junks off Chinchew, which chased her ten miles off the land, keeping up a sharp fire all the time. Their sails were a good deal cut, and one lascar badly wounded.

214. James Matheson in Macao to John Abel Smith in London,

25 July 1840

My dear Sir,

You will learn from our Circular that the first division of the Transports reached Macao Roads 21st instant and almost immediately proceeded to the Northward, whither the rest are to follow on arrival under convoy of *H.M.S. Larne* which is detained for the purpose. Having been interrupted in a confidential conversation with Captain Elliot yesterday, I have not much authentic information as to their respective movements; but I believe there is no doubt their destination is Chusan, after taking possession of which the plenipotentiaries (Admiral and Captain Elliot) will probably seek to open a communication with Pekin before attempting further hostilities. This tallies with Lord Palmerston's declaration in Parliament that the proposed operations will be more in the way of *Communications* than hostilities. Before the arrival of the fleet it was fully intended to take the Bogue Forts but I rather think the instructions

[140] The 'Inner Passage' referred to the indirect waterways amongst marshland, west of the main estuary (the Bogue) which linked Macao with the city of Canton. This was the slow passage which Lord Napier had been made to use on his fatal return to Macao.

[141] It is unclear whether this '*Black Joke*' is the same ship as the *Black Joke* which had previously suffered at the hands of Chinese pirates on 23 August, 1839. (See Letter **177**, note 80).

[142] The firm of two Parsee partners operating in Canton: Dadabhoy Rustomjee and Manackjee Rustomjee. (Several letters listed in the *BI*).

from home do not countenance this,[143] and should they be taken hereafter, which I much doubt unless the Chinese should provoke us to it by their aggressions, it will be on the Admiral's own responsibility.

This forbearance is a very general disappointment to every one from our Chief downwards and all seem to think it will tend with the smallness of our force (only 5,000 men) greatly to protract a final settlement which would have been far more hopeful from a bolder and more sudden course of action, that would have taken the authorities by surprise and rendered them panic struck by a signal display of the power of British arms.[144]

By the plan which to all appearance is proposed to be adopted they will have time to recover from their alarm, and to exercise their well-known ingenuity in getting the better of us by wily negotiation.[145] In short we look forward to its being a very longwinded affair; and I am now by no means so confident as before in the expectation I expected of Trade being practicable on the Coast which was entirely based on the supposition (no longer probable) that the Authorities would be so paralysed as to be unable to prevent their people from dealing with us. Still such is Elliot's eagerness for Trade and so great his boasting and self-congratulation on what has been already done in this way (no thanks to him !) that I am convinced Trade he *will* have at all hazards and by whatever means; and should no other plan be feasible between this and January, I shall not be surprised to see a relaxation of the Blockade or a licence system introduced to enable foreigners to recommence bringing Teas from Whampoa for the British shipping. This can only, however, be to a partial extent, probably not more than half the usual supply; as among other causes it is unlikely there will be much available shipping. The tonnage actually at and going up to Whampoa before the Blockade on the 28th will not suffice for more than about 15,000 chests; and under all

[143] Palmerston's instructions were indeed not to take the Bogue Forts but to sail immediately north to occupy Chusan and to deliver his letter of demands to the Emperor. Palmerston's strategy was influenced to a large extent by William Jardine's recommendations, particularly the idea of arranging for military pressure to bear close to Peking rather than in Canton. Competing voices had advised him to follow a different strategy, notably that of Sir John Barrow, second secretary at the Admiralty, who recommended in vain that force be applied primarily in the Gulf of Canton. (Fay, *The Opium War*, p. 215).

[144] This remark suggests that James Matheson, like Sir John Barrow in London and most of the British community in Canton (but contrary to William Jardine's opinion) would have preferred to see an immediate display of force in and around Canton which, they thought, would have swiftly brought the Chinese to the negotiating table.

[145] James Matheson's judgment was impeccable on this point and Captain Elliot's two-week long negotiations with Kishen from 30 August 1840 resulted in a truce which gave the Chinese a welcome breathing space, but brought nothing to the British except a temporary loss of advantage. (See Letters **219** and **220**). Eventually it was this error of judgment which caused Captain Elliot's recall as much as the insufficiently remunerating clauses of the failed 'convention' negotiated with Kishen at Chuenpee in January 1841. (See Letter **223**).

circumstances we see no reason to prevent the holder of Tea from continuing to maintain a fair market.

I have had the confidential perusal of a correspondence that the Portuguese have just had with the Chinese on the one hand and Elliot on the other by which in consideration of our not landing troops in the vicinity and of our having opened the inner passage for native craft between Canton and Macao, the Chinese engage not to molest the English, nor stop provisions at Macao. It is also stipulated that British goods may be landed and stored here [which], though a part of the objectionable temporizing policy, will tend greatly to our comfort as residents here, and will be convenient in giving inward vessels the option of landing their cargoes with some chance of a sale.

All the Americans had made up their minds to leave Canton immediately, but the unexpectedly pacific course of affairs will induce many of them to remain and some who had left are about to return.

I have not time to do more than briefly acknowledge your favours up to 4th March and repeat my most grateful thanks for your singular zeal and (I hope) success in the compensation cause. It is gratifying to observe by the April mail that [once] the preliminary step of obtaining a committee[146] had been carried I lost not a moment in using my influence with Elliot to have *Magniac Smith & Co.* nominated as Agents for any property that may be got from the Chinese in payment of the compensation.[147] He could not of course say anything definite, and you will be sorry to hear that he advocates the abandonment of claims against the Chinese on consideration of their surrendering Chusan. Hoping I may be able to advise a better aspect of affairs at some future day, I remain

With kind regards to yours partners,

Yours most sincerely,

215. James Matheson in Macao to William Jardine in London,

27 July 1840

My dear Jardine,

Excuse my troubling you to ask you who is to bear the loss on the Cornelians alluded to in the enclosed correspondence between Framjee Pestonjee[148] and us. It is likely to be heavy, say, including interest about 50 per cent, most of the Cornelians being still on hand, and at the risk of H.M. Government (under

[146] The Committee of the House of Commons which was supposed to recommend immediate partial payments to the opium merchants, but instead decided to report without comment. See Letter **208**, last paragraph.

[147] James Matheson, whilst at times extremely critical of Captain Elliot, was always urbane and often helpful in his private dealings with him. Not only had he become the British force's principal banker, he proved here particularly adroit in obtaining an official mandate for his London agents.

[148] On Framjee Pestonjee Cama, See Letter **108**, note 72.

Shillaber's charge) at Canton. You will know best what Her Majesty's guarantee is worth.[149] You may remember the advance was made or at his insistence to Hurjeerum Amtha[150], on the occasion of Framjee's last leaving China in January 1837. Framjee having an advance made on them which he had no mode of realizing, unless by getting the money on their security for us. If you think you did not look to Framjee as the responsible party, of course the house must bear the loss, otherwise we shall hold him liable. As far as I can learn from Heerjeebhoy,[151] it seems to have been a dirty attempt of Framjee's to pass off the Cornelians on us as security which he well knew not to be worth our advance.[152]

Yours sincerely,

216. William Jardine in Cheltenham to James Matheson in Macao,

3 August 1840

My Dear Matheson,

Grant, Johnstone and old Jardine[153] being a little unwell, or fancying themselves so, left town a fortnight ago for Leamington and Cheltenham. Johnstone left us in a few days and Grant and I return to London on Wednesday the 5th Instant, being now in good health. I had a letter from one of your Sisters a few days ago. Your Brother was with them, and they are all well. I shall pay them a visit in the course of this month, or early in September if possible.

Since my arrival here I have been favored with your letters of the 10th, 18th, and19th of March, for which many thanks. Alexander [Matheson] is in Scotland. He shall be, or rather has been informed, of what was going on among you, in the celestial regions.[154]

Your letters are satisfactory, and I am glad you had sent an express to Canton to purchase more teas. My feeling is in favor of Teas, being of opinion, that we cannot have 30 or 35, millions of pounds next season, even should the war be at an end in a month from the day the Troops arrive on the Coast of China; there must be a short supply from the Teas districts, and the stock in this country will be so much reduced that Congos are not likely to be lower than 2 shillings and 6 pence per pound for the next two years—if ever. Our market has been sadly bothered by our friends *Jamsetjee Jejeebhoy & Co.*, and *Baring and Co.* for some

[149] An incisive and untypically cynical remark on the part of James Matheson.

[150] Hurjeerum Amtha, or Herjeerum Amtha (Letter **229**) was not identified.

[151] On Herjeebhoy Rustomjee, see above, Letter **170**, note 29.

[152] An advance on the security of gem stones was highly untypical of the firm's practice. If it was sanctioned by a partner the advance is likely to have been made in order to assist a party who was then considered a friend.

[153] William Jardine was 56 when he wrote this Letter.

[154] A variation on a standard joke. The 'Celestials' was the traditional tongue-in-cheek way of referring to the Chinese.

months.[155] But the holders generally are firm. You will be pleased to hear that *Magniac Smith & Co.* have paid *Forbes Forbes & Co.* all we had engaged to remit to them, on Jamsetjee's account; and all the Teas, Silk, etc., shipped by you have been made over to the former firm. Jamsetjee Jejeebhoy wrote to me to send him out a ship, and he would load her with cotton and send her to *Magniac Smith & Co.* We chartered a vessel home, that was there on the way out, and have heard of her arrival out and of her cargo being ready for shipping; but he will not leave *Forbes, Forbes & Co.* while Sir Charles Forbes is alive.[156]

We shall be large holders of Tea, but it is safe property, and when we hear of hostilities having commenced, the Teas dealers will begin to calculate the probable supply and the consumption, more accurately than they have yet done. I have had much pleasure in hearing your management highly approved of, by those who had, and have goods in the hands of the firm. But shippers generally are rather unreasonable. When Teas advanced so very rapidly here, every one fancied they should have had Tea, even in opposition to their own instructions. They forget that after my arrival in England they might have purchased cheaper here than you could buy them down for; and yet they never blamed themselves for their own neglect in not purchasing; though they know more of the intentions of the ministers than you did.

I have had many applications from manufacturers and others to ask if I would take a share in a shipment to China, on advance on goods, or recommend the parties to ship to *Magniac Smith & Co.* I have discouraged shipments under existing circumstances, but have not advised any one decidedly. I have pointed out to them the mode of sending their goods to Singapore, or Manila, so as to be at hand when the ports of China are opened, and after giving them every information in my power, have left them to judge for themselves.

Macvicar, Lindsay, and many others, have been shipping largely; and some of them are still shipping. I confess freely, my nerves are not equal to such rash acts, and my judgment is against such proceedings; but I may be wrong.[157] Lord Palmerston says the blockade will be a swift one whenever it takes place; and my feelling is against an easy settlement, or rather I am of opinion that hostilities once commenced, in earnest, the war is likely to be a protracted one. At the same time I never doubted that, if Elliot had left China the moment he was at liberty the Chinese would have disgraced Lin, paid for the opium, and opened the Trade

[155] The two firms were selling large quantities of tea, which kept the price down.
[156] See above, Letter **182**, note 102. William Jardine and James Matheson had used their influence with Jamsetjee Jejeebhoy to persuade him to shift more of his London business from *Forbes, Forbes & Co.* to *Magniac Smith & Co.*
[157] Previous disappointments with British piece goods had made William Jardine sceptical about the ability of British exporters to make money in China. Although his experience had been similar, John Macvicar had not learned the same lesson.

on fair terms, rather than have risked all the consequences of a war with Great Britain.

Before leaving London I attended a meeting of John Abel Smith, Horsley Palmer, Crawford, and Freshfield, to deliberate on the best mode of bringing the opium question before the Commons. After much discussion, it was deemed advisable not to bring the question on—from a fear that the Conservatives might, during the debate, say something that would prevent them, *when in power* from making good the claims against the government.[158] I was for bringing the business on, at all hazards; as we cannot be worse off than we are at present. John Abel Smith had a leaning to my view of the case, but did not like to take the responsibility in opposition to the others. The truth is—we fall a sacrifice *to the state of things*. Both parties acknowledge the justice of our claims, the ministers are afraid to bring them forward, or to support them, and the opposition will not bring them forward. They would do anything to get H.M. Ministers into trouble, but are not honest enough to do us justice. Ministers have behaved ill—in fact they have acted dishonestly—and Elliot has disgraced himself beyond redemption by his letter number 4, I think, in the additional papers forming the blue Book.[159]

[158] The argument was disingenuous and signalled the near-paralysis of a political situation where the Whig government was holding to power with the thinnest majority in the Commons.

[159] The originality of Elliot's arguments in his letter to Palmerston dated 28 November 1839 makes it an interesting document. His view was that Lin's violent confiscation of the whole of the opium stock in 1839 in fact saved the opium traders from ruin, and ensured a healthy continuation of their trade. The following are extracts from this letter:

[. . .] The British trade is formally cut off at present; but I have never known it carried on with more vigour or advantage: and it is a striking comment upon what I have just said, that the leading American merchants have been constrained to live, for at least four months, not at Canton but at the station of the British merchants,—that is on shipboard, exposed to all manner of privations and danger. We are now in a situation to judge of the result of the Commissioner's policy for the suppression of the opium trade; and it may be pronounced to be a signal failure, and pregnant with the worst character of mischief to this empire, as it was always reasonable to suppose such an extravagant course of proceeding must prove to be.

He found the traffic stagnant; he has made it flourish in a degree and to an extent that it had never reached before.

When he arrived, and for four months before that date, there had been scarcely any deliveries. The great bulk of last year's supply had accumulated; and the immense stock of the current year was only commencing to come in. In China, prices had fallen to between two and three hundred per cent below the cost of production and charges; and at Calcutta and Bombay, on the very day that opium was surrendered in Canton, sales were either impossible of ruinous.

These results had been produced by steady adherence to measures of repression against the consumers; a character of proceeding to which the Chinese system of government and police is well adapted, when its strength is put forth: and my own measures of December last, against the river traffic, had pressed heavily upon the whole—both in the moral sense, as unequivocally separating Her Majesty's Government from the least countenance of it, and directly, because that channel remained to the last the best vent for the drug.

John Abel did all he could, and I feel deeply indebted to him. He was as much annoyed, as I was, at the result; and believe me, that was not little.[160] I have little doubt we shall get paid ultimately, and in the meanwhile even the saints have acknowledged that the firms in China were as highly respectable and honorable as any in the world. Poor consolation—we knew that before.

I hope your stock of opium may be small when the armament reaches; as it is possible the opium trade may be interrupted, as well as the regular trade; but time must determine these points, as H.M. Ministers keep us all in profound ignorance. The proceedings of the Commons, have so thoroughly disgusted me, that I should almost hesitate about taking a seat in the House, were it offered to me.

But, my Lord, the moment the Commissioner rejected all reasonable prospects for working out a solution of the difficult if not impracticable problem confided to him, and drove me to the necessity of ransoming my countrymen by the delivery of all British opium to China, it was clear to me that he could reap nothing but disappointment and difficulty.

The character of his measures was an acknowledgment of his own sense of helplessness against the smugglers themselves, either native or foreign. A proceeding of that kind upon a handful of defenceless men could never be repeated; and to take away 20,000 chests of opium, already nearly valueless from weight of stock, was not to extinguish the trade. It turns out, indeed, to be a measure nothing short of salvation to the opium trade, generally considered, whatever it might have been to the actual holder of the particular quantity taken away. But indeed, that very stock had already fallen to a point so far below its price, that it would be difficult to say, the proprietors would have been in a better condition if the Commissioner had given it to them again next morning. Certainly, looking at future operations it seems susceptible of proof, that the general market needed the full relief which the Commissioner gave to it before opium could recover such a price as would repay the mere cost of its production and other expenses of laying it down in China. But, looking still further forwards, and seeing that the traffic has been carried on with incessant vigour and immense advantages since the 24th March last, it must be admitted that the persons who have continued to pursue it are deeply indebted to his Excellency; and could indeed well afford to sacrifice the price they paid for the opium they surrendered, out of the profit of the opium they could never had sold otherwise, without total ruin. I believe that would be a moderate imposition upon present returns and present prospects; and whilst I am upon this subject I may presume to say, that the Commissioner has fallen upon the single device which left any hope of supporting the Company's opium returns of next year. If he had left the 20,000 chests of opium in the hands of the holders, the Company must have sacrifices their next year's supply. Under present circumstances, I see no reason to doubt that there will be a handsome income from that source. It is greatly to the honour of some of our principal merchants here, that they have steadily adhered to the voluntary pledge to relinquish this unworthy and lawless traffic under circumstances of intense temptation; and with regard to such of them as stand in that honourable situation, I cannot help expressing the sincere hope that Her Majesty's Government will find it practicable to relieve them from burdens which must press most heavily upon them, and carry out some effectual and comprehensive scheme for the protection of the lawful trade. [. . .] (*PP.* Vol. XXXVI, pp. 539–541).

160 'Annoyance' was a powerfully disruptive emotion for William Jardine. He used the word to describe his state of mind when he felt practically helpless in the pursuit of some objective, though morally vindicated. He often felt morally vindicated; but very rarely did he feel helpless. The chemistry between the two feelings usually erupted in an expression of disgust couched in powerful yet controlled language. (See the end of the next paragraph: 'The proceedings in the Commons, have so thoroughly disgusted me, that I should almost hesitate about taking a seat in the House, were it offered to me'). However, within a year of this statement he had sufficiently recovered from his disgust to seek and obtain a seat in the House of Commons as member for Ashburton. (See Letter **240**).

Be pleased to present my kind regards to all around you, say to Heerjeebhoy his letter has been received, and believe me,

My dear Matheson,

Yours very sincerely.

217. William Jardine in Cheltenham to Jamsetjee Jejeebhoy in Bombay, 3 August 1840

My dear Sir,

Tomorrow being the day for the overland Mail, I am unwilling to let slip the opportunity of addressing a few lines to you though without anything of importance to communicate. You will of course hear of the arrival of *Balcarras* and every particular from your London Friends. On my arrival there your [letter] will be delivered to the Captain and I shall strongly urge economy and despatch.

Previous to leaving London I attended a meeting of Mr. Crawford, Mr. H. Palmer, Mr. John Abel Smith, and Mr. Freshfield to deliberate on the best mode of bringing the opium claims before the Commons, the Committee having laid the evidence before the House without any comment or remarks from the Members. After a long discussion as to who would and who would not support the claims, the chances of a change of Ministry, etc., we determined not to bring the question before the House, Mr. Crawford and Mr. Palmer being of opinion that we run the risque[161] of the opposition Members saying something against the claims in the heat of the debate which might, *when in power*, prevent them from supporting our cause. I confess I had a different feeling and was and am still of opinion that we cannot be in a worse position than we are, and should therefore have preferred bringing on a discussion in the House. John Abel Smith had a leaning to my view of the question but did not wish to take the responsibility of bringing the business forward in opposition to the opinion of the other Parties interested, more particularly as Sir Robert Peel was of opinion we could not get a Majority and Mr. Gladstone had scruples of conscience about urging our claims, fearful such a proceeding might tend to induce Ministers to prosecute the War with more determination than they would, were the business allowed to rest as it is. With due deference to the Honorable Member, this appears to me extremely silly, as he admits most fully the justness of our claims, and anything done or *said here now* cannot in any way change our plans in China.[162] You will see from the Newspapers that many Members on both sides of the House admit our claims to be just, but still we can get nothing from them. The truth is our interests are sacrificed to the state of Parties.

[161] The two spelling, 'risk' and 'risque' (dating back to the seventeenth century), were still common at the time. (*OED*).

[162] William Jardine's logic seems much sounder that Gladstone's reported argument.

H.M. Ministers are afraid to move or to support the Claims and the opposition would do anything to embarrass them, but between them they have not sufficient honesty to do justice, a wretched state of things. I believe both sides of the house think we have a direct claim against the Government, and I have no doubt we shall get paid at last, but not for a long while, which is far from right.[163]

In hopes of hearing from you by the overland Mail in a few days and with kind regards to yours Sons and all Friends, I remain, my dear Sir,

Yours sincerely.

218. John Robert Morrison[164] on board *H.M.S. Melville*,[165] to James Matheson in Macao, 19 November 1840

My dear Mr. Matheson,

We are passing the entrance to Hongkong, and I may soon have an opportunity of sending you the enclosed letters, while I shall myself probably be unable to get down to Macao for a day or two. Elmslie has, I believe, some other letters for you, respecting which I will speak to him, should any opportunity of sending them occur before he himself goes down.

I saw Boyd, Donald [Matheson], David Jardine, etc.,[166] all well on board the *Syden*, on the evening of Friday the 13th, and Thom quitted us, also well, on the evening of Saturday. The *Nimrod* in which he was to return to Chusan, did not part company with us till Sunday morning, when we made a fair start from the south end of the archipelago. Our squadron is composed of the three lines of battle ships,[167] and the *Modeste*. The *Madagascar* will folllow us, but I do not know how long after. The *Columbine* will probably be the first vessel sent up. Your letters will tell you of the actual condition of things in Chusan.[168]

[163] Jardine's feeling of 'annoyance', so apparent when writing to an intimate friend and partner like James Matheson, has been suppressed and proper decorum restored in this Letter addressed to one of the firm's most important business constituents.

[164] John Robert Morrison was secretary and interpreter to the British Plenipotentiaries. For details on his short career, see Letter **49**, note 7.

[165] The *Melville*, the British force's flagship had come to harm in a mudflat on 6 July 1840, the day after reaching Chusan. It took several weeks to have her careened and her bottom mended. She was in service again from September1840. (*The Opium War*, pp. 225, 257).

[166] The associates and young partners sent to Chusan to conduct the firm's opium and exchange businesses. See Letter **211**, note 128, second paragraph.

[167] *HMS Bleinheim*, *HMS Wellesley* and *HMS Melville*.

[168] The island of Chusan had been occupied by the British since Tinghai had fallen with hardly any resistance in early July. Lieutenant Colonel Burrell set up his headquarters in the abandoned town on 20 July, accompanied by Lord Jocelyn, Carl Gutzlaff, Robert Thom and Captain Caine (the new civil magistrate and future Hong Kong official). Whilst the *Melville* was being repaired, the two British plenipotentiaries followed Palmerston's instructions and sailed north in the *Blenheim* to the Gulf of Chihli, reaching the mouth of the Peiho on 10 August 1840. (*The Opium War*, pp. 225–231).

Remember me kindly to Mr. Wright, [Andrew] Jardine, and all in your house.
Believe me, my dear Mr. Matheson,
Very sincerely yours.

219. Charles Elliot on board the *H.M.S. Melville* to James Matheson in Macao, 26 November 1840[169]

My dear Mr. Matheson,

I think you will be pleased to know as much of our movements, as I am in a situation to tell you.

The *Blenheim* has moved Bocca Tigris wards,[170] then [ ], and if we can fill the steamer[171] with coals, and finish up some other pressing business, I hope we shall sail her tomorrow.

It seems possible enough that our advent in those parts will draw the new Commissioner,[172] and assuredly he is too adroit a person to have [wanted us to

[169] On Elliot's difficult hand, see Letter **174**, note 66.

[170] From Toon Koo, where the ships of the line had anchored, Captain Elliot was planning to sail towards Canton, the 'Bocca Tigris' being half way to Whampoa.

[171] The 'Steamer' was the *Nemesis*, (Captain William Hall, R.N.). The 660-ton paddle steamer had been built on the Mersey in 1839 by John Laird for the Secret Committee of the East India Company. The steamer was built entirely of iron. She was 284 feet long 29 feet wide with a flat bottom, and had been sent secretly to China as a reinforcement of the force. The *Nemesis* arrived in Macao via the Cape the day before this Letter was written. (For the eventful progress of the *Nemesis* from Liverpool to Canton, see: Fay, *The Opium War*, pp. 261–264).

[172] The new Commissioner was Kishen. He was a cousin of the Doaguang Emperor and was viceroy of Chihli at the time of Captain Elliot's first meeting with him, on 30 August 1840. He was subsequently appointed plenipotenriary 'Commissioner' to deal with the foreigners. Kishen and the Captain Elliot parleyed repeatedly between the end of August and 10 September 1840. Elliot followed his instructions as far as delivering Palmerston's letter of demands to the Emperor; he also repeatedly spelt out these demands to Kishen. Meanwhile Kishen, who was anxious to see the British force move away from the vicinity of Peking adroitly managed to persuade Elliot to sail south to Canton where he intimated negotiations would resume.

Contrary to his instructions, Elliot then decided to move back to Canton with the fleet, while leaving Chusan occupied as a bargaining chip. On the way south, he stopped over in Ningpo, where a few British soldiers and citizen had been taken prisoners (including Captain Anstruther). There, on 6 November, he negotiated a truce with Ilipu, the viceroy of Kiangsu, Kiangsi and Anwhei. The truce endorsed the *status quo* until further negotiations: the British held on to Chusan, and the Chinese to their prisoners. (Fay, *Opium War*, pp. 231–236, 253–259, 262–266; Hoe, *The Taking of Hong Kong*, pp. 132–137).

This Letter **219** exemplifies Captain Elliot's over-optimistic belief that he could negotiate a Treaty with Kishen without having to spill blood. The arguments he developed here show that his mind tended to work by inducing Kinshen's motives and intentions from the generality of human behaviour, rather than deducing them from specific hard facts and past actions. Events were soon to prove him mistaken. Meanwhile he had written to Palmerston, asking permission to settle for less than he had been instructed to. (*Ibid.* p. 267).

lose sight] of his whereabouts, till the appearance of our preparation should justify his apparition with reasonable schemes of adjustments.[173]

The more we press the more satisfactorily will he be able to explain his concession policy. And I am very well convinced *that is his real policy*. He did not leave a balmy station in the Cabinet to come here and fight Barbarians. He knows well enough that peace is the wisest policy. He has pretty well guessed what price must be paid for it, and I do not believe he will be chagrined with us for enabling him to open the Ball with a Chop to the Court setting forth that he arrived just in time to prevent a great calamity and disgrace. In any event I feel confident that we are not far off one solution or the other to our long course of vexations in this country.

For my own part, it is no exaggeration to say, that a double headed shot from Kwang Tong[174] would be more welcome to me that a continuation of that state of overwhelming anxiety and misrepresentation which has been my lot these past 20 months.

Adieu, my dear Mr. Matheson. Be assured that I am not insensible of the consideration and friendliness you have always evinced towards me. And whenever you will do me the favour to write me a line it will be very acceptable to me.

Very sincerely yours,

220. James Matheson in Macao to William Jardine in London,

29 November 1840

My dear Jardine,

The news of the day is the advance of the *Blenheim 74* towards the Bogue on the 26th; but having stuck in the mud she had not made much progress by yesterday's accounts. She is to be followed by the *Wellesley* and *Melville 74s*, the *Druid 50*, steamers and about 600 sepoys. The object of this movement is to commence hostilities in case Kishen should not make the appearance to negotiate according to promise. But as the Chinese say he was at Fa Lee on the 26th and would make his formal entry at Canton on the 27th, I have no doubt he will soon reach the Bogue and then, for the present, prevent a recourse to fighting; though I have no doubt it will sooner or later be necessary.

Enclosed I have for your *private* perusal a confidential letter from Elliot setting forth his views.[175] I think you cannot but be struck with the flimsy fine drawn reasoning on which he is proceeding. He does throw out a hint as if he had some means of knowing Kishen's real sentiment, but I do not think he has any beyond

[173] Kishen did arrive in Canton to start negotiations on 29 November 1840.

[174] 'Kwang Tong': Canton. The sentence brings out the pathos of Elliot's untenable position as both Superintendent of Trade and Plenipotentiary.

[175] See Letter **219** immediately above.

his civil speeches, at their view at the Pei Ho.[176] Still I think there is a good deal of probability in the remark he makes that it is not to be supposed Kishen would have left his seat as leading member of the cabinet to come here and *fight* barbarians, whence the references that he must have come, *really* to *negotiate*. This, however, is forming an opinion on exceedingly flimsy grounds.

It appears to me, Jardine, that by the copies of letters I have sent you from those who should be best able to judge from their position behind the curtain, I have given you the materials for forming as correct an opinion as if you were on the spot;[177] and whatever conclusion you may arrive at I shall consider as entitled to far greater weight than my own, influenced as I must necessarily be by the local excitement of the moment. I decidedly agree with Elliot that the Chinese have made up their minds not to risk the hazards of a war, but he expects a settlement much sooner than I do. I cannot forget that with all Asiatic sovereigns, the usual course has been, in such circumstances, evasion as long as they are allowed to protract it,—then comes an insincere treaty or arrangement which some cause occurs to prevent being ratified, [and] this has been usually followed by a renewal of hostilities, and after every act of opposition has been tried in vain, they are at last obliged to put up with the real sincere treaty.[178] This was the course pursued by the Nepalese,[179] by the Burmese,[180] and two or three years ago by a very petty Raja of Joudpore near the Indus.[181] Why the Chinese should be less insincere, or should more readily, at once, succumb to us, it is not easy to divine; and I do not think it will be the case. I still have no doubt a very little fighting will bring them to terms; and though you will think me a bold man to venture on prophesying, it seems by no means unlikely that, after a few references to Pekin, a settlement may be come to, in the course of the next four or five months, a much shorter time than, not long since, I thought would be necessary.

It does not look like the usual well-weighed policy of the Chinese to suppose that they will re-open regular trade before we make a final settlement; seeing that they have hitherto fancied they have held us in check by tea or in other words by the necessity we are under of getting tea and rhubarb.[182] Captain Elliot and others are, however, sanguine of an immediate renewal of the regular trade—but

[176] Elliot's and Kishen's early September parleys had taken place on dry land, off the Peiho river.
[177] James Matheson probably sent enclosures with this Letter which contained assessment of the situation as seen from the Canton perspective by the firm's agents who were still working there.
[178] In this sentence, James Matheson again shows remarkable insight. What he describes in general terms is almost a template of future events.
[179] The border dispute with Nepal provoked the hard-fought war of 1814–1816 following which the British acquired the Kumaun Division. (*EWH*).
[180] The Burmese War was fought from 1824 to 1826 and led to the British acquisition of Assam, Arakan and Tensserim. King Bagyidaw lost his throne to his brother, Tharawaddi Min. (*EWH*)
[181] This reference to the Rajah of Jodhpur near the Indus was not identified.
[182] Mandarins were convinced that the British would die of constipation if deprived of rhubarb.

where—noone ventured to foresee. However myself doubtful on this point for the reason just mentioned I cannot doubt that, by some means or other, we shall soon have trade, indirect and by connivance, if not regular and authorized. But whether in 2 or 4 or 10 weeks it is impossible to foresee. I incline to think it will be shortly before or soon after the Chinese New Year on 23rd. January.

Captain Elliot is quite decided that we ought not, as a permanent system, to place ourselves again in the power of the Chinese at Canton. But while we have so overpowering a force here to keep them in check, I suspect indeed he said he would not much object to our going up as a *temporary* arrangement, for the sake of getting tea. Do not be surprised therefore if we should be soon again writing you from the Creek Hong.[183]

Some of our neighbours having written the Admiral[184] to inquire about the state of affairs, we are sending you extracts of their letter and of his reply; the only important points of which is that as the truce at Chusan is entirely local, it will not affect the blockade here, which will not at present be taken off.[185]

Mr. Coolidge has gone up with funds from us to operate for us in the Canton market. Two days afterwards some of *Russell & Co.* went up and today *Wetmore & Co.* are to follow. We are making retail sales of cotton at Toonkoo, at 11 Taels for good Bombay. George Armstrong's Long Cloths are also going off slowly. The *Fort William* is to go home as soon as teas can be got and probably daily expected.

I remain, with kind regards to all friends, particularly all around you of *Magniac Smith & Co.*, my dear Jardine,

Yours sincerely,

[183] The 'Creek Hong' was *Jardine, Matheson & Co.'s* Canton office in Factory Square. The Creek Hong premises were in fact rarely used by the firm after that date; see below, p. 463, n. 12.

[184] Admiral Sir George Elliot. The Admiral had been unwell for some time, suffering from heart palpitations. He landed at Macao from the *Melville* on the day James Matheson wrote this Letter (29 November 1840). He had just resigned on account of his health. On 7 December, he left for London on *HMS Volage* commanded by his son, Captain George Elliot. (Hoe, *The Taking of Hong Kong*, p. 139).

A few weeks later, Lord Auckland's sister, Emily Eden wrote her assessment of Admiral Elliot's mission to China: 'The Admiral has made a shocking mess of China—at least he has done nothing, and the force and the ships and the money have all been wasted, leaving things just as they were a year ago. Now he has given up the Command, writing most pitiable accounts of his being in in a dying state from disease of the heart, with no chance of reaching home alive. [. . .] and now, today, George (Lord Auckland) has a letter written on board his son's ship, saying [. . .] that he thought he had mistaken his complaint, which was now merely liver, and that he felt nearly well again. It is an unhappy bit of his career, and such weakness is rather odd in such a stern, stiff-looking man as G. Elliot. [Captain] Charles [Elliot] is now left sole Plenipotentiary. [. . .]' (*Ibid.*, p. 140).

[185] Of the 3,500 men who had landed at Chusan, 1,600 had either died of dysentery and malaria or were unfit for battle as a result of illness. Reinforcement of 900 troops reached China at the end of 1840. (*Opium War*, p. 252–260).

P.S. I have already mentioned that Captain Elliot does not mean to submit propositions to the Chinese, to avoid the scrape that Baynes, Millet, etc., fell into with their 8 propositions which you will recollect.[186] He will throw on them [instead] of proposing.

Alun Tzy and other linguists came down the other day from Howqua to ascertain from Elliot the purpose of the chop he wished to present at the Bogues! Their folly in expecting an answer and self-complacent strut with which they made their appearance clearly shows that these Canton worthies have yet to be disabused of their preposterous assumption. They did not see Elliot who had left for Toonkoo.

1841

221. James Matheson in Macao to Charles Lyall in Calcutta,

6 January 1841

My dear Lyall,

We are now again on the eve of a warlike crisis and it is hoped the Bogue Forts will be taken tomorrow.[1] Kishen's answer to Captain Elliot's proposals for the future management of foreign trade having been so unsatisfactory as to have induced his suspending negotiations and passing over the affair into the warlike hands of the Commodore.[2] It is quite a chance, however, whether Kishen will not again give in at the last, as he did when pressed in a recent instance.

John Lyall has just left for the Bogue to see the fun. We hope the *Kosciusko* will pass the 2nd Bar today.[3] She has already the Commodore's licences to pass

[186] The negotiations with the supercargoes Baynes and Millet dated back to pre-1834 days.

[1] Captain Elliot had spent the month of December 1840 negotiating with Kishen. By early Januray 1841, negotiations had stalled. Kishen had offered only 5 million dollars, and had refused to cede territory or to open new ports to the north. Captain Elliot then decided to prepare for an assault on the Bogue forts which defended the entrance of the river channel to Whampoa.

[2] Sir Gordon Bremer became Commodore upon the resignation of Admiral Sir George Elliot. He remained commander in chief of the fleet until August 1841, when he was succeeded by Sir William Parker.

[3] The *Kosciusko* (see Letter **183**, note 129) had been in Whampoa loading tea on behalf of *Jardine, Matheson & Co.* The first bar was the one closest to Whampoa; the second bar was some ten miles further down the river, but still another ten miles away from the Bogue forts where the assault was being planned. James Matheson hoped that the loaded ship would be able to leave the river before hostilities resumed. Unfortunately, at about the time when he was writing this Letter, the *Kosciusko* ran aground near the second bar, in Anson Bay. Meanwhile, Captain Elliot had given the order to prepare the assault. On 7 and 8 January, Sir Gordon Bremen successfully stormed the first group of Bogue forts (the Battle of Chuenpi). He was preparing to force the second group of forts when a cease-fire called for by the Chinese was agreed to by Captain Elliot. James Matheson who had immediately sailed to Anson Bay to protect the *Kosciusko*'s tea cargo reported that Captain Elliot was 'full of compunctious feelings, not perhaps unnatural at having to attack and slaughter beings so helpless' (*JMArch*, 13 January 1841, C5-6). On 9 January, the *Kosciusko* managed to reach the safety of Toon

out. We have fixed your interest in her Congo at about 40,000 dollars. Patna has declined to 390 dollars new. The old is unsaleable at 355 dollars. New Benares 360 [dollars]. Malwa 420 and 430 [dollars].

What in the name of goodness can have induced your speculating in *dear* opium at such a period, discountenanced as it was by our advices? I fear you are not yet cured of the mania of following the many in their opium purchases, against which I have so often and so strongly warned you. Let me again repeat, ACT *COUNTER* TO THE COURSE OF THE MANY IN YOUR DRUG PURCHASES, as the only safe plan;[4] which you will find to your cost in your recent consignment.

Yours in haste most sincerely,

222. *Jardine, Matheson & Co.* in Macao to *Magniac Smith & Co.* in London, 10 January 1841

Dear Sirs,

The demands of our Plenipotentiary not having been acceded to by the High Commissioner, the Chuenpee forts on the east side of the river about four miles below the Bogue and Tycocktow[5] on the west were taken possession of and destroyed by our sea and land forces on the morning of the 7th, with the loss of only one man killed and about twenty wounded. The line of battle ships then proceeded to take up their positions for attacking the Anunghoy and Wangtung Forts, and were ready to commence by noon of the 8th, when the Chinese begged to be allowed three days to communicate immediately with the High Commissioner at Canton, which was granted, and nothing further will be done till tomorrow at noon. The remaining Forts will then be taken if Captain Elliot's demands are not complied with.

General opinion is very much divided as to whether the Chinese have had enough of fighting or not. Their loss at Chuenpee was very great—600 to 700

Koo island in the delta, where the precious cargo of one and a half million pounds of Congo was transshipped to three smaller vessels bound for London. The ceasefire was thus providential for *Jardine, Matheson & Co.* in that it enabled the rescue of a cargo worth some £75,000 which might otherwise have been lost. The firm's rivals were quick to conclude that Captain Elliot had agreed to the cease fire as a commercial favour to the firm. Fay simply observes : 'Twice running Elliot had salvaged the trade of the seaon. It was something he valued above his reputation with the officers of the expedition, above his standing with Palmerston even. He meant to salvage it again. That was why he wanted a cease-fire and, if possible, an immediate settlement'. (On the *Kosciusko* episode and the battle of Chuenpi, see Fay, *TheOpium War*, pp. 271–275; Hoe, *The Taking of Hong Kong*, pp. 149–151).

[4] On *Lyall Matheson & Co.*'s frequent misunderstanding of instructions, see above Letters **146**, note 61, and **207**, note 92.

[5] Taikoktow to the west of the river channel, and Anunghoy and Chuenpi to the east, are the three large island where the Bogue forts were situated. Two small island in the middle of the river channel, North Wangtong and South Wangtong, were also fortified.

men were killed, 180 taken prisoners and only 20 or 30 escaped of the whole garrison which numbered 900 men.[6]

We are, dear Sirs,

Your Most Obedient Servants.

A similar letter sent to the following—viz: John Anderson, *Crawford, Colvin & Co., Forbes, Forbes & Co., Hyde Lennox & Co.*, Archibald Hasties, M.P., *Larkins & Co., Lyall Brothers & Co., N. M. Rothschild & Co., Walkinshaw & Co., Thompson Anderson & Co.*, Thomas Ripley,[7] George Armstrong, *Ewing & Co.*, J. N. Murphy,[8] *Manning & Anderson*,[9] *E. de Otadui & Co.*

223. James Matheson in Macao to William Jardine in London,

15 January 1841

My dear Jardine,

Our circular of today, the second by the *Prima Donna* will inform you of Captain Elliot having last night come here from Chuenpee; and he is more sanguine than ever of our immediate adjustment and recommencement of trade. I learn from him, very confidentially, that Kishen has agreed to the British having a possession of their own outside,[10] but objects to ceding Chuenpee; in lieu of which Captain Elliot has also proposed that the trade of the English with China shall be re-opened simultaneously with that of all other foreigners, within ten days after the New Year, or in other words within a fortnight, or rather 18 days from this date.

In consideration of our getting a possession, as above, the leave of trading at a port to the Northward,[11] which was to have been granted, is to be relinquished. This I must regret. And on the whole the prospect before us is to my mind far from satisfactory. Equal privileges and security for good treatment at places of trade *in China* are what I should have more desired. But I fear these will be in some measures lost sight [of] for the bait of a possession on the *borders only* of the Empire.

In a former letter some weeks ago I hinted at the possibility of our having to return to Canton to carry through this season's business, and I think this is going

[6] For the Battle of Chuenpi, see above, Letter **221**, note 3.

[7] Thomas Ripley 'of Liverpool' (see Letter **234**) was not further identified. Four letters from Thomas Ripley are listed in the *BI*.

[8] James Nicholas Murphy was a Cork tea merchant. See Letter **245**. (Six Letters are listed in the *BI*).

[9] Manning and Anderson: 'Merchants, 3 New Bank Buildings, London'. (*TLCD*).

[10] Captain Elliot confidentially outlined the main terms of the Chuenpi Convention which was then being negotiated with Kishen. (For the terms of the Chuenpi Convention, see Letter **224**).

[11] Freedom of trade at several northern ports had been one of the demands of Palmerston.

to be the case;[12] which I do not regret, though most of our neighbours do; but we need not be apprehensive of any evil consequences from it, while we have so powerful an armament in the river.

By letters of yesterday from Canton, it appears the Chinese are completely paralysed, and no longer believe the Bogue forts can be defended. In fact their soldiers declare they will not fight against our shells, rockets, etc., etc., which Howqua tells Colledge he thinks must have been invented by the devil himself.

In short, my dear Jardine, I am convinced both sides are equally desirous of an immediate peace and recommencement of trade, and this we shall have immediately, by hook or by crook, before the monsoon changes, you may be quite sure. I hope *Magniac Smith & Co.* have cleared off all our former tea consignments to be ready for the extensive ones which are to follow.[13]

Yours most sincerely,

224. James Matheson in Macao to William Jardine in London,

22 January 1841

My dear Jardine

My letter to you of the 15th and one to *Magniac Smith & Co.* of the 18th will have prepared you for the settlement announced in Elliot's enclosed circular of the 20th.[14] I really believe had it been ever so favourable it would have been impossible to please the cankered minds of our neighbours under the influence of *Dent & Co.* who are at violent animosity with Elliot. The principle you and I have followed has always been as you know to put up quietly with public events, as they arise and manage our own and constituents' interests in the best manner which these events may permit. We therefore do not complain; and in return for Elliot's firm and friendly conduct in regard to the egress of the *Kosciusko* I even try to defend his measures when it is possible to do so.[15] But in the present case, I must confess I find it a very uphill task. This, however, is in some degree owing to the want of sufficient explanation in his notices, and partly to a want of

[12] James Matheson went back temporarily to the old Canton Creek factory. Members of the firm were working there in April 1841. (Fay, *The Opium War*, p. 285).

[13] The one and a half million pounds of tea transhipped from the damaged *Kosciusko*.

[14] Elliot's circular of 20 January 1841 was not traced. Its contents outlined the terms of the Chuenpi Convention which he had negotiated with Kishen. The Chuenpi Convention was to be repudiated by both the Chinese and the British governments, a move accompanied by the recall of their respective plenipotentiaries. The agreement between Elliot and Kishen envisaged the outright cession of Hong Kong; the payment of a 6 million dollars indemnity over a six-year period; the opening of direct official intercourse between China and England; the resumption of trade. On 21 January, the day before this Letter was written, what remained of the Bogue forts was handed back to Admiral Kuan in an appropriate ceremony.

[15] On the *Kosciusko*'s episode and the interpretation of Captain Elliot's timely agreement to a cease-fire, see above, Letter **221**, note 3.

consideration, on the part of the unreflecting, to the very peculiar circumstances of the case. The liability to Chinese duty on commerce carried on at the British settlement of HongKong is perhaps the most open to objection. In the first place, however, these are to be merely Emperor's duties, without Canton's exactions and without measurement duties. Secondly they are not to be collected *on HongKong*. The Chinese must find out a way of collecting them, and must for this purpose erect a customs house on their own territory, not on HongKong. And it seems so complicated an arrangment that it will in all probability end in their not being collected at all. Meanwhile the stipulation as to duties has no doubt greatly tended to prevent Kishen from refusing so important a cession; and it would not have seemed well in the eyes of the world or in the eyes of reason had we continued warlike operations with the Chinese for the sake of obtaining a reduction of Canton duties.

HongKong is to be immediately occupied by our forces, and till Her Majesty's pleasure is known, will be garrisoned by about a thousand Europeans. So independent will be our tenure, Elliot says, that he sees no objection to our stowing opium there.[16] And as soon as the New Year holidays are over, I shall set about building[17]— but of course with every caution, etc., on a small scale till the pleasure of the home Government is known. Nor shall we remove our drug from the good security of our own vessels, until we see the most undoubted security for it on shore, which I doubt if we can know, before hearing from home. Rely on our caution in this respect.

Strange to say the subject of opium has been but once mentioned in Kishen's negotiations with Elliot, and from their slurring it over in a final settlement, it is quite clear they seem to connive at the trade being carried on with the same freedom as before—which, should Kishen continue in power, will no doubt be followed by legislation; but not for some time probably, lest it should appear to the world as the result of English dictation. Still, notwithstanding this prospect there being no activity of demand either here or on the Coast, we are unwilling to run the risk of holding, more especially as we have large supplies coming on. We therefore go on selling at present prices though low.

[16] The fact that the Chuenpi convention was never ratified meant that the colony of Hong Kong had no grounding in international law in the first two years and a half of its existence. The British officially took possession of Hong Kong on 26 January 1841 (see post-scriptum to Letter **226**), but the ratifications of the Treaty of Nanking were exchanged only on 26 June 1843. (King, *Trade and Diplomacy*, p. 110).

[17] The first land auction took place in Hong Kong on 7 June 1841 (Bard says 14 June). At that auction *Jardine, Matheson & Co.* bought the largest waterfront parcel available. The land was situated at East Point where the firm started building its godowns and living quarters. (Bard, *Traders of Hong Kong*, p. 120; Fay, *The Opium War*, p. 303; Letter **241**, 3rd paragraph; Evans, Dafydd Emrys, 'Jardine, Matheson & Co.'s first site in Hong Kong', *JRAS*, vol. 8, 1968, pp. 149–152).

The advantage of HongKong will be that the more the Chinese obstruct and trammel the trade of Canton with Consoo charges, exaction, etc., etc., the more will they drive trade to the new English settlement. Captain Elliot is therefore not particularly solicitous to stipulate *now* for much amelioration of intercourse at Canton, feeling confident that it will follow of itself from the natural order of things, more especially while Kishen continues here. And if any circumstances should occasion the reverse at Canton, so much the better for the new English settlement.

An emissary of Kishen has been today with Elliot for the purpose of concocting something of the opening of trade, slurring over past sores and details as much as possible, with a view to *save the face of both parties*, Chinese and English. The obnoxious opium bonds[18] will of course be no more heard of. To test this, I made application some days ago for a chop for us to go to Canton. Howqua at first hesitated and spoke of the opium bond. He apparently had not been in Kishen's confidence on this matter; but next day, both he and Mowqua signed the application for our chop. There, however, owing to the New Year holidays, the matter must for the present rest. To save Kishen and the emperor's face has been a leading point with Elliot throughout the negotiations. This prevented his taking possession of the Bogue which could have been done probably without bloodshed after the taking of Chuenpee. But had he done this, it would have endangered Kishen's position, in whose fall he should have lost the only statesman sufficiently enlightened to perceive the policy of coming to terms with us and avoiding all the evils (to both parties) of a protracted war. This was the more especially to be apprehended as we have had recent rumours of the war party having gained the ascendancy in Pekin.

You will be amused to hear the Chinese have applied for musters of Congreve Rockets[19] and shrapnell shells,[20] also for a steam boat—which Elliot will, I believe, recommend being presented by the British Government. This spirit of innovation will of course go on advancing.

What I regret most is the want of access to a northern port. This arose from Kishen having remarked in one of his chops: 'As we have granted you territory you do not have now to require another port.' And, as in the previous

[18] On the opium bonds, see Letter **170**, note 41.

[19] Sir William Congreve (1772–1828) was comptroller of the Woolwich Academy in 1814. The new rockets he had invented in 1808 were first used in the Napoleonic wars. (*CBD*).

One of the Congreve rockets used in the Battle of Chuenpi blew up a Chinese war junk in spectacular fashion when it landed in the junk's magazine. 'The junk blew up with a roar, scattering wreckage in all directions, and presenting to the astonished English a spectacle so dramatic that it naturally invited comparison with the destruction of the 120-gun *Orient* in Aboukir Bay forty three years before. (Fay, *The Opium War*, p. 274).

[20] Henry Shrapnel (1761–1842) served as a soldier in many parts of the world and invented the device that bears his name. He was made inspector of artillery in 1804. (*CBD*).

correspondence, this ambiguity of the Chinese language left some doubt whether he meant *really* to *grant territory* or merely a trading factory at HongKong. Elliot was so desirous of fixing this unequivocally to the former that he thought it of sufficient importance to induce his at once acquiescing in Kishen's own arrangement on the subject. I have a strong suspicion Kishen is very far from being aware of this extent of sacrifice he has made in ceding HongKong. He expects it perhaps to be as dependent as Macao and will be very much surprised when in a few days he sees a proclamation to the inhabitants taking them over as subjects of the British Crown, forts erecting, etc., etc.

If you ask how I expect the future to work, I shall do best by referring you to the concluding paragraph of our official [letter] of the 18th to *Magniac Smith & Co.* I expect a period of difficulty, misunderstanding, uneasiness and paralysation of vessels, but ultimately have every confidence of a favourable outturn.

We have a good deal of Tea engaged in Canton, besides [that] which is going in this *Gaunt* and *Charles Kerr* (now in the Roads) and the *Lloyds*, which will be down in two or three days. We think of loading home the *Fort Williams* and Heerjeebhoy's recent purchase the *Scaleby Castle* commanded by your shipmate Lowjee Johnston.[21] The best Nankin silk is held at 5 shillings which we are not apprehensive of much competition and do not meddle with it for the present.

As for the consignments per *John O Gaunt*, *Kerr* and *Lloyd*'s we shall wish them realized if they will pay about 5 shillings per dollar. And those of secondary quality which will not hold their ground in a falling market had better be sold at what they will fetch. In fact they cost us only 4 shillings and 8 pence and in mentioning 5 shillings, we do so *not* as a limit, but as a profit with which we shall be well satisfied. You must always do the best you can for us and not consider yourselves fettered by instructions.

The *Columbian* starts today with orders to evacuate Chusan.[22]

I have much to write you but am hampered for time and must conclude. Many thanks for your kind favours of 11th August and *Herald,* which is our latest; our August and September overlands not having yet reached. Kindest regards to *Magniac Smith & Co.* and all friends.

Yours most sincerely,

[21] Lowjee Johnston was not identified.

[22] Following his negotiation of the Convention of Chuenpi, Captain Elliot ordered the evacuation of Chusan which had been taken and occupied by British troops as a bargaining chip since July 1840 (see above, Letter **211**, note 128). Chusan was to be taken again in early October 1841 by order of Sir Henry Pottinger, the new British plenipotentiary.

225. William Jardine in London to James Matheson in Macao,
28 January 1841

My dear Matheson

It is possible you may be shocked by the announcement of our friend, Alexander Grant's death,[23] in the newspapers, before this reaches you. It was announced most unfeelingly in some of them, the *Morning Post* and others, though they only stated the [death].

He destroyed himself at Carnousie[24] in the night of the 18th instant by opening the jugular vein with his pen knife, and was found dead in the morning. It is impossible to describe to you the shock the intimation of it gave to us all here. We were completely horror struck [and at a loss] to account in any way for the rash and violent act. While writing I have received a letter, from little doctor Campbell of Aberdeen, saying he had been threatened with ague[25] and had taken blue pill[26] with opium and drank it with wine to keep off the fit. He went on to suppose he had become sleepy, had woken from a slumber in the hot stage of the fit [ ] and committed the act.

His accounts will be found in a very confused state, I fear. We have no accounts here [ ]. I fear his family will be badly off, unless the tea market improves.

[. . .] This melancholy affair [ ] will, I know, distress you very much.

Believe me, my dear Matheson,

226. James Matheson in Macao to William Jardine in London,
30 January 1841

My dear Jardine,

Elliot returned this morning after a meeting with Kishen at second Bar, at which everything was conducted in a highly satisfactory manner. A repast was provided for Elliot and his party—kishen returning on the ground of delicate health, having a cold and spitting of blood. The Quang chow foo and Quang[27] acted as attendants at this repast, and it was some time before our party could prevail upon them to sit down.

Next day was devoted to a business conference in Kinshen's boat, when the arrangements for conducting future business at Canton were brought under discussion; but as I warned Elliot before hand Kishen gave little or no hope of his conceding any important amelioration, putting him off with the oft-repeated commonplaces as to his unreasonableness of our wishing to alter the customs of

[23] For Captain Alexander Grant, see Letter **14**, note 28.

[24] Alexander Grant's estate in Scotland.

[25] Ague: 'a malarial fever, with paroxysms, consisting of a cold, a hot, and a sweating stage'. (*OED*).

[26] Blue pill: 'a mercurial antibilious pill'. (*Ibid.*).

[27] 'Quang Chow foo': the prefect of Canton.

China and impose our own, etc., etc. The result was that all details of trade are to be left for mutual arrangements between the British merchants and the Hong merchants, which latter body will, of course regulate every thing their own way. Elliot will, I hope and trust, stipulate for at least some declaration of a general nature to prevent our being trampled on quite so badly as before. He has today issued a circular stating that the negotiations are going on favourably and as he has heard that some British subjects contemplate proceeding immediately to Canton, warning them it will be at their own peril if they do so before he issues a declaration that he considers it safe and prudent.

The report in the community is that the second Bar negotiations are not favourable to an immediate re-opening of the trade, and it is very possible Elliot may not have let me fully in to his confidence on the subject. So much the better in such event for our recent shipments in *Kosciusko*[28]— and coupling the warning in the Circular with the enclosed extracts from ones of our latest Canton letters, there may be room for suspecting that we are not quite so near a final settlement as had been supposed. Still we do not wish our teas held for such a chance. I am convinced Elliot has been all along determined that this season's supply of tea should go home. And this will be done *coute que coute*.

With kindest regards to *Magniac Smith & Co.* and all friends, I remain,

Most sincerely,

P.S. I witnessed the hoisting of the British flag at HongKong on this 26th. Afterwards circumnavigated the Island.[29]

[28] On the *Kosciusko*, see Letter **221**, note 3.

[29] Captain Sir Edward Belcher (1799–1877), commander of HMS survey ship *Sulphur*, raised the Union Jack on 'Possession Point', Hong Kong island, on 26 January 1841. Captain Belcher subsequently published his *Narrative of a Voyage Round the World, Performed in Her Majesty's Ship Sulphur, During the Years 1836–1842, Including details of the Naval Operation in China, from Dec. 1840 to Nov. 1841, etc.*, 2 volumes, London, Henry Colburn, 1843.

In vol. 2, p. 157, Belcher writes : 'On the return of the Commodore on the 24th we were directed to proceed to Hong Kong and commence its survey. We landed on Monday the 26th at fifteen minutes past eight, and being 'bona fide' first possessors, Her Majesty's health was drunk with three cheers on Possession Mount. On 26th the squadron arrived; the marines were landed, the union hoisted on our post, and formal possession taken of the island by Commodore Sir J. G. Bremer, accompanied by the other officers of the squadron, under a feu de joie from the marines, and a royal salute from ships of war'. (Quoted by J. R. Jones in 'Who hoisted the Union Jack', *JRAS*, vol 12, 1972, p. 196).

227. James Matheson in Macao to William Jardine in London,
19 February 1841

My dear Jardine,

You will perceive from the accompanying circular that to all appearances hostilities are about to recommence,[30] to my great regret and disgust; every hour's delay in this realization of our large cotton consignments being now of the utmost possible detriment, in consequence of the heavy additional supplies which Elliot's premature circular of 20th ultimo will be the means of soon bringing in competition with us.

I fear you will put little value on my opinion as to the future, after having allowed myself to be humbugged into a belief in Elliot's fallacious hopes of a peaceful settlement. Still it is my duty to tell you what I think, however little weight it may deserve. On the whole I incline to believe the Chinese will not long hold out against a proper manifestation of our force; and I cannot swerve from this opinion I have always expressed that in any case we shall have [our] export of tea by some means or other, regular or irregular. This is at all events the *safest belief for holders of teas in England to entertain*,[31] and should recommend selling whenever saving prices can be obtained; which course I sincerely hope you will induce *Magniac Smith & Co.* to adopt with our teas. Hitherto the tea smuggling trade has been very much paralyzed by a belief that the regular exports of the article would soon recommence. If it should not do so, I have reason to think Elliot's efforts will be chiefly directed to the fostering of a forced trade—with which view the Bogue forts will be taken possession of, and such a demonstration made on Canton as to intimidate or drive away the authorities, give courage to smugglers and others who may be disposed to deal with us.

The American and native reports from Canton are so multifarious that it is scarcely worthwhile troubling you with them. One is that Kishen is displaced and Lin again Viceroy of this province. But this is certainly not true. It appears, however, the Emperor's nephew accompanied by three Commissioners has actually left Pekin and may be expected here in a month[32]—till when, they tell us, no progress can be made towards peace. Meanwhile, I have no doubt, Kishen is in constant communication and consultation with Lin and Iliang[33]. The square in

[30] After agreeing to the Chuenpi Convention orally on 20 January, Kishen was delaying putting his seal to the document. By mid-February, Captain Elliot was beginning to lose hope and preparing to renew hostilities. (Fay, *The Opium War*, pp. 277–278).

[31] It was 'safer' from a financial point of view to believe that the Opium War would not disrupt the tea supplies so as to avoid the temptation of undue speculation and of holding supplies in anticipation of rising prices.

[32] Kishen was recalled by the Emperor in April 1841, and three new officers were appointed to replace him: Yang Fang (a professional soldier), Ishan, and Lung-wen. (*The Opium War*, p. 286).

[33] Iliang: the governor of Canton.

front of the factories is covered with five mat houses about 50 by 100 feet deep; to occupy which they are enlisting 4,000 to 5,000 able bodied men. Wages 4 dollars per month if no fighting and 8 dollars if there should be. It is said Howqua looks very sad and declares there will not be an early settlement.

Elliot's solution of the warlike preparations is that they are to enable the authorities, (at the moment of closing) to save face with their own people, and make it appear that they are coercing us into submission—but if so, they have rather overdone their game.

The *Rose* from Bombay 26th November announces the arrival of the October mail, but that the letters were left at Malta—very unlucky !

With kind regards to all friends, I remain,

Yours very sincerely,

228. James Matheson in Macao to Jamsetjee Jejeebhoy in Bombay,

26 February 1841

My dear Sir,

It is with the deepest regret we have to announce a renewal of hostilities,[34] contrary to the sanguine expectations of our Plenipotentiary, to which I did not feel warranted in refusing the belief due to an official authority possessed of exclusive information, inaccessible to the rest of the world. Our circular explains all we know; and as for conjectures about the future, you will probably think it very idle troubling you with them, seeing they have hitherto proved so fallacious. I do not yet despair of peace on the arrival of the Commissioners mentioned in my letter of the 20th as expected from Pekin about three weeks hence.[35] I refer you to the *Canton Register* for the Emperor's Edicts censuring Kishen and the admiral for the defeat at Chuenpee.[36] It is remarkable that although punished with a reduction of rank neither of them is displaced from his situation and Kishen is still ordered to manage matters.

I do not think we have force enough to take possession of Canton,[37] even after the arrival of the troops expected from Chusan, and it is probable an armement will not for the present advance beyond the first Bar, which however it is hoped

[34] The new attack by the British forces was delivered on the day this Letter was written. The previously destroyed Bogue forts which had been given back to the Chinese were again occupied. Further forts upriver were stormed. Admiral Kuan died whilst defending the Anunghoi forts. By the evening of 27 February, the British controlled the river up to the first bar and Whampoa. The following few weeks were spent roaming the waterways of the delta. By 20 March 1841, the British were masters of the delta. *The Opium War*, pp. 278–279).

[35] See above, Letter **227**, note 32.

[36] 'The defeat at Chuenpee': the storming of the Bogue forts on 7 and 8 January 1841. See above, Letter **221**, note 3.

[37] The British forces did not actively prepare to take the city of Canton until May 1841. See below, Letter **235**.

will enable them to keep the river open for the natives to carry on an increasing trade with us in spite of the authorities; but this remains to be seen, and you will of course await further advices before acting on any such expectations.

Several junks have been seized by our men-of-war, some with valuable cargoes for Java; but I believe orders have been given to spare all coming to trade with foreigners, including of course the native drug vessels; but it is nevertheless to be feared, the dealers will not venture to trust their money afloat with the same confidence as before, lest it should be seized in mistake which it so easily may be. The demand for the drug continues pretty regular. Since my last we have had a heavy arrival of Malwa per *Corwallis* (on the 22nd) and the price has declined to 400 dollars. Patna, though the stock is becoming very limited, does not rise beyond 420 dollars. Benares 405 dollars. The *Ardaseer* and *Sultana* still keep out, as do the Bengal clippers.

We have incurred a heavy expense to obtain the services of the *Folkestone* (a remarkably fast sailer) for conveying the present news to you and our mutual friends in England, and sincerely hope it may be of use to you. We have ordered it to be sent from Madras by express. There was no object in making a private despatch, rather the contrary indeed. The *Folkestone* will proceed from Madras to load opium at Calcutta, and we shall feel obliged if you will request your friends to give her a preference.

Hoping to have the pleasure of again writing in a few days per *Waterwitch*, I remain with kind regards to Cursetjee and your other sons and partners, my dear Sir,

Yours most sincerely,

P.S. Mr. Bridgman, an American missionary here, has just written: 'I have had a long call this morning from an old Canton friend who left the city on Tuesday (23). He was at Kishen's office just before he left and gave me the impression that his Excellency would proceed immediately to the Bogue for an interview. I do not give up all hopes of peace'.

229. William Jardine in London to James Matheson in Macao,

3 March 1841

My Dear Matheson,

Since I had the pleasure of addressing you, by the last overland mail, nothing of importance has occurred here, in the mercantile or political world. Lord Jocelyn[38] has, since his arrival in this country, published a small book, of 155 pages, on the Chinese expedition, which he terms 'Six months with the Chinese

[38] Viscount Jocelyn (1816–1854): 'eldest son of the Earl of Roden, military secretary to the Chinese expedition and author of *Six months in China*. Conservative MP for Lynn Regis'. (*DPC*, 1843).

expedition' or 'Leaves from a soldier's notebook'[39]—and, in my humble opinion, he would have been conferring a benefit on H.M. subjects, or rather, sparing them from an infliction, had he committed the whole book to the flames.

I read the work between dinner time and bed time in hopes of finding something that would enable me to form an opinion as to the views of the Plenipotentiary, and the probable issue of the negotiations at Canton, but have been sadly disappointed, and from Captain Elliot's *most confidential* letter to you I can draw no inference whatever, farther than this mortifying conviction that he, and the Admiral[40] have mismanaged the business entrusted to them, and have hitherto been regularly humbugged by the Chinese.

Lord Jocelyn, Rees[41] says, expressed himself to the same effect on board the Steamer—in his book, page 138, he says: 'Thus to all appearances [ ] this Chinese war, if so it may be termed, seems drawing to a close'. For this opinion he offers reasons; but at the same time, admits the possibility of the negotiations failing. When speaking of the conference with Ki Shan,[42] he says it appeared, however, that another communication with the court would be necessary before any ultimate arrangement could be decided upon. With regard to the island of Chusan being retained, or given up, we can form no opinion from the book. He says: 'It would always require a force of 1,500 men, as a secure garrison, backed by a couple of corvettes.' His Lordship, p. 141, says: 'It should be remembered that there are mercantile houses in China, whose speculations give them an interest, in a long and tedious war, and who will be the first to pick some hole in the final arrangement.' He then goes on to give Elliot credit for getting teas of last season out—raves about the increased profits, and hints at the propriety of not paying for the opium[43]—in the same style that Elliot does in a letter, to Lord Palmerston, dated *Volage*, Tong koo, November 28th 1839. (Additional papers to the Blue Book, N° 4, page 49, letter n° 4).[44] A blackguard production, which I called your attention to long ago. Had Elliot been desirous of proving himself an

[39] Jocelyn, Robert, *Six Month with the Chinese Expedition; or, Leaves from a Soldier's Note-Book*, London, John Murray, 1841. William Jardine read the book shortly after it was first published. It was subsequently translated into French and Italian. (Lust, *Western Books on China*, p. 135).

[40] Admiral Sir George Elliot.

[41] Captain John Rees, one time commodore of the firm's opium fleet. (See Letter **81**, note 2).

[42] William Jardine's spelling for Kishen, the Chinese plenipotentiary .

[43] Viscount Jocelyn's suggestion that the opium traders needed no compensation for the loss of their contraband goods was shocking to William Jardine. The British opium traders always started from the premise that opium was definitely *not* contraband. See above, Letter **83**, note 17.

From his background and his family connection with the Mintos, Captain Charles Elliot's aristocratic sensibilities may have been closer closer to Jocelyn's than to Jardine's. His repeated and often criticized efforts to keep the China trade open, however, was motivated by what he saw as his duty as superintendent of British trade (a duty which often clashed with that of plenipotentiary in time of war) and not by any personal desire for gain or advantage.

[44] See above, Letter **216**, note 159.

unprincipled vagabond, he could not have adopted a better plan of doing so. And yet you are all on confidential terms with him, or fancy you are. I confess I do not understand this—unless on the principle of *holding the candle to the devil.*[45] So much for Lord Jocelyn's book.

In the tea market there had been little change. Company's Congo about 1 shilling and 7 pence per pound. Clearances go. Money market a little easier. Foreign exchange very slightly improved. And gold accumulating, in the Bank of England, very slowly. The conservatives did all they could to get a majority in the Commons, on Lord Morpeth's[46] Registration Bill for Ireland, but were beat by five. Had ministers been in the minority, it is generally believed they would have dissolved Parliament. Neither party are strong enough to carry on the business of the nation in the way it should be carried on; which is a great evil. Has Elliot ever thought of the necessity of getting out a full year's consumption of tea? If he does not and loses a season, the revenue will be in a worse condition, than it would have been had he at once blockaded the port of Canton, not permitting a single pound to be brought out , and pursued other decisive measures, so as to have settled the affair in the course of a few months. We must, however, wait patiently for the growth of the small twig he has in his portfolio.

Alexander [Matheson] is enjoying himself in Scotland, but is expected in London soon. I have not heard from your sisters lately; but have reason to believe they are well. I have hitherto omitted to write to you respecting your friend Purvis,[47] who must, ere now, have written to you himself, and told you the state of his affairs. I had consented, under a conviction that you would have done so had you been here, to pay to *Messrs. Gregson & Co.* four thousand pounds on his account on his sending me an engagement on the part of his firm to pay back two thousand pounds in four or five years, by annual installments, and selling his Singapore property to you or to me for 2.000 pounds sterling redeemable, by him, in five or six years, should he be able to redeem it. The rent would pay the interest on both sums; and, with the support of the Canton house and *Magniac Smith & Co.* here he ought soon to be able to pay off the 4.000 pounds sterling. He has however made a grand mistake in not sending me a letter from the firm binding themselves to pay the 2.000 pounds sterling, but a letter from himself expressing his gratitude, and consenting to the arrangement—adding that he has written to you to inquire to whom the property at Singapore shall be made over. This is very stupid, and I feel at a loss how to act; as, by the arrangement, *Gregson & Co.*

[45] The difference of opinion on Captain Elliot between William Jardine and James Matheson could not be more clearly emphasized than by this vivid image.

[46] George Howard, Viscount Morpeth (1802–1864) succeeded his father as seventh Earl of Carlisle in 1848. He was Chief Secretary for Ireland (1835–1841). His office became a Cabinet one on 20 Feb. 1839 (*BHF*). The Registration Bill was one of nine such measures for defining the Irish parliamentary franchise between 1835 and 1841. None succeeded and the issue was settled only in 1850.

[47] On John Purvis, see above, Letter **36**, note 4, and Letter **92**, note 62.

sacrifice twelve, or thirteen hundred pounds; which *Purvis & Co.* save. Purvis is not satisfied with Mr. Scott's management[48] during his absence, and announces his intention of bringing their partnership to a close [ ].

Since commencing this letter I have heard from Alexander [Matheson]. His better half has been confined to her bed, with a severe cold, at Burnside near Inverness, and her medical attendant says she will not be able to travel for a week, or ten days, which is annoying to him in more ways than one, he being anxious to be in London to prepare for leaving England by the April steamer.

I have to apologize for not having replied earlier to your letter of the 27th July on the subject of cornelians deposited with us by Framjee Pestonjee,[49] he having advanced a certain sum upon them to Herjeerum Amtha, a man none of us knew, (as far as I recollect), and certainly one whom none of us would have trusted. I have a distinct recollection of the transaction, my own aversion to having any concern with the said cornelians, and Mr. Wright's remonstrance on the subject; with my eruption of my having declined to receive them, on any other terms, than those of advancing the money to him, not to Herjeerum Amtha, and holding him responsible for any deficiency with interest. I think Mr. Wright must recollect the transaction. Nothing short of a written document signed by me, or in my own handwriting as a memorandum, could convince me that Framjee Pestonjee's statement is correct. I knew nothing of the value of cornelians, and made no particular inquiry [beyond those made] by Framjee Pestonjee, who represented them as worth more money than we advanced to him on them. Why should we have run any risk, when we could gain nothing? I had a great aversion to having anything to do with them, as had Mr Wright. In my opinion the loss is Framjee Pestonjee's, not ours.

The only letters from you unacknowledged are one in a shape of a P.S. to yours of the 12th or 13th of October, duplicate, and one of the 18th of October. Believe me, we are very anxious to have further news from Chusan, and Macao, but not sanguine about receiving anything of importance from either place by the mail now nearly due.

I have omitted to notice the exportation of teas, during the three last weeks. It has been very considerable to Canada, and some shipments have been made to the United States of America, and to Hamburg, and Holland. The home deliveries have also increased with the reduction of prices. Be pleased to present my kind regards to all around you, and believe me, my Dear Matheson,

Yours sincerely,

[48] Mr. Scott was not identified. The details of the transaction outlined in this paragraph remain obscure.

[49] On the transaction involving cornelians, see above, Letter **215**.

March 4th 1841
My Dear Matheson

The tea market is firm. Company's Congo 1 shilling and 7¾ pence per pound cash. *Magniac Smith & Co.* sold a small lot of Pekoe of ours yesterday at 3 shillings 4½ and ¾ pence per pound; for which they had never had a better offer than 3 shillings per pound when teas were at the highest. Cost price 38 or 40 Tales per picul. Such tea is [in demand] and wanted by the trade.

We have had bad account from the United States today. The Banks south of New York have been obliged to leave off paying in cash. Two small failures, one in New york, and one in Philadelphia. You could not be too cautious in taking bills drawn against American credits. *Howland & Aspinwall* have written privately to John Abel Smith, stating their perfect ease, and the ampleness of their means. *Magniac Smith & Co.* have no reason whatever to doubt this, but with all operations on credit in favour of these gentlemen, (*Messrs. Howland & Aspinwall*) suspended until you hear from them, or from me again. Our friend Mr. King[50] was here a day or two ago. He is not a favourite here. His manners and yankee[51] feelings, are objectionable in the eyes of all. I did not see him. Believe me,

Yours sincerely,

230. James Matheson in Macao to Jamsetjee Jejeebhoy in Bombay,
15 March 1841

My dear Sir,

I regret to say trade continues completely at a stand, and appearances exceedingly unfavourable as explained in our accompanying circular to which I refer for particulars.

On the 6th or 7th instant Captain Elliot had an interview with the Quang chow foo and Howqua, Mowqua, etc., near Canton; when he left them under an impression that in consideration of our sparing Canton (pending a reference to Pekin) and permitting American and neutral vessels to proceed to Whampoa for trade, the Chinese authorities would, on their side, connive at British vessels going also to Whampoa and trading on exactly the same footing as the rest. But no sooner were the Chinese relieved from immediate apprehension by the cessation of hostilities than they drew back from the arrangement, which appears to have been

[50] Charles William King, the American witness of the destruction of the opium stocks and the former partner of *Olyphant & Co.* was last mentioned in Letter **194**. The frequent use of the antiphrasis 'our / your friend' to describe someone he intensely disliked is one of William Jardine's stylistic signatures. Instances occur, however, when he used the phrase 'our / your friend' in the standard way.

[51] The substantive 'Yankee' (origin unknown) is recorded as of 1758 as 'a nickname for a New-Englander, or an inhabitant or native of the northern states generally'. As an adjective: 'pertaining to or characteristic of Yankees (often connoting cleverness, cunning, or cold calculation' (1781). (*OED*).

merely by word of mouth. Fighting has consequently resumed. Two days ago Captain Elliot left in the steamer *Nemesis* with the boats of H.M.S. *Samarang* to go up the inner passage[52] and attack the Mandarins at the large town of Heangshan, the capital of the district. Meanwhile, since Captain Elliot's departure, Mr. Delano, the american Vice Consul, has come from Canton with a message to him from Howqua that Canton is in a state of disorganization and becoming rapidly deserted by the inhabitants, with their property, and that unless an arrangement be speedily come to, matters will be in so bad a state as to prevent any trade whatever for a long time to come.

The arrangement which Howqua proposes (through Mr. Delano) is that the Commodore shall permit Americans and neutrals to trade at Whampoa, in consideration of which the Mandarins will connive at a smuggling trade being carried on with the British outside. But no chop is to be issued to this effect. It is to be a mere vague verbal promise, which they can at any time evade. And in my opinion Captain Elliot will not be justified in agreeing to a proposal so humiliating and insidious. Still the mere circumstance of Howqua sending down Mr. Delano with proposals is important; and as the proverb says: 'where there's a will, there's a way,' we may hope both parties being inclined for trade, some unobjectionable mode will be discovered for carrying it on. Meanwhile the position of parties having consignments on hand is one of indescribable anxiety and perplexity.

The *Rover* was the first Bengal clipper on the 7th. The *Mor* on the 10th. The *Poppy* ditto. The *Falcon* and *Sylph*, 13th. The *RobRoy* and *Ardaseer*, 15th. The *Charles Forbes* and *Orleana* arrived on 2nd. The *Java* on the 10th.[53]

The *Sylph* will be despatched on the 18th and by her I shall have the pleasure of replying to your several favours.

I now remain, my dear Sir,

Yours most sincerely.

[52] This Letter was written only three days before the British forces attacked the Canton city river front. In the shallow waters upstream from Whampoa, the principal assault ship was the flat-bottomed, iron-clad *Nemesis*. The assault on the Canton river front was the continuation of what James Matheson briefly describes here. 'The English,' Fay writes, 'carried all before them. On the 18th [of March 1841] they mounted a general assault upon the city's river front. A chain of raft was brushed aside; hundreds of river craft were sent flying, among them smug boats recently purchased for the water forces; the small forts on Honam [the large island opposite the city] and the mainland were silenced, the twenty-five guns on Dutch Folly [a small island in the middle of the river] overwhelmed and the tiny island occupied. Early in the afternoon marines and armed seamen landed on to the factory square, chased the ragged guard of Chinese soldiers behind their rattan shields. Then the English withdrew to their ships. On the 20th, however, they came back, the flag was raised, and from the great hall of the New English factory, Captain Elliot announced that hostilities were again suspended. Trade was to resume, this time positively and for certain'. (*The Opium War*, pp. 281–282).

[53] The mention of so many opium clippers in one single sentence suggests the drug business was continuing unabated. This is not surprising since the British were now in total control of the Pearl river delta.

231. James Matheson in Macao to William Jardine in London,
19 March 1841

My dear Jardine,

[ ] The {*Narrick Hall*} is loaded almost entirely by *Dent & Co.*, with smuggled[54] teas, at prices which appeared to us [so] exorbitant while there was any hope of a regular trade that we have declined meddling with them. But with the hopeless prospect now before us, we have commenced turning our attention to tea smuggling and shall be regulated by circumstances as to the extent we may embark in it.

I cannot express to you how deeply I am mortified at the turn affairs have taken—the more so as in giving any heed to Elliot's sanguine expectations I surrendered to him my own better judgment; in proof of which let me submit for your *confidential* perusal the enclosed copy of my letter to him of 19th December[55] which I think had some effect in bringing about the taking of Chuenpee, and now seems as if it were prophetic. You will say it is far too complimentary; but as official personages are proverbially jealous of interference with them, I thought my best chance of being influential was to present my sentiments in the garb in which they were most likely to find favourable acceptance. In listening to him I was further influenced by the consideration that in managing for others, we were not authorized from merely speculative notions, to run the risk of disregarding the opinions of the only one among us who had information and official documents inaccessible to the rest of the world,—preparations for peace having been moreover the *safest* course under any circumstances for ourselves and friends interested in the tea market.[56]

I have received your letters to 4th December and hope to reply by *H.M.S. Melville* to sail in a few days.[57] The Calcutta first sale has gone far too high at 800 Rupees, and buyers will lose unless we are relieved by some unexpected opening—sales being slack here at 400 dollars. The *Mor* has just arrived from Bombay with 1,600 chests and is about to return with a handsome treasure freight. We are all well, and I remain, with kindest regards to *Magniac Smith & Co.* and all friends,

Yours sincerely,

[54] 'Smuggled' in the sense explained by James Matheson in Letter **230**, 3rd paragraph.

[55] James Matheson's letter to Captain Elliot was not traced.

[56] In this paragraph of self-defence against what he anticipated would be William Jardine's criticism for his implicit trust in Captain Elliot, James Matheson reverts to the sound commercial argument he had used previously in Letter **227**, 2nd paragraph, and note 31).

[57] The *HMS Melville* needed more permanent repair than had been possible to arrange in Chusan. (See Letter **218**, note 165). Sir Gordon Bremer sailed home in the *Melville*. In his absence, Captain Sir Humphrey Le Fleming Senhouse became commodore of the British Fleet. At the time he took over the command he was sixty and had only three months to live. On the circumstances of his death, see below Letter **235**, 4th paragraph.

232. William Jardine in London to James Matheson in Macao,
2 May 1841[58]

My Dear Matheson,

This being Sunday and the second day of the month, while alone and [not pressed for time], I shall devote a few hours to writing to you, by the overland mail, of the 4th Instant. Your letters being in the City I shall not attempt to notice them separately but endeavour to convey to you my views of friend Elliot's management, or what in this country is generally termed mismanagement since the admiral left China.

In one of your letters you mention the cankered feeling that existed among your neighbours[59] against Captain Elliot's permitting the *Kosciusko* and the *Panama* to go out of the port of Canton with full cargoes and add that, in return for his kindness, on that occasion, you did all you could to defend him and his measures—a hard task, you acknowledge, owing to his want of detail in the documents announcing the signing of a preliminary treaty.

I admire your gratitude and should be sorry indeed to say one word against the principle on which you acted; as for the arguments used, I consider them, as in a great measure uninviting from the Plenipotentiary himself and as such shall comment on them freely.

The affair of the two ships[60] has not produced much sensation here and I hope for your sake, Elliot will easily get over that. H.M. ministers can scarcely blame him for letting out teas sufficient to load three ships for England after having themselves admitted the damaged teas for the [season] at a reduced duty and permitted them to be sold duty free. What duty was paid we know not, but there is reason to believe that some of the teas were the property of Howqua.

I cannot agree with the reasoning in Elliot's private note, and your letters. He appears to me to have lost sight of almost every object for which the expedition was fitted out. Not even an apology [ ] after the forts are restored 'the English Barbarians are now obedient to orders'—having restored Tinghae and [Chusan]. [. . .] [61]

[A mode of management which operates] by patching up a disgraceful peace, does appear to me the true mode to induce the war party to renew hostilities. I may be very ignorant on the subject, [ ] but it will afford me much pleasure to

[58] This Letter is one of the first which William Jardine wrote from his new residence at n° 6, Upper Belgrave Square, London.
[59] In this paragraph William Jardine refers directly to James Matheson's Letter **224** above.
[60] For the *Kosciusko*, see Letter **221**, note 3. The other ship involved was the *Panama*, an American ship. (*The Opium War*, p. 275). That may be the reason why 'the affair did not produce much sensation' in London.
[61] Five of the six pages of this letter are illegible.

find our country, and our countrymen, benefited by what appears to my weak mind sad mismanagement.

Since commencing this letter, I have had an interview with Lord Clare,[62] who is deeply interested for our friend Jamsetjee Jejeebhoy, and anxious to do everything in his power to forward the payment of the opium claims; but he is unfortunately on the wrong side of politics, and acknowledged his influence to be very limited.

Alexander [Matheson], poor fellow, has lost his wife—a sad melancholy event, which must distress him deeply.[63] I have not heard from him since the 28th of March, when she was sinking fast. I pray he will be in London ere long, and will of course write to you by this conveyance. I shall address you again tomorrow. In the meanwhile, believe me, my Dear Matheson,

Yours sincerely,

233. William Jardine in London to Jamsetjee Jejeebhoy in Bombay,

3 May 1841[64]

My dear Sir,

As the mail via Marseilles is to be made up tomorrow I shall now have the pleasure of acknowledging and replying to your esteemed favors of the 25th February and 1st March which reached me on the 10th ultimo; for the copies of letters therein contained accept my grateful thanks.

In your letter of the 25th February you appear to be under an impression that Lord Palmerston's instructions to Captain Elliot must have been mild and [of] an inactive tendency, but this I believe is incorrect. Mr. John Abel Smith has spoken with his Lordship respecting them again and again and has always been assured that the orders were plain and simple, leaving Elliot plenty of discretionary power and at the same time desiring him to take decided measures and settle the business as soon as possible. I have also heard from a gentleman who read them that they are very ably drawn up and if they had been attended to, Elliot would not have acted as he has done. Two millions sterling were to be received on account of the Opium surrendered, in two years if possible, but on no account to exceed three years. The Hong debts were to be recovered at an earlier period than that agreed upon by the Hong Merchants and the Creditors. Elliot has entirely overlooked the Hong debts and in the event of his succeeding in his plan of paying the Emperor's duty only, on Teas and other articles shipt off and landed at Hong Kong, he will destroy the source from whence the installments on the Hong debts

[62] On the second Earl of Clare, see above, Letter **211**, note 123.

[63] After the loss of his young wife, Alexander Matheson returned to Hong Kong and was taipan of *Jardine, Matheson & Co.* from 1842 (when James Matheson retired) to 1852.

[64] This letter is marked: 'A true copy, signed WJ'.

were derived. the Emperor's duty on tea is about one Tael 5 mace per pecul and on cotton about one mace five candarins per Pecul, and from these two articles about 8/10th of the instalments were derived. When I left china we paid 5 Taels per Pecul on Tea and one Tael five Mace or one Tael seven Mace per Pecul on Cotton and two Taels per pecul were paid into the Consoo fund *in cash* before the Tea could be shipped off.[65]

The want of the Ports to the Northward is another grand oversight which cannot be altered in the details.[66] Elliot has given them up entirely. When we had an interview with Lord Palmerston,[67] I pointed out all these things and many more but got very little out of him, in return he said they had not received the details of the Treaty. When telling him that the compensation was only half the amount due, I added unless Captain Elliot has put a high value on the Island of Hong Kong, and if he has, we shall be very happy to consider H.M. Government indebted to us for the other half. His Lordship laughed and said he supposed we would.[68]

I observe what you say respecting shipment of teas, etc., from China on your account and have brought them to Mr. John Abel Smith's notice in the manner you mentioned, and Company's Bills for 30,000 pounds sterling will be sent to you by this conveyance.

In this letter of the 25th February, you mention your having taken shares in the *Bank of Asia*[69] for which I have already thanked you in a letter written three or four days ago, but I revert back to the subject of the Bank with a view of explaining to you how we have been annoyed by the Court of Directors some of whom disliked our secretary while others were influenced by the Houses of Agency here who wished to keep the exchanges entirely to themselves. We have not got quit

[65] For the Consoo fund, see above Letter **143**, note 40, and Letter **141**, note 26.

[66] William Jardine continues to compare what Captain Elliot was instructed to obtain with the draft of the Chuenpi Convention which he had just received from James Matheson.

[67] The interview and its participants are described more fully in Letter **234** below, 2nd paragraph, although the date of the interview is not given.

[68] As usual, Palmerston is quite receptive to William Jardine's comments, served here with an additional touch of dry humour, but he does not let on any information about his intentions to recall Captain Elliot. There is some evidence to suggest that when the interview took place, Palmerston had already written his letter of recall to Elliot.

The letter of recall is dated 21 April 1841 (Blake, *Jardine, Matheson*, p. 100). And whilst he does not give the exact date of the interview, William Jardine writes in Letter **234** that it took place 'a short time before before [his] letters by the last mail were written', i.e. shortly before 2 May. Even if the interview took place before 21 April, the participants at the meeting were given no clue as to the Foreign Secretary's intentions.

[69] This is one of only two references to the *Bank of Asia* in this collection of Letters. (See Letter **244**). A fair amount of factual information can be pieced together from this paragraph, including that William Jardine was one of the bank's promoters (probably with John Abel Smith), and that failure to obtain a charter from the Court of directors of the East India Company somewhat reduced the ambitions of the promoters and the scope of the planned operation. The 'secretary' who was allegedly disliked by the Court of directors was not identified.

of our secretary and I hope we shall fill up our share list faster then we have hitherto done. We have not yet appointed an agent in Calcutta nor in Bombay: the Firms who receive subscriptions are only acting till the Bank is formed. Our plan is to have a Board of Shareholders at each Presidency to superintend the business of the Bank, but in the first instance while the business of the bank is limited we might, I think, get on with an agent only as a good deal of our business would be in Exchanges, which do not require much labour. In the event of our commencing in this way would it suit your *friends Messrs. B. & A. Hormusjee*[70] to act for the Bank for a time ? And they might possibly be continued as treasurer when the Bank got into full operation, that is, if it would answer their purpose. I mention these Points to you in confidence and shall feel obliged for you favoring me with your opinion on this and any other point connected with the working of the Bank. Had the Court of Directors granted us a charter which the Directors refused [but we had] in the first instance never doubted, we should have by this time been in full operation. They behaved very ill and assigned no reason for doing so which led to our determination to try what we could without a charter and I hope we shall ultimately succeed.

I had a long conversation with your friend Lord Clare[71] yesterday who is very anxious to see you paid your opium and willing to do every thing in his power to support the claims, but he is unfortunately on the wrong side of politics. Parties are so equally balanced that it is doubtful if ministers can retain their places and having the excuse of being still without details. Mr. Crawford[72] has postponed his motion till after the arrival of the next mail.

I shall not say much on the subject of the Tea market as I understand the firm have written to you fully on that subject. Prices are still low, though the consumption has been going on most rapidly, and the stock on hand is moderate. Should the negotiations have been broken off and the trade be again suspended (which I think possible) prices must advance, but I do not feel sanguine about them. I understand H.M. Ministers intend to ratify the Treaty as it is.[73] Be pleased to present my kind regards to your Sons and to all friends and believe me, my dear Sir,

Yours very sincerely,

[70] Bomanjee and Ardaseer Hormusjee, Parsee merchants and agents from Bombay. (*BI*).

[71] Jamsetjee Jejeebhoy knew Lord Clare from his time as governor of Bombay.

[72] On William Crawford, the writer of Letter **182**, see Letter **180**, note 95.

[73] By 'Treaty' William Jardine refers to the 'Chuenpi Convention'. His ignorance about decisions already taken (which was shared by all outside advisers to the government, including John Abel Smith) is another proof of how close to his chest Palmerston had kept his cards.

234. William Jardine in London to James Matheson in Macao,

16 May 1841[74]

My dear Matheson,

So much has transpired here, respecting China affairs, since the date of my last letter, that I am unwilling to put off writing to you, till the last moment, and so run the risk of having to apologize from a hurried, unsatisfactory letter, at a time when my correspondence ought to be full and explicit. For this reason I shall now commence, and finish about the time the mail is made up—the 4th Proximo.

In my letters, by the last mail, you were informed of the particulars of an interview we had with Lord Palmerston, a short time before they were written, on which occasion Mr. Crawford, the City Member, was the person appointed to open the discussion, a letter having, previously, been sent to his Lordship, numerously signed, asking for the interview. This letter was signed by *Magniac Smith & Co.*—but my name was not attached to it. John Abel Smith, after having read attentively your letter,[75] wherein you express ourselves tolerably well satisfied with the treaty, would have qualified the letter to Lord Palmerston, or withdrawn their signature, but it had been sent to his Lordship. The expression he wished altered, was one expressing the alarm the parties felt lest H.M. Ministers should ratify the treaty—unless they were in possession of information more explanatory and satisfactory than that before the public. I have been induced to mention these particulars, that you may be aware of all that was done here, previous to Captain Elliot being superseded.[76]

On my return from the City, about 7 p.m. on the 4th Instant, after having despatched my letters by the mail, I found a note on the table from Major General {Dyson},[77] informing me of the appointment of Sir Henry Pottinger to take charge of affairs in China, with full powers to act and to leave by the first steamer for Alexandria, and [I wrote] to Mr. John Abel Smith, who waited on Lord Palmerston to ask a few questions with the view of despatching a special messenger, after the mail, with letters for you, announcing the appointment, but found there was scarcely a chance of his reaching Marseilles in time.

Sir Henry is to leave by the June steamer, and the Bombay Government have been ordered to have a steamer or fast sailing vessel, ready to take him on to China; and as Alexander Matheson has taken his passage in the June steamer, they may possibly arrive in China together. Sir Henry expects to receive letters from

[74] This letter is marked: 'Received 10 August—so brought as the ship who brought Sir H. Pottinger'. (Sic).

[75] The letter William Jardine refers to here is Letter **224**, written by James Matheson to him.

[76] As usual, William Jardine is very meticulous in imparting all information necessary for his partner to be made fully aware of what happened.

[77] Jerry Francis Dyson entered the Bombay Army in 1797; was later colonel of the Bombay native infantry. He was made a general in 1854. He died in London in 1861. (*MEB*).

the Governor General at Bombay. You will see from the public papers, that orders have been sent out to retake Chusan, should our troops have been withdrawn.

It is difficult to say what effect our conversation with Lord Palmerston had—possibly very little.[78] The whole country were against the treaty, and against Elliot's half and half measures. Even the saints have left off railing against the opium war, and are quiet. But the ways and means are not in a state to admit of ministers making us an advance, so we must wait, I fear, till the Chinese hand over the cash.[79]

We must very soon have a change of ministers. The Whigs cannot carry on the business of the country. They wish to resign. The Queen insists on their dissolving, and, I believe, ministers, themselves, do not think which way to act. Most of the party wish to resign. The Queen is said to be positive—and so matters are at present, but the point may probably be settled before the departure of the mail. A great many men, of both sides, are anxious to see Sir Robert Peel and Lord john Russell acting together, which, you may remember, I predicted long ago,[80] but Innes[81] and you laughed at me saying I had no time to read the debates.

I am still desirous of seeing a strong and efficient ministry, whether by a mixture of parties, or otherwise; and really care very little for which party is in place. Place and power bury the great objects with both sides of the House. I am afraid neither party will make good our claims, though both admit the justice of them. Reports are abroad that Elliot continues to advise ministers not to pay them; but I am unwillling to believe this. How dreadfully he must be mortified when he receives notice to quit. What will his dear friend Ki-shen, say to his friend Elliot, being so harshly treated ? It is ridiculous enough to find the Emperor blaming

[78] On the question of influencing Palmerston regarding the recall of Elliot, see above, Letter **233**, note 68.

[79] On the question of early payments on the opium receipts, William Jardine had previously refused to give up hope.

[80] The remark makes it plain that the mercantile community in Canton never ceased to follow political developments at home as closely as distance and the pressure of trade allowed. It also shows that Matheson was politically the more perceptive, since the union of Peel and Lord John Russell was implausible. The difference between ministers resigning and dissolution was that the latter step had to lead to a general election. In the event, the Conservatives under Sir Robert Peel were to win the 1841 general election by a handsome margin. See Letter **237**, 3rd paragraph.

[81] James Innes, Jardine's and Matheson's notorious friend (see Letter **9**, note 48, and Letter **63**, note 83) was very ill at the time when William Jardine was writing this Letter. He was to die six weeks later in Macao, on 1 July 1841 after a protracted illness. (*JMArch.*, *C5-7*, Letter to James Innes's brother, Cosmo Innes in Edinburgh, dated 2 July 1841; extract from this letter are quoted in Fay, *The Opium War*, p. 304; for details on James Innes's illness and death, see also Ride, *East India Company Cemetery*, p. 224).

Ki-shen for yielding too much, while our ministers blame Elliot for having been satisfied with too little. But people are never contented in this wicked world.[82]

The news from your side had not much effect on the tea market here; but the announcements, made in both houses of Parliament, had the effect of advancing prices considerably. Congo advanced 3 or 4 pence per pound and the market is firm. Green teas did not advance much, the stock of them being heavy. We are availing ourselves of the rise to lessen our stock, at about saving prices, say 1 shilling and 9 pence or 1 shilling and 10 pence and 2 shilling and twopence per pound for middling and tolerably good Congos, of which I trust you will approve.

Were we certain of your not getting out more, than 15 or 20 millions of pounds this season, prices would rule much higher, but Elliot has evinced such an anxiety for trade, on any terms, that noone has he slightest confidence in what he does, or says. I cannot help fancying that Lin and Iliang will advise the trade to be put a stop to, when they see Elliot so much bent on having teas.[83] They will think of the old plan, of stopping tea and rhubarb. We know they can prevent smuggling, to any great extent, when they deem it of great importance so to do. I feel more anxious for a rise on account of poor Alexander Grant's family, who must be badly off, should teas not advance; but at present prices, they will be better than we at one time expected.

I had a letter from their grandmamma yesterday, begging me to endeavour to get a writership for the boy, which we must do if possible. The mother, is about Aberdeen, and little Doctor Campbell told me not long since, he, the boy, was rather disposed to attach himself to her. He will soon be of age, when he can act as he may deem best, but I should be sorry to hear of his taking so foolish a step.[84]

[82] A statement with religious overtones rarely found in William Jardine's business correspondence.

The parallel discontent of Peking and London with their respective plenipotentiaries was striking. From the British point of view, however, the recall of Captain Elliot and the appointment of Sir Henry Pottinger was a mere change of personnel. Palmerston saw no need to alter his China policy, and the British financial, commercial and political advantages to be gained from the Opium war remained unaltered. Unlike that of his predecessor, Pottinger's resolve was undivided by any consideration of trade nor was it mollified by any Chinese sympathies. His single-mindedness of approach helped him reach Britain's objectives as embodied by the Treaty of Nanking in a swift twelve months campaign, from August 1841 to August 1842.

[83] This discussion directly refers to the content of Letter **227**.

[84] On Alexander Grant and his family, see Letter **111**, note 121, and Letter **225**. The suggestion is that, according to the early Victorian code of behaviour, Alexander Grant's wife, or at least the 'mother' of his children, was not socially acceptable. This could have been for a variety of reason, including that she was of Chinese origin. (On Eurasian children, see also Letter **40**, note 30).

May 31st. 1841[85]

Since writing the foregoing, I have been down in Devonshire canvassing the Borough of Ashburton,[86] in expectation of a dissolution of Parliament, which is expected in the course of next month. It was expected sooner, and the present member, Charles Lushington,[87] gave notice of his intention not to come forward again, at the same time recommending me to go down immediately. There are 280 or 290 voters. I waited on nearly the whole of them, whigs, Tories, Radicals, and doubtfuls, with fully as much success as we expected. My opponent is Mr. McKillop,[88] who arrived the day before I left. I have not heard of his success, but do not expect him to get more than 60, or 70 positive promises. I got 118, and upwards of twenty electors declared positively they would not vote against me. There were a good many, who said that they had not promised, and would not promise till the last moment. It is not difficult to interpret such language, but I trust we shall have not occasion for their votes.

Alexander [Matheson] took leave of me yesterday, and has, by this time, left for Southampton. I have just sent to Sir Henry Pottinger, a letter of introduction to you. He is desirous of knowing you, and of benefiting by your advice. You will find him straightforward. His powers are ample, and the admiral[89] cannot interfere with him; but has orders to obey him. If the force has been dispersed before he arrive at Bombay, he intends to proceed to Calcutta, and remain there till another force is collected.

I have had two or three conferences with him, of a very satisfactory nature, and he has spared no trouble to gain information. He had a conversation with Captain Rees on Saturday last. On Friday he dined with me—no one present but Alexander [Matheson], John Abel Smith joined us about 10 p.m. We had the chart of the coast of China before us, and discussed many knotty points, no doubt most ably. I intend to send him a few hints on paper through the Foreign Office on the 4th Proximo.

[85] This section of the Letter was written at the time when, at the other end of the world, the City of Canton was being spared from a British attack by Captain Charles Elliot. (See Letter **235**).

[86] Ashburton was a pocket borough controlled by Lord Clinton. It had 198 voters after the 1832 Act. Lord Clinton was a major Devonshire Landowner (14,000 acres). (See: Gash, Norman, *Politics in the Age of Peel, A Study in the Technique of Parliamentary Representation*, London, New York, Longman, Green, & Co.1953; Bateman, J., *The Great Landowners of Great Britain and Ireland*, (1876, 1878), Leicester, Leicester University Press, 1971.

[87] Several Lushingtons were connected with the East India Company. One Charles Lushington had served in the Bengal Board of Revenue and had been a member of the Madras Council. (*EIRD*).

[88] A partner of the East India agency *Cruttenden McKillop & Co.*

[89] The new commodore of the China fleet was Sir William Parker, commander-in-chief, East India station. He was appointed in April 1841. The other senior officer appointed to assist Sir Henry Pottinger in his mission was Sir Hugh Gough, who was confirmed as head of the armed forces. (*The Opium War*, p. 311).

Your sisters are in London, but I have not spoken to them; though I passed two of them in Regent's Street on saturday. I had returned to Town on Friday, and was not aware that they were in London. We looked hard at each other. They must have recognized me, but as I was passing them quickly, they could only see my back till I turned around. I thought it was them, but not till I had had time to think. On inquiring of Alexander [Matheson] he told me they had arrived in Town during my absence, and gave me their address. I shall call tomorrow or next day if possible.

Mr. Goddard[90] wrote to you some time ago, respecting some funds he remitted to *Lyall Matheson & Co.*, Calcutta, to be by them invested in opium to your consignment. They advanced the money on *respondentia*[91] on opium, contrary to orders, *he says*, and he naturally feels annoyed, as if they acted as he instructed them he would have gained a few thousand dollars in pounds sterling. He is averse to legal proceedings, and more averse to doing anything that could, by any possibility, annoy you. He wrote to them, their reply was not satisfactory to him, and I may say to me, as far as my memory serves me. I believe he has written again, offering to leave the affair to your decision. He has suffered by [other agents'] roguery, which makes him feel the loss, I am writing about, more severely. You should, under any circumstances, read them a severe lecture on the liberties they take with the orders of their constituents. I have had several complaints about them, and hints that, but for *Jardine, Matheson & Co.*, they would have had more than one action brought against them. They are foolish to act in such manner.

3 Lombard Street, May 31st.

Since my arrival here I have received a note from Ashburton saying 'we cannot make out that Mackillop has had more than 70 promises at the utmost.'

I shall say nothing about tea till the 4th Proximo. We have a sale tomorrow. A letter from Mr. Ripley[92] of Liverpool, just received, mentions some extensive shipment of piece goods to the house by the *Mary Ann Webb*. Armstrong[93] and [ ] are very much pleased with the teas you sent them per *John of Gaunt*. They sold at 2 shillings 2 pence per pound. In haste,

Yours sincerely,

[90] James Goddard: one of the signatories of Letter **151**. For James Matheson's firm reply to his complaints, see Letters **249** and **250**.

[91] On *Respondentia* bonds, see Letter **15**, note 33.

[92] Mr Ripley, of Liverpool, was not identified. Four letters are listed in the *BI*.

[93] George Armstrong was not identified. Several Letters mention his name. See Letter **188**, note 151.

235. James Matheson in Macao to William Jardine in London, 19 May 1841

My dear Jardine,

Affairs are hastening to a war-like crisis.[94] The *Paradox* left Canton yesterday morning, when Elliot was about to arrive in the *Nemesis* steamer. All was then quiet, but the native inhabitants were still leaving in crowds. Andrew [Jardine] writes me 17th, 'we have been scarcely able to hear ourselves speak all the morning in consequence of the noise they are making in the Creek'. Heerjeebhoy who left the evening before last says the heads of streets were ordered by the authorities to warn the inhabitants to lay in stocks of provisions, also supplies of water to be at hand in case of fire. This however may possibly be in consequence of their having perhaps heard of rumours of Captain Elliot's intention to starve out the place by an embargo, in the event of their refusing to order away the Northern soldiers. But Heerjeebhoy also states they were making warlike preparations near Fa-tee.[95] On the other hand they have evacuated a fort at Sha-meen[96] the

[94] Hostilities were last suspended on 20 March, following an assault on the Canton river front. By the end of March, the British controlled the delta (see Letter **230**, note 52). In March and April, trade was revived, and many British merchants returned to their Canton factories, including Andrew Jardine mentioned in the paragraph. Kishen was recalled to Peking in April 1841 at about the time when his successors, Yang Fang (the head of the military), Ishan and Lungwen made their way to Canton. Chinese troops arrived in large numbers to defend the city. On 11 May, whilst inspecting the British troops at Canton, Captain Elliot shelved his plan to recapture Amoy and decided instead to occupy the heights of Canton. With this in mind, the whole force sailed up the river. Palmerston's decision to recall Elliot was taken in early May (see Letter **234**), but Elliot did not know this until August, and he was therefore still in charge, and, as many thought, still bungling.

In the night of 21 to 22 May, the Chinese launched a surprise attack, using fireboats against the British ships. (This Letter **235** was written two days before the fireboat attack which, though spectacular and potentially dangerous, failed to harm the British fleet).

On 24 May, Major General Hugh Gough directed a flanking movement of the British troops and positioned his two thousand men on the hills immediately to the north of the Canton city walls. Meanwhile, Sir Le Fleming Senhouse controlled the river. The Chinese residents of Canton who had not fled the city were preparing for the worst. Elliot had given Gough orders to threaten the city but to stay 'without the walls'. On 26 May, a mandarin waved a white flag from the city's walls, but to no effect as Gough went ahead and finalized preparations. On 27, as the troops were ready to attack the city, an officer delivered a message from Captain Elliot agreeing to a truce.

The men and their officers were angry to have been robbed of a battle many had looked forward to. Senhouse in particular was extremely vexed by Elliot's decision. He soon caught the 'Hong Kong fever' and died two weeks later, on 13 June 1841. He was buried with full honours in the Macao Protestant cemetery. (Ride, *An East India Company Cemetery*, pp. 220–222). Meanwhile, Elliot sat down once more to the negotiating table with the mandarins. On 5 June, he announced the terms of the 'Canton Settlement' (see Letter **239**).

(For this summary of military events from April to June 1841, see: Fay, *The Opium War*, pp. 284–295).

[95] Fa-tee or Fati: a village near Canton. (Garrett, *Heaven is High*, p. 53)

[96] Shameen: an area immediately upriver from the Canton Factories. Shameen was to become the exclusive foreign concession of Canton later in the 19th century. (*Ibid.*, 1860 map, p. 28).

re-arming of which was one of Elliot's ground of complaints. Accounts of yesterday from HongKong state our forces were just beginning to move up the river, and I cannot help thinking the intelligence of this will have a wonderful effect in cooling the belligerent ardour of the authorities.

As already stated we have shipped teas enough to be nearly a sell-off against the cotton we have deposited with the Hong Merchants. So that I feel quite easy as to the aspect of affairs. The *Fort William* and *Scaleby* are fully laden and the *Clare* nearly so, the former and latter consigned to *Forbes, Forbes & Co.*

The *Appolline* (recommended to us by *Magniac Smith & Co.*) and *George Armstrong* are just arrived.

Yours most sincerely,

P.S. A February overland newspaper notices Grant's dreadful end. But no letters yet.

236. William Jardine in London to James Matheson in Macao,
31 May 1841[97]

My Dear Matheson,

It affords me much pleasure to have the opportunity of introducing to you Sir Henry Pottinger, who has been appointed to take charge of our affairs in China, and, if possible, to correct the errors of our friend, Captain Elliot, and put our intercourse with the Chinese on a satisfactory footing, after having received satisfaction for the insults, and injuries hitherto heaped upon us, by the inhabitants of the 'central nation'.

I have assured Sir Henry that you will have much pleasure in being in any way useful to him, and I am satisfied that it is unnecessary to say more—in contributing to the comfort, and success, of Sir Henry and his friends, you will confer a favour on,

My Dear Matheson,

Yours most sincerely,[98]

[97] This letter is addressed to James Matheson, in 'Macao or elsewhere in China'. It was written on the same day as the end of Letter **234**.

[98] As William Jardine was writing this Letter, Captain Elliot was in the last stages of negotiating the 'Canton Settlement' with Chinese mandarins. The terms of the Canton Settlement were announced on 5 June. They included the payment of 6 million dollars within six days against the withdrawal of British troops from Canton and the resumption of trade. The silver was paid promptly into the British Canton treasury. Half the amount was shipped to India, the other half to the Royal Mint in London. (*The Opium War*, pp. 298, 305).

237. William Jardine in London to James Matheson in Macao, 5 July 1841

My dear Matheson,

The last mail brought us nothing new from China, only a few letters by the Madagascar Steamer, which were too late for the previous mail.

This want of news has a good effect on the Tea market, and Company's Congo advanced a penny or twopence per pound on the day the letters were delivered, the 2nd of July, but the following day being Saturday, and the excitement of the General election not yet subsided, we have had no opportunity of judging whether this rise is to be maintained, or a greater one established on a firm footing. The stock on hand is moderate, and if importers are firm, we should have prices a good deal higher than they are now. Company's congo is quoted at 2 shillings and one penny to 2 shillings and 2 pence per pound. Nothing doing in free trade teas, the holders being unwillling to sell at the prices offered. Should any change take place, in the course of the day, you shall be informed thereof. We must have an advance ere long, if affairs in your quarter continue unsettled, and the trade remains suspended. I have no doubt you will get out a certain quantity of Teas, whether the trade is opened or not; but the quantity must be comparatively small, probably five or ten millions of pounds. But this quantity ought not to depress the market.

In consequence of the Parliament being dissolved[99] the whole country has been in a state of very great excitement for the last fortnight; and will not be in a quiet state till the county elections are over. You will see from the newspapers, that Mr. MacKillop and Mr. Jardine canvassed Ashburton. The former, who boasted not a little of being certain of success, found it unnecessary to withdraw on the day of nomination, and the latter was returned as a matter of course.

T. Dent laughed at the idea of my even expecting to be returned, and alluded to the opposition in the East, saying Mr. Jardine appeared to be doomed to oppose his partners. In my opinion MacKillop never had anything like a fair chance of being returned, and I have no doubt you will be glad to hear that we have maintained our position here as well as in China.[100] John Abel as before without opposition. Thomas Weeding beat for Berwick.

[99] Parliament was dissolved after the Whig government lost a vote of censure on 4 June 1841.The general election gave a convincing victory to Sir Robert Peel who formed a government on 30 August. The Earl of Aberdeen succeeded Palmerston at the Foreign Office. The affairs of China, however, were transferred to the Department of War and the Colonies headed by Lord Stanley. The Earl of Haddington succeeded Lord Minto at the Admiralty. Lord Ellenborough headed the Board of Control for a brief month before being appointed Governor General of India in October in place of Lord Auckland. (*BHF*).

[100] This unexpected use of 'we' provides William Jardine with a charming way of associating James Matheson to his electoral victory. William Jardine was to sit in the conservative Parliament until his death on 27 February 1843. A few days later, on 2 March 1843, James Matheson made the journey to

I was surprised a few days ago by a hurried note from Andrew Johnstone of Halleaths, announcing the sudden death of his brother David,[101] but without any particulars. I have, however, heard since, that he fell a sacrifice to his dissipated habits. I have not seen Andrew since, but expect him in London in a few days.

I have had so little time to spare, since my return from Ahburton, that I am unable to say how your sister is, not having [seen] any of them. The invalid had left London a few days before I left it, and thought herself a little better; but you must have letters, by this conveyance, from your brother, who was in town when I left. I have not seen Lanrick[102] since it was purchased, but hope to be able to pay a short visit to that part of the world before Parliament meet.

Captain Vaux[103] has called to say he intends leaving the river on the 1st and Portsmouth on the 6th Proximo, in a very fast sailing vessel of 450 tons, called '*Anonyma*', which he has purchased, and proposes employing her in the drug trade under your auspices. He has, by the advice of J. H. Gledstanes arranged for removing his account from *Gledstanes & Co.* to *Magniac Smith & Co.*, and he hopes you may be able to promote his views in the East. I have seen the vessel, and like her much. She was one of the fastest yachts in this country. He proposes touching at Bombay on his way to China, and I have no doubt Jamsetjee Jejeebhoy will do all he can for him. Bear him in mind, should you be able to assist him.

The *Earl of Hardwick*, *Carnatic*, and *Tartar* are taken up to carry troops to China; and will be consigned to you; but I have no doubt Captain Young[104] has written to you respecting them. My time and paper are both near a close; so I shall beg to be kindly remembered to all friends around you, and remain,

My Dear Matheson,

Yours sincerely,

238. William Jardine in London to James Matheson in Macao, 5 July 1841

My Dear Matheson,

This will be handed to you by Mr. Rolfe, son of my dedicated friend Robert Rolfe,[105] formerly of the East India Company's service, who is about to embark

---

Ashburton and introduced himself to its electors. He subsequently took his former partner's seat in Parliament. See Letters **257** and **258**.

[101] David Johnstone is not entered in the Jardine Family tree provided by Keswick. (See Keswick, *The Thistle and the Jade*, p. 262). Being called 'David' like his father, he probably was the eldest son of the family.

[102] Lanrick: the estate William Jardine bought in Scotland.

[103] Captain Vaux had commanded the *Balcaras* in 1839. Eight of his letters are listed in the *BI*.

[104] On Captain Young, see Letter **205**, note 83.

[105] Robert Rolfe was not further identified. Eight of his letters are listed in the *BI*.

with our friend Captain Scanlan[106] for China—there to push his fortune under your auspices. And I hope you will be able to find employment for him in the office.

He has a small sum become due to him here, in the course of a few months, the amount I know not, but he will be able to inform you respecting this small sum, and should you think it advisable for him to have it in China, I shall feel obliged by your favouring him with your advice as to the best mode of getting it out.

I think you will find Mr. Rolfe obedient, and willing to make himself useful; he knows something of teas, and is highly spoken of by the gentlemen in whose office he has been.

Having said so much, I commit the youth to your good care, trusting he will conduct himself so as to merit your patronage, and remain, my Dear Matheson,

Yours sincerely,

239. James Matheson in Macao to James Abel Smith in London,
15 July 1841

My dear Sir,

Although the *Bombay Castle* is not likely to Take our latest news for the Suez mail, I am unwilling to let her sail without writing you a few lines on the state of affairs here. Captain Elliot has lately returned from a trip to Canton, which he undertook in order to recover compensation for property destroyed in the Factories amounting to about 310,000 dollars of which he has recovered a third, and is to receive the remainder in a fortnight. He also had in view to induce the authorities to remove the restrictions on the transit of building materials etc., to HongKong, in which I hope he has succeeded.

The Viceroy sent a message by the Quangchowfoo expressing regret that he could not visit Captain Elliot from fear of being exposed to the false charges of bribery and corruption which the Chinese impute to Ki-Shen. He also sent a chop announcing the emperor's approval of the re-opening of British trade; in consequence of which Captain Elliot will soon probably issue a declaration that he no longer considers British subjects and ships unsafe at Canton and Whampoa. We therefore expect ere long to see British trade again going on there as usual, and a fresh impetus given to exports of tea to Britain. I think, however, that for the next six months at least they will be on a scale sufficiently moderate to prevent any uneasiness respecting our own and friends' teas under your firm's management. But it seems always best to realize when saving prices are obtainable, and we are particularly desirous you should do so with our teas, as it will enable us with the greater confidence to go on making further shipments; which we cannot so well

[106] Anthony Scanlan had a long association with the firm and was captain of the *Hellas* in 1838.

do with the apprehension before us of an accumulating stock held on, with speculative views from year's end to year's end. I shall revert to this interesting subject when more at leisure.

I may here add that on the recommencement of warlike operations to the northward[107] we shall have no confidence in the continuance of safe and peaceful trade at Canton. But as regard our tea in your hands, we shall prefer your acting, as if there were no doubt of exports going on regularly on a moderate scale. Captain Elliot is strongly of opinion the Emperor is sick of the war and that we are not far from a final settlement. But his opinions are so often erroneous as not to be entitled to much weight and we do not agree with his sanguine anticipations. He has *entre nous* pretty well made up his mind his successor is not far off.

Captain Young of the *Tartar* left here a Mr. Rishton[108]—as a youth in whom you take an interest. He has been for some time on the Coast but has just returned, he and his captain not liking each other. He wishes to go home or to Van Dieman's Land,[109] but I recommend his staying here. With kindest regard to all [in] your firm, I remain,

Yours most sincerely,

[P.S.] The movement to the North is delayed till the arrival of reinforcements and steamers from India.[110]

240. William Jardine in London to James Matheson in Macao,

1 August 1841

My Dear Matheson,

We have received a telegraphic dispatch from Paris announcing the arrival of the overland mail from India, at Marseilles, but without any important intelligence from China, which is annoying enough to those who are anxious about their friends and the state of affairs there.

[107] It had been Captain Elliot's intention to retake Amoy (See Letter **235**, note 94). Following the Canton Settlement of 5 June, the idea was revived, but more troops were needed than were currently available.

[108] Mr. Rishton was not identified.

[109] Van Dieman's Land: today's Tasmania.

[110] On 21 July, a week after James Matheson wrote this Letter, a most severe typhoon hit the Canton delta, creating havoc everywhere. The British fleet suffered serious damage. Captain Elliot himself and his cutter *Louisa* disappeared during the storm. His ship master was washed overboard. Elliot took over the ship and steered the *Louisa* to a creek where she broke up on the rocks. Elliot was the last to leave the sinking ship. The shipwrecked party was 'rescued' by Chinese villagers who stripped them of everything. Eventually a boat was hired and Captain Elliot made his way back to Macao where he reappeared in the morning of 24 July dressed in 'a manila hat, a jacket, no shirt, a pair of striped trousers and shoes'. (Hoe, *The Taking of Hong Kong*, pp. 186–188; for Fay's account of the same episode, see: *Opium War*, pp. 305–307).

We expect our letters tomorrow, and hope some of our friends [are right to] entertain a hope that you may have got a letter onto Bombay; though there is no notice of any arrival in the telegraphic announcement. From the last day of March to the 19th June, is a long time for the good folks in Bombay to be without an arrival from China. There is therefore some little chance of hearing from you, but I am not sanguine about it, knowing May and June to be tedious passage months down the China sea, and on to Bombay. If anything important had been done Elliot would have sent a steamer, or clipper to Calcutta, to set the governor General's mind at rest.

Teas will, I think, advance, even if there is no news from China, but were we to hear that none had been shipped off in all April, prices ought to improve a good deal.

Our elections are now over, and the Conservatives must have a strong majority when Parliament meets; but they are not very much united, and doubts are entertained whether Sir Robert Peel will be able to satisfy his party in the division of the houses [ ]. The little Queen would prefer having the Whigs in office, but she cannot help herself, and I hope she will yield with a good grace. Sir Robert will not interfere with the Maids of Honour or Ladies of the Household. He is wiser than he was some years ago.[111]

Many of our politicians calculate on the ministry being of short duration, but I confess, I can see no good reason why they should not remain in power for many years—say three, four, or five—that is, if they [manage affairs] well.

Our friend John Abel Smith, has been suffering from bilious fever for several weeks, is much reduced, and about to leave England for Ems[112] to recover his strength and spirits, which are very low. He intends staying on the Continent for a month, and I hope most sincerely he may return restored to health and strength. His family are to accompany him.

Aug, 4th.

Our friend John Abel Smith left on Sunday morning for Ems, much disappointed in having no advices from China, or letter from you to Jamsetjee Jejeebhoy of Bombay, copied there, and sent [. . .]

One report says Ke-shin was put to death on his way to Pekin by order of Lin—[and that] officers of *H.M.S. Blenheim*, had been found covered with wounds of every description. These reports are generally believed, and in consequence Teas have advanced a penny or two pence per pound with a brisk demand. [ ] I

[111] William Jardine alludes to the 'bedchamber episode' in 1839. Melbourne's government had resigned on the Jamaica question. The young Queen Victoria summoned Peel to form a cabinet and approved his list. But when Peel recommended that some of the ladies of the bedchamber should be superseded, the Queen balked and the Melbourne government resumed office. (*DNB*).

[112] Bad Ems, east of Koblenz, was a well-known spa town.

doubt the accuracy of the *Arithus*'s report and have advised our friends *Magniac Smith & Co.* to go [on] realizing such teas as are yielding a handsome profit, taking care not to depress the market.

Money continues rather tight, and mercantile men are afraid of the Bank of England suddenly clapping on the screw and so placing them in a difficult situation should they speculate beyond their means. This has, all along, tended to keep Teas down and is likely to continue to do so. Add to this the distress prevalent in the manufacturing district, and you will probably agree with me, as to the propriety of realizing at a fair profit. *Dent & Co.*'s smuggled teas are of very inferior quality. Those you got out in the *Huskisson* have been pronounced very good.

It will be satisfactory for you to know, that I ascertained, at the foreign office yesterday that Government had submitted the question of the *drug ships* to H.M. legal advisers and received their legal opinion in favour of these vessels being, under the circumstances, permitted to leave the port of Canton in the manner they did. Captain Douglas after having received so many [congratulations] and honors from H.M. Ministers, has turned round upon them and demanded 15,000 pounds sterling for the detention of his ship in China, his losses, etc., etc.; and threatens, if not paid, to have his claim brought before Parliament. {At these proceedings} H.M. Ministers are much enraged.[113]

I intend running over to Boulogne tonight or tomorrow morning, and for what purpose do you suppose ? To try and settle William Magniac's debts,[114] and relieve his wife and family from difficulties and misery. Holly[115] has done so two or three times, and gave him notice last time that he would not assist him again if he got into debt. This was after having given him a clean allowance of 800 pounds sterling per annum. [But he has continued overspending and] his debts now amount to nearly 2,000 sterling. I shall clear him this time and have made up my mind never to give him another farthing. I have told him this in very plain terms. Considering what I gained by his folly, I should not have felt comfortable, had I not acted as I have done. My mind will, after this is settled, be at ease on the subject, and should he play the fool again, I shall have no hesitation in refusing to render him the slightest aid. The Smiths tell me I am throwing my money away, but I think you will approve of the plan I have adopted.

[113] On Captain Douglas and the *Cambridge*, see above, Letter **172**, note 61.

[114] This is the first reference to 'William' Magniac. He may have been a younger brother of Hollingworth Magniac, the other two brothers previously mentioned being Charles Magniac and Daniel Magniac. (For Daniel Magniac and his situation, see Letter **11**, note 6, and Letter **40**, note 3). 'William' Magniac's predicament as described here, however, closely mirrors that of Daniel Magniac, and 'William' could therefore be a slip of the pen for 'Daniel' or a second christian name.

[115] Short for Hollingworth Magniac.

I have not heard from your sisters lately. I believe they are in Scotland. I shall keep this open till I reach N° 3, in case there should be City news. Kind regards to all around you. Believe me, My Dear Matheson,

Yours very sincerely,

3 Lombard Street. August 4th 1841

Nothing new today. Teas have continued in demand, and prices are rather on the advance than the decline, and I have just instructed Mr. Fraser[116] to sell about 700 chests that poor Grant and I purchased long ago, to support the market. They yield from 2 shillings to 4 shillings and threepence per pound after paying all charges, interest, etc.

241. James Matheson in Macao to William Jardine in London,
23 August 1841

My dear Jardine,

The May mail arrived 23 July and the June mail, with Sir Henry Pottinger, the admiral[117] and Alexander Matheson on the night of the 9 Instant:[118] ours being the first house they entered on landing, to see Sir Hugh Gough, then living with us. Sir Henry delivered your letter of introduction and we gave him a dinner to meet the commercial community, on all of whom and ourselves he has made a favourable impression. He lost no time in sending Major Malcolm[119] with Thom in the *Nemesis*, to announce his appointment at Canton, where their appearance occasioned great consternation, causing some of the most timid dealers to leave the place. Soon after the Guangchowfoo came to Macao, but was not received by Sir Henry and saw only Major Malcolm, whom he endeavoured to dissuade from the proposed movement to the North, saying it would lose the emperor's face and would compel the authorities to renew our troubles here; to which Malcolm replied that, if so, we must retaliate, and should not again spare Canton. It was reported he had offered 10 millions of dollars, to make peace but this is not the case.

[116] Mr Fraser was not identified. He was probably a manager in *Magniac Smith & Co.*'s tea department.

[117] 'The admiral': Sir William Parker.

[118] Sir Henry Pottinger and Sir William Parker had left London with the June Mail. They stopped over at Bombay and there decided to go straight to China without stopping at Calcutta. They arrived at Macao in the *Sesostris*, a new steam frigate, on 9 August 1841. (Fay, *The Opium War*, 312).

[119] Major (later Colonel) George Alexander Malcolm (1810–1880) was secretary to Sir Henry Pottinger during the negotiations of the Treaty of Nanking. He sailed back to London with a copy of the treaty at the end of August 1842 to have it ratified. (*Ibid.*, p. 360); Major Malcolm is also mentioned in Letters **261** and **262**).

Sir Henry and suite left yesterday for HongKong, whence it is supposed the expedition will move today; leaving only a very small invalid force to protect the new British Settlement, under the military command of that notable *imbecile*, General Burrell,[120] and the Civil Government, of Johnston.[121] This is not using us well, and it is fortunate therefore we are able to send up to Whampoa much of the cotton we had stored there. The only thing known for certain is that a light squadron is to revisit the Peiho; Chusan is also to be reoccupied; but whether Amoy is to be attacked *en route* is uncertain. Report says this is a point depending on the discretion of the Admiral and General, Sir Henry Pottinger's authority going no further than to request them to make war, leaving it to them to determine how.

The Plenipotentiary speaks of being back here in three months but it cannot be supposed there is the least chance, within that time, of prevailing on the Emperor to accede to the severe terms which will no doubt be required. His friends therefore hint that if he finds the Emperor as obstinate as we expect, he will take advantage of the comparative inaction of the winter months to visit Calcutta and consult with the Governor General. On the whole there seems every probability we shall not have a peace for nearly a year to come.[122] But in this we may be mistaken, and if teas can be sold at saving rates in your market, I should not be disposed to hold for more. I have no doubt such a peace as would have satisfied Elliot could have been got this season—liberal in regard to money, but short of the public expectation in other respects. The Canton authorities are thoroughly humbled, as a proof of which I may mention that on Thom handing the Quangchoofoo his chair here, the latter said to him, 'pray do not take the trouble, we are humble now, and you in the ascendant.'

As to the prospect of the English doing business at Canton next winter, it is difficult to give my opinion with any confidence. We have the *Balcarres* and other ships at Whampoa, but shall not be free from anxiety about them, on hostilities recommencing, more especially if this should be so near as Amoy. Both English and Chinese authorities will no doubt be desirous to avoid a re-establishment of the blockade; but there is no saying what unforeseen and undesired consequences may ensue, should irritation get up between them. With the utmost peace and freedom of trade at Canton, I do not think we need fear the supply of tea will be excessive; while on the other hand, under the relaxed system which has lately been gaining ground, it is not probable the utmost degree of restrictions will prevent tea from oozing out pretty freely through Macao, where it is now compara-

[120] Old General Burrell (he was 64 in 1841) had acquired a reputation of weakness and inefficiency during the July 1840 Chusan campaign. (*Ibid.*, pp. 221–223)

[121] On Alexander Johnston, see Letter **106**, note 59.

[122] This assessment was to prove entirely correct. The Treaty of Nanking was signed on 29 August 1842.

tively abundant. The heavy Consoo charge of 10 Taels (some say even 12 Taels) per picul on tea will tend to encourage a smuggling trade.

HongKong.[123] I fear Elliot's unpopularity will in some degree descend on his petchild, HongKong, but I have earnestly to beg you will use your influence, if not for its retention, at least for the retention of some place near this river, where alone the English are known and multitudes of natives are ready to become our subjects and trade with us, in place of being scared away as at Chusan and elsewhere. I lament to say we have not yet been able to commence any trade but opium at HongKong, and were it not for the excellence of its harbour some spot on the Macao side of the river would perhaps have been better for commercial purposes for the sake of proximity to the Inner passage: but I know not where else we could have got a harbour equally good and more especially for large vessels, and I cannot suppose its distance from the Inner passage would be a serious obstruction, were we able to settle on it in right earnest under the acknowledged and *irrevocable* protection of the British Government. While doubt exists on this point, it cannot do otherwise than languish. Once thoroughly protected roads made and settlers encouraged it could hardly fail to become a considerable emporium. Our outlays in building an extensive godown etc. at HongKong will by and bye amount to perhaps 20,000 dollars—so that I am not disinterested in advocating its retention. Many prefer Cowloon Peninsula, but we ought to have both.[124]

Elliot goes per *Atalanta*. He says you will be one of the first he will see in London and that he hopes under the favour of your port wine, to convince you that you were *talking* wrong as a member of the deputation to Lord Palmerston though he is sure you would have been one of the last to *act* so, had you been here on the spot. 'It is very easy', he says, 'for merchants to tell Lord Palmerston to disregard trade while their returns are going home with the same regularity as if there was no troubles. But reverse this—suppose no trade and merchants tottering for want to returns what then would be the cry?' But I will not undetake the arduous task of his defense, and, to say the honest truth, I have been so completely engrossed with anxiety for the goods consigned to us, as not to have a thought to spare on the general impolicy of otherwise of Elliot's measures. We have been so placed as to have compelled us to consider trade or no trade as the sole test of his merits in my eyes. And as the arrangement for opening Canton trade in March last was an inexpressible relief to us, so it is that I cannot help

[123] This impassioned appeal for the retention of Hong Kong may have cut little ice with William Jardine. It certainly would have had little effect on ministers at home who were set against it. Hong Kong would probably not have been retained if Pottinger himself had not grown fond of the new colony and exceeded his orders by negotiating for its retention in the Treaty of Nanking. (See last paragraph of the Introduction).

[124] This wish was to be realized by the Treaty of Tientsin signed by Lord Elgin on 3 July 1858, following the second Opium War. (Hanes III, W. Travis, and Sanello Frank, *The Opium Wars*, p. 223).

viewing it as a master stroke of *commercial* policy,[125] and far better than the turmoil, destruction of property, claims and counterclaims, as well as wide individual ruin and disruption of all commercial confidence that would have ensued had we attempted to seize the teas by force without giving a consideration for them.

My intercourse with Elliot has been regulated on the simple plan of taking him as I found him. Such as he is, he was appointed to be our Superintendent, and I felt I could not improve him by thwarting him or offering him advice in an unpalatable form that would prevent his following it. Certain it is the extraordinary malignity with which he has been assailed by certain parties[126] here has been much exasperated by the tendency which some of his measures had to benefit our business operations—especially his letting out the blockaded vessel *Kosciusko*[127] when the clamour raised against him might not unreasonably have caused a man of less nerve to falter in his purpose, to our great (*possible*) detriment. But he persevered manfully against the fiercest opposition, even to the length of taking all the responsibility on himself, when he saw the Commodore hesitate. I had before begged him not to mind our interest in the matter, for we would rather submit to the inconvenience of having the vessel detained in [the Bogue] than be the means of getting him into a scrape [ ]. He had before exasperated the same parties in September 1839 by assembling [the force for] the intended blockade which they had hoped would have stopped our transshipping operations. This was in fact the commencement of the schism between him and them. On the whole I trust you will excuse my bespeaking as much of your countenance and aid as you can consistently give him towards making good his case in the eyes of the people in England.[128] I will not defend his letter to Lord Palmerston of 28th

[125] A strong phrase in a sentence which generally commends Captain Elliot for his humane qualities and expresses James Matheson's tiredness with war and its trail of destruction.

[126] James Matheson refers here to the firm's archrival, *Dent & Co.* and its partners.

[127] For the *Kosciusko*, see Letter **221**, note 3.

[128] This paragraph contains James Matheson's final personal assessment of Captain Charles Elliot. His explicit desire to 'make good [Captain Elliot's] case with the English people' was based on his recognition of the plenipotentiary's qualities of personal courage and intelligence as a superintendent of British trade. In view of the critical comments he also often made in his letters, it is clear that in his send-off James Matheson chose to emphasize the good points of this much-criticized historical figure rather than dwell on his shortcomings as a military and diplomatic plenipotentiary. And yet these good points, emphasized here by one of the co-founders of *Jardine, Matheson & Co.*, one of the firms which benefited most from Captain Elliot's commercial actions and from the taking and subsequent retention of Hong Kong, have to this day failed to be recognized by historians (with the exception of Suzanna Hoe). Robert Blake himself, the firm's official historian, presents a very negative picture of Elliot, and one which perhaps could well have been drawn by William Jardine, though not by James Matheson. It is interesting to note that history has tended to endorse the view of one of the firm's partners (Jardine's) and to dismiss the view of the other (Matheson's).

Commenting on the beginning of the whole Opium War episode, Blake writes: 'The Chief Superintendent had put his head in a trap. It was folly to have gone to Canton at all without the backing of a far larger naval force than he had at his disposal. // Folly tends to produce further folly. Elliot

November 1839.[129] On me it made a less unfavourable impression that upon others, because it was but an echo of what he had been dinning into my ears in repeated conversations and contained a good deal of truth though decked out with his characteristic exaggeration, but such truth as he ought to have been the last man to lay unmasked before the Government. He says, however, it is a mere private gossiping letter which Lord Palmerston ought not to have published.

Reverting to Elliot's general policy I may add that the unpopularity of our cause in England, the smallness of our force and the inefficiency of its heads were so many reasons that moderated my expectations of a favourable result and led me to put up with almost any sort of settlement, were it only for the sake of its furnishing us with a better *Casus Belly*[130] on some future occasion. If Sir Henry Pottinger can obviate this by making a *good* settlement at once, it will, of course, be infinitely better.

Excuse the length of this prosy epistle and believe me always

Yours most sincerely,

242. James Matheson in Macao to Jamsetjee Jejeebhoy in Bombay,
24 August 1841

My dear Sir,

Our friend Captain Charles Elliot being a passenger to Bombay per *Atalanta*, I cannot omit the opportunity of expressing to you how much we feel indebted for the important aid which his measures have at times afforded us in the management of our concerns. I am all the more desirous of bringing this to your notice, being convinced that to the tendency which some of his measures had to benefit our commercial operations is attributable much of our neighbours violent rancour

panicked. In fact the condition of life in the factories under Lin's embargo was by no means disagreeable. [. . .] It was all rather like a picnic. In London at the end of the year, the so-called 'siege' of the factories was blown up by Jardine's propaganda machine into something like the 'Black Hole of Calcutta'. In reality the only danger to the beseiged was obesity from too much food and too little exercise. Elliot decided to surrender abjectly and completely'(*Jardine Matheson*, p. 91). As against this assessment, James Matheson himself was 'inclined to regard [the surrender of the opium] as a large and statesmanlike measure'. (Letter **170**).

Commenting on the agreement by Elliot to a truce just as the British troops were poised to attack Canton on 26 May 1841, Blake writes: 'Elliot was at a loss what to do. He had become convinced that Canton was irrelevant, that a foray to the north to pressurize Peking was needed and he made plans for it, but he was out of sympathy with Palmerston's enthusiasm for the northern ports. The truth is that Elliot was at heart a 'mandarin'. Just as the real mandarins looked down on the Co-hong, so Elliot disliked the Jardines, the Mathesons and the Dents of this world'. (*ibid.*, p. 102). This is a view which is difficult to reconcile with James Matheson's own assessment that some of Elliot's actions were 'master strokes of *commercial* policy', and with his assertions that Elliot's had repeatedly shown his personal concern for the trade in general, and in particular for *Jardine, Matheson & Co.*'s trade.

[129] See Letter **216**, note 159, and Letter **229**, note 44.

[130] An amusing slip of the pen.

towards him, which communicated to their London correspondents, and widely disseminated by both organs of our public press, without any means of explanation or counteraction on his part, has no doubt greatly contributed to bring about his present downfall.[131]

His schism with the parties alluded to commenced in September 1839 when he annulled the intended blockade which they hoped would have extinguished our transhipping operations. But his crowning offence in their eyes, was letting out the blockaded vessel, *Kosciusko*, when the violent clamour raised against him might not unreasonably have caused a less resolute man to pause, to our great (possible) detriment and that our of constituents; but he persevered against the fiercest opposition, even to the length of taking all the responsibility on himself when he saw the Commodore hesitate.

I have no wish to justify Captain Elliot's general policy and, to say the truth, our attention was so completely engrossed by anxiety for the consignments we had in hand, as not to have a thought to spare for any other consideration; and our position compelled us to view Trade or no trade as almost the sole test of his deserts. The arrangement for opening Canton trade in March last was an immense relief to our constituents as well as most fortunate in its result, and I cannot help thinking it far better that the destruction of property, wide spread ruin of our Chinese customers, and entire disruption of commercial confidence that would have ensued had we attempted to seize the teas by force without giving value for them. Under all circumstances I hope you will give captain Elliot a friendly reception and I shall feel much obliged for any public or private countenance you can show him.

I have also to bespeak your influence with your friends in favour of the retention of HongKong, which is it to be feared, may suffer in public estimation from the unpopularity of its founder. It is far the best harbour for large ships in the vicinity of Canton River. It is in this part of China only that the English are yet well known, and many natives have already become our subjects at HongKong, in place of being frightened away as at Chusan and elsewhere. So that, though it is undoubtedly desirable to have likewise a settlement to the North, HongKong would advance much faster in prosperity than any other, if it were known that the British Government are determined to retain it.

I remain, My dear Sir,

Yours most sincerely,

[131] James Matheson articulates here the most extended argument to date in an effort to account for Captain Elliot's bad press. But the argument is probably too one-sided and too closely tied up to commercial rivalries to be entirely convincing.

Similar letters to: J. W. Henderson Esq.,[132] Bombay; John Abel Smith, Esq. London,

P.S. I refer you to Jardine and our Circular for all news—no one seems to know whether Amoy is to be the first place of attack or a more northern position. I hope the latter. It is impossible to foresee the probable extent of the ensuing export of tea supposing the Chinese at Canton to be quiet and enter into trade without molestation (which can hardly be expected). I do not think the supply will be excessive, nor on the other hand will the utmost extent of Chinese restriction prevent a good deal of tea from going home via Macao. On the whole we still wish you to sell ours whenever fair remunerating prices can be got, but in a contrary event, we shall not be afraid of your holding.

243. William Jardine in London to James Matheson in Macao

6 September 1841

My Dear Matheson,

On the 4th Instant I was favoured with your anxiously looked for letters of 1st, 21st of April, 3rd,[133] 15th, and 19th[134] of May, for which accept my grateful acknowledgements.

I confess the state of affairs in Canton puzzles me very much, and I have no confidence in the Chinese authorities. Fear of consequences may keep them quiet and prevent treachery while our fleet is in the vicinity of HongKong or the Bocca Tigris; but had Elliot been foolish enough to send the outer force to Amoy, I should have preferred Macao to Canton; as I have no opinion of the protection, that the inner force could afford the merchants, were the Chinese to make a night attack upon the force, and the factories at the same moment. Numbers must prevail, when courage and determination urge them on, even against superior discipline in the ranks of the smaller party. There is no use, however, in speculating on such results, as I sincerely hope and trust, you are all, ere long, in a state of safety.

I note what you say in your letter of 1st April, respecting your previous communication to Alexander [Matheson] and myself, dated 21st November; and, from your saying nothing to the contrary, I sincerely hope Mr. William Stewart[135] continues to fill Boyd's place to your satisfaction.

I shall here take an opportunity of explaining, to you, a conversation, I had with Alexander [Matheson], respecting [William] Stewart, being fearful one

[132] For J. W. Henderson, a partner in *Remington & Co.*, see Letter **183**, note 122.
[133] See above, Letter **233**.
[134] See above, Letter **235**.
[135] William Stewart was one of William Jardine's young relatives, the son of James Stewart of Gillienbierigg. See Letter **38**.

observation of mine may have been misunderstood, and may operate unfavourably to his interests. When conversing about admitting partners, after your retirement, Alexander [Matheson] named Mr. Stewart as if he fancied he had a promise or a claim, and would be admitted as a matter of course. I said immediately no—he has no promise of being made a partner and must depend on his good conduct and exertions, for getting on, adding some other observations of similar description. Now, it has struck me since, that Alexander [Matheson] may have attached more meaning to my observations than I intended he should; and, for this reason, I wish you all to be aware, that I should be highly gratified to learn that Stewart has so conducted himself as to make one and all of you deem him worthy of being admitted as a partner when the proper time comes. I was certainly dissatisfied with his selfish extravagance in squandering his money on himself, when he should have made a point of sending a small sum to his father, but I trust his visit to this country has done him good, and that he has now more consideration. He does not want for ability—if he will only make a good use of it. Having said so much I leave him in the hands of the firm, not wishing to influence any of you improperly, and, as I have not mentioned the subject to any of the others, I shall feel obliged by your communicating as much of this letter as you may deem fit and right.[136]

I am afraid our friend Shillaber,[137] did himself harm in the estimation of *Magniac Smith & Co.* the other day, by circulating [ ] a report of news from China—not real news, but such as he wished, and probably believed, might prove true, some future day—he wrote to them, in my absence, and enclosed a letter for America, which they hesitated about forwarding; but I convinced them we were bound to forward it—the hoax letter[138] was without a name. The papers here swallowed it greedily. Shillaber is now in, or near Paris.

I shall say nothing about Tea, having written on that subject to Andrew [Jardine]. Thanks for the remittance you are making me—Tea, Bills, or Silk, any of them will answer my purpose. I give you great credit for the manner in which you have placed your cotton, etc., etc., as well as for your general management of weighty matters under your charge.

I believe John Abel Smith has returned from the Continent, in good health, but I have not yet seen him.

5 p.m. I have just seen John Abel, he is much better but still looking rather thin. The *Herald* has arrived. I have received your duplicate of the 21st April by her.

[136] William Stewart became a partner of *Jardine, Matheson & Co.* in 1842. (Keswick, *The Thistle and the Jade*, p. 264).

[137] On John Shillaber, see Letter **49**, note 3.

[138] This hoax letter circulated to the papers was not traced.

I shall write to James Duncan, informing him what you say respecting the *Herald*.[139]

Kind regards to all our friends, including Mr. Wright, and Boyd if still with you.

Believe me,

Yours sincerely,

244. William Jardine in London to Jamsetjee Jejeebhoy in Bombay,
6 September 1841

My dear Sir,

Many thanks for you letter of the 19th July and its enclosures; which bring our news from China down to the 20th of May, at which date our friend were in anything but a satisfactory position.

I am not afraid of the Chinese attacking the factories, or being guilty of any gross treachery, while our outer squadron is in the vicinity of HongKong; but had Elliot moved that division of the force to Amoy, as he intended to have done, I cannot help thinking the Troops in Canton would have made an attack on the small force in the inner waters.

If there are forty thousand troops in Canton and its vicinity, there is, I think, some risk of their becoming troublesome, and urging the Authorities to allow them to drive the foreign force from the river. A night attack, at a time when our small force did not expect it, would prove a serious affair.[140] Let us hope for the best, but I do not feel comfortable about our friends in Canton; and I shall be glad to hear of their being safe afloat, or at Macao.

The Tea market has suffered severely. Congos have fallen in price 6 pence to 10 pence per pound; but prices are firmer today, and we hope for a return to something like former prices, say 2 shillings to 2 shillings and 6 pence or 2 shillings and 8 pence per pound for Congos, according to quality.

There is a public sale tomorrow, which will have the effect of testing the feelings and views of the Trade.

I know not what you say respecting remittances, and shall communicate your wishes to our friend John Abel Smith, who has returned from the Continent in good health, but I have not yet seen him.

I have heard nothing from our friend Framjee Cowasjee, respecting the account I sent him; but Mr. Alexander Matheson informs me he saw him, and he was making many kind enquiries after my health , etc., etc. I wish the business settled, and

139 On the *Herald* and James Duncan of Leith, see below, Letter **245**, 4th paragraph.

140 The remark shows William Jardine's remarkable knowledge of the Chinese. A surprise night attack by fireboats was indeed launched on 22 May, two days after the date of the latest news he had received from China. (See above, Letter **235**, note 94).

should wish to know his objections to the account sent, if he has any. Mr Weeding made it out, and Framjee has one of the Arbitrators, in the settlement with Mr. Weeding, in Bombay, so that he can refer to him if necessary. My account is made out on the same principle, as far as the affairs of the *Sarah* are concerned.[141]

The Governor General's letter respecting the *Bank of Asia's* Charter,[142] is still before the Court of Directors of the East India Company. The Chair and Deputy Chair are granting us a charter, many of the others, influenced by the Houses of Agency, opposed us. Our friend Mr. Crawford is doing all he can to prevent our getting a charter. We shall know the result ere long, I hope. I am sick of unfair opposition for selfish ends.[143] Kind regards to your Sons. In haste,

Yours sincerely,

245. William Jardine in London to James Matheson in Macao,

4 October 1841

My Dear Matheson,

To prevent interruption I shall address a few lines to you before going into the City, this being Mail day.

You may suppose we are all very anxious to receive the news by the inward mail, considering the unpleasant position you are placed in, when the last account of the 19th of May left you.[144] It was gratifying to me, to observe that you were under no apprehension about the safety of our friends at Canton, but still their position was an unsafe one, and I shall be glad to find your views of the case confirmed.

There is little passing here that is worth noticing. The crops are now nearly all off the ground, and, I believe, the supply of food is not very far from an average one; though many statements of a different description have been published in the newspapers.

The Tea market has been tolerably steady, during the last month, and holders appear determined not to sacrifice their Teas at losing prices. The cargo of the *Herald* was put up for sale, at Leith, on the 30th Ultimo, and yielded a fair profit to the importers, but the particulars have not been received, or rather had not been received on Saturday. You will no doubt have the result of the sale from Leith, as well as from N°3 Lombard Street. About four fifth were sold.

I shall be satisfied with similar prices for all my Teas, if 20, or 30 millions of pounds are imported; for, though prices may, and ought to, rule higher before we receive the Teas of next market season, still I prefer realizing, and getting out of

[141] On the content of this paragraph, see also Letter **206**, note 91.

[142] On the *Bank of Asia* Charter, see also Letter **233** above.

[143] A classic Jardine sentence in its abrupt expression of annoyance.

[144] See Letter **235**.

debt. Money is far from being plentiful, and is occasionally very scarce. I hope Sir Henry Pottinger may succeed in obtaining early payment from Elliot's disgraced paper,[145] and I should prefer taking the sum I shall have to put into the house of *Magniac Smith & Co.* from that source,[146] to bothering you remitting at a time when it may be inconvenient to you. Magniac is unwell at Harrowgate, where he is ordered to remain till the middle or end of this month.

I have had another visit from Mr. Murphy of Cork.[147] Their Teas have been nearly all landed, and the quality pronounced good. So far they are satisfied, but he would have been more so, had you sent them a larger quantity. He said, after many apologies, that you had done better for Mr. Carr,[148] who did not send you so much money as his firm did. His friend sent a credit on *Barclay & Co.*, which you used, but did not use his credit on *Magniac Smith & Co.*, which he wished you had used. I told him I should mention the circumstance, but I had no doubt you would assign a sufficient reason for what you had done; and hinted at the possibility of some striking difference in the terms of the two orders of Tea. Mr. Murphy is one of those men, who pride themselves on their wealth, having an income of eleven hundred per annum, as he is fond of complaining. All the while very polite, and very desirous of keeping the connection with the China Firm. He has sent out an order for Teas, and intended to have sent Company's bills by this mail. I told him he might wait till we heard from China, and send the bills by next mail, and promised to mention this to you, that you may be prepared to purchase the Tea, should you deem it advisable so to do, trusting to the bills being sent by the November mail. He wishes you to write more frequently. Now, I have done my duty,[149] and I have no doubt you will say enough of Mr. Murphy.

The new ministry, you will observe, are very unwilling to do anything rashly; and wish for five months leisure time to deliberate. It is generally believed they are not unanimous in their opinion, and Sir Robert is in hopes time, or accident, may change the opinion of some of them.

I mentioned to Alexander [Matheson] that Thacker,[150] alias Jawing Jack, is going to Sydney to join *Hunter & Co.*, and a Mr. de Sales may possibly accompany him, but this is not finally arranged—de Sales[151] is hesitating. Edwards[152]

[145] 'Elliot's disgraced paper': the 1839 opium receipts which were still pending settlement.

[146] William Jardine's allusion to his joining the *Magniac Smith & Co.* partnership.

[147] James Nicholas Murphy: see Letter **222**, note 8).

[148] 'Mr. Carr': possibly William Carr, 'merchant, 65 Old Broad Street'. (*TLCD*).

[149] A characteristic remark from William Jardine. From the mention about his 'eleven hundred per annum', Murphy was a small-time tea merchant or speculator. But as a customer of the firm, he was given time to air his complaints which William Jardine had undertaken to pass them on to Canton in the full knowledge that they would not feature high on James Matheson's priority list.

[150] On Captain John Thacker, see above, Letter **83**, note 25.

[151] 'de Sales' was not identified.

[152] For Mr and Mrs Edwards, see Letter **128**, note 2.

is in London. Mrs. Edwards at Hastings, unwell. Colledge[153] has purchased a house, and settled in Cheltenham, as a physician, or general practitioner.

Present my kind regards to all around you, and believe me, my Dear Matheson,
Yours sincerely,

246. William Jardine in Scotland to James Matheson in Macao,
2 November 1841[154]

My dear Matheson,

Here I am on my way farther north. [Andrew] Johnstone (who desires to be kindly remembered to you all) and I leave this at 8 a.m. tomorrow for Lanrick,[155] where we propose remaining for a fortnight, or three weeks. We take a carriage and saddle horses with us, and we hope to have some amusement.

The last despatches from China, did not much please me. With so few troops, it might have been imprudent to take possession of Canton; but why allow the troops, from the North, to march out with their drums, and colours, to claim a victory? which the vagabonds will do.[156]

Many thanks for your letters by the last mail, and for the remittance you had made, and were making to me. The teas to Leith made a good remittance, and I do not intend parting with any of the others unless they yield 5 shillings per dollar; and when out of debt,[157] I shall hold on for 5 shillings 6 pence, or 6 shillings per dollar.

Silk I do not think so favourably of, the price, in China, is too high to admit of its meeting the best Italian silk in this market. I determined, therefore, to sell, at once, at the best prices procurable, and had it put up at the first sale, ten or twelve days ago, when 17 bales of the best were sold at 22 shillings to 22 shillings and 5 pence per pound. 5 bales of second quality at 20 shillings, and 11 bales more or less damaged, at from 14 shillings and 8 pence to 18 shillings and 6 pence per

[153] For Dr Thomas Richardson Colledge, see Letter **128**, note 3.

[154] This letter was written from Halleaths, Andrew Johnstone's estate.

Whilst this Letter was being written, a new phase of the Opium War had started under the direction of Sir Henry Pottinger. Amoy was taken on 25 August 1841. On 1 October Tinghai was retaken. On 13 October, Ningpo fell. This is where the troops spent the winter months, awaiting the decisive Yangtze campaign which started in May 1842. (Fay, *The Opium War*, pp. 308–321).

Meanwhile Sir Henry Pottinger returned to Hong Hong in February 1842 and moved his superinendency from Macao to the infant colony. Roads, bazaars, godowns and barracks were being built; a magistracy organized, a prison planned, and missionary schools were soon opening. (*Ibid.*, 322–338).

[155] For Lanrick, see above, Letter **237**, note 102.

[156] William Jardine refers here to the Chinese troops.

[157] Debt had been incurred for the purchase of Lanrick and No 6 Upper Belgrave Square. William Jardine had his capital remitted from Canton only as and when profitable means of doing so presented themselves.

pound. The demand was almost entirely confined to the finer descriptions, but *Magniac Smith & Co.* hoped to place some of the others by the bye, when they wrote to me on the 27th Ultimo.

The newspapers say *Dent & Co.* were paid 63,000 pounds sterling for their dishonoured bills. It this is true, and Elliot did not pay you, at the same time, and in a similar manner, for the drug you purchased and gave up, without demanding bills on the Treasury,[158] he ought to be sent to Coventry for ever.[159]

I am afraid the mail, now daily expected, will not bring us anything of importance from China. We are anxious for later accounts. Referring to our London friends for mercantile information, I remain, with kindest regards to all around you, my Dear Matheson,

Yours very sincerely,

1842

247. James Matheson in Macao to Jamsetjee Jejeebhoy in Bombay,

10 January 1842

My dear Sir,

I am now to have the pleasure of replying to your esteemed favours received by the two last despatches.

– *1841*, August 11th, received 23 November, requests my attention to a remittance of 9,500 dollars due 23 Instant on account of Colonel Daly,[1] which shall be remitted to England, on the most favourable terms, probably 5 shillings per dollar.

– September 3rd, received 28 October, enclosed Accounts Sales and Invoices of returns for Opium per *Cornwallis* and *Ardaseer* by *Messrs. Dent & Co.* and *Macvicar & Co.*, exhibiting results considerably more favourable than our sales, owing to their having been enabled to avail of an unusually favourable chance on the East Coast. To counterbalance this, however, our returns were remitted much more promptly than theirs. You will recollect that in 1840 we made great exertions to keep up the price of Malwa; but having learnt from you that our Constituents disliked the delay which this occasioned in remitting the returns, our chief attention was subsequently directed to making sales and returns with the least possible delay, which object, it will readily occur to you, could not be

[158] On the drug especially purchased for delivery to Captain Elliot, see above, Letter **198**, note 23, and Letter **170**, note 36.

[159] The phrase 'to be sent to Coventry' referred to army officers whose offences were not considered bad enough for a court-martial. The Coventry gaol was mentioned as an alternative. (Partridge, Eric, and Grose, Francis, (eds.), *A Classical Dictionary of the Vulgar Tongue*, 1963).

[1] Colonel Daly was not identified.

accomplished without some sacrifice in the price. The Coast markets are exceedingly uncertain. One voyage may be successful as in the case of our neighbours which you bring to our notice; while another may be a total failure, as happened the other day to a vessel that went with Malwa to Chusan and after being out several months, without making sales, has brought it all back again. Prices are in some measure regulated by the expected average result of the good and bad adventures to the Coasts; and as our Constituents have none of the risks, it will sometimes unavoidably happen that they do not participate in the full benefit of the highest prices that may be unexpectedly obtained. We are much obliged to you for so kindly pointing out to us those cases where our neighbours are enabled to do better for their constituents than we do, and we trust you will continue to favour us with similar information. It will be our earnest study to combine promptitude of remittance with the fullest benefit of the markets within our reach; and I confidently trust that the Malwa sales we are now making will be found considerably more advantageous than most others.

– September 6th point out an overcharge in our Commission on the *Fort William's* freight for which we credit your firm 5 per cent on your portion of her cargo, 705 tons at 7.10 ; 4,537.10 pounds sterling; 220.17.6 pounds sterling at 5 shillings per dollars equals 967.50 dollars.[2]

It must be superfluous for me to say that we are fully as much aggrieved as yourself, by the unfavourable result of you last season's cotton consignments; which is owing to the quantity imported having been so much greater than could have been anticipated in a state of war, and to the reopening of the trade having been delayed so much longer than was expected by those best informed on the subject; while it would not have suited you, had we attempted getting rid of yours by small barter sales, on credit, to parties whom we could not trust, and who had no security to give, which is the only mode of selling cotton at Macao. As for the Bazar rumours of *Messrs. Russell & Co.*'s quick and advantageous returns for cotton, I think we may be justified in doubting their veracity, after the exposure we sent you of the falsehood of similar rumours in regard to *Messrs. Lindsay & Co.*

The Sycees sent per *Charles Forbes* at 7 per cent was in advance for opium, just received and not realized. For opium realized we sent by her sycee at only

[2] As this Letter shows, it was not unknown for the correspondence between the senior partners of two of the largest trading firms at the time to go into details which more junior managers might normally have been expected to handle. But Parsee merchants in general and Jamsetjee Jejeebhoy in particular always loved to get involved in minutiae in business correspondence. He had a perfect eye for the odd clerical or accounting error, and he expected the senior partner of his correspondent agent to notice all his points, challenges and criticisms. James Matheson conscientiously and adroitly played his correspondent's game and was thus able to deflect much criticism which a less experienced and less personable partner would not have handled so elegantly and efficiently. Jamsetjee Jejeebhoy was to receive the news of his knighthood (the letters patent were dated 2 March 1842) only a few weeks after receiving this Letter. (*MEB*).

5½ per cent premium. The expense of ship room and insurance for keeping on hand our stock of sycee is, as you know, considerable. Sometimes by buying from parties who are pushed for cash, it may be procured cheaper than we send it, as in the case of Mr. Henderson, which you lately brought to my notice. But when the low rate becomes general, in place of being confined to one or two isolated instances, we are then obliged to send our constituents sycee at a loss to ourselves, which is the case at present; as it costs on the Coast 4 per cent, besides freight and insurance, but only circulated here at par, thereby saddling us with a very heavy loss.

– October 9th, received 24th December, announced the satisfactory intelligence of the *Bombay Castle's* arrival, and alludes to a consignment of 50 chests [of] drug per *Isabella*, which claims a repetition of our thanks, and shall be cared for on that vessel's arrival. I am much obliged for the perusal of Messrs. D. and M. Rustomjee's Account[3] Sale, on the Coast, which I perceive they represent to you as higher than the average of any other vessel, and it is therefore another instance of fortunate chance such as I have already alluded to in this letter. I may, however, observe to you that their charge of 10 per cent seems inadequate to cover the expense of demurrage[4] besides the Captain's commission and their own, considering the long period generally required to effect sales, and the expensive fitting out of the ships. Two dollars charged by them for shroffing[5] 15,075 dollars is also very inadequate; a Shroff's wages being usually 35 dollars per month besides a small fee on every chest delivered. On the whole it looks very much as if our worthy neighbours were willing to suffer loss on the charges for the sake of attracting constituents.

– October 18th alludes to the unfavourable outturn of our shipments of China goods which we very much regret, as also the inferiority in our sycee,[6] which we do all we can to guard against; but it is impossible to be always successful in preventing small adulterations.

I read with great concern what you state as to our London friends[7] not complying with your wishes for early sales and accounts. I have written to them on the subject and confidently hope that you will have no more cause of complaint. We were induced to send them, the larger share of your goods from knowing that Mr. Jardine in such an event would be able to look after the sale of them, than whom I am sure none can be more zealous in your service. We had also an eye to the advantage likely to be derived, in the London market, from concentrating in

[3] Dadabhoy and Manackjee Rustomjeee had two vessels selling opium up the coast at the time. (Bard, *Traders of Hong Kong*, p. 45).

[4] Goods sold had to be collected from the warehouse by buyers within a specified number of days. Past that time, a *per diem* demurrage fee was due on the goods stored.

[5] A shroff was a Chinese money counter.

[6] For 'sycee' see above Letter **21**, note 37.

[7] *Magniac Smith & Co.*

one hand as much as possible on particular kinds of tea and also of Nankin silks. But I will not conceal from you, that in preferring our own London friends, we were also influenced by the evident disposition which *Messrs. Forbes, Forbes & Co.* appear to have to find fault with our consignments to them, on your account; which as we are accountable for our proceedings to you alone, and in no way to them, seems to us to be going beyond their province, and to evince a disaffection calculated to weaken our confidence in their impartiality.

If, however, you should still find that *Magniac Smith & Co.* are not equally successful in realizing your goods, you will find us ever ready to consign to whatever other parties you may prefer.

I need not revert to the subject of Malwa sales except to say that you may depend on our availing of every opening whether on the Coast or elsewhere to do the best we can for you; and I do not think you will be soon again annoyed by seing better account sales from others than from us.

Many kind thanks for your consignment of 100 chests per *Sir H. Compton*, which we are now getting rid of by barter.

I learn some of the new Gujerat [ ] drug turns out good, but some of it also inferior; on which heads I shall make you a special report as soon as we get further information.

You ask my opinion as to the effect of the Emperor legalizing the opium trade. It will no doubt lead to an increase of consumption and a rise of prices. But though there is little doubt of its ultimately taking place, it is very uncertain at what period. I know Sir Henry Pottinger is very much bent on gaining this point;[8] but it cannot be, until we have peace, and we are not likely to have peace, without a considerably larger force to compel compliance with our demands. The hope of legalization has so often raised prices in India to the loss of speculators, that the less said about it before it occurs the better.

[8] The subject of legalizing opium was periodically re-examined by the Chinese. A few months after this Letter was written, as he was negotiating the Treaty of Nanking, (which eventually did not as much as mention the subject of opium), Sir Henry Pottinger tried to discuss the subject with the two Chinese plenipotentiaries, Ilipu and Kiying. Their conversation is reported by Fay, quoting Grenville Gower Loch (1813–1853) in his *The Closing events of the Campaign in China: The Operations in the Yang-Tze-Kiang; and The Treaty of Nanking*, London, John Murray, 1843, p. 172. '[The Chinese plenipotentiaries] declined entering upon the subject until Sir Henry assured them he did not wish to speak of it but as a topic of private conversation'. Fay continues : 'They then showed considerable interest. They wanted to know why the English did not stop the cultivation of the poppy in their Indian dominions. Pottinger gave the stock answer: 'If your people are virtuous, they will desist from the evil practice; and if your officers are incorruptible, and obey their orders, no opium can enter your country'. As neither was the case, would it not be better to legalize the drug, put a duty on it, and at least benefit the treasury? It was a point Pottinger felt strongly about, it was a point his government had much on its mind—and he pressed it warmly. But it was clear the Chinese were not going to follow his advice'. (Fay, *Opium War*, p. 361).

– October 20th enclosed sketches of the accounts of your European Friends and, also of *Forbes and Forbes*'s Friends, which have [our] attention. The small sycee which is put in to complete the weight of each box is generally of the lower touch than the large. We are much obliged to you for pointing out this and also the lower premium charged by W. Henderson.[9]

– October 20th respecting the deficiency of about 3 per cent in the weight of sycee to Dinshaw Dadabhoy Ghandy which we exceedingly regret. We have a certificate of 50 Taels short weight in sycee silver sent to Rutingur Ramgar and of 200 Taels short to Gopaldoss Joolseydoss Moody;[10] to all three we are forwarding in reply certificates of full weight having been packed. Whence it is to be inferred this deficiency must have been occasioned by plunder on board, or in the boats conveying the silver to or from the ships; a risk to which you will admit we ought not to be liable. None of the certificates states that the seals were perfect and unbroken, when the boxes were opened, which seems an essential requisite to fix the responsibility on us; as without this we should be laying ourselves open to endless claims however they might arise from plunder or carelessness during the voyage, or even from differences in the weights used. We shall write to *Messrs. Remington & Co.* on the subject and shall be very willing to do in the matter, whatever you and they think right.

– October 24th communicates your view about sending the *Bombay Castle* to Manila, but as we had previously arranged for the *Balcarras* taking that voyage, I conclude we shall have to send the *Bombay Castle* to Bombay direct, I hope with a good freight. Your sugar would have been very late in reaching Bombay had we detained it for her, and would probably have met the same fate as the *Castle Huntly's* in 1840.

You may rely on our doing all we can to give effect to your plans to the benefit of the *Reliance*; but as she will not probably arrive till March, it is yet too early to anticipate what prospects there may be for her. Allow me to observe, however, that the period of 15 days allowed [by] you before commencing to unload is far too short. Even if Canton trade were going on without any chance of interruption, the regulation of the port in times of peace would not allow us to commence unloading till at least ten days after getting her pilot. The *Castle Huntly's* charter party allowed you 4 weeks before commencing to unload which is little enough.

I feel very grateful to you for you great kindness to our late Superintendent Captain Elliot and for your very handsome letter to him, of which you are good enough to send me a copy. It will be of the greatest use to him in London.[11]

[9] W. Henderson: probably the same J. W. Henderson mentioned earlier in paragraph 6 this Letter. See Letter **183**, note 122.

[10] Dinshaw Dadabhoy Ghandy, Rutingur Ramgar, and Gopaldoss Joolseydoss Moody were not identified.

[11] The copy of the letter was not traced, but it is clear that Jamsetjee Jejeebhoy had honoured James Matheson's request and given Captain Elliot a very friendly send-off in Bombay. (See Letter **242**).

I very much regret the heavy loss of 50,000 Rupees which you report on your 1,200 chests of Malwa. I cannot but feel sanguine, however, that it will be much more than made up by the profit on your returns to London.

With sincerest wishes that this may be the case, and kindest remembrances to your sons and partners, I remain, my dear Sir,

Most sincerely yours,

248. James Matheson in Macao to William Jardine in London,

25 January 1842[12]

My dear Jardine,

As the three Misses Ullman[13] are going to England in the *Parkfield*, to join Mr. and Mrs, Veiga[14] in Portugal, I write these few lines to explain to you how they are situated in money matters.

	(dollars)
Their original fund amounted to	2,900
each, or for the three	8,700
but Mrs. Veiga gives her sisters the interest of her share	2,900
making a total of principal	11,600
besides which there was on 1st instant a saving of past interest	2,215
amounting to total	13,815
but as we are remitting 300 pounds sterling, say	1,200
out of this to provide for their first year's expenses in Europe, there will remain at interest only about	12,615

or say about 1,000 dollars per annum, which we shall remit for them from time to time, to *Messrs Magniac Smith & Co.* In our office letter of credit, we state their probable income at about 220 pounds sterling per annum; but it will generally be greater, more or less according to the rate of exchange.

The proceeds of their furniture and of a recovery from Samqua[15] pay for their passage and outfit home.

It is, I know, superfluous for me to recommend the Ladies to your kind offices and care.

Yours very sincerely,

[12] The Letterbook C6-2 where this Letter was found is described in the *JMArch.* catalogue as 'Alexander Matheson's Letterbook. This letter, however, as well as several others, are clearly copies of letters written by *James* Matheson prior to his departure home around 11 March 1842.

[13] On J. G. Ullman, the father of the Misses Ullman and the firm's old book-keeper, see Letter **11**, note 12. On his retirement fund, see Letter **56**, note 40.

[14] One of the four Ullman sisters was married to Mr. Veiga, probably a son of Joaquim José Ferreira Veiga. (see Letter **7**, note 37). Of the three unmarried sisters, Anna Margarita, Roza Maria, and Maria Francesca, the latter subsequently married a Mr. Bristow. (*BI*).

[15] Samqua: a bankrupt Hong merchant.

249. James Matheson in Macao to James Goddard in London, 26 January 1842[16]

Dear Goddard,

It is some time since I received the copy of your letter of 3rd June last to *Lyall Matheson & Co.*, Calcutta; but I have been so taken up with the labours and anxieties of business that it is only now I am able to give attention to the matter.

After very carefully examining the subject in all its bearings, I think I can satisfy you, that far from being liable to the blame you suppose, they, on the contrary, acted with that prudent discretion which agents at such a distance, could hardly have omitted to exercise, in the unparalleled and critical state of affairs in China, at the time your remittances and orders to purchase reached Calcutta.

I may premise that among our friends the chief inducement for preferring the agency of *Lyall Matheson & Co.* is the knowledge they possess, as our confidential agents, of our views and opinions respecting the China market for opium; which our friends generally expect, shall in some measure serve as a guide for the price and extent to which they may safely venture in their purchases not only for ourselves, but for them. And in your case this was still more imperative as they knew the remittances which *Magniac Smith & Co.* made them for buying opium on your account, originated in advances furnished by them under our guarantee.

In consequence of the unexampled rigour and success of the new measures adopted by the Chinese Government for the utter extinction of opium smoking, we became so convinced of the increased hazards of the trade and of the unprofitability of realizing what we had already on hand, that we determined to cancel the extensive orders for the article which we had before given *Lyall Matheson &Co.*, and accordingly wrote them on 22 December 1838 (as per accompanying extract)[17] not to purchase any more opium for us, and should they have already done so, to keep it back for our future instructions. This letter, however, arrived too late, as they had already purchased a considerable quantity, for ourselves and friends, which as we prohibited them from shipping it, remained for many months in their hands. Although the accounts which they subsequently received were of a still more disastrous and determined nature, they were tempted by the

[16] This business Letter was called for by the recriminations of James Goddard mentioned in William Jardine's Letter **234**. Goddard had sent money and instructed *Lyall Matheson & Co* to invest in opium at the time of the 1839 crisis. *Lyall Matheson & Co.* invested only half the amount, thus reducing Goddard's risk, but also, it turned out, his profit. James Matheson took time to research the case, and although he generally thought that *Lyall Matheson & Co* were prone to misinterpret his own instructions, he made up his mind about the lack of merit of Goddard's case from the evidence at his disposal. The Letter is in the same vein as Letter **247** to Jamsetjee Jejeebhoy. It provides an idiosyncratic mixture of urbanity and tough business sense, and is a typical illustration of James Matheson's talent for rational argument.

[17] The extract was not traced, but would have quoted events similar to those mentioned in note 85 of Letter **168**.

unprecedented low prices of the April sale to invest your first remittance through *Magniac Smith & Co.* of 14,117.10.4 Calcutta Rupees in the purchase of 30 chests of opium on your account; retaining them for the chance of any favourable change that might afterwards occur. And they had them still on hand, totally at a loss what to do with them, when on the 6th July 1839, they received from the same parties a remittance of 14,117.10.4 Calcutta Rupees on your account. But having also in the interval received intelligence from China of [an event of] a still more appalling and unprecedented nature, they wrote us, that they could not venture to interest you deeper in a speculation apparently so very desperate and had therefore arranged for remitting this further sum in a bill on ourselves, on the security of the *opium they had previously purchased.*

The China intelligence which I allude to as having deterred them must be familiar to all; and after I have cursorily glanced at the leading events, I will put it to any one, whether it would not have been almost an act of madness to have gone on increasing their constituent's stock of opium.

There was:

First, the order of Captain Elliot, Chief Superintendent of British Trade, requiring British subjects to surrender all opium to him or the Chinese Government, for the purpose of being destroyed, *which surrender was accordingly made*, and though Captain Elliot pledged the guarantee of the British Government to make good its value, *it has not yet been paid for*, and no compensation received, as you are aware.

Secondly, to enforce the above surrender, all foreigners in Canton were placed in durance, under a strong guard, with drawn swords, threatened with starvation for a period of six weeks to two months, *and were compelled to sign a pledge no longer to deal in drug,*—while the punishment of death was announced against all who should be concerned in the article.

Captain Elliot publicly proclaimed to Chinese and English his desire to concur in suppressing the trade and to interdict it to his countrymen; so that *Lyall Matheson & Co.* not only found that your intended market was closed against them; but that we, your intended consignees, had in common with all our neighbours (to all appearance) bound ourselves no longer to sell opium. How we afterwards came to resume our dealings, I will presently show; but in the meantime, the fulfillment of your instructions became (as far as they could then see) an impossibility. There was no consignee even to whom they could have sent your opium, supposing they had had the hardihood to ship it; we to whom you had ordered it, having disqualified ourselves from acting for you.

That Lyall's views were concurred in by the Calcutta community generally is susceptible of the amplest proof. The greatest consternation was excited there by the news of the opium having been surrendered, etc., which reached on 25th May. The fourth sale was to come on, on the 27th, and considerable efforts were made by influential parties to induce Government to postpone it, on the ground that the disastrous accounts 'from China led them to apprehend most serious consequences from it, to the British Community there'.

Let us now see to what perils your opium would have been exposed, had it come to China. The burning of the Brig *Bilbaino*, by the mandarins in the Typa,[18] or outer anchorage of Macao, on the mere suspicion of having opium, (though unfounded) must be fresh in your recollection; and not less so, several battles, on the East and West Coasts, in which the mandarins were more than once very near succeeding in the capture of an opium vessel which, had it occurred, we had no means of recovering the loss, it being a risk excepted against by all underwriters in India and China.

I may also mention that when two or three vessels entered to do opium business on a small scale at Hong Kong in September 1839 Captain Elliot peremptorily ordered them out of the anchorage, though it was in the middle of the typhoon season, and there was no other safe anchorage they could resort to. The sad catastrophe of the *Bilbaino* and *Black Joke* having occurred only a few days before.[19] An attempt was them made to carry on the trade in a Portuguese vessel at Hong Kong; but Captain Elliot immediately instigated our men of war to seize her, which led to a heavy sacrifice on the property, though it was subsequently released. He also instigated our men of war to molest the opium vessels, on the plea of their having an unlicensed number of guns on board, for self-defence; while he intimated to the Chinese authorities that he would not interfere with their seizing any vessel they might discover having opium on board. Finally when he concluded an abortive arrangement with the Chinese authorities for reopening British trade at Chuenpee, it was a leading stipulation that no British merchant should be allowed to trade till he deposited with him an engagement that neither himself, not partners, nor assistants would be trading in the drug directly or indirectly.

I have entered into this long explanation to show you that the hazards which *Lyall Matheson & Co*. had to consider in acting for you, were great and imminent and far from being light or imaginary.

It remains to notice the manner in which you 30 chests were finally realized. On our release from durance we sent the *Red Rover*, in June 1839, to Calcutta for the purpose of bringing to Manila, the drug, previously bought on account of ourselves and constituents. We were in hopes the China junks would go there to buy opium, and enable us to make sales without the risk to persons and property from which we had suffered and were apprehensive of further suffering here. To give effect to this plan, Mr. Andrew Jardine proceeded to Manila to establish a branch of our house. But our hopes of doing business there were frustrated, and it became

[18] The Spanish brig *Bilbaino* had been mistaken for an English opium carrier. (Fay, *The Opium War*, p. 176).
[19] On the Black Joke murders, see above, Letter **177**, note 80.

necessary to bring the drug to China, where it yielded you a handsome profit. It was not without the most eminent risks, so much so that almost all our neighbours shrunk from encountering them.

The Chinese Government which promised imunities and forgetfulness of the past, on the surrender of our drug, having broken faith and expelled us, we considered ourselves justified, after some hesitation, on being no longer restrained by the pledge we had given to abstain from Opium business.[20]

On the whole, although the result proves, that you would have gained more by 60 chests than by the 30 that were bought, I think you ought to be satisfied with the very handsome profit actually accruing to you from a crisis of so much danger and difficulty.

I remain,

Sincerely yours,

250. James Matheson in Macao to William Jardine in London,

26 January 1842

My dear Jardine,

With reference to your letter of 5th June last alluding to Goddard's controversy with *Lyall & Co.*, for their having invested only the half, instead of all his funds in opium to China, in the alarming year of 1839, I enclose my letter on the subject, open for your perusal, after which kindly forward it. I hope you will agree with me, that under the circumstances they acted with prudent discretion on the occasion. Goddard has adopted a peremptory and offensive style of writing to them, which were there no obstacle, would of itself operate as a bar to their attempting to compromise the matter with him. Besides the amount at stake is too large for this; and their only safe course is to resist it, which I think they can do with success.

[etc.,]

251. James Matheson in Macao to William Jardine in London,

7 February 1842

My dear Jardine,

We are all quiet and in *Statu quo.*

Sir Henry Pottinger reached HongKong per Bleinheim on 2nd Instant and we expect him tomorrow.[21] Mr. Morrison is already in Macao, and we learn with

[20] This might well be the weakest argument in the whole letter.

[21] Having retaken Ningpo and Chusan, the British force, under the command of its senior officers, spent the winter holding its positions. (See Letter **246**, note 154; see also Gough's remarks in the following paragraph).

much satisfaction that Sir Henry disapproved of all objectionable proceedings that have been going on in his absence, more especially the Junk captures which are already discontinued. Whether he will attack the Chinese defences up the river is not yet determined. I suspect not; for in consequence of the Emperor refusing to treat with us, it is said Sir Henry is now for doing all he can to open the Ports and promote intercourse and trade with the natives along the whole line of coast. It is not likely therefore that he will interrupt trade at Canton. HongKong, Chusan and Amoy are to be declared free Ports, it is said.

I have a few lines from Sir Hugh Gough at Ningpo, of which the following extract is rather significant: 'We are in an extraordinary position here, one which the Home or India Government never contemplated and which may make it necessary to change the line of policy hitherto pursued. The Emperor, it would appear, is prepared to set his kingdom on the issue. Never was a gamester more certain of defeat.'

What he alludes to as extraordinary is that the Chinese troops are too timid to fight us and the inhabitants [in] no wise reluctant to submit to our rule.

No sooner has Mr. B. A Barretto resumed his duties in the office than Mr. William Stewart the head of the correspondence department has been seized with the small Pox severely at first, but going on favourably. You may believe it puts us to much inconvenience, and when I shall be able to get away,[22] (if at all), it is impossible to foresee—certainly not for a month. Kindly mention Stewart's illness, as the cause to any complaints as to remissness in correspondence.

Yours in haste,
very sincerely,

Sir Henry Pottinger returned to Hong Kong in February 1842 and stayed there until the end of June, when he joined the final Yangtze campaign. He moved the British Superintendency of trade from Macao to Hong Kong in recognition of the fact that the new settlement had started resembling a colony. Land sales had been effected, (though this had been done prior to his arrival and without any sound basis in international law), and new buildings had been erected. In May 1842, he received the home government's disapproval of the offices of Land Officer, Surveyor and Colonial Surgeon, and he therefore abolished these offices. He also received new instructions from Lord Aberdeen who 'refused to countenance any cessions of territory at the expense of China'. Pottinger then wrote back to say that the only step he had taken was the removal of the Superintendency of Trade from Macao to Hong Kong and that 'even that was forced on me by the extraordinary and unparalleled progress which this settlement has made. [. . .] I had no predilection for raising a colony at Hong Kong or at any other place in China, [. . .but] this settlement has already advanced too far to admit of its ever being restored to the authority of the Emperor'. (Quoted by Endacott, *History of Hong Kong*, pp. 33–34).

[22] A rare indication of James Matheson's impatience to retire and sail back home, after three particularly stressful years since March 1839.

252. James Matheson in Macao to Lieutenant General Sir Hugh Gough in Hong Kong, 5 March 1842

My dear Sir,

I have now the pleasure to enclose a statement of your Account Current, showing at your debit Spanish Dollars 1,362 dollars and a half, which I hope you will find correct; and you can repay the amount in any manner most convenient to you, either by an order on the Paymaster here, or on Madras or England, any of these modes will be quite the same to us. Accompanying are four statements of the little shipments we have made to you for Madras.

I have arranged with my friend, Mr. Coolidge of Canton to have your Tea pot, milk Vase, etc., etc., etc., made; and feel assured they will be completed in the best taste. For the milk Vase we have selected the model of a much admired Chinese Bronze highly ornamented with Dragons etc., and all will be in Chinese taste.

I am sorry to say the Doctors have suddenly ordered me off to England on account of my health,[23] and I propose embarking in a few days per *Tartar* for Bombay and Suez; so that I shall not again have the honour of writing to you from hence. But my nephew Alexander Matheson will be most happy to attend to any commands, which your Excellency or Major Gough may confide to him and he hopes you will do him the honour to occupy your former quarters in our house whenever you may return to Macao; which I feel assured, will be an occasion of triumph and rejoicing no less to yourself than to our country and all your friends; for the War in your hands cannot fail to come to an honourable conclusion.[24]

[23] This Letter **252** is the last letter recorded in the *JMArch.* out-correspondence to have been written by James Matheson from China. A letter written on 9 March 1842 by Alexander Matheson informs its reader that his uncle was sailing back home on 11 March. As a result, the correspondence of the two founding partners as preserved in the *JMArch.* virtually came to an end in March 1842.

The exchange of letters between James Matheson and William Jardine came to a complete stop, since they now both lived in London and saw each other frequently. As to the letters addressed to, or written by, either of them, they are few and far between in the in-correspondence. There was indeed rarely a need for copies of such letters to be sent to Hong Kong, where the Archive was left to accumulate from the date of the firm's foundation to the 1930s.

[24] The decisive campaign which concluded the Opium War was to come a few months later and is known as the 'Yangtze campaign'. Reinforcements arrived from England and India. By early summer, Gough commanded 10,000 men. On 18 May, Chapu (on the north side of the Hangchow Bay) was taken after fierce resistance. On 16 June, Woosung, at the mouth of the Yangtze river, was attacked and fell. Three days later, it was Shanghai's turn to fall. On 4 July the forces started the long and slow progress up the Yangtze towards Chinkiang which controlled the Grand Canal and the food supply to Peking and the north of the country. The Battle for Chinkiang was fought on 21 July. It was a major engagement where two thousand of the best Chinese bannermen fought bitterly to the death. The disaster of Chinkiang alarmed Peking. With its entire force in the Yangtze, the British controlled China's principal waterways. The country was throttled. The emperor realized he had to come to terms. He sent two plenipotentiaries, Ilipu and Kiying, to negotiate with the British. An initial meeting between he two sides was arranged on 9 August. But in order to avoid a repetition of any delaying tactics or of

May I beg you to present my kind regards and cordial congratulations to Major Gough[25] on his promotion.

I have the honour to remain, etc., etc.

253. William Jardine in London to Jamsetjee Jejeebhoy in Bombay, 29 September 1842[26]

My dear Sir Jamsetjee,[27]

I have been requested by one of my oldest and best friends in the Company's service to introduce to your [good] and kind offices [captain] John Campbell of the Ship *Scotia* which vessel he has commanded since she was launched, but owing to change of owners and other [circumstances] he is now out of employ with a numerous family and very slender means to provide for them. He is, however, an active, able, and trustworthy Commander, in good health, well-known to your friends in Bombay, to the Lyalls in Calcutta, and to our friends in China. Under these circumstances, destitute at home though willing to work, he intends embarking by the October mail for Bombay, and I beg most earnestly to bring him under your notice and bespeak for him as early employment as through you and other kind friends can possibly be procured.

---

agreements being subsequently reneged, Sir Henry Pottinger firmly refused to negotiate with anyone until documents showing their plenipotentiary powers were produced and found acceptable. The Chinese soon realized that the British force was ready and determined to attack Nanking (the former capital) if negotiations did not start in earnest. On 17 August, hostilities were suspended. On 19 Aug., a copy of the Treaty was sent to the emperor. On 27 Aug., Peking's permission to sign reached Kiying. The Treaty of Nanking was signed by the plenipotentiaries on board the *Corwallis* on 29 August. With China being forced to open to foreign influence, a page of history was turning.

The main stipulations of the Treaty were the following: the payment by the Chinese of an indemnity of £4,375,000 (21,000,000 dollars) in addition to the ransom of £1,250,000 (6,000,000 dollars) already surrendered; the opening of the ports of Canton, Amoy, Fouchow, Ningpo and Shanghai to British merchants, with permission for consular officers to reside there; the cession of Hong Kong island in perpetuity; the correspondence between the two governments to be conducted on terms of perfect equality; the island of Chusan to be held until full payment was received.

News of the treaty reached London at the end of November. Not unlike other newspapers, the *Illustrated London News*, chose to stress the commercial value of the Treaty: '[The Treaty of Nanking] secures us a few round millions of dollars and no end of refreshing tea. It gives an impetus to trade, cedes us one island in perpetuity, and in short puts that sort of climax to the war which satisfies our interests more than our vanity and rather gives over glory a preponderance to gain'.

(For details on the Yangtze campaign, the negotiation of the Treaty of Nanking, and London reactions to it, see Fay, *Opium War*, pp. 339–371. For the text of the Nanking Treaty, see **Appendix X**.

[25] Sir Hugh Gough's son.

[26] This letter is signed '*per pro* William Jardine'. By September 1842 William Jardine could no longer write his own letters, owing to his illness.

[27] Jamsetjee Jejeebhoy had recently been knighted. See Letter **247**, note 2.

Were I not satisfied, my dear Sir Jamsetjee, that you will derive as much pleasure aiding my friend as I have in introducing him, I should apologize for doing so. But I deem this unnecessary, and trusting to your warm heart and generous disposition, I have the pleasure to describe myself,

My dear Sir Jamsetjee,

Yours very sincerely,

P.S. I have to apologize for having employed my nephew, Mr. Andrew Johnstone, who is leaving with me a fair copy of the above. The fact is, I cannot write without a good deal of pain;[28] and I am sure you do not wish to add to what I already suffer. With Kind regards to Lady Jamsetjee and family, believe me,

254. William Jardine in Glasgow to Jamsetjee Jejeebhoy in Bombay,

2 December 1842[29]

My dear Sir,

I have been favored with your letters of 28th September and 13th October for which and their accompaniments accept my best thanks. The latter communicates the most unexpected News of Peace with China. What the commercial consequences of this may be it is difficult to foresee. It has excited the most extraordinary ferment and most sanguine hopes among our manufacturers and exporters. I cannot but think, however, that all forbids the expectation of a favourable result with the first rush of competition that inevitably occurs to any market newly opened or reopened.

The late pacification cannot be expected to make any sudden change in the long experience and deeply rooted dispositions of the Chinese officials to practise every sort of hidden extortion on Foreign trade, which their well-trained ingenuity will easily enable their doing without giving us a handle for the renewal of war, but short of this every chicane and evasion will be successfully resorted to to thwart and nullify the trading advantages to be expected from the Treaty. Hong Kong and the smugglers will, to be sure, be powerful engines of counteraction, on our part, but if slow operations, and not to the extent of preventing much loss and disappointment to speculators, what the future fate of the opium Trade is to be is a question of much interest. It will probably have been decided ere you receive this. I would be inclined to be in any case very timid and cautious in speculating in the drug at the high prices that will no doubt prevail with you.

[28] This is the first we hear of William Jardine's illness. His health must have started failing quite some time before James Matheson's arrival home. He was only fifty eight, but was not to recover from this debilitating and painful illness. See Letter **256** below.

[29] The Letter bears the marks: 'A true copy' of Jardine's letter' and below: '(signed) James Matheson'. See the Post Scriptum to the Letter.

You may rely on my most earnest endeavour in the compensation cause, and as my health is now greatly better, I propose proceeding to London three days hence for the purpose of looking after this and other affairs.

The pending Tea sales having opened with tolerable firmness, I think there will be a material reduction in that article, though we must have a considerable diminution of the stock on hand ere the market can resume a wholesome and satisfactory aspect. I should think low teas will become again the most precarious.

With kind regards to Cursetjee and your other sons and partners, Believe me, etc.,

P.S. I am deeply grieved that Mr. Jardine's symptoms are becoming more unfavorable and it is feared he cannot hold out long.[30]

1843

255. George Canning[1] in London to George Larpent, Bart.,[2] in London

3 January 1843

Sir,

I am directed by the Earl of Aberdeen to acknowledge the receipt of the letter which you addresssed to his Lordship on the 31st December on behalf of the Committee of the East India and China Association, requesting to be made acquainted with such provisions of the Treaty signed by Sir Henry Pottinger with the Chinese Plenipotentiaries on the 29th August as may have reference to the regulations of the future commercial intercourse between this country and China. His Lordship directs me to state to you in reply, that although Her Majesty has been pleased to ratify the Treaty signed by Sir Henry Pottinger it would be inconsistent with the general practice officially, to make known the contents of that Treaty until Her Majesty's Ratification shall have been exchanged against the Ratification of the Emperor of China, and the treaty cannot be considered, to be finally, concluded until that exchange has taken place.[3]

Lord Aberdeen, however, regrets the less that he is precluded from giving you officially the information that you request, as the accounts contained in the Public Prints of the late negotiations in China are substantially correct, and his Lordship desires me to state to you that Her Majesty's Government trust that the stipulations of the Treaty, and the arrangement which have to be made for giving full effect to it, will place the intercourse between the two countries on a satisfactory

[30] James Matheson added the ominous *Post Scriptum*.

[1] Viscount Canning was Under Secretary at the Foreign Office.

[2] For George Larpent, see Letter **182**, note 105.

[3] The exchange of ratification took place on 26 June 1843. See Letter **224**, note 16.

footing. Her Majesty's Government will spare no exertion to protect and promote the legal Trade of Her Majesty's subjects resorting to China, but Her Majesty's Government feel that the advantages which Her Majesty's subjects may derive from the trade with China must after all depend in a great measure on the manner, in which that trade shall be conducted by the parties who may engage in it. Her Majesty's Government would therefore call the attention of all such parties to the expediency of impressing upon those whom they may employ, that, at the commencement of the new era which is about to open to British Trade in China, it is of the utmost importance that the feelings and prejudices of the Chinese Authorities and people should as far as possible be respected, and that every endeavour should be made to conciliate the goodwill of the inhabitants of the country, and to inspire them with a favorable opinion of the British Character.

I am, Sir,

Yours most obedient and humble servant,

256. John Abel Smith in London to Jamsetjee Jejeebhoy in Bombay, 6 January 1843

My dear Sir,

I take the liberty to wish you many many happy returns of the New Year and to express my hearty desire that all prosperity and happiness may attend you.

Mr. Jardine remains in the same state nearly as when I wrote to you a month ago except that his bodily strength and physical powers are much reduced. He is now wholly confined to the Water Bed and has somewhat rallied since he was compelled by sheer weakness to give up the standing and kneeling positions, which he had kept for many weeks. I think of the certainty of the result just as I did, but I think it may be delayed for a few weeks if he is able to get sleep as he now does on the water couch.[4]

His resignation and fortitude are most extraordinary and really almost heroic.

I have taken the liberty to send you by a private hand a small parcel containing a book which I think possibly has not reached Bombay and which is the most beautiful specimen yet produced in England of that kind of Typography.[5] I hope you will think it creditable to English art and will allow it a place on your table.

Mr. Matheson tells me that he has written to you fully about opium claims. We shall doubtless by next mail be able to tell you the intentions of HM Government and though I am not sanguine in this matter I do certainly expect the immediate distribution of the six millions dollars last paid in China. This business will

[4] The symptoms alluded to here and in Letter **258** do not allow the reader to form a precise view of William Jardine's terminal illness. He may have suffered from a form of pulmonary oedema.

[5] This special volume was not identified.

engage all my attention as soon as Sir Robert Peel returns to Town after the Christmas holidays.[6]

The falling of the Quarter's Revenue excites a good deal of discussion but not much surprise. I attribute it less to the stagnation of Trade than to the fear, and apprehension, and general retrenchments in private expenses produced by the Income Tax.[7] The state of the country generally is improving.

I am, my dear Sir,

Your most faithful and obliged Servant,

257. James Matheson in Ashburton to the Electors of Ashburton

2 March 1843[8]

Gentlemen,

The unanimous resolution passed at a crowded and influential meeting of the Electors of this Borough, last evening, approving of my Political Principles, and the numerous assurances of support I have already received, embolden me to announce myself as a Candidate for your suffrages at the approaching Election.

I present myself to you as the friend and former partner of your late lamented Member, Mr. Jardine. My Political opinions are favorable to every measure of practicable and progressive Reform, and I profess myself the zealous and ardent friend of Civil, Religious, and Commercial Freedom.

My mercantile connexions will, I trust, enable me to promote the Prosperity of the staple Trade of your Town,[9] and if returned as your Representative, it will be my earnest endeavour, to discharge, with zeal and assiduity, every duty attached to so honorable and important a Trust.

It is my intention to pay my personal Respects to every Elector, which is fixed for Tuesday, the 7th Instant.

I have the honor to remain, Gentlemen,

Your most obedient Servant,

258. James Matheson in Ashburton to Jamsetjee Jejeebhoy in Bombay,

3 March 1843

My dear Sir,

You will hear by this conveyance the melancholy intelligence of the decease of our ever to be lamented Friend Mr. Jardine which took place without suffering at

[6] Payment by the government on the opium receipts was to be effected from 25 August 1843, over seven months after this Letter was written. See Letter **263**.

[7] The Income Tax of 1799 was abolished in 1816. Peel reintroduced the tax in an 'improved' form in his 1842 budget.

[8] Letter **258** immediately below should be read before this Letter.

[9] The manufacture of woollen cloth.

4 p.m. on the 27th ultimo from effusion of water in the chest. For the last few weeks his sufferings had become considerably alleviated and his mind continued clear and composed to the last.[10]

Immediately on the occurrence of the sad event I was suddenly called away to this place to canvas for the seat in Parliament held by our late Friend, an honor which I in the first instance declined but on its being represented to me that my presence in the House of Commons might be of use to the Opium Compensation cause, I could no longer hesitate in submitting to all the sacrifice of personal inconvenience which it entails upon me. Being now in the midst of a laborious canvas I regret being unable to reply to your valued favors by last Mail but hope you will kindly excuse me till next opportunity in the assurance that the furtherance of all your wishes and interests occupies my constant attention and will continue to do so. Our friends in Lombard Street will send you a copy of our Second representation to Sir Robert Peel respecting Opium compensation and hope you will again approve it.[11] No answer has been received up to the date of my leaving London.

I enclose a copy of my address to the Electors of this place[12] and hope there is no doubt of my success.

With kind regards to Cursetjee and your other sons and partners I remain, my dear Sir,

Yours most sincerely,

259. Sir Jamsetjee Jejeebhoy in Bombay to Alexander Matheson in Macao, 4 June 1843

My dear Matheson,

Since my last of the 25th Ultimo I have received your favors of the 1st, 5th and 8th of April and thank you for your kind attention in advising the sales of Cotton and Opium that the former is very miserable indeed. I never saw before such prices. However whatever you had done for us is satisfactory. I thank you for completing your undertaking on our behalf to our London friends. I expected at one time that you would make bill remittance to *Messrs. Magniac, Jardine & Co.*[13] for the remainder. The only object I have in view is the sale very slow, that the account you kindly sent us is very satisfactory that the only item of the half proceed of Cotton per *Tartar*, amounting to 28,481 dollars, you credit us instead of *Jamsetjee Jejeebhoy & Co's* European friends. Please carry the same in proper

[10] William Jardine was buried 'at his home town of Lochmaben in Dumfriesshire'. (Keswick, *The Thistle and the Jade*, p. 25).

[11] A copy of the 'representation' was not traced.

[12] See Letter **257** immediately above.

[13] *Magniac Smith & Co.* had become *Magniac Jardine and Co.* when William Jardine became a partner of the firm in 1842.

head and remit the amount to me as requested. We hope to expect shortly the supplementary account to enable us to close many adventures account and request your early attention if not already forwarded the same.

We will see what account of the Tea Market the next Mail will bring but what I am annoyed to see a sale of a few Boxes at a time. I hope you will attend to my wishes in regard of new understanding on our behalf to the both Houses far better to divide it in three different modes is suggested in my letter to you.[14]

The *Fort William* is now ready to start as soon as the Weather permit. On safe arrival please to do the needful. You may hold as long as you please the cargoes she now carries to your consignment. A large quantity put back to Northward and we have about 7,00 Bales among them.

We will dispatch the *Charlotte* about the end of this month. On safe arrival please to unload her and send her early to Manila if the sugar be ready provided for her, or if not send her immediately by the 1st october direct to Bombay with such Freight as you can procure as we have ready cargo provided for her and request your attention.

In reference to our N° 39 of the 30th May you will observe what we then anticipated respecting the 4th Opium sale, that the average Rupees 1,515. I have a private note from Mr. J. Lyall in which he states his opinion, the extract goes for your perusal. You will observe what he says that very small quantity will be exported for three months, to come to your place and he hopes prices will improve at your market and this was the case with us here after the departure of *Mor* and the *Inglis* but carry large quantities but after them none went to any consequence that the holder decline of selling at any price and if they sell it will be small quantity and raise a price to every 10 chests and much difficulty in buying 50 to 100 chests at a time and I apprehend in securing the *Anonyma*'s Cargo. Price now asked 1,030 Rupees for 5 chests and no seller of large quantity. A large quantity will remain here for ensuing season. All this will satisfy you. The ships to China are without Opium under these circumstances. Your better take good care of our property as well as belonging to our Friends under your charge and not to part unless you secure very good prices. All the petty shippers now cease of buying here in the face of 550 dollars. This will be another advantage in favour of holding any quantity remain with you unsold for most advantageous prices and request your particular attention. You better send a few hundred chests to the Coast as I had shown you the difference of what you rendered the Account Sale of 50 Chests Patna Opium per *Rover* and 25 Chests per same ship by *Rustomjee & Co.* of Calcutta. This Hint enough and I don't wish to say more on the subject hoping you will now render us favourable Account Sales.

[14] By 'the both Houses', Jamsetjee Jejeebhoy refers to his two principal agents in London, *Forbes, Forbes & Co.* and *Magniac Jardine & Co.* The letter explaining the 'three modes of dividing' the tea was not traced.

Thank you for the attention you paid in granting occasionably bills on England to Cowasjee Saporjee Taback[15] and hope your Patronage will be continued when he had occasion for. I have shipped some more young men in the *Fort William* to be exchanged and request your usual good office.

No appearance of *Good Success* yet. She was seen on the 19 Ultimo but she must have gone to Western. We hope hourly expected. She will have quick dispatch on arrival.

On regard of *Mor*'s return voyage if you deem advisable to send her to Bengal instead of Bombay I think do well according to Mr. Lyall's suggestions, if we could not put our hands at reasonable prices we have ample means to advance upon shipment. Think this and determine on the subject and now remain with great regard and esteem, My dear Matheson,

Your's Sincerely,

Extract of a letter from Mr. J. Lyall Esq. to Sir Jamsetjee Jejeebhoy dated 22nd May 1843

'You will be no less surprised than I am myself at the outrageously absurd proceedings of the Opium Dealers at today's Sale. [ ] extensive purchases gave rise to a scene of competition amongst the petty Brokers of the most [unprecedented] description and the biddings were kept up with a rapidity which the almost total absence of shipping Houses tended in no degree to check. Of the whole quantity sold today a very small portion was bought for immediate shipment and the probability is that nearly the whole will be held on hand until towards the close of the year when it will either be forced upon the Market at reduced rates or go on to China under advances though to effect the latter will be somewhat difficult since few will I expect be found to advance beyond 1,000 to 1,200 Rupees per Chest in the face of the very heavy supply we are to have next year. My own idea is that prices in China will rule highest about September and October from the very limited quantity that will go forward from hence during the next three months. We did not ourselves today buy a chest nor did any of the regular shipping Houses, prices being so much above the limits assigned by Parties in China; the few Chests I have orders to buy.'

260. Alexander Matheson in Macao to Sir Jamsetjee Jejeebhoy in Bombay, 24 June 1843

My dear Sir,

I think it best to acknowledge separately your esteemed favor of the 15th Ultimo.

[15] Cowasjee Saporjee Taback was not identified.

It is with sincere regret we have learnt the determination of the British Government with regard to the Opium claim.[16] Our own loss, I need not tell you, will be very considerable, but we are far more grieved for the losses which the unjust conduct of the present administration will entail on our constituents. They must do us the justice however to admit that the then senior members of our Firm did all in their power to protect their interests in China, a duty attended with no ordinary amount of personal fatigue and mental anxiety, and in England their exertions have been unremitting ever since the spoliation at Canton to obtain redress from the British Government.

In addition to this the then head of our Firm, Mr. Jardine, is now no more, and as any refund of commission[17] now made by us would to a certain extent involve a sacrifice on the part of those interested in his Estate, we feel it a more difficult matter to meet your suggestions.

My uncle states in his letter to you of 6th April, that he will adjust in England the refund of commissions on certain consignments made by you to Mr. Jardine's Firm,[18] on your favouring him with a list of them.

He has not written to me on the subject, and until I know his sentiments, you will at once see that I who was then a Junior partner, cannot with propriety enter upon a subject involving so much the interests of my seniors.

[16] The government was delaying payment on the Opium receipts, although 6,000,000 dollars had been earmarked for that purpose from the funds already received from China. The final parliamentary debate about the opium compensation question took place on 4 August 1843 (see Letter **263**). In the meantime, few weeks passed without the subject being raised in Parliament by various Members.

On 24 February, Lord John Russell 'wished to ascertain the causes of the delay which had taken place in the payment of the indemnity for the opium surrender to the Chinese. [. . .] The Chancellor of the Exchequer said that until the ratification of the Treaty with China, it was impossible that the government could act on the stipulations therein contained. The ratification on our part has been sent out from this country: it would probably be exchanged with the Chinese government, and then HM's government would be enabled to take the steps in fulfilment of the conditions of the treaty [. . .] so anxious was the government to prevent any delay in the settlement of the just claims of the opium holders, that reference had been made to India and China, and when the inquiry into the claims was completed, reports would be received from both these quarters, on which HM's government would be able maturely to form their judgment'. (*Hansard*, 1843, vol. 66, p. 1277).

Further similar questions were asked on 1 March. On 3 March, John Abel Smith asked the same question again and said that 'the papers of claim had been sent from China and India to London'; whereupon the Chancellor of the Exchequer replied that he had different information. On 6 March, John Abel Smith raised the question yet again. Sir Robert Peel replied that 'all papers would be produced about the price of opium'. (Ibid., vol. 67, pp. 265, 298).

[17] By asking for a refund of commission in order to mitigate his losses on his opium delivered to Captain Elliot, Jamsetjee Jejeebhoy shows that the honours which had now come his way had not gone to his head, nor had in any way blunted his hard-nosed business sense.

[18] By agreeing to compensate Jamsetjee Jejeebhoy by adjusting commissions charged in London by *Magniac Jardine & Co.* (a firm which he was soon to join as principal partner and which, as a result, changed its name to *Matheson & Co.*) James Matheson shows once more his flexibility and diplomatic sense.

I remain, my dear Sir,
Yours most sincerely,

261. Alexander Matheson in Macao to John Abel Smith in London

3 July 1843

My dear Sir,

I must not allow the *Mor* to take her departure without thanking you for your esteemed favors of 4th March and 6th April though from various arrivals and departures to day, I am more than usually pressed for time.

All those here interested in the Opium compensation question, are, with ourselves, deeply sensible of your unwearied exertion in their cause,[19] and while they regret that the result is not more favorable, they are quite satisfied that their friends have done all that was possible for them under the circumstances. We hope to learn by the next mail that Government have commenced paying the miserable sum[20] that has been with so much difficulty squeezed out of them.

I am happy to say that the Opium trade still continues to flourish here. The demand is brisk, and the prices for Malwa very remunerating, so that our Bombay friends will have a profitable season of it, in the event of our Government giving us no trouble.

We send you under a separate cover, copy of the proclamations issued by Sir Henry Pottinger after the ratification of the treaty. It is expected that the Tariff will be settled early next month,[21] after which a steamer will be despatched with Colonel Malcolm,[22] direct to Suez.

Sir Henry is quite silent even to his friends as to his intentions respecting Opium. My opinion is that he will not interfere with the trade so long as the Chinese anthorities do not press the subject upon him, and make no complaint of

[19] See above, Letter **260**, note 16.

[20] The government was to pay £64 on average per opium chest. See below, Letter **263**.

[21] Following the signature of the Treaty of Nanking, not less than a year of preparations and negotiations was necessary to reach the Treaty Tariff and general regulations of 22 July 1843 and the Supplementary Treaty of 8 October 1843.

The scale of duties was drawn up by Robert Thom, (*Jardine, Matheson & Co.*'s former manager of the piece-good department—see Letter **72**, note 41). In his letters to Lord Aberdeen, Sir Henry Pottinger mentioned that the scale of duties was 'in almost every instance more advantageous to the [British] importer that even the merchants themselves' had dared suggest. Similarly, 'the rates on exports proposed by Mr Thom are considerably lower than those of the merchants'. (See Fairbank, *Trade and Diplomacy*, p. 118, quoting Pottinger's letter to Aberdeen of 11 March 1843, 'Private'. FO 17/68, encl. 21 and 22).

[22] On Colonel Malcolm, previously referred to as 'Major' Malcolm, see Letter **241**, note 119.

the trade being still carried on.[23] I have often heard him say that if he were a merchant, there is no branch of commerce he would sooner engage in.

There is nothing doing in the way of Tea shipments, the stock remaining at Canton being very limited. I have a strong presentiment that Teas will, for the future, be dearer and more difficult to procure in any quantity than during the existence of the Hongs. We shall also be more exposed to fraud in every shape. We learn that nearly the whole of a cargo of tea shipped at Amoy, last Season, has turned out false packed.

I hope you and my uncle have fallen upon some plan for increasing your proportion of Tea sales. Sir Jamsetjee send us regularly your and *F. Forbes & Co.*'s monthly sales on his account and we are always surprised at the larger quantity they manage to get rid of. They are also more successful in getting higher valuations from the Brokers of the Teas consigned to them. It would be worthwhile trying to ascertain how they manage this. In addition to Jamsetjee's they have a large portion of Howqua's Teas[24] to dispose of, and we have lately ascertained at Canton that they are more successful in selling his Teas also than *Baring Brothers & Co.* I mean to have some conversation with David Jardine,[25] who has just landed from the *Red Rover*, on this subject.

If you can put any business in the way of *Matheson & Scott* [26] of Liverpool, I shall feel much obliged.

[23] The Supplementary Treaty of 8 October 1843 was 'the keystone of the legal arch supporting the new British order'. The document dealt 'with the most difficult points in the general settlement' Among these points was the prevention of smuggling (art. XII), the status of Hong Kong (art. XIII-XVI), and the local Hong Kong-Canton trade. (*Ibid.*, p. 121).

Fairbank's chapter 'The opium settlement of 1843' (*Ibid.*, pp. 133–151) gives a detailed account of the insurmountable difficulties faced by Sir Henry Pottinger in his attempts to negotiate an opium settlement. In the end the Chinese refused to legalize the opium trade, and the British would not agree to suppress it. The official impasse was as complete as it had been before the Opium war. In practice, the opium trade continued to expand, unregulated and unchecked, in this legal vacuum left in the Treaty of Nanking and the Supplementary Treaty. The practical compromise which was reached—with Chinese officials turning a blind eye to the traffic, and British officials in Hong Kong and in the Treaty ports offering no overt protection to the opium traders—was a virtual return to the *status quo ante*. As Fairbank puts it: 'By general agreement among officials of both governments and the opium merchants, the drug trade could flourish within certain limits, even though it remained beyond the reach of the law and of official tax-collector'. The 'opium settlement' thus undermined the official British effort to establish its entire foreign trade with China upon a sound legal basis. This anomaly was to continue until the Treaty of Tienstin in 1858, when the opium trade was finally legalized and taxed. (*Ibid.*, p. 151).

[24] Not surprisingly, the 'aged' Howqua, the senior Hong merchant, was thoroughly opposed to the new tariff regulations which, because there were no longer a prerogative of the Chinese, meant the end of the Co-hong. He died on 3 September 1843. (*Ibid.*, p. 117).

[25] David Jardine, (1819–1853), the eldest son of William Jardine's sister Margaret, later founded the tea trading firm of *Jardine, Skinner & Co.* in Calcutta. (22 index cards of letters are listed in the *BI*).

[26] *Matheson & Scott* was listed as 'Tea broker' in Liverpool. (*PODL*). The firm was founded by Hugh Matheson (1805–1875), a brother of the writer of this Letter, previously of *Lyall Matheson & Co*, Calcutta) in partnership with Charles Lyall. (See *BI* under 'Matheson, Hugh').

With kind regards to all friends, I remain, my dear Sir,
Yours very truly,

262. Alexander Matheson in Macao to John Abel Smith, Esq., MP in London

31 July 1843

My dear Sir,

I have now the pleasure of addressing you by the *Acbar* and beg to thank you most sincerely for your three kind letters of 6th May. I shall reply separately to that which relates to Mr. Lewes' vessels.[27]

Colonel Malcolm takes home the new Tariff and port regulations[28] which are really very moderate and favorable, and if strictly adhered to by the Chinese, our trade with England is sure to increase very much. I have however my misgivings, but we shall be better able to form an opinion as to the working of the new system after it has been in operation for a few months. We learn that the Hongs are still to be retained and that all vessels belonging to nations not having consuls in China, and probably also American ships, will still be secured by them, and the duties paid through them to the Government and the expenses of shipping off sea under the new system, added to the new duty, will be nearly 5 taels per pecul, or about equal to the old duty and Consoo charges.

The new Congos are arriving in Canton and David Jardine proceeds there in a few days to remain and superintend our Tea purchases.[29] Our present intention is to go on fine Congos, but we do not expect to secure them under last year's rates.

I long much to hear that you have commenced the system of holding small sales every week or fortnight, and always selling a certain portion at each sale. I am convinced it is the only way in which you can secure for us a fair proportion of the London sales and taking one sale with another we should always have the average of the prevailing prices throughout the year.[30] I trust the plan is ere now in active operations and that our stock of tea will never again be allowed to accumulate as heretofore in London. We shall lose heavily by our shipments in 1841–1842 ; though other parties realized a handsome profit on theirs sent to London in the same vessels—the *General Kyd*, for instance. David Jardine thinks that if we were to send home Mr. Humpston[31] to you he would be found very use-

[27] Mr. Lewes was not identified.

[28] On the new tariff and port regulations, see above, Letter **261**, note 21.

[29] On David Jardine's subsequent career, see above, Letter **261**, note 25.

[30] The plan advocated here by Alexander Matheson for his tea sales is a seller's early variant of the 'dollar-averaging' investment method, where regular, periodic sales were meant to iron out price fluctuations.

[31] Gervas Humpston, the firm's tea-taster had arrived in Canton with David Jardine in 1838. See above, Letter **156**, and Letter **166**, note 76. (*BI*).

ful in your Tea Department, and we can easily spare him, more particularly after the arrival of Joseph Jardine.[32]

The drug trade continues to prosper. On the new Tariff coming into operation all the Opium vessels under the British flag left Whampoa, but they are not interfered with outside the Bogue. Sir Henry Pottinger will do nothing adverse to the trade so long as it is not forced on his notice at the five ports. I trust therefore that it will continue to prosper for some years to come.

The trade in British manufactures (more particularly cotton) is daily on the increase at Chusan and Amoy, and unless the shipments to this country have been have been very great they are sure to answer. The demand is much greater than we looked for a year ago. In short, there will be an immense trade between Great Britain and China, in a few years, if the amicable relations now established between the two countries remain undisturbed. The only object now to be particularly desired, is the legalization of the Opium trade, and of that there is no hope during the reign of the present Emperor. Until it is legalized, the next thing to be desired, is that is should be carried on by parties of respectability as at present and not be driven into the hands of desperadoes and pirates,[33] as would inevitably be the case were Lord Ashley[34] and his friends to succeed in carrying their measures. No one is more conscious of this than Sir Henry Pottinger, who of course communicates his sentiments to Sir Robert Peel.

The final dividends from the Bankrupt Hongs are now in the course of payment, and we shall have to remit to you about 60,000 pounds sterling on account of Mr. Jardine's estate, as soon as our Exchange improves, say in November next. Bills are now scarce at 4 shillings and 5 pence and in order to avail of this favorable rate, we may probably be induced to draw on you somewhat in excess of our assets in your hands, but we shall make a point of placing you in funds by early tea shipments.

[32] Joseph Jardine (1822–1861): another nephew of Wiliam Jardine, and a son of David Jardine (of Muirhousehead). Joseph Jardine was a partner of *Jardine, Matheson & Co.* from 1845 to 1860. (Keswick, *The Thistle and the Jade*, pp. 262, 264).

[33] Continued control of the opium business by 'parties of respectability' was, on balance, what the 'opium settlement of 1843' achieved. As the Hong Kong colonial government afforded no protection to the traders, the opium firms had to arrange for their own protection against pirates, and continued the practice of arming their ships and using their arms in self-defence. The Victorian idea of 'respectability' when applied to firms included not only financial self-sufficiency, but also the ability to bear any economic pain with fortitude and in silence.

[34] On 4 April 1843, Lord Ashley, MP, had moved a resolution in Parliament for the suppression of the opium trade. The motion incorporated the principal arguments of petitions received by Parliament from the Wesleyan Missionary Society, the Baptist Missionary Society, and the London Missionary Society. However, the motion was adjourned, and it was subsequently withdrawn. (See *Hansard*, vol. 68, pp. 362–474)

Colonel Malcolm has been a most obliging and useful friend to us, during his stay in China, and should you ever have opportunities of paying him attentions or forwarding his views you will hereby be conferring a favour upon us.

With kind regards to all friends around you, I remain, my dear Sir,

Yours very sincerely,

263. James Matheson in Leamington[35] to Jamsetjee Jejeebhoy in Bombay, 4 August 1843

My dear Sir,

I have much pleasure in acknowledging your esteemed favour of 17th June, from which I am very glad to learn the welfare of yourself and family. Having been rather poorly in health for some time back, I have been chiefly residing at Brighton and this place, since I had last the pleasure of writing you; which has had the good effect of producing a complete recovery, and I am now preparing to rejoin my family in the North of Scotland, with whom I propose passing the next two months during what is called our sporting season; after which it is probable I shall travel on the Continent.

After various most unexpected delays, the Opium debate is to come on tonight, which I trust will be followed by the immediate payment of the very inadequate compensation the Government has agreed to grant.[36]

[35] The medicinal value of the spring water at Leamington Spa was discovered in the late eighteenth century. The town grew and became a fashionable resort. Queen Victoria granted the Royal prefix to the town in 1838.

[36] In the evening of 4 August 1843, Parliament voted at last on the following motion: 'That a sum not exceeding 1,281,211 £ be granted to Her Majesty to make good to certain holders of opium surrendered in China in March 1839, the amount of compensation due to them under the 4th Art. of the treaty of peace with China'. The members divided. There were 74 Ayes, 27 Noes, and the motion was carried by a majority of 47. (*HPD*, vol. 71, p. 283). Palmerston and John Abel Smith both voted 'no'. (*Ibid.*, p. 296).

Prior to the division, several speeches were heard, including one by John Abel Smith who expressed criticism at the amount of compensation (*ibid.*, pp 268–272). The debate had started with a speech on behalf of the government by Sir G. Clerk, the First Secretary to the Treasury. 'The Chinese paid to England 6,000,000 of dollars', he said, '[which] when brought to the Mint and assayed, was 1,315,158 £. The produce thereof now for the holders of opium was 1,281,211 £. The difference between the two sums being a deduction of 500 chests, which was procured from certain parties in Canton, to make up the quantity required. The whole of the amount paid by the Chinese government was in accordance with the 4th article of the treaty. It was now intended to pay the full amount of what had been received from China, under the articles of the treaty, to the holders of opium, as compensation, and as that compensation would amount to about 64 £ the chest of opium, he thought that the committee would approve of it as a fair compensation'. (*Ibid.*, p. 242).

The average compensation approved by Parliament of £64 per chest corresponded approximately to the sale price of the drug (250–300 dollars) in the spring of 1839, a time when the opium market was at its most depressed.

The tea market is rallying a little, and will, I trust, continue gaining strength as the season's imports appear to be more moderate than was expected.

I am much pleased to notice the satisfaction you express with one of my nephews having joined *Messrs. Magniac Jardine & Co.*s office, but am grieved to say the delicate state of his health will, I fear, prevent his remaining with them; which is a great disappointment to me.[37] I trust, however, you will henceforth have better reason to be pleased with our London friends than heretofore. You may depend on my doing all the good I can in your friend's affair, concerning which you have written in your private note of the 17th accompanying certain documents under a separate cover.

With kindest regards to all your family and partners, I remain,

My dear Sir,

Yours most sincerely,

P.S. I am much obliged to your kind promise to do all you can for the *Lanrick*.[38] She sailed 27th ultimo. Her figurehead is [a] copy of the marble bust of Mr. Jardine; and I am now having one carved in marble for you.

It is interesting to note that the 'difference' of £ 33,947 referred to above and relating to the additional chests 'procured from certain parties in Canton', was essentially owed to *Jardine, Matheson & Co., Dent & Co.* having already received its compensation in the form of a £63,000 payment on a bill drawn by Captain Elliot on the additional chests the firm had delivered to him. (See Letter **246**, note 158).

Actual payments to holders of opium receipts started being made by the Treasury on 25 August 1843. (Keswick, *The Thistle and the Jade*, p. 73).

[37] The nephew of James Matheson who had then briefly joined *Magniac Jardine & Co.* has not been identified.

[38] The ship was named after William Jardine's Scottish estate.

APPENDIX I

Out-correspondence

(Relevant material in *italics*)

Sub-Series	Number of volumes	Period	Origination and content
C1	4*	1818–1821	R. Taylor and James Matheson
C2	*5**	*1822–1830*	*Yrisarri & Co.*
C3	*4**	*1835–1847*	*Employees JM&Co.*
C4	*7**	*1830–1839*	*William Jardine — Private*
C5	*7**	*1831–1841*	*James Matheson — Private*
C6	*4**	*1841–1846*	*Alexander Matheson — Private*
C7	1*	1845–1848	Donald Matheson — Private
C8	8*	1844–1855	Hong Kong to Canton — Private
C9	10*	1846–1885	Hong Kong to India — Private
C10	*67**	*1800–1883*	*Canton, Macao, Hong Kong to India*
C11	*60**	*1810–1898*	*Canton, Macao, Hong Kong to Europe*
C12	2*	1868–1883	Hong Kong to London (Piece Goods)
C13	*31**	*1839–1883*	*Macao, Hong Kong to Coast*
C14	*14**	*1842–1882*	*Macao, Hong Kong — Local*
C15	*8**	*1842–1859*	*Hong Kong — Insurance*
C16	5	1881–1905	Hong Kong to India & Straits
C17	3	1870–1887	Hong Kong to Great Britain
C18	16	1878–1899	Hong Kong — General Foreign
C19	1	1883–1885	Hong Kong to Australia
C20	8	1877–1898	Hong Kong to America
C21	41	1871–1896	Hong Kong to Coast
C22	25	1871–1896	Hong Kong to Coast (Shipping)
C23	7	1871–1901	Hong Kong — Local
C24	9	1881–1819	Hong Kong — Book Office
C25	1	1887–1903	Hong Kong — Contracts
C26	1	1890–1902	Hong Kong — Properties
C27	1	1890–1902	Hong Kong — Shares, Dividends
C28	2	1893–1899	Hong Kong — Charbonnages
C29	1	1879–1883	Hong Kong — Swatow Sugar
C30	4	1880–1913	Hong Kong — China Sugar
C31	3	1874–1876	Hong Kong — Hong Kong Times
C32	9	1883–1901	Hong Kong — Indo-China Steam Navigation

*An asterisk denotes a bound volume of copied out-letters. Where there is no asterisk the letters are unbound press copies.

Sub-Series	Number of volumes	Period	Origination and content
C33	3	1900–1902	Hong Kong — China Mutual Steam Navigation
C34	1	1881–1896	Hong Kong — *Hong Kong Ice Co.*
C35	*2**	*1820–1838*	*Canton Insurance Company*
C36	*36**	*1835–1894*	*Canton Insurance Office*
C37	11	1874–1891	Hong Kong — *Hong Kong Fire Insurance Co.*
C38	1	1859–1860	Alexander Bird — Private
C39	1*	1880	J. J. Keswick — Private
C40	2*	1863–1868	Danish Consulate — Private
C41	14	1876–1895	Shanghai to Hong Kong — Private
C42	6	1872–1892	Shanghai to Coast — Private
C43	2	1873–1890	Shanghai – Local — Private
C44	1	1872–1879	Shanghai to Japan — Private
C45	1	1884	Shanghai to Korea — Private
C46	36*	1858–1908	Shanghai — General
C47	5*	1847–1870	Shanghai to Hong Kong
C48	6*	1855–1868	Shanghai to Coast
C49	2*	1859–1869	Shanghai to Japan
C50	1*	1854–1859	Shanghai Insurance
C51	5	1889	Shanghai — Piece Goods
C52	4	1870–1891	Shanghai — Book Office
C53	1	1881–1883	Shanghai — China Coast Steam Navigation
C54	3*	1847–1853	Canton — General
C55	1*	1865–1867	Hankow to Shanghai — Private
C56	1	1882	Manila to Hong Kong — Private
C57	1	1883–1884	Korea — General
C58	11	1865–1872	*Augustine Heard & Co.*
C59	3	1865–1868	*Thomas Hunt & Co.*

APPENDIX II

In-correspondence

(Relevant material in *italics*)

Sub-Series	Number of[1] letters	Period	Origination/Content
B1–B11: Unbound Series			
B1 'Private, Non-Local'			
B1–1	*8*	*1813–1838*	*Africa, with surrounding islands*
B1–2	*85*	*1813–1869*	*America*
B1–3	*31*	*1837–1882*	*Australasia*
B1–4	*283*	*1828–1871*	*Bombay*
B1–5	*390*	*1815–1867*	*Calcutta*
B1–6	*188*	*1813–1882*	*East Indies, Siam, Malaya*
B1–7	9	1828–1882	Europe, excluding Great Britain
B1–8	*171*	*1829–1873*	*Great Britain, excluding London*
B1–9	*69*	*1820–1867*	*India, excluding Bombay, Calcutta & Madras*
B1–10	*203*	*1814–1882*	*London*
B1–11	*11*	*1838–1850*	*Madras*
B2 'Private, Local'			
B2–1	104	1845–1872	Amoy
B2–2	*2,492*	*1813–1872*	*Canton*
B2–3	9	1865–1885	Chefoo
B2–4	9	1868–1879	Chiukiang
B2–5	*5*	*1835–1841*	*Chuenpee*
B2–6	*63*	*1837–1843*	*Chusan*
B2–7	*291*	*1813–1867*	*Coast*
B2–8	2	1865	Donkaloo
B2–9	626	1854–1880	Foochow
B2–10	41	1865–1872	Hankow
B2–11	331	1858–1867	Honam
B2–12	*1,090*	*1829–1886*	*Hong Kong*
B2–13	*15*	*1831–1837*	*Kapsingmun*
B2–14	7	1865–1868	Kienning, Kiungfoo
B2–15	25	1865–1872	Kiukiang
B2–16	34	*1835–1842*	*Kumsingmun*
B2–17	*51*	*1824–1838*	*Lintin*
B2–18	*665*	*1813–1872*	*Macao*
B2–19	*92*	*1834–1839*	*Namoa*

[1] The number of letters is given only for the unbound series B1 to B11.

Sub-Series	Number of letters	Period	Origination/Content
B2–20	2	1860	Nanzing
B2–21	5	1865–1870	Ningpo
B2–22	2	1872–1875	Pekin
B2–23	1,411	1844–1888	Shanghai
B2–24	1	1867	Swatow
B2–25	2	1870–1872	Taku
B2–16	9	1858–1872	Tientsin
B2–27	*27*	*1839–1840*	*Toon Koo*
B2–28	*17*	*1837–1867*	*Whampoa*
B2–29	23	1848–1853	Woosung
B3 'Private, Formosa'			
B3–1	1	1864	Keelung
B3–2	14	1863–1873	Taiwanfoo (Tainan)
B3–3	8	1864	Takao (Kaohiung)
B3–4	12	1864–1878	Tamsui (Tanshui)
B3–5	1	1872	Twatutia
B4 'Private, Japan'			
B4–1	11	1863–1870	Hakodate
B4–2	5	1870–1872	Kobe
B4–3	13	1859–1867	Nagasaki
B4–4	2	1872	Tokyo
B4–5	196	1859–1887	Yokohama
B5 'Private, Unplaced'			
B5–1	*84*	*1806–1886*	*Unplaced*
B6 'Non-Local'			
B6–1	185	1825–1881	Africa with surrounding islands
B6–2	*5,102*	*1821–1898*	*America*
B6–3	4,874	1894–1898	Australasia
B6–4	*13,191*	*1822–1881*	*Bombay*
B6–5	*8,560*	*1818–1893*	*Calcutta*
B6–6	11,166	*1821–1898*	*East Indies, Siam and Malaya*
B6–7	6,168	*1820–1891*	*Europe, excluding Great Britain*
B6–8	*8,192*	*1822–1898*	*Great Britain, excluding London*
B6–9	*1,604*	*1819–1898*	*India, excluding Bombay, Calcutta & Madras*
B6–10	*20,814*	*1814–1898*	*London*
B6–11	*2,153*	*1823–1881*	*Madras*
B7 'Local'			
B7–1	*4,298*	*1833–1898*	*Amoy*
B7–2	*12,924*	*1814–1904*	*Canton*
B7–3	*1*	*1842*	*Chapoo*
B7–4	810	1859–1901	Chefoo
B7–5	*600*	*1833–1863*	*Chin Chew*
B7–6	14	1853–1863	Chinhai

Sub-Series	**Number of letters**	**Period**	**Origination/Content**
B7–7	1,146	1863–1901	Chiukiang
B7–8	*8*	*1840*	*Chuenpee*
B7–9	*24*	*1840–1860*	*Chusan*
B7–10	*935*	*1825–1893*	*Coast*
B7–11	4,299	1846–1890	Foochow and River Min
B7–12	1,948	1861–1901	Hankow
B7–13	49	1876–1881	Hoihow
B7–14	352	1858–1869	Honam
B7–15	*14,713*	*1833–1905*	*Hong Kong*
B7–16	1	1883	Ichang
B7–17	1	1869	Kahing
B7–18	2	1876–1878	Kalgan
B7–19	*24*	*1830–1891*	*Kapsingmun*
B7–20	3	1861–1864	Kienning
B7–21	3	1863–1864	Kienyang
B7–22	1,266	1861–1886	Kiukiang
B7–23	*9*	*1837–1900*	*Kowloon*
B7–24	*1,355*	*1835–1856*	*Kumsingmun*
B7–25	*120*	*1823–1843*	*Lintin*
B7–26	74	1847–1854	Lookong (Luhwang)
B7–27	*8,313*	*1813–1898*	*Macao*
B7–28	1	891	Mukden
B7–29	27	1844–1860	Namoa
B7–30	470	1861–1901	Newchwang (Yingtze)
B7–31	1,052	1844–1883	Ningpo
B7–32	3	1855–1888	Pagoda Island
B7–33	52	1877–1880	Pakhoi
B7–34	29	1860–1901	Pekin
B7–35	1	1886	Pingtu
B7–36	3	1886–1901	Port Arthur
B7–37	10,820	1844–1891	Shanghai
B7–38	1	1861	Shung-van
B7–39	4	1857–1863	Suichune
B7–40	1	1869	Suyeada
B7–41	3	1861	Suykut
B7–42	2,910	1853–1894	Swatow
B7–43	5	1851–1856	Taitan
B7–44	5	1860–1871	Taku
B7–45	1,166	1860–1901	Tientsin
B7–46	*109*	*1839–1840*	*Toon Koo*
B7–47	1	1864	Tsingsan
B7–48	3	1901	Tsingtau
B7–49	4	1850	Wei-hai-wei
B7–50	2	1877–1878	Wenchow
B7–51	1,253	*1825–1885*	*Whampoa*

Sub-Series	**Number of letters**	**Period**	**Origination/Content**
B7–52	646	1844–1871	Woosung
B7–53	2	1883–1884	Wuhu
B8 'Formosa'			
B8–1	1	1865	Ao
B8–2	1	1855	Chochea
B8–3	64	1864–1881	Keelung
B8–4	1	1860	Penghu (Pescadores)
B8–5	56	1860–1901	Taiwanfoo (Tainan)
B8–6	209	1856–1881	Takao (Kaohiung)
B8–7	941	1860–1898	Tamsui (Tanshui)
B8–8	1	1861	Tungshan
B8–9	2	1872–1879	Twatutia
B9 'Korea'			
B9–1	118	1883–1884	Chemulpo
B9–2	25	1883–1884	Foong Tung
B9–3	3	1883–1884	Fusan
B9–4	1	1883	Fusan
B9–5	35	1883–1884	Seoul
B9–6	3	1884	Wanchichow
B9–7	4	1884	Wonsan
B9–8	2	1883	Unplaced
B10 'Japan'			
B10–1	54	1859–1873	Hakodate
B10–2	553	1868–1881	Kobe
B10–3	3	1879	Hirado
B10–4	1,527	1859–1886	Nagasaki
B10–5	9	1869–1870	Niigata
B10–6	36	1868–1870	Osaka
B10–7	19	1870–1886	Tokyo
B10–8	1	1869	Yagamuti
B10–9	3,668	1859–1892	Yokohama
B11 'Unplaced'			
B11–1	*5,723*	*1813–1900*	*Unplaced*

B12–B31: Bound Volumes Series

B12 'America – Hong Kong'			
B12–1		1897–1912	America
B13 'Calcutta – Hong Kong'			
B13–1		1893–1896	Calcutta
B14 'Amoy – Hong Kong'			
B14–1		1885–1887	Amoy – *Russell & Co.*
B14–2		1885–1886	Amoy – *Fearon Low & Co.*
B14–3		1887–1888	Amoy – *Fearon Low & Co.*

Sub-Series	Number of letters	Period	Origination/Content
B14–4		1889–1892	Amoy – *Fearon Low & Co.*
B14–5		1888	Amoy – *Fearon Low & Co.* – Tea
B14–6		1888–1889	Amoy – *Fearon Low & Co.* – Tea
B14–7		1890	Amoy – *Fearon Low & Co.* – Tea
B14–8		1892	Amoy – *JM&Co.*
B14–9		1892–1893	Amoy – *JM&Co.*
B14–10		1893–1895	Amoy – *JM&Co.*
B15 'Canton – Hong Kong'			
B15–1		1885	Canton
B15–2		1886–1887	Canton
B15–3		1887	Canton
B15–4		1887	Canton
B15–5		1888	Canton
B15–6		1889	Canton
B15–7		1889–1890	Canton
B15–8		1890–1891	Canton
B15–9		1891–1892	Canton
B15–10		1892–1894	Canton
B15–11		1894–1895	Canton
B16 'Canton & Macao – Hong Kong'			
B16–1		1888–1890	Canton and Macao – *Herbert Dent & Co.*
B17 'Coast Miscellaneous – Hong Kong'			
B17–1		1884–1887	Coast
B17–2		1887–1889	Coast
B17–3		1889–1890	Coast
B17–4		1890–1894	Coast
B17–5		1894–1895	Coast
B18 'Coast Reports – Hong Kong'			
B18–1		1898–1900	Coast
B19 'Foochow – Hong Kong'			
B19–1		1885	Foochow
B19–2		1885	Foochow
B19–3		1886–1887	Foochow
B19–4		1887–1888	Foochow
B19–5		1888–1890	Foochow
B19–6		1890–1893	Foochow
B19–7		1893–1895	Foochow
B19–8		1888	Foochow – Tea
B19–9		1888–1889	Foochow – Tea
B19–10		1890	Foochow – Tea
B20 'Local – Hong Kong'			
B20–1		1885–1886	Local

Sub-Series	Number of letters	Period	Origination/Content
B20–2		1886–1887	Local
B20–3		1888–1889	Local
B20–4		1890–1891	Local
B21 'Macao – Hong Kong'			
B21–1		1885–1887	Macao – *Margesson & Co.*
B22 'Shanghai – Hong Kong'			
B22–1		1885	Shanghai
B22–2		1885–1886	Shanghai
B22–3		1886–1887	Shanghai
B22–4		1887–1888	Shanghai
B22–5		1888–1889	Shanghai
B22–6		1889–1890	Shanghai
B22–7		1890–1891	Shanghai
B22–8		1891–1892	Shanghai
B22–9		1892–1894	Shanghai
B22–10		1894–1895	Shanghai
B22–11		1895	Shanghai
B23 'Swatow – Hong Kong'			
B23–1		1885–1886	Swatow
B23–2		1886–1888	Swatow
B23–3		1892–1894	Swatow
B24 'Formosa – Hong Kong'			
B24–1		1884–1887	Formosa – *Bain & Co., Dodd & Co.*
B24–2		1888–1890	Formosa – *Dodd & Co.*
B25 'Kobe – Hong Kong'			
B25–1		1888–1890	Kobe – *JM&Co.*
B25–2		1890–1893	Kobc – *JM&Co.*
B25–3		1885–1886	Kobe – *Browne & Co.*
B25–4		1886–1889	Kobe – *Browne & Co.*
B26 'Nagasaki – Hong Kong'			
B26–1		1887–1888	Nagasaki – *JM&Co.*
B26–1		1889–1894	Nagasaki – *Browne & Co.*
B27 'Yokohama – Hong Kong'			
B27–1		1885	Yokohama
B27–2		1886–1887	Yokohama
B27–3		1887–1888	Yokohama
B27–4		1888–1890	Yokohama
B27–5		1890–1892	Yokohama
B27–6		1892–1894	Yokohama
B27–7		1899–1902	Yokohama – *Canton Insurance Office*
B27–8		1891–1893	Yokohama – shipping

Sub-Series	Number of letters	Period	Origination/Content
B28 '*Indo-China Steam Navigation Company*'			
B28–1		1886–1889	*Indo-China Steam Navigation Company*
B29 '*Hong Kong Ice Co. Ltd.*'			
B29–1		1886–1901	*Hong Kong Ice Co. Ltd.*
B30 '*London & Pacific Petroleum Co. Ltd.*'			
B30–1		1890–1894	*London & Pacific Petroleum Co. Ltd.*
B31 'Semi-Official Correspondence to New York' (G. L. Montgomery, agent *JM&Co.*)			
B31–1		1886–1896	Yokohama – W. B. Walter (deposited 1950)
B31–2		1891–1899	Calcutta – *Jardine Skinner & Co.* (deposited 1950)
B31–3		1891–1894	Hong Kong – J. J. Keswick (deposited 1950)
B31–4		1888–1910	London – W. Keswick (deposited 1950)
B31–5		1891–1903	London – W. Keswick (deposited 1950)
B31–6		1897–1912	Miscellaneous: Chicago (*Fitch and Howland*) – Lyons (*Morel & Co.*) – Shanghai (J. Mackie, *JM&Co*) – London (*African Traders Co. Ltd.*) – *Commercial Bank of Scotland Ltd.*

APPENDIX III

Letter References

1827

1.	27.02.14	James Matheson to *Magniac & Co.*	*JMArch.*, C2–5, pp. 171–173
2.	27.03.01	James Matheson to John Purvis	*JMArch.*, C2–5, p. 219
3.	27.04.14	*Fairlie Bonham & Co.* to *Magniac & Co.*	*JMArch.*, B6–10, L.152
4.	27.04.16	J. H. Gledstanes to William Jardine,	*JMArch.*, B6–10, L.155
5.	27.04.16	J. H. Gledstanes to William Jardine,	*JMArch.*, B6–10, L. 160
6.	27.04.27	*Fairlie Bonham & Co.* to *Magniac & Co.*	*JMArch.*, B6–10, L. 162
7.	27.10.28	Alexander Matheson to James Matheson	*JMArch.*, B2–2, P.37
8.	27.11.09	Alexander Matheson to James Matheson	*JMArch.*, B2–2, P.41
9.	27.11.16	Alexander Matheson to James Matheson	*JMArch.*, B2–2, P.44

1828

10.	28.01.01	James Matheson to *Gregson Melville Knight & Co.*	*JMArch.*, C2–5, p. 361
11.	28.01.10	William Jardine to Hollingworth Magniac	*JMArch.*, B2–2, P.61
12.	28.08.22	William Jardine to Howqua	*JMArch.*, B11–1, P.35
13.	28.11.16	William Jardine to Hollingworth Magniac	*JMArch.*, B2–2, P.67
14.	28.12.06	Alexander Grant to William Jardine	*JMArch.*, B11–1, P.36
15.	28.12.29	James Matheson to *L. Calvo & Co.*	*JMArch.*, C2–5, pp. 11–12

1829

16.	29.02.25	William Jardinc to Hollingworth Magniac	*JMArch.*, B2–2, P.68
17.	29.04.21	*Fairlie Bonham & Co.* to *Magniac & Co.*	*JMArch.*, B6–10, L. 259
18.	29.04.12	*Finlay Hodgson & Co.* to *Magniac & Co.*	*JMArch.*, B6–10, L. 264
19.	29.05.29	*Spode & Copeland* to William Jardine	*JMArch.*, B6–10, L. 270
20.	29.09.15	James Matheson to William Jardine	*JMArch.*, B2–2. P.69
21.	29.09.17	James Matheson to William Jardine	*JMArch.*, B2–2, P.70
22.	29.12.22	Jamsetjee Jejeebhoy to William Jardine	*JMArch.*, A8–98[1]

1830

23.	30.03.21	William Jardine to Andrew Johnstone	*JMArch.*, C4–1, pp. 7–8
24.	30.04.14	William Jardine to Hollingworth Magniac	*JMArch.*, C4–1, pp. 32–34
25.	30.04.30	Thomas Weeding to *Magniac & Co.*	*JMArch.*, B6–10, L.361
26.	30.05.11	H. J. and R. Barton to *Magniac & Co.*	*JMArch.*, B6–8, L.52

[1] Series A8–98 contains 'Loose letters to Magniac & Co., January 1823 to April 1830'.

27.	30.07.13	W. Mathieson to *Fairlie Bonham & Co.*	*JMArch.*, B6–8, L.57e
28.	30.09.08	William Jardine to James Matheson	*JMArch.*, B2–2, P.78
29.	30.09.11	William Jardine to James Matheson	*JMArch.*, B2–2, P.80
30.	30.10.16	*Magniac & Co.* to *Fergusson & Co.*	*JMArch.*, C10–11, pp. 220–222
31.	30.11.16	William Jardine to Hollingworth Magniac	*JMArch.*, C4–1, pp. 48–50
32.	30.12.07	William Jardine to Thomas Weeding	*JMArch.*, C4–1, pp. 53–54
33.	30.12.24	James Matheson to Charles Thomas	*JMArch.*, C10–11, pp. 460–461
34.	30.12.30	William Jardine to Jamsetjee Jejeebhoy	*JMArch.*, C10–11, pp. 492–493
35.	30.12.31	*Magniac & Co.* to *Biny & Co.*	*JMArch.*, C10–11, pp. 498–500

1831

36.	31.01.17	James Matheson to W. R. Paton	*JMArch.*, C5–1, p. 1
37.	31.01.17	William Jardine to Hollingworth Magniac	*JMArch.*, B2–2, P.89
38.	31.01.28	William Jardine to James Stewart	*JMArch.*, C4–1, p. 78
39.	31.03.10	James Matheson to H. P. Haddow	*JMArch.*, C5–1, pp. 15–18
40.	31.05.25	Hollingworth Magniac to James Matheson	*JMArch.*, B1–10, P.7
41.	31.06.23	William Jardine to James Matheson	*JMArch.*, B2–2, P.90
42.	31.06.26	William Jardine to James Matheson	*JMarch.*, B2–2, P.91
43.	31.07.30	*Magniac & Co.* to *Carnegy & Co.*	*JMArch.*, B2–2, P.92
44.	31.10.17	William Jardine to Hollingworth Magniac	*JMArch.*, B2–2, P.95.
45.	31.10.17	William Jardine to Hollingworth Magniac	*JMArch.*, B2–2, P.96
46.	31.10.20	John Macvicar to *Magniac & Co.*	*JMArch.*, B6–8, L.122
47.	31.11.14	James Matheson to Hugh Matheson	*JMArch.*, C5–1, pp. 42–43
48.	31.11.04	James Matheson to Hugh Matheson	*JMArch.*, C5–1, pp. 44–46

1832

49.	32.01.28	William Jardine to James Matheson	*JMArch.*, B2–2, P.97
50.	32.02.24	*Baring Bros.* to *Magniac & Co.*	*JMArch.*, B6–10, L. 609
51.	32.02.29	Charles Millet to William Jardine	*JMArch.*, B2–2, P.98
52.	32.03.[?]	James Matheson to Hollingworth Magniac	*JMArch.*, B11–1, P.78
53.	32.03.02	William Jardine to Hollingworth Magniac	*JMArch.*, C4–2, pp. 3–6
54.	32.03.10	James Matheson to H. P. Haddow	*JMArch.*, C5–1, pp. 73–76
55.	32.03.11	James Matheson to John White	*JMArch.*, C5–1, pp. 79–80
56.	32.03.15	James Matheson to Mr Pearson	*JMArch.*, C5–1, p. 73

57.	32.03.18	James Matheson to Da Costa	*JMarch.*, C5–1, pp. 76–78
58.	32.04.07	James Matheson to Hugh Matheson	*JMArch.*, C5–1, pp. 98–101
59.	32.04.09	William Jardine to Alexander Grant	*JMArch.*, C4–1, p. 88
60.	32.04.17	*Smith Elder & Co.* to *Magniac & Co.*	*JMArch.*, B6–10, L.638
61.	32.08.10	William Jardine to de Vitre	*JMArch.*, C4–2, pp. 35–37
62.	32.09.02	John Macvicar to William Jardine and James Matheson	*JMArch.*, B6–8, L.242
63.	32.12.07	James Innes to James Matheson	*JMArch.*, B7–10, L.27
64.	32.12.10	*Canton Insurance Co.* to *Lyall Matheson & Co.*	*JMArch.*, C35–2, pp. 1–2

1833

65.	33.01.04	*Canton Insurance Co.* to *Fairlie Clarke Innes & Co.*	*JMArch.*, C35–2, pp. 5–6
66.	33.01.24	*Canton Insurance Co.* to Charles Thomas	*JMArch.*, C35–2, pp. 9–10
67.	33.03.27	Jamsetjee Jejeebhoy to William Jardine	*JMArch.*, B6–4, L.2868
68.	33.04.04	William Jardine to Thomas Weeding	*JMArch.*, C4–2, pp. 32–133
69.	33.04.04	William Jardine to Hollingworth Magniac	*JMArch.*, C4–2, pp. 130–132
70.	33.04.06	William Jardine to James Matheson	*JMArch.*, C4–2, pp. 34–135
71.	33.04.08	W. J. Thompson to *Jardine, Matheson & Co.*	*JMArch.*, B6–10, L.850
72.	33.04.29	John Macvicar to William Jardine and James Matheson	*JMArch.*, B6–10, L.889
73.	33.05.28	W. MacKay to William Jardine and James Matheson	*JMArch.* B7–10, L.32
74.	33.06.07	Horatio Hardy to *Jardine, Matheson & Co.*	*JMArch.*, A7–214
75.	33.06.26	Horatio Hardy to *Jardine, Matheson & Co.*	*JMArch.*, A7–214
76.	33.08.06	Carl Gutzlaff to William Jardine	*JMArch.*, B2–7, L. P4
77.	33.09.06	John Innes to *Jardine, Matheson & Co.*	*JMArch.*, B6–8, L.244
78.	33.10.10	Horatio Hardy to *Jardine, Matheson & Co.*	*JMArch.*, A7–214
79.	33.10.10	*East India & China Co.* to Investors	*JMArch.*, A7–215
80.	33.11.26	*Fergusson & Co.* to *Jardine, Matheson & Co.*	*JMArch.*, B6–5, L.1714

1834

81.	34.01.13	William Jardine to Carl Gutzlaff	*JMArch.*, B2–2, P.105
82.	34.03.11	Cursetjee Jamsetjee to William Jardine	*JMArch.*, B6–4, L.3211
83.	34.04.20	William Jardine to Thomas Weeding	*JMArch.*, C4–3, pp. 105–108

84.	34.04.23	William Jardine to John Thacker	*JMArch.*, C4–3, pp. 108–110
85.	34.04.26	William Jardine to W. T. Copeland	*JMArch.*, C4–3, pp. 110–113
86.	34.05.02	*Lyall Matheson & Co.* to *Jardine, Matheson & Co.*	*JMArch.*, B6–5, L.1839
87.	34.05.09	William Jardine to John Macvicar	*JMArch.*, C4–3, pp. 116–118
88.	34.06.20	Carl Gutzlaff to William Jardine	*JMArch.* B2–2, P.108
89.	34.07.02	Carl Gutzlaff to William Jardine	*JMArch.*, B11–1, P.127
90.	34.08.08	H. P. Hadow to James Matheson	*JMArch.*, B6–4, L.3419
91.	34.08.20	William Jardine in Canton to John Macvicar in Manchester,	*JMArch.*, C4–3, pp. 150–153
92.	34.09.25	James Matheson to John Purvis	*JMArch.*, C5–2, pp. 1–3
93.	34.10.09	Canton Chamber of Commerce to HM Government	*JMArch.*, B6–8, L.498
94.	34.10.10	James Matheson to James Scott	*JMArch.*, C5–2, pp. 6–7
95.	34.10.23	William Jardine to John Macvicar	*JMArch.*, C4–3, pp. 165–166
96.	34.10.24	James Matheson to HM Superintendents	*JMArch.*, B6–8, L.498
97.	34.11.01	James Matheson to Charles Lyall	*JMArch.*, C5–2, pp. 8–10
98.	34.11.27	Horatio Hardy to *Jardine, Matheson & Co.*	*JMArch.*, A7–214
99.	34.12.18	*Canton Insurance Co.* to Timothy Wiggin	*JMArch.*, C35–2, pp. 49–50

1835

100.	35.01.27	F. P. Alleyn to William Jardine	*JMArch.*, B7–10, L.71
101.	35.01.31	James Matheson to Lancelot Dent	*JMArch.*, C35–2, pp. 55–56
102.	35.02.25	William Jardine to Hollingworth Magniac	*JMArch.*, C4–4, pp. 8–11
103.	35.02.27	William Jardine to Thomas Weeding	*JMArch.*, C4–4, pp. 11–12
104.	35.03.09	William Jardine to Captain Rees	*JMArch.*, C4–4, pp. 19–21
105.	35.03.18	Manchester Ch. of Com. to *Jardine, Matheson & Co.*	*JMArch.*, B6–8, L.498
106.	35.04.10	Henry Wright to William Jardine	*JMArch.*, B2–2, P.111
107.	35.04.11	William Mackay to William Jardine	*JMArch.*, B11–1, P.143
108.	35.05.10	William Jardine to James Matheson	*JMArch.*, C4–4, pp. 52–53
109.	35.05.22	William Jardine to John Macvicar	*JMArch.*, C4–4, pp. 56–58
110.	35.05.23	John Macvicar to William Jardine	*JMArch.*, B6–8, L.498

111.	35.07.08	James Matheson to William Jardine	*JMArch.*, B1–10, P.15
112.	35.07.11	James Matheson to William Jardine	*JMArch.*, B1–10, P.14
113.	35.07.12	Hollingworth Magniac to James Matheson	*JMArch.*, B1–10, P.15
114.	35.07.15	John Macvicar to *Jardine, Matheson & Co.*	*JMArch.*, B6–8, L.607
115.	35.07.17	Lady Napier to *Jardine, Matheson & Co.*	*JMArch.*, B6–8, L.616
116.	35.07.21	William Jardine to Captain Jauncey	*JMArch.*, C4–4, pp. 80–81
117.	35.07.31	James Matheson to William Jardine	*JMArch.*, B1–10, P.16
118.	35.08.01	James Matheson to William Jardine	*JMArch.*, B1–10, P.18
119.	35.08.24	James Matheson to William Jardine	*JMArch.*, B1–8, P.6
120.	35.09.05	William Jardine to H. P. Haddow	*JMArch.*, C4–4, pp. 145–146
121.	35.09.05	William Jardine to G. J. Gordon	*JMArch.*, C4–4. p. 118
122.	35.09.07	William Jardine to Captain Ovenstone	*JMArch.*, C4–4, pp. 119–120
123.	35.10.29	Hollingworth Magniac to James Matheson	*JMArch.*, B1–10, P.19
124.	35.11.10	William Jardine to Captain Clifton	*JMArch.*, C4–4, pp. 160–161
125.	35.11.24	William Jardine to James Matheson	*JMArch.*, C4–4, pp. 173–174
126.	35.12.30	John Macvicar to James Matheson	*JMArch.*, B6–8, L.665
127.	35.12.30	William Jardine to John Macvicar	*JMArch.*, C4–4, pp. 190–191

1836

128.	36.02.16	William Jardine to J. H. Gledstanes	*JMArch.* C4–4, pp. 204–206
129.	36.04.16	William Jardine to George Moffat	*JMArch.*, C4–5, pp. 27–28
130.	36.04.26	William Jardine to John Macvicar	*JMArch.*, C4–5, pp. 32–33
131.	36.08.13	William Jardine to Green and Wetmore	*JMArch.*, C4–5. p. 91
132.	36.10.10	William Jardine to Macvicar	*JMArch.*, C4–5, pp. 112–115
133.	36.11.04	William Jardine to Howqua	*JMArch.*, C4–5, pp. 131–132
134.	36.11.22	William Jardine to Henry Templer	*JMArch.*, C4–5, pp. 144–145
135.	36.12.07	James Matheson to John Macvicar	*JMArch.*, C5–2, pp. 24–25
136.	36.12.12	James Matheson to Captain Larkins	*JMArch.*, C5–2, pp. 25–26
137.	36.12.24	William Jardine to John Macvicar	*JMArch.*, C5–2, pp. 35–36

1837

138.	37.01.21	William Jardine to Sir John Tobin	*JMArch.*, C4–5, pp. 163–164
139.	37.01.31	William Jardine to John Shillaber	*JMArch.*, C4–5, pp. 167–169
140.	37.05.03	James Matheson to John Abel Smith	*JMArch.*, C5–3, pp. 18–22
141.	37.08.11	William Jardine to John Shillaber	*JMArch.*, C4–6, pp. 78–79
142.	37.08.19	William Jardine to Captain Rees	*JMArch.*, C4–6, pp. 81–82
143.	37.08.26	William Jardine to Hollingworth Magniac	*JMArch.*, C4–6, pp. 86–88
144.	37.09.09	James Matheson to John Abel Smith	*JMArch.*, C5–2, pp. 89–90
145.	37.10.12	James Matheson to John Shillaber	*JMArch.*, C5–2, pp. 102–104
146.	37.10.18	James Matheson to Charles Lyall	*JMArch.*, B2–2, P.118
147.	37.10.20	James Matheson to Alexander Grant	*JMArch.*, C5–2, pp. 105–107
148.	37.10.20	William Jardine to Thomas Weeding	*JMArch.*, C4–6, p.109
149.	37.12.09	James Matheson to William Lyall	*JMArch.*, C5–2, pp. 134–136
150.	37.12.11	James Matheson to John Abel Smith	*JMArch.*, C5–2, pp. 136–140

1838

151.	38.01.02	*East India and China Association* to the Public	*JMArch.*, A7–215
152.	38.01.09	James Matheson to Robert Smith	*JMArch.*, C5–2, pp. 155–157
153.	38.01.23	James Matheson to John Abel Smith	*JMArch.*, B2–2, P.122
154.	38.01.24	James Matheson to John Macvicar	*JMArch.*, C5–2, pp. 170–171
155.	38.01.24	William Jardine to Captain Jauncey	*JMArch.*, C4–7, pp. 4–5
156.	38.02.12	James Matheson to John Abel Smith	*JMArch.*, B2–2, P.123
157.	38.02.13	William Jardine to Captain Rees	*JMArch.*, C4–7, pp. 9–11
158.	38.02.16	Warren Delano to James Matheson	*JMArch.*, B2–2, P.124
159.	38.02.28	James Matheson to George Moffat	*JMArch.*, C5–3, pp. 44–45
160.	38.03.13	William Jardine to Jamsetjee Jejeebhoy	*JMArch.*, C4–7, pp. 26–28
161.	38.06.18	James Matheson to Alexander Grant	*JMArch.*, C5–3, pp. 83–84
162.	38.07.06	William Jardine to Captain Parry	*JMArch.*, C4–7, p. 73

163.	38.07.27	James Matheson to John Abel Smith	*JMArch.*, C5–3, pp. 95–99
164.	38.08.10	James Matheson to William Jardine	*JMArch.*, B7–15, L.5
165.	38.10.06	James Matheson to Jamsetjee Jejeebhoy	*JMArch.*, C5–3, p. 107–109
166.	38.11.19	James Matheson to John Abel Smith	*JMArch.*, B2–2, P.139
167.	38.12.03	William Jardine to Thomas Weeding	*JMArch.*, C4–7, pp. 128–129
168.	38.12.05	William Jardine to Jamsetjee Jejeebhoy	*JMArch.*, C4–7, p. 131

1839

169.	39.02.15	Nathaniel Wallich to *Jardine. Matheson & Co.*	*JMArch.*, B6–5, L.2272
170.	39.05.01	James Matheson to William Jardine	*JMArch.*,C5–4, pp. 35–47
171.	39.06.13	James Matheson to William Jardine	*JMArch.*, C5–4, pp. 62–63
172.	39.06.23	James Matheson to Jamsetjee Jejeebhoy	*JMArch.*, C5–4, pp. 67–71
173.	39.06.25	James Matheson to Lady Napier	*JMArch.*, C5–4, pp. 66–67
174.	39.09.05	Charles Elliot to James Matheson	*JMArch.*, B11–1, P.193
175.	39.09.09	James Matheson to John Abel Smith	*JMArch.*, C5–4, pp. 131–134
176.	39.09.14	Palmerston to John Abel Smith	*JMArch.*, B1–8, P.12
177.	39.09.24	James Matheson to John Abel Smith	*JMArch.*, C5–4, pp. 137–141
178.	39.09.24	James Matheson to John Abel Smith	*JMArch.*, C5–4. p.140
179.	39.09.25	William Jardine to James Matheson	*JMArch.*, B6–10, L.2239
180.	39.09.25/27	William Jardine to James Matheson	*JMArch.*, B6–10, L.2240
181.	39.09.25/28	William Jardine to James Matheson	*JMArch.*, B6–10, L.2241
182.	39.10.14	W. Crawford to R.W. Crawford	*JMArch.*, B1–10. P.38
183.	39.10.16	James Matheson to J. W. Henderson	*JMArch.*, C5–4, pp. 143–146
184.	39.10.17	James Matheson to H. W. Hubbell	*JMArch.*, C5–5, p. 142
185.	39.10.21	William Jardine to James Matheson	*JMArch.*, B6–10, L.2246
186.	39.10.31	James Matheson to John Abel Smith	*JMArch.*, C5–4, pp. 154–155
187.	39.11.21	James Matheson to Mrs Turner	*JMArch.*, C5–4, pp. 163–164
188.	39.11.24	James Matheson to W. Jardine and J. Abel Smith	*JMArch.*, C5–4, pp. 181–184

189.	39.12.01	James Matheson to Charles Lyall	*JMArch.*, C5–4, p. 176
190.	39.12.03	William Jardine to James Matheson	*JMArch.*, B6–8, L.719
191.	39.12.14	James Matheson to Charles Lyall	*JMArch.*, C5–4, pp. 177–179
192.	39.12.14	James Matheson to John Abel Smith	*JMArch.*, C5–4, p. 179

1840

193.	40.02.06	William Jardine to James Matheson	*JMArch.*, B6–10, L.2251
194.	40.02.17	James Matheson to William Jardine	*JMArch.*, C5–5, pp. 15–17
195.	40.02.29	James Matheson to John Abel Smith	*JMArch.*, C5–5, pp. 23–24
196.	40.03.04	William Jardine to James Matheson	*JMArch.*, B6–10, L.2252
197.	40.03.09	William Jardine to James Matheson	*JMArch.*, B6–10, L.2253
198.	40.03.21	James Matheson to Jamsetjee Jejeebhoy	*JMArch.*, C5–5, p. 45
199.	40.03.27	William Jardine to James Matheson	*JMArch.*, B6–10, L.2254
200.	40.04.02/04	William Jardine to James Matheson	*JMArch.*, B6–10, L.2255
201.	40.04.11	'Santiago Thomasen' to James Ryan in Canton	*JMArch.*, B11–1, P.220
202.	40.04.26	James Matheson to William Jardine and A. Matheson	*JMArch.*, C5–5. pp. 79–80
203.	40.04.28	James Matheson to Carl Gutzlaff	*JMArch.*, C5–5, p. 47
204.	40.05.02	William Jardine to James Matheson	*JMArch.*, B6–10, L.2256
205.	40.05.04	James Matheson to Andrew Johnstone	*JMArch.*, C5–5, pp. 48–49
206.	40.05.04	William Jardine to Jamsetjee Jejeebhoy	*JMArch.*, B1–10, P.43
207.	40.05.11	James Matheson to Charles Lyall	*JMArch.*, C5–5, pp. 52–54.
208.	40.06.03	William Jardine to James Matheson	*JMArch.*, B6–10, L.2275(2)
209.	40.06.04	William Jardine to Jamsetjee Jejeebhoy	*JMArch.*, B1–10, P.45
210.	40.06.25	James Matheson to W. Jardine and A. Matheson	*JMArch.*, C5–5, pp. 105–106
211.	40.07.01	James Matheson to Jamsetjee Jejeebhoy	*JMArch.*, C5–5, pp. 101–102
212.	40.07.04	William Jardine to James Matheson	*JMArch.*, B6–10, L.2261
213.	40.07.19	James Matheson to J.W. Henderson	*JMArch.*, C5–5, pp. 113–114
214.	40.07.25	James Matheson to John Abel Smith	*JMArch.*, C5–5, pp. 106–109

215.	40.07.27	James Matheson to William Jardine	*JMArch.*, C5–5, p. 124
216.	40.08.03 a	William Jardine to James Matheson	*JMArch.*, B6–8, L.720
217.	40.08.03b	William Jardine to Jamsetjee Jejeebhoy	*JMArch.*, B1–8, P.13
218.	40.11.19	J. R. Morrison to James Matheson	*JMArch.*, B7–10, L.134
219.	40.11.26	Charles Elliot to James Matheson	*JMAch.*, B7–10, L.135
220.	40.11.29	James Matheson to William Jardine	*JMArch.*, C5–6, pp. 13–15

1841

221.	41.01.06	James Matheson to Charles Lyall	*JMArch.*, C5–6, pp. 42–43
222.	41.01.10	*Jardine, Matheson & Co.* to *Magniac Smith & Co.*	*JMArch.*, C5–6, pp. 46–47
223.	41.01–15	James Matheson to William Jardine	*JMArch.*, C5–6, pp. 51–52
224.	41.01.22	James Matheson to William Jardine	*JMArch.*, C5–6, pp. 58–61
225.	41.01.28	William Jardine to James Matheson	*JMArch.*, B6–10, L.2267
226.	41.01.30	James Matheson to William Jardine	*JMArch.*, C5–6, pp. 64–65
227.	41.02.19	James Matheson to William Jardine	*JMArch.*, C5–6, pp. 75–77
228.	41.02.26	James Matheson to Jamsetjee Jejeebhoy	*JMArch.*, C5–6, pp. 80–82
229.	41.03.03	William Jardine to James Matheson	*JMArch.*, B6–10, L.2269
230.	41.03.15	James Matheson to Jamsetjee Jejeebhoy	*JMArch.*, C5–6, pp. 104–105
231.	41.03.19	James Matheson to William Jardine	*JMArch.*, C5–6, pp. 107–109
232.	41.05.02	William Jardine to James Matheson	*JMArch.*, B6–10, L.2271
233.	41.05.03	William Jardine to Jamsetjee Jejeebhoy	*JMArch.*, B1–10, P.53
234.	41.05.16	William Jardine to James Matheson	*JMArch.*, B6–10, L.2272
235.	41.05.19	James Matheson to William Jardine	*JMArch.*, C5–7, pp. 8–9
236.	41.05.31	William Jardine to James Matheson	*JMArch.*, B6–10, L.2273
237.	41.07.05	William Jardine to James Matheson	*JMArch.*, B6–10, L.2276
238.	41.07.05	William Jardine to James Matheson	*JMArch.*, B6–10, L.2277
239.	41.07.15	James Matheson to James Abel Smith	*JMArch.*, C5–7, pp. 65–67
240.	41.08.01	William Jardine to James Matheson	*JMArch.*, B6–10, L.2278

241.	41.08.23	James Matheson to William Jardine	*JMArch.*, C5–7, pp. 121–125
242.	41.08.24	James Matheson to Jamsetjee Jejeebhoy	*JMArch.*, C5–7, pp. 118–119
243.	41.09.06	William Jardine to James Matheson	*JMArch.*, B6–10, L.2282
244.	41.09.06	William Jardine to Jamsetjee Jejeebhoy	*JMArch.*, B1–10, P.58
245.	41.10.04	William Jardine to James Matheson	*JMArch.*, B6–10, L.2284
246.	41.11.02	William Jardine to James Matheson	*JMArch.*, B6–8, L.722

1842

247.	42.01.10	James Matheson to Jamsetjee Jejeebhoy	*JMArch.*, C6–2, pp. 5–10
248.	42.01.25	James Matheson to William Jardine	*JMArch.*, C6–2, p. 24
249.	42.01.26	James Matheson to James Goddard	*JMArch.*, C6–2, pp. 26–30
250.	42.01.26	James Matheson to William Jardine	*JMArch.*, C6–2, p. 36
251.	42.02.07	James Matheson to William Jardine	*JMArch.*, C6–2, pp. 40–41
252.	42.03.05	James Matheson to L. Gen. Sir Hugh Gough	*JMArch.*, C6–2, p. 66
253.	42.09.29	William Jardine to Jamsetjee Jejeebhoy	*JMArch.*, B6–10, L.2297
254.	42.12.02	William Jardine / James Matheson to J. Jejeebhoy	*JMArch.*, B6–8, L.722

1843

255.	43. 01.03	Canning to Sir George de H. Larpent	*JMArch.*, B1–10, P.64
256.	43.01.06	John Abel Smith to Jamsetjee Jejeebhoy	*JMArch.*, B1–10, P.67
257.	43.03.02	James Matheson to the Electors of Ashburton	*JMArch.*, B6–8, L.724
258.	43.03.03	James Matheson to Jamsetjee Jejeebhoy	*JMArch.*, B6–8, L.725
259.	43.06.04	Jamsetjee Jejeebhoy to Alexander Matheson	*JMArch.*, B6–4, L.3997
260.	43.06.24	Alexander Matheson to Jamsetjee Jejeebhoy	*JMArch.*, C6–3, pp. 198–199
261.	43.07.03	Alexander Matheson to John Abel Smith	*JMArch.*, C6–3, pp. 209,216
262.	43.07.31	Alexander Matheson to John Abel Smith	*JMArch.*, C6–3, pp. 223–225
263.	43.08.04	James Matheson to Jamsetjee Jejeebhoy	*JMArch.*, B6–8, L.727

APPENDIX IV

Canton Petition, 24th December 1830

To the Honourable the Commons of the United Kingdom of Great Britain and Ireland in Parliament Assembled.
The Humble Petition[1] *of the Undersigned British Subjects in China*

Humbly sheweth,

That your petitioners having long submitted in silence to the oppressive and corrupt rule of the Chinese Government, consider it a duty alike owing to their country and to themselves to bring their grievances to the notice of your Honourable House, at this important crisis, when the regulation of British intercourse with China engages the attention of the legislature, in consequence of the approaching termination of the East India Company's charter.

While British intercourse with other considerable states in the world is regulated by international treaties, that with the Chinese Empire is abandoned to the arbitrary control of the local authorities of Canton, a venal and corrupt class of persons, who having purchased their appointments, study only the means of amassing wealth by extortion and injustice, equally unrestrained by their own, and unopposed by the governments whose subjects they oppress. For the attainment of this end, severe burdens are imposed upon commerce, unsanctioned by, and frequently in defiance of, commands from the Imperial Government at Peking; to which the most erroneous reports are made of occurrences in this remote province, while no means of counteraction by opposing statements, are in any way afforded to your petitioners.

From the earliest period of British subjects resorting to this Empire, trade has been the sole subject, a desire to promote which, and sometimes, (it must be admitted,) a nervous anxiety for its preservation, have subjected foreigners to privations and treatment to which it would be difficult to find a parallel in any part of the world. China was too remote from England, and the commerce was too limited to render it, in former years, a subject of much national interest; but during the whole course of the eighteenth, and still more during the present century, it has been gradually increasing, in defiance of Chinese restrictions, until it has reached a point of such important magnitude, as, your petitioners feel satisfied, will raise the anxiety of your Honourable House to place it, if it be possible, upon a permanent and honourable basis.

Your petitioners entertain the firm belief that much may be obtained from the fears, but that nothing will ever be conceded by the goodwill, of the Chinese

[1] Source: *The Canton Register*, Vol. III, 18 Dec. 1830, Issue No 25.

government. In confirmation of this opinion the attention of your Honourable House need only be entreated to the total failure of both the Embassies to the Court of Peking in every respect, except the high principle which was maintained in the refusal to acquiesce in humiliating and degrading requisitions; which your petitioners are convinced produced, a moral effect of the most beneficial tendency upon the minds of the Chinese. That these embassies were undertaken with a view to the improvement of the condition of British subjects in China, your petitioners are deeply sensible, and indeed find this expressed in the instructions from His Majesty's ministers to Lord Macartney. 'Under these circumstances it would become the dignity and character of His Majesty, to extend his paternal regard to these, his distant subjects, even if the commerce and prosperity of the nation were not concerned in their success, and to claim the Emperor of China's particular protection of them, with that weight which is due to the requisition of one great sovereign to another.' Your petitioners trust that His Majesty's government may ever be influenced by similar opinions. It is with considerable regret however that your petitioners make another brief extract from the same instructions, unhappily still descriptive of the condition in which they remain. 'Hitherto however Great Britain has been obliged to pursue the trade with that country, under circumstances the most discouraging, hazardous to its agents employed in conducting it, and precarious to the various interests involved in it. The only place where His Majesty's subjects have the privilege of a factory is at Canton: the fair competition of the market is there destroyed by associations of the Chinese. Our supercargoes are denied open access to the tribunals of the country and to the equal execution of its laws, and are kept altogether in a most arbitrary state of depression, ill suited to the importance of the concerns which are entrusted to their care, and scarcely compatible with the regulations of civilized society.'

The result of two British Embassies, in common with those of all other European governments, will forcibly suggest to your Honourable House, how little is to be gained in China, by any of the refinements of diplomacy. The whole history of the foreign intercourse with this country demonstrates that a firm opposition to the arrogance and unreasonable pretensions of its government, even with imperfect means, has, sooner or later, been followed by an amicable and conciliatory disposition. While the Portuguese of Macao maintained this independence, they were treated by the Chinese government with respect, and carried on an extensive and advantageous commerce, but when they adopted a servile course of policy, they were regarded with contempt, and a flourishing colony has gradually sunk into misery and decay. Even violence has frequently received friendly treatment at the hands of this Government, while obedience and conformity of it's[2] arbitrary laws, have met only with the return of severity and oppression. In the

[2] (Sic). This text contains several instances of the possessive 'its' being spelt in this way.

history of English commerce with China, many instances of this description exist. When Admiral Drury, in compliance with the reiterated commands of the Canton Government yielded up possession of Macao, which for several months had been garrisoned by a British force, the most contumelious and threatening proclamations were issued against him; and he was declared to have fled from a dread of the punishment which awaited him. About the same period, after a horde of pirates well-known by the name of 'Ladrones' had, for a succession of years, ravaged the southern coasts of the Empire, and committed numerous atrocities, their leader, a man of bold and determined character, was received in person by the Viceroy with every mark of respect, invested with a robe of honour, and ultimately nominated to an important official situation.

A British Admiral for his forbearance was despised and treated with indignity; the leader of pirates and banditti was, in reward of his atrocities, received with the most ceremonious attention, and was ranked among the nobility of the land. It is with no wish to advocate deeds of violence that these statements are made; but such is the people and such the Government of the Chinese Empire. This submissive spirit was exhibited in the most striking manner which can indicate the character of a nation when, at the last Tartar conquest this most ancient Empire of the world, containing so many millions of comparatively civilized human beings was subdued by its bitterest enemies, and yielded implicit obedience to a tribe of rude and ignorant barbarians.

Your petitioners earnestly entreat the consideration of your Honourable House to the fact, that the merciless and indiscriminating laws of China, as applied to foreigners, make no distinction between manslaughter and murder. In those cases (happily few) of the death of a native by the hand of a foreigner, the life of an individual of the same nation (it being immaterial whether the offender or not) is invariably demanded, without reference to the palliating circumstances recognized by Chinese law, as modifying the offence and its punishment, where natives alone are concerned. On all such occasions the Chief of the nation, supposed to be implicated, is required to find out the guilty person, to point out his name and deliver him up, that the local magistrate may try and punish him, which having been proved by melancholy experience to mean nothing else than summary execution, he is in fact required to select and surrender a victim for strangulation, to appease the sanguinary malice of this Government. Such a requisition admits of but one reply, since no foreigners in China have authority from their own governments to judge or deliver up even a guilty fellow subject: and, on the other hand, non-compliance is sure to be followed by a total suspension of trade with the nation concerned. The necessity of thus permitting the guilty to escape, in order to secure the safety of the innocent, is an evil deeply to be lamented, and loudly calling for the interposition of your Honourable House. It is much to the honour of the British Factory that, since the year 1784, when an innocent man was seized and executed by the Government of Canton, a firm and effectual resistance has been made against the enforcement of this unjust requisition, though such resistance has invariably given rise to suspension of commercial intercourse, and long protracted discussions with the Government.

While your petitioners acknowledge it is an undeniable principle, that foreigners should yield obedience to the law of the country in which they reside, they submit that this doctrine cannot be maintained in favour of a government which, like the Chinese, withholds from foreigners the protection of its laws, and whose power is felt only in a system of unceasing oppression pursued on the avowed principle of considering every people as placed many degrees below its own in the scale of humans beings.

Your petitioners will now briefly advert to some of the principal commercial disabilities to which they are subjected. English ships were formerly admitted to trade at various ports; Amoy, Ningpo, and the islands of Chusan and Formosa: but of late, the entire foreign commerce of this vast Empire has been restricted to the single port of Canton, where the exorbitant harbour dues operate as a virtual exclusion of the smaller class of shipping while the privilege of dealing with foreigners is confined to some ten or twelve licensed native merchants, such is the oppressive conduct of the local authorities towards these individuals, by a systematic course of constantly recurring exactions and generally harsh treatment, that respectable and wealthy men cannot be prevailed on to accept the privilege, though earnestly urged by the Government to do so, for the purpose of supplying vacancies arising from death and bankruptcies. The Government being thus unable to maintain, in an efficient state, the limited medium of intercourse which they have established, and prohibiting foreigners from renting warehouses, in which to deposit their cargoes, there is no adequate competition, nor any chance of obtaining a fair market value of a commodity; an evil the more deeply felt in consequence of nearly all imports for the year necessarily arriving about the same time, during the few months when the periodical winds are favourable in the China sea. From the moment a foreign vessel arrives, her business is liable to be delayed by the underlings of the Customs house, on frivolous pretexts, for the sake of extorting unauthorized charges – the duty on her import cargo is levied in an arbitrary manner by low unprincipled men, who openly demand bribes, – it is consequently of uncertain amount, and, by the addition of local exactions, exceeds by many times, the rates, prescribed by the Imperial Tariff, which appear to be in general, moderate, although so little attended to in practice, that is is scarcely possible to name any fixed charge except on a very few articles.

It is unnecessary to occupy the time of your Honourable House, by dwelling on the individual and national loss arising from this oppressive and corrupt system. It would be equally out of place to enter into a detail of the many studied indignities heaped upon foreigners by acts of this Government, and by the contumelious edicts placarded on the walls of their very houses, representing them as addicted to the most revolting crimes, with no other object than to stamp them in th eyes of the people as a barbarous, ignorant, and depraved race, everyway inferior to themselves, thereby exciting the lower orders to treat them with habitual insolence. Suffice it to say that no privation or discomfort, is too minute to escape notice, in the pursuit of this ever present purpose. Free air and exercise are curtailed, by precluding access to the country, or beyond the confined streets in the immediate vicinity of their habitations. Even the sacred ties of domestic life are disregarded, in the separation of husband and wife, parent and child, regarded unavoidable by a capricious prohibition of foreign ladies residing in Canton, for which there appears to be no known law, and not other authority than the plea of usage.

Your petitioners consider it a duty which they owe to truth and justice to declare to your Honourable House, that they attribute the evils which have been enumerated to the nature and character of the Chinese Government, and not to any want of proper spirit and firmness in the Agents of the East India Company, who have on various occasions opposed effectual resistance to many of them, which could not have been attempted by individuals pursuing their separate interests, and unconnected by any bond of union. The servants of the Company have insisted on being heard by the Government, and have maintained the right of addressing it in the Chinese language, when that has been denied to other foreigners. Privileges have thus been repeatedly gained, and the most serious evils averted.

The influence which the East India Company has acquired by its extensive dealings, furnishes the strongest evidence of the importance of foreign commerce to this self sufficient people. Your petitioners are however of opinion that, to place the commercial interests of Great Britain on that fair and equitable footing to which they are entitled, a higher authority is required, emanating directly from His Majesty, as a medium of communication with the Canton Government as well as with the Imperial Court at Peking; which would remove the impression prevalent among the Chinese authorities, that foreigners in China have forfeited the protection of their own sovereigns, as in the case with natives of China who leave this country. Your petitioners would anticipate the most beneficial results from the permanent residence at Peking of a representative of His Majesty instructed to act with becoming spirit in protecting the interests of his countrymen; an arrangement which, they believe, was considered of such importance as to be one of the principal objects of the last Embassy. And as the Russians, who conduct the trade on the frontiers between that Empire and China, have long had the privilege of resorting to Peking, to acquire the language in a college expressly established for the purpose, it is reasonable to suppose that the residence of British subjects would, if insisted on, be also tolerated, more particularly as they would no longer have to contend with the religious and political jealousy of the Roman Catholic Missionaries formerly established at Peking but now dismissed.

The successful termination of the Burmese war and the approximation of British dominion in India to the confines of China are well known in this country, and a remonstrance from the British Government would, your petitioners have reason to believe, be received with a deference and attention never yet accorded to any Embassy, all of which have been conducted on the erroneous principle of attempting to negotiate for that which, if firmly demanded, could not have been withheld, while the Ambassadors have been designated 'Tribute bearer' and recognized in no other light than that of public officers deputed by inferiors Princes to offer presents and acknowledge vassalage to the supreme Sovereign of the earth. But your petitioners cannot deny to the Chinese Government the credit of having hitherto successfully triumphed over European power and dignity. The ruler of the most ancient Empire has seen the representatives of the Monarchs of other countries bear tribute to his throne, and, in many instances, prostrate themselves in the dust before him, while he has treated their abject and submissive spirit with the general indifference which it deserved.

Unless through the direct intervention of His Majesty's Government, in communication with the Court at Peking, your petitioners fear that no material extension of British commerce, or effectual amelioration of the humiliating conditions of British subjects, in China, can be expected. If unattainable by the course suggested, your petitioners indulge a hope that the Government of Great Britain, with the sanction of the legislature, will adopt a resolution worthy of the nation, and, by the acquisition of an insular possession near the coast of China, place British commerce, in this remote quarter of the globe, beyond the reach of future despotism and oppression.

Your petitioners therefore humbly pray, that your Honourable House will take the premises into your consideration, and grant such relief as to our wisdom may appear expedient.

And your petitioners will ever pray, &c.

CANTON, CHINA, 24th December, 1830

Thomas Beale,	William Jardine,	A. Grant,
Jas. H. Rodgers,	James Matheson,	John Crockett,
William Dallas,	John Macvicar,	James Boucaut,
J.R. Morrison Junr.	James Innes,	J. Rees,
William Haylett,	John C. Whiteman,	Wm. McKay,
H. Wright,	R. Turner,	D.Wilson,
Thomas Allport,	C. Fearon,	H. Tudor,
Arthur S. Keating,	A. P. Boyd,	Richard A. J. Roe,
Fs. Hollingworth,	John Templeton,	Edward Parry,
Thomas C. Beale,	W. H. Harton,	Chas. Markwick,
Alexander Matheson,	J. W. H. Ilbery,	L. Just Junr.

Henry S. Robinson,
D. Manson,
R. Browne,
George Horback,
Burjorjee Manuckjee,
J. Henry,
R. Markwick,
G.R. Johnson,
Nasserwanjee Framjee,
Burborjee Framjee,
Jehangier Cursetjee,
Framjee Pestonjee,
Sorabjee Cowasjee,
Marvanjee Hormajee,

APPENDIX V

Canton Petition, 9th December 1834

To the King's most Excellent Majesty in Council, the petition of the undermentioned British subjects at Canton,[1]

Humbly showeth,

That we are induced, by the extraordinary position in which we feel ourselves placed in relation to the Chinese government, to petition Your Majesty in Council to take such measures as may be adapted alike to maintain the honour of our country, and the advantages which a safe and uninterrupted commerce with China is calculated to yield to the revenues of Great Britain, and to the important classes interested in its arts and manufactures.

We beg humbly to represent, that at the present moment, the commissioners appointed by Your Majesty to superintend the affairs of British subjects trading at Canton, are not acknowledged by the constituted authorities of this country, and that they are not permitted to reside within the limits to which their jurisdiction is, by their commission, strictly confined; while they are forbidden by their instructions to appeal to the imperial government at Peking, and are perfectly powerless to resent the indignities offered to their late Chief superintendent, or to compel reparation for the injuries done to Your Majesty's subjects by the late unprovoked stoppage of their trade.

Your petitioners are well persuaded that the powers vested in Your Majesty's commissioners were thus restricted with the express object of avoiding, as far as possible, all occasions of collision with the Chinese authorities; while it was hoped that, by maintaining a direct intercourse with the principal officers of government, instead of indirectly communicating through the Hong merchants, a sure way would be opened for the improvement of the present very objectionable footing on which foreign merchants stand in this country, and for security against the many wrongs and inconveniences which they have had to suffer in the present state of commercial avocations.

Your petitioners, however, beg most earnestly to submit to Your Majesty in Council, their thorough conviction, founded on the invariable tenor of the whole history of foreign intercourse with China, as well as of its policy on occasions of internal commotion, down to the present moment, that the most unsafe of all courses that can be followed in treating with the Chinese government, or any of its functionaries, is that of quiet submission to insult, or such unresisting

[1] Source: Matheson, James, *Present Position and Future Prospects of the China Trade, etc.* London, Smith Elder, 1836. Annexes.

endurance of contemptuous or wrongful treatment, as may compromise the honour, or bring into question the power of our country. We cannot, therefore, but deeply deplore that such authority to negotiate, and such force to protect from insult, as the occasion demands, were not entrusted to Your Majesty's commissioners, confident as we are, without a shadow of doubt, that, had the requisite powers, properly sustained by an armed force, been possessed by Your Majesty's late first commissioner, the lamented Lord Napier, we should not have to deplore the degraded and insecure position in which we are placed, in consequence of the representative of our Sovereign having been compelled to retire from Canton, without having authority to offer any remonstrance to the supreme government, or to make a demonstration of a resolution to obtain reparation at once, for the insults wantonly heaped upon him by the local authorities.

Your petitioners, therefore, humbly pray that Your Majesty will be pleased to grant powers plenipotentiary to such person of suitable rank, discretion and diplomatic experience, as Your Majesty, in your wisdom, may think fit and proper to be entrusted with such authority; and your petitioners would suggest that he be directed to proceed to a convenient station on the east coast of China, as near to the capital of the country as may be found most expedient, in one of Your Majesty's ships of the line, attended by a sufficient maritime force, which we are of opinion need not consist of more that two frigates, and three or four armed vessels of light draft, together with a steam vessel, all fully manned; that he may, previously to landing, require in the first instance, in the name of Your Majesty, ample reparation for the insults offered by the governor of Kwangtung and Kwanse in his edicts published on the occasion of Lord Napier's arrival at Canton, and the subsequent humiliating conduct pursued towards his Lordship, to which the aggravation of his illness and death may be attributed; as well as for the arrogant and degrading language used towards Your Majesty and our country in edicts emanating from the local authorities, wherein Your Majesty was represented as the 'reverently submissive' tributary of the Emperor of China, and Your Majesty's subjects as profligate barbarians, and that they be retracted, and never again employed by Chinese functionaries; that he may also demand reparation for the insult offered to Your Majesty's flag by firing on Your Majesty's ships of war from the forts at the Bogue, and that remuneration shall be made to Your Majesty's subjects for the losses they have sustained by the detention of their ships during the stoppage of their trade. After these preliminaries shall have been conceded, (as your petitioners have no doubt they will be,) and not till then, your petitioners humbly suggest that it will be expedient for Your Majesty's plenipotentiary to propose the appointment of commissioners on the part of the Chinese government, to adjust with him, on shore, such measures as may be deemed most effectual to the prevention of future occasion of complaint and misunderstanding, and for the promotion and extension of the trade generally, to the mutual advantage of both countries. Your petitioners believe, that if these matters shall be fairly represented, so as to do away with all reasonable objection, and the favourable inclination of the Chinese commissioners be gained, there will be found little disposition on the part of the supreme government to withhold its assent, and every desirable object will thus have been attained.

Your petitioners would humbly entreat Your Majesty's favourable view of these suggestions, in the confidence that they may be acted upon, not only with every prospect of success, but without the slightest danger to the existing commercial intercourse, inasmuch, as even with a force not exceeding that which we have proposed should be placed at the disposal of Your Majesty's plenipotentiary, there would be no difficulty, should proceedings on a compulsory nature be required, in putting a stop to the greater part of the external and internal commerce of the Chinese empire; – in intercepting its revenues in their progress to the capital, and in taking possession of all the armed vessels of the country. Such measures would not only be sufficient to evince both the power and spirit of Great Britain to resent insult, but would enable Your Majesty's plenipotentiary to secure indemnity for any injury that might, in the first instance, be offered to the persons or property of Your Majesty's subjects; and would speedily induce the Chinese government to submit to just and reasonable terms. We are, at the same time, confident, that resort to such measures as these, far from being likely to lead to more serious warfare, an issue which both our interest and inclinations alike prompt us to deprecate, would be the surest course for avoiding the danger of such collision.

You petitioners beg to submit that the mere restoration of the liberty once possessed of trading to Amoy, Ningpo, and Chusan, would be followed by the most beneficial consequences, not merely in the more extended field thereby opened for commercial enterprise, but in the rivalry which would be excited as formerly, in the officers of government at these several ports, to attract the resort of foreign merchants, and thus extend their own opportunities of acquiring emoluments from the trade.

With respect, however, to this point, or any other commercial interest that it would be expedient to make the subject of negotiation, your petitioners would humbly suggest that Your Majesty's minister in China should be instructed to put himself in communication with the merchants of Canton, qualified as they must be in a certain degree by their experience and observation to point out, in what respect the benefits that might be reaped under a well regulated system of commercial intercourse, are curtailed or lost in consequence of the restrictions to which the trade is at present subjected, and the arbitrary and irregular exactions to which it is exposed either directly, or no less severely because indirectly, through the medium of the very limited number of merchants licensed to deal with foreigners. As an instance of the latter, your petitioners may state the fact, that the whole expense of the immense preparations lately made by the local government to oppose the expected advance towards Canton of your Majesty's frigates after they had passed the Bogue, has been extorted from the Hong merchants; and as but a few of them are in a really solvent state, they have no other means of meeting their demand, but by combining to tax both the import and export trade.

We would further humbly, but urgently, submit that as we cannot but trace the disabilities and restrictions under which our commerce now labours, to a long acquiescence in the arrogant assumption of supremacy over the monarchs and peoples of other countries, claimed by the Emperor of China for himself and his subjects, we are forced to conclude that no essentially beneficial result can be expected to arise out of negotiations, in which such pretensions are not decidedly repelled. We most seriously apprehend, indeed, that the least concession or waiving of this point under present circumstances, could not fail to leave us as much as ever subject to a repetition of the injuries of which we have now to complain.

We would, therefore, humbly beseech Your Majesty not to be induced by a paternal regard for your subjects trading to this remote empire, to leave it to the discretion of any future representative of Your Majesty, as was permitted in the case of the embassy of Lord Amherst, to swerve in the smallest degree from a direct course of calm and dispassionate, but determined maintenance of the true rank of Your Majesty's empire in the scale of nations, well assured as we feel, that any descent from such just position, would be attended with worse consequences than if past events were to remain unnoticed, and we were to be left for the future to conduct our concerns with the Chinese functionaries, each as best he may.

It would ill become Your Majesty's petitioners to point to any individual as more competent than another to undertake the office of placing on a secure and advantageous footing our commercial relations with this country. We may, however, perhaps be permitted to suggest the inexpediency of assigning such a task to any person previously known in China as connected with commerce conducted under the trammels and degradations to which it has hitherto been subjected, or to anyone, in short, who has had the misfortune, either in a public or private capacity, to endure insult or injury from Chinese authorities. Equally inexpedient would it be, as appears to our petitioners, to treat with any functionary not specially nominated by the Imperial cabinet, whose constant course of corrupt and oppressive conduct forms a prominent ground of complaint; or to permit any future commissioner to set foot on the shore of China, until ample assurance is afforded of a reception and treatment suitable to the dignity of a minister of Your Majesty, and the honour of an empire that acknowledges no superior on earth.

And your petitioners shall ever pray, &c. . .

Canton, 9th December, 1834.

[Signed by thirty five of about forty five individuals, composing the resident British trading Community, by all the Commanders of the East India ships who revisited Canton after the opening of the trade, and by several other commanders and traders, – making in all eighty-eight signatures.]

APPENDIX VI
Glasgow Petition, 2nd June 1835

Unto the Right Hon. Lord Viscount Melbourne, First Lord of his Majesty's Treasury, &c.&c.&c.
The memorial of the Glasgow East India Association[1]

Respectfully Sheweth,

That while your memorialists feel deeply sensible of the value of the great measure of Parliament, by which the China seas were opened to the enterprise of the British Nation, they feel themselves called upon to represent to your Lordship the importance of having trade with China placed on a more secure footing than it at present enjoys.

Your memorialists lament the unfortunate result of the late Lord Napier's mission to China, by which the position of Great Britain with that nation has not been improved. Now as formerly, personal liberty is quite insecure, and the British merchant possesses no kind of control over the sale or realization of his property. The goods of British traders must be passed for sale wholly out of the hands of the owner into those of the Hong merchants upon whom the owner possesses no check whatever. The trade is subjected to numerous duties and heavy exactions, to rate and the mode of charging which are arbitrary, and for the payment of a large proportion of which the Hong merchants are held responsible by the Chinese government, thus placing in jeopardy the whole property of British subjects and others, for debts due to government by these Hong merchants, the majority of whom it is notorious are in arrears for years past, and are in an insolvent state.

These and other grievances will prevent the free trade of Great Britain and China from expanding itself with the rapidity and to the extent which the immense scope afforded by the latter country, and the liberty lately granted by the British legislature, would otherwise not fail to induce.

Your memorialists therefore submit to your Lordship, that it would be of incalculable benefit to this country and our Indian possessions, were it practicable to devise means of establishing such a treaty of amity and commerce as would remove the disadvantages under which the trade at present labours; including also, if possible, a restoration of the privileges formerly possessed of trading to Amoy and other ports on the east coast of China.

While your memorialists forbear recommending any particular method of attaining this end, surrounded as the question is with difficulty, they cannot omit

[1] Source: see **Appendix V**.

stating to your Lordship, that in their opinion the object intended is much more likely to be accomplished by a direct application to the Court at Pekin, than by negotiation through inferior officers of the Chinese government.

Your memorialists presume further to suggest to your Lordship, that failing a satisfactory arrangement with the Chinese government, it would be of the greatest advantage to British trade in that part of the world were His Majesty's government to obtain one or more of the islands near to China, as an emporium for carrying on commerce free from the exaction, control or annoyance of the Chinese government. In the conviction that this important subject will receive due consideration from your lordship, the memorialists, as in duty bound, will ever pray.

Signed on behalf of the East India Association of the City of Glasgow.

Kirkman Finlay, Chairman.
2nd June 1835.

APPENDIX VII
Liverpool Petition, February 1836

To the Right Honourable The Lord Viscount Melbourne, First Lord of his Majesty's Treasury:
The memorial of the Liverpool East India Association[1]

Respectfully Sheweth,

That your memorialists view, with serious uneasiness, the unprotected state in which the extensive trade between this country and China is placed, especially since the failure of the mission of Lord Napier.

This trade labours under two great evils, from which arise most of the other grievances by which it is oppressed: – first, the imposition, by the Canton local officers, of unauthorized and arbitrary duties, greatly exceeding the established tariff. And secondly, the restriction of the trade to ten or twelve Chinese, under the name of Hong merchants, most of whom are in embarrassed circumstances. To these Hong merchants all imports must be passed for sale, wholly out of the owner's custody and control, and [whilst] they thus monopolize the trade of British subjects, they are invested with the inconsistent power of governing them under the plea that Europeans are a barbarian and degraded race, unfit to be placed within the pale of Chinese law, and therefore not to be allowed to approach the tribunals and established authorities of the country. Hence results a systematic denial of justice, accompanied by an endless train of wrongs and disabilities, which greatly hinders the natural progress of trade, which they assume the right to suspend entirely at any moment, whenever they may be desirous of enforcing the submission of the foreigners to their irregular proceedings. This power they recently exercised with the late Lord Napier, on the mere ground of his Lordship residing in Canton; a proceeding which it is important to distinguish from the more serious events which followed on His Majesty's ships returning fire of the Chinese ports when on their progress to join the merchant shipping at Whampoa.

Should these indignities offered to His Majesty's representative, terminating in his Lordship's death, and the severe losses occasioned to British merchants and shipowners, from the stoppage of trade which then occurred, be allowed to pass without effectual remonstrance on the part of His Majesty's government, your memorialists apprehend not only a material aggravation of existing evils, but the strongest probability of constant collisions and interruptions of trade, equally prejudicial to British merchants, as to the immense revenue derivable from that source to His Majesty's Exchequer.

[1] Source: See **Appendix V**.

From the professions of goodwill towards foreigners, uniformally expressed in Imperial edicts, and the redress afforded in the rare instances in which an appeal to the supreme government was formerly practicable, your memorialists are impressed with a conviction that the grievances under which the trade is suffering, are attributable, rather to the corrupt administration of the Canton local officers, than to any adverse feeling on the part of the Imperial cabinet.

Your memorialists will only add, that trade for which they thus solicit protection, employs about six millions sterling of British capital, and ninety thousand tons of shipping, besides yielding and annual revenue of four to five millions sterling, on the single commodity of tea; while it supplies to a great extent the article of raw silk, now become indispensable to a rising and important branch of British manufactures.

Your memorialists, therefore, earnestly pray, that your Lordship will adopt such measure as may secure for British commerce and British subjects in China, the same degree of protection, which His Majesty's government extends to them in other foreign countries.

Liverpool, February 1836

APPENDIX VIII

Manchester Petition, February 1836

To the Right Honourable The Lord Viscount Melbourne, First Commissioner of his Majesty's Treasury, &c., and
The Right Honourable the Lord Palmerston, M.P., His Majesty's Secretary of State for Foreign Affairs, &c.,&c.,

The memorial of the President, Vice President, and Directors, of the Chamber of Commerce and Manufacturers at Manchester,[1]

Sheweth,

That your memorialists beg to draw your Lordships attention to the great importance of the trade to China, to the mercantile, manufacturing, and shipping interests of Great Britain, and to the unprotected situation of our commerce in that country, and of our fellow-subjects resident in China, through whose medium the trade is conducted.

That the trade appears to your memorialists, to be capable of great extension and of increased advantages to this country. Its present importance may be briefly brought to your Lordships notice.

It affords employment for nearly one hundred thousand tons of British shipping. It affords a market for the manufactures of this country to a large and rapidly increasing amount, and for the production of our Indian possessions, to the extent, it is believed, of upwards of three millions sterling per annum, which enables our Indian subjects to consume our manufactures on a largely increased scale.

That no country presents to us the basis of a more legitimate and mutually advantageous trade than China; for the productions of that country, are as admirably suited to our wants and necessities, as ours are to theirs. The returns which China presents to us, for these large imports from Great Britain and India, are principally teas and raw silk. That the value of raw silk imported from China, exceeds one million of pounds sterling per annum, the want of which would greatly paralyse a most important and growing manufacture.

That your memorialists cannot contemplate without the most serious alarm, the uncertain and unprotected state, in which this most important trade is placed, more particularly since the failure of Lord Napier's mission.

That this large and valuable trade is, at the present moment, without any protection, and subjected to the arbitrary exactions of the Hong merchants, (a body

[1] Source: see **Appendix V**.

of men through whom alone our transactions are permitted to be conducted, nearly all of them in embarrassed circumstances, and many of them insolvent,) and of the corrupt local officers at Canton, whose exactions, it is believed, are contrary to the laws of the empire, and to the wishes of the government.

That the trade is liable at any moment to be stopped by the caprice of the Hong merchants and the local government, whose exactions, beyond what the law authorizes, are frequent.

That British property is daily in jeopardy; our countrymen daily subjected to insult; our Sovereign, in the person of his representative, the late Lord Napier, has been subjected to indignity; our industry is liable to be paralysed; our revenue exposed to the loss of from four to five millions sterling a-year. This accumulation of evils your memorialists beg most respectfully, but most earnestly to submit, calls for the protecting influence of the British government, which it is believed, will prove more effective, if directed to the supreme government, than through the corrupt and distant medium of the inferior officers at Canton.

Your memorialists, therefore, humbly pray that your Lordships will take into your early and serious consideration, the nature of our political relations with China, and that your Lordships will adopt such measure, as, in your wisdom may be considered most effectual, for the protection of British subjects resident in China, and the property entrusted to their care.

And as in duty bound they will ever pray.

Manchester, February, 1836.

APPENDIX IX

East India Company Ships, their Managing Owners and Commanders 1829–1830[1]

Name of ship	tonnage	Managing owner	Commander
Tho. Coutts	1,334	S. Marjoribanks	Alex Chrystie
Duchess of Atholl	1,330	W. E. Ferrers	E. M. Daniell
Dunira	1,325	Geo. Palmer	J. P. Wilson
William Fairlie	1,348	Joseph Hare	Thomas Blair
Abercr. Robinson	1,330	H. Bonham	John Innes
Macqueen	1,333	John Campbell	Robert Lindsay
Orwell	1,335	Matthew Isacke	Robert Isacke
Reliance	1,416	John F. Timins	C. S. Timms
General Harris	1,283	James Sims	Joseph Stanton
Marquis Camden	1,261	W. C. Drysdale	Thomas Larkins
Edinburgh	1,325	H. Bonham	Henry Bax
Berwickshire	1,332	S. Marjoribanks	F. Madan
London	1,332	Company's ship	Timothy Smith
Castle Huntly	1,322	J. H. Gledstanes	H. A. Drummond
George IV	1,329	Company's ship	T. W. Barrow
Lord Lowther	1,332	H. Blanshard	R. C. Fowler
Earl of Balcarras	1,417	Company's ship	B. Broughton
Sir David Scott	1,324	Joseph Hare	D. J. Ward
Canning	1,326	Company's ship	Philip Baylis
Astell	871	S. Marjoribanks	J. Lawrence
Bengal Merchant	503	*Sedgwick & Co.*	G. R. Fox
Lady Kendway	583	G. F. Young	L. W. Moncrieff
Susan	572	Thos. Ward	Geo. Holiday
Protector	511	Geo Waugh	Geo. Waugh
Lady East	648	Wm. Richardson	Geo. Denny
Ann & Amelia	586	Joseph Somes	W. Richards
Malcolm	605	R. W. Eyles	James Eyles
Marquis of Hastings	452	Joseph Somes	Joseph Short
Henry Porcher	485	G, F, Young	G. F. Redman
Recovery	493	John Chapman	H. C. Chapman
Stakesby	437	Aaron Chapman	J. Johnson
Roxburgh Castle	599	*Wigram & Co.*	T. Buttershaw
Maitland	648	Joseph Somes	J. J. Brown
Buckinghamshire	1,369	Company's ship	R. Glasspoole
Marquis of Huntley	1,348	Thomas Ward	John Hine
Lady Melville	1,263	O. Wigram	Robert Clifford
Thames	1,330	Henry Blanshard	James K. Forbes

[1] *EIRD*, 1831, (viii–ix)

Name of ship	**tonnage**	**Managing owner**	**Commander**
Duke of Sussex	1,336	S. Marjoribanks	W. H. Whitehead
Farquharson	1,326	John C. Lochner	J, Cruickshank
General Kyd	1,286	Robert Small	Alex Nairn
Repulse	1,334	John Timms	Henry Gribble
Vansittart	1,273	Joseph Hare	Robert Scott
Herefordshire	1,279	John Locke	Wm. Hope
Hythe	1,333	S. Marjoribanks	Thos. Sheperd
Warren Hasings	1,068	Geo. Reed	H. B. Ararne
Rose	1,024	John Milroy	T. Marquis
Duke of York	1,327	S. Marjoribanks	Robert Locke
Inglis	1,321	R. Borradaile	Joseph Dudman
Waterloo	1,325	Company's ship	n/a
Scaleby Castle	1,242	Company's ship	W. R. Blakeley
Winchelsea	1,330	Wm. Moffat	P. H. Hart
Bombay	1,242	Henry Templer	n/a
Lowther Castle	1,427	John Pirrie	n/a
Minerva	978	George Palmer	George Probyn
Thomas Grenville	886	Company's ship	Charles Shea

APPENDIX X

Text of the Treaty of Nanking[1]

Treaty between Her Majesty the Queen of Great Britain and the Emperor of China, signed in the English and Chinese languages, at Nanking, August 29th, 1842.

Her Majesty, the Queen of the United Kingdom of Great Britain and Ireland, and His Majesty the Emperor of China, being desirous of putting an end to the misunderstandings and consequently hostilities which have arisen between the two countries, have resolved to conclude a treaty for that purpose, and have therefore named as their plenipotentiaries, that is to say: Her Majesty the Queen of Great Britain and Ireland, Sir Henry Pottinger, Bart., a Major General in the Service of the East India Company, &c., &c., ; and His Imperial Majesty the Emperor of China, the high commissioners Keying, a member of the Imperial House, a guardian of the Crown Prince, and General of the garrison of Canton; and Ilípú, of the Imperial Kindred, graciously permitted to wear the insignia of the first rank, and the distinction of a peacock's feather, lately minister and Governor-General, &c., and now Lieutenant-General commanding at Chàpú: Who, after having communicated to each other their respective full powers, and found them to be in good and due form, have agreed upon and concluded the following articles:

Art. I. There shall henceforward be peace and friendship between Her Majesty the Queen of the United Kingdom of Great Britain and Ireland, and His Majesty the Emperor of China, and between their respective subjects, who shall enjoy full security and protection of their persons and property within the dominion of each other.

Art. II. His Majesty the Emperor of China agrees, that British subjects, with their families and establishments, shall be allowed to reside, for the purpose of carrying on their mercantile pursuits, without molestation or restraint, at the cities and towns of Canton, Amoy, Fuchaufú, Ningpo, and Shanghai; and Her Majesty the Queen of Great Britain, &c., will appoint superintendents, or consular officers, to reside at each of the abovenamed cities or towns, to be the medium of communication between the Chinese authorities and the said merchants, and to see that the just duties and other dues of the Chinese Government, as hereafter provided for, are duly discharged by Her Britannic Majesty's subjects.

[1] As printed in the *Hongkong Almanack* for the year 1846

Art. III. It being obviously necessary and desirable that British subjects should have some port whereat they may careen and refit their ships when required, and keep stores for that purpose, His Majesty the Emperor of China cedes to Her Majesty the Queen of Great Britain, &c., the island of Hongkong, to be possessed in perpetuity by Her Britannic Majesty, Her Heirs and Successors, and to be governed by such laws and regulations as Her Majesty the Queen of Great Britain, &., shall see fit to direct.

Art. IV. The Emperor of China agrees to pay the sum of six millions of dollars, as the value of the Opium which was delivered up at Canton in the month of March 1839, as a ransom for the lives of Her Britannic Majesty's superintendent and subjects, who had been imprisoned and threatened with death by the Chinese high officers.

Art. V. The Government of China having compelled the British merchants trading at Canton to deal exclusively with certain Chinese merchants, called hong-merchants (or co-hong,) who had been licensed by the Chinese Government for that purpose, the Emperor of China agrees to abolish that practice in future at all ports where British merchants may reside, and to permit them to carry on their mercantile transactions with whatever persons they please; and His Imperial Majesty further agrees to pay to the British Government the sum of three millions of dollars, on accounts of debts due to British subjects by some of the said hong-merchants, or co-hong, who have become insolvent, and who owe very large sums of money to subjects of her Britannic Majesty.

Art. VI. The Government of Her Britannic Majesty having been obliged to send out an expedition to demand and obtain redress for the violent and unjust proceedings of the Chinese high authorities towards Her Britannic Majesty's officer and subjects, the Emperor of China agrees to pay the sum of twelve millions of dollars, on account of the expenses incurred; and Her Britannic Majesty's plenipotentiary voluntarily agrees, on behalf of Her Majesty, to deduct from the said amount of twelve millions of dollars, any sums which may have been received by Her Majesty's combined forces, as ransom for cities and towns in China subsequent to the 1st day of August, 1841.

Art. VII. It is agreed, that the total amount of twenty-one millions of dollars, described in the three preceding articles, shall be paid as follows:

Six millions immediately. Six millions in 1843; that is, three millions on or before the 30th of the month of June, and three millions on or before the 31st of December. Five millions in 1844; that is, two millions and a half on or before the 30th of June, and two millions and a half on or before 31st of December. Four millions in 1845, that is, two millions on or before the 30th June, and two millions on or before the 31st of December.

And it is further stipulated, that interest, at the rate of 5 per cent per annum, shall be paid by the Government of China on any portion of the above sums that are not punctually discharged at the periods fixed.

Art. VIII. The Emperor of China agrees to release, unconditionally, all subjects of her Britannic Majesty (whether natives of Europe or India) who may be in confinement at this moment in any part of the Chinese Empire.

Art. IX. The Emperor of China agrees to publish and promulgate, under His Imperial Sign Manual and Seal, a full and entire amnesty and act of indemnity to all subjects of China, on account o their having resided under, or having had dealings or intercourse with, or having entered the service of, Her Britannic Majesty, or of Her Majesty's officers; and His Imperial Majesty further engages to release all Chinese subjects who may be at this moment in confinement for similar reasons.

Art. X. His Majesty the Emperor of China agrees to establish at all the ports which are, by the second article of this Treaty, to be thrown open for the resort of British merchants, a fair and regular tariff of export and import customs and other dues, which tariff shall be publicly notified and promulgated for general information; and the Emperor further engages, that when British merchandise shall have once been paid at any of the said ports the regulated customs and dues, agreeable to the tariff to be hereafter fixed, such merchandise may be conveyed by Chinese merchants to any province of city, in the interior of the Empire of China, on paying a further amount as transit duties, which shall not exceed per cent [ ][2] on the tariff value of such goods.

Art. XI. It is agreed that Her Britannic Majesty's chief high officer in China shall correspond with the Chinese high officers, both at the capital and in the provinces, under the term 'communication'; the subordinate British and Chinese officers in the provinces, under the terms 'statement', on the part of the former, and on the part of the latter, 'declaration'; and the subordinates of both countries on a footing of perfect equality; merchants and others not holding official situations, and therefore not included in the above, on both sides, to use the term 'representation' in all papers addressed to, or intended for the notices of the respective Governments.

Art. XII. On the assent of the Emperor of China to this Treaty being received, and the discharge of the first instalment money, Her Britannic Majesty's forces will retire from Nanking and the Grand Canal, and will no longer molest or stop the trade of China. The military post at Chinhâi will also be withdrawn; but the islands of Kúlang-zú and of Chusan will continue to be held by Her Majesty's

[2] Left blank in the printed text.

forces until the money payments, and the arrangements for opening the ports to British merchants, be completed.

Art. XIII. The ratification of this treaty by Her Majesty of Queen of Britain, &c., and His Majesty the Emperor of China, shall be exchanged as soon as the great distances which separates England from China will admit; but, in the meantime, counterpart copies of it, signed and sealed by the plenipotentiaries on behalf of their respective sovereigns, shall be mutually delivered, and all its provisions and arrangements shall take effect.

Done at Nanking, and signed and sealed by the plenipotentiaries on board Her Britannic Majesty's Ship *Cornwallis*, this twenty-ninth day of August, 1842; corresponding with the Chinese date, twenty fourth day of the seventh month, in the twenty-second year of Táukwáng.

Approved and ratified by the Emperor on the 24th day of the 9th month, in the 22nd year of his reign, (October 27th, 1842).

Note:—This treaty was ratified by Her Majesty, and the great seal affixed, on the 31st of December 1842. The ratifications were exchanged at Hongkong, June 26th, 1843.

APPENDIX XI

The Principal Characters in the Letters

Alleyn, Frederick P. A close friend of William Jardine. Former surgeon on EIC ships. He died in Jardine's Macao house in October 1837.

Barretto, Bartolomeu Antonio. Son of an established Portuguese merchant in Macao, and one of the firm's bookkeepers.

Beale, Chay. Nephew of Thomas Beale. One of the firm's bookkeepers.

Beale, Thomas. A partner in a predecessor firm to *Jardine, Matheson & Co.* and an old friend of the Magniacs. Famed for his garden in Macao.

Bonham, Henry. Co-founder of *Fairlie-Bonham & Co*, the firm's principal London banking correspondent until 1834.

Chipnowe family. Family of William Jardine's sister, Margaret.

Clifton, Captain William. One of William Jardine's favourite captains. Famed for sailing the *Red Rover* from India with the first opium of the season.

Cowasjee, Framjee. Bombay Parsee merchant. First business partner of William Jardine with Thomas Weeding.

Davis, Sir John Francis. British Official. Succeeded Lord Napier as First Superintendent of British Trade in Canton in October 1834. In 1843, he succeeded Sir Henry Pottinger as second governor of Hong Kong.

Dent, Thomas. Senior partner in *Dent & Co., Jardine, Matheson & Co.* principal rival firm.

Dent, Lancelot. A relation of Thomas Dent and a partner in *Dent & Co.*

De Vitre, Mathias, Theosodius, Denis. A close business friend of William Jardine and a partner in the Bombay firm *Remington & Co.*

Elliot, Captain Charles. First Superintendent of British Trade in succession to Sir George Best Robinson. Plenipotentiary during the Opium War until his recall by Palmerston in 1841.

Elliot, Admiral Sir George. Joint plenipotentiary during the Opium War until his resignation in November 1840 on account of ill health.

Graham, Sir James Robert George. MP for Dorchester. Mover of the motion of no confidence in the Commons debate on the China question in April 1840.

Grant, Captain Alexander. Trusted friend and business partner of the founders. In charge of the receiving ships.

Gutzlaff, Reverend Carl. Pomeranian Protestant missionary. Interpreter for the firm on several coastal missions. Subsequently an official in the administration of the colony of Hong Kong.

Haddow, H. P. A partner in the Bombay Agency of *Remington & Co* and a close business friend of the founders.

Hardie, Horatio. Keeper of the *Jerusalem Coffee House* in Cornhill and an important source of intelligence during the 1833 India Bill debate.

Hengtai, One of the principal hong merchants with whom the firm traded in the mid-1830s.

Hine, Captain John. A former EIC supercargo and a close friend of William Jardine's.

Hollingworth, Francis. A young relation of Hollingworth Magniac who failed to be made a member of the firm.
Howqua. The richest and most respected of the hong merchants.
Innes, Captain James. A free trader and notorious opium merchant.
Jejeebhoy, Jamsetjee (later Sir). A Parsee from Bombay and the firm's principal business partner throughout the period. After accumulating the largest commercial fortune in India, he became the most generous philanthropist and was knighted by Queen Victoria.
Jamsetjee Cursetjee. Jamsetjee Jejeebhoy's son and partner.
Jardine, William. Co-founder of *Jardine, Matheson & Co.* and partner of the firm from 1832 to 1840.
Jardine, Andrew. Eldest son of William Jardine's elder brother, David. A partner in the firm from 1839 to 1843.
Jardine, David. A brother of Andrew Jardine, and a partner in the firm from 1843 to 1856.
Johnstone, Andrew. Son of William Jardine's eldest sister, Janet. A partner in the firm from 1835 to 1836.
Kishen. Chinese plenipotentiary in succession to Commissioner Lin. In 1841 negotiated the abortive Chuenpi Convention with Captain Elliot which ceded Hong Kong to the British Crown.
Kiying. Chinese plenipotentiary in succession to Kishen and the negotiator of the Treaty of Nanking with Sir Henry Pottinger.
Lin, Commissioner. Chinese plenipotentiary holder of an imperial commission to eradicate the opium trade in 1839.
The Lyalls. A family of East India merchants trading in London and Calcutta. Several brothers (Charles, Robert, William) were business partners of James Matheson.
Mackay, Captain William. A first cousin of James Matheson and the captain of one of the opium ships. He tragically met his fate at the hands of pirates in the China seas.
Macvicar, John. A syndicator of British textile exports from the Midlands to China and a business partner of the founders.
Magniac, Charles. Founding partner of *Magniac & Co.*, the predecessor firm to *Jardine, Matheson & Co.*
Magniac, Daniel. A brother of Charles Magniac who did not work in the family firm.
Magniac, Hollingworth. Brother of Charles Magniac. Senior partner of *Magniac & Co.* after his brother's death in 1824. He invited William Jardine to join his firm in 1825. In 1832 the firm's name was changed to *Jardine, Matheson & Co.*
Matheson, Alexander (later Sir). One of James Matheson's nephews. A partner of the firm from 1835, and senior partner from 1842 to 1852.
Matheson, James, (later Sir). Co-founder of *Jardine, Matheson & Co.* and partner of the firm from 1832 to 1842.
Matheson, Hugh. Brother of Alexander Matheson. Co-founder of *Lyall Matheson & Co.*, the firm's principal Calcutta correspondent.
Moffat, George. London tea trader, and a friend of James Matheson.
Morrison, Dr Robert. The first protestant missionary in China and a Chinese scholar. Chief interpreter to Lord Napier in 1834.
Morrison, John Robert. Son of Dr. Robert Morrison. Chief interpreter and translator to Sir Henry Pottinger during the Opium War.
Moorhousehead family. The family of William Jardine's older brother, David.
Mowqua. One of the hong merchants with whom the firm traded.

Napier, Lord. First Superintendent of British Trade in China. Died in Macao in October 1834, having failed in his mission to open diplomatic relations with the Chinese authorities in Canton.
Palmerston, Viscount. Foreign Secretary at the start of the Opium War and key decision maker on Britain's China policy.
Pottinger, Sir Henry. Succeeded Captain Charles Elliot as British Plenipotentiary. He successfully completed his mission with the signature of the Treaty of Nanking in August 1842 and started administering the new colony of Hong Kong.
Robinson, Sir George, Best. Succeeded Sir John Francis Davis as First Superintended of British Trade. In 1836 he was recalled by Palmerston. Captain Charles Elliot succeeded him.
Smith, John Abel. Grand-son of the founder of the banking firm *Smith, Payne & Smith.* Business partner of Hollingworth Magniac in London, and subsequently close business friend of William Jardine and James Matheson.
Smith, T. C. Former EIC supercargo and a business friend of Hollingworth Magniac.
Smith, James Warley. First tea-taster for the firm in Canton.
Thom, Robert. Head of the firm's piece-good department. Subsequently British Consul at Ningpo.
Ullman, J. G. The firm's head bookkeeper in the early 1830s.
Weeding, Thomas. Former EIC supercargo and William Jardine first business partner.
Wright, Henry. Former Purser on EIC ships and a trusted friend of William Jardine. Became manager of the firm's opium department and was a partner from 1835 to 1841.
Yrisarri, Xavier de. James Matheson's previous partner in the Canton firm *Yrisarry & Co.* After his death in 1826, James Matheson joined William Jardine and Hollingworth Magniac in *Magniac & Co.*

GLOSSARY

Agency House. A counting house located in India or China, executing sale and purchase orders on commission on behalf of third parties.
Ague. A malarial fever.
Almira. Anglo-Indian for a cupboard or chest of drawers.
Artificer. A craftsman.
Average. In maritime insurance, a clause requiring that the sums paid upon loss or damage of property be shared equitably between the parties insured.
Barque. A masted ship with fore and main masts square-rigged.
Bill of Exchange. A written order by a drawer to a drawee to pay a certain sum on a specified date to the drawer or to a named payee.
Block. An encumbered ship.
Blockade. In the context of the Canton trade and of the Opium War, the shutting up of the Pearl River at the instigation of either the Chinese or the British authorities, with a view to stopping the trade.
Board of Control. The government-appointed body supervising the operations of the East India Company following the India Act of 1784
Bonded warehouse. A warehouse under the control of H. M. Excise and Duty where imported goods may leave bond only after duty has been paid. Bonded warehouses were first used in 1834 for tea imports.
Bottomry bond. A loan contract whereby the owner of a ship borrowed money against the security of his ship.
Broken dollar. A Spanish or Latin American gold coin which was worn, chipped or broken, and which needed to be weighed for an assessment of its real weight and value.
Cambric. White linen originally made at Cambray in Flanders, and subsequently manufactured in Lancashire.
Camlet. Imitation of a costly eastern fabric made of various combinations of wool, silk, hair, cotton or linen.
Candarin/candareen. A Chinese money of account, of about six grains Troy in weight.
Carolus. A variety of Spanish dollar coin.
Cassia. The root, bark, and wood of the cassia tree used as a tonic, stomachic, antiseptic and febrifuge.
Catty. A measure of weight equivalent of 16 taels [q.v.], or 1,33 lbs.
Celestials. Early nineteenth century tongue-in-cheek way of referring to the Chinese.
Chest. Wooden container used to ship tea and opium.
Clipper. A type of fast sailing ship originally designed by American shipbuilders.
Chop. 1 – A licensed light boat for transporting goods.
2 – An official seal or stamp on a document.
3 – A parcel of goods of identical quality (e.g. 'a chop of tea').
Cochineal. A dye-stuff consisting of the dried bodies of the insect *Coccus Cacti*.
Combination. Association of workers outlawed by the *Combination Acts* of the early 1800s, subsequently repealed in 1824.
Commission. *Ad valorem* percentage charged by Agency houses to their customers as remuneration for their brokerage services.

Comprador. Chinese or Eurasian servant entrusted with the responsibility of keeping a foreign firm's accounts for all domestic and household transactions.
Co-hong (or **Cohong**). The official body formed by the hong merchants [q.v.].
Congo. A quality of black tea particularly popular at the time the Letters were written.
Consoo Administration of the Canton port duties and taxes, under the supervision of the Hoppo [q.v.].
Consoo Fund. An insurance fund administered by the Hoppo to repay foreigners the debts due by failed hong merchants [q.v.].
Contractor. A supplier to the Army and Navy.
Court of Directors (of the EIC). The body of people managing the affairs of the East India Company.
Court of Proprietors. The body of people owning East India Company stock and voting at General Meetings.
Crape/crepe. A thin silk fabric, often dyed black and used for mourning.
Cumshaw. Compulsory gratuity or baksheesh.
Damaun. A quality and provenance of Indian opium shipped to China from the port of Daman or Damao, south of Surat.
Dollar. Short for 'Spanish dollar', the currency most frequently used in the early nineteenth century by foreign merchants trading in the East.
Doubloon. Spanish gold coin worth two pistols.
Dunnage. Loose wood laid on the bottom of a ship's hold to keep the cargo out of bilge water, or wedged between parts of the cargo to keep them steady.
Eight Regulations. Code of Chinese rules meant to be strictly observed by foreigners trading at Canton, but in practice largely disregarded at the time the Letters were written.
Endorsement. (of bills of exchange) The signing on the back of a bill of exchange by its current owner to make over his right in the instrument.
Exchange rate. The rate at which a currency is exchanged for another. (e.g. During the period covered by the Letters, the rate of exchange between Spanish dollars and pounds sterling fluctuated between 4 and 5 dollars to 1 pound).
Factory. In Canton, the building and establishment where foreign merchants both conducted their business and had their living quarters.
Fag. To work hard at one's business.
Favour. A letter.
Ferdinand. A variety of Spanish dollar coin.
Finance committee. After 1834, the rump of the East India Company left to operate in Canton.
H.C.S. Initials standing for 'Honourable Company's Ship' and preceding the name of a ship belonging to, or chartered by, the East India Company.
Hong. Chinese name for a warehouse and trading business. In Canton the word referred specifically to the businesses of the hong merchants [q.v].
Hong merchant. An exclusive group of Canton merchants (usually 12) licensed to trade with foreigners and who held a monopoly over Chinese imports and exports. Together, the hong merchants formed the cohong [q.v.].
Hoppo. Important Chinese official. As head of the Superintendency of Maritime customs he was responsible for the collection of all fees due in connection with the activities of the port of Canton.
Humbug. Insincere, manipulative behaviour.

Indigo. Blue dye from the *indigofera* plant cultivated in Bengal.
Kinchae. Chinese for 'by imperial decree'. The term was applied to Commissioner Lin in 1839 and to his successors as Chinese plenipotentiaries.
Lac/Lakh. Anglo-Indian for 'one hundred thousand'.
Lascar. East Indian sailor.
Linguist. In Canton, a Chinese translator of official documents. By extension: an interpreter and translator.
Long ell. A variety of long cloth from the Lancashire manufactures.
Mace. A weight and money of account equal to one-tenth of a tael.
Malwa. A variety and quality of opium cultivated and manufactured in the north-west of India and shipped to China from Bombay.
Mandarin. European name for a ranked Chinese official.
Maund. A measure of weight current in India and Western Asia equivalent to 100 lbs troy, or 82⅔ avoirdupois.
Monopoly. A system of trading where freedom and competition were legally curtailed (e.g. the East India Company monopoly on tea purchases and sales until 1834).
Musk. A very strong scented substance, found under the belly of the *moschus mosciferus* male goat.
Nankeen. A kind of cotton cloth originally made at Nanking from a yellow variety of cotton.
Opium bond. A pledge signed during the Opium War by a foreign merchant (usually American) who wanted to continue trading at the port of Canton (Whampoa) and who agreed to abstain from dealing in opium under penalty of death.
Opium receipt. A receipt issued by Captain Charles Elliot to an owner of opium against delivery of his stocks in May 1839. As evidence of claims against the British government, opium receipts were valuable financial instruments.
Overland route. The route from England to India developed in the 1830s via the Mediterranean and Suez, as opposed to the traditional, longer route, via the Cape of Good Hope.
Overtrade. To trade in excess of one's capital or the needs of the market.
Packet. In the absence of a regular postal service, East India Company ships carried general correspondence to India and China and back to London in containers known as 'Company Packets'.
Parsee. A member of the Zaroastrian Community based in and around Bombay and active in the China Trade at the time of the Letters.
Patna. A variety and quality of opium cultivated and processed in Bengal under the official control of the East India Company. It was auctioned off in Calcutta and then shipped privately to Canton.
Pensioner. The recipient of a private pension or endowment.
Petition. A written request sent by a group of people to a sovereign or his officials. This was the standard method of communication in Canton between foreign merchants and Chinese officials, and in England between various interest groups and Parliament.
Picul. A Chinese measure of weight equal to 100 catties [q.v.], i.e. about 133⅓ lbs avoirdupois.
Pidgin. Jargon of English words used between Chinese and Europeans .
Piece goods. Export products from British textile manufactures.
Poplar fund. Relief fund set up by the East India Company to compensate impecunious ship commanders for loss of voyages.

Primage. An allowance made by a shipper to the master and crew for loading and taking care of the cargo.
Private trade. Privileges granted by the East India Company to its officers, allowing them to trade in restricted items like tea and silk.
Procurador. In Macao, the head of the Portuguese administration.
Protection. (of bills) The payment or acceptance by friendly parties of bills of exchange coming due, particularly in periods of financial stress or turmoil.
Quang chow foo/Quangchoofoo. The Canton senior magistrate, or prefect.
Receiving ship. A ship serving as floating warehouse.
Remittance. The shipment of goods, negotiable financial instruments, or bullion to a correspondent, with a view to balancing a firm's accounts in said correspondent's books.
Respondentia. A type of loan where the lender was secured on the cargoes shipped.
Rupee. Generally, the currency of account used in India. However, the Sicca Rupee used in Bombay, the Current rupee used in Calcutta, and the Pagoda used in Madras, all had different exchange rates [q.v.].
Sanguine. Hopeful, confident and optimistic.
Speculation. A financial or commercial venture where the amount of profit or loss is uncertain until the transactions are finally unwound.
Screw. A mechanical implement used to pack raw cotton tightly into bales prior to shipping.
Select Committee. In Canton, the executive committee of the East India Company.
Shroff. A Chinese money counter.
Silk privilege. See: 'Private trade'.
Supercargo. A commander of an East India Company ship who was also responsible for managing the sale of outward cargo and the purchase of return goods.
Superintendent (of British Trade). A British official appointed by the Crown as one of the heads of the British trading community in Canton, following the East India Act of 19th June 1833 and the abolition of the East India Company Select Committee [q.v.].
Supreme Council. The executive council of the British Governor General in Bengal.
Sycee. Chinese uncoined silver used as a medium of exchange, in the form of lumps of various sizes, usually having an assayer's stamp on them.
Tael/Tale. Chinese name for an ounce. Hence, Chinese unit of account. The silver tael coin weighed one tael of standard silver.
Tape. A narrow woven strip of stout linen, cotton or silk used as a string for tying garments, etc.
Taysaam. One of two common types of woven Chinese silk.
Tea. The market recognised nine different varieties of black teas and six of green teas. The black teas came in the following varieties: Congo [q.v] (or Congou), Campoi, Ankoi, Souchong, Pouchong, Pekoe (spelt in a variety of ways), Orange Pekoe, Hong Moi, and Flowery Pekoe. The green teas came in the following varieties: Singlo, Hyson, Hyson skin, Young Hyson, Imperial and Gunpowder.
Tea Taster. A professional employed by a tea firm to assess of the quality of teas available in the market prior to purchase.
Touchstoner. An expert at testing the quality of gold and silver alloys.
Tsatlee. One of the two qualities of Chinese silk piece goods.
Tsoo Yuen. A Chinese official responsible for grain transport.
Vagabond. In early nineteenth century parlance, a disreputable person, a rascal.
Viceroy. European title for the governor of the Canton Province.

Index of Names

Prepared by Gerard M-F Hill

Italics are illustrations. (Parentheses are alternative forms.) [Brackets are editorial.] Companies are filed by the first family name, so Timothy Wiggin & Co. is filed at W, but Alexander, Turner & Co. is filed at A. The definite article is ignored, so The Bogue is filed at B.

Index of Topics

Prepared by Gerard M-F Hill

Italics are illustrations. (Parentheses are alternative forms.) [Brackets are editorial.]

www.ingramcontent.com/pod-product-compliance
Ingram Content Group UK Ltd.
Pitfield, Milton Keynes, MK11 3LW, UK
UKHW020223290926